THEORIES OF
PERSONALITY

THEORIES OF PERSONALITY

THIRD EDITION

CALVIN S. HALL
University of California
Santa Cruz, California

GARDNER LINDZEY
Center for Advanced Study in the Behavioral Sciences
Stanford, California

JOHN WILEY & SONS

New York · Chichester · Brisbane · Toronto · Singapore

Cover photo: Tibetan mandala from the collection of Jane Werner.

Library of Congress Cataloging in Publication Data:

Hall, Calvin Springer, 1909–
　Theories of personality.

　Bibliography: p.
　1. Personality.　I. Lindzey, Gardner, joint
author.　II. Title.
BF698.H33　1978　　　155.2　　　77-26692
ISBN 0-471-34227-0

Printed and bound by Malloy Lithographing, Inc.

30

TO OUR TEACHERS AND FRIENDS

Gordon W. Allport
Henry A. Murray
Edward C. Tolman

PREFACE

This edition of *Theories of Personality* contains a number of new features. Most prominent of these are two new chapters, one on Contemporary Psychoanalytic Theory; the other on Eastern Psychology. The former describes some of the changes that have taken place in psychoanalytic theory and research since the death of its founder, Sigmund Freud. Particular attention is paid to the important contributions of Erik H. Erikson in this chapter.

Because of the growing interest in Eastern thought, we considered it appropriate and timely to present an overview of Eastern personality theory and its influence on Western psychology. We were fortunate to have Daniel Goleman, an authority on Eastern psychology, draft this chapter for us.

Another innovation is a change in the order of the chapters. Clinically oriented theories are grouped together in the first half of the book; the more experimental and quantitative theories are grouped together in the second half of the book.

Chapters that appeared in the second edition have undergone varying amounts of revision, amplification, and condensation. In every case we have tried to discuss all major theoretical or research contributions published since our last edition.

Our publishers have made every effort to produce an attractively designed book, one that has clearly emphasized headings and subheadings for easier reading. Photographs appear in the book for the first time.

We have received significant assistance from a number of individuals. Erik Erikson read the section of Chapter 3 devoted to his views and made numerous helpful suggestions for improving it. Medard Boss provided us with new information about his activities since 1970, and Jason Aronson and Paul J. Stern made available to us the manuscripts of English translations of two recent books by Boss. Raymond B. Cattell and B. F. Skinner have identified what they consider their major recent contributions. Once again John Loehlin and Janet T. Spence have provided essential services in the revision of the Factor Theory and S-R Theory chapters respectively. Jim Mazur provided a comparable service in connection with the chapter dealing with Operant Theory.

William McGuire of Princeton University Press and Janet Dallett of the C. G. Jung Clinic, Los Angeles, were helpful in the revision of the Jung chapter. Vernon J. Nordby assisted in the preparation of the new chapter on Contemporary Psychoanalytic Theory. Ruth Wylie provided us with unpublished material for use in the chapter on Rogers. Rosemary Wellner provided skillful editorial advice and Gen Carter was very helpful in the final preparation of much of the manuscript. Gardner Lindzey's contributions were facilitated by the Center for Advanced Study in the Behavioral Sciences.

Calvin S. Hall
Gardner Lindzey

PREFACE TO THE FIRST EDITION

In spite of the deepening interest of psychologists in personality theory, there is no single source to which the student can turn for a survey of existing theories of personality. The present volume is intended to correct this shortcoming. It provides compact yet comprehensive summaries of the major contemporary theories of personality written at a level of difficulty that is appropriate for undergraduate or graduate instruction. From this book the student can secure a detailed overview of personality theory and at the same time he can prepare himself to read original sources with more appreciation and greater facility. It is our hope that this volume will serve a function in the area of personality similar to that served by Hilgard's *Theories of Learning* in the area of learning.

What theories should be included in a volume on personality theory? Although it is not easy to specify precisely what a theory of personality is, it is even more difficult to agree as to what are the most important of these theories. As set forth in the first chapter, we are willing to accept any general theory of behavior as a theory of personality. In judging importance we have relied primarily upon our evaluation of the degree of influence the theory has had upon psychological research and formulation. Also involved in this complex judgment is the matter of distinctiveness. When two or more theories have appeared to us to be very similar, we have either treated them in a single chapter or selected one theory to focus upon to the exclusion of the others. Given these broad criteria of importance and distinctiveness, there will probably be little objection to the particular theories we have elected to include in the volume. There may be less unanimity, however, concerning our decision to omit certain theories from consideration. Notable among the omissions are McDougall's Hormic Theory, Role Theory, Guthrie's Contiguity Theory, Tolman's Purposive Behaviorism, and some of the recently developed positions such as David McClelland's, Julian Rotter's, and George Kelly's.

We originally planned to include both McDougall's Hormic Theory and Role Theory but limitations of space forced us to reduce the number of chapters and these were the theories we judged to be most expendable. Hormic Theory was omitted because its influence is somewhat more indirect than in the case of the other theories. Although we regard McDougall as a theorist of great importance, his contemporary impact is largely mediated by more recent theorists who have borrowed features of his theory. Role Theory, it seems to us, is less systematically developed than most of the other positions we elected to include. It is true that the theory contains a leading idea of considerable value and importance but this idea has not as yet been incorporated into a network of concepts which deal comprehensively with human behavior. Guthrie and Tolman were omitted in favor of Hull's reinforcement theory simply because there has been less extensive research application of these theories outside of the area of learning. McClelland, Rotter, and Kelly were not included because of their recency and because, in some respects, their positions resemble theories or combinations of theories that we have included.

Having decided upon what theories to include, we were still faced with the problem of how to organize and describe these positions. Some consistency in mode of presentation seemed desirable; yet at the same time we wished to preserve the integrity of the individual theories. Our compromise consisted of providing general categories in terms of which the theories could be described while permitting ourselves a good deal of latitude within these categories so as to present each theory in the manner that seemed most natural. Even these general categories were not adhered to rigidly. In some instances new ones were necessary in order to represent a particular theory adequately, and in one or two cases it seemed advisable to combine categories. Typically, however, each theory is introduced with an Orientation section which recounts briefly the personal history of the theorist, outlines the main lines of influence upon the theory, and provides a summary of the salient features of the theory. Next the reader will find a section on the Structure of Personality in which are included the concepts designed to represent the acquisitions or enduring portions of personality. Following this is a section on Dynamics of Personality which sets forth the motivational or dispositional concepts and principles espoused by the theorist. Then comes a section on Development of Personality which deals with growth and change as represented by the theory. A section on Characteristic Research and Research Methods follows, in which representative investigations and empirical techniques are presented. There is a concluding section entitled Current Status and Evaluation which outlines briefly the present state of the theory and summarizes the major contributions of the theory as well as the chief criticisms it has elicited. At the end of each chapter is a brief list of Primary Sources which represents the most important of the original sources concerning the theory. All of the publications referred to in the text are brought together in a final section at the end of each chapter entitled References.

We have attempted to present each theory in a positive light, dwelling upon those features of the theory that seem to us most useful and suggestive. Although we have included a brief critique of each theory it has not been our primary intention to evaluate these theories. Rather, we have attempted to present them in expository terms that will demonstrate what they are good for or what promise they hold for the individual who adopts them. The length of a chapter does not reflect our judgment of the relative importance of the theory. Each theory is written in what seemed to us the smallest number of pages necessary to represent its essential features accurately and comprehensively. The reader will observe that in some chapters there appears to be more detailed and personal information concerning the theorist and the development of his theory than in other chapters. This was determined solely by availability of information. In those instances where we knew a good deal about the theorist, we decided to include as much of this information as seemed vital even though this would result in some chapters appearing more personalized than others.

In the preparation of this volume we sought and received invaluable assistance from a number of colleagues. It is with deep gratitude and appreciation that we acknowledge the personal contribution made by many of the theorists whose work is presented here. They clarified our thinking upon a number of points and made numerous suggestions both as to form and content which greatly improved the manuscript. Whatever merit this book possesses must be attributed in large measure to the meticulous care with which each of the following theorists read and criticized the chapter devoted to his theory: Gordon W. Allport, Raymond B. Cattell, H. J. Eysenck, Kurt Goldstein, Carl Jung, Neal E. Miller, Gardner Murphy, Henry A. Murray, Carl Rogers, Robert R. Sears, and William Sheldon. In addition to illuminating comments concerning the chapter dealing with his own theory, Gordon Allport provided us with penetrating criticisms and generative suggestions concerning all of the remaining chapters. He also used many of the chapters in his undergraduate and graduate courses and provided us with the comments and suggestions of these students. We are greatly indebted not only to these Harvard and Radcliffe students but also to many students at Western Reserve University who read and commented upon the chapters. We are pleased to acknowledge our further indebtedness to the following individuals, each of whom read and improved by their suggestions one or more chapters in this book: John A. Atkinson, Raymond A. Bauer, Urie Bronfenbrenner, Arthur Combs, Anthony Davids, Frieda Fromm-Reichmann, Eugene L. Hartley, Ernest Hilgard, Robert R. Holt, Edward E. Jones, George S. Klein, Herbert McClosky, George Mandler, James G. March, A. H. Maslow, Theodore M. Newcomb, Helen S. Perry, Stewart E. Perry, M. Brewster Smith, Donald Snygg, S. S. Stevens, Patrick Suppes, John Thibaut, Edward C. Tolman, and Otto A. Will, Jr. We are indebted to Heinz and Rowena Ansbacher for providing us with page proof of their book *The Individual Psychology of Alfred Adler* prior to its publication. It was very helpful to us in writing the section on Adler's theory of personality. In the final preparation of the manuscript we received invaluable assistance from Virginia Caldwell, Marguerite Dickey, and Kenneth Wurtz.

The completion of this volume was greatly facilitated by a half-year leave of absence granted by Western Reserve University to Calvin S. Hall and by a fellowship at the Center for Advanced Study in the Behavioral Sciences granted to Gardner Lindzey. The writing was also facilitated by the permission granted Lindzey to use the facilities of the Dartmouth College Library during the summer of 1954.

Calvin S. Hall
Gardner Lindzey

PREFACE TO THE SECOND EDITION

In the thirteen years that have intervened between the first edition of *Theories of Personality* and the present edition, a number of changes in personality theory have taken place. Death has diminished the roll of the major theorists: Angyal (1960), Jung (1961), Goldstein (1965), and Allport (1967). Some of the theories have been substantially revised and elaborated by their originators. All of the theories to a greater or lesser extent, have stimulated additional empirical activities. More importantly, new viewpoints have appeared on the scene that merit attention.

Let us reflect on the new viewpoints. It was difficult to decide which of the new theories that have emerged since 1957 should be discussed here. Few readers will object strenuously to the choices we made. Friend and foe alike will agree that B. F. Skinner's viewpoint (dare we call it a theory?) has become a major influence in American psychology and should not be omitted from consideration. Nor could we ignore an important European contribution to personality theory. Existential psychology has acquired an impressive constituency in the past ten years, not only in its European homeland but also in the United States. It is one of the mainstreams of the flourishing humanist movement. Although there may be little disagreement with these choices, we anticipate complaints about the omissions, notably Piaget and cognitive theory. Both were given careful consideration and both would have been included if space had permitted. The final decision was based on the criterion of their centrality for the psychology of personality. Skinner and existential psychology seemed to us to meet this criterion somewhat better than does either Piaget's developmental theory or cognitive theory.

Space limitations also required some excisions. Cattell emerged as the principal representative of factor theory. Eysenck, who shared the stage with Cattell in the first edition, has been increasingly involved in behavior theory and appears in the stimulus response theory chapter (Chapter Eleven) as well as in the factor theory chapter (Chapter Ten). Murphy's biosocial theory was reluctantly sacrificed on the grounds that it is an eclectic theory and, as such, its main concepts are adequately represented in other chapters. All of the remaining chapters have been updated. Some of the chapters (particularly those that deal with Allport, factor theory, S-R theory, and Rogers) were extensively revised. Other chapters needed fewer alterations.

The format of the chapters has not been changed. All of the viewpoints are still presented in a positive light. We have made every effort to depict with clarity and accuracy the essential features of each theory.

We were extremely fortunate to have B. F. Skinner and Medard Boss, whose positions are represented in the two new chapters (Chapters Twelve and Fourteen), read and comment on what we had written concerning their viewpoints. Preparation of the new chapter on Skinner's operant reinforcement theory and revision of the chapters on S-R theory and factor theories were greatly facilitated by the detailed and substantial contributions of Richard N. Wilton, Janet T. Spence, and John C. Loehlin. Also we are grateful to G. William Domhoff, Kenneth MacCorquodale, and Joseph B. Wheelwright, who made critical contributions to the revision. Florence Strong and Allen Stewart were diligent proofreaders and indexers.

Calvin S. Hall
Gardner Lindzey

CONTENTS

THEORIES OF
PERSONALITY

THE NATURE OF PERSONALITY THEORY

In this volume we will present an organized summary of the major contemporary theories of personality. In addition to providing a digest of each theory we will discuss relevant research and provide a general evaluation of the theory. Before proceeding, however, something should be said about what personality theories are as well as how the various personality theories can be distinguished from one another. Further, we will place these theories in a general context, relating them to what has gone on historically in psychology as well as locating them in the contemporary scene.

In this chapter we begin with a very general and somewhat informal outline of the role of personality theory in the development of psychology, followed by a discussion of what is meant by the terms personality and theory. From these considerations it is an easy step to the question: what constitutes a personality theory? We will also consider very briefly the relation between personality theory and other forms of psychological theory, and present a number of dimensions by means of which personality theories can be compared with one another. These dimensions can be considered to represent the major theoretical issues in this area, while the theories themselves may be considered to represent the scientific viewpoints, attitudes, or images of humans available to the person who wishes to study and understand human behavior broadly.

PERSONALITY
THEORY AND
THE HISTORY OF
PSYCHOLOGY

A comprehensive view of the development of personality theory must surely begin with conceptions of man advanced by the great classical scholars such as Hippocrates, Plato, and Aristotle. An adequate account would also be obligated to deal with the contributions of dozens of thoughtful individuals, for example, Aquinas, Bentham, Comte, Hobbes, Kierkegaard, Locke, Nietzsche, and Machiavelli who lived in the intervening centuries and whose ideas are still detected in contemporary formulation. It is not our intention here to attempt any such general reconstruction. Our goal is much more limited. We shall merely consider in broad terms the general role personality theory has played in the development of psychology during the past six or seven decades.

To begin with, let us examine some relatively recent sources of influence upon personality theory. A tradition of *clinical observation* beginning with Charcot and Janet but including most importantly Freud, Jung, and McDougall has done more to determine the nature of personality theory than any other single factor. In a moment we shall examine some of the effects of this movement. A second path of influence stems from the *Gestalt tradition* and William Stern. These theorists were tremendously impressed with the unity of behavior and consequently were convinced that the segmental or fragmented study of small elements of behavior could never prove enlightening. As we shall discover, this point of view is deeply embedded in current personality theory. There is also the more recent impact of *experimental psychology* in general and *learning theory* in particular. From this avenue has come increased concern with carefully controlled empirical research, a better understanding of the nature of theory construction, and a more detailed appreciation of how behavior is modified. A fourth determinant is represented by the *psychometric tradition* with its focus upon the measurement and study of individual differences. This source has provided increasing sophistication in scaling or measuring dimensions of behavior and the quantitative analysis of data. There are numerous other paths of influence upon personality theory including genetics, logical positivism, and social anthropology but none of these seems, thus far, to have had such far-reaching implications as the four determinants we have just outlined.

The specific background out of which each of the theories presented in this book emerged is briefly discussed in the following chapters. General discussions of the development of contemporary personality theory will be found in Allport (1937, 1961) and Boring (1950). The current status of personality theory and research is summarized in a series of chapters appearing in the *Annual Review of Psychology* commencing in 1950 (for example, (Carlson, 1975; Dahlstrom, 1970; Edwards, and Abbott, 1973; Holzman, 1974; Phares and Lamiell, 1977; Sarason and Smith, 1971; Sechrest, 1976; Singer and Singer, 1972.) There are also a number of worthwhile substantive treatments of the field including Byrne (1966), Geen (1976), Maddi (1976), Mischel (1976), Sanford (1963), Sarnoff (1962), and Sarason (1966).

Let us turn now to some of the distinctive features of personality theory. Although this body of theory is manifestly a part of the broad field of psychology, there are still appreciable differences between personality theory and research, and research and theory in other areas of psychology. These differences are particularly pronounced in regard to personality theory in its early stages of development and they exist in spite of a great deal of variation among personality theories themselves. The striking differences among personality theories, however, imply that almost any statement that applies with detailed accuracy to one theory of personality will be somewhat inaccurate when applied to many other theories. In spite of this, there are modal qualities or central tendencies inherent in most personality theories and it is upon these that we shall focus our discussion.

Granted that there are important congruences in the streams of influence that determined the early paths of general psychology and of personality theory, still there are significant differences. It is true that Darwin was a potent factor in the development of both positions and it is also true that physiology of the nineteenth century had its influence upon personality theorists as well as a marked effect upon general psychology. Nevertheless the broad flavor of the factors influencing these two groups during the past three quarters of a century has been distinguishably different. While personality theorists were drawing their leading ideas primarily from clinical experience, experimental psychologists were paying heed to the findings of the experimental laboratory. Where the names Charcot, Freud, Janet, McDougall, and Stern are in the forefront of the work of early personality theorists, we find Helmholtz, Pavlov, Thorndike, Watson, and Wundt cast in a comparable role in experimental psychology. The experimentalists derived their inspirations and their values from the natural sciences while personality theorists remained closer to clinical data and their own creative reconstructions. One group welcomed intuitive feelings and insights but scorned the trappings of science with its restriction upon the imagination and its narrow technical skills. The other applauded the rigor and precision of delimited investigation and shrank in distaste from the unrestrained use of clinical judgment and imaginative interpretation. In the end it was clear that early experimental psychology had little to say concerning problems of interest to the personality theorist and that the personality theorist had little respect for problems of central importance to the experimental psychologist.

It is well known that psychology developed in the late nineteenth century as the offspring of philosophy and experimental physiology. The origin of personality theory owes much more to the medical profession and to the conditions of medical practice. In fact, the early giants in this area (Freud, Jung, and McDougall) were not only trained in medicine but practiced as psychotherapists. This historical link between personality theory and practical application has remained evident throughout the development of psychology and provides an important distinction between this brand of theory and certain other types of psychological theory.

Consistent with what we have said thus far are two generalizations concerning personality theory. First, it is clear that *personality theory has occupied a dissident role in the development of psychology*. Personality theorists in their own times have been rebels. Rebels in medicine and in experimental science, rebels against conventional ideas and usual practices, rebels against typical methods and respected techniques of research, and most of all rebels against accepted theory and normative problems. The fact that personality theory has never been deeply embedded in the mainstream of academic psychology has had several important implications. On the one hand, it tended to free personality theory from the deadly grip of conventional modes of thought and preconceptions concerning human behavior. By being relatively uninvolved in the ongoing institution of psychology it was easier for personality theorists to question or reject assumptions that were widely accepted by psychologists. On the other hand, this lack of involvement also freed them from some of the discipline and the responsibility for reasonably systematic and organized formulation that is the heritage of the well-socialized scientist.

A second generalization is that *personality theories are functional in their orientation*. They are concerned with questions that make a difference in the adjustment of the organism. They center about issues of crucial importance for the survival of the individual. At a time when the experimental psychologist was engrossed with such questions as the existence of imageless thought, the speed with which nerve impulses travel, specifying the content of the normal-conscious-human-mind, deciding whether there was localization of function within the brain, the personality theorist was concerned with why it was that certain individuals developed crippling neurotic symptoms in the absence of organic pathology, the role of childhood trauma in adult adjustment, the conditions under which mental health could be regained, and the major motivations that underlay human behavior. Thus, it was the personality theorist, and only the personality theorist, who in the early days of psychology dealt with questions that to the average person seem to lie at the core of a successful psychological science.

The reader should not construe what has just been said as an indictment of general psychology and a eulogy of personality theory. It is still not clear whether the path to a comprehensive and useful theory of human behavior will proceed most rapidly from the work of those who have aimed directly at such a goal, or whether it will eventually owe more to the efforts of those who have focused upon relatively specific and limited problems. The strategy of advance in science is never easy to specify and the general public is not usually considered an adequate final court for deciding what problems should be focused upon. In other words, while it is a statement of fact that personality theorists have dealt with issues that seem central and important to the typical observer of human behavior, it remains to be seen whether this willingness to tackle such issues will prove to advance the science of psychology.

As we have implied, there is no mystery concerning why personality theories were broader in scope and more practical in orientation than the formulations of most other psychologists. The great figures of academic psychology in the nineteenth century were men such as Wundt, Helmholtz, Ebbinghaus, Titchener, and Külpe who carried out their work within university settings with few pressures from the outside world. They were free to follow their own intellectual inclinations with little or no compulsion to deal with what others considered important or significant. In fact, they were able to define what was significant largely by their own interests and activities. In contrast the early personality theorists were practitioners as well as scholars. Faced with the problems of everyday life, magnified by neurosis or worse, it was natural that they should address themselves to formulations that had something to contribute to these problems. A set of categories for the analysis of emotions that could be applied by trained subjects in a laboratory setting was of scant interest to a therapist who daily observed the operation of emotions that were hampering, disabling, and even killing fellow humans. Thus, the strong functional flavor of personality theories, their concern with problems of significance to the survival of the organism, seems a natural outgrowth of the setting in which these theories developed.

It is clear that *personality theorists* have customarily *assigned a crucial role to the motivational process*. At a time when many psychologists ignored motivation or attempted to minimize the contribution of such factors in their studies, the personality theorist saw in these same variables the key to understanding human behavior. Freud and Mc-Dougall were the first to give serious consideration to the motivational process. The wide gap between the arena of life and the theory developed by laboratory psychologists is pictured by McDougall as he justifies his attempts to develop an adequate theory of social behavior (which was more of a theory of personality than it was a theory of social behavior):

The department of psychology that is of primary importance for the social sciences is that which deals with the springs of human action, the impulses and motives that sustain mental and bodily activity and regulate conduct; and this, of all the departments of psychology, is the one that has remained in the most backward state, in which the greatest obscurity, vagueness, and confusion still reign (McDougall, 1908, pp. 2–3).

Thus, variables that were primarily of nuisance value to the experimental psychologist became a matter for intensive study and focal interest for the personality theorist.

Related to this interest in the functional and motivational is the personality theorist's conviction that *an adequate understanding of human behavior will evolve only from the study of the whole person.* Most personality psychologists insisted that the subject should be viewed from the vantage of the entire functioning person in their natural habitat. They pleaded strongly for the study of behavior in context, with each behavioral event examined and interpreted in relation to the rest of the individual's behavior. Such a point of view was a natural derivative of clinical practice where the entire person presented him or her self for cure and where it was indeed difficult to limit consideration to one sense modality or a limited array of experience.

If we accept the intent of most personality theorists to promote the study of the whole, unsegmented person, it is easy to understand why many observers have considered that *one of the most distinctive features of personality theory is its function as an integrative theory.* Although psychologists in general have shown increased specialization, leading to the complaint that they were learning more and more about less and less, the personality theorist accepted at least partial responsiblity for bringing together and organizing the diverse findings of specialists. The experimentalist might know a great deal about motor skills, audition, perception, or vision but usually knew relatively little about the way in which these special functions related to one another. The personality psychologist was, in this sense, more concerned with reconstruction or integration than with analysis or the segmental study of behavior. From these considerations comes the somewhat romantic conception of the personality theorist as the individual who will put together the jigsaw puzzle provided by the discrete findings of separate studies within the various specialties that make up psychology.

In broad terms, then, *what has distinguished personality theorists from traditional psychological theorists?* They are more speculative and less tied to experimental or measuremental operations. The stiffening brush of positivism has spread much more lightly over the personality psychologist than over the experimental psychologist. They develop theories that are multidimensional and more complex than those fashionable within general psychology and, consistently, their theories tend to be somewhat more vague and less well specified than the experimentalist's theories. They are willing to accept any aspect of behavior that possesses functional significance as legitimate data for their theoretical mill whereas most experimental psychologists are content to fix their attention upon a limited array of observations or recordings. They insist that an adequate understanding of individual behavior can be achieved only when it is studied in a broad context that includes the total, functioning person. The personality theorist sees motivation, the "why" or underlying impellents of behavior, as *the* crucial empirical and theoretical problem whereas experimentalists see this as one of many problems and deal with it by means of a small number of concepts closely linked to physiological processes.

Thus far we have proceeded as though the reader and the writers were in good agreement concerning what the term personality means. Although this may be the case, it is by no means certain and before proceeding further it seems wise to examine the meaning of this term.

WHAT IS PERSONALITY?

There are few words in the English language that have such a fascination for the general public as the term personality. Although the word is used in various senses, most of these popular meanings fall under one of two headings. The first use equates the term to social skill or adroitness. An individual's personality is assessed by the effectiveness with which he or she is able to elicit positive reactions from a variety of persons under different circumstances. It is in this sense that schools that specialize in glamorizing the American intend the term when they refer to courses in "personality training." Likewise, the teacher who refers to a student as presenting a personality problem is probably indicating that his social skills are not adequate to maintain satisfactory relations with his fellow students and the teacher. The second use considers the personality of the individual to consist of the most outstanding or salient impression that he or she creates in others. A person may thus be said to have an "aggressive personality" or a "submissive personality" or a "fearful personality." In each case the observer selects an attribute or quality that is highly typical of the subject and that is presumably an important part of the over-all impression created in others and the person's personality is identified by this term. It is clear that there is an element of evaluation in both usages. Personalities as commonly described are good and bad.

While the diversity in ordinary use of the word personality may seem considerable, it is overshadowed by the variety of meanings with which the psychologist has endowed this term. Allport (1937) in an exhaustive survey of the literature extracted almost fifty different definitions that he classified into a number of broad categories. Here we will concern ourselves with only a few of these definitions.

It is important initially to distinguish between what Allport calls biosocial and biophysical definitions. The *biosocial definition* shows a close correspondence with the popular use of the term as it equates personality to the "social stimulus value" of the individual. It is the reaction of other individuals to the subject that defines the subject's personality. One may even assert that the individual possesses no personality but that provided by the response of others. Allport objects vigorously to the implication that personality resides only in the "responding-other" and suggests that a *biophysical definition* that roots the personality firmly in characteristics or qualities of the subject is much to be preferred. According to the latter definition, personality has an organic side as well as a perceived side and may be linked to specific qualities of the individual that are susceptible to objective description and measurement.

Another important type of definition is the rag-bag or *omnibus definition*. This definition embraces personality by enumeration. The term personality is used here to include everything about the individual and the theorist ordinarily lists the concepts considered of primary importance in describing the individual and suggests that personality consists of these. Other definitions place primary emphasis upon the *integrative* or organizational function of personality. Such definitions suggest that personality is the organization or pattern that is given to the various discrete responses of the individual or else they suggest that the organization results from the personality that is an active force within the individual. Personality is that which gives order and congruence to all the different kinds of behavior in which the individual engages. A number of theorists have chosen to emphasize the function of personality in mediating the *adjustment* of the individual. Personality consists of the varied and yet typical efforts at adjustment that are carried out by the individual. In other definitions, personality is equated to the *unique* or individual aspects of behavior. In this case, it is a term to designate those things about the individual that are distinctive and set him or her apart from all other persons. Finally, some theorists have considered personality to represent the *essence* of the human condition. These definitions suggest that personality refers to that part of the individual that is most representative of the person, not only in that it differentiates the individual from others, more important, because it is what he or she actually is. Allport's suggestion that "personality is what a man really is" illustrates this type of definition. The implication here is that personality consists of what, in the final analysis, is most typical and deeply characteristic of the person.

We could profitably spend much more time dealing with the problem of defining personality if we did not know that in the ensuing chapters the reader will encounter many detailed definitions of personality in their natural context. Furthermore, it is our conviction that *no substantive definition of personality can be applied with any generality.* By this we mean simply that the way in which given individuals will define personality will depend completely upon their particular theoretical preference. Thus, if the theory places heavy emphasis upon uniqueness and the organized, unified qualities of behavior, it is natural that the definition of personality will include uniqueness and organization as important attributes of personality. Once the individual has created or adopted a given theory of personality, their definition of personality will be rather clearly implied by the theory. Thus, we submit that *personality is defined by the particular empirical concepts that are a part of the theory of personality employed by the observer.* Personality consists concretely of a set of scores or descriptive terms that describe the individual being studied in terms of the variables or dimensions that occupy a central position within the particular theory utilized.

If this seems an unsatisfactory definition, let the reader take consolation in the thought that in the pages to follow a number of specific definitions will be encountered. Any one of these will become the reader's if he or she adopts that particular theory. In other words, what we have said is that it is impossible to define personality without coming to agreement concerning the theoretical frame of reference within which personality will be viewed. If we were to attempt a single substantive definition now, we would be settling implicitly many of the theoretical issues that we intend to explore.

WHAT IS A THEORY?

Just as everyone knows what a personality consists of, so everyone knows what a theory is! The most common conviction is that a theory exists in opposition to a fact. A theory is an unsubstantiated hypothesis or a speculation concerning reality that is not yet definitely known to be so. When the theory is confirmed it becomes a fact. There is a grain of correspondence between this view and the usage we will advocate here, for it is agreed that theories are not known to be true. There is also an element of disagreement as the commonsense view asserts that a theory will become true or factual when the appropriate data have been collected if these data are confirmatory. In our view, theories are never true or false although their implications or derivations may be either.

The passages to follow represent a relatively conventional summary of the thinking of methodologists or logicians of science. There is by no means complete agreement concerning all of the issues discussed but the point of view presented is intended to be modal rather than original. The beginning student may find it a little difficult to grasp fully some of these ideas and it is only fair to indicate that an understanding of them is not essential in order to read and appreciate the remainder of the volume. On the other hand, if the reader is seriously interested in the field and has not yet been immersed in this area of scholarship, it would be well to acquaint oneself with methodology much more extensively than one can hope to do in this brief section. There are a number of excellent sources that provide a detailed treatment of these matters (for example, Conant, 1947; Feigl and Brodbeck, 1953; Feigl and Sellars, 1949; Frank, 1949; Hanson, 1958; Hempel, 1952; Kuhn, 1962; Lakatos and Musgrave, 1974; Suppe, 1974; Turner, 1967).

Let us commence by considering what a theory is and subsequently turn to the more important question of what are the functions of a theory. To begin with, a theory is a *set of conventions* created by the theorist. Viewing a theory as a "set of conventions" emphasizes the fact that theories are not "given" or predetermined by nature, the data, or any other determinant process. Just as the same experiences or observations may lead a poet or novelist to create any one of a multitude of different art forms, so the data of investigation may be incorporated in any of countless different theoretical schemes. The theorist in choosing one particular option to represent the events in which he or she is interested is exercising a free creative choice that is different from the artist's only in the kinds of evidence upon which it focuses and the grounds upon which its fruitfulness will be judged. We are emphasizing here the creative and yet arbitrary manner in which theories are constructed and this leads naturally to the observation that we can specify how a theory should be evaluated or appraised but we cannot specify how a theory should be constructed. There is no formula for fruitful theory construction any more than there is a formula for making enduring literary contributions.

The fact that a theory is a conventional choice, rather than something that is inevitable or prescribed by known empirical relations, emphasizes the lack of appropriateness of truth or falsity as attributes to be ascribed to a theory. A theory is only *useful or not useful* and these qualities are defined, as we shall see, primarily in terms of how efficiently the theory can generate predictions or propositions concerning relevant events that turn out to be verified (true).

Let us be somewhat more specific concerning what a theory is. Just what does a theory, in its ideal form, consist of? It should contain a cluster of relevant assumptions systematically related to each other and a set of empirical definitions!

The *assumptions* must be relevant in that they bear upon the empirical events with which the theory is concerned. If it is a theory of audition the assumptions must have something to do with the process of hearing; if it is a theory of perception the assumptions must bear upon the perceptual process. Ordinarily the nature of these assumptions represents the distinctive quality of the theory. The good theorist is the person who can ferret out useful or predictive assumptions concerning the empirical events within a domain of interest. Depending upon the nature of the theory these assumptions may be very general or quite specific. A behavioral theorist might choose to assume that all behavior is motivated, that events taking place early in life are the most important determinants of adult behavior, that the behavior of different animal species is governed by the same general principles; or the theorist might assume that increased anxiety leads to a decrement in motor performance or that a particular variable has a normal distribution within a given population. These assumptions may also vary in form from the precision of mathematical notation to the relative inexactness of most of the assumptions we have just used as illustrations.

Not only must the assumptions be stated clearly but also the assumptions and the elements within the theory must be explicitly combined and related to one another. That is, there must be rules for the systematic interaction between the assumptions and their embedded concepts. To give the theory logical consistency and permit the process of derivation, these internal relations must be clear. Without such specification it would be difficult or impossible to extract empirical consequences from the theory. Because of their similarity to the rules of grammar these statements are sometimes referred to as the *syntax* of the theory. We have already suggested that one might choose to assume that an increase in anxiety would lead to a decrement in motor performance. In addition, it might be assumed that an increase in self-esteem would lead to an improvement in motor performance. If we knew nothing more than this, the relation between these two assumptions would be clearly indeterminant as we need to find out something about the relation between anxiety and self-esteem before we can make any predictions concerning what may take place under circumstances where both variables are involved. An adequate statement of the theoretical assumptions would provide the user of the theory with a clear specification of the relation between these two assumptions.

The *empirical definitions* (coordinating definitions) permit the more or less precise interaction of certain terms or concepts within the theory with empirical data. Thus, by means of these definitions the theory at certain prescribed places comes into definite contact with reality or observational data. These definitions are frequently called operational definitions as they attempt to specify operations by means of which the relevant variables or concepts can be measured. Emphasis upon empirical definitions is the mark of an investigative intent and it is safe to say that if a theory is eventually to make a contribution in an empirical discipline it must possess some means for empirical translation. On the other hand, it should be clear that these definitions exist on a continuum ranging from complete and exact specification to a very general and qualitative statement. Although the more precision the better, an early insistence upon complete specification can destroy many fruitful paths of inquiry. Defining intelligence as simply "what intelligence tests measure" or equating anxiety solely to certain physiological changes as measured by the galvanometer may be exact, but neither definition alone seems likely to lead to much productive thought or inquiry. The proper attitude toward empirical definitions is that they should be as precise as present conditions within the relevant field permit.

We have now seen, in general terms, of what a theory consists. The next question is, What does it do? First, and most important, it leads to the collection or *observation of relevant empirical relations not yet observed*. The theory should lead to a systematic expansion of knowledge concerning the phenomena of interest and this expansion ideally should be mediated or stimulated by the derivation from the theory of specific empirical propositions (statements, hypotheses, predictions) that are subject to empirical test. In a central sense, the core of any science lies in the discovery of stable empirical relationships between events or variables. The function of a theory is to further this process in a systematic manner. The theory can be seen as a kind of proposition mill, grinding out related empirical statements which can then be confirmed or rejected in the light of suitably controlled empirical data. It is only the derivations or propositions or ideas derived from the theory which are opened to empirical test. The theory itself is assumed and acceptance or rejection of it is determined by its *utility,* not by its truth or falsity. In this instance, utility has two components—verifiability and comprehensiveness. *Verifiability* refers to the capacity of the theory to generate predictions that are confirmed when the relevant empirical data are collected. *Comprehensiveness* refers to the scope or completeness of these derivations. We might have a theory that generated consequences that were often confirmed but which dealt with only a few aspects of the phenomena of interest. Ideally the theory should lead to accurate predictions that deal very generally or inclusively with the empirical events that the theory purports to embrace.

It is important to distinguish between what may be called the systematic and the heuristic generation of research. It is clear that in the ideal case the theory permits the derivation of specific testable propositions and these in turn lead to specific empirical studies. However, it is also manifest that many theories, for example, Freud's and Darwin's, have had a great effect upon investigative paths without the mediation of explicit propositions. This capacity of a theory to generate research by suggesting ideas or even by arousing disbelief and resistance may be referred to as the *heuristic influence of the theory*. Both types of influence are of great importance and at the present stage of development within psychology are to be valued equally.

A second function that a theory should serve is that of permitting the *incorporation of known empirical findings* within a logically consistent and reasonably simple framework. A theory is a means of organizing and integrating all that is known concerning a related set of events. An adequate theory of psychotic behavior should be able to arrange all that is known concerning schizophrenia and other psychoses in an understandable and logical framework. A satisfactory learning theory must embrace in a consistent manner all the dependable findings dealing with the learning process. Theories always commence with that which has thus far been observed and reported and in this sense begin in an inductive phase and are guided and to some extent controlled by what is known. However, if the theories did nothing more than make consonant and orderly what was presently known they would serve only a very minor function. Under such circumstances the dogged investigator would be justified in the conviction that theories are mere verbal fluff floating in the wake of the experimenter who has done the real business of science. The empiricist who insists that theories are mere after-the-fact rationalizations of what the investigator has already reported fails to appreciate the main function of the theory—which is to point out new and, as yet, unobserved relations. The productiveness of the theory is tested before the fact not after the fact.

Simplicity or, as it is sometimes called, parsimony is also of importance but only after matters of comprehensiveness and verifiability have been settled. It becomes an issue only under circumstances where two theories generate exactly the same consequences. As long as the theories differ in the derivations that can be made concerning the same empirical events, the choice of the theory should be decided in terms of the extent to which these predictions differ in verification. Thus, it is only when you have a tautology—two theories arriving at the same conclusions from different terms—that simplicity becomes an important question. There are few examples of such a state of affairs in science and none, to our knowledge, in psychology. Simplicity as opposed to complexity becomes, consequently, a matter of personal value or preference in personality theorizing, rather than an attribute that is necessarily to be prized or sought after.

Another function that a theory should serve is that of *preventing the observer from being dazzled by the full-blown complexity of natural or concrete events.* The theory is a set of blinders and it tells its wearer that it is unnecessary to worry about all of the aspects of the event one is studying. To the untrained observer any reasonably complex behavioral event seems to offer countless different possible means for analyzing or describing the event—and indeed it does. The theory permits the observer to go about abstracting from the natural complexity in a systematic and efficient manner. Abstract and simplify one will, whether one uses a theory or not, but if one does not follow the guidelines of an explicit theory the principles determining one's view will be hidden in implicit assumptions and attitudes of which one is unaware. The theory specifies to the user a limited number of more or less definite dimensions, variables, or parameters that are of crucial importance. The other aspects of the situation can to a certain extent be overlooked from the point of view of this problem. A useful theory will detail rather explicit instructions as to the kinds of data that should be collected in connection with a particular problem. Consequently, as might be expected, individuals occupying drastically different theoretical positions may study the same empirical event and share little in the way of common observations.

In recent years a growing number of psychologists have adopted the theoretical reasoning and terminology of Thomas Kuhn (1962) who, in an engaging, if oversimplified, monograph, has suggested that scientific advance may be depicted most accurately as consisting of a series of revolutionary steps, each of them accompanied by its own characteristic and dominant *paradigm.* According to Kuhn, every scientific field emerges in a sprawling and uncoordinated manner, with the development of disparate lines of investigation and theoretical ideas that preserve their autonomous and competitive positions, until a particular set of ideas assumes the status of a paradigm. He suggests that these paradigms serve to:

. . . define the legitimate problems and methods of a research field for succeeding generations of practitioners. They were able to do so because they shared two essential characteristics. Their achievement was sufficiently unprecedented to attract an enduring group of adherents away from competing modes of scientific activity. Simultaneously, [they were] . . . sufficiently open-ended to leave all sorts of problems for the redefined group of practitioners to resolve. . . . These are the traditions which the historian describes under such rubrics as 'Ptolemaic astronomy' (or 'Copernican'), 'Aristotelian dynamics' (or 'Newtonian'), 'corpuscular optics' (or 'wave optics'), and so on (p. 10).

It is interesting to speculate concerning the paradigmatic status of personality theory and research. For those who adopt this idiom, it seems easiest to view this area as in a preparadigmatic state. That is, while there are plentiful sets of systematic, or somewhat systematic, ideas, none of these has gained a position of real dominance. There is no single theory that serves as a "paradigm" to order known findings, determine relevance, provide an establishment against which rebels may struggle, and dictate the major path of future investigation. If Kuhn's historical analysis is accurate, it remains for the future to develop a systematic position that will sweep all, or most, of the field with it for at least an academic generation.

A THEORY OF PERSONALITY

We have agreed that personality is defined by the particular concepts contained within a given theory that are considered adequate for the complete description or understanding of human behavior. We have also agreed that a theory consists of a set of related assumptions concerning the relevant empirical phenomena, and empirical definitions to permit the user to move from the abstract theory to empirical observation. By simple addition we have the implication that a theory of personality must be a set of assumptions relevant to human behavior together with the necessary empirical definitions. There is the further requirement that the theory must be relatively comprehensive. It must be prepared to deal with, or make predictions concerning, a wide range of human behavior. In fact, the theory should be prepared to deal with any behavioral phenomenon that can be shown to possess significance for the individual.

What has been said to this point possesses a formal validity that, however, cannot be sustained upon close scrutiny of existing theories of personality. Our discussion is of value in identifying the qualities toward which all theorists aspire and it also gives some idea of what, eventually, personality theories should look like. It is clear, nevertheless, that at the present time they do not look like this. A word should be said concerning the manner in which they fail to resemble the ideal both in structure and in function.

First of all, as we shall see, most of them lack explicitness. It is generally very hard to get at the assumptions or the axiomatic base of these theories. Personality theories are frequently packaged in a great mass of vivid word images that may serve very well as a means of persuading the reluctant reader but which frequently serve to cloak and conceal the specific assumptions that underlie the theory. In other words, most of the theories are not presented in a straightforward and orderly manner and many of them seem more oriented toward persuasion than exposition. Related to this lack of definiteness is a frequent confusion between that which is given or assumed and that which is stated empirically and open to test. As we have already agreed, it is only the derivations or the predictions generated by the theory that are open to empirical test. The remainder of the theory is assumed or given and is not to be judged on grounds of confirmation or disconfirmation but rather in terms of how successfully it generates verified propositions. In general, then, the distinction between the personality theory itself and its implications or derivations is very poorly maintained.

An inevitable consequence of the lack of explicitness concerning the nature of the assumptions underlying the theory is the existence of serious confusion in the process of deriving empirical statements from the theory. Thus, there is the possibility that different individuals using the same theory will arrive at conflicting derivations. Actually, the derivation process in most personality theories is haphazard, obscure, and inefficient. This is not only a reflection of the lack of explicitness of these theories but also of the fact that most personality theorists have been oriented toward after-the-fact explanation rather than toward the generation of new predictions concerning behavior. Finally, it is clear that although personality theories vary in how carefully they specify empirical definitions, none of these theories achieves a very high standard in absolute terms.

The statements we have just made concerning the formal status of personality theories may seem sufficiently discouraging to warrant abandoning attempts to construct such theories at this time. Would it not be better at present to forget about theories and focus upon empirical tools and specific empirical findings? Emphatically no! Such a decision does not involve giving up inadequate theory for no theory but rather involves the substitution of implicit theory for explicit theory. There is no such thing as "no theory"; consequently, the moment we attempt to forget about theory "for the present" we are really using implicit, personally determined and perhaps inconsistent assumptions concerning behavior and these unidentified assumptions will determine what will be studied and how. The observation of any concrete empirical event is carried out under the dictates of some "theory"—that is, certain things are attended to and certain things are overlooked—and one of the purposes of theorizing is to make explicit the rules determining this abstraction process. The possibility of improving upon the assumptions that are controlling research is eliminated the moment one gives up the attempt to define the theoretical base from which one operates.

Poor though personality theories may be when compared to the ideal, they still represent a considerable step forward when compared to the thinking of the naive observer who is convinced that he or she is embracing or viewing reality in the only way in which it can reasonably be viewed. Even though personality theories do not possess the degree of explicitness that one might wish, their mere existence makes it possible to work toward this goal in a systematic manner. In fact, it is clear that the present state of personality theory represents a considerable improvement over its formal status twenty years ago.

Granted that personality theories do not ordinarily permit as explicit a derivation process as we might wish, just what function do they serve for the individual who wields them? At the very least they represent a cluster of attitudes (assumptions) concerning behavior that in a broad way limits the kinds of investigation to be considered crucial or important. In addition to stimulating certain general kinds of research, they also provide specific parameters or dimensions that are considered important in the exploration of these problems. Thus, even if the theory does not provide an exact proposition for test, it orients the theorist toward certain problem areas and indicates that particular variables are of central importance in studying these problems. Moreover, there is the heuristic value of these theories to be considered. Taken as a group, personality theories are highly provocative and, as we shall discover, they have led to large quantities of research even though relatively little of this has been the result of a formal derivation process. In other words, the capacity of these theories to generate ideas, to stimulate curiosity, to stir doubts, or to lead to convictions has resulted in a healthy flourishing of investigation in spite of their lack of formal elegance.

Our discussion thus far has led us to the conclusion that a theory of personality should consist of a set of assumptions concerning human behavior together with rules for relating these assumptions and definitions to permit their interaction with empirical or observable events. At this point the question may be asked reasonably whether this definition in any way differentiates personality theories from other psychological theories. In answering this question it will be helpful to

PERSONALITY THEORY AND OTHER PSYCHOLOGICAL THEORIES

begin with a distinction between two types of psychological theory.

It is evident that certain psychological theories appear ready to deal with any behavioral event that can be shown to be of significance in the adjustment of the human organism. Other theories specifically limit themselves to behavior as it occurs under certain carefully prescribed conditions. These theories profess an interest in only limited aspects of human behavior. A theory that attempts to deal with all behavioral phenomena of demonstrated significance may be referred to as a *general theory of behavior* and those theories that restrict their focus to certain classes of behavioral events are called *single-domain theories*.

Clearly, personality theories fall into the first category; they are general theories of behavior. This simple observation serves to separate personality theory from the bulk of other psychological theories. Theories of perception, audition, rote memory, motor learning, discrimination, and the many other special theories within psychology are single-domain theories and can be distinguished from personality theory on grounds of scope or comprehensiveness. They make no pretense at being a general theory of behavior and are content to develop concepts appropriate for the description and prediction of a limited array of behavioral events. Theories of personality, however, have generally accepted the challenge of accounting for or incorporating events of the most varied nature so long as they possess demonstrated functional significance for the individual.

The question remains whether there are general theories of behavior that would not ordinarily be called personality theories. One possibility is that what has usually been called motivational theory may be a general theory of behavior and yet distinct from personality theory. Actually, insofar as the theory deals exclusively with the motivational process it is not a general theory, although, in fact, what are usually referred to as theories of motivation are also theories of personality, for example, psychoanalysis, hormic psychology, Murray's theory. As we shall discover, the motivational portion of theories of personality is of central importance to these theories. Thus, if the theory deals only with motivation it is a single-domain theory; if it is more embracive it is simply a type of personality theory.

A second possibility is that learning theory may in some instances be sufficiently generalized so that it constitutes a general theory of behavior. This is clearly the case and, as we shall see in detail later, a number of theorists have attempted to generalize learning theories so that they are comparable in comprehensiveness to any other general theory of behavior. In such instances, the theory of learning ceases to be merely a learning theory and becomes a personality theory or, if you like, a general theory of behavior. It is true that such generalized models possess certain distinctive characteristics that are reminiscent of their origin, but in intent and in logical properties they are no different from any other theory of personality.

This lumping together of theories that have had their origins in the animal laboratories and theories that originated in the therapist's chambers may appear forced to many observers. However, if we consider the theories from the point of view of what they intend to do and their general structure, rather than from the point of where they come from or the detailed assumptions they make about behavior, it is clear that any general theory of behavior is the same as any other. In this sense all general theories of behavior are personality theories and vice versa. Within this large group of theories, of course, many distinctions can be made and the following section will deal with a number of attributes in terms of which theories of personality can be differentiated or compared. One could set up numerous subgroups or classifications on the basis of these dimensions.

It is evident that when bodies of formulation as numerous and complex as personality theories are examined there are many qualities by which they can be compared and distinguished. Here we shall point to only a few of the more important of these to provide a basis for whatever generalizations may eventually seem worthwhile concerning the state of contemporary personality theory. These dimensions also serve to identify the main issues or options confronting the personality theorist today. The attributes divide naturally into those concerned with matters of formal adequacy and those concerned with the substantive nature of the theory.

THE COMPARISON OF THEORIES OF PERSONALITY

Here we are interested in how adequately the structure of the theory is developed and presented. There is a definite evaluative aura to each of these qualities as they represent an ideal and the closer the theory comes to reaching this ideal the more effectively it can be used.

Formal Attributes

The question of *clarity and explicitness* is of huge importance. This is a matter of how clearly and precisely the assumptions and embedded concepts that make up the theory are presented. In the limiting case the theory may be stated in terms of mathematical notation, with a precise definition of all but the primitive terms, so that the person who has been adequately trained can employ the theory with a minimum of ambiguity. Under such circumstances different individuals employing the theory independently will arrive at highly similar formulations or derivations. At the other extreme, we find theories presented with such a rush of vivid and complex description that it is extremely difficult for the individual who would employ the theory to be certain of just what he or she is grappling with. Under these circumstances there is little likelihood that individuals using the theory independently will arrive at the same formulations or derivations. It will become clear as we progress that there is no theory of personality that approaches very far toward the ideal of mathematical notation; still, granted the free use of verbal description, we shall find that there is considerable variation among personality theories in the clarity of their exposition.

A further question is the matter of *how well the theory is related to empirical phenomena.* Here we are concerned with the explicitness and practicality of the definitions proposed to translate theoretical conceptions into measuremental operations. At one extreme we find theories that prescribe relatively exact operations for assessing or measuring each of the empirical terms within the theory, whereas in other cases the theorist appears to assume that the name assigned to the concept is a sufficient defining operation by itself.

Perhaps this is an appropriate place to emphasize again our conviction that all matters of formal adequacy pale alongside the question of *what empirical research is generated by the theory.* However vague and poorly developed the theory, and however inadequate its syntax and empirical definitions, if it can be shown to have had a generative effect upon significant areas of research we would have to conclude that it passes the crucial test. Thus, the payoff question that overrides, and actually makes trivial, all questions of formal adequacy is the matter of how much important research the theory has produced. True, it is not easy to agree upon what is important research, particularly since importance will largely be determined by the theoretical position of the judge. It is also true that it is not always easy to say just what the process was which led to a particular investigation being conducted and thus the generative role of the theory may be difficult to assess. In spite of this there are clear and perceptible differences between theories of personality in the extent to which they have been translated into investigations that are of general interest.

Substantive Attributes   While the formal attributes we have just described all present a normative or valued standard in terms of which each theory can be compared, the following attributes posses no such evaluative implication. They are neutral in regard to good and bad and merely reflect the particular assumptions concerning behavior that the theory embraces.

Differences between personality theories in content naturally reflect the major issues that currently exist in this area. Thus, in the following pages we shall not only be outlining dimensions that can be used for the comparison of personality theories but we shall also be pointing to the major options that face a theorist in this area. We could with perfect appropriateness label this section "issues in modern personality theory."

Older than the history of psychology is the question of whether human behavior should be viewed as possessing *purposive or teleological qualities*. Some theories of behavior create a model of the individual in which goal-striving, purpose, and seeking are viewed as essential and central aspects of the individual's behavior. Other theories assume that the striving and seeking aspects of behavior are unimportant and believe that behavior can be accounted for adequately without such an emphasis. The latter theorists consider the subjective elements of striving and seeking as an epiphenomenon, accompanying behavior but not playing a determinant role in its instigation. Generally, theories that minimize the importance of purpose or teleology are labeled "mechanistic" although this term has come to have a disparaging quality, which is undesirable when, after all, we are simply considering matters of theoretical option.

Another ancient debate is concerned with the relative importance of conscious and *unconscious determinants of behavior*. In its archaic form this issue would be phrased in terms of the relative rationality or irrationality of human behavior. The term unconscious is used here simply to refer to determinants of behavior of which the individual is unaware and unable to bring to awareness except under special conditions. Theories of personality range from those that explicitly reject any consideration of unconscious determinants of behavior, or refuse to accept the existence of such determinants, to theories that consider them the most important or powerful determinants of behavior. A middle ground is occupied by those theorists who are willing to assign a central role to unconscious determinants in the behavior of disturbed or abnormal individuals while claiming that for the normal individual conscious motives are the ruling forces.

The relative importance of *hedonism, reward, or effect* is likewise a question that has engrossed students of human behavior for centuries. In its earlier formulations, such as those of the utilitarians, Bentham and J. S. Mill, it was a question of whether man was primarily motivated by seeking pleasure and avoiding pain. Its contemporary form is the "law of effect." This law states that only those responses that are accompanied by a reward or reinforcement will be retained or learned. In either case the question is one of how important are reward or pleasure as determinants of behavior. Again we find that theories vary from those in which the crucial role of reward or reinforcement is the dominant assumption to those that minimize the importance of reward or subsume its operation under other theoretical principles.

Just as some theorists place the law of effect at the core of their theory, so others consider the *principle of association* (contiguity) to be of first importance. These theorists consider that more important than the reward or effect that follows a given response is the exact stimulus configuration accompanying the response. In other words, it is the simultaneous or near-simultaneous occurrence of a stimulus and a response that leads to learning, rather than the reward or reinforcement that follows the response. Obviously these principles need not be mutually exclusive and, as we shall learn, there are theorists who have assigned to both principles a central role within the same theory.

A fundamental distinction between theories of personality has to do with the extent to which the *learning process,* or the modification of behavior, is a matter for detailed and explicit attention. Some personality theorists see in the understanding of the learning process the key to all behavioral phenomena whereas for other theorists learning is an important but secondary problem. Although no personality theorist would deny the significance of learning, we shall find that some theorists prefer to focus upon the acquisitions or outcomes of learning rather than on the process itself. This issue thus becomes a matter of disagreement between those who propose to deal primarily with the process of change and those who show themselves most interested in the stable structures or *acquisitions of personality* at a given time.

Closely related to the relative emphasis upon the learning process versus description of personality organization or structure is the distinction between theories that deal extensively with the *content of behavior* and its description *as opposed to* those that deal chiefly with *general principles, laws, and formal analysis.* Largely, this is a matter of whether theorists concentrate upon the concrete details of experience and behavior or whether they are principally concerned with laws or principles that can be very widely generalized. Typically, the more abstract the theory, the less the concern with the content or concrete details of behavior.

An issue as old as man's thoughts about man is the question of the relative importance of genetic or *hereditary factors* in determining behavior. Almost no one will deny that hereditary factors have some implications for behavior, but there are still many personality theorists who have dramatically undercut their importance, insisting that all the major behavioral phenomena can be understood without recourse to the biological and genetic. In America the role of hereditary factors has generally been played down in favor of some brand of environmentalism but there is still considerable variation as to how much and how explicitly the various theorists are willing to deal with genetic factors.

An additional dimension in terms of which personality theories show considerable variation has to do with the relative importance of *early developmental experiences*. This is a question of whether the theory assigns a strategic and critical importance to events taking place in infancy and childhood that is not matched in importance by events taking place at later stages of development. As we shall discover, there are some theories that imply the key to adult behavior is to be found in events that have taken place in the earliest years of development, while other theories state quite explicitly that behavior can be understood and accounted for solely in terms of contemporary or ongoing events. Related to this question is the extent to which theorists consider the personality structure at a given point in time to be autonomous or functionally distinct from the experiences that have preceded this point. For certain theorists the understanding of behavior in terms of *contemporaneous factors* is not only possible but the only defensible path to understanding. For others a reasonable understanding of the present must always depend partly upon some knowledge of events that have taken place in the past. Naturally, those who emphasize the contemporaneous point of view are convinced of the functional independence of the personality structure at any particular point in time, while those who emphasize the importance of past or early experience are less convinced of the freedom of present structure from the influence of past events.

Closely related to the preceding issue is the question of the *continuity or discontinuity* of behavior at different stages of development. Most theories that emphasize the learning process and/or the importance of early developmental experiences tend to view the individual as a continuously developing organism. The structure that is observed at one point in time is related in a determinant manner to the structure and experiences that occurred at an earlier point. Other theories tend to consider the organism as going through stages of development that are relatively independent and functionally separated from the earlier stages of development. The latter point of view may lead to the construction of drastically different theories for infant behavior and adult behavior.

A major difference between personality theories lies in the extent to which they embrace *holistic principles*. That is, do they consider it legitimate to abstract and analyze so that at a given time, or in a particular study, only a small part of the individual is being examined? The individuals who adopt a holistic position consider behavior to be understandable only in context, so that the total, functioning person together with the significant portions of his or her environment must be given simultaneous consideration if there is to be a fruitful outcome. Other theories accept the fact that the very nature of science and investigation necessitates analysis and these positions usually show no special concern over violation to the integrity of the whole organism that may be involved in segmental studies.

This emphasis upon the wholeness of the individual and the environment can be broken down into two rather distinct forms. The first is usually referred to as an *organismic position*. Here there is great stress upon the interrelatedness of everything the individual does, upon the fact that each act performed can be understood only against the background provided by the person's other acts. Not only is there an implication that all behavior is essentially interrelated and not susceptible to techniques of analysis but also there is usually an interest in the organic underpinnings of behavior. Consequently, behavior should be viewed against the perspective provided by the individual's other acts as well as the perspective offered by accompanying physiological and biological processes. All of the person's behavior and biological functioning make up an organic whole that is not to be understood if it is studied segmentally.

The second holistic position is usually referred to as a *field emphasis*. Here the theory is primarily concerned with the inextricable unity between a given behavioral act and the environmental context within which it occurs. To attempt to understand a given form of behavior without specifying in detail the "field" within which it occurs is to strive for understanding with a large proportion of the significant factors missing. Although behavior is partially a result of determinants that inhere in the individual, there are equally compelling forces that act upon the person from without. It is only when the individual's significant environment is fully represented that these forces acting outside of the person can be given their due. There is a strong tendency for theorists who emphasize the importance of the "field" to minimize the importance of hereditary factors as well as events taking place early in development. This is not a logical necessity but in practice most theorists who have focused strongly upon the environmental context of the individual have emphasized the present rather than the past and have been more interested in what is "out there" rather than what inheres in the individual.

Related to the issue of holism is the matter of *uniqueness* or individuality. Certain theories place a heavy emphasis upon the fact that each individual and, in fact, each act is unique and not to be duplicated by any other individual or act. They point out that there are always distinctive and important qualities that set off the behavior of any single individual from the behavior of all other persons. In general, the individual who strongly embraces a field or organismic point of view tends to stress uniqueness also. This follows naturally from the fact that if you broaden sufficiently the context that must be considered in connection with each behavioral event, the event will come to have so many facets that it is bound to display distinct differences in comparison to all other events. Some theories accept the fact that each individual is unique but propose that this uniqueness can be accounted for in terms of differences in the patterning of the same underlying variables. Other theories maintain that individuals cannot even be compared fruitfully in terms of common or general variables as these distort and misrepresent the individual's uniqueness. Personality theories vary from those that make no special mention of uniqueness to those where this is one of the most central assumptions.

Intimately associated with the issues of holism and uniqueness is the *breadth of the unit of behavior* employed in the analysis of personality. Those theorists who are relative or absolute holists choose to analyze behavior only at the level of the complete person while other personality theorists employ constructs of varying degrees of specificity or elementalism. On occasion this has been referred to as a choice between a molar (general) versus a molecular (specific) approach to the study of behavior. At the most segmental end of this continuum is the theorist who believes that behavior should be analyzed in terms of reflexes or specific habits; at the other extreme is the observer who is unwilling to view behavior at any level more molecular than the entire functioning person.

Some theories of personality demonstrate a primary concern for the operation of self-regulating mechanisms that serve to maintain a steady or balanced psychological state. Such theories see the operation of *homeostatic mechanisms* as one of the most significant and characteristic aspects of human behavior. This process is conceived of as a vital, automatic tendency that disposes the individual to maintain unity, integrity or psychological equilibrium in much the same manner as the physiological mechanisms that control essential functions such as temperature control and hormonal secretions. Generally those theories that place a heavy emphasis upon change and the learning process are not likely to focus upon the tendency of the organism to make extensive use of self-correcting tendencies that return the individual to a previous state of balance and adaptation.

We shall discover that certain personality theorists have centered their theoretical position about the importance of the *psychological environment* or the subjective frame of reference. This is a matter of emphasizing that the physical world and its events can affect individuals only as they perceive or experience them. Thus, it is not objective reality that serves as a determinant of behavior but rather objective reality as it is *perceived* or assigned meaning by the individual. It is the psychological environment, not the physical environment, which determines the manner in which the individual will respond. In contrast, there are theoretical positions that assume a firm theory of behavior can never be built on the shifting sands of subjective report or the complicated inferences needed to infer "meaning" from physical events. Such theories maintain that greater progress can be achieved through largely overlooking individual differences in the manner in which the same objective event is experienced and focusing upon relations involving external and observable events.

A further distinction between personality theorists has to do with whether or not they find it necessary to introduce a *self-concept*. For certain theorists the most important single human attribute is the view or perception the individual has of himself or herself and this self-viewing process is often seen as the key to understanding the multitude of puzzling behavioral events displayed by any single person. There are other theories where no such concept is elaborated and where the subject's perception of himself is considered of little general significance.

Personality theorists show great variation in the extent to which they explicitly emphasize cultural or *group membership determinants* of behavior. In some theories these factors are assigned a primary role in shaping and controlling behavior; in others the emphasis is almost exclusively upon determinants of behavior that operate independently of the society or cultural groups to which the individual is exposed. In general, theorists who are characterized by a heavy organismic emphasis tend to play down the role of group-membership determinants while those who emphasize the field within which behavior occurs are more sympathetic to the role of sociocultural or group-membership determinants. The extreme examples of this position, usually referred to as examples of cultural determinism, are found among anthropological and sociological theorists although psychological theorists also show considerable variation on this issue.

Related to the questions of hereditary determination and cultural determination is the more general question of how explicitly personality theorists attempt to relate their theory to the theorizing and empirical findings in neighboring disciplines. This might be referred to as a question of *interdisciplinary anchoring*. Some personality theorists are relatively content to deal with behavioral phenomena in terms of psychological concepts and findings with little or no attention to what is going on in neighboring disciplines. Others feel that psychological theorizing should lean heavily upon the formulations and findings of other disciplines. The "other-oriented" personality psychologists can be neatly divided into two basic types: those who look toward the natural sciences (biology, physiology, neurology, genetics) for guidance and those who look toward the social sciences (sociology, anthropology, economics, history) for guidance.

Theories of personality show a great deal of variation in *the number of motivational concepts* they employ. In some cases one or two such concepts are considered to lie at the base of all behavior; for other theories there is an extremely large number of hypothesized motives; and for still others the number is theoretically limitless. There is also considerable difference between theories in how much attention is paid to primary or innate motives as opposed to secondary or acquired motives. Further, some theories provide a relatively detailed picture of the process whereby acquired motives develop while others show very little interest in the derivation or acquisition of motives.

Closely associated with the multiplicity of motives utilized by the theory is its preference for what Gordon Allport has referred to as *simple and sovereign mechanisms* rather than pluralistic mechanisms. The primary issue here is whether behavior is to be understood largely by means of a single overarching principle (for example, law of effect, functional autonomy, striving for superiority) or whether a large number of related principles are necessary to shed much light on human behavior. As we will observe, current theories of personality show substantial variation in their complexity and the extent to which they invoke multiple mechanisms.

A further respect in which personality theories show considerable variation is the extent to which they deal with evaluative or *normative aspects of behavior*. Some theorists provide a rich description of the positive or ideal components of personality while others limit themselves to an objective or factual description with no effort to indicate the positive and negative or even the normal and abnormal. Some theorists are much concerned with the characteristics of the mature or ideal person while others are reluctant to consider one form of adjustment as necessarily superior to another.

Some personality theories are derived from and have great relevance for the description of *abnormal or pathological behavior*. Other theories and theorists are focused on the normal or better-than-normal. Clearly those theories whose origins lie in psychiatric clinics, counselling centers, and therapists' offices tend to have more to say about deviant or abnormal behavior while those that derive more heavily from the study of children and college students are more descriptive and representative of the relatively normal range of personality.

We have now completed our list of dimensions for the comparison of theories of personality but we hope readers will not put them from their minds. The very brief guide provided here can be given richer meaning and greater significance if these issues are considered while reading the chapters describing the individual theories of personality. It will also become clear that the most distinctive features of these theories have evolved from decisions concerning the issues we have just discussed. In the final chapter we shall reconsider these dimensions in the light of the specific theories of personality that by then will have been arrayed.

This brings us to the close of our introductory discussion and we can now proceed to the essence of this volume—the theories of personality themselves. If the reader is to retain a lone thought from what has been said to this point, let it be the simple impression that personality theories are attempts to formulate or represent significant aspects of human behavior and that the fruitfulness of these attempts is to be judged primarily by how effectively they serve as a spur to research.

BIBLIOGRAPHY

Allport, G. W. *Personality: a psychological interpretation*. New York: Holt, 1937.

Allport, G. W. *Pattern and growth in personality*. New York: Holt, Rinehart and Winston, 1961.

Boring, E. G. *A history of experimental psychology*. 2nd ed. New York: Appleton-Century-Crofts, 1950.

Byrne, D. *An introduction to personality*. Englewood Cliffs, N.J.: Prentice-Hall, 1966.

Carlson, R. Measurement of personality traits: theory and technique. In P. H. Mussen and M. R. Rosenzweig (Eds.), *Annual review of psychology, Vol. 26,* Stanford, Calif., Annual Reviews, 1975, pp. 393–414.

Conant, J. B. *On understanding science*. New Haven: Yale Univ. Press, 1947.

Dahlstrom, W. G. Personality. In P. H. Mussen and M. R. Rosenzweig (Eds.), *Annual review of psychology, Vol. 21.* Stanford, Calif.: Annual Reviews, 1970, pp. 1–48.

Edwards, A. L., and Abbott, R. D. Measurement of personality traits: theory and technique. In P. H. Mussen and M. R. Rosenzweig (Eds.), *Annual review of psychology, Vol. 24,* Stanford, Calif.: Annual Reviews, 1973, pp. 241–278.

Feigl, H., and Brodbeck, May. *Readings in the philosophy of science*. New York: Appleton-Century-Crofts, 1953.

Feigl, H., and Sellars, W. *Readings in philosophical analysis*. New York: Appleton-Century-Crofts, 1949.

Frank P. *Modern science and its philosophy*. Cambridge, Mass.: Harvard Univ. Press, 1949.

Geen, G. *Personality: the skein of behavior*. St. Louis, Mo.: Mosby, 1976.

Hanson, N. R. *Patterns of discovery*. Cambridge, Eng.: Cambridge Univ. Press, 1958.

Hempel, C. G. *Fundamentals of concept formation in empirical science*. Chicago: Univ. of Chicago Press, 1952.

Holzman, P. S. Personality. In M. R. Rosenzweig and L. W. Porter (Eds.), *Annual review of psychology, Vol. 25,* Stanford, Calif.: Annual Reviews, 1974.

Kuhn, T. S. *The structure of scientific revolutions.* Chicago: Univ. of Chicago Press, 1962.

Lakatos, I., and Musgrave, A. E. (Eds.). *Criticism and the growth of knowledge.* Cambridge: Cambridge Univ. Press, 1970.

McDougall, W. *An introduction to social psychology.* Boston: Luce, 1908.

Maddi, R. *Personality theories: a comparative analysis,* 3rd ed. Homewood, Ill.: Dorsey Press, 1976.

Mischel, W. *Introduction to personality,* 2nd ed. New York: Holt, Rinehart & Winston, 1976.

Phares, E. J., and Lamiell, J. T. Measurement of personality traits: theory and technique. In M. R. Rosenzweig and L. W. Porter (Eds.), *Annual review of psychology, Vol. 28,* Stanford, Calif.: Annual Reviews, 1977, pp. 113–140.

Sanford, N. Personality: its place in psychology. In S. Koch (Ed.) *Psychology: a study of a science. Vol. 5.* New York: McGraw-Hill, 1963, pp. 488–579.

Sarason, I. G. *Personality: an objective approach.* New York: Wiley, 1966.

Sarason, I. G., and Smith, R. E. Personality. In P. H. Mussen and M. R. Rosenzweig (Eds.), *Annual review of psychology, Vol. 22,* Stanford, Calif.: Annual Reviews, 1971, pp. 393–446.

Sarnoff, I. *Personality dynamics and development.* New York: Wiley, 1962.

Sechrest, L. Measurement of personality traits: theory and technique. In M. R. Rosenzweig and L. W. Porter (Eds.), *Annual review of psychology, Vol. 27,* Stanford, Calif.: Annual Reviews, 1976, pp. 1–28.

Singer, J. L., and Singer, D. G. Personality. In P. H. Mussen and M. R. Rosenzweig (Eds.), *Annual review of psychology, Vol. 23,* Stanford, Calif.: Annual Reviews, 1972, pp. 375–412.

Suppe, F. *The structure of scientific theories,* Urbana, Ill.: Univ. of Illinois Press, 1974.

Turner, M. *Philosophy and the science of behavior.* New York: Appleton-Century-Crofts, 1967.

FREUD'S CLASSICAL PSYCHOANALYTIC THEORY

2

When psychology emerged as an independent scientific discipline in Germany during the middle of the nineteenth century, it defined its task as the analysis of consciousness in the normal, adult human being. It conceived of consciousness as being made up of structural elements that were closely correlated with processes in the sense organs. Visual sensations of color, for example, were correlated with photochemical changes in the retina of the eye, and tones with events taking place in the inner ear. Complex experiences resulted from the joining together of a number of elementary sensations, images, and feelings. The task of psychology was to discover the basic elements of consciousness and to determine how they formed compounds. Psychology was often referred to as mental chemistry.

Objections to this kind of psychology came from many directions and for a variety of reasons. There were those who opposed the exclusive emphasis on structure and who insisted with considerable vigor that the outstanding characteristics of the conscious mind are its active processes and not its passive contents. Sensing and not sensations, thinking and not ideas, imagining and not images—these processes, it was asserted, should be the principal subject matter of the science of psychology. Others protested that conscious experience could not be dissected without destroying the very essence of experience, namely, its quality of wholeness. Direct awareness, they said, consists of patterns or configurations, and not of elements joined together. Another large and vocal group asserted that mind is not amenable to investigation by the methods of science because it is too private and too subjective. They urged instead that psychology be defined as the science of behavior.

Freud's attack upon the traditional psychology of consciousness came from quite a different direction. He likened the mind to an iceberg in which the smaller part showing above the surface of the water represents the region of consciousness while the much larger mass below the water level represents the region of unconsciousness. In this vast domain of the unconscious are to be found the urges, the passions, the repressed ideas and feelings—a great underworld of vital, unseen forces that exercise an imperious control over the conscious thoughts and deeds of individuals. From this point of view, a psychology that limits itself to the analysis of consciousness is wholly inadequate for understanding the underlying motives of human behavior.

For over forty years, Freud explored the unconscious by the method of free association and developed what is generally regarded as the first comprehensive theory of personality. He mapped the contours of its topography, penetrated to the headwaters of its stream of energy, and charted the lawful course of its growth. By performing these incredible feats, he became one of the most controversial and influential figures in modern times. (For an account of the status of the unconscious before Freud see Whyte, 1962.)

Sigmund Freud was born in Moravia, May 6, 1856, and died in London, September 23, 1939. For nearly eighty years, however, he resided in Vienna and left that city only when the Nazis overran Austria. As a young man he decided that he wanted to be a scientist and with this goal in mind he entered the medical school of the University of Vienna in 1873 from which he graduated eight years later. Freud never intended to practice medicine but the scanty rewards of scientific work, the limited opportunities for academic advancement for a Jew, and the needs of a growing family forced him to enter private practice. In spite of his practice, he found time for research and writing, and his accomplishments as a medical investigator earned him a solid reputation.

Freud's interest in neurology caused him to specialize in the treatment of nervous disorders, a branch of medicine that had lagged behind in the forward march of the healing arts during the nineteenth century. In order to improve his technical skills Freud studied for a year with the famous French psychiatrist, Jean Charcot, who was using hypnosis in the treatment of hysteria. Although Freud tried hypnosis with his patients, he was not impressed by its efficacy. Con-

Sigmund Freud

sequently, when he heard about a new method that had been devised by a Viennese physician, Joseph Breuer, a method by which the patient was cured of symptoms by talking about them, he tried it out and found it effective. Breuer and Freud collaborated in writing up some of their cases of hysteria that had been treated by the talking-out technique (1895).

However, the two men soon parted company over the importance of the sexual factor in hysteria. Freud felt that sexual conflicts were the cause of hysteria while Breuer held a more conservative view. Thereafter, Freud worked pretty much alone developing the ideas that were to form the foundation of psychoanalytic theory and which culminated in the publication of his first great work, *The interpretation of dreams* (1900). Other books and articles soon brought his views to the attention of physicians and scientists throughout the world, and it was not long before Freud was surrounded by a group of disciples from various countries, among them Ernest Jones of England, Carl Jung of Zurich, A. A. Brill of New York, Sandor Ferenczi of Budapest, Karl Abraham of Berlin, and Alfred Adler of Vienna. Jung and Adler later withdrew from the circle and developed rival viewpoints.

It is impossible within the brief space permitted us to cover even the highlights of Freud's intellectual and personal life: the early years as a

Freud's consulting room.

medical student and investigator; the decisive influence of the great German physiologist, Ernst Brücke, who was one of the leaders in the Helmholtz School of Medicine and from whom Freud learned to regard the individual as a dynamic system subject to the laws of nature (Amacher, 1965); his marriage to Martha Bernays and his lifelong devotion to her and to his six children, one of whom, Anna, followed her father's calling; the stimulating year with Charcot in Paris; his searching self-analysis begun in the 1890s and continuing throughout his life; the abortive attempt to account for psychological phenomena in terms of cerebral anatomy; the years of isolation from the medical community of Vienna; the invitation from G. Stanley Hall, the eminent American psychologist and president of Clark University, to address the meetings commemorating the founding of that university; the establishing of the International Psychoanalytic Association and the secession of such important disciples as Jung, Adler, Rank, and Stekel; the influence of World War I upon Freud's thinking and his thoroughgoing revision of the basic tenets of psychoanalytic theory; the application of psychoanalytic concepts in all fields of human endeavor; Freud's personal characteristics and the long torment of cancer of the jaw; and finally his melodramatic escape from the clutches of the Nazis. Fortunately, every nook and cranny of Freud's long life has been surveyed by the foremost English psychoanalyst, Ernest Jones, and brilliantly related in a three-volume biography (1953, 1955, 1957).

Nor does space permit us to list the published works of Freud. Beginning with *The interpretation of dreams* in 1900 and terminating in the posthumously published *Outline of psychoanalysis* in 1940, Freud's psychological writings fill twenty-four volumes in the definitive, standard English edition (1953–1974). For the reader who is unfamiliar with Freud's theory of personality, the following books are recommended: *The interpretation of dreams* (1900), *The psychopathology of everyday life* (1901), *General introductory lectures on psycho-analysis* (1917), *New introductory lectures on psychoanalysis* (1933), and *An outline of psychoanalysis* (1940).

In the following account of Freud's ideas we shall have to limit ourselves to those matters that pertain to Freud's theory of personality, and exclude from consideration the psychoanalytic theory of neurosis, which, in any event, has been covered so well by Otto Fenichel (1945), the techniques of psychoanalysis, and the far-flung applications of Freudian psychology in the social sciences (see Hall and Lindzey, 1968), the arts, and the humanities. Nor shall we be able to take notice of the evolution of Freud's thinking with respect to the basic concepts of his personality theory; it will have to suffice to present Freud's final word on such concepts as we shall discuss. In the next chapter, we will discuss some of the additions to and modifications of Freud's classical theory by his followers. The dissenting theories of Jung and Adler who started out as proponents of psychoanalysis are presented in Chapters 4 and 5.

THE STRUCTURE OF PERSONALITY

The personality is made up of three major systems: the *id,* the *ego,* and the *superego*. Although each of these provinces of the total personality has its own functions, properties, components, operating principles, dynamisms, and mechanisms, they interact so closely with one another that it is difficult if not impossible to disentangle their effects and weigh their relative contribution to human behavior. Behavior is nearly always the product of an interaction among these three systems; rarely does one system operate to the exclusion of the other two.

The Id

The id is the original system of the personality; it is the matrix within which the ego and the superego become differentiated. The id consists of everything psychological that is inherited and that is present at birth, including the instincts. It is the reservoir of psychic energy and furnishes all the power for the operation of the other two systems. It is in close touch with the bodily processes from which it derives its energy. Freud called the id the "true psychic reality" because it represents the inner world of subjective experience and has no knowledge of objective reality. (For a discussion of the id, see Schur, 1966.)

The id cannot tolerate increases of energy that are experienced as uncomfortable states of tension. Consequently, when the tension level of the organism is raised, either as a result of external stimulation or of internally produced excitations, the id functions in such a manner as to discharge the tension immediately and return the organism to a comfortably constant and low energy level. This principle of tension reduction by which the id operates is called the *pleasure principle*.

To accomplish its aim of avoiding pain and obtaining pleasure, the id has at its command two processes. These are *reflex action* and the *primary process*. Reflex actions are inborn and automatic reactions like sneezing and blinking; they usually reduce tension immediately. The organism is equipped with a number of such reflexes for dealing with relatively simple forms of excitation. The primary process involves a somewhat more complicated psychological reaction. It attempts to discharge tension by forming an image of an object that will remove the tension. For example, the primary process provides the hungry person with a mental picture of food. This hallucinatory experience in which the desired object is present in the form of a memory image is called *wish-fulfillment*. The best example of the primary process in normal people is the nocturnal dream, which Freud believed always represents the fulfillment or attempted fulfillment of a wish. The hallucinations and visions of psychotic patients are also examples of the primary process. Autistic or wishful thinking is highly colored by the action of the primary process. These wish-fulfilling mental images are the only reality that the id knows.

Obviously, the primary process by itself is not capable of reducing tension. The hungry person cannot eat mental images of food. Consequently, a new or secondary psychological process develops, and when this occurs the structure of the second system of the personality, the ego, begins to take form.

The ego comes into existence because the needs of the organism   *The Ego* require appropriate transactions with the objective world of reality. The hungry person has to seek, find, and eat food before the tension of hunger can be eliminated. This means that the person has to learn to differentiate between a memory image of food and an actual perception of food as it exists in the outer world. Having made this crucial differentiation, it is then necessary to convert the image into a perception, which is accomplished by locating food in the environment. In other words, the person matches the memory image of food with the sight or smell of food as they come to the person through the senses. The basic distinction between the id and the ego is that the id knows only the subjective reality of the mind whereas the ego distinguishes between things in the mind and things in the external world.

The ego is said to obey the *reality principle* and to operate by means of the *secondary process*. The aim of the reality principle is to prevent the discharge of tension until an object that is appropriate for the satisfaction of the need has been discovered. The reality principle suspends the pleasure principle temporarily although the pleasure principle is eventually served when the needed object is found and the tension is thereby reduced. The reality principle asks in effect whether an experience is true or false—that is, whether it has external existence or not—while the pleasure principle is only interested in whether the experience is painful or pleasurable.

The secondary process is realistic thinking. By means of the secondary process the ego formulates a plan for the satisfaction of the need and then tests this plan, usually by some kind of action, to see whether or not it will work. The hungry person thinks where he or she may find food and then proceeds to look in that place. This is called *reality testing*. In order to perform its role efficiently the ego has control over all the cognitive and intellectual functions; these higher mental processes are placed at the service of the secondary process.

The ego is said to be the executive of the personality because it controls the gateways to action, selects the features of the environment to which it will respond, and decides what instincts will be satisfied and in what manner. In performing these highly important executive functions, the ego has to try to integrate the often conflicting demands of the id, the superego, and the external world. This is not an easy task and often places a great strain upon the ego.

It should be kept in mind, however, that the ego is the organized portion of the id, that it comes into existence in order to forward the aims of the id and not to frustrate them, and that all of its power is derived from the id. It has no existence apart from the id, and it never becomes completely independent of the id. Its principal role is to mediate between the instinctual requirements of the organism and the conditions of the surrounding environment; its superordinate objectives are to maintain the life of the individual and to see that the species is reproduced.

The Superego The third and last system of personality to be developed is the superego. It is the internal representative of the traditional values and ideals of society as interpreted to the child by its parents, and enforced by means of a system of rewards and punishments imposed upon the child. The superego is the moral arm of personality; it represents the ideal rather than the real and it strives for perfection rather than pleasure. Its main concern is to decide whether something is right or wrong so that it can act in accordance with the moral standards authorized by the agents of society.

The superego as the internalized moral arbiter of conduct develops in response to the rewards and punishments meted out by the parents. To obtain the rewards and avoid the punishments, the child learns to guide its behavior along the lines laid down by the parents. Whatever they say is improper and punish the child for doing tends to become incorporated into its *conscience,* which is one of the two subsystems of the superego. Whatever they approve of and reward the child for doing tends to become incorporated into its *ego-ideal,* the other subsystem of the superego. The mechanism by which this incorporation takes place is called *introjection.* The child takes in or introjects the moral standards of the parents. The conscience punishes the person by making him or her feel guilty, the ego-ideal rewards the person by making him or her feel proud. With the formation of the superego, self-control is substituted for parental control.

The main functions of the superego are (1) to inhibit the impulses of the id, particularly those of a sexual or aggressive nature, since these are the impulses whose expression is most highly condemned by society, (2) to persuade the ego to substitute moralistic goals for realistic ones, and (3) to strive for perfection. That is, the superego is inclined to oppose both the id and the ego, and to make the world over into its own image. However, it is like the id in being nonrational and like the ego in attempting to exercise control over the instincts. Unlike the ego, the superego does not merely postpone instinctual gratification; it tries to block it permanently. (A historical analysis of the superego has been made by Turiell, 1967.)

In concluding this brief description of the three systems of the personality, it should be pointed out that the id, ego, and superego are not to be thought of as manikins that operate the personality. They are merely names for various psychological processes that obey different system principles. Under ordinary circumstances these different principles do not collide with one another nor do they work at cross purposes. On the contrary, they work together as a team under the administrative leadership of the ego. The personality normally functions as a whole rather than as three separate segments. In a very general way, the id may be thought of as the biological component of personality, the ego as the psychological component, and the superego as the social component.

THE DYNAMICS OF PERSONALITY

Freud was brought up under the influence of the strongly deterministic and positivistic philosophy of nineteenth century science and regarded the human organism as a complex energy system, which derives its energy from the food it consumes and expends it for such various purposes as circulation, respiration, muscular exercise, perceiving, thinking, and remembering, Freud saw no reason to assume that the energy that furnishes the power for breathing or digesting is any different, save in form, from the energy that furnishes the power for thinking and remembering. After all, as nineteenth century physicists were firmly insisting, energy has to be defined in terms of the work it performs. If the work consists of a psychological activity such as thinking, then it is perfectly legitimate, Freud believed, to call this form of energy *psychic energy*. According to the doctrine of the conservation of energy, energy may be transformed from one state into another state but can never be lost from the total cosmic system; it follows from this that psychic energy may be transformed into physiological energy and vice versa. The point of contact or bridge between the energy of the body and that of the personality is the id and its instincts.

Instinct

An instinct is defined as an inborn psychological representation of an inner somatic source of excitation. The psychological representation is called a *wish,* and the bodily excitation from which it stems is called a *need.* Thus, the state of hunger may be described in physiological terms as a condition of nutritional deficit in the tissues of the body whereas psychologically it is represented as a wish for food. The wish acts as a motive for behavior. The hungry person seeks food. Instincts are considered therefore to be the propelling factors of personality. Not only do they drive behavior but they also determine the direction that the behavior will take. In other words, an instinct exercises selective control over conduct by increasing one's sensitivity for particular kinds of stimulation. The hungry person is more sensitive to food stimuli, the sexually aroused person is more likely to respond to erotic stimuli.

Parenthetically, it may be observed that the organism can also be activated by stimuli from the external world. Freud felt, however, that these environmental sources of excitation play a less important role in the dynamics of personality than do the inborn instincts. In general, external stimuli make fewer demands upon the individual and require less complicated forms of adjustment than needs. One can always flee from an external stimulus but it is imposible to run away from a need. Although Freud relegated environmental stimuli to a secondary place, he did not deny their importance under certain conditions. For example, excessive stimulation during the early years of life when the immature ego lacks the capacity for binding large amounts of free energy (tension) may have drastic effects upon the personality, as we shall see when we consider Freud's theory of anxiety.

An instinct is a quantum of psychic energy or as Freud put it "a measure of the demand made upon the mind for work" (1905a, p. 168). All the instincts taken together constitute the sum total of psychic energy available to the personality. As previously pointed out, the id is the reservoir of this energy and it is also the seat of the instincts. The id may be considered to be a dynamo that furnishes psychological power for running the manifold operations of personality. This power is derived, of course, from the metabolic processes of the body.

An instinct has four characteristic features: a *source,* an *aim,* an *object,* and an *impetus.* The source has already been defined as a bodily condition or a need. The aim is the removal of the bodily excitation. The aim of the hunger instinct, for example, is to abolish the nutritional deficiency, which is accomplished, of course, by eating food. All of the activity that intervenes between the appearance of the wish and its fulfillment is subsumed under the heading of *object.* That is, object refers not only to the particular thing or condition that will satisfy the need but also includes all the behavior that takes place in securing the necessary thing or condition. For instance, when a person is hungry he or she usually has to perform a number of actions before reaching the final goal of eating.

The impetus of an instinct is its force or strength, which is determined by the intensity of the underlying need. As the nutritional deficiency becomes greater, up to the point where physical weakness sets in, the force of the instinct becomes correspondingly greater.

Let us briefly consider some of the implications in this way of conceptualizing an instinct. In the first place, the model that Freud provides is a tension-reduction one. The behavior of a person is activated by internal irritants and subsides as soon as an appropriate action removes or diminishes the irritation. This means that the aim of an instinct is essentially *regressive* in character since it returns the person to a prior state, one that existed before the instinct appeared. This prior state to which the personality returns is one of relative quiescence. An instinct is also said to be *conservative* because its aim is to conserve the equilibrium of the organism by abolishing disturbing excitations. Thus, we can picture an instinct as a process that repeats as often as it appears a cycle of events starting with excitement and terminating with repose. Freud called this aspect of an instinct *repetition compulsion*. The personality is compelled to repeat over and over again the inevitable cycle from excitation to quiescence. (The term repetition compulsion is also employed to describe perseverative behavior that occurs when the means adopted for satisfying the need are not completely appropriate. A child may perseverate in sucking its thumb when it is hungry.)

According to Freud's theory of instincts, the source and aim of an instinct remain constant throughout life, unless the source is changed or eliminated by physical maturation. New instincts may appear as new bodily needs develop. In contrast to this constancy of source and aim, the object or means by which the person attempts to satisfy the need can and does vary considerably during the lifetime of the person. This variation in object choice is possible because psychic energy is *displaceable;* it can be expended in various ways. Consequently, if one object is not available either by virtue of its absence or by virtue of barriers within the personality, energy can be invested in another object. If that object proves also to be inaccessible another displacement can occur, and so forth, until an available object is found. In other words, objects can be substituted for one another, which is definitely not the case with either the source or the aim of an instinct.

When the energy of an instinct is more or less permanently invested in a substitute object, that is, one that is not the original and innately determined object, the resulting behavior is said to be an *instinct derivative*. Thus, if the first sexual object choice of the baby is the manipulation of its own sex organs and it is forced to give up this pleasure in favor of more innocuous forms of bodily stimulation such as sucking the thumb or playing with the toes, the substitute activities are derivatives of the sexual instinct. The aim of the sexual instnct does not change one whit when a substitution takes place; the goal sought is still that of sexual gratification.

The displacement of energy from one object to another is the most important feature of personality dynamics. It accounts for the apparent plasticity of human nature and the remarkable versatility of human behavior. Practically all of the adult person's interests, preferences, tastes, habits, and attitudes represent the displacements of energy from original instinctual object-choices. They are almost all instinct derivatives. Freud's theory of motivation was based solidly on the assumption that the instincts are *the* sole energy sources for human behavior. We shall have a great deal more to say about displacement in subsequent sections of this chapter.

NUMBER AND KINDS OF INSTINCTS. Freud did not attempt to draw up a list of instincts because he felt that not enough was known about the bodily states upon which the instincts depend. The identification of these organic needs is a job for the physiologist, not the psychologist. Although Freud did not pretend to know how many instincts there are, he did assume that they could all be classified under two general headings, the *life* instincts and the *death* instincts.

The life instincts serve the purpose of individual survival and racial propagation. Hunger, thirst, and sex fall in this category. The form of energy by which the life instincts perform their work is called *libido*.

The life instinct to which Freud paid the greatest attention is that of sex, and in the early years of psychoanalysis almost everything the person did was attributed to this ubiquitous drive (Freud, 1905a). Actually, the sex instinct is not one instinct but many. That is, there are a number of separate bodily needs that give rise to erotic wishes. Each of these wishes has its source in a different bodily region referred to collectively as *erogenous zones*. An erogenous zone is a part of the skin or mucous membrane that is extremely sensitive to irritation and which when manipulated in a certain way removes the irritation and produces pleasurable feelings. The lips and oral cavity constitute one such erogenous zone, the anal region another, and the sex organs a third. Sucking produces oral pleasure, elimination anal pleasure, and massaging or rubbing genital pleasure. In childhood, the sexual instincts are relatively independent of one another but when the person reaches puberty they tend to fuse together and to serve jointly the aim of reproduction.

The death instincts, or, as Freud sometimes called them, the destructure instincts, perform their work much less conspicuously than the life instincts, and for this reason little is known about them, other than that they inevitably accomplish their mission. Every person does eventually die, a fact that caused Freud to formulate the famous dictum, "the goal of all life is death" (1920a, p. 38). Freud assumed specifically that the person has a wish, usually of course unconscious, to die. He did not attempt to identify the somatic sources of the death instincts although one may wish to speculate that they reside in the catabolic or breaking-down processes of the body. Nor did he assign a name to the energy by which the death instincts carry on their work.

Freud's assumption of a death wish is based upon the constancy principle as formulated by Fechner. This principle asserts that all living processes tend to return to the stability of the inorganic world. In *Beyond the pleasure principle* (1920a), Freud made the following argument in favor of the concept of the death wish. Living matter evolved by the action of cosmic forces upon inorganic matter. These changes were highly unstable at first and quickly reverted to their prior inorganic state. Gradually, however, the length of life increased because of evolutionary changes in the world but these unstable animate forms always eventually regressed to the stability of inanimate matter. With the development of reproductive mechanisms, living things were able to reproduce their own kind, and did not have to depend upon being created out of the inorganic world. Yet even with this advance the individual member of a species inevitably obeyed the constancy principle, since this was the principle that governed its existence when it was endowed with life. Life, Freud said, is but a roundabout way to death. Disturbed out of its stable existence, organic matter strives to return to a quiescent state. The death wish in the human being is the psychological representation of the constancy principle.

An important derivative of the death instincts is the *aggressive drive*. Aggressiveness is self-destruction turned outward against substitute objects. A person fights with other people and is destructive because the death wish is blocked by the forces of the life instincts and by other obstacles in the personality that counteract the death instincts. It took the Great War of 1914–1918 to convince Freud that aggression was as sovereign a motive as sex. (This view that the Great War stimulated Freud's interest in aggression has been disputed by Stepansky, 1977.)

The life and death instincts and their derivatives may fuse together, neutralize each other, or replace one another. Eating, for example, represents a fusion of hunger and destructiveness that is satisfied by biting, chewing, and swallowing food. Love, a derivative of the sex instinct, can neutralize hate, a derivative of the death instinct. Or love can replace hate, and hate love.

Since the instincts contain all the energy by which the three systems of the personality perform their work, let us turn now to consider the ways in which the id, ego, and superego gain control over and utilize psychic energy.

The Distribution and Utilization of Psychic Energy

The dynamics of personality consists of the way in which psychic energy is distributed and used by the id, ego, and superego. Since the amount of energy is a limited quantity, there is competition among the three systems for the energy that is available. One system gains control over the available energy at the expense of the other two systems. As one system becomes stronger the other two necessarily become weaker, unless new energy is added to the total system.

Originally the id possesses all of the energy and uses it for reflex action and wish-fulfillment by means of the primary process. Both of these activities are in the direct service of the pleasure principle by which the id operates. The investment of energy in an action or image that will gratify an instinct is called an instinctual *object-choice* or *object-cathexis*.

The energy of the id is in a very fluid state, which means that it can easily be shunted from one action or image to another action or image. The displaceable quality of this instinctual energy is due to the id's inability to form fine discriminations between objects. Objects that are different are treated as though they were the same. The hungry baby, for instance, will take up almost anything that it can hold and put it to its lips.

Since the ego has no source of power of its own, it has to borrow it from the id. The diversion of energy from the id into the processes that make up the ego is accomplished by a mechanism known as *identification*. This is one of the most important concepts in Freudian psychology, and one of the most difficult to comprehend. It will be recalled from a previous discussion that the id does not distinguish between subjective imagery and objective reality. When it cathects an image of an object it is the same as cathecting the object itself. However, since a mental image cannot satisfy a need, the person is forced to differentiate between the world of the mind and the outer world. He has to learn the difference between a memory or idea of an object that is not present and a sensory impression or perception of an object which is present. Then, in order to satisfy a need, the person must learn to match what is in his or her mind with its counterpart in the external world by means of the secondary process. This matching of a mental representation with physical reality, of something that is in the mind with something that is in the outer world, is what is meant by identification.

Since the id makes no distinction between any of the contents of the mind, whether they be perceptions, memory images, ideas, or hallucinations, a cathexis may be formed for a realistic perception as readily as for a wish-fulfilling memory image. In this way, energy is diverted from the purely subjective psychological processes of the id into the objective, logical, ideational processes of the ego. In both cases, energy is used for strictly psychological purposes, but in the case of the id no distinction is made between the mental symbol and the physical referent, whereas in the case of the ego this distinction is made. The ego attempts to make the symbol accurately represent the referent. In other words, identification enables the secondary process to supersede the primary process. Since the secondary process is so much more successful in reducing tensions, more and more ego cathexes are formed. Gradually the more efficient ego obtains a virtual monopoly over the store of psychic energy. This monoply is only relative, however, because if the ego fails to satisfy the instincts, the id reasserts its power.

Once the ego has trapped enough energy, it can use it for other purposes than that of gratifying the instincts by means of the secondary process. Some of the energy is used to bring the various psychological processes such as perceiving, remembering, judging, discriminating, abstracting, generalizing, and reasoning to a higher level of development. Some of the energy has to be used by the ego to restrain the id from acting impulsively and irrationally. These restraining forces are known as *anticathexes* in contradistinction to the driving forces or cathexes. If the id becomes too threatening, the ego erects defenses against the id. These defense mechanisms, which will be discussed in a later section, may also be used to cope with the pressures of the superego upon the ego. Energy, of course, is required for the maintenance of these defenses.

Ego energy may also be displaced to form new object-cathexes, so that a whole network of derived interests, attitudes, and preferences is formed within the ego. These ego-cathexes may not directly satisfy the basic needs of the organism but they are connected by associative links with objects that do. The energy of the hunger drive, for example, may fan out to include such cathexes as an interest in collecting recipes, visiting unusual restaurants, and selling chinaware. This spreading of cathexes into channels that are only remotely connected with the original object of an instinct is made possible by the greater efficiency of the ego in performing its fundamental job of gratifying the instincts. The ego has a surplus of energy to use for other purposes.

Finally, the ego as the executive of the personality organization uses energy to effect an integration among the three systems. The purpose of this integrative function of the ego is to produce an inner harmony within the personality so that the ego's transactions with the environment may be made smoothly and effectively.

The mechanism of identification also accounts for the energizing of the superego system. This, too, is a complex matter and takes place in the following way. Among the first object-cathexes of the baby are those of the parents. These cathexes develop early and become very firmly entrenched because the baby is completely dependent upon its parents or parent-substitutes for the satisfaction of needs. The parents also play the role of disciplinary agents; they teach the child the moral code and the traditional values and ideals of the society in which the child is raised. They do this by rewarding the child when it does the right thing and punishing it when it does the wrong thing. A reward is anything that reduces tension or promises to do so. A piece of candy, a smile, or a kind word may be an effective reward. A punishment is anything that increases tension. It may be a spanking, a disapproving look, or a denial of some pleasure. Thus, the child learns to identify, that is, to match its behavior with the sanctions and prohibitions laid down by the parents. The child introjects the moral imperatives of its parents by virtue of the original cathexes it has for them as need-satisfying agents. It cathects their ideals and these become its ego-ideal; it cathects their prohibitions and these become its conscience. Thus, the superego gains access to the reservoir of energy in the id by means of the child's identification with the parents.

The work performed by the superego is often, although not always, in direct opposition to the impulses of the id. This is the case because the moral code represents society's attempt to control and even to inhibit the expression of the primitive drives, especially those of sex and aggression. Being good usually means being obedient and not saying or doing "dirty" things. Being bad means being disobedient, rebellious, and lustful. The virtuous person inhibits his or her impulses, the sinful person indulges them. However, the superego can sometimes be corrupted by the id. This happens, for example, when a person in a fit of moralistic fervor takes aggressive measures against those considered wicked and sinful. The expression of aggression in such instances is cloaked by the mantle of righteous indignation.

Once the energy furnished by the instincts has been channeled into the ego and the superego by the mechanism of identification, a complicated interplay of driving and restraining forces become possible. The id, it will be recalled, possesses only driving forces or cathexes whereas the energy of the ego and the superego is used both to forward and to frustrate the aims of the instincts. The ego has to check both the id and the superego if it is to govern the personality wisely, yet it must have enough energy left over to engage in necessary intercourse with the external world. If the id retains control over a large share of the energy, the behavior of the person will tend to be impulsive and primitive in character. On the other hand, if the superego gains control of an undue amount of energy, the functioning of the personality will be dominated by moralistic considerations rather than by realistic ones. The anticathexes of the conscience may tie up the ego in moral knots and prevent action of any sort, while the cathexes of the ego-ideal may set such high standards for the ego that the person is being continually frustrated and may eventually develop a depressing sense of failure.

Moreover, sudden and unpredictable shifts of energy from one system to another and from cathexes to anticathexes are common, especially during the first two decades of life before the distribution of energy has become more or less stabilized. These shifts of energy keep the personality in a state of dynamic flux. Freud was pessimistic about the chances of psychology ever becoming a very exact science because, as he pointed out, even a very small change in the distribution of energy might tip the scale in favor of one form of behavior rather than its opposite (Freud, 1920b). Who can say whether the person poised on the window ledge is going to jump or not, or whether the batter is going to strike out or hit a winning home run?

In the final analysis, the dynamics of personality consist of the interplay of the driving forces, cathexes, and the restraining forces, anticathexes. All the conflicts within the personality may be reduced to the opposition of these two sets of forces. All prolonged tension is due to the counteraction of a driving force by a restraining force. Whether it be an anticathexis of the ego opposed to a cathexis of the id or an anticathexis of the superego opposed to a cathexis of the ego, the result in terms of tension is the same. As Freud was fond of saying, psychoanalysis is "a dynamic [conception], which traces mental life back to an interplay between forces that favour or inhibit one another" (1910b, p. 213).

Anxiety

The dynamics of personality is to a large extent governed by the necessity for gratifying one's needs by means of transactions with objects in the external world. The surrounding environment provides the hungry organism with food, the thirsty one with water. In addition to its role as the source of supplies, the external world plays another part in shaping the destiny of personality. The environment contains regions of danger and insecurity; it can threaten as well as satisfy. The environment has the power to produce pain and increase tension as well as to bring pleasure and reduce tension. It disturbs as well as comforts.

The individual's customary reaction to external threats of pain and destruction with which it is not prepared to cope is to become afraid.

The threatened person is ordinarily a fearful person. Overwhelmed by excessive stimulation that the ego is unable to bring under control, the ego becomes flooded with anxiety.

Freud recognized three types of anxiety: *reality* anxiety, *neurotic* anxiety, and *moral* anxiety or feelings of guilt (1926b). The basic type is reality anxiety or fear of real dangers in the external world; from it are derived the other two types. Neurotic anxiety is the fear that the instincts will get out of control and cause the person to do something for which he or she will be punished. Neurotic anxiety is not so much a fear of the instincts themselves as it is a fear of the punishment likely to ensue from instinctual gratification. Neurotic anxiety has a basis in reality, because the world as represented by the parents and other authorities does punish the child for impulsive actions. Moral anxiety is fear of the conscience. People with well-developed superegos tend to feel guilty when they do something or even think of doing something that is contrary to the moral code by which they have been raised. They are said to feel conscience-stricken. Moral anxiety also has a realistic basis; the person has been punished in the past for violating the moral code and may be punished again.

The function of anxiety is to warn the person of impending danger; it is a signal to the ego that unless appropriate measures are taken the danger may increase until the ego is overthrown. Anxiety is a state of tension; it is a drive like hunger or sex but instead of arising from internal tissue conditions it is produced originally by external causes. When anxiety is aroused it motivates the person to do something. He or she may flee from the threatening region, inhibit the dangerous impulse, or obey the voice of conscience.

Anxiety that cannot be dealt with by effective measures is said to be traumatic. It reduces the person to a state of infantile helplessness. In fact, the prototype of all later anxiety is the *birth trauma*. The neonate is bombarded with stimuli from the world for which it is not prepared and to which it cannot adapt. The baby needs a sheltered environment until its ego has had a chance to develop to the point where it can master strong stimuli from the environment. When the ego cannot cope with anxiety by rational methods it has to fall back upon unrealistic ones. These are the so-called *defense mechanisms* of the ego that will be discussed in the following section.

THE
DEVELOPMENT
OF PERSONALITY

Freud was probably the first psychological theorist to emphasize the developmental aspects of personality and in particular to stress the decisive role of the early years of infancy and childhood in laying down the basic character structure of the person. Indeed, Freud felt that personality was pretty well formed by the end of the fifth year, and that subsequent growth consisted for the most part of elaborating this basic structure. He arrived at this conclusion on the basis of his experiences with patients undergoing psychoanalysis. Inevitably, their mental explorations led them back to early childhood experiences that appeared to be decisive for the development of a neurosis later in life. Freud believed that "the child is father of the man." It is interesting in view of this strong preference for genetic explanations of adult behavior that Freud rarely studied young children directly. He preferred to reconstruct the past life of a person from evidence furnished by adult recollections.

Personality develops in response to four major sources of tension: (1) physiological growth processes, (2) frustrations, (3) conflicts, and (4) threats. As a direct consequence of increases in tension emanating from these sources, the person is forced to learn new methods of reducing tension. This learning is what is meant by personality development. (For a lucid discussion of Freud's theory of learning, see Hilgard and Bower, 1975.)

Identification and *displacement* are two methods by which the individual learns to resolve frustrations, conflicts, and anxieties.

Identification

This concept was introduced in an earlier section to help account for the formation of the ego and superego. In the present context, identification may be defined as the method by which a person takes over the features of another person and makes them a corporate part of his or her own personality. One learns to reduce tension by modeling one's behavior after that of someone else. Freud preferred the term *identification* to the more familiar *imitation* because he felt that imitation denotes a kind of superficial and transient copying behavior whereas he wanted a word that would convey the idea of a more or less permanent acquisition to personality.

We choose as models those who seem to be more successful in gratifying their needs than we are. The child identifies with its parents because they appear to be omnipotent, at least during the years of early childhood. As children grow older, they find other people to identify with whose accomplishments are more in line with their current wishes. Each period tends to have its own characteristic identification figures. Needless to say, most of this identification takes place unconsciously and not, as it may sound, with conscious intention.

It is not necessary for a person to identify with someone else in every respect. One usually selects and incorporates just those features that he or she believes will help achieve a desired goal. There is a good deal of trial and error in the identification process because one is usually not quite sure what it is about another person that accounts for their success. The ultimate test is whether the identification helps to reduce tension; if it does the quality is taken over, if it does not it is discarded. One may identify with animals, imaginary characters, institutions, abstract ideas, and inanimate objects as well as with other human beings.

Identification is also a method by which one may regain an object that has been lost. By identifying with a loved person who had died or from whom one has been separated, the lost person becomes reincarnated as an incorporated feature of one's personality. Children who have been rejected by their parents tend to form strong identifications with them in the hope of regaining their love. One may also identify with a person out of fear. The child identifies with the prohibitions of the parents in order to avoid punishment. This kind of identification is the basis for the formation of the superego.

The final personality structure represents an accumulation of numerous identifications made at various periods of the person's life, although the mother and father are probably the most important identification figures in anyone's life.

Displacement   When an original object-choice of an instinct is rendered inaccessible by external or internal barriers (anticathexes), a new cathexis is formed unless a strong repression occurs. If this new cathexis is also blocked, another displacement takes place, and so on, until an object is found that yields some relief for the pent-up tension. This object is then cathected until it loses its power to reduce tension, at which time another search for an appropriate goal object is instituted. Throughout the series of displacements that constitute, in such large measure, the development of personality, the source and aim of the instinct remain constant; it is only the object that varies.

A substitute object is rarely if ever as satisfying or tension-reducing as the original object, and the more dissimilar the substitute object is from the original one the less tension is reduced. As a consequence of numerous displacements, a pool of undischarged tension accumulates that acts as a permanent motivating force for behavior. The person is constantly seeking new and better ways of reducing tension. This accounts for the variability and diversity of behavior, as well as for human restlessness. On the other hand, the personality does become more or less stabilized with age owing to the compromises that are made between the urging forces of the instincts and the resistances of the ego and superego.

As we have written in another place (Hall, 1954):

Interests, attachments, and all the other forms of acquired motives endure because they are to some degree frustrating as well as satisfying. They persist because they fail to yield complete satisfaction. . . . Every compromise is at the same time a re-nunciation. A person gives up something that he really wants but cannot have, and accepts something second or third best that he can have (p. 104).

Freud pointed out that the development of civilization was made possible by the inhibition of primitive object-choices and the diversion of instinctual energy into socially acceptable and culturally creative channels (1930). A displacement that produces a higher cultural achievement is called a *sublimation*. Freud observed in this connection that Leonardo da Vinci's interest in painting Madonnas was a sublimated expression of a longing for intimacy with his mother from whom he had been separated at a tender age (1910a). Since sublimation does not result in complete satisfaction, any more than any displacement does, there is always some residual tension. This tension may discharge itself in the form of nervousness or restlessness, conditions which Freud pointed out were the price that humans paid for their civilized status (1908).

The direction taken by a displacement is determined by two factors. These are (1) the resemblance of the substitute object to the original one, and (2) the sanctions and prohibitions imposed by society. The factor of resemblance is actually the degree to which the two objects are identified in the mind of the person. Da Vinci painted Madonnas rather than peasant women or aristocrats because he conceived of his mother as resembling the Madonna more than any other type of woman. Society acting through the parents and other authority figures authorizes certain displacements and outlaws others. The child learns that it is permissible to suck a lollipop but not to suck its thumb.

The ability to form substitute object-cathexes is the most powerful mechanism for the development of personality. The compelx network of interests, preferences, values, attitudes, and attachments that characterize the personality of the adult human being is made possible by displacement. If psychic energy were not displaceable and distributive, there would be no development of personality. The person would be merely a mechanical robot driven to perform fixed patterns of behavior instinctually.

Under the pressure of excessive anxiety, the ego is sometimes forced to take extreme measures to relieve the pressure. These measures are called defense mechanisms. The principal defenses are repression, projection, reaction formation, fixation, and regression (Anna Freud, 1946). All defense mechanisms have two characteristics in common :

The Defense Mechanisms of the Ego

(1) they deny, falsify, or distort reality, and (2) they operate unconsciously so that the person is not aware of what is taking place.

REPRESSION. This is one of the earliest concepts of psychoanalysis. Before Freud arrived at his final formulation of personality theory in terms of the id, ego, and superego, he divided the mind into three regions: consciousness, preconsciousness, and unconsciousness. The preconscious consisted of psychological material that could become conscious when the need arose. Material in the unconscious, however, was regarded by Freud as being relatively inaccessible to conscious awareness; it was said to be in a state of repression.

When Freud revised his theory of personality, the concept of repression was retained as one of the defense mechanisms of the ego, (Gill, 1963, points out that Freud gave up a topography of the mind in terms of conscious, preconscious, and unconscious for a structural view in terms of id, ego, and superego because repression and what was repressed could not be in the same system. He assigned repression to the ego, and what was repressed to the id. See also, Arlow and Brenner, 1964). Repression is said to occur when an object-choice that arouses undue alarm is forced out of consciousness by an anticathexis. For example, a disturbing memory may be prevented from becoming conscious or a person may not see something that is in plain sight because the perception of it is repressed. Repression can even interfere with the normal functioning of the body. Someone may become sexually impotent because he is afraid of the sex impulse, or he may develop arthritis as a consequence of repressing feelings of hostility.

Repressions may force their way through the opposing anticathexes or they may find expression in the form of a displacement. If the displacement is to be successful in preventing the reawakening of anxiety it must be disguised in some suitable symbolic form. A son who has repressed his hostile feelings towards his father may express these hostile feelings against other symbols of authority.

Repressions once formed are difficult to abolish. The person must reassure himself that the danger no longer exists, but he cannot get such reassurance until the repression is lifted so that he can test reality. It is a vicious circle. That is why adults carry around with them a lot of childish fears; they never get a chance to discover that these fears have no basis in reality.

PROJECTION. Reality anxiety is usually easier for the ego to deal with than either neurotic or moral anxiety. Consequently, if the source of the anxiety can be attributed to the external world rather than to the individual's own primitive impulses or to the threats of conscience, the person is likely to achieve greater relief for the anxious condition. This mechanism by which neurotic or moral anxiety is converted into an objective fear is called projection. This conversion is easily made because the original source of both neurotic and moral anxiety is fear of punishment from an external agent. In projection, one simply says "She hates me" instead of "I hate her," or "He is persecuting me" instead of "My conscience is bothering me." Projection often serves a dual purpose. It reduces anxiety by substituting a lesser danger for a greater one, and it enables the projecting person to express his impulses under the guise of defending himself against his enemies.

REACTION FORMATION. This defensive measure involves the replacement in consciousness of an anxiety-producing impulse or feeling by its opposite. For example, hate is replaced by love. The original impulse still exists but it is glossed over or masked by one that does not cause anxiety.

The question often arises as to how a reaction formation may be distinguished from a genuine expression of an impulse or feeling. For instance, how can reactive love be differentiated from true love? Usually, a reaction formation is marked by extravagant showiness—the person protests too much—and by compulsiveness. Extreme forms of behavior of any kind usually denote a reaction formation. Sometimes the reaction formation succeeds in satisfying the original impulse that is being defended against, as when a mother smothers her child with affection and attention.

FIXATION AND REGRESSION. In the course of normal development, as we shall see in the next section, the personality passes through a series of rather well-defined stages until it reaches maturity. Each new step that is taken, however, entails a certain amount of frustration and anxiety and if these become too great, normal growth may be temporarily or permanently halted. In other words, the person may become fixated on one of the early stages of development because taking the next step is fraught with anxiety. The overly dependent child exemplifies defense by fixation; anxiety prevents it from learning how to become independent.

A closely related type of defense is that of regression. In this case, a person who encounters traumatic experiences retreats to an earlier stage of development. For example, a child who is frightened by the first day at school may indulge in infantile behavior, such as weeping, sucking the thumb, hanging onto the teacher, or hiding in a corner. A young married woman who has difficulties with her husband may return to the security of her parents' home, or a man who has lost his job may seek comfort in drink. The path of regression is usually determined by the earlier fixations of the person. That is, people tend to regress to a stage upon which they have been previously fixated. If they were overly dependent as children, they will be likely to become overly dependent again when their anxiety increases to an unbearable level.

Fixation and regression are ordinarily relative conditions; a person rarely fixates or regresses completely. Rather the personality tends to include infantilisms, that is, immature forms of behavior, and predispositions to display childish conduct when thwarted. Fixations and regressions are responsible for the unevenness in personality development.

Stages of Development

The child passes through a series of dynamically differentiated stages during the first five years of life, following which for a period of five or six years—the period of latency—the dynamics become more or less stabilized. With the advent of adolescence, the dynamics erupt again and then gradually settle down as the adolescent moves into adulthood. For Freud, *the first few years of life are decisive for the formation of personality.*

Each stage of development during the first five years is defined in terms of the modes of reaction of a particular zone of the body. During the first stage, which lasts for about a year, the mouth is the principal region of dynamic activity. The *oral* stage is followed by the development of cathexes and anticathexes around the eliminative functions, and is called the *anal* stage. This lasts during the second year and is succeeded by the *phallic* stage in which the sex organs become the leading erogenous zones. These stages, the oral, anal, and phallic, are called the pregenital stages. The child then goes into a prolonged latency period, the so-called quiet years, dynamically speaking. During this period the impulses tend to be held in a state of repression. The dynamic resurgence of adolescence reactivates the pregenital impulses; if these are successfully displaced and sublimated by the ego, the person passes into the final stage of maturity, the *genital* stage.

THE ORAL STAGE. The principal source of pleasure derived from the mouth is that of eating. Eating involves tactual stimulation of the lips and oral cavity, and swallowing or, if the food is unpleasant, spitting out. Later when the teeth erupt the mouth is used for biting and chewing. These two modes of oral activity, incorporation of food and biting, are the prototypes for many later character traits that develop.

Pleasure derived from oral incorporation may be displaced to other modes of incorporation such as the pleasure gained from acquiring knowledge or possessions. A gullible person, for example, is one who is fixated on the oral incorporative level of personality; such a person will swallow almost anything he or she is told. Biting or oral aggression may be displaced in the form of sarcasm and argumentativeness. By displacements and sublimations of various kinds, as well as by defenses against the primitive oral impulses, these prototypic modes of oral functioning provide the basis for the development of a vast network of interests, attitudes, and character traits.

Furthermore, since the oral stage occurs at a time when the baby is almost completely dependent upon its mother for sustenance, when it is cradled and nursed by her and protected from discomfort, feelings of dependency arise during this period. These feelings of dependency tend to persist throughout life, in spite of later ego developments, and are apt to come to the fore whenever the person feels anxious and insecure. Freud believed that the most extreme symptom of dependency is the desire to return to the womb.

THE ANAL STAGE. After the food has been digested, the residue accumulates in the lower end of the intestinal tract and is reflexly discharged when the pressure upon the anal sphincters reaches a certain level. The expulsion of the feces removes the source of discomfort and produces a feeling of relief. When toilet training is initiated, usually during the second year of life, the child has its first decisive experience with the external regulation of an instinctual impulse. It has to learn to postpone the pleasure that comes from relieving anal tensions. Depending upon the particular method of toilet training used by the mother and her feelings concerning defecation, the consequences of this training may have far-reaching effects upon the formation of specific traits and values. If the mother is very strict and repressive in her methods, the child may hold back its feces and become constipated. If this mode of reaction generalizes to other ways of behaving, the child will develop a retentive character. It will become obstinate and stingy. Or under the duress of repressive measures the child may vent its rage by expelling feces at the most inappropriate times. This is the prototype for all kinds of expulsive traits—cruelty, wanton destructiveness, temper tantrums, and messy disorderliness, to mention only a few. On the other hand, if the mother is the type of person who pleads with her child to have a bowel movement and who praises the child extravagantly when it does, the child will acquire the notion that the whole activity of producing feces is extremely important. This idea may be the basis for creativity and productivity. Innumerable other traits of character are said to have their roots laid down in the anal stage.

THE PHALLIC STAGE. During this stage of personality development sexual and aggressive feelings associated with the functioning of the genital organs come into focus. The pleasures of maturbation and the fantasy life of the child that accompanies autoerotic activity set the stage for the appearance of the *Oedipus complex*. Freud considered the identification of the Oedipus complex to be one of his greatest discoveries. The Oedipus complex is named for the king of Thebes who killed his father and married his mother.

Briefly defined, the Oedipus complex consists of a sexual cathexis for the parent of the opposite sex and a hostile cathexis for the parent of the same sex. The boy wants to possess his mother and remove his father, the girl wants to possess her father and displace her mother. These feelings express themselves in the child's fantasies during masturbation and in the alternation of loving and rebellious actions toward his parents. The behavior of the three- to five-year-old child is marked to a large extent by the operation of the Oedipus complex, and although it is modified and suffers repression after the age of five it remains a vital force in the personality throughout life. Attitudes toward the opposite sex and toward people in authority, for instance, are largely conditioned by the Oedipus complex.

The history and fate of the Oedipus complex differ for males and females. To begin with, both sexes love the mother because she satisfies their needs and resent the father because he is regarded as a rival for the mother's affections. These feelings persist in the boy but change in the girl. Let us consider first the sequence of events that characterize the development of the male Oedipus complex.

The boy's incestuous craving for the mother and his growing resentment toward the father bring him into conflict with his parents, especially the father. He imagines that his dominant rival is going to harm him, and his fears may actually be confirmed by threats from a resentful and punitive father. His fears concerning what the father may do to him center around harm to his genital organs because they are the source of his lustful feelings. He is afraid that his jealous father will remove the offending organs. Fear of castration or, as Freud called it, *castration anxiety* induces a repression of the sexual desire for the mother and hostility toward the father. It also helps to bring about an identification of the boy with his father. By identifying with the father, the boy also gains some vicarious satisfaction for his sexual impulses toward the mother. At the same time, his dangerous erotic feeling for the mother is converted into harmless tender affection for her. Lastly, the repression of the Oedipus complex causes the superego to undergo its final development. In Freud's words, the superego is the heir of the male Oedipus complex. It is the bulwark against incest and aggression.

The sequence of events in the development and dissolution of the female Oedipus complex is more involved. In the first place, she exchanges her original love object, the mother, for a new object, the father. Why this takes place depends upon the girl's reaction of disappointment when she discovers that a boy possesses a protruding sex organ, the penis, while she has only a cavity. Several important consequences follow from this traumatic discovery. In the first place, she holds her mother responsible for her castrated condition which weakens the cathexis for the mother. In the second place, she transfers her love to the father because he has the valued organ which she aspires to share with him. However, her love for the father and for other men as well is mixed with a feeling of envy because they possess something she lacks. Penis envy is the female counterpart of castration anxiety in the boy, and collectively they are called the *castration complex*. She imagines that she has lost something valuable, while the boy is afraid he is going to lose it. To some extent, the lack of a penis is compensated for when a woman has a baby, especially if it is a boy baby.

In the girl the castration complex initiates the Oedipus complex by weakening her cathexis for the mother and instituting a cathexis for the father. Unlike the boy's Oedipus complex, which is repressed or otherwise changed by castration anxiety, the girl's Oedipus complex tends to persist although it undergoes some modification due to the realistic barriers that prevent her from gratifying her sexual desire for the father. But it does not fall under the strong repression that the boy's does. These differences in the nature of the Oedipus and castration complexes are the basis for many psychological differences between the sexes.

Freud assumed that every person is inherently bisexual; each sex is attracted to members of the same sex as well as to members of the opposite sex. This is the constitutional basis for homosexuality, although in most people the homosexual impulses remain latent. This condition of bisexuality complicates the Oedipus complex by inducing sexual cathexes for the same sex parent. Consequently, the boy's feelings for his father and the girl's feelings for her mother are said to be ambivalent rather than univalent in character. The assumption of bisexuality has been supported by investigations on the endocrine glands which show rather conclusively that both male and female sex hormones are present in each sex.

The emergence and development of the Oedipus and castration complexes are the chief events of the phallic period, and leave a host of deposits in the personality.

THE GENITAL STAGE. The cathexes of the pregenital periods are narcissistic in character. This means that the individual obtains gratification from the stimulation and manipulation of his or her own body and other people are cathected only because they help to provide additional forms of body pleasure to the child. During adolescence, some of this self-love or narcissism becomes channeled into genuine object choices. The adolescent begins to love others for altruistic motives and not simply for selfish or narcissistic reasons. Sexual attraction, socialization, group activities, vocational planning, and preparations for marrying and raising a family begin to manifest themselves. By the end of adolescence, these socialized, altruistic cathexes have become fairly well stabilized in the form of habitual displacements, sublimations, and identifications. The person becomes transformed from a pleasure-seeking, narcissistic infant into a reality-oriented, socialized adult. However, it should not be thought that the pregenital impulses are displaced by genital ones. Rather, the cathexes of the oral, anal, and phallic stages become fused and synthesized with the genital impulses. The principal biological function of the genital stage is that of reproduction; the psychological aspects help to achieve this end by providing a certain measure of stability and security.

In spite of the fact that Freud differentiated four stages of personality growth, he did not assume that there were any sharp breaks or abrupt transitions in passing out of one stage into another. The final organization of personality represents contributions from all four stages.

CHARACTERISTIC
RESEARCH AND
RESEARCH
METHODS

The empirical data upon which Freud based his theories consisted principally of the verbalizations and expressive behavior of patients undergoing psychological treatment. Although Freud was schooled in the precise methods of nineteenth century science and had established a substantial reputation as a medical investigator before turning his attention to psychology, he did not employ experimental or controlled observational techniques in his investigations of the human mind. Freud was not a part of the movement of experimental psychology that had been initiated by Fechner in 1860 and developed into a science by Wundt during the following two decades. He was, of course, familiar with this movement and Fechner's philosophy influenced him, but Freud was not an experimental psychologist. He did not perform controlled psychological experiments, nor did he collect data and analyze them quantitatively as other psychologists of the nineteenth century were doing. One looks in vain for a table or graph in his extensive writings. Nor did Freud ever employ a diagnostic test or any other kind of objective appraisal of personality. His theories germinated as he listened to the facts and fancies verbalized by troubled personalities.

Yet it would be a serious mistake to say that the verbalizations of people in treatment were the only ingredients out of which Freud fashioned his theories. Certainly as important as these raw data was the rigorously critical attitude that Freud brought to the analysis of his patients' free associations. Today we would say that he analyzed his raw material by the method of internal consistency. Inferences made from one part of the material were checked against evidence appearing in other parts, so that the final conclusions drawn from a case were based upon an interlocking network of facts and inferences. Freud proceeded in his work in much the same way as a detective assembling evidence or a lawyer summing up a case to the jury. Everything had to fit together coherently before Freud was satisfied that he had put his finger upon the correct interpretation. It should be remembered, moreover, that the material produced by one case who was seen five hours a week for as long as two or three years was of immense proportions, and that Freud had ample opportunity to check and recheck his hunches scores of times before deciding upon the final interpretation. By contrast, the subject in the typical psychological experiment performed under controlled conditions is observed or tested for only one or two hours on the average. Certainly two of Freud's most important contributions to research strategy were the intensive study of the single case and the use of the method of internal consistency for testing hypothesis.

Again and again Freud was forced to revise his theories because new discoveries could not be accounted for adequately by his current theories. Freud was reluctant to abandon a systematic position once it had been formulated, but the history of the psychoanalytic theory of personality from its inception in the 1890s down to the late 1920s demonstrates quite conclusively that Freud's views were determined eventually by the weight of the evidence *as he saw it*. Although his close associates may have had some influence in shaping his ideas, it seems to be reasonably clear that the ultimate test of the validity of his theories was largely that of Freud's own self-criticism and his willingness to be guided by new evidence. The storm of indignant attacks upon psychoanalysis that began as soon as Freud had enunciated his theory of the sexual etiology of hysteria and which continued for the rest of his life did not influence his thinking. There were few times in life when he replied to his critics. Nor did the disaffection of some of his closest associates cause Freud to alter his theories. Freud seems to have been endowed with an abundance of intellectual autonomy, which is without doubt one of the prerequisites for greatness.

Freud's Scientific
Credo

Freud's views on the way in which the scientist works to develop a science are succinctly set forth in one of his rare pronouncements on this topic. He writes:

> We have often heard it maintained that sciences should be built up on clear and sharply defined basic concepts. In actual fact no science, not even the most exact, begins with such definitions. The true beginning of scientific activity consists rather in describing phenomena and then in proceeding to group, classify and correlate them. Even at the stage of description it is not possible to avoid applying certain abstract ideas to the material in hand, ideas derived from somewhere or other but certainly not from the new observations alone. Such ideas—which will later become the basic concepts of the science—are still more indispensable as the material is further worked over. They must at first necessarily possess some degree of indefiniteness; there can be no question of any clear delimitation of their content. So long as they remain in this condition, we come to an understanding about their meaning by making repeated references to the material of observation from which they appear to have been derived, but upon which, in fact, they have been imposed. Thus, strictly speaking, they are in the nature of conventions—although everything depends on their not being arbitrarily chosen but determined by their having significant relations to the empirical material, relations that we seem to sense before we can clearly recognize and demonstrate them. It is only after more thorough investigation of the field of observation that we are able to formulate its basic scientific concepts with increased precision, and progressively so to modify them that they become serviceable and consistent over a wide area. Then, indeed, the time may have come to confine them in definitions. The advance of knowledge, however, does not tolerate any rigidity even in definitions. Physics furnishes an excellent illustration of the way in which even 'basic concepts' that have been established in the form of definitions are constantly being altered in their content (1915, p. 117).

By choice, then, Freud preferred the more open, informal type of inductive theory-building that stays reasonably close to the empirical supports upon which it rests to the more formal deductive type of theory that starts with sharply defined concepts and carefully phrased postulates and corollaries from which testable hypotheses are derived and subsequently tested. Moreover, as this quotation shows, Freud was fully aware of the importance of the "prepared mind" of the scientist in enabling him or her to make maximum use of empirical data. These "abstract ideas" might come from various sources; in Freud's case, from wide reading in the classics and other literature, from his hobby of archeology, from his observations as the father of six children, from everyday experiences of all kinds, and most of all, perhaps, from his lifelong habit of self-analysis.

Let us turn now to a consideration of some of the special data-collecting techniques employed by Freud. They were used, of course, in the therapeutic situation because this is where Freud gathered his data.

After a brief tryout of the method of hypnosis (1887–1889) which was then very much in vogue, especially in France, Freud learned about a new method that had been used successfully by his friend and colleague, Dr. Joseph Breuer, in the treatment of a case of hysteria. This method which Breuer called catharsis or the "talking cure" consisted of the patient relating the details of the first appearance of each of the symptoms, following which the symptoms disappeared. Out of this method, Freud gradually evolved his own unique free-association method which Ernest Jones has called "one of the two great deeds of Freud's scientific life," the other being Freud's self-analysis.

Free Association and Dream Analysis

In essence, the free-association method requires the patient to say everything that comes into consciousness, no matter how ridiculous or inappropriate it may sound. Unlike the cathartic method, the free-association method does not stop with the origin of symptoms; it allows—indeed it demands—that patients talk about everything and anything that occurs to them without restraint and without any attempt to produce a logical, organized, meaningful discourse. The role of the therapist is, to a great extent, a passive one. The therapist sits and listens, prods occasionally by asking questions when the verbal flow of the patient dries up, but does not interrupt when the patient is talking. In order to reduce the influence of external distractions to a minimum, the patient ordinarily reclines on a couch in a quiet room.

Freud observed that when these conditions prevail, the patient eventually begins to talk about memories of early childhood experiences. These memories provided Freud with his first real insight into the formation of the personality structure and its subsequent development. This method of reconstructing the past from current verbalizations may be contrasted with the developmental method of observing the growth of personality from infancy to adulthood.

Perhaps Freud's most original insight about the undisciplined wanderings of his patients' verbalizations was that each statement is associated in some meaningful, dynamic manner with the preceding statement, so that a continuous chain of associations exist from first to last. Everything that the patient says is related, without exception, to what has previously been said. There may be numerous circumlocutions and verbal blockages, but eventually the history of the person's mind and its present organization will be divulged to the listener by following the chain of associations through the verbal maze.

The analysis of dreams is not a separate method from that of free association; it is a natural consequence of the instruction to patients that they talk about everything that comes to their minds. Freud's early patients spontaneously recalled their dreams and then proceeded to give free associations to them. Freud soon realized that these reported dreams and the accompanying free associations were especially rich sources of information about the dynamics of human personality. As a result of this insight, which he tested on his own dreams, Freud formulated the famous theory that states that the dream is an expression of the most primitive workings and contents of the human mind (1900). The primitive process that creates the dream Freud called the primary process. As we have seen, the primary process attempts to fulfill a wish or discharge a tension by inducing an image of the desired goal. By having his patients free-associate to their dreams, Freud was able to penetrate into the most inaccessible regions of the human mind and to discover the bedrock of personality.

Freud's Case Studies   The vast amount of raw material from which Freud fashioned his theory of personality will never be known. The few case histories that Freud chose to publish represent only an infinitesimal fraction of the cases he treated. Professional ethics partially restrained Freud from presenting his cases to the world since there was always the danger that the identity of his patients might be guessed by a curious public.

Aside from the case histories appearing in *Studies in hysteria* (1895) that he wrote in collaboration with Breuer before psychoanalytic theory had taken definite shape in Freud's mind, he published only six accounts of cases. One of these, the so-called Schreber case (1911), was not a patient of Freud's. Freud based his analysis upon a autobiographical account of a case of paranoia written by Judge Daniel Schreber. Another case study concerned a phobia in a five-year-old boy, Little Hans (1909a) which was treated by the boy's father, himself a physician, under Freud's guidance and instructions. In the other four cases, Freud was the therapist. These are referred to as "Dora" (1905b), the "Rat Man" (1909b), the "Wolf Man" (1918), and a case of female homosexuality (1920b). Each of these cases was presented to bring out the salient features of one or more of Freud's theoretical concepts.

Dora was published, Freud says, in order to show how the analysis of dreams enables one to ferret out the hidden and repressed parts of the human mind and to demonstrate that hysterical symptoms are motivated by the sexual impulse. Following a fairly lengthy account of the background factors and the current clinical picture, Freud presents a detailed analysis of two of Dora's dreams. Much of the material consists of a verbatim account of Dora's free associations and Freud's interpretations, and gives a remarkably lucid picture of the exact manner in which dreams are interpreted. In this case history, as in the others, we see how Freud wove the patterned fabric of personality out of the tangled verbal threads of a suffering person, and we obtain glimpses of Freud's unusual talent for seeing relationships between widely disparate utterances. Operating on the assumption that everything that the person says or does is meaningful and fits into the total picture of the personality organization, Freud was a vigilant observer; the most commonplace statement or act was scrutinized for a deeper meaning.

Freud did not regard his talent for observation as being in any way unusual, as the following quotation indicates.

When I set myself the task of bringing to light what human beings keep hidden within them, not by the compelling power of hypnosis, but by observing what they say and what they show, I thought the task was a harder one than it really is. He that has eyes to see and ears to hear may convince himself that no mortal can keep a secret. If the lips are silent, he chatters with his finger tips; betrayal oozes out of him at every pore. And thus the task of making conscious the most hidden recesses of the mind is one which it is quite possible to accomplish (1905b, pp. 77–78).

Freud's remarkable ability to draw inferences of great significance from commonplace behavior is seen to best advantage in what is probably the most popular of all of his writings, *The psychopathology of everyday life* (1901). This book is replete with examples of the dynamic import of simple slips of the tongue, errors of memory, accidents, and mistakes of various kinds.

The case of Little Hans afforded Freud his first opportunity to verify his theory of infantile sexuality, which had been formulated on the basis of the adult memories, by observations made on a young child. Hans was afraid that a horse would bite him should he venture out in the street. From the careful notes kept by the boy's father, many of which are presented verbatim in the published account, Freud was able to show that this phobia was an expression of the two most important sexual complexes of early childhood: the Oedipus complex and the castration complex. The case of Little Hans exemplifies and corroborates the theory of infantile sexuality set forth by Freud in 1905.

In the case of the Rat Man, who suffered from the revolting obsession that his girl friend and his father would each be punished by having a potful of ravenous rodents fastened to their buttocks, Freud pieced together the involved dynamics and thought connections of an obsessional neurotic. Although the presentation is only fragmentary, this case clearly illustrates how Freud went about resolving the apparent contradictions, distortions, and absurdities in the disconnected ramblings of a sick personality, and made them into a logically coherent pattern. In reporting this case, Freud tells us that it is based upon notes made on the evening of the day of the treatment and not upon notes made during the analytic session. Freud was opposed to any note-taking by the therapist during the treatment period because he felt that the withdrawal of the therapist's attention would interfere with the progress of therapy. He believed in any event that the therapist would remember the important material and forget the trivial details.

Freud's analysis of the Schreber case was based upon Schreber's own account of his mental illness which was diagnosed as paranoia. Freud justified his use of this autobiographical book on the grounds that paranoia is a type of disorder in which the written case history is as satisfactory as personal acquaintance with the case. The characteristic symptom of paranoia is the tortuous delusional system that the patient constructs. Schreber's delusions consisted of thinking that he was the Redeemer and that he was being transformed into a woman. In an intricate analysis of these two delusions Freud showed that they were related, and that the motive power for both of them as well as for the other aspects of the case was that of latent homosexuality. In this case study, Freud set forth his famous hypothesis of the causal relationship between homosexuality and paranoia. Freud's penchant for deriving a generalization of far-reaching power from a mass of particular facts is beautifully portrayed in the Schreber case.

The Wolf Man is an account of an infantile neurosis that was brought to the surface during the analysis of a young man, and was shown to be related dynamically to the present condition of the patient. Freud observed that the analysis of an experience that took place some fifteen years earlier has its advantages as well as its disadvantages when compared with the analysis of an event shortly after it occurs. The principal disadvantage is that of the unreliability of memory for early experiences. On the other hand, if one tries to analyze very young children there is the drawback that they cannot express themselves verbally. The Wolf Man is the adult counterpart of Little Hans and both approaches, the reconstructive and the genetic, are shown to be valuable sources of empirical evidence for the theories of psychoanalysis. The principal feature of this case history is a lengthy analysis of a dream of wolves that the patient remembered from his early childhood, and which was interpreted as being caused by the child's reaction to the *primal scene,* Freud's term for the child's observation or fantasy of seeing his parents engage in sexual intercourse. (For a discussion of this case see Gardner, 1971.)

The last case reported by Freud was one that he had to break off because the resistance of the patient to giving up her homosexuality was so strong that no progress could be made. Nevertheless, as the published case history shows, Freud was able to arrive at a complete understanding of the origin and development of homosexuality. Homosexuality in both sexes is due to two primary factors, an inherent bisexuality in all living things and a reversal of the Oedipus complex. Instead of loving the father and identifying with the mother, this woman identified with the father and cathected the mother. In the case of male homosexuality, there would be an identification with the mother and a love for the father. This case also contains some of Freud's views on suicide, since the reason for the woman's coming to Freud in the first place was an attempt at self-destruction.

It is impossible to say with any assurance that these particular case histories that Freud chose to make public were the actual empirical sources for the theories that they exemplified, or whether they were merely convenient and clear-cut examples of theoretical formulations that had already taken shape in Freud's mind. It really does not make much difference whether the Schreber case, for example, was *the* case that revealed to Freud the dynamics of paranoia, or wehther he had made the fundamental discovery on the basis of prior cases and merely applied them to this particular case. In any event, the type of material that Freud collected, the kind of techniques he employed, and the way in which he thought are revealed in these six case studies. Anyone who wishes to get close to the raw material with which Freud worked should read them.

One should not confuse these case histories with the application of psychoanalytic theory for the better understanding of literature and the arts or for the purposes of social criticism. Freud did not learn about sublimation from his study of the life of Leonardo da Vinci and he did not discover the Oedipus complex by reading Sophocles, Shakespeare, or Dostoevsky. Nor did he fathom the basic irrationality of human thinking by observing human religious or political behavior. The interpretation of a literary work or the analysis of a social institution using the insights of psychoanalytic theory may have helped to confirm the usefulness of the insights and even to validate their authenticity and universality, but the literary and artistic productions and the social institutions themselves did not constitute any part of Freud's empirical data.

Freud's Self-analysis   The material dredged up from his own unconscious constituted an important source of empirical data for Freud. As related by Ernest Jones (1953), Freud began his own self-analysis in the summer of 1897 with the analysis of one of his dreams. From this searching self-scrutiny, Freud confirmed to his own satisfaction the theory of dreams and the theory of infantile sexuality. He found in his own personality those conflicts and contradictions and irrationalities that he had observed in his patients, and this experience perhaps more than any other convinced him of the essential correctness of his views. In fact, Freud was reluctant to accept the validity of any hypothesis until he had tested it out on himself. Freud continued his self-analysis throughout his life, reserving the last half hour of each day for this activity.

Criticisms   No other psychological theory has been subjected to such searching and often such bitter criticism as has psychoanalysis. From every side and on every conceivable score, Freud and his theory have been attacked, reviled, ridiculed, and slandered. The only comparable case in modern science, in which both the theory and the theorist have been so ardently vilified, is that of Charles Darwin whose evolutionary doctrine shocked Victorian England. Freud's chief offenses consisted of ascribing lustful and destructive wishes to the baby, attributing incestuous and perverted urges to all human beings, and explaining human behavior in terms of sexual motivation. "Decent" people were infuriated by Freud's view of the individual and called him a libertine and a pervert.

In recent years, Freudian theory has been criticized as being too closely allied with the mechanistic and deterministic outlook of nineteenth century science, and that consequently it is not sufficiently humanistic. The theory is regarded by many today as painting too bleak a picture of human nature. Feminists have vigorously attacked Freud's speculations about the psychology of women, particularly the concept of penis envy, although one prominent figure in the women's movement (Mitchell, 1975) has come to Freud's defense.

It is not our intention to review the criticism that has been leveled at psychoanalysis. Much of it was scarcely more than the sound and fury of overwrought people. A lot of the criticism has been outdated by subsequent developments in Freud's thinking. And a sizable portion of the criticism, it can be seen now, was based upon misinterpretations and distortions of psychoanalysis. A philosopher, Jerry Canning (1966), has made a logical analysis of the criticisms leveled at psychoanalysis and concludes that "of the many criticisms considered *none* is found to be meaningful *and* reasonable in terms of scientific ideals, *and* adequately supported by evidence." Moreover, to review the criticisms of psychoanalysis in an adequate manner would require a book at least as large as the present one. Instead, we shall discuss several types of criticisms that have been leveled repeatedly at psychoanalysis and are still widely discussed.

One type of criticism asserts that there are grave shortcomings in the empirical procedures by which Freud validated his hypotheses. It is pointed out that Freud made his observations under uncontrolled conditions. Freud acknowledged that he did not keep a verbatim record of what he and the patient said and did during the treatment hour, but that he worked from notes made several hours later. It is impossible to say how faithfully these notes reflected the events as they actually occurred but judging from experiments on the reliability of testimony it is not unlikely that distortions and omissions of various kinds crept into the record. Freud's assumption that the significant material would be remembered and the trivial incidents forgotten has never been proved and seems improbable.

Critics of Freud's methods have also objected to his accepting at face value what a patient said without attempting to corroborate it by some form of external evidence. They believed he should have secured evidence from relatives and acquaintances, documents, test data, and medical information. However, Freud maintained that what was important for understanding human behavior was a thorough knowledge of the unconscious that could only be obtained from free association and dream analysis.

Given then what was surely an incomplete record and more than likely an imperfect one, Freud proceeded to draw inferences and reach conclusions by a line of reasoning that was rarely made explicit. For the most part what we find in Freud's writings is the end result of his thinking—the conclusions without the original data upon which they were based, without an account of his methods of analysis, and without any systematic presentation, either qualitative or quantitative, of his empirical findings. The reader is asked to take on faith the validity of his inductive and deductive operations. Consequently, it is practically impossible to repeat any of Freud's investigations with any assurance that one is proceeding in accordance with the original design. This may help to explain why other investigators have reached quite different conclusions, and why there are so many interpretations of ostensibly the same phenomenon.

Freud eschewed any quantifying of his empirical data, which makes it impossible to weigh the statistical significance and reliability of his observations. In how many cases, for example, did he find an association between paranoia and homosexuality, between hysteria and fixation on the oral stage, between a wish and a phobia, between the primal scene and adult instability? How many cases of a particular type did he study and from what classes and backgrounds did these cases come? What measures and criteria were used for assigning a case to a particular clinical category? Did Freud ever check his interpretations against those of another competent psychoanalyst to establish the reliability of his judgment? These and numerous other questions of a similar nature trouble the quantitatively oriented psychologist.

Freud's disinclination to follow the conventions of full scientific reporting of his data leaves the door open for many doubts regarding the scientific status of psychoanalysis (Hook, 1960). Did Freud read into his cases what he wanted to find there? Were his inferences guided more by his biases than by the material at hand? Did he select only that evidence that was in agreement with his hypotheses and disregard negative instances? Were the free associations of his patients really free or were they telling Freud what he wanted to hear? Did Freud rear an elaborate theory of personality that was alleged to hold for all people on inferences drawn from the verbal utterances of a relatively small number of atypical patients? How much solid evidence did Freud really have to support his grandiloquent speculations? What safeguards did he employ against the insidious influence of bias? Questions of this kind have cast doubts upon the validity of psychoanalytic theory.

Lawrence Kubie, a prominent psychoanalyst, has summarized the limitations of psychoanalysis as a basic science in the following way.

In general, they [the limitations] can be summarized by saying that the basic design of the process of analysis has essential scientific validity, but that the difficulties of recording and reproducing primary observations, the consequent difficulty in deriving the basic conceptual structure, the difficulties in examining with equal ease the circular relationship from unconscious to conscious and from conscious to unconscious, the difficulties in appraising quantitatively the multiplicity of variables, and finally the difficulty of estimating those things which increase and those things which decrease the precision of its hypotheses and the validity of its predictions are among the basic scientific problems which remain to be solved (1953, pp. 143–144).

Another type of criticism attacks the theory itself, and says in effect that the theory is "bad" because many parts of it do not have and cannot be made to have empirical consequences. For example, it is impossible to derive any empirical propositions from the postulation of a death wish. This being so, the death wish "remains shrouded in metaphysical darkness" and has no meaning for science. Although one may use the death wish to "explain" certain phenomena, such as suicide or accidents, such after-the-fact explanations mean very little. It is like betting on a horse after the race has been run. A good theory, on the other hand, is one that enables its user to predict in advance what is going to happen. Some people may prefer to bring together and organize a mass of apparently unrelated data under the single heading of the death wish, but preferences of this sort merely indicate the interests of the systematizer and not the "truth" of the heading. Used in this way, the death wish is scarcely more than a slogan.

Freudian theory is markedly deficient in providing a set of relational rules by which one can arrive at any precise expectations of what will happen if certain events take place. What exactly is the nature of the relationship between traumatic experiences, guilt feelings, repression, symbol formation, and dreaming? What connects the formation of the superego with the Oedipus complex? These and a thousand other questions have still to be answered regarding the tangled web of concepts and assumptions that Freud conjured up.

The theory stands silent on the knotty problem of how the interplay of cathexes and anticathexes are to be measured quantitatively. In fact, there is no specification of how one is to go about estimating, even in the roughest terms, differences in quantity. How intense does an experience have to be before it is traumatic? How weak must the ego be before it can be overridden by an instinctual impulse? In what ways do the various quantities interact with one another to produce a given result? And yet everything depends in the final analysis upon just such specifications. Lacking them no laws can be derived.

If one concedes that psychoanalytic theory is guilty of at least two serious faults, first that it is a "bad" theory and second that it has not been substantiated by scientifically respectable procedures (and also mindful of the fact that many other criticisms might have been cited), the question then arises as to why psychoanalytic theory is taken seriously by anybody, and why it was not relegated to oblivion long ago. How are we to account for its dominant and influential status in the world today?

The fact of the matter is that all theories of behavior are pretty poor theories and all of them leave much to be desired in the way of scientific proof. Psychology has a long way to go before it can be called an exact science. Consequently, the psychologist must select the theory he or she intends to follow for reasons other than those of formal adequacy and factual evidence.

What does psychoanalytic theory have to offer? Some people like the picturesque language that Freud uses to project his ideas. They are attracted by the skillful way in which he employs literary and mythological allusions to put across fairly abstruse notions and his talent for turning a phrase or creating a figure of speech to illuminate a difficult point for the reader. His writing has an exciting literary quality that is rare among scientists. The style is matched by the excitement of the ideas. Many people find Freud's concepts fascinating and sensational. Of course, sex is an alluring topic and has a sensation value even when it is discussed in scientific works. Aggression and destructiveness are almost as absorbing as sex. It is only natural, then, the people are attracted by Freud's writings.

But a fine literary style and an exciting subject matter are not the main reasons for the great esteem in which Freud is held. Rather it is because his ideas are challenging, because his conception of the indivual is both broad and deep, and because his theory has relevance for our times. Freud may not have been a rigorous scientist nor a first-rate theoretician, but he was a patient, meticulous, penetrating observer and a tenacious, disciplined, courageous, original thinker. Over and above all of the other virtues of his theory stands this one—it tries to envisage full-bodied individuals living partly in a world of reality and partly in a world of make-believe, beset by conflicts and inner contradictions, yet capable of rational thought and action, moved by forces of which they have little knowledge and by aspirations that are beyond their reach, by turn confused and clearheaded, frustrated and satisfied, hopeful and despairing, selfish and altruistic; in short, a complex human being. For many people, this picture of the individual has an essential validity.

BIBLIOGRAPHY
PRIMARY SOURCES

Freud, S. *The standard edition of the complete psychological works.* J. Strachey (Ed.). London: Hogarth Press, 1953–1974.

Freud, S. The interpretation of dreams. In *Standard edition.* Vols. 4 and 5. London: Hogarth Press, 1953. (First German edition, 1900.)

Freud, S. The psychopathology of everyday life. In *Standard edition.* Vol. 6. London: Hogarth Press, 1960. (First German edition, 1901.)

Freud, S. Three essays on sexuality. In *Standard edition.* Vol. 7. London: Hogarth Press, 1953. (First German edition, 1905a.)

Freud, S. Introductory lectures on psycho-analysis. In *Standard edition.* Vols. 15 and 16. London: Hogarth Press, 1963. (First German edition, 1917.)

Freud, S. Beyond the pleasure principle. In *Standard edition.* Vol. 18. London: Hogarth Press, 1955. (First German edition, 1920a.)

Freud, S. Inhibitions, symptoms, and anxiety. In *Standard edition.* Vol. 20. London: Hogarth Press, 1959. (First German edition, 1926b.)

Freud, S. New introductory lectures on psycho-analysis. In *Standard edition.* Vol. 22. London: Hogarth Press, 1964. (First German edition, 1933.)

Freud, S. An outline of psycho-analysis. In *Standard edition.* Vol. 23. London: Hogarth Press, 1964. (First German edition, 1940.)

Amacher, P. Freud's neurological education and its influence on psychoanalytic theory. *Psychol. Issues,* 1965, **4** (4), 1–93.

Arlow, J. B., and Brenner, C. *Psychoanalytic concepts and the structural theory.* New York: International Universities Press, 1964.

Breuer, J., and Freud, S. Studies on hysteria. In *Standard edition*. Vol. 2. London: Hogarth Press, 1955. (First German edition, 1895.)

Canning, J. W. *A logical analysis of criticisms directed at Freudian psychoanalytic theory.* Ph.D. Dissertation, University of Maryland, 1966.

Fenichel, O. *The psychoanalytic theory of neurosis.* New York: Norton, 1945.

Freud, A. *The ego and the mechanisms of defence.* New York: International Universities Press, 1946.

Freud, S. *The standard edition of the complete psychological works.* J. Strachey (Ed.). London: Hogarth Press, 1953–1974.

Freud S. The interpretation of dreams. In *Standard edition*. Vols. 4 and 5. London: Hogarth Press, 1953. (First German edition, 1900.)

Freud, S. Psychopathology of everyday life. In *Standard edition*. Vol. 6. London: Hogarth Press, 1960. (First German edition, 1901.)

Freud, S. Three essays on sexuality. In *Standard edition*. Vol. 7. London: Hogarth Press, 1953. (First German edition, 1905a.)

Freud, S. Fragment of an analysis of a case of hysteria. In *Standard edition*. Vol. 7. London: Hogarth Press, 1953. (First German edition, 1905b.)

Freud, S. Jokes and their relation to the unconscious. In *Standard edition*. Vol. 8. London: Hogarth Press, 1960. (First German edition, 1905c.)

Freud, S. Jensen's 'Gradiva'. In *Standard edition*. Vol. 9. London: Hogarth Press, 1959. (First German edition, 1906.)

Freud, S. "Civilized" sexual morality and modern nervous illness. In *Standard edition,* Vol. 9. London: Hogarth Press, 1959. (First German edition, 1908.)

Freud, S. Analysis of a phobia in a five-year-old boy. In *Standard edition*. Vol. 10. London: Hogarth Press, 1955. (First German edition, 1909a.)

Freud, S. Notes upon a case of obsessional neurosis. In *Standard edition*. Vol. 10. London: Hogarth Press, 1955. (First German edition, 1909b.)

Freud, S. Leonardo da Vinci: a study in psychosexuality. In *Standard edition*. Vol. 11. London: Hogarth Press, 1957. (First German edition, 1910a.)

Freud, S. The psycho-analytic view of psychogenic disturbance of vision. In *Standard edition*. Vol. 11. London: Hogarth Press, 1957. (First German edition, 1910b.)

Freud, S. Psycho-analytic notes on an autobiographical account of a case of paranoia (dementia paranoides). In *Standard edition*. Vol. 12. London: Hogarth Press, 1958. (First German edition, 1911.)

Freud, S. Totem and taboo. In *Standard edition*. Vol. 13. London: Hogarth Press, 1955. (First German edition, 1913.)

Freud, S. Instincts and their vicissitudes. In *Standard edition*. Vol. 14. London: Hogarth Press, 1957. (First German edition, 1915.)

Freud, S. Introductory lectures on psycho-analysis. In *Standard edition*. Vols. 15 and 16. London: Hogarth Press, 1963. (First German edition, 1917.)

Freud, S. From the history of an infantile neurosis. In *Standard edition*. Vol. 17. London: Hogarth Press, 1955. (First German edition, 1918.)

Freud, S. Beyond the pleasure principle. In *Standard edition*. Vol. 18. London: Hogarth Press, 1955. (First German edition, 1920a.)

Freud, S. The psychogenesis of a case of homosexuality in a woman. In *Standard edition*. Vol. 18. London: Hogarth Press, 1955. (First German edition, 1920b.)

Freud, S. The question of lay analysis. In *Standard edition*. Vol. 20. London: Hogarth Press, 1959. (First German edition, 1926a.)

Freud, S. Inhibitions, symptoms and anxiety. In *Standard edition*. Vol. 20. London: Hogarth Press, 1959. (First German edition, 1926b.)

Freud, S. Future of an illusion. In *Standard edition*. Vol. 21. London: Hogarth Press, 1961. (First German edition, 1927.)

Freud, S. Civilization and its discontents. In *Standard edition*. Vol. 21. London: Hogarth Press, 1961. (First German edition, 1930.)

Freud, S. New introductory lectures on psycho-analysis. In *Standard edition*. Vol. 22. London: Hogarth Press, 1964. (First German edition, 1933.)

Freud, S. Analysis terminable and interminable. In *Standard edition*. Vol. 23. London: Hogarth Press, 1964. (First German edition, 1937.)

Freud, S. Moses and monotheism. In *Standard edition*. Vol. 23. London: Hogarth Press, 1964. (First German edition, 1939.)

Freud, S. An outline of psychoanalysis. In *Standard edition*. Vol. 23. London: Hogarth Press, 1964. (First German edition, 1940.)

Gardner, M. (Ed.) *Wolfman: with the case of wolf-man by Sigmund Freud*. New York: Basic Books, 1971.

Gill, M. M. Topography and systems in psychoanalytic theory. *Psychol. Issues,* 1963, **3**, (2), 1–179.

Hall, C. S. *A primer of Freudian psychology*. Cleveland: World Publishing Co., 1954.

Hall, C. S., and Lindzey, G. The relevance of Freudian psychology and related viewpoints for the social sciences. In G. Lindzey and E. Aronson (Eds.). *Handbook of social psychology,* Vol. 1. Cambridge: Addison-Wesley, 1968.

Hilgard, E. R., and Bower, G. *Theories of learning*. New York: Prentice-Hall, 1975.

Hook, S. (Ed.). *Psychoanalysis, scientific method and philosophy*. New York: Grove, 1960.

Jones, E. *The life and work of Sigmund Freud*. New York: Basic Books, Vol. 1, 1953; Vol. 2, 1955; Vol. 3, 1957.

Kubie, L. S. Psychoanalysis as a basic science. In Franz Alexander and Helen Ross (Eds.). *20 years of psycho-analysis*. New York: Norton, 1953, pp. 120–154.

Mitchell, J. *Psychoanalysis and feminism: Freud, Reich, Laing, and women.* New York: Pantheon, 1974.

Schur, M. The id and the regulatory principles of mental functioning. *J. Amer. Psychoanal. Assoc., Monograph series,* 1966, No. 4, 1–220.

Stepansky, P. A history of aggression in Freud. *Psychol. Issues,* Vol. X, No. 3, Monogr. 39. New York: International Univ. Press, 1977.

Turiell, E. A historical analysis of the Freudian concept of the superego. *Psychoanal. Rev.,* 1967, **54**, 118–140.

Whyte, L. L. *The unconscious before Freud.* Garden City, N.Y.: Doubleday, 1962.

CONTEMPORARY PSYCHOANALYTIC THEORY

3

What has happened to Freud's theory of personality since his death in 1939? This is the question we will address ourselves to in the present chapter. Before beginning the discussion, it should be noted that a lot happened to psychoanalytic theory during Freud's lifetime. In order to see this, one has only to compare the *Introductory lectures* published in 1916–1917 with the *New introductory lectures* published in 1933. In 1916, there were no id, ego, or superego. Nor were there any death instinct and its derivatives, aggression and self-destruction. In 1916, anxiety was the *result* of repression; in 1933, it was the *cause* of repression. By 1933, Freud had evolved a new theory of the female Oedipus complex. It would be wrong, however, to conclude from these comparisons that psychoanalytic theory was in continual flux and change during Freud's lifetime. Many of the original concepts remained the same. The steady elaboration and extension of the basic ideas rather than radical revisions marked the course of Freud's work.

There are those who feel that Freud became more speculative as he grew older and that his speculations about the origins, structures, and dynamics of the mind—what Freud called "metapsychology"—were a far cry from his theoretical formulations, which were closely tied to data obtained from the direct clinical observation of patients. Others point out, however, that the seeds of his metapsychology were already planted in the *Project for a scientific psychology* (1895) and Chapter 7 of *The interpretation of dreams* (1900), and that Freud was always interested in arriving at a general theory of the mind or personality and not in merely conceiving a theory of neurosis.

Although Freud was surrounded by a number of stimulating men and women, he was the master builder of psychoanalytic theory during his lifetime. He laid the foundations, guided the course of its development, and assumed sole responsibility for its major revisions. Freud was receptive to ideas advanced by his associates in the psychoanalytic movement and often credited them with new insights, but he was adamant about preserving the conceptual pillars upon which psychoanalysis was based. Anyone who attempted to undermine these pillars or to replace them was no longer considered a part of the psychoanalytic enterprise. Inevitably, a number of psychoanalysts seceded and developed their own theories. Notable among these were Adler, Jung, Rank, and Reich. It would be incorrect, however, to say, as some have done, that Freud was dictatorial or that he was personally vindictive toward those who dissented. In Jung's case, for example, the correspondence between Freud and Jung (McGuire, 1974) reveals that Freud made a great effort, and a kindly one, to persuade Jung of the incorrectness of his (Jung's) views. (Parenthetically, it may be observed that it was fortunate Freud did not succeed in persuading Jung.) A theory is, after all, the brainchild of one person; it cannot be conceived by a committee.

Upon the death of Freud in 1939, his followers were faced with the difficult task of deciding what should be done regarding the future development of psychoanalytic theory. The course many chose was to amplify aspects of Freud's system, to make more explicit some of Freud's postulates, to sharpen the definitions of some of the basic concepts, to extend the range of phenomena covered by psychoanalytic explanations, and to employ observational methods other than the psychoanalytic interview to validate propositions derived from Freudian theory. Changes in psychoanalytic therapy have also been instituted, but this aspect of psychoanalysis lies outside the scope of the present volume.

In much of the psychoanalytic literature, both past and present, the opening paragraphs of an article or chapter in a book are devoted to a presentation of what Freud had to say concerning the topic under consideration. This is followed by the writer's amplification of the topic, and the presentation of new evidence or arguments. Freud's writings are the primary authority, and quotations from them are sprinkled throughout the article or book to justify the points made by the writer. In spite of this strong allegiance to Freud's ideas on the part of his followers—and their understandable tendency to treat the formidable corpus of his published works as sacred writings—some new trends can be detected in the psychoanalytic literature since Freud's death. We shall discuss some of these trends.

We shall also take note of the growing *rapprochement* of psychology and psychoanalysis. It is no secret that most psychologists were hostile toward Freud's ideas prior to World War II, but, for reasons to be discussed in this chapter, this hostility has been steadily diminishing although it has not completely disappeared. Not only have Freud's ideas permeated psychology but also psychologists have made theoretical and empirical contributions to psychoanalysis.

The chief focus of the chapter will fall on the writings of Erik Erikson. He, probably more than any other contemporary figure, best exemplifies the ways in which classical psychoanalysis has been elaborated, extended, and applied. His extensive writings have also provided a bridge between psychology and psychoanalysis.

Easily the most striking development in psychoanalytic theory since Freud's death is the emergence of a new theory of the ego, sometimes referred to as ego psychology. Although Freud regarded the ego as the executive of the total personality, at least in the case of the healthy person, he never granted it an autonomous position; it always remained subservient to the wishes of the id. In what was to be his final pronouncement on psychoanalytic theory, Freud (1940) reiterated what he had said so many times before, "This oldest portion [the id] of the mental apparatus remains the most important throughout life" (p. 14). The id and its instincts express "the true purpose of the individual organism's life." There is no question as to how Freud felt regarding the relationship of the ego and the id: the id is the dominant member of the partnership.

In contrast to Freud's position is that of some psychoanalytic theorists to enhance the role of the ego in the total personality. The leader of the new ego theory is Heinz Hartmann (1958, 1964). This new ego theory not only embraces such topics as the development of the reality principle in childhood, the integrative or synthesizing functions of the ego, the ego's auxiliary processes of perceiving, remembering, thinking, and acting, and the defenses of the ego but, more important, it has put forward the concept of the autonomy of the ego. Discussions of the autonomous functions of the ego usually begin by quoting from one of Freud's last articles in which he wrote, "But we must not overlook the fact that id and ego are originally one, and it does not imply a mystical over-valuation of heredity if we think it credible that, even before the ego exists, its subsequent lines of development, tendencies and reactions are already determined" (Freud, 1937, pp. 343–344). Proceeding from this quotation, Hartmann pos-

EGO PSYCHOLOGY

tulates that there is an undifferentiated phase early in life during which both the id and the ego are formed. The ego does not emerge out of an inborn id, but each system has its origin in inherent predispositions and each has its own independent course of development. Moreover, it is asserted that the ego processes are operated by neutralized sexual and aggressive energies. The aims of these ego processes can be independent of purely instinctual objectives.

Ego defenses do not have to be pathological or negative in character; they may serve healthy purposes in the formation of personality. Hartmann believes that a defense may become independent of its origin in combating the instincts and serve the functions of adjustment and organization. Ego theorists also attribute a conflict-free sphere to the ego. This means that some processes of the ego are not in conflict with the id, the superego, or the external world. These ego processes may, of course, be incompatible with one another so that the person has to decide which is the best of several ways to solve a problem or make an adaptation.

Parallel to the emergence of this new conception of an autonomous ego has been a growing interest in the adaptive functions of the ego, that is, the nondefensive ways in which the ego deals with reality, or with what Freud called "reality testing." For making effective adaptations to the world, the ego has at its disposal the cognitive processes of perceiving, remembering, and thinking. One consequence of this new emphasis on the ego's cognitive processes has been to draw psychoanalysis closer to psychology, a trend discussed in the next section of this chapter. Among the leaders of this adaptational viewpoint are Rapaport (1960), Gill (1959), and Klein (1970).

The Harvard psychologist, Robert White (1963), has proposed that the ego not only has its own intrinsic energy, but that there are also intrinsic ego satisfactions independent of id or instinctual gratifications. These autonomous ego satisfactions are things such as exploration, manipulation, and effective competence in performing tasks.

An even more radical version of ego psychology has been put forth by the British psychoanalyst, Ronald Fairbairn (1952). He believes that the ego is present at birth, it has its own dynamic structure, and it is the source of its own energy. In fact, there is only the ego; there is no id. The ego's main functions are to seek, find, and establish relations with objects in the external world. These functions can be observed in infants soon after birth as the observations of Melanie Klein and her associates (1955) show. If there is no id to conflict with the ego, what is the source of conflict according to this object-relations theory? Conflicts arise from disparate experiences a person has with objects. The baby's interactions with the mother, for example, are sometimes satisfying and sometimes frustrating. Consequently, the child develops ambivalent or conflictful feelings about the mother. Ambivalence characterizes many of our relations with objects in the world.

This trend of treating the ego as an autonomous system whose origin is parallel with the id and which is endowed with autonomous functions and energy sources has not gone unchallenged by other psychoanalysts. Nacht (1952), for example, deplores this new "ego psychology," which he considers sterile and regressive. The psychologist, Robert R. Holt (1965), has made a critical evaluation of the concept of ego autonomy as presented in the writings of Hartmann and Rapaport, and concludes that it will not come to occupy an important place in psychoanalytical thinking. Holt writes, "One would instead be mainly concerned to describe the relative roles of drive, external stimuli and press, and various inner structures in determining behavior, and the complex interactions between them" (p. 157). It might be pointed out that this is precisely what Freud was saying and doing throughout his life.

This new ego theory has appealed to many psychologists because it focusses on the traditional subject-matter of psychology—namely, perception, memory, learning, and thinking. It also has an appeal because it emphasizes the characteristic processes and behavior of the normal person in contradistinction to the deviant processes and behavior of a patient population. Furthermore, ego theory tends to place more emphasis on the rational, conscious, constructive aspects of human personality in contrast to the emphasis placed on the unconscious and irrational by classical psychoanalysis. Finally, ego theory is said to be more "humanistic" than orthodox psychoanalytic theory.

THE MERGING OF PSYCHOANALYSIS AND PSYCHOLOGY

Psychoanalysis and psychology have a common background in nineteenth century science, but they remained independent of one another for a number of years because of their different interests. In its early years, psychology was concerned with investigating the elements and processes of consciousness. Sensation, perception, memory, and thinking were its chief topics of interest. Psychoanalysis, on the other hand, was a psychology of the unconscious; its interests were in the areas of motivation, emotion, conflict, neurotic symptoms, dreams, and character traits. Moreover, the science of psychology grew up in an academic and laboratory setting, whereas psychoanalysis developed in a clinical setting; so representatives of the two disciplines had little contact with each other.

Gradually, the gap between the two disciplines began to diminish and, following World War II, the interpenetration of psychology and psychoanalysis has grown at an accelerated rate. Freudian psychology is now one of the dominant viewpoints in academic psychology. Shakow and Rapaport (1964) and Hall and Lindzey (1968) discuss the reasons why psychology and psychoanalysis have grown closer together in recent years. On the one hand, psychoanalysis, which Freud always regarded as being a branch of psychology, has shown more interest in "normal" behavior, culminating in the construction of an ego psychology. The extent to which the "psychologizing" of psychoanalysis has progressed is indicated by the title of a book of essays honoring the father of ego psychology, Heinz Hartmann. It is called *Psychoanalysis: a general psychology* (Loewenstein, Newmann, Schur, and Solnit, 1966.) Labeling psychoanalysis "a general psychology" goes beyond what Freud claimed for it—a part and not the whole of psychology.

Psychology for its part began to take an interest in motivation and personality, and the field of clinical psychology burgeoned during and following World War II. Psychologists found much that was relevant to its new concerns in psychoanalysis. Even prior to the war, individual psychologists such as Kurt Lewin and Henry Murray conducted empirical research that was related to, and in part inspired by psychoanalysis. During the late thirties the efforts that were made to bring about a rapprochement between Hull's reinforcement theory and aspects pf psychoanalysis by such psychologists as Neal Miller, Hobart Mowrer, and Robert Sears brought more experimentalists into contact with Freud's conceptions of personality. More recently, some psychologists have found in Piaget a useful bridge to psychoanalysis (Wolff, 1960; Cobliner, 1967).

On the theoretical side, David Rapaport (1959, 1960) drew up a conceptual model of psychoanalysis that is closely interwoven with a number of traditional psychological concepts. In fact, Rapaport has been one of the key figures in the growing interpenetration between psychoanalysis and psychology. Klein, Erikson, and others have acknowledged Rapaport's great influence on their thinking. Symposia that included both psychologists and psychoanalysts interested in examining the mutual relations between the two fields were also helpful in reducing the communication gap (Frenkel-Brunswik, Richfield, Scriven, and Skinner, 1954; Pumpian-Mindlin, 1952; Bellak, 1959).

Surely one of the most important factors in bringing about a closer relationship between psychology and psychoanalysis was the opportunity offered psychologists to obtain competent training in psychoanalysis from qualified psychoanalysts. Psychoanalytic institutes and places like the Menninger Clinic in Topeka, Kansas, and the Austen Riggs Center in Stockbridge, Massachusetts, opened their doors to selected post-doctoral psychologists in the years following World War II. Prior to that time, psychoanalytic training was available only to persons with a medical degree. At least, this was the case in the United States. The monopolizing of psychoanalysis by the medical profession is ironical in view of the fact that Freud himself was strongly opposed to psychoanalysis becoming exclusively a medical specialty, and argued vigorously for an open-door policy in the training of psychoanalysts (1926). Many of the early psychoanalysts were not physicians.

Psychologists who received psychoanalytic training returned then to universities where they were able to offer their students a better and more sympathetic understanding of psychoanalysis. They also initiated research programs that had a psychoanalytic orientation. Nor should the role played by the National Institute of Mental Health of the Department of Health, Education, and Welfare be overlooked. This Institute has provided large sums of money for training and research in psychoanalytically oriented psychology. Without this financial support it is doubtful whether such great strides could have been made in uniting the two fields.

George Klein

George Klein may be taken as an exemplar of those psychologists who in the post-war years combined a traditional education in psychology with training in psychoanalysis. These individuals brought to psychoanalysis the values of laboratory experimentation and quantification and a respect for theory-building as well as a firm grounding in cognitive processes. They received from psychoanalysis the kind of theoretical orientation and insights into the person that were lacking in their educational background. That psychoanalysis is no longer considered to be alien to academic psychology is due in large part to the pioneer efforts of these psychologists.

Klein received his graduate training in psychology at Columbia University where he did experimental investigations on animal behavior and human perception, highly respectable areas of psychology. After being discharged from the Air Force in 1946, he went to the Menninger Clinic, one of the few places in the United States where psychologists could obtain psychoanalytically oriented training in clinical psychology. Klein like many other psychologists of that period underwent a personal psychoanalysis and later graduated from the New York Psychoanalytic Institute. His principal identification remained with psychology, however. As a professor of psychology and one of the founders of the Research Center for Mental Health at New York University, Klein in collaboration with other psychologists and graduate students carried on an extensive research program on topics heavily influenced by psychoanalytic thought. In 1959, Klein founded a monograph series, *Psychological Issues,* which has provided a forum for the presentation of research findings and theoretical issues relevant to psychoanalysis.

Klein's principal contributions to the fusion of psychology and psychoanalysis were fourfold. First, he and his associates demonstrated that clinically derived hypotheses could be investigated in the laboratory under rigorously controlled conditions. Second, he and his associates provided an opportunity for doctoral candidates in psychology interested in psychoanalysis to pursue their studies in a research-oriented environment. Third, by virtue of the fact that Klein was himself a recognized and acceptable member of traditional psychology, his writings helped to weaken the hostility many psychologists felt toward what they considered to be "unscientific" psychoanalysis. Finally, Klein made important contributions to psychoanalytic theory, contributions that also helped to make the theory more palatable to psychologists.

As we said earlier, Klein was only one psychologist among many who were instrumental in breaking down the barriers between psychology and psychoanalysis. As noted in another chapter, Henry Murray and his many brilliant students at Harvard were a strong force, perhaps the strongest, in introducing psychoanalysis into the mainstream of academic psychology. Murray was medically trained and a psychoanalyst, however, and not a traditionally trained psychologist. Moreover, he evolved a theory of personality that, although strongly influenced by psychoanalysis, was uniquely his own theory. Klein, on the other hand, and many like him were and remained psychologists despite their training in psychoanalysis. Not only did they labor to make psychoanalysis more scientific but they also contributed to the elaboration and modification of classical psychoanalysis. They were not concerned with formulating a new theory.

Although Klein's research activities embraced a number of areas, he is probably best known for his studies of the different ways in which we perceive a situation, remember a past event, or solve a problem. "Our focus has been the perceiver and how he organizes experience in his own way" (Klein, 1970, p. 142).

In one series of perceptual studies, it was found that some people employed the strategy of "leveling" their perceptions whereas others employed the strategy of "sharpening" their perceptions. Levelers compared with sharpeners, for instance, were poorer at making correct estimates of the sizes of squares that were gradually increased in size. Levelers tended to make the same estimate of size for large squares as they did for small ones. They did not notice the difference.

Sharpeners varied their estimates so they were much more accurate. These strategies Klein called *cognitive controls* or *attitudes*. In subsequent experiments, it was found that people behaved consistently in different types of tasks. People who were levelers in estimating size were less able to discover hidden faces in a picture because they were less aware of small differences in the picture than sharpeners. This personal consistency in the use of a particular strategy is called *cognitive style*. A number of other cognitive strategies have been identified (Gardner and others, 1959).

For Klein, needs, motives, drives, and emotions are not the only processes that direct and control behavior. Indeed, they may not even be the most important ones. The way in which a person's cognitive structure is organized, that is, for example, whether he or she is a leveler or a sharpener, also directs and controls behavior, and thereby helps to determine its effectiveness in adapting to the world.

Although Klein acknowledged that his research on cognitive processes was motivated by the ego theory of Hartmann and others, it may be pointed out that these studies are more in the tradition of academic psychology than in the tradition of psychoanalysis. They could have been planned and executed without recourse to psychoanalytic ego theory.

Psychologists trained in psychoanalysis have not only made laboratory investigations of Freudian hypotheses but they have also engaged in dissecting and reformulating psychoanalytic theory. George Klein, to take one example, devoted the last years of his life to disentangling what he called the clinical theory of psychoanalysis from its metapsychology (Klein, 1976; also Gill and Holzman, 1976). Metapsychology refers to speculations about the structure, dynamics, origins, and development of personality. Freud's metapsychology, Klein claims, is based on a natural science conception of humans. It treats the individual as a biological system, that is, an organism, consisting of structures (id, ego, and superego) charged with instinctual energies. The energies in the different structures come into conflict with one another (cathexis versus anticathexis), resulting in the accumulation of tensions. The aim of the organism is to discharge these tensions and return to a state of rest. In attempting to realize this aim, the instinctual energies undergo what Freud called vicissitudes of various kinds including repression, displacement, projection, and reaction formation. Metapsychology is, in Klein's view, impersonal and mechanistic.

Freud's clinical theory as described by Klein is a theory of the person rather than one of the organism. It is personal and humanistic. It tries to understand *this* individual's problems and to interpret his or her experience and behavior in terms of *his* or *her* aims, intentions, directions, and purposes. It looks for reasons rather than causes. Klein feels that the two theories, the clinical and the metapsychological, should be sharply differentiated—which he says Freud did not do—because they present quite different views of the individual, the former psychological and human, the latter biological and physical. In fact, Klein would dispense with metapsychology entirely because it serves no useful purpose for the psychologist and may even be a detriment to the proper understanding of the individual. Since Freud has been repeatedly criticized by psychologists for his depersonalized model, Klein's rejection of metapsychology has eliminated from psychoanalytic theory this major impediment to its acceptance by psychologists. Klein has been joined in this endeavor by Gill (1976) who asserts defiantly "metapsychology is not psychology."

Other psychologists who have contributed to the reformation of psychoanalytic theory are White (1963), Schafer (1976), and Holt (1976).

EXPERIMENTAL VALIDATION OF PSYCHOANALYTIC HYPOTHESES

We have already observed that one result of the development of a closer relationship between psychology and psychoanalysis is the laboratory testing of hypotheses derived from psychoanalytic theory. Let us consider this development in greater detail.

Investigations in this area were surveyed by Sears (1943, 1944), Hilgard (1952), and Blum (1953). These reviews, however, are primarily of historical value because much of the early research was done using an inappropriate methodology and an insufficient understanding of psychoanalytic theory (Horwitz, 1963). Kline (1972) has made a more up-to-date survey of some 700 references. Kline concluded that "far too much that is distinctively Freudian has been verified for the rejection of the whole psychoanalytic theory to be possible" (p. 350). Hans Eysenck, an implacable foe of psychoanalysis, in collaboration with Glenn Wilson, reexamined the data on which Kline based his conclusion and assert "there is no evidence at all for psychoanalytic theory" (1974, p. 385). The most recent book to survey the evidence is by Fisher and Greenberg (1977). They feel the evidence, generally speaking, favors Freud. An annual review entitled *Psychoanalysis and contemporary science* edited by Holt and Peterfreund has been appearing since 1972.

Rather than attempting to review all the experimental tests of psychoanalytic propositions that have been made in recent years, we shall instead devote our attention to two research programs considered models of theoretical and experimental sophistication. These programs have been in existence since the mid-1960s and are still very active. Dozens of experiments have been performed and the results are consistent in confirming psychoanalytic hypotheses. One program is being conducted at the Research Center for Mental Health of New York University by Lloyd Silverman and co-workers, the other at Michigan State University by Joseph Reyher and co-workers. Both sets of investigations are clearly described by Silverman (1976).

The hypotheses tested in both programs center around the general Freudian notion that abnormal or deviant behavior can be increased or reduced by stirring up or diminishing conflicts over unconscious sexual and aggressive wishes. The programs differ in two important respects: the method used for inducing unconscious conflicts and the type of subjects tested. The New York researchers use the method of subliminal stimulation and groups of people displaying obvious pathological or deviant behavior. The Michigan investigastors use the method of hypnotic suggestion and groups of individuals (college students) who display no obvious forms of abnormal or deviant behavior.

The New York Studies

The method of subliminal stimulation involves showing a person a picture or printed phrase so briefly that he or she is unable to recognize what it is. This brief exposure (.004 seconds) is done by an instrument called a tachistoscope. It has been clearly demonstrated in a number of investigations that although a person is not aware of what has been presented tachistoscopically, nevertheless the material shown may affect feelings and behavior in demonstrable ways.

As an example of the methodology, we will describe experiments on depressed people. According to psychoanalytic theory, depression is produced by turning unconscious aggressive feelings toward others inward against one's self. If this hypothesis is correct, a depressed person should feel even more depressed when unconscious aggressive wishes are activated. To stimulate such wishes depressed individuals were shown an aggressive picture, for instance, a snarling man holding a dagger or a verbal message, for instance, CANNIBAL EATS PERSON. Aggressive pictures or messages were each exposed to the subject, it will be recalled, for only 4/1000 of a second. Prior to and after the presentation the individual made self-ratings of his feelings. The same subjects, in a different session, were shown subliminally a neutral picture, for example, a person reading a newspaper or a verbal message, for example, PEOPLE ARE WALKING, and they were asked to make self-ratings before and after the presentation. Silverman (1976) writes: "The subliminal presentation of content designed to stimulate aggressive wishes led to an intensification of depressive feelings that were not in evidence after the subliminal presentation of neutral content" (p. 627).

In order to show that the effect of the material was specific to the aggressive content, as the psychoanalytic theory of depression demands, and could not be produced by a different type of emotional material, the Silverman group performed the following experiment. Depressed patients were shown subliminally an aggressive picture on one occasion and a picture of a person defecating on another. The latter picture is supposed to stimulate conflictful anal wishes, which according to Freudian theory are linked with stuttering. The depressives became more depressed following the presentation of the aggressive picture but not following the presentation of the anal picture. The opposite effect was shown by a group of stutterers. They stuttered more after being shown the anal picture subliminally but not after the aggressive picture.

The New York group also demonstrated that abnormal symptoms could be *reduced* by diminishing conflictful wishes. For these experiments, schizophrenic patients were tested. They are shown tachistoscopically a printed message MOMMY AND I ARE ONE. Their abnormal symptoms were reduced by this subliminal message, and not by other control messages. Why does the MOMMY message have a beneficial effect? For three reasons, Silverman says. First, the oneness with mother wards off unconscious hostile feelings toward her. Second, the fantasy of oneness implies an uninterrupted supply of nurturance (mothering) from the mother. And third, the fantasy diminishes separation anxiety. By contrast, when schizophrenics were shown messages that contained hostility toward the mother or fears of losing her their abnormal symptoms increased.

The reader may wonder what would happen if the messages that were designed to activate unconscious wishes were shown under normal conditions, that is, where the subject could clearly recognize and understand the message. The answer is that consciously perceived messages had no effect on the symptoms of the patients. Apparently, unconscious wishes can only be stirred up by something of which the person is not aware.

The Michigan Studies   Reyher and associates use hypnosis to implant aggressive or sexual conflicts in college students who have no obvious psychiatric disturbance. For example, a hypnotized person is told a story in which he (the subject) is nearly seduced by a very attractive older woman. This story is designed to arouse unconscious oedipal feelings in young men. While the person is still under hypnosis, it is suggested to him first that he will not remember anything about the story (this is called inducing *posthypnotic amnesia*) and second that he will have strong sexual feelings whenever certain words are mentioned after he has been awakened. This is called *posthypnotic suggestion*. He is then brought out of the hypnotic state and presented visually with a list of words. Some of the words are connected with the story, others are not. He is asked how he feels after each word is presented. A number of indications of disturbance appeared when the critical words were seen but not when the neutral ones were seen. Disturbances included nausea, sweating, trembling, confusion, disorientation, and feelings of guilt, shame, and disgust. The Michigan studies—and there have been a number of them—corroborate the New York findings despite differences in method and subjects.

A number of experimental studies that have failed to verify Freudian hypotheses could be cited. These failures may be due to a number of circumstances including improper derivation from the theory of the hypothesis to be tested, inappropriate methodology, and inadequate controls. Or the hypothesis tested may simply be wrong.

In any event, it appears that we have entered a new era in the testing of psychoanalytic hypotheses. It is an era in which experimental ingenuity is linked with theoretical sophistication.

ERIK H. ERIKSON

The choice of Erik H. Erikson as the central figure in this chapter on contemporary psychoanalytic theory is an obvious one. No other person since the death of Sigmund Freud has worked so conscientiously to elaborate and extend the structure of psychoanalysis laid down by Freud, and to reformulate its principles for an understanding of the modern world. The world changes, and unless a theory keeps abreast of these changes, it eventually stagnates and becomes irrelevant. One has only to read Freud chronologically to see how he kept his views abreast of the changing times. Since Freud's death, Erikson more than any other person discussed in this chapter has performed that function. He has breathed new life into psychoanalytic theory.

Some critics may say that Erikson's elaborations deviate so markedly from the letter and the spirit of psychoanalysis that they fall outside of the Freudian tradition. It is not our intention, however, to make an exhaustive comparison of Erikson's views with those of Freud's to determine whether he is or is not a true Freudian. The question, in any event, is a trivial one. The reader may find, if desired, one version of the differences between Erikson and Freud in Roazen (1976). Whatever others may say, Erikson considers himself a Freudian psychoanalyst. Trained in psychoanalysis at its very vortex, Vienna, analyzed by Anna Freud, a longtime practitioner of psychoanalysis, a member of its official organizations, and a training psychoanalyst for 35 years, Erikson feels that his views are consonant with the basic doctrine of psychoanalysis laid down by Freud. If Erikson has to be pinned down by a name, he would probably prefer to be called a post-Freudian.

Clearly, the most significant contributions Erikson has made fall under two major headings: (1) a psychosocial theory of development from which emerges an expanded conception of the ego and (2) psychohistorical studies that exemplify his psychosocial theory in the lives of famous individuals.

It is important for the reader to bear in mind what is meant by psychosocial when used in conjunction with development. It means specifically that the stages of a person's life from birth to death are formed by social influences interacting with a physically and psychologically maturing organism. In Erikson's words, there is a "mutual fit of individual and environment—that is, of the individual's capacity to relate to an ever expanding life space of people and institutions, on the one hand, and, on the other, the readiness of these people and institutions to make him part of an ongoing cultural concern" (1975, p. 102).

Erikson does not intend for his psychosocial theory to replace either Freud's psychosexual theory or Piaget's theory of cognitive development. He recognizes that they were concerned with other aspects of development. It should also be noted that while the theories of Freud and Piaget stop short of adulthood, as does Sullivan's interpersonal theory of development (see Chapter 5), Erikson's extends into old age. It should also be noted that Erikson's scheme like those of Freud, Piaget, and Sullivan is a *stage* theory, which means that there are more or less clearly defined ages at which new forms of behavior appear in response to new social and maturational influences. All theories of development are not necessarily stage theories. Skinner's operant conditioning theory, for example, assumes that development is continuous rather than stepwise.

Erikson's own life history is one that he feels has had a distinct bearing upon the development of his theoretical outlook. He apparently experienced many of the conflicts, confusions, and crises that later he was to write about. His life and work has been the subject of two full-length books, one by Robert Coles (1970) who is a former co-worker and great admirer of Erikson, the other by Paul Roazen (1976) who is more critical in his analysis. Erikson has referred to his own life history in some of his writings.

Born in Frankfurt, Germany, June 15, 1902, of Danish parents—his mother's family were Jewish—Erikson never knew his real father because his parents were separated before he was born. His mother married a Karlsruhe pediatrician, Dr. Homburger, who adopted Erikson

Erik H. Erikson

and whose name Erikson took. It was only much later in 1939 when he became an American citizen that Erikson added the name by which he is now known—Erik Homburger Erikson.

Upon completing his education at the gymnasium Erikson was undecided what he wanted to do. Like many young Germans at the time, he spent a year wandering through Europe searching for some inspiration or direction as to what he should become. He finally decided on art, for which he had the talent and the inclination. At this point in his life (he was then twenty-five years old), something happened that was to change it drastically. He was invited to teach in a small private school in Vienna. This school had been established as a place where children could be educated while they and/or their parents were being psychoanalyzed. It was a progressive school and the teachers and pupils were given complete freedom in developing the curriculum. Erikson became so interested in the education of children that he enrolled in and graduated from a school for the training of teachers in the Montessori method. The Montessori method stresses the development of the child's own initiative through play and work. This experience had a lasting influence on Erikson.

An even more profound influence was his inevitable exposure to psychoanalysis. He became acquainted with the Freud circle, underwent a training psychoanalysis with Anna Freud, and studied psychoanalysis at the Vienna Psychoanalytic Institute from which he graduated in 1933. He had now found his professional identity.

While studying psychoanalysis and teaching at the school, Erikson married Joan Serson, a Canadian-born dancer and fellow teacher. They decided to move to Denmark but when that did not work out satisfactorily, they came to the United States, settling in Boston in 1933. Erikson became the first child psychoanalyst in that city. He was also given a position at the Harvard Medical School and acted as a consultant to various agencies as well. While in Boston Erikson became associated with Henry A. Murray at the Harvard Psychological Clinic where he did research. After three years in Boston Erikson accepted a position in the Yale University Institute of Human Relations and an instructorship in the Medical School. In 1938 an invitation to observe Indian children at the Sioux reservation in South Dakota proved irresistible. In 1939 Erikson went to California where he became associated with the Institute of Child Welfare at the University of California in Berkeley which was conducting a large-scale longitudinal study of child development. He also resumed his work as a psychoanalyst, taking time off to observe the Yurok Indians of Northern California.

During these years in California he wrote his first book *Childhood and Society* (1950, revised edition, 1963). This book had an immediate and far-reaching impact. Although Erikson has published seven other books since then, *Childhood and Society* is generally regarded as the most significant since it lays down the themes that were to preoccupy Erikson for the rest of his life.

After resigning from his first professorship at the University of California as a protest against a special loyalty oath required of faculty members (it was later declared unconstitutional), Erikson took a position at the Austen Riggs Center in Stockbridge, Massachusetts, a leading center of residential psychiatry. In 1960, Erikson was appointed a professor at Harvard where his course on the Life Cycle became very popular with students. Erikson retired in 1970 and moved to a suburb of San Francisco where he continues to write and acts as a consultant for the Mount Zion Hospital and the Health and Medical Sciences Program in the University of California.

Now let us turn to a discussion of Erikson's theoretical formulations.

Development, as we have pointed out, proceeds by stages—eight in all, according to Erikson's timetable. The first four stages occur during infancy and childhood, the fifth stage during adolescence, and the last three stages during the adult years up to and including old age. In Erikson's writings, particular emphasis is placed on the adolescent period because it is then that the transition between childhood and adulthood is made. What happens during this stage is of the greatest significance for adult personality. *Identity, identity crises,* and *identity confusion* are undoubtedly the most familiar of Erikson's concepts.

These consecutive stages, it should be noted, are not laid out according to a strict chronological timetable. Erikson feels that a given child has its own timetable, and therefore it would be misleading to specify an exact duration for each stage. Moreover, each stage is not passed through and then left behind. Instead, each stage contributes to the formation of the total personality. In Erikson's words, ". . . anything that grows has a ground plan, and that out of this ground plan the parts arise, each part having its time of special ascendancy, until all parts have arisen to form a functioning whole" (1968, p. 92). This is known as the *epigenetic principle,* a term borrowed from embryology.

In describing the eight stages of psychosocial development, we have brought together and paraphrased material from four sources. In *Childhood and Society* (1950, 1963), and later in *Identity: Youth and Crisis* (1968) Erikson set forth the stages in terms of the basic *ego quality* that emerges during each stage. In *Insight and Responsibility* (1964) he discussed the *virtues* or ego strengths that appear during successive

THE PSYCHOSOCIAL THEORY OF DEVELOPMENT

stages. In his most recent book *Toys and Reasons* (1976), he describes the *ritualization* peculiar to each stage. By ritualization Erikson means a playful and yet culturally patterned way of doing or experiencing something in the daily interplay of individuals. The basic purpose of these ritualizations is to turn the maturing individual into an effective and familiar member of a community. Unfortunately, ritualizations can become rigid and perverted and turn into *ritualisms*.

I. Basic Trust vs. Basic Mistrust   The earliest basic trust is established during the oral-sensory stage and is demonstrated by the infant by its capacity to sleep peacefully, to take nourishment comfortably, and to excrete relaxfully. Each day, as its wakeful hours increase, the infant becomes more familiar with sensual experiences, and their familiarity coincides with a sense of feeling good. Situations of comfort and the people responsible for these comforts become familiar and identifiable to the infant. Because of the infant's trust in and familiarity with the maternal person, it achieves a state of acceptance in which that person may be absent for awhile. This initial social achievement by the infant is possible because it is developing an inner certainty and trustfulness that the maternal person will return. Daily routines, consistency, and continuity in the infant's environment provide the earliest basis for a sense of psychosocial identity. Through continuity of experiences with adults the infant learns to rely on them and to trust them; but perhaps even more importantly it learns to trust itself. Such assurance must outbalance the negative counterpart of basic trust—namely, basic mistrust which, in principle, is essential for human development.

The proper ratio of trust and mistrust results in the ascendance of *hope*. "Hope is both the earliest and the most indispensable virtue inherent in the state of being alive" (1964, p. 115). The foundation of hope relies on the infant's initial relations with *trustworthy maternal parents* who are responsive to its needs, who provide such satisfying experiences as tranquility, nourishment, and warmth. All the verifications of hope originate in the mother-child-world. Through an ever increasing number of experiences in which the infant's hope is verified, it receives inspiration for new hopefulness. Simultaneously, it develops a capability to abandon disappointed hopes and to foresee hope in future goals and prospects. It learns what hopes are within the realm of possibility and directs its expectations accordingly. As it matures, it finds that hopes that were once high priority are superseded by a higher level or more advanced set of hopes. Erikson states, "Hope is the enduring belief in the attainability of fervent wishes, in spite of the dark urges and rages which mark the beginning of existence" (1964, p. 118).

This first stage of life, infancy, is the stage of the *numinous* ritualization. What Erikson means by numinous is the baby's sense of the hallowed presence of the mother, her looking, holding, touching, smiling, feeding, naming, and otherwise "recognizing" him. These repeated interactions are highly personal and yet culturally ritualized. Recognition of the infant by the mother affirms and certifies the infant and its mutuality with the mother. Lack of recognition can cause *estrangement* in the infant's personality; a sense of *separation* and *abandonment*.

Each of the early stages establishes a ritualization that is continued on into childhood and there contributes to the society's rituals. The perverted form of the numinous ritual is expressed in adult life by idolatrous hero worship, or *idolism*.

II. Autonomy vs. Shame and Doubt

During the second stage of life (the anal-muscular stage in the psychosexual scheme) the child learns what is expected of it, what its obligations and privileges are along with what limitations are placed upon it. The child's striving for new and more activity-oriented experiences places a dual demand upon it: a demand for self-control, and a demand for the acceptance of control from others in the environment. Adults in order to tame the child's willfulness will utilize the universal and necessary human propensity for shame; yet they will encourage the child to develop a sense of autonomy and to eventually stand on its own two feet. Adults that exercise control must also be firmly reassuring. The child should be encouraged to experience situations that require the autonomy of free choice. Excessive shamefulness will only induce the child to be shameless or force it to attempt to get away with things by being secretive, sneaky, and sly. This is the stage that promotes freedom of self-expression and lovingness. A sense of self-control provides the child with a lasting feeling of good will and pride; however, a sense of loss of self-control can cause a lasting feeling of shame and doubt.

The virtue of *will* emerges during this second stage of life. Trained self-will and the example of superior will displayed by others are the two origins from which the virtue of will develops. The child learns from itself and from others what is expected and what is expectable. Will is responsible for the child's gradual acceptance of lawfulness and necessity. The elements of will are increased gradually through experiences involving awareness and attention, manipulation, verbalization, and locomotion. Will is the ever-increasing strength to make free choices, to decide, to exercise self-restraint, and to apply oneself.

Erikson calls the ritualization of this stage *judicious,* because the child begins to judge itself and others and to differentiate between right and wrong. It develops a sense of the rightness or wrongness of certain acts and words, which prepares the experience, in the next stage, of feeling guilty. The child also learns to distinguish between "our kind" and others judged to be different; therefore others that are not like its own kind can be automatically assessed as wrong or bad. This is the ontogenetic basis of the worldwide estrangement that is called a *divided species*. In other writings, Erikson labels this *pseudospecies,* the origin of intra-human prejudice.

This period of judicious ritualization in childhood is the origin within the life cycle of the *judicial* ritual in adulthood exemplified by the courtroom trial and the procedures by which guilt or innocence is established.

The perverted ritualism of this stage is *legalism,* which is the victory of the letter of the law over the spirit, retribution for compassion. The legalistic person achieves satisfaction in having the convicted punished and humiliated, whether or not that was the intention of the law.

III. Initiative vs. Guilt
The third psychosocial stage of life, corresponding to the genital-locomotor stage of psychosexuality, is that of initiative, an age of expanding mastery and responsibility. The child during this stage presents itself as being decisively more advanced and more "together" both physically and mentally. Initiative combines with autonomy to give the child a quality of pursuing, planning, and determination of achieving tasks and goals. The danger of this stage is the feeling of guilt that may haunt the child for an overzealous contemplation of goals, including genital fantasies, and the use of aggressive, manipulative means of achieving these goals. The child is eager to learn and learns well at this age; it strives to grow in the sense of obligations and performances.

Purpose is the virtue that ascends during this developmental stage. The child's major activity at this age is playing, and purpose results from its playing, explorations, attempts and failures, and experimentation with its toys. In addition to physical games it undertakes mental games by assuming roles of parents and other adults in a make-believe world. By imitating these adult images it realizes to some degree what it is like to be like them. Play provides the child with an intermediate reality; it learns what the purpose of things are, the connection between an inner and outer world, and how memories of the past apply to goals of the future. Thus, imaginative and uninhibited play are vitally important to the child's development. "Purpose, then, is the courage to envisage and pursue valued goals uninhibited by the defeat of infantile fantasies, by guilt and by the foiling fear of punishment" (1964, p. 122).

This age of play is characterized by *dramatic* ritualization. The child actively participates in playacting, wearing costumes, imitating adult personalities, and pretending to be anything from a dog to an astronaut. This early stage of ritualization contributes to the dramatic element to be found in rituals (such as drama as a ritual of its own) throughout the remainder of its life. The inner estrangement that may ensue from this stage of childhood is a sense of *guilt*.

The negative counterpart of dramatic ritualization is the ritualism of *impersonation* throughout life. The adult plays roles or acts in order to present an image that is not representative of one's true personality.

During this fourth stage of the epigenetic process (in Freud's scheme, the latency period) the child must submit to controlling its exuberant imagination and settling down to formal education. It develops a sense of industry and learns the rewards of perseverance and diligence. The interest in toys and play is gradually superseded by an interest in productive situations and the implements and tools used for work. The hazard of this stage is that the child may develop a sense of inferiority if it is (or is made to feel it is) unable to master the tasks that it undertakes or which are set for it by teachers and parents.

IV. Industry vs. Inferiority

The virtue of *competence* emerges during the industry stage. Virtues of the previous stages (hope, will, and purpose) provided the child with a view of future tasks, although not a very specific view. The child now needs specific instruction in fundamental methods to become familiar with a technical way of life. It is ready and willing to learn about and use the tools, machines, and methods preparatory for adult work. As soon as it has developed sufficient intelligence and capacities for work, it is important that it apply itself to this work to prevent feelings of inferiority and regression of the ego. Work, in this sense, includes many and varied forms, such as attending school, doing chores at home, assuming responsibilities, studying music, learning manual skills, as well as participating in skillful games and sports. The important thing is that the child must apply its intelligence and abounding energy to *some* undertaking and direction.

A sense of competence is achieved by applying oneself to work and to completing tasks, which eventually develops *workmanship*. The fundamentals of competence prepare the child for a future sense of workmanship; without it the child would feel inferior. During this age the child is eager to learn the techniques of productivity. "Competence, then, is the free exercise of dexterity and intelligence in the completion of tasks, unimpaired by infantile inferiority" (1964, p. 124).

School age is the stage of *formal* ritualization, when the child learns how to perform methodically. Watching and learning methods of performance provides the child with an over-all sense of quality for craftsmanship and perfection. Whatever the child does—whether skills in school or tasks at home—it does it the proper way.

The distorted ritualism in adulthood is that of *formalism,* which consists of the repetition of meaningless formalities and empty rituals.

V. Identity vs.
Identity Confusion
During adolescence the individual begins to sense a feeling of his own or her own identity, a feeling that one is a unique human being and yet prepared to fit into some meaningful role in society whether this role is adjustive or innovating. The person becomes aware of individual inherent characteristics, such as likes and dislikes, anticipated goals of the future, and the strength and purpose to control one's own destiny. This is a time in life when one wishes to define what one is at the present and what one wants to be in the future. It is a time for making vocational plans.

The activating inner agent in identity formation is the ego in its conscious and unconscious aspects. The ego at this stage has the capacity to select and integrate talents, aptitudes, and skills in identification with likeminded people and in adaptation to the social environment, and to maintain its defenses against threats and anxiety, as it learns to decide what impulses, needs, and roles are most appropriate and effective. All of these ego-selected characteristics are assembled and integrated by the ego to form one's psychosocial identity.

Because of the difficult transition from childhood to adulthood, on the one hand, and of a sensitivity to social and historical change, on the other, the adolescent during the stage of identity formation is likely to suffer more deeply than ever before or ever again from a confusion of roles, or *identity confusion.* This state can cause one to feel isolated, empty, anxious, and indecisive. The adolescent feels he or she must make important decisions, but is unable to do so. Adolescents may feel that society is pushing them to make decisions, thus they become even more resistant. They are deeply concerned with how others view them, and are apt to display a lot of self-consciousness and embarrassment.

During identity confusion, the adolescent may feel he is regressing rather than progressing, and, in fact, a periodical retreat to childishness appears to be a pleasant alternative to the complex involvement required of him in an adult society. The adolescent's behavior is inconsistent and unpredictable during this chaotic state. At one moment he has an inner reservation not to commit himself to anyone in fear of being rejected, disappointed, or misled. The very next moment he may want to be a follower, a lover, or disciple, no matter what the consequences of such a commitment may be.

The term *identity crisis* refers to the necessity to resolve the transitory failure to form a stable identity, or a confusion of roles. Each successive stage, in fact, "is a potential crisis because of a radical change in perspective" (1968, p. 96). The identity crisis, however, may seem particularly dangerous because the whole future of the individual as well as the next generation appears to depend on it.

Especially disturbing also is the development of a *negative identity*, that is, a sense of possessing a set of potentially bad or unworthy characteristics. The most common way of dealing with one's negative identity is to project the bad characteristics onto others. "They are bad, not me." Such projection can result in a lot of social pathology including prejudice and crime, and discrimination against various groups of people, but it is also an important part of the adolescent's readiness for ideological involvement.

At this adolescent age the virtue of *fidelity* develops. Although now sexually mature and in many ways responsible, he or she is not yet adequately prepared to become a parent. The ego-balance is confronted with a precarious situation; on the one hand one is expected to assimilate oneself into an adult pattern of life, but, on the other hand, one must deny oneself the sexual freedom of an adult. Behavior shuttles back and forth from impulsive, thoughtless, sporadic actions, to that of compulsive restraint. During this difficult time, however, the youth seeks an inner knowledge and understanding of his or herself and attempts to formulate a set of values. The particular set of values that emerges is what Erikson calls fidelity. "Fidelity is the ability to sustain loyalties freely pledged in spite of the inevitable contradictions of value systems" (1964, p. 125).

Fidelity is the foundation upon which a continuous sense of identity is formed. The substance for fidelity is acquired through the "confirmation" of ideologies and truths, and also through the affirmation of companions. The evolution of identity is based upon the human's inherent need to feel that he or she belongs to some particular or "special" kind of people. For example, one needs to know that one belongs to a special ethnic group or religious group in which one may participate in its customs, rituals, and ideologies, or, indeed, that one prefers to participate in movements destined to change or renew the social structure. The youth's identity gives definition to his or her environment.

The ritualization concurrent with the adolescent stage is that of *ideology*. Ideology is the solidarity of conviction that incorporates ritualizations from previous life stages into a coherent set of ideas and ideals. The estrangement that results from a lack of any integrated ideology is identity confusion.

The perversion of the ideology ritualization that may occur is *totalism*. Totalism is the fanatic and exclusive preoccupation with what seems to be unquestionably right or ideal.

VI. Intimacy vs. Isolation
In this stage, young adults are prepared and willing to unite their identity with others. They seek relationships of intimacy, partnerships, and affiliations, and are prepared to develop the necessary strengths to fulfill these commitments despite the sacrifices they may have to make. Now, for the first time in their life, the youth can develop true sexual *genitality* in mutuality with a loved partner. Sex life in previous stages was restricted to a searching for sexual identity and a striving for transitory intimacies. For genitality to be of lasting social significance it requires someone to love and to have sexual relations with, and with whom one can share in a trusting relationship. The hazard of the intimacy stage is isolation, which is the avoidance of relationships because one is unwilling to commit oneself to intimacy. A transitory sense of isolation, too, is a necessary condition for making choices, but, of course, can also result in severe personality problems.

The virtue of *love* comes into being during the intimacy stage of development. The dominant virtue of the universe, love, appears in many forms throughout earlier stages beginning with the infant's love for its mother, then the adolescent's infatuations, and finally the love one exhibits in caring for others as an adult. Although love is apparent in the earlier stages, the development of true intimacy transpires only *after* the age of adolescence. Young adults are now capable of committing themselves to a joint relationship in which their mode of life is mutually shared with an intimate partner. Erikson writes, "Love, then, is mutuality of devotion forever subduing the antagonisms inherent in divided function" (1964, p. 129). Although one's individual identity is maintained in a joint intimacy relationship, one's ego-strength is dependent upon the mutual partner who is prepared to share in the rearing of children, the productivity, and the ideology of their relationship.

The corresponding ritualization of this stage is the *affiliative,* that is, a sharing together of work, friendship, and love. The corresponding ritualism, namely, *elitism,* is expressed by the formation of exclusive groups that are a form of communal narcissism.

VII. Generativity vs. Stagnation
The stage of generactivity is characterized by the concern with what is generated—progeny, products, ideas, and so forth—and the establishment and setting forth of guidelines for up-coming generations. This transmission of social values is a necessity for both the psychosexual and psychosocial aspects of personality enrichment. When generativity is weak or not given expression the personality regresses, and takes on a sense of impoverishment and stagnation.

The virtue of *care* develops during this stage. Care is expressed by one's concern for others, by wanting to take care of those who need it and to share one's knowledge and experience with them. This is accomplished through childrearing and teaching, demonstrating, and supervising. Humans as a species have an inherent need to teach, a need common to those of every vocation. Humans achieve satisfaction and fulfillment by teaching children, adults, employees, and even animals. Facts, logic, and truths are preserved throughout generations by this passion to teach. Caring and teaching are responsible for the survival of cultures, through reiteration of their customs, rituals, and legends. The advancement of every culture owes its progression to those who care enough to instruct and to live exemplary lives. Teaching also instills in humans a vital sense of feeling needed by others, a sense of importance, which deters them from becoming too engrossed and absorbed with themselves. During one's lifetime a multitude of experience and knowledge is accumulated, such as education, love, vocation, philosophy, and style of life. All these aspects of livelihood must be preserved and protected, for they are cherished experiences. The preservation of these experiences is accomplished by transcending or passing them on to others. "Care is the widening concern for what has been generated by love, necessity, or accident; it overcomes the ambivalence adhering to irreversible obligation" (1964, p. 131).

The ritualization of this stage is the *generational,* which is the ritualization of parenthood, production, teaching, healing and so forth, roles in which the adult acts as a transmitter of ideal values to the young.

Distortions of the generational ritualization are expressed by the ritualism of *authoritism*. Authoritism is the seizure or encroachment of authority incompatible with care.

VIII. Integrity vs. Despair

The last stage of the epigenetic process of development is labeled integrity. It can best be described as a state one reaches after having taken care of things and people, products and ideas, and having adapted to the successes and failures of existence. Through such accomplishments individuals may reap the benefits of the first seven stages of life, and perceive that their life has some *order and meaning* within a *larger order*. Although one who has reached a state of integrity is aware of various life styles of others, he or she preserves with dignity their own style of life and defends it from potential threats. This style of life and the integrity of culture thus become the "patrimony of the soul."

The essential counterpart of integrity is a certain despair over the vicissitudes of the individual life cycle, as well as over social and historical conditions, not to speak of the nakedness of existence in the face of death. This can aggravate a feeling that life is meaningless, that the end is near, a fear of—and even a wish for—death. Time is now too short to turn back and attempt alternative styles of life.

Wisdom is the virtue that develops out of the encounter of integrity and despair in the last stage of life. Physical and mental activity of everyday functions are slowing down by this time in the life cycle. Simple wisdom maintains and conveys the integrity of accumulated experiences of previous years. "Wisdom, then, is detached concern with life itself, in the face of death itself" (1964, p. 133).

That the aging person is less adaptable to changing situations does not preclude a certain playfulness and curiosity that permits a closure of experience, as accrued from years of knowledge and judgment. Those in the stage of wisdom can represent to younger generations a style of life characterized by a feeling of wholeness and completeness. This feeling of wholeness can counteract the feeling of despair and disgust, and the feeling of being finished as present life situations pass by. The sense of wholeness also alleviates the feeling of helplessness and dependence that can mark the very end of life.

The ritualization of old age may be called *integral;* this is reflected in the wisdom of the ages. In search of a corresponding ritualism Erikson suggests *sapientism:* "the unwise pretense of being wise."

A NEW CONCEPTION OF THE EGO

Freud, it will be recalled, conceived of the ego as the executive of the personality, an executive whose duties are to satisfy the impulses of the id, to deal with the social and physical exigencies of the external world, and to try to live up to the perfectionistic standards of the superego. Beleaguered from three sides, the ego resorts to various defenses to avoid being overwhelmed. This concept of a defensive ego, originated by Freud and elaborated by Anna Freud (1946) was modified by Hartmann and others (see pp. 77–79) to include adaptive and integrative functions.

As the foregoing discussion of Erikson's stages of life demonstrates, he has endowed the ego with a number of qualities that go far beyond any previous psychoanalytic conception of the ego. Such qualities as trust and hope, autonomy and will, industry and competence, identity and fidelity, intimacy and love, generativity and care, and integrity, although recognized human qualities, are not usually discussed in the psychoanalytic literature. When they are, the discussion usually consists of tracing such qualities back to infantile origins. Erikson scoffs at the exclusive emphasis on *originology* as he calls it, or *reductionism* as others have labeled it.

Erikson asserts that he is aware of the "idealistic" connotations of such words as trust, hope, fidelity, intimacy, integrity, and so forth. He chose them because they connote, in a variety of languages, universal human values that in primitive and ancient cultures as well as in modern life hold together three spheres essential to each other: the individual life cycle, the sequence of generations, and the basic social structure.

The kind of ego that Erikson describes may be called the *creative ego,* although he does not use that word. It can and does find creative solutions to the new problems that beset it at each stage of life. It knows at each stage to use a combination of inner readiness and outer opportunity and does so with vigor, and even with a sense of joy. When thwarted, the ego reacts with renewed effort instead of giving up. The ego appears to be immensely robust and resilient. The powers of recovery, Erikson notes, are inherent in the young ego. The ego, in fact, thrives on conflict and crisis. It can be and usually is the master and not the slave of the id, the external world, and the superego. Indeed, Erikson says very little about the id and the superego, or about unconscious motivation and irrational strategies.

As a practicing psychoanalyst, Erikson is, of course, aware of the vulnerability of the ego, the irrational defenses it erects, and the devastating consequences of trauma, anxiety, and guilt. But he also sees more often than not, that the patient's ego is capable of dealing effectively with its problems with some help from the psychotherapist. This concentration on the potential strength of the ego characterizes all of Erikson's writings.

Erikson's conception of the ego is a very socialized and historical one. In addition to the genetic, physiological, and anatomical factors that help to determine the nature of the individual's ego, there are also important cultural and historical influences. It is this placing of the ego in a cultural and historical context—a space-time frame—that is one of Erikson's most creative contributions to ego theory.

Erikson has also speculated about the dimensions a new ego identity might take (1974). An identity, he feels, must be anchored in three aspects of reality. The first is that of *factuality* "a universe of facts, data, and techniques that can be verified with the observational methods and the work techniques of the time" (1974, p. 33). Then there is a *sense of reality* that can also be called *universality* because it combines the practical and concrete in a visionary world image. Ghandi, for one, had such a sense of reality. The third dimension is *actuality,* "a new way of relating to each other, of activating and invigorating each other in the service of common goals" (1974, p. 33). But then, perhaps with tongue in cheek, Erikson adds a fourth dimension, luck or chance. This new ego identity would, at the same time, bring into existence a new world image in which a wider sense of common identity will gradually overcome the pseudospeciation that has helped to cause prejudice, discrimination, hate, crime, war, poverty, and enslavement. Only time will tell whether such a world image is attainable but without the vision, Erikson might say, no new actuality can come into existence.

CHARACTERISTIC
RESEARCH AND
RESEARCH
METHODS

Observations made of patients in treatment constitute the main source of data for psychoanalytic theorists. Although Erikson derives his formulations from such observations, for the most part, he has also observed normal children and adolescents in play situations, made several forays into Indian territory, and studied the lives of historical figures. He is probably best known for his psychohistorical studies, and his books on Luther (1958) and Ghandi (1969) are widely read.

Case Histories

Although Erikson has not published many case studies of his patients, the few that have appeared (1963) display a rare insight into the dynamics of personality and a compassion for disturbed people, especially children in trouble. His remarkable talent for establishing rapport with his patients is clearly evident, and his polished style makes these case studies literary events as well as scientific works.

Play Situations

In doing psychotherapy with children, Erikson—as have others—discovered that children could often reveal their concerns better when playing with toys than they could in words. This led Erikson to develop a standardized play situation making use of toys and blocks which he employed in a nonclinical study of 150 boys and 150 girls between the ages of ten and twelve. "I set up a play table and a random selection of toys and invited the boys and girls of the study, one at a time to come in and to imagine that the table was a movie studio and the toys, actors and sets. I then asked them 'to construct on the table an exciting scene out of an imaginary moving picture'" (1963, p. 98). The child was then asked to tell a story about the scene he or she had constructed.

In studying a variety of connections between play-configurations and the life-history of these children, Erikson was astonished by the clear-cut differences in the use of play space in the scenes constructed by boys and girls. Boys, in general, built tall structures out of the blocks, girls tended to use the table as the interior of a house in which they placed furniture and people. They rarely used the blocks for constructing walls or structures. The boys' scenes included a lot of implied action—traffic moving through streets, police officers who blocked the moving traffic, animals, and Indians. The girls' scenes were more peaceful although often the tranquility was disturbed by an intruding animal, boy, or man—never a girl or woman. Girls did not attempt to block these intrusions by erecting walls or closing doors. Erikson remarks that "the majority of these intrusions have an element of humor or pleasurable excitement" (1963, p. 105). Erikson observes that girls accentuate inner space and boys outer space.

In interpreting these differences between the sexes, Erikson tends to emphasize what he calls "the ground plan of the body"—meaning that at least in these prepubertal children the anatomical configuration of the maturing sexual organs strongly influence the playful use of space in elaborating on exterior and interior configurations. These, of course, contain themes strongly influenced by traditional sex roles. These interpretations seem to agree with Freud's dictum that "anatomy is destiny," with the implication that sex differences are inborn and resistant to change.

Recently Erikson (1975) has discussed objections raised by feminist critics to these interpretations. He points out that he never said psychological similarities or differences between the sexes were determined solely by biological facts. Biology, while demarcating vital potentials, interacts with cultural and psychological variables to produce a given behavioral effect. Consequently, what males do and what females do with their masculine and feminine potentials is not rigidly controlled by their respective anatomies and physiologies but is amenable to differences in personality, social roles, and aspirations.

Play situations serve about the same role in child analysis that dreams do in adult analysis. Although Erikson does not emphasize dreams in his writings, he has written one very important theoretical paper on dreams (1954), using one of Freud's own dreams to illustrate Erikson's views.

Erikson is one of only a few psychoanalysts who has studied the relation of adult character traits to the ways in which children are brought up in primitive groups. In 1937, Erikson accompanied a field representative of the Commissioner of Indian Affairs to South Dakota to try to find out why Sioux children displayed such marked apathy. He discovered that the Sioux child was trapped in the dilemma of trying to reconcile the traditional tribal values inculcated in him or her during early training with the white man's values taught in the schools run by the Indian Service. Unable to effect a reconciliation, many children simply avoided the issue by withdrawing into a state of apathy.

Later, Erikson went to the Klamath River in Northern California where the Yurok Indians live. He was especially interested in making correlations between childhood training practices and the character-

Anthropological Studies

istic personality traits of these fishermen living along a river as compared to the hunters on the plains. For example, the acquisition and retention of possessions was a continuing preoccupation of the Yuroks. Reinforcement of this behavior began very early in life by teaching the child to be abstemious, to subordinate impulses to economic considerations, and to engage in fantasies about catching salmon and making money.

Psychohistory   In one of his writings (1974) Erikson defines psychohistory as "the study of individual and collective life with the combined methods of psychoanalysis and history" (p. 13). His book on Luther (1958) is subtitled *A Study in Psychoanalysis and History.*

Erikson's interest in "psychoanalyzing" famous individuals began with his chapters on Hitler's childhood and Maxim Gorky's youth in *Childhood and society* (1950, 1963). These initial essays were followed by two full-length books *Young man Luther* (1958) and *Ghandi's truth* (1969). He has also written about George Bernard Shaw (1968), Thomas Jefferson (1974), William James (1968) and, in many of his writings, Freud, although, regrettably, he has not yet put together a full-length study of Freud. Freud himself probed the lives of famous people including Leonardo da Vinci (1910), Daniel Schreber, a German jurist (1911), Dostoevsky (1928), Moses (1939), and Woodrow Wilson in collaboration with William Bullitt (1967). This last volume has been the subject of considerable dispute as to just how much of a role Freud played in the collaboration. Erikson (1975) has expressed his opinions of this controversial issue.

CASE HISTORY AND LIFE HISTORY. Erikson took a giant methodological step in the study of historical figures when he envisioned that it was possible to apply the same methods used for reconstructing the past of a patient in psychoanalysis to reconstructing the past of a historical person. Case history becomes life history. But he also realized in making the transition from case history to life history that the psychoanalyst needs to take into consideration what patients do in the world outside the clinic, what their world is like, and what restraints their world places on them as well as what opportunities it offers them. What can patients do given the world as it is, he asks. As a consequence of his thinking about the lives of historical figures he realized that the techniques of psychoanalysis "must supplement its clinical findings with the study of psycho-social functioning" (1975, p. 105).

Great men and women differ from patients, however, since they change the world by formulating a new world view that seizes the imagination of people and stirs them to action. One major difference between the life history of a famous person and the case history of a patient is as follows. In a case history, one tries to explain why a person fell to pieces; in a life history, one tries to explain how a person manages to stay together in spite of conflicts, complexes, and crises. This, of course, is an immensely important question. There must be many Hitlers roaming the streets or confined in mental or penal institutions, but there has only been one or possibly several successful (at least, for a time) Hitlers in modern times. Why does the same conflict or crisis break one person and make another?

In studying historical figures like Luther and Ghandi, Erikson is not interested in their childhood traumas as such, nor does he consider their adult behavior merely a fixation on or a regression to their infantile complexes. Instead he tries to show how the traumas of early life are reenacted in a transformed version in the deeds of adult life. It is simple enough to establish that Ghandi or Luther or any other man for that matter experienced conflicts and guilt over sensual feelings for his mother and hostile ones for his father. For Erikson the Oedipus complex or crisis is only the infantile form of a generational conflict. It is how this conflict is acted out in various forms throughout life that is important. Great men seem to be able to act it out in such a manner that it inspires and motivates many others to become their followers. Ghandi was an inspiration for millions of Indians who aspired to be free from British rule, as was Luther 400 years earlier for millions of Europeans who aspired to be free of the authority of Rome. In psychohistorical studies of great individuals one tries to show how the vicissitudes of their individual development history change the course of history.

What the great man does is to personify and to offer to people an integrating and liberating world view that, at the same time, is necessary for his own grandiosely conflicted identity and provides them with a sense of a new and wider collective identity. A common world view welds people together into an effective force for change. Luther's personality and world view led to the Reformation, Ghandi's to the liberation of India, Jefferson's to American democracy, Lenin's to Russian communism, and Mao's to Chinese communism.

PSYCHOHISTORICAL METHODOLOGY. Erikson has laid down fairly stringent rules as to how a psychohistorical study should proceed (1975). First, it is essential to bear in mind that the interpretation of any statement a person makes about his or her life must take into consideration several questions. At what point in their life did the person make the statement? How does the statement made at a particular moment fit into the whole life history? What was going on in their world at the time the information was recorded? How do these contemporary world events articulate with the whole historical process? For example, Erikson had to face these questions when he analyzed and interpreted Ghandi's autobiography written when he was in his late fifties.

Moreover, in judging the validity of an interpretation of an event in a life history whether recorded by the person himself or by another, it should be *"compatible with the developmental stage* at which it is said to have occurred" (1975, p. 128) and also be plausible with respect to the whole continuity of a person's life. The probability of an event having actually happened in the life of a person is strengthened if it can be shown that it occurs commonly *"within the contemporary culture* of the community and . . . *within the history of that culture"* (1975, pp. 132–133). Thus, it is as important for the biographer to be knowledgeable about the society, past and present, in which the person lives as it is for him or her to be informed about the events in the person's life. The person is made by history as well as making it.

The psychohistorian's interpretations are inevitably influenced by one's mood at the time one made the interpretations and by the intellectual tradition in which one has been trained. As the last part of this statement suggests Erikson is a relativist which he openly avows insisting, however, that this refers to relativity, not to relativism. This means that if someone else of a different intellectual persuasion—say a Jungian or an existentialist—should write a life of Luther or Ghandi, it is to be expected that their interpretations would differ from those of Erikson. (The same diversity, of course, is also to be found in the interpretations of patients' behavior by people of differing theoretical allegiances.) Even two Freudians do not agree in their interpretations as the contrasting account of Luther by Norman O. Brown (1959) and Erikson (1958) show. (See Domhoff, 1970 for an interesting comparison of these "two Luthers.")

Erikson also points out that any psychohistorian "projects . . . on the men and the times he studies some unlived portions and often the unrealized selves of his own life . . ." (1975, p. 148). This observation suggests that the psychohistorian just as the psychotherapist should himself be psychoanalyzed to become aware of his own conflicts and complexes before writing or judging biographies.

As a consequence of Erikson's seminal psychohistorical studies, psychohistory has become a discipline in its own right with numerous pratitioners. Erikson feels somewhat ambivalent about this new "industry" of which he is the entrepeneur.

Erikson's current status as a thinker, scholar, teacher, and writer is a very prestigious one not only within the academic and professional circles with which he is associated but also in the world at large. Erikson's name is as familiar as those of Piaget and Skinner. Unlike his mentor, Freud, and unlike another Harvard professor, B. F. Skinner, Erikson is not a controversial figure. His writings are singularly free of adverse criticisms of other viewpoints—in fact, they have a strong ecumenical flavor—nor have his views been subjected to very much adverse criticism. There is something very charismatic about the man and his writings that affect many people.

Erikson's reputation among psychologists derives almost entirely from his account of psychosocial development throughout the span of life from infancy to senility, in particular his concepts of identity and identity crisis. Psychologists, by and large, prefer Erikson's stages to Freud's psychosexual stages. They feel Erikson has done for personality development what Piaget has done for intellectual development. But Erikson's reputation does not rest solely upon his theoretical formulations. He is also greatly admired for his acute observations and sensible interpretations, for the literary merits of his writings, and for his deep compassion for everything human.

Erikson has been criticized for his overly optimistic view of humans just as Freud was, and still is, criticized for his pessimistic view. Although the terms, optimism and pessimism, deserve no place in the evaluation of a scientific viewpoint, since whatever is is despite our feelings, Erikson has answered this criticism by pointing out that "for each psychosocial step I posit a crisis and a specific conflict denoting . . . a lifelong . . . anxiety . . ." (1975, p. 259). But then he goes on to draw the conclusion that without anxiety, conflict, and crisis there would be no human strength.

Erikson has been reproached for watering down Freudian theory by concentrating on the strengths of the ego, the rational, and the conscious at the expense of the id, the irrational, and the unconscious. Even if this reproach were justified, it is really not pertinent. The mere fact that Erikson may diverge significantly from Freud, a fact Erikson himself would deny, does not justify a repudiation of Erikson's views. Freud's theories are not the ultimate measures of truth, nor did he ever contend they were. Erickson's formulations regarding psychosocial development must be evaluated in terms of the evidence, pro and con, and not in terms of their deviation from or agreement with any other theory.

A more subtle type of allegation charges Erikson with supporting the status quo when he says the individual must learn to conform or adjust to the institutions of the society in which he grows up. Actu-

CURRENT STATUS AND EVALUATION

ally, Erikson says that people must find their *identity* within the potentials (for stability *or* change) of their society, while their *development* must mesh with the requirements of society, or suffer the consequences.

Whether Erikson is a conservative and a traditionalist has no bearing upon the validity of his ideas. It is interesting, however, that Erikson chose to exemplify his psychosocial developmental scheme by a close examination of the lives of two men, Luther and Ghandi, who were hardly to be called conformists since they radically changed the societies in which they lived. Moreover, Erikson in his personal life has taken a strong stand against social injustice, notably in the University of California loyalty oath controversy. The reader may also be interested in reading the conversations between Erikson and the radical Black Panther leader, Huey Newton (K. T. Erikson, 1973).

A criticism with more merit than the foregoing ones focuses on the quality of the empirical foundations upon which the theory is based. No one can question the tremendous variety of observational data Erikson has assembled. He has been for years a psychoanalyst in private practice as well as on the staff of numerous hospitals and clinics. He has observed the play of normal children under standardized conditions. He has made firsthand observations of two Indian cultures. And he has explored in detail the lives of two historical figures. As an artist as well as a scientist, Erikson has a trained eye.

Despite these qualities, however, description based upon personal observation, although constituting the raw data of any scientific undertaking, is not sufficient. It is well recognized—indeed Erikson recognizes it himself—that observation can be very subjective. A person may choose to see what he or she wants to see. Nor does agreement among a lot of observers, known technically as consensual validation, constitute proof. The history of science offers many examples of the pitfalls of consensual validation.

Observation and description should lead one to measurement and controlled experimentation, and this Erikson has not done with the possible exception of his studies of children's play. He is, of course, not alone in this regard. Few theories of personality are supported by a solid foundation of quantitative and experimental data. Much of what Erikson has written appears to have face validity, that is, it seems to ring true to the average reader. Who can deny the reality of identity crisis and confusion during adolescence, for example? Moreover, Erikson's formulations do provide a rich source of hypotheses that can be and are being quantified and tested experimentally. This, in itself, is a major accomplishment.

Erikson, E. H. *Childhood and society*. New York: Norton, 1950, 2nd ed. revised and enlarged, 1963.

Erikson, E. H. *Insight and responsibility*. New York: Norton, 1964.

Erikson, E. H. *Identity: youth and crisis*. New York: Norton, 1968.

Erikson, E. H. *Dimensions of a new identity*. New York: Norton, 1974.

Erikson, E. H. *Life history and the historical moment*. New York: Norton, 1975.

Erikson, E. H. *Toys and reasons*. New York: Norton, 1976.

Klein, G. S. *Perception, motives, and personality*. New York: Knopf, 1970.

Klein, G. S. *Psychoanalytic theory: an exploration of essentials*. New York: International Universities Press, 1976.

Silverman, L. H. Psychoanalytic theory: "the reports of my death are greatly exaggerated." *American Psychologist,* 1976, **31,** 621–637.

Bellak, L. (Ed.). Conceptual and methodological problems in psychoanalysis. *Annals N.Y. Acad. of Science,* 1959, **76,** 971–1134.

Blum, G. S. *Psychoanalytic theories of personality*. New York: McGraw-Hill, 1953.

Brown, N. O. *Life against death*. Middletown, Conn: Wesleyan University Press, 1959.

Cobliner, W. G. Psychoanalysis and the Geneva school of genetic psychology: parallels and counterparts. *Int. J. Psychiat.,* 1967, **3,** 82–129.

Coles, R. *Erik H. Erikson: the growth of his work*. Boston: Little, Brown, 1970.

Domhoff, G. W. Two Luthers; the orthodox and heretical in psychoanalytic thinking. *Psychoanal. Rev.* 1970, **57,** 5–17.

Erikson, E. H. *Childhood and society*. New York: Norton, 1950, 2nd ed. revised and enlarged, 1963.

Erikson, E. H. The dream specimen of psychoanalysis. *Journal of the American Psychoanalytic Association,* 1954, **2,** 5–56.

Erikson, E. H. *Young man Luther*. New York: Norton, 1958.

Erikson, E. H. *Insight and responsibility*. New York: Norton, 1964.

Erikson, E. H. *Identity: youth and crisis*. New York: Norton, 1968.

Erikson, E. H. *Ghandi's truth*. New York: Norton, 1969.

Erikson, E. H. *Dimensions of a new identity*. New York: Norton, 1974.

Erikson, E. H. *Life history and the historical moment*. New York: Norton, 1975

Erikson, E. H. *Toys and reasons*. New York: Norton, 1976.

Erikson, K. T. (Introducer). *In search of common ground: conversations with Erik H. Erikson and Huey P. Newton*. New York: Norton, 1973.

Eysenck, H. J., and Wilson, G. D. *The experimental study of Freudian theories*. New York: Barnes & Noble, 1974.

Fairbairn, W. R. D. *Psycho-analytic studies of the personality*. New York: Basic Books, 1952.

Fisher, S., and Greenberg, R. P. *The scientific credibility of Freud's theories and therapy*. New York: Basic Books, 1977.

Frenkel-Brunswik, Else, Richfield, J., Scriven, M., and Skinner, B. F. Psychoanalysis and scientific method. *Sci. Mon.,* 1954, **79,** 293–310.

Freud, Anna. *The ego and the mechanisms of defense*. New York: International Universitias Press, 1946.

Freud, S. Project for a scientific psychology. In *Standard edition*. Vol. 1. London: Hogarth Press, 1966. (Written in 1895; first German edition, 1950).

Freud, S. The interpretation of dreams. In *Standard edition*. Vols. 4 and 5. London: Hogarth Press, 1953. (First German edition, 1900.)

Freud, S. Leonardo da Vinci and a memory of his childhood. In *Standard edition*. Vol. 11. London: Hogarth Press, 1957. (First German edition, 1910.)

Freud, S. Psycho-analytic notes on an autobiographical account of a case of paranoia (dementia paranoides). In *Standard edition*. Vol. 12. London: Hogarth Press, 1958. (First German edition, 1911.)

Freud, S. The question of lay analysis. In *Standard edition*. Vol. 20. London: Hogarth Press, 1959 (First German edition, 1926.)

Freud, S. Dostoevsky and parricide. In *Standard edition*. Vol. 21. London: Hogarth Press, 1961. (First German edition, 1928.)

Freud, S. Analysis terminable and interminable. In *Standard edition*. Vol. 23. London: Hogarth Press, 1964. (First German edition, 1937.)

Freud, S. Moses and monotheism. In *Standard Edition*. Vol. 23. London: Hogarth Press, 1964. (First German edition, 1939.)

Freud, S. An outline of psychoanalysis. In *Standard edition*. Vol. 23. London: Hogarth Press, 1964. (First German edition, 1940.)

Freud, S., and Bullitt, W. C. *Thomas Woodrow Wilson: twenty-eighth president of the United States. A psychological study*. Boston: Houghton Mifflin, 1967.

Gardner, R. W., Holzman, P. S., Klein, G. S., Linton, H. B., and Spence, D. P. Cognitive control: a study of individual consistencies in cognitive behavior. *Psychol. Issues,* Monogr. 4. New York: International Universities Press, 1959.

Gill, M. M. The present state of psychoanalytic theory. *J. abn. soc. Psychol.,* 1959, **58,** 1–8.

Gill, M. M. Metapsychology is not psychology. In Psychology versus metapsychology: psychoanalytic essays in memory of George S. Klein (Gill, M. M. and Holzman, P. S. eds.) *Psychol. Issues,* Monogr. 36. New York: International Universities Press, 1976.

Gill, M. M. and Holzman, P. S. (Eds.) Psychology versus metapsychology: psychoanalytic essays in memory of George S. Klein. *Psychol. Issues,* Monogr. 36. New York: International Universities Press, 1976.

Hall, C. S., and Lindzey, G. The relevance of Freudian psychology and related viewpoints for the social sciences. In G. Lindzey and E. Aronson (Eds.). *Handbook of social psychology,* Vol. 1. Cambridge: Addison-Wesley, 1968, pp. 245–319.

Hartmann, H. *Ego psychology and the problem of adaptation.* New York: International Universities Press, 1958.

Hartmann, H. *Essays on ego psychology: selected problems in psychoanalytic theory.* New York: International Universities Press, 1964.

Hilgard, E. R. Experimental approaches to psychoanalysis. In E. Pumpian-Mindlin (Ed.). *Psychoanalysis as science.* Stanford, Calif.: Stanford Univ. Press, 1952, pp. 3–45.

Holt, R. R. Ego autonomy re-evaluated. *Int. J. Psychiat.,* 1965, **46,** 151–167.

Holt, R. R. Drive or wish? A reconsideration of the psychoanalytic theory of motivation. In Psychology versus metapsychology: psychoanalytic essays in memory of George S. Klein (Gill, M. M. and Holzman, P. S. eds.) *Psychol. Issues,* Monogr. 36. New York: International Universities Press, 1976.

Horwitz, L. Theory construction and validation in psychoanalysis. In M. H. Marx (Ed.), *Theories in contemporary psychology.* New York: Macmillan, 1963, pp. 413–434.

Klein, G. S. *Perception, motives, and personality.* New York: Knopf, 1970.

Klein, G. S. *Psychoanalytic theory: an exploration of essentials.* New York: International Universities Press, 1976.

Klein, Melanie, Heimann, Paula, and Money-Kyrle, R. E. (Eds.). *New directions in psycho-analysis: the significance of infant conflict in the pattern of adult behaviour.* London: Tavistock Publications, 1955.

Kline, P. *Fact and fancy in Freudian theory.* London: Methuen, 1972.

Loewenstein, R., Newmann, Lottie M., Schur, M., and Solnit, A. J. (Eds.). *Psychoanalysis-a general psychology: essays in honor of Heinz Hartmann,* New York: International Universities Press, 1966.

McGuire, W. (Ed.). *Freud/Jung letters.* Princeton, N.J.: Princeton Univ. Press, 1974.

Nacht, S. Discussion of "The mutual influences in the development of ego and id." In Anna Freud *et al.* (Eds.), *The psychoanalytic study of the child.* Vol. 7. New York: International Universities Press, 1952, pp. 54–59.

Pumpian-Mindlin, E. (Ed.). *Psychoanalysis as science.* Stanford, Calif.: Stanford Univ. Press, 1952.

Rapaport, D. The structure of psychaoanalytic theory: a systematizing attempt. In S. Koch (Ed.), *Psychology: a study of a science.* Vol. 3. New York: McGraw-Hill, 1959, pp. 55–183.

Rapaport, D. The structure of psychoanalytic theory: a systematizing attempt. *Psychol. Issues,* Monogr. 6. New York: International Universities Press, 1960.

Roazen, P. *Erik H. Erikson: the power and limits of his vision.* New York: Free Press, 1976.

Schafer, R. *A new language for psychoanalysis.* New Haven, Conn.: Yale Univ. Press, 1976.

Sears, R. R. Survey of objective studies of psychoanalytic concepts. *Soc. Sci. Res. Council Bull.,* 1943, No. 51.

Sears, R. R. Experimental analyses of psychoanalytic phenomena. In J. McV. Hunt (Ed.). *Personality and the behavior disorders.* Vol. 1. New York: Ronald Press, 1944, pp. 306–332.

Shakow, D. and Rapaport, D. *The influence of Freud on American psychology.* New York: International Universities Press, 1964.

Silverman, L. H. Psychoanalytic theory: "the reports of my death are greatly exaggerated." *American Psychologist,* 1976, **31,** 621–637.

White, R. W. Ego and reality in psychoanalytic theory: a proposal regarding independent ego energies. *Psychol. Issues,* Mongr. No. 11. New York: International Universities Press, 1963.

Wolff, P. H. The developmental psychologies of Jean Piaget and psychoanalysis. *Psychol. Issues,* Mongr. 5. New York: International Universities Press, 1960.

JUNG'S ANALYTIC THEORY

Carl Jung was a young psychiatrist in Zurich when he read Freud's *Interpretation of dreams* soon after it was published in 1900. Greatly impressed by Freud's ideas, which he used and verified in his own practice, Jung sent Freud copies of his writings that, in general, upheld the Freudian viewpoint. In 1906 a regular correspondence began between the two men, and the following year Jung paid his first visit to Freud in Vienna when they talked continuously for thirteen hours! Freud decided that Jung was to be his successor, "his crown prince" as he wrote to Jung. When the International Psychoanalytic Association was founded in 1910, Jung became its first president, a position he held until 1914. In 1909, Freud and Jung traveled together to Clark University in Worcester, Massachusetts, both having been invited to deliver a series of lectures at the celebration of the twentieth year of the founding of the university. Three years later, however, the personal relationship between Freud and Jung began to cool until finally in early 1913 they terminated their personal correspondence, and a few months later their business correspondence. In April, 1914, Jung resigned his presidency of the association, and in August, 1914, he withdrew as a member. The break was then complete. Freud and Jung never saw one another again.

There have been many accounts of the relationship between Freud and Jung including those of the two participants (Freud, 1914, 1925; Jung, 1961), Freud's biographer, Ernest Jones (1955), and others

(Weigert, 1942; Dry, 1961). The articles published by Jung while he was still influenced by Freud, and his subsequent criticisms of Freudian psychoanalysis have been brought together in Volume 4 of the *Collected works*. Two other articles on Freud are included in Volume 15. The 359 letters that passed between Freud and Jung during the years 1906–1913 have been published (McGuire, 1974).

Although the causes for the rupture in the once intimate relationship were complex and "overdetermined," involving as they did both personal and intellectual incompatibilities, one important reason was Jung's rejection of Freud's pansexualism. "The immediate reason was that Freud . . . identified his method with his sex theory, which I deemed to be inadmissible" (personal communication from Jung, 1954). Jung then proceeded to forge his own theory of psychoanalysis and his own method of psychotherapy, which became known as *analytical psychology,* the lines of which had been laid down before he met Freud and which he had been working on consistently during the period of his association with Freud (Jung, 1913).

Before discussing the salient and distinctive characteristics of Jung's viewpoint, let us briefly review some aspects of his life. Carl Gustav Jung was born in Kesswyl, a town on Lake Constance in the Canton of Thurgau, Switzerland, July 26, 1875, and grew up in Basel. His father was a pastor in the Swiss Reformed Church. Jung entered the University of Basel with the intention of becoming a classical philologist and if possible an archeologist, but a dream is supposed to have aroused his interest in the study of the natural sciences and thus incidentally in medicine. After obtaining his medical degree from the University of Basel he became an assistant in the Burghölzli Mental Hospital, Zurich, and the Psychiatric Clinic of Zurich and thus embarked upon a career in psychiatry. He assisted and later collaborated with Eugen Bleuler, the eminent psychiatrist who developed the concept of schizophrenia, and studied briefly with Pierre Janet, Charcot's pupil and successor in Paris. In 1909 he gave up his work at the Burghölzli and in 1913 his instructorship in psychiatry at the University of Zurich in order to devote full time to private practice, training, research, traveling, and writing. For many years he conducted a seminar in English for English-speaking students, and following his retirement from active teaching a training institute named for him was started in Zurich. In 1944 a chair of medical psychology was founded especially for Jung at the University of Basel, but poor health required his resigning the chair after a year. He died June 6, 1961, in Zurich at the age of 85. No full length biography of Jung comparable to Ernest Jones' biography of Freud has been published yet. In the year of Jung's death there was published an autobiography, *Memories, dreams, reflec-*

tions (1961), which was in part directly written by Jung and in part recorded and edited by his confidential secretary, Aniela Jaffé, and supplemented by material from talks given by Jung. *Memories, dreams, reflections* is primarily an inner or spiritual autobiography, although it also contains a great deal of information about the external events in Jung's life. The tone of the book is set by the first sentence, "My life is a story of self-realization of the unconscious." Biographical material for Jung can be found in Frieda Fordham (1953), Bennet (1961), Dry (1961), Jaffé (1971), Wehr (1971), von Franz (1975), Hannah (1976),

Carl Gustav Jung

Stern (1976), and van der Post (1976). None of these books, however, can be regarded as a definitive biography.

Carl Jung is acknowledged to be one of the foremost psychological thinkers of the twentieth-century. For sixty years, he devoted himself with great energy and with a singularity of purpose to analyzing the far-flung and deep-lying processes of human personality. His writings are voluminous and the extent of his influence incalculable. He is known not only to psychologists and psychiatrists but to educated people in all walks of life. Many honors were bestowed upon him, among them honorary degrees from Harvard University and Oxford University. He often lectured in the United States and has many followers and admirers in this country. Virtually the entire body of Jung's writings is now available in a 20 volume English language edition (Jung, 1953–1978). In addition to the Freud/Jung letters previously mentioned, two volumes of Jung's letters have been published (Jung, 1973b, 1975). There is also a volume containing interviews and encounters with Jung (McGuire, 1977).

Although Jung's theory of personality is usually identified as a psychoanalytic theory because of the emphasis that it places upon unconscious processes, it differs in some notable respects from Freud's theory of personality. Perhaps the most prominent and distinctive feature of Jung's view of humans is that it combines teleology with causality. Human behavior is conditioned not only by individual and racial history (causality) but also by aims and aspirations (teleology). Both the past as actuality and the future as potentiality guide one's present behavior. Jung's view of personality is prospective in the sense that it looks ahead to the person's future line of development and retrospective in the sense that it takes account of the past. To paraphrase Jung, "the person lives by aims as well as by causes." This insistence upon the role of destiny or purpose in human development sets Jung clearly apart from Freud. For Freud, there is only the endless repetition of instinctual themes until death intervenes. For Jung, there is constant and often creative development, the search for wholeness and completion, and the yearning for rebirth.

Jung's theory is also distinguished from all other approaches to personality by the strong emphasis that it places upon the racial and phylogenetic foundations of personality. Jung sees the individual personality as the product and container of its ancestral history. Modern humans have been shaped and molded into their present form by the cumulative experiences of past generations extending far back into the dim and unknown origins of humans. The foundations of personality are archaic, primitive, innate, unconscious, and probably universal.

Freud stresses the infantile origins of personality whereas Jung emphasizes the racial origins of personality. Humans are born with many predispositions that have been bequeathed to them by their ancestors; these predispositions guide their conduct and determine in part what they will become conscious of and respond to in their own world of experience. In other words, there is a racially preformed and collective personality that reaches out selectively into the world of experience and is modified and elaborated by the experiences that it receives. An individual's personality is a resultant of inner forces acting upon and being acted upon by outer forces.

This great respect for a person's racial past and the bearing that it has upon people today meant that Jung, more than any other psychologist, probed into human history to learn what he could of the racial origins and evolution of personality. He studied mythology, religion, ancient symbols and rituals, the customs and beliefs of primitive people, as well as dreams, visions, the symptoms of neurotics, and the hallucinations and delusions of psychotics, in his search for the roots and developments of human personality. His learning and erudition, both as to breadth of knowledge and depth of understanding, are probably unsurpassed among present-day psychologists.

Dry (1961) has identified some of the important intellectual developments of the nineteenth century that presumably influenced Jung. First, there were the philosophers, particularly Schopenhauer, von Hartmann, and Nietzsche, with their conceptions of the unconscious, of polarity working toward unity, and the substitution of will or intuition for reasoning in comprehending reality. Then there was

the newly developed German and French psychiatry . . . ; the scientific discoveries of other fields, especially biology; the widespread acceptance of evolutionary theory . . . ; the application of evolutionary ideas to man, including the study of his social organization and religion, and the controversy between the proponents of psychic unity and cultural diffusion in exploring similarities [among different societies]; the imagination-stirring finds of archeology; and the great literary, historical and theological traditions of Germany, with a strong tincture of Romanticism (pp. 19–20).

Dry also feels that the neutrality and stability of Switzerland favored a life of thought and solitude.

We will now present the principal features of Jung's theory of personality. Although theoretical formulations are found throughout his voluminous writings, Volumes 7, 8, and 9, Part 1 of the *Collected works* contain the most systematic statements of his position.

THE STRUCTURE OF PERSONALITY

The total personality or psyche, as it is called by Jung, consists of a number of differentiated but interacting systems. The principal ones are the *ego,* the *personal unconscious* and its *complexes,* the *collective unconscious* and its *archetypes,* the *persona,* the *anima* and *animus,* and the *shadow.* In addition to these interdependent systems there are the *attitudes* of introversion and extraversion, and the *functions* of thinking, feeling, sensing, and intuiting. Finally, there is the *self* which is the center of the whole personality.

The Ego

The ego is the conscious mind. It is made up of conscious perceptions, memories, thoughts, and feelings. The ego is responsible for one's feeling of identity and continuity, and from the viewpoint of the individual person it is regarded as being at the center of consciousness.

The Personal Unconscious

The personal unconscious is a region adjoining the ego. It consists of experiences that were once conscious but which have been repressed, suppressed, forgotten, or ignored and of experiences that were too weak in the first place to make a conscious impression upon the person. The contents of the personal unconscious, like those of Freud's preconscious material, are accessible to consciousness, and there is a great deal of two-way traffic between the personal unconscious and the ego.

COMPLEXES. A complex is an organized group or constellation of feelings, thoughts, perceptions, and memories that exist in the personal unconscious. It has a nucleus that acts as a kind of magnet attracting to it or "constellating" various experiences (Jung, 1934).

Consider, for example, the *mother complex* (Jung, 1954a). The nucleus is derived in part from racial experiences with mothers and in the part from the child's experiences with its mother. Ideas, feelings, and memories relating to the mother are attracted to the nucleus and form a complex. The stronger the force emanating from the nucleus the more experiences it will pull to itself. Thus, someone whose personality is dominated by their mother is said to have a strong mother complex. Their thoughts, feelings, and actions will be guided by the conception of the mother, what she says and what she feels will mean a great deal to the person, and her image will be uppermost in his mind. A complex may behave like an autonomous personality that has a mental life and a motor of its own. It may seize control of the personality and utilize the psyche for its own ends, as Tolstoy is said to have been dominated by the idea of simplification and Napoleon by the lust for power.

The nucleus and many of the associated elements are unconscious at any particular time, but any of the associations can and often do become conscious.

The concept of a collective or *transpersonal* unconscious is one of the most original and controversial features of Jung's personality theory. It is the most powerful and influential system of the psyche, and in pathological cases overshadows the ego and the personal unconscious (Jung, 1936, 1943, 1945).

The Collective Unconscious

The collective unconscious is the storehouse of latent memory traces inherited from one's ancestral past, a past that includes not only the racial history of humans as a separate species but their prehuman or animal ancestry as well. The collective unconscious is the psychic residue of human evolutionary development, a residue that accumulates as a consequence of repeated experiences over many generations. It is almost entirely detached from anything personal in the life of an individual and it is seemingly universal. All human beings have more or less the same collective unconscious. Jung attributes the universality of the collective unconscious to the similarity of the structure of the brain in all races of humans and this similarity in turn is due to a common evolution.

Racial memories or representations are not inherited as such; rather we inherit the *possibility* of reviving experiences of past generations. They are predispositions that set us to react to the world in a selective fashion. These predispositions are projected on the world. For example, since human beings have always had mothers, every infant is born with the predisposition to perceive and react to a mother. The individually acquired knowledge of the mother is a fulfillment of an inherited potentiality that has been built into the human brain by the past experiences of the race. Just as humans are born with the capacity for seeing the world in three dimensions and develop this capacity through experience and training, so humans are born with many predispositions for thinking, feeling, and perceiving according to definite patterns and contents that become actualized through individualized experiences. Humans are predisposed to be afraid of the dark or of snakes because it may be assumed primitive humans encountered many dangers in the dark and were victims of poisonous snakes. These latent fears may never develop in modern humans unless they are strengthened by specific experiences, but nonetheless the tendency is there and makes one more susceptible to such experiences. Some ideas are easily formed, such as the idea of a Supreme Being, because the disposition has been firmly imprinted in the brain and needs very little reinforcement from individual experience to make it emerge into consciousness and influence behavior. These latent or potential memories depend upon inherent structures and pathways that have been engraved on the brain as a result of the cumulative experiences of mankind. To deny the inheritance of these primordial memories, Jung asserts, is to deny the evolution and inheritance of the brain.

The collective unconscious is the inherited, racial foundation of the whole structure of personality. Upon it are erected the ego, the personal unconscious, and all other individual acquisitions. What a person learns as a result of experiences is substantially influenced by the collective unconscious that exercises a guiding or selective influence over the behavior of the person from the very beginning of life. "The form of the world into which he is born is already inborn in him as a virtual image" (Jung, 1945, p. 188). This virtual image becomes a concrete perception or idea by identifying itself with objects in the world that correspond to the image. One's experiences of the world are shaped to a large extent by the collective unconscious, although not completely so for otherwise there could be no variation and development.

The two unconscious regions of the mind, the personal and the collective, can be of immense service to humans. "It [the unconscious] holds possibilities which are locked away from the conscious mind, for it has at its disposal all subliminal contents, all those things which have been forgotten or overlooked, as well as the wisdom and experience of uncounted centuries, which are laid down in its archetypal organs" (Jung, 1943, p. 114). On the other hand, if the wisdom of the unconscious is ignored by the ego, the unconscious may disrupt the conscious rational processes by seizing hold of them and twisting them into distorted forms. Symptoms, phobias, delusions, and other irrationalities stem from neglected unconscious processes.

ARCHETYPES. The structural components of the collective unconscious are called by various names: *archetypes, dominants, primordial images, imagoes, mythological images,* and *behavior patterns* (Jung, 1943). An archetype is a universal thought form (idea) that contains a large element of emotion. This thought form creates images or visions that correspond in normal waking life to some aspect of the conscious situation. For example, the archetype of the mother produces an image of a mother figure that is then identified with the actual mother. In other words, the baby inherits a preformed conception of a generic mother that determines in part how the baby will perceive *its* mother. The baby's perception is also influenced by the nature of the mother and by the infant's experiences with her. Thus, the baby's experience is the joint product of an inner predisposition to perceive the world in a certain manner and the actual nature of that world. The two determinants usually fit together compatibly because the archetype itself is a product of racial experiences with the world, and these experiences are much the same as those that any individual living in any age and in any part of the world will have. That is to say, the nature of mothers—what they do—has remained pretty much the same throughout the history of the race, so that the mother archetype which the baby inherits is congruent with the actual mother with whom the baby interacts.

How does an archetype originate? It is a permanent deposit in the mind of an experience that has been constantly repeated for many generations. For instance, countless generations have seen the sun make its daily excursion from one horizon to the other. The repetition of this impressive experience eventually became fixed in the collective unconscious as an archetype of the sun-god, the powerful, dominating, light-giving, heavenly body that humans deified and worshipped. Certain conceptions and images of a supreme deity are offshoots of the sun archetype.

In a similar manner, humans have been exposed throughout their existence to innumerable instances of great natural forces— earthquakes, waterfalls, floods, hurricanes, lightning, forest fires, and so forth. Out of these experiences there has developed an archetype of energy, a predisposition to perceive and be fascinated by power and a desire to create and control power. The child's delight in firecrackers, the young person's preoccupation with fast cars, and the adult's obsessive interest in releasing the hidden energies of atoms have their roots in the archetype of energy. Humans are *driven* by this archetype to seek new sources of energies. Our present age of energy represents the ascendance of the energy archetype. That is, archetypes function as highly charged autonomous centers of energy that tend to produce in each generation the repetition and elaboration of these same experiences. Berger (1977) has suggested that archetypes are the human equivalents of feature detectors which have recently been discovered in lower animals.

Archetypes are not necessarily isolated from one another in the collective unconscious. They interpenetrate and interfuse with one another. Thus, the archetype of the hero and the archetype of the wise old man may blend together to produce the conception of the "philosopher king," a person who is responded to and revered because he is both a hero leader and a wise seer. Sometimes, as seemed to be the case with Hitler, there is a fusion of the demon and hero archetypes so that one gets a satanic leader.

As we have already seen, the nucleus of a complex may be an archetype that draws experiences to it. The archetype can then penetrate into consciousness by way of these associated experiences. Myths, dreams, visions, rituals, neurotic and psychotic symptoms, and works of art contain a great deal of archetypal material, and constitute the best source of knowledge regarding archetypes. Jung and his associates have done a prodigious amount of work on archetypal representations in religions, myths, and dreams.

There are presumed to be numerous archetypes in the collective unconscious. Some of the ones that have been identified are archetypes of birth, rebirth, death, power, magic, unity, the hero, the child, God, the demon, the old wise man, the earth mother, and the animal.

Although all archetypes may be thought of as autonomous dynamic systems that can become relatively independent of the rest of the personality, some archetypes have evolved so far as to warrant their being treated as separate systems within the personality. These are the *persona,* the *anima* and *animus,* and the *shadow*.

The Persona   The persona is a mask adopted by the person in response to the demands of social convention and tradition and to his or her own inner archetypal needs (Jung, 1945). It is the role assigned to one by society, the part that society expects one to play in life. The purpose of the mask is to make a definite impression upon others and it often, although not necessarily, conceals the real nature of the person. The persona is the *public* personality, those aspects that one displays to the world or that public opinion fastens on the individual as contrasted with the *private* personality that exists behind the social facade.

If the ego identifies with the persona, as it frequently does, the individual becomes more conscious of the part that he is playing than he is of his genuine feelings. He becomes alienated from himself and his whole personality takes on a flat or two-dimensional quality. He becomes a mere semblance of a human, a reflection of society instead of an autonomous human being.

The nucleus from which the persona develops is an archetype. This archetype, like all archetypes, originates out of the experiences of the race; in this case, the experiences consist of social interactions in which the assumption of a social role has served a useful purpose to humans throughout their history as social animals. (The persona resembles Freud's superego in some respects.)

The Anima and the   It is fairly well recognized and accepted that a human is essentially a
Animus   bisexual animal. On a physiological level, the male secretes both male and female sex hormones, as does the female. On the psychological level, masculine and feminine characteristics are found in both sexes.

Homosexuality is just one of the conditions, but perhaps the most striking one, that has given rise to the conception of human bisexuality.

Jung ascribes the feminine side of man's personality and the masculine side of woman's personality to archetypes. The feminine archetype in man is called the *anima,* the masculine archetype in woman is called the *animus* (Jung 1945,1954b). These archetypes, although they may be conditioned by the sex chromosomes and the sex glands, are the products of the racial experiences of man with woman and woman with man. In other words, by living with woman throughout the ages man has become feminized; by living with man woman has become masculinized.

Not only do these archetypes cause each sex to manifest characteristics of the other sex but they also act as collective images that motivate each sex to respond to and understand members of the other sex. Man apprehends the nature of woman by virtue of his anima, and woman apprehends the nature of man by virtue of her animus. But the anima and animus may also lead to misunderstanding and discord if the archetypal image is projected without regard for the real character of the partner. That is, if a man tries to identify his idealized image of woman with an actual woman, and does not take into account sufficiently the discrepancies between the ideal and the real, he may suffer bitter disappointment when he realizes that the two are not identical. There has to be a compromise between the demands of the collective unconscious and the actualities of the external world for the person to be reasonably well adjusted.

The shadow archetype consists of the animal instincts that humans inherited in their evolution from lower forms of life (Jung, 1948a). Consequently, the shadow to begin with typifies the animal side of human nature. As an archetype the shadow is responsible for our conception of original sin; when it is projected outward it becomes the devil or an enemy.

The Shadow

The shadow archetype is also responsible for the appearance in consciousness and behavior of unpleasant and socially reprehensible thoughts, feelings, and actions. These then may either be hidden from public view by the persona or repressed into the personal unconscious. Thus the shadow-side of personality that owes its origin to an archetype permeates the private aspects of the ego and a large part of the contents of the personal unconscious as well.

The shadow with its vital and passionate animal instincts gives a full-bodied or three-dimensional quality to the personality. It helps to round out the whole person. (The reader will have noted a resemblance between the shadow and Freud's concept of the id).

The Self   In his earlier writings Jung considered the self to be equivalent to the psyche or total personality. However, when he began to explore the racial foundations of personality and discovered the archetypes, he found one that represented human striving for unity (Wilhelm and Jung, 1931). This archetype expresses itself through various symbols, the chief one being the *mandala* or magic circle (Jung, 1955a). In his book *Psychology and alchemy* (1944), Jung develops a psychology of totality based upon the mandala symbol. The main concept of this psychology of total unity is the *self*.

The self is the mid-point of personality, around which all of the other systems are constellated. It holds these systems together and provides the personality with unity, equilibrium, and stability.

If we picture the conscious mind with the ego as its centre, as being opposed to the unconscious, and if we now add to our mental picture the process of assimilating the unconscious, we can think of this assimilation as a kind of approximation of conscious and unconscious, where the centre of the total personality no longer coincides with the ego, but with a point midway between the conscious and unconscious. This would be the point of a new equilibrium, a new centering of the total personality, a virtual centre which, on account of its focal position between conscious and unconscious, ensures for the personality a new and more solid foundation (Jung, 1945, p. 219).

The self is life's goal, a goal that people constantly strive for but rarely reach. Like all archetypes, it motivates human behavior and causes one to search for wholeness especially through the avenues provided by religion. True religious experiences are about as close to selfhood as most humans will ever come, and the figures of Christ and Buddha are as highly differentiated expressions of the self archetype as one will find in the modern world. It is not surprising to learn that Jung discovered the self in his studies and observations of the religions of the Orient, in which the striving for unity and oneness with the world through various ritualistic practices such as Yoga is further advanced than in western religions.

Before a self can emerge it is necessary for the various components of the personality to become fully developed and individuated. For this reason, the archetype of the self does not become evident until the person has reached middle age. At this time, he or she begins to make a serious effort to change the center of personality from the conscious ego to one that is midway between consciousness and unconsciousness. This midway region is the province of the self.

The concept of the self is probably Jung's most important psychological discovery and represents the culmination of his intensive studies of archetypes.

Jung distinguishes two major attitudes or orientations of personality, the attitude of *extraversion* and the attitude of *introversion*. The extraverted attitude orients the person toward the external, objective world; the introverted attitude orients the person toward the inner, subjective world (1921).

The Attitudes

These two opposing attitudes are both present in the personality but ordinarily one of them is dominant and conscious while the other is subordinate and unconscious. If the ego is predominantly extraverted in its relation to the world, the personal unconscious will be introverted.

There are four fundamental psychological functions: *thinking, feeling, sensing,* and *intuiting.* Thinking is ideational and intellectual. By thinking humans try to comprehend the nature of the world and themselves. Feeling is the evaluation function; it is the value of things, whether positive or negative, with reference to the subject. The feeling function gives humans their subjective experiences of pleasure and pain, of anger, fear, sorrow, joy, and love. Sensing is the perceptual or reality function. It yields concrete facts or representations of the world. Intuition is perception by way of unconscious processes and subliminal contents. The intuitive person goes beyond facts, feelings, and ideas in their search for the essence of reality.

The Functions

The nature of the four functions may be clarified by the following example. Suppose that a person is standing on the rim of the Grand Canyon of the Colorado river. If the feeling function predominates she will experience a sense of awe, grandeur, and breath-taking beauty. If she is controlled by the sensation function she will see the Canyon merely as it is or as a photograph might represent it. If the thinking function controls her ego she will try to understand the Canyon in terms of geological principles and theory. Finally, if the intuitive function prevails the spectator will tend to see the Grand Canyon as a mystery of nature possessing deep significance whose meaning is partially revealed or felt as a mystical experience.

That there are exactly four psychological functions, no more and no fewer, "I arrived at" Jung writes, "on purely empirical grounds."

But as the following consideration will show, these four together produce a kind of totality. Sensation establishes what is actually present, thinking enables us to recognize its meaning, feeling tells us its value, and intuition points to possibilities as to whence it came and whither it is going in a given situation. In this way we can orient ourselves with respect to the immediate world as completely as when we locate a place geographically by latitude and longitude (1931b, pp. 540–541).

Thinking and feeling are called rational functions because they make use of reason, judgment, abstraction, and generalization. They enable humans to look for lawfulness in the universe. Sensation and intuition are considered to be irrational functions because they are based on the perception of the concrete, particular, and accidental.

Although a person has all four functions they are not necessarily equally well developed. Usually one of the four functions is more highly differentiated than the other three, and plays a predominant role in consciousness. This is called the *superior* function. One of the other three functions usually acts in an auxiliary capacity to the superior function. If the superior function is prevented from operating, the auxiliary function automatically takes its place.

The least differentiated of the four functions is called the *inferior* function. It is repressed and unconscious. The inferior function expresses itself in dreams and fantasies. The inferior function also has an auxiliary function associated with it.

If the four functions are placed equidistant from each other on the circumference of a circle, the center of the circle represents the synthesis of the four fully differentiated functions. In such a synthesis there are no superior or inferior functions and no auxiliaries. They are all of equal strength in the personality. Such a synthesis can only occur when the self has become fully actualized. Since complete actualization of the self is impossible, the synthesis of the four functions represents an ideal goal toward which the personality strives.

Interactions Among the Systems of Personality

The various systems and the attitudes and functions that go to make up the total personality interact with each other in three different ways. One system may *compensate* for the weakness of another system, one system may *oppose* another system, or two or more systems may *unite* to form a synthesis.

Compensation may be illustrated by the interaction of the contrasting attitudes of extraversion and introversion. If extraversion is the dominant or superior attitude of the conscious ego, then the unconscious will compensate by developing the repressed attitude of introversion. This means that if the extraverted attitude is frustrated in some way, the unconscious inferior attitude of introversion will seize hold of the personality and exert itself. A period of intense extraverted behavior is ordinarily followed by a period of introverted behavior. Dreams are also compensatory so that the dreams of a predominantly extraverted person will have an introverted quality, and conversely, the dreams of an introvert will tend to be extraverted.

Compensation also occurs between functions. A person who stresses thinking and feeling in their conscious mind will be an intuitive, sensation type unconsciously. Likewise, the ego and the anima in a man and the ego and the animus in a woman bear a compensatory relationship to each other. The normal male ego is masculine while the anima is feminine and the normal female ego is feminine while the animus is masculine. In general, all of the contents of the conscious mind are compensated for by the contents of the unconscious mind. The principle of compensation provides for a kind of equilibrium or balance between contrasting elements that prevents the psyche from becoming neurotically unbalanced.

Virtually all personality theorists of whatever creed or persuasion assume that the personality contains polar tendencies that may come into conflict with one another. Jung is no exception. He believes that a psychological theory of personality must be founded on the principle of opposition or conflict because the tensions created by conflicting elements are the very essence of life itself. Without tension there would be no energy and consequently no personality.

Opposition exists everywhere in the personality; between the ego and the shadow, between the ego and the personal unconscious, between the persona and the anima or animus, between the persona and the personal unconscious, between the collective unconscious and the ego, and between the collective unconscious and the persona. Introversion opposes extraversion, thinking opposes feeling, and sensation opposes intuition. The ego is like a shuttlecock that is batted back and forth between the outer demands of society and the inner demands of the collective unconscious. As a result of this struggle a persona or mask develops. The persona then finds itself under attack from other archetypes in the collective unconscious. The woman in man, that is, the anima, invades the male's masculine nature and the animus chips away at the femininity of woman. The contest between the rational and irrational forces of the psyche never ceases. Conflict is a ubiquitous fact of life.

Must personality always be a house divided against itself? Jung believes not. Polar elements not only oppose one another, they also attract or seek one another. The situation is analogous to a husband and wife who quarrel with each other yet are held together by the very differences that provoke the disagreements. The union of opposites is accomplished by what Jung calls the *transcendent function* (see below). The operation of this function results in the synthesis of contrary systems to form a balanced, integrated personality. The center of this integrated personality is the *self*.

AN EXAMPLE OF INTERACTION AMONG THE SYSTEMS OF PERSONALITY. To illustrate the kinds of interactions that take place within the psyche, let us consider the relations between the anima and the other systems of personality. Jung says "the whole nature of man presupposes woman . . . his system is tuned in to woman from the start . . ." (Jung, 1945, p. 188). The male infant, equipped with his archetype of woman, is instinctively attracted to the first woman he experiences, who is usually his mother. The establishing of a close relationship is nurtured, in turn, by the mother. However, as the child grows older these maternal bonds become restrictive and frustrating, if not actually dangerous to the child, so that the mother complex that has been formed in the ego is repressed into the personal unconscious.

At the same time that this development is taking place, feminine traits and attitudes that have been implanted in the ego by the anima are also repressed because they are alien to the role that society expects him to play as a male. In other words, his inborn femininity is repressed by a counterforce emanating from the persona and other archetypes.

As a result of these two acts of repression, the child's feelings for his mother and his femininity are driven from the ego into the personal unconscious. Thus, man's perception of women and his feelings and behavior toward them are directed by the combined forces of the personal and the collective unconscious.

The integrative task imposed upon the ego as a consequence of these vicissitudes of the mother archetype and the feminine archetype (the anima) is to find a woman who resembles the mother *imago* and who also fulfills the needs of his anima. If he chooses a woman who is at variance with either or both of these unconscious models, he is headed for trouble, because his conscious positive feelings for her will be disturbed by unconscious negative feelings. They will make him dissatisfied with her and he will blame her for various fancied faults and shortcomings without becoming aware of the real reasons for his discontent. If the transcendent function is operating smoothly it will unite all of his contradictory impulses and cause him to select a mate with whom he can be happy.

All of the important decisions in life require that due consideration be given unconscious as well as conscious factors if they are to be successful. Jung says that a great deal of maladjustment and unhappiness is due to a one-sided development of personality that ignores important facets of human nature. These neglected facets create personality disturbances and irrational conduct.

For Jung, the personality is an exceedingly complex structure. Not only are there numerous components—the number of possible archetypes and complexes, for example, is legion—but the interactions between these components are intricate and involved. No other personality theorist has evolved such a rich and complex description of the structure of personality.

Jung conceives of the personality or psyche as being a partially closed energy system. It is said to be incompletely closed because energy from outside sources must be added to the system, for example, by eating, and energy is subtracted from the system, for example, by performing muscular work. It is also possible for environmental stimuli to produce changes in the distribution of energy within the system. This happens, for instance, when a sudden change in the external world reorients our attention and perception. The fact that the personality dynamics are subject to influences and modifications from external sources means that the personality cannot achieve a state of perfect stabilization, as it might if it were a completely closed system. It can only become relatively stabilized.

THE DYNAMICS OF PERSONALITY

The energy by which the work of the personality is performed is called *psychic energy* (Jung, 1948b). Psychic energy is a manifestation of life energy that is the energy of the organism as a biological system. Psychic energy originates in the same manner as does all vital energy, namely, from the metabolic processes of the body. Jung's term for life energy is *libido* but he also uses libido interchangeably with psychic energy. Jung does not take a positive stand on the relation of psychic energy to physical energy but he believes that some kind of reciprocal action between the two is a tenable hypothesis.

Psychic Energy

Psychic energy is a hypothetical construct; it is not a concrete substance or phenomenon. Consequently, it cannot be measured or sensed. Psychic energy finds concrete expression in the form of actual or potential forces. Wishing, willing, feeling, attending, and striving are examples of actual forces in the personality; dispositions, aptitudes, tendencies, inclinations, and attitudes are examples of potential forces.

PSYCHIC VALUES. The amount of psychic energy invested in an element of the personality is called the *value* of that element. Value is a measure of intensity. When we speak of placing a high value upon a particular idea or feeling, we mean that the idea or feeling exerts a considerable force in instigating and directing behavior. A person who values truth will expend a great deal of energy on the search for it. One who places great value upon power will be highly motivated to obtain power. Conversely, if something is of trivial value it will have little energy attached to it.

The absolute value of an idea or feeling cannot be determined, but its relative value can be. One simple although not necessarily accurate way of determining relative values is to ask a person whether he or she prefers one thing more than another. The order of their preferences can be taken as a rough measure of the relative strengths of their values. Or an experimental situation can be devised to test whether an individual will work harder for one incentive than for another. Observing someone closely for a period of time to see what he or she does yields quite a fair picture of their relative values. If they spend more time reading than playing cards, then it can be assumed that reading is more highly valued than card-playing.

THE CONSTELLATING POWER OF A COMPLEX. Such observations and tests, useful though they may be for the determination of conscious values, do not shed much light upon the unconscious values. These have to be determined by evaluating the "constellating power of the nuclear element of a complex." The constellating power of a complex consists of the number of groups of items that are brought into association by the nuclear element of the complex. Thus, if one has a strong patriotic complex it means that the nucleus, love of one's country, will produce constellations of experiences around it. One such constellation may consist of important events in the history of one's nation, while another may be a positive feeling toward national leaders and heroes. A very patriotic person is predisposed to fit any new experience into one of the constellations associated with patriotism.

What means are available for assessing the constellating power of a nuclear element? Jung discusses three methods: (1) direct observation plus analytical deductions, (2) complex indicators, and (3) the intensity of emotional expression.

Through observation and inference one can arrive at an estimate of the number of associations that are attached to a nuclear element. A person who has a strong mother complex will tend to introduce his mother or something associated with his mother into every conversation whether it is appropriate or not. He will prefer stories and movies in which mothers play a prominent role and he will make a great deal out of Mother's Day and other occasions on which he can honor his mother. He will tend to imitate his mother by adopting her preferences and interests, and will be attracted to her friends and associates. And he will prefer older women to women his own age.

A complex does not always manifest itself publicly. It may appear in dreams or in some obscure form so that it is necessary to employ circumstantial evidence to discover the underlying significance of the experience. This is what is meant by analytical deduction.

A complex indicator is any disturbance of behavior that indicates the presence of a complex. It may be a slip of the tongue, for instance, when a man says "mother" when he intended to say "wife." It may be an unusual blockage of memory as happens when a person cannot remember the name of a friend because the name resembles that of his mother or something associated with his mother. Complex indicators also appear in the word association test.

Jung discovered the existence of complexes in 1903 by experiments using the word association test (Jung, 1973a). This test, now so widely employed in the evaluation of personality, consists of a standard list of words that are read one at a time to the person being tested. The subject is instructed to reply with the first word that enters his or her mind. If a person takes an unusually long time to reply to a particular word, this indicates that the word is connected in some manner with a complex. Repetition of the stimulus word and an inability to respond at all are also complex indicators.

The intensity of one's emotional reaction to a situation is another measure of the strength of a complex. If the heart beats faster, the breathing becomes deeper, and the blood drains from the face, these are pretty good indications that a strong complex has been tapped. By combining physiological measures such as the pulse, respiration, and electrical changes in the conductivity of the skin with the word association test, it is possible to make a fairly accurate determination of the strength of a person's complexes.

The Principle of Equivalence

Jung bases his view of psycho-dynamics upon two fundamental principles, the principle of equivalence and that of entropy (Jung, 1948b). The principle of equivalence states that if energy is expended in bringing about a certain condition, the amount expended will appear elsewhere in the system. Students of physics will recognize this principle as the first law of thermodynamics or the principle of the conservation of energy as propounded by Helmholtz. As applied to psychic functioning by Jung, the principle states that if a particular value weakens or disappears, the sum of energy represented by the value will not be lost from the psyche but will reappear in a new value. The lowering of one value inevitably means the raising of another value. For example, as the child's valuation of its family decreases, its interest in other people and things will increase. A person who loses their interest in a hobby will usually find that another one has taken its place. If a value is repressed, its energy can be used to create dreams or fantasies. It is possible, of course, for the energy lost from one value to be distributed among several other values.

In terms of the functioning of the total personality, the principle of equivalence states that if energy is removed from one system, for example the ego, it will appear in some other system, perhaps the persona. Or if more and more values are repressed into the shadow-side of personality, it will grow strong at the expense of other personality structures. Likewise, the de-energizing of the conscious ego is accompanied by the energizing of the unconscious. Energy is continuously flowing from one system of personality into other systems. These redistributions of energy constitute the dynamics of personality.

Of course, the principle of the conservation of energy cannot apply in any strict manner to a system like the psyche that is only partially closed. Energy is added to or subtracted from the psyche, and the rate at which it is added or subtracted can and probably does vary considerably. Consequently, the rise or fall of a value may be due not only to a transfer of energy from one part of the system to another but it may depend also upon the addition of energy from sources external to the psyche or by the subtraction of energy when muscular work is performed. One is invigorated mentally as well as physically after eating a meal or taking a rest, and one becomes mentally and physically tired after a period of work or exercise. It is these exchanges of energy between the psyche and the organism or the external world as well as the redistribution of energy within the psyche itself that are of great interest to Jung and to all dynamic psychologists.

The Principle of Entropy   The principle of entropy or the second law of thermodynamics states, in effect, that when two bodies of different temperatures are placed in contact with one another heat will pass from the hotter to the colder body. Another example is that of the flow of water that is always in the direction of moving from a higher level to a lower level when a channel is available. The operation of the principle of entropy results in an equilibrium of forces. The warmer object loses thermal energy to the colder one until the two objects have the same temperature. At that point, the energy exchange stops and the two objects are said to be in thermal balance.

The principle of entropy as adapted by Jung to describe personality dynamics states that the distribution of energy in the psyche seeks an equilibrium or balance. Thus, to take the simplest case, if two values (energy intensities) are of unequal strength, energy will tend to pass from the stronger value into the weaker value until a balance is reached. However, since the psyche is not a closed system, energy may be added to or subtracted from either of the opposing values and upset the equilibrium. Although a permanent balance of forces in the personality can never be established, this is the ideal state toward which the distribution of energy always strives. This ideal state in which the total energy is evenly distributed throughout the various fully developed systems is the *self*. Consequently, when Jung asserts that self-realization is the goal of psychic development he means among other things that the dynamics of personality move toward a perfect equilibrium of forces.

The directed flow of energy from a center of high potential to one of low potential is a fundamental principle governing the distribution of energy among the systems of personality. The operation of this principle means that a weak system attempts to improve its status at the expense of a strong system and in so doing creates tension in the personality. If the conscious ego, for example, is greatly overvalued relative to the unconscious, a great deal of tension will be generated in the personality by the attempt on the part of the energy to move from the conscious system into the unconscious. Likewise, the energy of the superior attitude, whether it be extraversion or introversion, tends to move in the direction of the inferior attitude. An overdeveloped extravert is under pressure to develop the introverted part of his or her nature. It is a general rule in Jungian psychology that any onesided development of personality creates conflict, tension, and strain, and an even development of all the constituents of personality produces harmony, relaxation, and contentment.

However, as Jung points out, a state of perfect balance would be one in which no energy was being produced because the production of energy requires differences in potential between the various components of a system. A system runs down and stops when all parts of it are in even balance, or perfect entropy as it is called. Therefore, it is impossible for a living organism to reach complete entropy.

The Use of Energy

The total psychic energy available to the personality is used for two general purposes. Some of it is expended in performing work that is necessary for the maintenance of life and for the propagation of the species. These are the inforn, instinctive functions, as exemplified by hunger and sex. They operate according to natural biological laws. Any energy in excess of that needed by the instincts may be employed in cultural and spiritual activities. According to Jung, these activities constitute the more highly developed purposes of life. As the person becomes more efficient in satisfying their biological needs, more energy becomes available for the pursuit of cultural interests. Moreover, as the aging body makes fewer demands on energy, more energy is available for psychic activities.

THE
DEVELOPMENT
OF PERSONALITY

The most salient feature of Jung's theory of personality, aside from his conception of the collective unconscious with its archetypes, is the emphasis that he places upon the forward-going character of personality development. Jung believes that humans are constantly progressing or attempting to progress from a less complete stage of development to a more complete one. He also believes that mankind as a species is constantly evolving more differentiated forms of existence.

What is the goal of development? Toward what end are humans and mankind striving? The ultimate goal is summed up by the term *self-realization*. Self-realization means the fullest, most complete differentiation and harmonious blending of all aspects of a human's total personality. It means that the psyche has evolved a new center, the *self*, that takes the place of the old center, the ego. All of evolution, as it manifests itself in psychic development, from the first primitive organisms to the appearance of humans is a parade of progress. Progress did not stop with the creation of humans; just as humans represent an advance over all other species of animals, so does civilized man represent an improvement over primitive man. Even civilized man still has far to go before he will reach the end of his evolutionary journey. It is the future of humans that Jung finds so interesting and challenging, and about which he has so much to say in his extensive writings.

*Causality Versus
Teleology*

The idea of a goal that guides and directs human destiny is essentially a teleological or finalistic explanation. The teleological viewpoint explains the present in terms of the future. According to this viewpoint, human personality is comprehended in terms of where it is going, not where it has been. On the other hand, the present may be explained by the past. This is the viewpoint of causality that holds that present events are the consequences or effects of antecedent conditions or causes. One looks into a person's past in order to account for their present behavior.

Jung maintains that both standpoints are necessary in psychology if a complete understanding of personality is sought. The present is not only determined by the past (causality) but it is also determined by the future (teleology). Psychologists in their quest for understanding have to be Janus-faced. With one face they look into a person's past, with the other they look into the person's future. The two views when combined yield a complete picture of the person.

Jung admits that causality and teleology are merely arbitrary modes of thinking employed by the scientist for ordering and understanding natural phenomena. Causality and teleology are not themselves found in nature. Jung points out that a purely causal attitude is likely to produce resignation and despair in humans since from the standpoint of causality they are prisoners of their past. They cannot undo what has already been done. The finalistic attitude, on the other hand, gives humans a feeling of hope and something to live for.

Late in his life, Jung (1952a) proposed a principle that was neither causality or teleology. He called it the *principle of synchronicity*. This principle applies to events that occur together in time but that are not the cause of one another; for example, when a thought corresponds with an objective event. Nearly everyone has experienced such coincidences. One is thinking of a person and the person appears, or one dreams about the illness or death of a friend or relative and later hears the event took place at the exact time of the dream. Jung points to the vast literature on mental telepathy, clairvoyance, and other types of paranormal phenomena as evidence for the principle of synchronicity. He believes that many of these experiences cannot be explained as chance coincidences; instead they suggest that there is another kind of order in the universe in addition to that described by causality. Synchronistic phenomena are attributed to the nature of archetypes. An archetype is said to be *psychoid* in character; that is, it is both psychological and physical. Consequently, an archetype can bring into consciousness a mental image of a physical event even though there is no direct perception of the physical event. The archetype does not cause both events; rather it possesses a quality that permits sychronicity to occur. The principle of synchronicity would appear to be an improvement upon the notion that a thought *causes* the materialization of the thing thought about. [There is a fine essay on synchronicity in Aneila Jaffé's *From the life and work of C. G. Jung* (1971). See also Progoff (1973).]

Synchronicity

Heredity is assigned an important role in Jungian psychology. In the first place, it is responsible for the biological instincts that serve the purposes of self-preservation and reproduction. The instincts constitute the animal side of human nature. They are the links with an animal past. An instinct is an inner impulsion to act in a certain manner when a particular tissue condition arises. Hunger, for example, evokes food-seeking activities and eating. Jung's views on instincts are no different from those held by modern biology (Jung 1929, 1948c).

Heredity

However, Jung deviates sharply from the position of modern biology when he asserts that there is, in addition to an inheritance of biological instincts, an inheritance of ancestral "experiences." These experiences, or to speak with greater accuracy, the potentiality of having the same order of experiences as one's ancestors, are inherited in the form of *archetypes*. As we have already seen, an archetype is a racial memory that has become a part of human heredity by being frequently and universally repeated over many generations. By accepting the notion of cultural inheritance Jung aligns himself with the doctrine of acquired characters, a doctrine whose validity has been questioned by most contemporary geneticists.

Stages of Development   Jung does not specify in detail, as Freud does, the stages through which the personality passes from infancy to adulthood. In the very early years, libido is invested in activities that are necessary for survival. Before the age of five, sexual values begin to appear, and reach their height during adolescence. In one's youth and early adult years, the basic life instincts and vital processes are in ascendance. The young person is energetic, vigorous, impulsive, and passionate, and is still to a great extent dependent upon others. This is the period of life when the person is learning a vocation, getting married and having children, and becoming established in the life of the community.

When an individual reaches the late thirties or early forties a radical transvaluation occurs. Youthful interests and pursuits lose their value and are replaced by new interests that are more cultural and less biological. The middle-aged person becomes more introverted and less impulsive. Wisdom and sagacity take the place of physical and mental vigor. The person's values are sublimated in social, religious, civic, and philosophical symbols. He or she becomes more spiritual.

This transition is the most decisive event in a person's life. It is also one of the most hazardous because if anything goes amiss during the transference of energy the personality may become permanently crippled. This happens, for example, when the cultural and spiritual values of middle age do not utilize all of the energy formerly invested in instinctual aims. In that case, the excess energy is free to upset the equilibrium of the psyche. Jung had a great deal of success treating middleaged people whose energies had failed to find satisfying outlets (Jung, 1931a).

Progression and Regression   Development may follow either a progressive, forward movement or a regressive, backward movement. By progression, Jung means that the conscious ego is adjusting satisfactorily both to the demands of the external environment and to the needs of the unconscious. In normal progression, opposing forces are united in a coordinated and harmonious flow of psychical processes.

When the forward-going movement is interrupted by a frustrating circumstance, the libido is thereby prevented from being invested in extraverted or environment-oriented values. As a consequence, the libido makes a regression into the unconscious and invests itself in introverted values. That is, objective ego values are transformed into subjective values. Regression is the antithesis of progression.

However, Jung believes that a regressive displacement of energy does not necessarily have a permanently bad effect upon adjustment. In fact, it may help the ego find a way around the obstacle and move forward again. This is possible because the unconscious, both personal and collective, contains the knowledge and wisdom of the individual and racial past that have either been repressed or ignored. By performing a regression the ego may discover useful knowledge in the unconscious that will enable the person to overcome the frustration. Humans should pay particular attention to their dreams because they are revelations of unconscious material. In Jungian psychology, a dream is regarded as a signpost that points the way forward to the development of potential resources.

The interaction of progression and regression in development may be exemplified by the following schematic example. A young man who has detached himself from dependence upon his parents meets an insurmountable barrier. He looks to his parents for advice and encouragment. He may not actually return to his parents in a physical sense, but rather his libido may make a regression into the unconscious and reactivate the parental imagoes that are located there. These parental images may then provide him with the knowledge and encouragment that he needs to overcome the frustration.

The Individuation Process

That personality has a tendency to develop in the direction of a stable unity is a central feature of Jung's psychology. Development is an unfolding of the original undifferentiated wholeness with which humans are born. The ultimate goal of this unfolding is the realization of selfhood.

In order to realize this aim it is necessary for the various systems of personality to become completely differentiated and fully developed. For if any part of the personality is neglected, the neglected and less well-developed systems will act as centers of resistance that will try to capture energy from more fully developed systems. If too many resistances develop, the person will become neurotic. This may happen when the archetypes are not allowed to express themselves through the medium of the conscious ego or when the wrappings of the persona become so thick that they smother the rest of the personality. A man who does not provide some satisfying outlet for his feminine impulses or a woman who stifles her masculine inclinations is storing up trouble because the anima or animus under these conditions will tend to find indirect and irrational ways of expressing themselves. To have a healthy, integrated personality, every system must be permitted to reach the fullest degree of differentiation, development, and expression. The process by which this is achieved is called the *individuation process* (Jung, 1939, 1950).

The Transcendent Function

When diversity has been achieved by the operation of the individuation process, the differentiated systems are then integrated by the *transcendent function* (Jung, 1916b).

This function is endowed with the capacity to unite all of the opposing trends of the several systems and to work toward the ideal goal of perfect wholeness (selfhood). The aim of the transcendent function is the revelation of the essential person and "the realization, in all of its aspects, of the personality originally hidden away in the embryonic germplasm; the production and unfolding of the original, potential wholeness" (Jung, 1943, p. 108). Other forces in the personality, notably repression, may oppose the operation of the transcendent function, yet in spite of any opposition the forward, unifying propulsion of development will take place, if not at a conscious level then at an unconscious one. The unconscious expression of a desire for wholeness is found in dreams, myths, and other symbolic representations. One such symbol that is always cropping up in myths, dreams, architecture, religion, and the arts is the mandala symbol. Mandala is a Sanskrit word meaning circle. Jung has made exhaustive studies of the mandala because it is the perfect emblem of complete unity and wholeness in Eastern and Western religions.

Sublimation and Repression

Psychic energy is displaceable. This means that it can be transferred from one process in a particular system to another process in the same or different system. This transference is made according to the basic dynamic principles of equivalence and entropy. If the displacement is governed by the individuation process and the transcendent function, it is called *sublimation*. Sublimation describes the displacement of energy from the more primitive, instinctive, and less differentiated processes to higher cultural spiritual, and more differentiated processes. For example, when energy is withdrawn from the sex drive and invested in religious values, the energy is said to have been sublimated. Its form has been changed in the sense that a new type of work is being performed; in this case, religious work replaces sexual work.

When the discharge of energy either through instinctual or sublimated channels is blocked, it is said to be *repressed*. Repressed energy cannot just disappear; it has to go somewhere according to the principle of the conservation of energy. Consequently, it takes up its residence in the unconscious. By adding energy to unconscious material, the unconscious may become more highly charged than the conscious ego. When this happens, energy from the unconscious will tend to flow into the ego, according to the principle of entropy, and disrupt the rational processes. In other words, highly energized unconscious processes will try to break through the repression, and if they succeed, the person will behave in an irrational and impulsive fashion.

Sublimation and repression are exactly opposite in character. Sublimation is progressive, repression is regressive. Sublimation causes the psyche to move forward, repression causes it to move backward. Sublimation serves rationality, repression produces irrationality. Sublimation is integrative, repression is disintegrative.

However, Jung asks us to bear in mind that since repression is regressive it may enable individuals to find the answers to their problems in their unconscious and thus move forward again.

A symbol in Jungian psychology has two major functions. On the one hand, it represents an attempt to satisfy an instinctual impulse that has been frustrated; on the other hand, it is an embodiment of archetypal material. The development of the dance as an art form is an example of an attempt to satisfy symbolically a frustrated impulse such as the sex drive. A symbolic representation of an instinctual activity can never be entirely satisfying, however, because it does not attain the real object and discharge all of the libido. Dancing does not take the place completely of more direct forms of sexual expression; consequently, more adequate symbolizations of thwarted instincts are constantly being sought. Jung believes that the discovery of better symbols, that is, symbols that discharge more energy and reduce more tension, enables civilization to advance to higher and higher cultural levels.

Symbolization

However, a symbol also plays the role of a resistance to an impulse. As long as energy is being drained off by a symbol, it cannot be used for impulsive discharge. When one is dancing, for example, one is not engaging in a direct sexual activity. From this standpoint a symbol is the same as a sublimation. Both involve displacements of libido.

The capacity of a symbol to represent future lines of personality development, especially the striving for wholeness, plays a highly significant role in Jungian psychology. It represents a distinctive and original contribution to the theory of symbolism. Jung returns again and again to a discussion of symbolism in his writings and has made it the subject of some of his most important books. The essence of Jung's theory of symbolism is found in this quotation: "The symbol is not a sign that veils something everybody knows. Such is not its significance: on the contrary, it represents an attempt to elucidate, by means of analogy, something that still belongs entirely to the domain of the unknown or something that is yet to be" (Jung, 1916a, p. 287).

Symbols are representations of the psyche. They not only express the stored-up racial and individually acquired wisdom of mankind but they can also represent levels of development that are far ahead of humanity's present status. A person's destiny, the highest evolution of his or her psyche, is marked out for them by symbols. The knowledge contained in a symbol is not directly known to humans; they must decipher the symbol to discover its important message.

The two aspects of a symbol, one retrospective and guided by the instincts, the other prospective and guided by the ultimate goals of mankind, are two sides of the same coin. A symbol may be analyzed from either side. The retrospective type of analysis exposes the instinctual basis of a symbol, the prospective type reveals the yearnings of mankind for completion, rebirth, harmony, purification, and the like. The former is a causal, reductive type of analysis, the latter a teleological, finalistic type of analysis. Both are necessary for a complete elucidation of the symbol. Jung believes that the prospective character of a symbol has been neglected in favor of the view that a symbol is solely a product of frustrated impulses.

The psychic intensity of a symbol is always greater than the value of the cause that produced the symbol. By this is meant that there is both a driving force and an attracting force behind the creation of a symbol. The push is provided by instinctual energy, the pull by transcendental goals. Neither one alone suffices to create a symbol. Consequently, the psychic intensity of a symbol is the combined product of causal and finalistic determiners and is therefore greater than the causal factor alone.

CHARACTERISTIC RESEARCH AND RESEARCH METHODS

Jung was both a scholar and a scientist. He found his facts everywhere: in ancient myths and modern fairy tales; in primitive life and modern civilization; in the religions of the Eastern and Western worlds; in alchemy, astrology, mental telepathy, and clairvoyance; in the dreams and visions of normal people; in anthropology, history, literature, and the arts; and in clinical and experimental research. In scores of articles and books, he set forth the empirical data upon which his theories are based. Jung insists that he is more interested in discovering facts than he is in formulating theories. "I have no system, I talk of facts" (personal communication to the authors, 1954).

Since it is completely impossible to review the vast amount of empirical material that Jung brought together in his numerous writings, we will have to resign ourselves to the presentation of a minute portion of Jung's characteristic research.

Jung's first studies to attract the attention of psychologists made use of the word association test in conjunction with physiological measures of emotion (Jung, 1973). In the word association test, a standard list of words is read to the subject one at a time and the person is instructed to respond with the first word that comes to mind. The time taken to respond to each word is measured by a stop watch. In Jung's experiments, changes in breathing were measured by a pneumograph strapped to the chest of the subject and changes in the electrical conductivity of the skin by a psychogalvanometer attached to the palm of the hand. These two measures give additional evidence of emotional reactions that may appear to specific words in the list since it is well known that breathing and skin resistance are affected by emotion.

Experimental Studies of Complexes

Jung utilized these measures to uncover complexes in patients. A long period of delay in responding to the stimulus word plus respiratory and skin resistance changes indicates that a complex has been touched off by the word. For example, if a person's breathing becomes irregular, his or her resistance to an electric current decreases because of sweating of the palms and the response to the word "mother" is unusually delayed, these factors suggest the presence of a mother complex. If other words related to "mother" are reacted to in a similar manner, it substantiates the existence of such a complex.

As noted in a preceding chapter, Freud published six long case studies. In each of these studies, Freud attempted to characterize the dynamics of a specific pathological condition, for example, Dora and hysteria, Schreber and paranoia. With the exception of a few short case studies published prior to his break with Freud, Jung did not write any case studies comparable to those of Freud. In *Symbols of transformation* (1952b), Jung analyzed the fantasies of a young American woman whom he knew only through an article by the Swiss psychologist, Theodore Flournoy. This is in no sense a case study; nor is the analysis of a long dream series in *Psychology and alchemy* (1944) or the analysis of a series of paintings made by a patient in *A study in the process of individuation* (1950). In these cases, Jung used the comparative method employing history, myth, religion, and etymology to show the archetypal basis of dreams and fantasies. Following his rupture with Freud, the comparative method provided Jung with his basic data and the principal support for his concepts. The reader may not be able to assimilate such arcane volumes as *Psychology and alchemy* (1944), *Alche-*

Case Studies

mical studies (1942–1957), *Aion* (1951), and *Mysterium coniunctionis* (1955b). The reader will find, however, in *Flying saucers: a modern myth of things seen in the sky* (1958), which Jung wrote late in his life, an easily digestible example of Jung's comparative methodology.

Comparative Studies of Mythology, Religion, and the Occult Sciences

Since the evidence for archetypes is difficult to secure from contemporary sources alone, Jung devoted a great deal of attention to researches in mythology, religion, alchemy, and astrology. His investigations took him into areas that few psychologists have explored and he acquired a vast amount of knowledge of such abstruse and complex subjects as Hindu religion, Taoism, Yoga, Confucianism, the Christian Mass, astrology, psychical research, primitive mentality, and alchemy.

One of the most impressive examples of Jung's attempt to document the existence of racial archetypes is found in *Psychology and alchemy* (1944). Jung believes that the rich symbolism of alchemy expresses many, if not all, of the archetypes of humans. In *Psychology and alchemy* he examines an extensive dream series collected from a patient (not one of Jung's) against the intricate tapestry of alchemical symbolism, and concludes that the same basic features appear in both. It is a *tour de force* of symbolical analysis that has to be read in its entirety in order to be appreciated. The few examples that we will present are merely to give the reader some idea of Jung's method.

The clinical material consists of over a thousand dreams and visions obtained from a young man. The interpretation of a selection of these dreams and visions occupies the first half of the book. The rest of the book is taken up with a scholarly account of alchemy and its relation to religious symbolism.

In one dream a number of people are walking to the left around a square. The dreamer is not in the center but stands at one side. They say that a gibbon is to be reconstructed (p. 119). The square is a symbol of the work of the alchemist that consisted of breaking down the original chaotic unity of the primal material into four elements preparatory to their being recombined into a higher and more perfect unity. Perfect unity is represented by a circle or mandala that appears in this dream as walking around a square. The gibbon or ape stands for the mysterious transforming substance of alchemy, a substance that transforms base material into gold. This dream signifies, therefore, that the patient must displace his conscious ego from the center of his personality in order to permit the repressed primitive urges to be transformed. The patient can only achieve inner harmony by integrating all of the elements of his personality just as the alchemist could only reach his goal (which he never did) by the proper mixing of basic elements. In another dream, a glass filled with a gelatinous mass stands on a table before the dreamer (p. 168). The glass corresponds to the alchemical apparatus used for distillation and the contents to the amorphous substance which the alchemist hopes to turn into the *lapis* or philosopher's stone. The alchemical symbols in this dream indicate that the dreamer is trying or hoping to transform himself into something better.

When the dreamer dreams of water it represents the regenerative power of the alchemist's *aquavitae;* when he dreams of finding a blue flower the flower stands for the birthplace of the *filius philosophorum* (the hermaphroditic figure of alchemy); and when he dreams of throwing gold coins on the ground he is expressing his scorn for the alchemist's ideal. When the patient draws a wheel Jung sees a connection between it and the alchemist's wheel which stood for the circulating process within the chemical retort by which the transformation of material was supposed to take place. In a similar vein, Jung interprets a diamond that appears in the patient's dream as the coveted *lapis* and an egg as the chaotic *prima material* with which the alchemist began his labors.

Throughout all the dreams of the series, as Jung demonstrates, there are strong parallels between the symbols employed by the dreamer to represent his problems and his goals and the symbols devised by medieval alchemists to represent their endeavors. The striking feature of the dream series is the more or less exact portrayal in them of the material aspects of alchemy. Jung is able to point to exact duplications of objects in the dreams and in the illustrations found in old alchemical texts. He concludes from this that the personality dynamics of the medieval alchemist as projected into his chemical investigations and those of the patient are precisely the same. This exact correspondence of the images proves the existence of universal archetypes. Moreover, Jung, who has carried on anthropological investigations in Africa and other parts of the world, finds the same archetypes expressed in the myths of primitive races. They are also expressed in religion and art, both modern and primitive. "The forms which the experience takes in each individual may be infinite in their variations, but, like the alchemical symbols, they are all variants of certain central types, and these occur universally" (Jung, 1944, p. 463).

Dreams

Jung, like Freud, paid a great deal of attention to dreams. He considered them to be prospective as well as retrospective in content, and compensable for aspects of the dreamer's personality that have been neglected in waking life. For example, a man who neglects his anima will have dreams in which anima figures appear. Jung also differentiated between "big" dreams in which there is much archetypal imagery, and "little" dreams whose contents are more closely related to the dreamer's conscious preoccupations.

THE METHOD OF AMPLIFICATION. This method was devised by Jung to explicate certain elements in dreams that are thought to be of rich symbolic significance. It contrasts with the method of free association. In free associating, the person ordinarily gives a linear series of verbal responses to a dream element. The dream element is merely the starting point for the subsequent associations, and the associations may and usually do move away from the element. In the method of amplification, the dreamer is required to stand by the element and to give multiple associations to it. The responses he or she makes form a constellation around a particular dream element, and constitute the many-faceted meanings of it for the dreamer. Jung assumes that a true symbol is one that has many faces, and that it is never completely knowable. Analysts can also assist in amplifying the element by contributing what they know about it. They may consult ancient writings, mythology, fairy tales, religious texts, ethnology, and etymological dictionaries to extend the meanings of the symbolic element. There are many examples of amplification in Jung's writings, for example the fish (1951) and the tree (1954c).

THE DREAM SERIES METHOD. Freud, it will be recalled, analyzed dreams one at a time by having the patient free-associate to each successive component of the dream. Then, by using the dream material and the free associations, Freud arrived at an interpretation of the meaning of the dream. Jung, while not disavowing this approach, has developed another method for interpreting dreams. In place of a single dream, Jung utilizes a series of dreams obtained from a person.

. . . they [the dreams] form a coherent series in the course of which the meaning gradually unfolds more or less of its own accord. The series is the context which the dreamer himself supplies. It is as if not one text but many lay before us, throwing light from all sides on the unknown terms, so that a reading of all the texts is sufficient to elucidate the difficult passages in each individual one. . . . Of course, the interpretation of each individual passage is bound to be largely conjecture, but the series as a whole gives us all the clues we need to correct any possible errors in the preceding passages (1944, p. 12).

In psychology, this is called the method of internal consistency, and is widely employed with qualitative material like dreams, stories, and fantasies. The use that Jung has made of it is displayed to advantage in his book *Psychology and alchemy* (1944) in which an extremely long dream series is analyzed.

THE METHOD OF ACTIVE IMAGINATION. In this method, the subject is required to concentrate his or her attention on an impressive but unintelligible dream image, or on a spontaneous visual image, and observe what happens to the image. The critical faculties must be suspended and the happenings observed and noted with absolute objectivity. When these conditions are faithfully observed, the image will usually undergo a series of changes that bring to light a mass of unconscious material. The following example is taken from Jung and Kerenyi's *Essays on a science of mythology* (1949):

I saw a white bird with outstretched wings. It alighted on the figure of a woman, clad in blue, who sat there like an *antique statue*. The bird perched on her hand, and in it she had a *grain of wheat*. The bird took it in its beak and flew into the sky again (p. 229).

Jung points out that drawing, painting, and modeling can be used for representing the flow of images. In the foregoing example, the person painted a picture to accompany the verbal description. In the picture, the woman was portrayed as having large breasts which suggested to Jung that the vision represented a mother figure. [A fascinating series of 24 pictures drawn by a woman during her analysis is reproduced in Jung (1950).]

The fantasies produced by active imagination usually have better form than do nocturnal dreams because they are received by a waking consciousness rather than a sleeping one.

CURRENT STATUS AND EVALUATION

Jungian psychology has a number of devoted admirers and proponents throughout the world. Many of these are practicing psychoanalysts who use Jung's method of psychotherapy and who have accepted his fundamental postulates regarding personality. Some are theoreticians who have elaborated Jung's ideas. Among these are Gerhard Adler (1948), Michael Fordham (1947), Esther Harding (1947), Erich Neumann (1954, 1955), Herbert Read (1945), Jolande Jacobi (1959), and Frances Wickes (1950). Jung also had powerful lay supporters like Paul Mellon of the Pittsburgh Mellons, who is president of the Bollingen Foundation (named for Jung's country residence on Lake Zurich). The Bollingen Foundation sponsors the publication of Jungian books through the Princeton University Press. The most ambitious project of the Bollingen Foundation to date is the translation and publication of Jung's collected works in English under the editorial supervision of Read, Fordham, and Adler. Finally, centers of influence for the dissemination of Jung's ideas are to be found in the Jungian Institutes which have been established in a number of cities.

Jung's influence outside of the fields of psychiatry and psychology has been considerable. Arnold Toynbee, the historian, acknowledges that he is indebted to Jung for opening up "a new dimension in the realm of life." Philip Wylie, the writer, is a great admirer of Jung, as are Lewis Mumford, the author and critic, and Paul Radin, the anthropologist. Hermann Hesse also admired Jung (Serrano, 1966). Perhaps Jung's greatest impact has been upon modern religious thought (Progoff, 1953). Jung was invited to give the Terry lectures at Yale University on *Psychology and religion* (1938). Jung was severely criticized for supporting Nazism (Feldman, 1945), although he and his followers vigorously deny the charges and claim that Jung has been misrepresented (Harms, 1946; *Saturday Review,* 1949; Jaffé, 1971; Cohen, 1975).

Jung has been attacked by psychoanalysts of the Freudian school beginning with Freud himself. Ernest Jones (1959) opined that after Jung's "great studies in association and dementia praecox, he had descended into a pseudo-philosophy out of which he has never emerged" (p. 165). Glover (1950), the English psychoanalyst, has made what is probably the most comprehensive assault upon analytical psychology. He ridicules the concept of archetypes as being metaphysical and incapable of proof. He believes that archetypes can be fully accounted for in terms of experience and that it is absurd to postulate racial inheritance. Glover says that Jung has no developmental concepts by which to explain the growth of the mind. Glover's principal criticism, however, and one that he reiterates a number of times, is that Jung's psychology is a retreat back to an outmoded psychology of consciousness. He accuses Jung of tearing down the Frudian concept of the unconscious and erecting a conscious ego in its place. Glover does not pretend to be impartial or detached in his evaluation of Jungian psychology. (For another comparison of the views of Freud and Jung, see Gray, 1949; also Dry, 1961.) Selesnick (1963) argues that Jung, during his association with Freud, influenced Freud's thinking in a number of significant ways.

What influence has Jung's theory of personality had upon the development of scientific psychology? Very little that one can directly perceive, except for the word association test and the concepts of introversion and extraversion. The word association test was not original with Jung. Galton is usually credited with the invention of the test, and it was introduced into experimental psychology by Wundt. Consequently, when Jung lectured on the word association method at Clark University in 1909 it did not sound strange and alien to the psychologists in his audience. Moreover, Jung's studies on word association employed a quantitative, experimental methodology that was bound to win favor with psychologists who prided themselves on being scientific. The use of the word association test is discussed in a number of surveys of clinical psychology and projective techniques (Bell, 1948; Levy, 1952; Rotter, 1951; Anastasi, 1968).

It is less easy to account for psychology's interest in Jung's typology. A number of tests of introversion-extraversion have been constructed and there is much psychological literature on the subject. Eysenck (1947), by means of factor analysis, identified introversion-extraversion as one of the three primary dimensions of personality, the other two being *neuroticism* and *psychoticism*. He considers his findings to represent an essential confirmation of Jung's ideas. Other factor analysis studies of Jung's typology have been done by Gorlow, Simonson, and Krauss (1966) and Ball (1967). Tests that assess the four psychological functions of thinking, feeling, sensing, and intuiting in conjunction with the attitudes of introversion and extraversion have been constructed by Gray and Wheelwright (1964) and Myers and Briggs (1962). [For a critical and understanding discussion of introversion-extraversion, see Murphy (1947), Chapter 25; see also Carrigan (1960).]

Analytical psychology has not been subjected to the searching criticism accorded Freudian psychoanalysis by psychologists. Nor has it found a substantial place in the standard histories of psychology. Boring in his *History of experimental psychology* devotes six pages to Freud and four *lines* to Jung. Peters in his revision and abridgment of Brett's *History of psychology,* after giving a rather full discussion of Freud, devotes a page each to Adler and Jung. He finds Jung's later work to be so mysterious as to be almost undiscussable. Flugel's *A hundred years of psychology* spends more time on Jung but most of it has to do with the word association test and typology. Murphy's *Historical introduction to modern psychology* devotes six pages to Jung as compared to a chapter of twenty-four pages given over to Freud, and those six pages come in a chapter entitled "The Response to Freud." When 45 teachers of the history of psychology were asked to rate those who had made significant contributions to psychological theory, Jung stood thirtieth on the list (flanked by Guthrie and Rogers) that was headed by Freud. (Coan and Zagona, 1962).

Why has psychology ignored Jung's analytical psychology when the world at large accords him so much respect and honor? One major reason is that Jung's psychology is based upon clinical findings and historical and mythical sources rather than upon experimental investigations. It has appealed to the toughminded experimentalist no more than Freudianism. In fact, Jung has had far less appeal than Freud because there is so much discussion of occultism, mysticism, and religion in Jung's writings that it apparently repels many psychologists. [This criticism infuriated Jung. He insisted that his interest in the occult sciences of alchemy and astrology and in religion does not imply, in any sense, an acceptance of these beliefs. They are studied and appear in his writings because they provide evidence for his theory. Whether God exists or not is not for Jung to say; that most people believe in God is as true as a fact as that water runs downhill. "God is an obvious psychic and non-physical fact, i.e., a fact that can be established psychically but not physically" (1952c, p. 464).] Moreover, he accepts such out-of-fashion ideas as acquired characters and teleology. Jung's style of presenting his ideas has been found baffling, obscure, confusing, and disorganized by many psychologists. [Suggestions for reading Jung will be found in Hall and Nordby's *A primer of Jungian psychology* (1973).] As a consequence, Jung's theories seem to have stimulated very little interest among psychologists and even less research.

The fact that Jung is thought of as a psychoanalyst has also contributed to the neglect of his system by psychology. When one thinks of psychoanalysis one usually thinks of Freud and only secondarily of Jung and Adler. Freud's olympian stature in psychoanalysis diverts attention away from other luminaries in the field. The publication of Jung's collected works in English could change the situation although the simultaneous publication of Freud's collected writings may cancel out the effect.

Although Jung has not had much direct influence upon psychology, it may be that some recent developments in psychology owe more to Jung than is realized. Indirect influences are hard to evaluate because ideas that come into circulation may be due either to the influence of one person or they may arise more or less spontaneously in the minds of a number of people at about the same time due to the prevailing intellectual climate. It cannot be denied that many of Jung's ideas are now in common circulation, whether he is responsible or not. Take, for example, the conception of self-realization. It or similar concepts are found in the writings of Goldstein, Rogers, Angyal, Allport, and Maslow, to name only those psychologists whose views are presented in this book. In no instance do we find Jung being credited with developing the conception. This in itself does not mean that Jung has had no influence, whether directly or indirectly, upon these men. They may have borrowed from Jung unconsciously, or borrowed from others who were influenced by Jung. Or consider the idea of development as proceeding from a global to a differentiated to an integrated state, which one finds in both Jung and Murphy. Did Jung influence Murphy (the opposite is not tenable since Jung's views were enunciated before Murphy's) or did Jung influence someone else who did influence Murphy or is there no connection between the two men other than their being contemporary figures living in Western civilization? There is no evidence one way or the other. Is the optimism that characterizes many recent views, for example, those of Rogers and Allport, a reflection of Jung's optimism or a reflection of the times? Has Jung's emphasis upon goal-directed behavior set the stage for other purposive theories, or is purpose as a theoretical concept fashionable right now because nineteenth century science was so mechanistic? These are hard questions to answer and we cannot answer them.

What Jungian theory needs to make it more acceptable to scientifically minded psychologists is for hypotheses derived from the theory to be tested experimentally. We have in mind not the clinical type of study (Adler, 1949; Fordham, 1949; Hawkey, 1947; Kirsch, 1949) nor type studies (for example, Eysenck, Gray and Wheelwright, and Myers-Briggs) but a more experimental approach as found in the work of Bash (1952), Melhado (1964), Meier (1965), and Dallett (1973). When more studies of this type are done the status of Jung's theories among psychologists will tend to improve because psychologists favor theories that generate testable hypotheses and instigate research. It will take a good deal of ingenuity to formulate empirical propositions from the welter of Jungian theory.

When all is said and done, Jung's theory of personality as developed in his prolific writings and as applied to a wide range of human phenomena stands as one of the most remarkable achievements in modern thought. The originality and audacity of Jung's thinking have few parallels in recent scientific history, and no other person aside from Freud has opened more conceptual windows into what Jung would choose to call "the soul of man." It appears likely that with the growing trend in Western society, especially among young people, toward introversion, phenomenology, existentialism, meditation, spirituality, mysticism, occultism, expansion of consciousness, individuation, transcendence, unity, and self-fulfillment, Jung will come to be recognized as the spiritual and intellectual leader of this "revolutionary" movement. It is evident that more college students are reading and reacting favorably to Jung today than was the case a few years ago. His popularity appears to be greater even than Freud's. Certainly his ideas merit the closest attention from any serious student of psychology.

BIBLIOGRAPHY
PRIMARY SOURCES

Jung, C. G. *Collected works.* H. Read, M. Fordham, and G. Adler (Eds.). Princeton: Princeton Univ. Press, 1953–1978.

Jung, C. G. The structure and dynamics of the psyche. In *Collected works.* Vol. 8. Princeton: Princeton Univ. Press, 1960. (First German edition, 1926–1958.)

Jung, C. G. The archetypes and the collective unconscious. In *Collected works.* Vol. 9, Part I. Princeton: Princeton Univ. Press, 1959. (First German edition, 1936–1955.)

Jung, C. G. The psychology of the unconscious. In *Collected works.* Vol. 7. Princeton: Princeton Univ. Press, 1953. (First German edition, 1943.)

Jung, C. G. The relations between the ego and the unconscious. In *Collected Works.* Vol. 7. Princeton: Princeton Univ. Press, 1953. (First German edition, 1945.)

REFERENCES

Adler, G. *Studies in analytical psychology.* New York: Norton, 1948.

Adler, G. A discussion on archetypes and internal objects. III. A contribution of clinical material. *Brit. J. Med. Psychol.,* 1949, **22,** 16–22.

Anastasi, A. *Psychological testing.* (3rd ed.) New York: Macmillan, 1968.

Ball, E. D. A factor analytic investigation of the personality typology of C. G. Jung. *Diss. Abst.* 1968, **28,** (10-B), 4277–4278.

Bash, K. W. Zur experimentellen Grundlegung der Jungschen Traumanalyse. (On the laying of an experimental foundation of Jung's dream analysis.) *Schweiz. Z. Psychol. Anwend.,* 1952, **11,** 282–295.

Bell, J. E. *Projective techniques.* New York: Longmans, 1948.

Bennet, E. A. *C. G. Jung.* London: Barrie and Rockliff, 1961.

Berger, R. *Psyclosis: the circularity of experience.* San Francisco: Freeman, 1977.

Carrigan, P. M. Extraversion-introversion as a dimension of personality: a reappraisal. *Psychol. Bull.,* 1960, **57,** 329–360.

Coan, R. W., and Zagona, S. V. Contemporary ratings of psychological theorists. *Psychol. Rec.,* 1962, **12,** 315–322.

Cohen, E. D. *C. G. Jung and the scientific attitude.* New York: Philosophical Library, 1975.

Dallett, J. O. *The effect of sensory and social variables on the recalled dream: complementarity, continuity, and compensation.* Unpublished doctoral dissertation. University of California, Los Angles Library, 1973.

Dry, A. M. *The psychology of Jung.* New York: Wiley, 1961.

Eysenck, H. J. *Dimensions of personality.* London: Routledge and Kegan Paul, 1947.

Feldman, S. S. Dr. C. G. Jung and National Socialism. *Amer. J. Psychiat.,* 1945, **102,** 263.

Fordham, F. *An introduction to Jung's psychology.* London: Penguin Books, 1953.

Fordham, M. S. M. *The life of childhood.* London: Routledge and Kegan Paul, 1947.

Fordham, M. S. M. A discussion on archetypes and internal objects. I. On the reality of archetypes. *Brit. J. Med. Psychol.,* 1949, **22,** 3–7.

Freud, S. The history of the psychoanalytic movement. In *Standard edition,* Vol. 14. London: Hogarth Press, 1957. (First German Edition, 1914.)

Freud, S. An autobiographical study. In *Standard edition.* Vol. 20. London: Hogarth Press, 1959. (First German edition, 1925.)

Glover, E. *Freud or Jung.* New York: Norton, 1950.

Gorlow, L., Simonson, N. R., and Krauss, H. An empirical investigation of the Jungian typology. *Brit. J. Soc. Clin. Psychol.,* 1966, **5,** 108–117.

Gray, H. Freud and Jung: their contrasting psychological types. *Psychoanal. Rev.,* 1949, **36,** 22–44.

Gray, H. and Wheelwright, J. B. *Jungian type survey.* San Francisco: Society of Jungian Analysts of Northern California, 1964.

Hall, C. S., and Nordby, V. J. *A primer of Jungian psychology.* New York: New American Library, 1973.

Hannah, B. *Jung: his life and work.* New York: Putnam, 1976.

Harding, M. E. *Psychic energy, its source and goal.* New York: Pantheon Books, 1947.

Harms, E. Carl Gustav Jung—defender of Freud and the Jews. *Psychiat. Quart.,* 1946, **20,** 199–230.

Hawkey, M. L. The witch and the bogey: archetypes in the case study of a child. *Brit. J. Med. Psychol.,* 1947, **21,** 12–29.

Jacobi, J. *Complex, archetype, symbol in the psychology of C. G. Jung.* New York: Pantheon Books, 1959.

Jaffé, A. *From the life and the work of C. G. Jung.* New York: Harper and Row, 1971.

Jones, E. *The life and work of Sigmund Freud.* Vol. 2. New York: Basic Books, 1955.

Jones, E. *Free associations.* London: Hogarth Press, 1959.

Jung, C. G. The theory of psychoanalysis. In *Collected works.* Vol. 4. Princeton: Princeton Univ. Press, 1961. (First German edition, 1913.)

Jung, C. G. The structure of the unconscious. In *Collected works.* Vol. 7. Princeton: Princeton Univ. Press, 1953. (First German edition, 1916a.)

Jung, C. G. The transcendent function. In *Collected works.* Vol. 8. Princeton: Princeton Univ. Press, 1960. (First German edition, 1916b.)

Jung, C. G. Psychological types. In *Collected works.* Vol. 6. Princeton: Princeton Univ. Press, 1971. (First German edition, 1921.)

Jung, C. G. The structure and dynamics of the psyche. In *Collected works.* Vol. 8. Princeton: Princeton Univ. Press, 1960. (First German edition, 1926–1958.)

Jung, C. G. The significance of constitution and heredity in psychology. In *Collected works.* Vol. 8. Princeton: Princeton Univ. Press, 1960. (First German edition, 1929.)

Jung, C. G. The stages of life. In *Collected works.* Vol. 8. Princeton: Princeton Univ. Press, 1960. (First German edition, 1931a.)

Jung, C. G. A psychological theory of types. In *Collected works.* Vol. 6. Princeton: Princeton Univ. Press, 1971. (First German edition, 1931b.)

Jung, C. G. A review of the complex theory. In *Collected works*. Vol. 8. Princeton: Princeton Univ. Press, 1960. (First German edition, 1934.)

Jung, C. G. The concept of the collective unconscious. In *Collected works*. Vol. 9, Part I. Princeton: Princeton Univ. Press, 1959. (Originally published in English, 1936.)

Jung, C. G. The archetypes and the collective unconscious. In *Collected works*. Vol. 9, Part I. Princeton Univ. Press, 1959. (First German edition, 1936–1955.)

Jung, C. G. Psychology and religion. In *Collected works*. Vol. 11. Princeton: Princeton Univ. Press, 1958. (Originally published in English, 1938.)

Jung, C. G. Conscious, unconscious, and individuation. In *Collected works*. Vol. 9, Part I. Princeton: Princeton Univ. Press, 1959. (Originally published in English, 1939.)

Jung, C. G. Alchemical studies. In *Collected works*. Vol. 13. Princeton: Princeton Univ. Press, 1967. (First German edition, 1942–1957.)

Jung. C. G. The psychology of the unconscious. In *Collected works*. Vol. 7. Princeton: Princeton Univ. Press, 1953. (First German edition, 1943.)

Jung, C. G. Psychology and alchemy. In *Collected works*. Vol. 13. Princeton: Princeton Univ. Press, 1953. (First German edition, 1944.)

Jung, C. G. The relations between the ego and the unconscious. In *Collected works*. Vol. 7. Princeton: Princeton Univ. Press, 1953. (First German edition, 1945.)

Jung, C. G. The shadow. In *Collected works*. Vol. 9, Part II. Princeton: Princeton Univ. Press, 1959. (First German edition, 1948a.)

Jung, C. G. On psychic energy. In *Collected works*. Vol. 8. Princeton: Princeton Univ. Press, 1960. (First German edition, 1948b.)

Jung, C. G. Instinct and the unconscious. In *Collected works*. Vol. 8. Princeton: Princeton Univ. Press, 1960. (First German edition, 1948c.)

Jung, C. G. A study in the process of individuation. In *Collected works*. Vol. 9, Part I. Princeton: Princeton Univ. Press, 1959. (First German edition, 1950.)

Jung, C. G. Aion. In *Collected works*. Vol. 9, Part II. Princeton: Princeton Univ. Press, 1959. (First German edition, 1951.)

Jung, C. G. Synchronicity: an acausal connecting principle. In *Collected works*. Vol. 8. Princeton: Princeton Univ. Press, 1960. (First German edition, 1952a.)

Jung, C. G. Symbols in transformation. In *Collected works*. Vol. 5. Princeton: Princeton Univ. Press, 1956. (First German edition, 1952b.)

Jung, C. G. Answer to Job. In *Collected works*. Vol. 11. Princeton: Princeton Univ. Press, 1958. (First German edition, 1952c.)

Jung, C. G. *Collected works*. H. Read, M. Fordham, and G. Adler (Eds.). Princeton: Princeton Univ. Press, 1953–1978.

Jung, C. G. Psychological aspects of the mother archetype. In *Collected works*. Vol. 9, Part I. Princeton: Princeton Univ. Press, 1959. (First German edition, 1954a.)

Jung C. G. Concerning the archetypes, with special reference to the anima concept. In *Collected works*. Vol. 9, Part I. Princeton: Princeton Univ. Press, 1959. (First German edition, 1954b.)

Jung, C. G. The philosophical tree. In *Collected works*. Vol. 13. Princeton: Princeton Univ. Press, 1967. (First German edition, 1954c.)

Jung, C. G. Mandalas. In *Collected works*. Vol. 9, Part I. Princeton: Princeton Univ. Press, 1959. (First German edition, 1955a.)

Jung. C. G. Mysterium coniunctionis. In *Collected works*. Vol. 14. Princeton: Princeton Univ. Press, 1963. (First German edition, 1955b.)

Jung, C. G. Flying saucers: a modern myth of things seen in the skies. In *Collected works*. Vol. 10. Princeton: Princeton Univ. Press, 1964. (First German edition, 1958.)

Jung, C. G. *Memories, dreams, reflections*. New York: Random House, 1961.

Jung, C. G. Experimental researches. In *Collected works*. Vol. 2. Princeton: Princeton Univ. Press, 1973a.

Jung, C. G. *Letters: 1906–1950*. Vol. 1. Princeton: Princeton Univ. Press, 1973b.

Jung, C. G. *Letters: 1951–1961*. Vol. 2. Princeton: Princeton Univ. Press, 1975.

Jung, C. G., and Kerenyi, C. *Essays on a science of mythology*. New York: Pantheon Books, 1949.

Kirsch, J. The role of instinct in psychosomatic medicine. *Amer. J. Psychother.*, 1949, **3**, 253–260.

Levy, S. Sentence completion and word association tests. In D. Brower and L. E. Abt (Eds.). *Progress in clinical psychology*. Vol. 1. New York: Grune and Stratton, 1952, 191–208.

McGuire, W. (Ed.). *The Freud/Jung letters: the correspondence between Sigmund Freud and C. G. Jung*. Princeton: Princeton Univ. Press, 1974.

McGuire, W. *C. G. Jung speaking*. Princeton: Princeton Univ. Press, 1977.

Meier, C. A. Clinic and Research Centre for Jungian Psychology, Zurich. *J. analyt. Psychol.*, 1965, **10**, 1–6.

Melhado, J. J. *Exploratory studies in symbolism*. Ph.D. dissertation. Univ. of Texas, 1964.

Murphy, G. *Personality*. New York: Harper, 1947.

Myers, Isabel B. *The Myers-Briggs Type Indicator*. Princeton: Educational Testing Service, 1962.

Neumann, E. *The origins and history of consciousness*. New York: Pantheon Books, 1954.

Neumann, E. *The great mother*. London: Routledge and Kegan Paul, 1955.

Progoff, I. *Jung's psychology and its social meaning*. New York: Julian, 1953.

Progoff, I. *Jung, synchronicity, and human destiny*. New York: Julian, 1973.

Read, H. E. *Education through art*. New York: Pantheon Books, 1945.

Rotter, J. B. Word association and sentence completion methods. In H. H. Anderson and Gladys L. Anderson (Eds.). *An introduction to projective techniques*. Englewood Cliffs, N.J.: Prentice-Hall, 1951, 279–311.

Saturday Review. Various writers. 1949, **32**, July 9, p. 25; July 16, pp. 21, 23; July 30, pp. 6–8; Sept. 10, p. 27; Oct. 15, pp. 23–25.

Selesnick, S. T. C. G. Jung's contribution to psychoanalysis. *Amer. J. Psychiat.,* 1963, **120,** 350–356.

Serrano, M. *C. G. Jung and Hermann Hesse.* London: Routledge and Kegan Paul, 1966.

Stern, P. J. *C. G. Jung: the haunted prophet.* New York: Braziller, 1976.

van der Post, L. *Jung and the story of our time.* New York: Pantheon, 1975.

von Franz, M-L. *C. G. Jung: his myth in our times.* New York: Putnam, 1975.

Wehr, G. *Portrait of Jung: an illustrated biography.* New York: Herder and Herder, 1971.

Weigert, E. V. Dissent in the early history of psychoanalysis. *Psychiatry,* 1942, **5,** 349–359.

Wickes, Frances G. *The inner world of man.* London: Methuen, 1950.

Wilhelm, R. and Jung, C. G. *The secret of the golden flower.* New York: Harcourt, Brace & World, 1931.

SOCIAL PSYCHOLOGICAL THEORIES: ADLER, FROMM, HORNEY, AND SULLIVAN

5

The psychoanalytic theories of personality formulated by Freud and Jung were nurtured by the same positivistic climate that shaped the course of nineteenth century physics and biology. An individual was regarded primarily as a complex energy system that maintains itself by means of transactions with the external world. The ultimate purposes of these transactions are individual survival, propagation of the species, and an ongoing evolutionary development. The various psychological processes that constitute the personality serve these ends. According to the evolutionary doctrine some personalities are better fitted than others to perform these tasks. Consequently, the concept of variation and the distinction between adjustment and maladjustment conditioned the thinking of the early psychoanalysts. Even academic psychology was swept into the orbit of Darwinism and became preoccupied with the measurement of individual differences in abilities and with the adaptive or functional value of psychological processes.

At the same time, other intellectual trends that were at variance with a purely biophysical conception of humans were beginning to take shape. During the later years of the nineteenth century, sociology and anthropology began to emerge as independent disciplines and their rapid growth during the present century has been phenomenal. While sociologists studied humans living in a state of advanced civilization and found them to be products of class and caste, institutions and folkways, anthropologists ventured into remote areas of the world where they found evidence that human beings are almost infinitely malleable. According to these new social sciences, an individual is chiefly a product of the society in which he or she lives. One's personality is shaped more by social circumstances than by biological factors.

Gradually, these burgeoning social and cultural doctrines began to seep into psychology and psychoanalysis and to erode the nativistic and physicalistic foundations of the sciences. A number of followers of Freud who became dissatisfied with what they considered to be his myopia regarding the social conditioners of personality withdrew their allegiance from classical psychoanalysis and began to refashion psychoanalytic theory along lines dictated by the new orientation developed by the social sciences. Among those who provided psychoanalytic theory with the twentieth century look of social psychology are the four people whose ideas form the content of the present chapter— Alfred Adler, Karen Horney, Erich Fromm, and Harry Stack Sullivan. Of these four, Alfred Adler may be regarded as the ancestral figure of the "new social psychological look" because as early as 1911 he broke with Freud over the issue of sexuality, and proceeded to develop a theory in which social interest and a striving for superiority became two of its most substantial conceptual pillars. No less an authority than Fromm acknowledged that Adler was the first psychoanalyst to emphasize the fundamental social nature of humans. Later, Horney and Fromm took up the cudgels against the strong instinctivist orientation of psychoanalysis and insisted upon the relevance of social psychological variables for personality theory. Finally, Harry Stack Sullivan in his theory of interpersonal relations consolidated the position of a personality theory grounded in social processes. Although each of the theories has its own distinctive assumptions and concepts, there are numerous parallels among them which have been pointed out by various writers (James, 1947; Ruth Munroe, 1955; and H. L. and R. R. Ansbacher, 1956).

Our choice of the major figure for this chapter, Harry Stack Sullivan, is dictated primarily by our belief that he brought his ideas to a higher level of conceptualization and consequently has been a more pervasively influential theorist. Sullivan was considerably more independent of prevailing psychoanalytic doctrines; although he earlier used the Freudian framework, in his later work he developed a theoretical system that deviated markedly from the Freudian one. He was profoundly influenced by anthropology and social psychology. Both Horney and Fromm, on the other hand, kept well within the province of psychoanalysis in their thinking; Adler, although a separatist from the Freudian school, continued to show the impact of his early association with Freud throughout his life. Horney and Fromm are usually referred to as revisionists or neo–Freudians although Fromm objects to these labels. Neither of them engaged in developing a new theory of personality; rather they regarded themselves as renovators and elaborators of an old theory. Sullivan was much more of an innovator. He was a highly original thinker who attracted a large group of devoted disciples and developed what is sometimes called a new school of psychiatry.

ALFRED ADLER

Alfred Adler was born in Vienna in 1870 of a middle-class family and died in Aberdeen, Scotland, in 1937 while on a lecture tour. He received a medical degree in 1895 from the University of Vienna. At first he specialized in ophthalmology and then, after a perioid of practice in general medicine, he became a psychiatrist. He was one of the charter members of the Vienna Psychoanalytic Society and later its president. However, Adler soon began to develop ideas that were at variance with those of Freud and others in the Vienna Society, and when these differences became acute he was asked to present his views to the society. This he did in 1911 and as a consequence of the vehement criticism and denunciation of Adler's position by other members of the society, Adler resigned as president and a few months later terminated his connection with Freudian psychoanalysis (Colby, 1951; Jones, 1955; H. L. and R. R. Ansbacher, 1956, 1964).

He then formed his own group, which came to be known as Individual Psychology and which attracted followers throughout the world. During the First World War, Adler served as a physician in the Austrian army and after the war he became interested in child guidance and established the first guidance clinics in connection with the Viennese school system. He also inspired the establishment of an experimental school in Vienna that applied his theories of education (Furtmüller, 1964).

In 1935 Adler settled in the United States where he continued his practice as a psychiatrist and served as Professor of Medical Psychology at the Long Island College of Medicine. Adler was a prolific writer and an indefatigable lecturer. He published a hundred books and articles during his lifetime. *The practice and theory of individual psychology* (1927) is probably the best introduction to Adler's theory of personality. Shorter digests of Adler's views appear in the *Psychologies of 1930* (1930) and in the *International Journal of Individual Psychology* (1935). Heinz and Rowena Ansbacher (1956, 1964) have edited and annotated two volumes containing an extensive selection from Adler's writings. These two volumes are the best source of information about Adler's Individual Psychology. Two book length biographies of Adler have been published (Bottome, 1939; Orgler, 1963). A recent perspective on Adler will be found in a book by Sperber (1974). Adler's ideas are promulgated in the United States by the American Society of Adlerian Psychology with branches in New

Alfred Adler

York, Chicago, and Los Angeles and through its journal, *The American Journal of Individual Psychology*.

In sharp contrast to Freud's major assumption that human behavior is motivated by inborn instincts and Jung's principal axiom that human conduct is governed by inborn archetypes, Adler assumed that humans are motivated primarily by social urges. Humans are, according to Adler, inherently social beings. They relate themselves to other people, engage in cooperative social activities, place social welfare above selfish interest, and acquire a style of life that is predominantly social in orientation. Adler did not say that humans become socialized merely by being exposed to social processes; social interest is inborn although the specific types of relationships with people and social institutions that develop are determined by the nature of the society into which a person is born. In one sense, then, Adler is just as biological in his viewpoint as are Freud and Jung. All three assume that a person has an inherent nature that shapes his or her personality. Freud emphasized sex, Jung emphasized primordial thought patterns, and Adler stressed social interest. This emphasis upon the social determinants of behavior that had been overlooked or minimized by Freud and Jung is probably Adler's greatest contribution to psychological theory. It turned the attention of psychologists to the importance of social variables and helped to develop the field of social psychology at a time when social psychology needed encouragement and support, especially from the ranks of psychoanalysis.

Adler's second major contribution to personality theory is his concept of the creative self. Unlike Freud's ego, which consists of a group of psychological processes serving the ends of inborn instincts, Adler's self is a highly personalized, subjective system that interprets and makes meaningful that experiences of the organism. Moreover, it searches for experiences that will aid in fulfilling the person's unique style of life; if these experiences are not to be found in the world the self tries to create them. This concept of a creative self was new to psychoanalytic theory and it helped to compensate for the extreme "objectivism" of classical psychoanalysis, which relied almost entirely upon biological needs and external stimuli to account for the dynamics of personality. As we shall see in other chapters, the concept of the self has played a major role in recent formulations regarding personality. Adler's contribution to this new trend of recognizing the self as an important cause of behavior is considered a very significant one.

A third feature of Adler's psychology that sets it apart from classical psychoanalysis is its emphasis upon the uniqueness of personality. Adler considered each person to be a unique configuration of motives, traits, interests, and values; every act performed by the person bears the stamp of his or her own distinctive style of life. In his respect, Adler belongs to the tradition of William James and William Stern who are said to have laid the foundation for personalistic psychology.

Adler's theory of the person minimized the sexual instinct that in Freud's early theorizing had played an almost exclusive role in the dynamics of behavior. To this Freudian monologue on sex, Adler added other significant voices. Humans are primarily social and not sexual creatures. They are motivated by social and not by sexual interest. Their inferiorities are not limited to the sexual domain, but may extend to all facets of being, both physical and psychological. They strive to develop a unique style of life in which the sexual drive plays a minor role. In fact, the way in which one satisfies sexual needs is determined by one's style of life and not vice versa. Adler's dethroning of sex was for many people a welcome relief from the monotonous pansexualism of Freud.

Finally, Adler considered consciousness to be the center of personality, which makes him a pioneer in the development of an ego-oriented psychology. Humans are conscious beings; they are ordinarily aware of the reasons for their behavior. They are conscious of their inferiorities and conscious of the goals for which they strive. More than that, humans are self-conscious individuals capable of planning and guiding their actions with full awareness of their meaning for their own self-realization. This is the complete antithesis of Freud's theory, which had virtually reduced consciousness to the status of a nonentity—a mere froth floating on the great sea of the unconscious.

Alfred Adler, like other personality theorists whose primary training was in medicine and who practiced psychiatry, began his theorizing in the field of abnormal psychology. He formulated a theory of neurosis before broadening his theoretical scope to include the normal personality, which occurred during the 1920s (H. L. and R. R. Ansbacher, 1956). Adler's theory of personality is an extremely economical one in the sense that a few basic concepts sustain the whole theoretical structure. For that reason, Adler's viewpoint can be rather quickly sketched under a few general rubrics. These are: (1) fictional finalism, (2) striving for superiority, (3) inferiority feelings and compensation, (4) social interest, (5) style of life, and (6) the creative self.

FICTIONAL FINALISM   Shortly after Adler dissociated himself from the circle that surrounded Freud, he fell under the philosophical influence of Hans Vaihinger whose book *The philosophy of "as if"* (English translation, 1925) had been published in 1911. Vaihinger propounded the curious and intriguing notion that humans live by many purely fictional ideas that have no counterpart in reality. These fictions, for example, "all men are created equal," "honesty is the best policy," and "the end justifies the means," enable humans to deal more effectively with reality. They are auxiliary constructs or assumptions and not hypotheses that can be tested and confirmed. They can be dispensed with when their usefulness has disappeared.

Adler took over this philosophical doctrine of idealistic positivism and bent it to his own design. Freud, it will be recalled, laid great stress upon constitutional factors and experiences during early childhood as determiners of personality. Adler discovered in Vaihinger the rebuttal to this rigid historical determinism; he found the idea that humans are motivated more by their expectations of the future than by experiences of the past. These goals do not exist in the future as a part of some teleological design—neither Vaihinger nor Adler believed in predestination or fatality—instead they exist subjectively or mentally here and now as strivings or ideals that affect present behavior. If a person believes, for example, that there is a heaven for virtuous people and a hell for sinners, this belief, it may be presumed, will exercise considerable influence on their conduct. These fictional goals were, for Adler, the subjective causation of psychological events.

Like Jung, Adler identified Freud's theory with the principle of causality and his own with the principle of finalism.

Individual Psychology insists absolutely on the indispensability of finalism for the understanding of all psychological phenomena. Causes, powers, instincts, impulses, and the like cannot serve as explanatory principles. The final goal alone can explain man's behavior. Experiences, traumata, sexual development mechanisms cannot yield an explanation, but the perspective in which these are regarded, the individual way of seeing them, which subordinates all life to the final goal, can do so (1930, p. 400).

This final goal may be a fiction, that is, an ideal that is impossible to realize but which is nonetheless a very real spur to human striving and the ultimate explanation of conduct. Adler believed, however, that the normal person could free him or her self from the influence of these fictions and face reality when necessity demanded, something that the neurotic person is incapable of doing.

What is the final goal toward which all humans strive and which gives consistency and unity to personality? By 1908, Adler had reached the conclusion that aggression was more important than sexuality. A little later, the aggressive impulse was replaced by the "will to power." Adler identified power with masculinity and weakness with femininity. It was at this stage of his thinking (circa 1910) that he set forth the idea of the "masculine protest," a form of overcompensation that both

STRIVING FOR SUPERIORITY

men and women indulge in when they feel inadequate and inferior. Later, Adler abandoned the "will to power" in favor of the "striving for superiority," to which he remained committed thereafter. Thus, there were three stages in his thinking regarding the final goal of humans: to be aggressive, to be powerful, and to be superior.

Adler makes it very clear that by superiority he does not mean social distinction, leadership, or a pre-eminent position in society. By superiority, Adler means something very analogous to Jung's concept of the self or Goldstein's principle of self-actualization. It is a striving for perfect completion. It is "the great upward drive."

I began to see clearly in every psychological phenomenon the striving for superiority. It runs parallel to physical growth and is an intrinsic necessity of life itself. It lies at the root of all solutions of life's problems and is manifested in the way in which we met these problems. All our functions follow its direction. They strive for conquest, security, increase, either in the right or in the wrong direction. The impetus from minus to plus never ends. The urge from below to above never ceases. Whatever premises all our philosophers and psychologists dream of—self-preservation, pleasure principle, equalization—all these are but vague representations, attempts to express the great upward drive (1930, p. 398).

Where does the striving for superiority or perfection come from? Adler says that it is innate; that it is a part of life; in fact, that it is life itself. From birth to death, the striving for superiority carries the person from one stage of development to the next higher stage. It is a prepotent dynamic principle. There are no separate drives, for each drive receives its power from the striving for completion. Adler acknowledges that the striving for superiority may manifest itself in a thousand different ways, and that each person has his or her own concrete mode of achieving or trying to achieve perfection. The neurotic person, for example, strives for self-esteem, power, and self-aggrandizement—in other words, for egoistic or selfish goals—whereas the normal person strives for goals that are primarily social in character.

Precisely how do the particular forms of the striving for superiority come into being in the individual? In order to answer this question it is necessary to discuss Adler's concept of inferiority feelings.

INFERIORITY FEELINGS AND COMPENSATION   Very early in his career, while he was still interested in general medicine, Adler put forth the idea of organ inferiority and overcompensation (English translation, 1917). At that time, he was interested in finding the answer to the perennial question of why people, when they become sick or suffer some affliction, become sick or afflicted in a particular region of the body. One person develops heart trouble, another lung trouble, and a third arthritis. Adler suggested that the reason for the site of a particular affliction was a basic inferiority in that region, an inferiority that existed either by virtue of heredity or because of some developmental abnormality. He then observed that a person with a defective organ often tries to compensate for the weakness by strengthening it through intensive training. The most famous example of compensation for organ inferiority is that of Demosthenes who stuttered as a child and became one of the world's greatest orators. Another more recent example is that of Theodore Roosevelt who was a weakling in his youth and developed himself by systematic exercise into a physically stalwart man.

Shortly after he had published his monograph on organ inferiority Adler broadened the concept to include any feelings of inferiority, those that arise from subjectively felt psychological or social disabilities as well as those that stem from actual bodily weakness or impairment. At this time, Adler equated inferiority with unmanliness or femininity, the compensation for which was called "the masculine protest." Later, however, he subordinated this view to the more general one that feelings of inferiority arise from a sense of incompletion or imperfection in any sphere of life. For example, the child is motivated by its feelings of inferiority to strive for a higher level of development. When it reaches this level, it begins to feel inferior again and the upward movement is initiated once more. Adler contended that inferiority feelings are not a sign of abnormality; they are the cause of all improvement in the human lot. Of course, inferiority feelings may be exaggerated by special conditions such as pampering or rejecting the child, in which case certain abnormal manifestations may ensue, such as the development of an inferiority complex or a compensatory superiority complex. But under normal circumstances, the feeling of inferiority or a sense of incompleteness is the great driving force of mankind. In other words, humans are pushed by the need to overcome their inferiority and pulled by the desire to be superior.

Adler was not a proponent of hedonism. Although he believed that inferiority feelings were painful he did not think that the relief of these feelings was necessarily pleasurable. Perfection, not pleasure, was for him the goal of life.

SOCIAL INTEREST

During the early years of his theorizing when he was proclaiming the aggressive, power-hungry nature of humans and the idea of the masculine protest as an overcompensation for feminine weakness, Adler was severely criticized for emphasizing selfish drives and ignoring social motives. Striving for superiority sounded like the war cry of the Nietzschean superman, a fitting companion for the Darwinian slogan of survival of the fittest.

Adler, who was an advocate of social justice and a supporter of social democracy, enlarged his conception of humans to include the factor of social interest (1939). Although social interest takes in such matters as cooperation, interpersonal and social relations, identification with the group, empathy, and so forth, it is much broader than all of these. In its ultimate sense, social interest consists of the individual helping society to attain the goal of a perfect society. "Social interest is the true and inevitable compensation for all the natural weaknesses of individual human beings" (Adler, 1929b, p. 31).

The person is embedded in a social context from the first day of life. Cooperation manifests itself in the relationship between the infant and the mother, and henceforth the person is continuously involved in a network of interpersonal relations that shape the personality and provide concrete outlets for striving for superiority. Striving for superiority becomes socialized; the ideal of a perfect society takes the place of purely personal ambition and selfish gain. By working for the common good, humans compensate for their individual weaknesses.

Adler believed that social interest is inborn; that humans are social creatures by nature, and not by habit. However, like any other natural aptitude, this innate predisposition does not appear spontaneously but has to be brought to fruition by guidance and training. Because he believed in the benefits of education Adler devoted a great deal of his time to establishing child guidance clinics, to improving the schools, and to educating the public regarding proper methods of rearing children.

It is interesting to trace in Adler's writings the decisive although gradual change that occurred in his conception of humans from the early years of his professional life when he was associated with Freud to his later years when he had achieved an international reputation. For the young Adler, humans are driven by an insatiable lust for power and domination in order to compensate for a concealed deep-seated feeling of inferiority. For the older Adler, humans are motivated by an innately given social interest that causes them to subordinate private gain to public welfare. The image of the perfect person living in a perfect society blotted out the picture of the strong, aggressive person dominating and exploiting society. Social interest replaced selfish interest.

STYLE OF LIFE   This is the slogan of Adler's personality theory. It is a recurrent theme in all of Adler's later writings (for example, 1929a, 1931) and the most distinctive feature of his psychology. Style of life is *the* system principle by which the individual personality functions; it is the whole that commands the parts. Style of life is Adler's chief idiographic principle; it is the principle that explains the uniqueness of the person. Everyone has a style of life but no two people develop the same style.

Precisely what is meant by this concept? This is a difficult question to answer because Adler had so much to say about it and because he said different and sometimes conflicting things about it in his various writings. Then, too, it is difficult to differentiate it from another Adlerian concept, that of the *creative self*.

Every person has the same goal, that of superiority, but there are innumerable ways of striving for this goal. One person tries to become superior through developing the intellect, while another bends all of his or her efforts to achieving muscular perfection. The intellectual has one style of life, the athlete another. The intellectual reads, studies, thinks; he or she lives a more sedentary and more solitary life than the active person does. The intellectual arranges the details of existence, domestic habits, recreations, daily routine, relations to family, friends, and acquaintances, social activities, in accordance with the goal of intellectual superiority. Everything done is done with an eye to this ultimate goal. All of a person's behavior springs from his or her style of life. The person perceives, learns, and retains what fits the style of life, and ignores everything else.

The style of life is formed very early in childhood, by the age of four or five, and from then on experiences are assimilated and utilized according to this unique style of life. Attitudes, feelings, apperceptions become fixed and mechanized at an early age, and it is practically impossible for the style of life to change thereafter. The person may acquire new ways of expressing his or her unique style of life, but these are merely concrete and particular instances of the same basic style found at an early age.

What determines the individual's style of life? In his earlier writings, Adler said that it is largely determined by the specific inferiorities, either fancied or real, that the person has. The style of life is a compensation for a particular inferiority. If the child is a physical weakling, its style of life will take the form of doing those things that will produce physical strength. The dull child will strive for intellectual superiority. Napoleon's conquering style of life was determined by his slight physical stature, and Hitler's rapacious craving for world domination by his sexual impotence. This simple explanation of human conduct that appealed to so many of Adler's readers and which was widely applied in the analysis of character during the 1920s and 1930s did not satisfy Adler himself. It was too simple and too mechanistic. He looked for a more dynamic principle and found the creative self.

THE CREATIVE SELF

This concept is Adler's crowning achievement as a personality theorist. When he discovered the creative power of the self, all his other concepts were subordinated to it; here at last was the prime mover, the philosopher's stone, the elixir of life, the first cause of everything human for which Adler had been searching. The unitary, consistent, creative self is sovereign in the personality structure.

Like all first causes, the creative power of the self is hard to describe. We can see its effects, but we cannot see it. It is something that intervenes between the stimuli acting upon the person and the responses the person makes to these stimuli. In essence, the doctrine of a creative self asserts that humans make their own personalities. They construct them out of the raw material of heredity and experience.

Heredity only endows him [man] with certain abilities. Environment only gives him certain impressions. These abilities and impressions, and the manner in which he 'experiences' them—that is to say, the interpretation he makes of these experiences—are the bricks, or in other words his attitude toward life, which determines this relationship to the outside world (Adler, 1935, p. 5).

The creative self is the yeast that acts upon the facts of the world and transforms these facts into a personality that is subjective, dynamic, unified, personal, and uniquely stylized. The creative self gives meaning to life; it creates the goal as well as the means to the goal. The creative self is the active principle of human life, and it is not unlike the older concept of soul.

In summary, it may be said that Adler fashioned a humanistic theory of personality that was the antithesis of Freud's conception of the individual. By endowing humans with altruism, humanitarianism, cooperation, creativity, uniqueness, and awareness, Adler restored to humans a sense of dignity and worth that psychoanalysis had pretty largely destroyed. In place of the dreary materialistic picture that horrified and repelled many readers of Freud, Adler offered a portrait of humans that was more satisfying, more hopeful, and far more complimentary to humans. Adler's conception of the nature of personality coincided with the popular idea that individuals can be the masters, and not the victims, of their fate.

CHARACTERISTIC RESEARCH AND RESEARCH METHODS

Adler's empirical observations were made largely in the therapeutic setting and consist for the most part of reconstructions of the past as remembered by the patient and appraisals of present behavior on the basis of verbal reports. There is space to mention only a few examples of Adler's investigative activities.

Order of Birth and Personality

In line with his interest in the social determiners of personality, Adler observed that the personalities of the oldest, middle, and youngest child in a family were likely to be quite different (1931, pp. 144–154). He attributed these differences to the distinctive experiences that each child has as a member of a social group.

The first-born or oldest child is given a good deal of attention until the second child is born; then it is suddenly dethroned from its favored position and must share its parents' affections with the new baby. This experience may condition the oldest child in various ways, such as hating people, protecting him or her self against sudden reversals of fortune, and feeling insecure. Oldest children are also apt to take an interest in the past when they were the center of attention. Neurotics, criminals, drunkards, and perverts, Adler observes, are often first-born children. If the parents handle the situation wisely by preparing the oldest child for the appearance of a rival, the oldest child is more likely to develop into a responsible, protective person.

The second or middle child is characterized by being ambitious. It is constantly trying to surpass its older sibling. It also tends to be rebellious and envious but by and large is better adjusted than either the older or younger sibling.

The youngest child is the spoiled child. Next to the oldest child it is most likely to become a problem child and a neurotic maladjusted adult.

Although early tests of Adler's birth-order theory failed to lend much support to it (Jones, 1931), the more sophisticated work of Schachter (1959) has provided impressive confirmation of the Adlerian thesis and has opened the subject for an immense amount of research. For example, one survey (Vockell, Felker, and Miley, 1973) lists 272 new studies of birth order published between 1967 and 1972.

Early Memories

Adler felt that the earliest memory a person could report was an important key to understanding one's basic style of life (1931). For example, a girl began an account of her earliest memory by saying, "When I was three years old, my father . . ." This indicates that she is more interested in her father than in her mother. She then goes on to say that the father brought home a pair of ponies for an older sister and her, and that the older sister led her pony down the street by the halter while she was dragged along in the mud by her pony. This is the fate of the younger child—to come off second best in the rivalry with an older sibling—and it motivates her to try to surpass the pacemaker. Her style of life is one of driving ambition, an urge to be first, a deep feeling of insecurity and disappointment, and a strong foreboding of failure.

A young man who was being treated for severe attacks of anxiety recalled this early scene. "When I was about four years old I sat at the window and watched some workmen building a house on the opposite side of the street, while my mother knitted stockings." This recollection indicates that the young man was pampered as a child because his memory includes the solicitous mother. The fact that he is looking at others who are working suggests that his style of life is that of a spectator rather than a participant. This is borne out by the fact that he becomes anxious whenever he tries to take up a vocation. Adler suggested to him that he consider an occupation in which his preference for looking and observing could be utilized. The patient took Adler's advice and became a successful dealer in art objects.

Adler used this method with groups as well as individuals and found that it was an easy and economical way of studying personality. Early recollections are now being used as a projective technique (Mosak, 1958).

Childhood Experiences   Adler was particularly interested in the kinds of early influences that predispose the child to a faulty style of life. He discovered three important factors: (1) children with inferiorities, (2) spoiled children, and (3) neglected children. Children with physical or mental infirmities bear a heavy burden and are likely to feel inadequate in meeting the tasks of life. They consider themselves to be, and often are, failures. However, if they have understanding, encouraging parents they may compensate for their inferiorities and transform their weakness into strength. Many prominent people started life with some organic weakness for which they compensated. Over and over again Adler spoke out vehemently against the evils of pampering for he considered this to be the greatest curse that can be visited upon the child. Pampered children do not develop social feeling; they become despots who expect society to conform to their self-centered wishes. Adler considered them to be potentially the most dangerous class in society. Neglect of the child also has unfortunate consequences. Badly treated in childhood, as adults they become enemies of society. Their style of life is dominated by the need for revenge. These three conditions—organic infirmity, pampering, and rejection—produce erroneous conceptions of the world and result in a pathological style of life.

ERICH FROMM

Erich Fromm was born in Frankfurt, Germany, in 1900 and studied psychology and sociology at the Universities of Heidelberg, Frankfurt, and Munich. After receiving a Ph.D. degree from Heidelberg in 1922, he was trained in psychoanalysis in Munich and at the famous Berlin Psychoanalytic Institute. He came to the United States in 1933 as a lecturer at the Chicago Psychoanalytic Institute and then entered private practice in New York City. He has taught at a number of universities and institutes in this country and in Mexico. Fromm now resides in Switzerland. His books have received considerable attention not only from specialists in the fields of psychology, sociology, philosophy, and religion but also from the general public.

Fromm has been heavily influenced by the writings of Karl Marx, particularly by an early work *The economic and philosophical manuscripts* composed in 1844. This work in an English translation by T. B. Bot–

Erich Fromm

tomore is included in Fromm's *Marx's concept of man* (1961). In *Beyond the chains of illusion* (1962), Fromm compares the ideas of Freud and Marx, noting their contradictions and attempting a synthesis. Fromm regards Marx as a more profound thinker than Freud and uses psychoanalysis mainly to fill in the gaps in Marx. Fromm (1959) wrote a highly critical, even polemical, analysis of Freud's personality and influence and, by way of contrast, an unconditional eulogy of Marx (1961). Although Fromm could be accurately called a Marxian personality theorist, he himself prefers the label *dialectic humanist*. Fromm's writings are inspired by his extensive knowledge of history, sociology, literature, and philosophy.

The essential theme of all of Fromm's writings is that a person feels lonely and isolated because he or she has become separated from nature and from other people. This condition of isolation is not found in any other species of animal; it is the distinctive human situation. The child, for example, gains freedom from the primary ties with its parents with the result that it feels isolated and helpless. The serf eventually secured his freedom only to find himself adrift in a predominantly alien world. As a serf, he belonged to someone and had a feeling of being related to the world and to other people, even though he was not free. In his book, *Escape from freedom* (1941), Fromm develops the thesis that as humans have gained more freedom throughout the ages they have also felt more alone. Freedom then becomes a negative condition from which they try to escape.

What is the answer to this dilemma? A person can either unite with other people in the spirit of love and shared work or can find security by submitting to authority and conforming to society. In the one case, humans use their freedom to develop a better society; in the other, they acquire a new bondage. *Escape from freedom* was written under the shadow of the Nazi dictatorship and shows that this form of totalitarianism appealed to people because it offered them a new security. But as Fromm points out in subsequent books (1947, 1955, 1964), any form of society that humans have fashioned, whether it be that of feudalism, capitalism, fascism, socialism, or communism, represents an attempt to resolve the basic contradiction of humans. This contradiction consists of a person being both a part of nature and separate from it, of being both an animal and a human being. As an animal one has certain physiological needs that must be satisfied. As a human being one possesses self-awareness, reason, and imagination. Experiences that are uniquely human are feelings of tenderness, love, and compassion; attitudes of interest, responsibility, identity, integrity, vulnerability, transcendence, and freedom; and values and norms

(1968). The two aspects of a person being both animal and human constitute the basic conditions of human existence. *"The understanding of man's psyche must be based on the analysis of man's needs stemming from the conditions of his existence"* (1955, p. 25).

What are the specific needs that rise from the conditions of human existence? There are five needs: the need for relatedness, the need for transcendence, the need for rootedness, the need for identity, and the need for a frame of orientation. The need for relatedness (also called the frame of devotion in *Revolution of hope,* 1968) stems from the stark fact that humans in becoming human have been torn from the animal's primary union with nature. "The animal is equipped by nature to cope with the very conditions it is to meet" (1955, p. 23) but humans with their power to reason and imagine has lost this intimate interdependence with nature. In place of those instinctive ties with nature that animals possess humans have to create their own relationships, the most satisfying being those that are based upon productive love. Productive love always implies mutual care, responsibility, respect, and understanding.

The urge for transcendence refers to a person's need to rise above his or her animal nature, to become a creative person instead of remaining a creature. If the creative urges are thwarted, a person becomes a destroyer. Fromm points out that love and hate are not antithetical drives; they are both answers to a person's need to transcend his or her animal nature. Animals can neither love nor hate, but humans can.

Humans desire natural roots; they want to be an integral part of the world, to feel that they belong. As children, they are rooted to their mothers but if this relationship persists past childhood it is considered to be an unwholesome fixation. A person finds the most satisfying and healthiest roots in a feeling of kinship with other men and women. But one wants also to have a sense of personal identity, to be a unique individual. If one cannot attain this goal through individual creative effort, he may obtain a certain mark of distinction by identifying with another person or group. The slave identifies with the master, the citizen with the country, the worker with the company. In this case, the sense of identity arises from belonging to someone and not from being someone.

Finally, humans need to have a frame of reference, a stable and consistent way of perceiving and comprehending the world. The frame of reference that they develop may be primarily rational, primarily irrational, or it may have elements of both.

For Fromm these needs are purely human and purely objective. They are not found in animals and they are not derived from observing what humans say they want. Nor are these strivings created by society; rather they have become embedded in human nature through evolution. What then is the relation of society to the existence of humans? Fromm believes that the specific manifestations of these needs, the actual ways in which a person realizes inner potentialities, are determined by "the social arrangements under which he lives" (1955, p. 14). One's personality develops in accordance with the opportunities that a particular society offers one. In a capitalistic society, for example, a person may gain a sense of personal identity by becoming rich or develop a feeling of rootedness by becoming a dependable and trusted employee in a large company. In other words, a person's adjustment to society usually represents a compromise between inner needs and outer demands. He or she develops a social character in keeping with the requirements of the society.

Fromm has identified and described five social character types that are found in today's society: receptive, exploitative, hoarding, marketing, and productive. These types represent the different ways in which individuals can relate to the world and to each other. Only the last of these is considered by him to be healthy and express what Marx called "free conscious activity." Any given individual is a blend of these five types or orientations toward the world, although one or two of the orientations may stand out more prominently than the others. Thus, it is possible for a person to be either a productive-hoarding type or a nonproductive-hoarding type. A productive-hoarding type might be a person who acquires land or money in order to be more productive; a nonproductive-hoarding type may be a person who hoards just for the sake of hoarding without any benefit to society.

More recently, Fromm (1964) has described a sixth pair of character types, the *necrophilous* who is attracted to death versus the *biophilous* who is in love with life. Fromm notes that what might be considered a parallel between this formulation and Freud's life and death instincts is actually not a parallel. For Freud, both life and death instincts are inherent in the biology of humans, whereas for Fromm, life is the only primary potentiality. Death is merely secondary and only enters the picture when the life forces are frustrated.

From the standpoint of the proper functioning of a particular society it is absolutely essential that the child's character be shaped to fit the needs of society. The task of the parents and of education is to make the child want to act as it has to act if a given economic, political, and social system is to be maintained. Thus, in a capitalistic system the desire to save must be implanted in people so that capital is available for an expanding economy. A society that has evolved a credit system must see to it that people will feel an inner compulsion to pay their bills promptly. Fromm gives numerous examples of the types of character that develop in a democratic, capitalistic society (1947).

By making demands upon humans that are contrary to their nature, society warps and frustrates humans. It alienates them from their "human situation" and denies them the fulfillment of the basic conditions of existence. Both capitalism and communism, for example, try to make an individual into a robot, a wage slave, a nonentity, and they often succeed in driving the person into insanity, antisocial conduct or self-destructive acts. Fromm does not hesitate to stigmatize a whole society as being sick when it fails to satisfy the basic needs of humans (1955).

Fromm also points out that when a society changes in any important respect, as occurred when feudalism changed into capitalism or when the factory system displaced the individual artisan, such a change is likely to produce dislocations in the social character of people. The old character structure does not fit the new society, which adds to a person's sense of alienation and despair. One is cut off from traditional ties and until one can develop new roots and relations one feels lost. During such transitional periods, a person becomes a prey to all sorts of panaceas that offer a refuge from loneliness.

The problem of a person's relations to society is one of great concern to Fromm, and he returns to it again and again. Fromm is utterly convinced of the validity of the following propositions: (1) humans have an essential, inborn nature, (2) society is created by humans in order to fulfill this essential nature, (3) no society that has yet been devised meets the basic needs of human existence, and (4) it is possible to create such a society.

What kind of a society does Fromm advocate? It is one

. . . in which man relates to man lovingly, in which he is rooted in bonds of brotherliness and solidarity . . . ; a society which gives him the possibility of transcending nature by creating rather than by destroying, in which everyone gains a sense of self by experiencing himself as the subject of his powers rather than by conformity, in which a system of orientation and devotion exists without man's needing to distort reality and to worship idols (1955, p. 362).

Fromm even suggests a name for this perfect society: Humanistic Communitarian Socialism. In such a society everyone would have equal opportunity to become fully human. There would be no loneliness, no feelings of isolation, no despair. People would find a new home, one suited to the "human situation." Such a society would realize Marx's goal of transforming a person's alienation under a system of private property into an opportunity for self-realization as a social, productively active human being under socialism. Fromm has extended the blueprint of the ideal society by spelling out how our present technological society can be humanized (1968). Fromm's views have been sharply criticized by Schaar (1961).

Although Fromm's views grew out of his observations of individuals in treatment and his wide reading in history, economics, sociology, philosophy, and literature, he has undertaken one large-scale empirical investigation. In 1957 Fromm initiated a social-psychological study of a Mexican village to test his theory of social character. He trained Mexican interviewers to administer an in-depth questionnaire that could be interpreted and scored for important motivational and characterological variables. This questionnaire was supplemented by the Rorschach Ink Blot Method, which reveals more deeply repressed attitudes, feelings, and motives. By 1963 data-collection had been completed, and in 1970 the findings were published (Fromm and Maccoby, 1970).

Three main social character types were identified: the productive-hoarding, the productive-exploitative, and the unproductive-receptive. The productive-hoarding type are the landowners, the productive-exploitative the business people, and the unproductive-receptive the poor workers. Since people with similar character structures tend to intermarry, the three types constitute a fairly rigid class structure in the village.

Before the influence of technology and industrialization reached the village, there were only two main classes: the landowners and the peasants. The productive-exploitative type existed only as a deviant type. It was this type, however, that took the initiative in making the fruits of technology available to the villagers, becoming thereby symbols of progress and leaders of the community. They provided cheap entertainment in the form of movies, radio, and television, and factory-made commodities. As a consequence, the poor peasants were weaned away from their traditional cultural values without gaining many of the material advantages of a technological society. What they did gain was shoddy in comparison with what they had formerly: movies replaced festivals, radio replaced local bands, ready-made clothes replaced handwoven garments, and mass-produced utensils and furniture replaced handmade ones. The main focus of the study, however, is to illustrate Fromm's thesis that character (personality) affects and is affected by social structure and social change.

KAREN HORNEY

Karen Horney was born in Hamburg, Germany, September 16, 1885, and died in New York City, December 4, 1952. She received her medical training at the University of Berlin and was associated with the Berlin Psychoanalytic Institute from 1918 to 1932. She was analyzed by Karl Abraham and Hans Sachs, two of the pre-eminent training analysts in Europe at that time. Upon the invitation of Franz Alexander, she came to the United States and was Associate Director of the

Karen Horney

Chicago Psychoanalytic Institute for two years. In 1934 she moved to New York where she practiced psychoanalysis and taught at the New York Psychoanalytic Institute. Becoming dissatisfied with orthodox psychoanalysis, she and others of similar convictions founded the Association for the Advancement of Psychoanalysis and the American Institute of Psychoanalysis. She was Dean of this institute until her death. For a recent appraisal of Horney's work see Martin (1975).

Horney conceives of her ideas as falling within the framework of Freudian psychology, not as constituting an entirely new approach to the understanding of personality. She aspires to eliminate the fallacies in Freud's thinking—fallacies that have their root, she believes, in his mechanistic, biological orientation—in order that psychoanalysis may realize its full potentialities as a science of humans. "My conviction, expressed in a nutshell, is that psychoanalysis should outgrow the limitations set by its being an instinctivistic and a genetic psychology" (1939, p. 8).

Horney objects strongly to Freud's concept of penis envy as the determining factor in the psychology of women. Freud, it will be recalled, observed that the distinctive attitudes and feelings of women and their most profound conflict grew out of their feeling of genital inferiority and their jealousy of the male. Horney believes that feminine psychology is based on lack of confidence and an overemphasis of the love relationship, and has very little to do with the anatomy of her sex organs. [Horney's views on feminine psychology have been brought together and published posthumously (1967).]

Regarding the Oedipus complex, Horney feels that it is not a sexual-aggressive conflict between the child and his parents but an anxiety growing out of basic disturbances, for example, rejection, overprotection, and punishment, in the child's relationships with his mother and father. Aggression is not inborn as Freud stated, but is a means by which humans try to protect their security. Narcissism is not really self-love but self-inflation and overevaluation owing to feelings of insecurity. Horney also takes issue with the following Freudian concepts: repetition compulsion, the id, ego, and superego, anxiety, and masochism (1939). On the positive side, Horney asserts that Freud's fundamental theoretical contributions are the doctrines of psychic determinism, unconscious motivation, and emotional, nonrational motives.

Horney's primary concept is that of basic anxiety, which is defined as

. . . the feeling a child has of being isolated and helpless in a potentially hostile world. A wide range of adverse factors in the environment can produce this insecurity in a child: direct or indirect domination, indifference, erratic behavior, lack of respect for the child's individual needs, lack of real guidance, disparaging attitudes, too much admiration or the absence of it, lack of reliable warmth, having to take sides in parental disagreements, too much or too little responsibility, overprotection, isolation from other children, injustice, discrimination, unkept promises, hostile atmosphere, and so on and so on (1945, p. 41).

In general, anything that disturbs the security of the child in relation to its parents produces basic anxiety.

The insecure, anxious child develops various strategies by which to cope with its feelings of isolation and helplessness (1937). It may become hostile and seek to avenge itself against those who have rejected or mistreated it. Or he may become overly submissive in order to win back the love that it feels it has lost. It may develop an unrealistic, idealized picture of itself in order to compensate for its feelings of inferiority (1950). The child may try to bribe others into loving it, or may use threats to force people to like it. It may wallow in self-pity to gain people's sympathy.

If the child cannot get love, it may seek to obtain power over others. In that way, it compensates for its sense of helplessness, finds an outlet for hostility, and is able to exploit people. Or the child becomes highly competitive, in which the winning is far more important than the achievement. It may turn its aggression inward and belittle itself.

Any one of these strategies may become a more or less permanent fixture in the personality; a particular strategy may, in other words, assume the character of a drive or need in the personality dynamics. Horney presents a list of ten needs that are acquired as a consequence of trying to find solutions for the problem of disturbed human relationships (1942). She calls these needs "neurotic" because they are irrational solutions to the problem.

1. *The neurotic need for affection and approval.* This need is characterized by an indiscriminate wish to please others and to live up to their expectations. The person lives for the good opinion of others and is extremely sensitive to any sign of rejection or unfriendliness.

2. *The neurotic need for a "partner" who will take over one's life.* The person with this need is a parasite. He or she overvalues love, and is extremely afraid of being deserted and left alone.

3. *The neurotic need to restrict one's life within narrow borders.* Such a person is undemanding, content with little, prefers to remain inconspicuous, and values modesty above all else.

4. *The neurotic need for power.* This need expresses itself in craving power for its own sake, in an essential disrespect for others, and in an

indiscriminate glorification of strength and a contempt for weakness. People who are afraid to exert power openly may try to control others through intellectual exploitation and superiority. Another variety of the power drive is the need to believe in the omnipotence of will. Such people feel they can accomplish anything simply by exerting will power.

5. The neurotic need to exploit others.

6. The neurotic need for prestige. One's self-evaluation is determined by the amount of public recognition received.

7. The neurotic need for personal admiration. People with this need have an inflated picture of themselves and wish to be admired on this basis, not for what they really are.

8. The neurotic ambition for personal achievement. Such persons want to be the very best and drive themselves to greater and greater achievements as a result of their basic insecurity.

9. The neurotic need for self-sufficiency and independence. Having been disappointed in their attempts to find warm, satisfying relationships with people, the person sets him or herself apart from others and refuses to be tied down to anyone or anything. They become "loners."

10. The neurotic need for perfection and unassailability. Fearful of making mistakes and of being criticized, people who have this need try to make themselves impregnable and infallible. They are constantly searching for flaws in themselves so that they may be covered up before they become obvious to others.

These ten needs are the sources from which inner conflicts develop. The neurotic's need for love, for example, is insatiable; the more the neurotic gets the more he or she wants. Consequently, they are never satisfied. Likewise, their need for independence can never be fully satisfied because another part of their personality wants to be loved and admired. The search for perfection is a lost cause from the beginning. All of the foregoing needs are unrealistic.

In a later publication (1945), Horney classifies these ten needs under three headings: (1) moving toward people, for example, need for love, (2) moving away from people, for instance, need for independence, and (3) moving against people, for example, need for power. Each of the rubrics represents a basic orientation toward others and oneself. Horney finds in these different orientations the basis for inner conflict. The essential difference between a normal and a neurotic conflict is one of degree. ". . . the disparity between the conflicting issues is much less great for the normal person than for the neurotic" (1945, p. 31). In other words, everyone has these conflicts but some people, primarily because of early experiences with rejection, neglect, overprotection, and other kinds of unfortunate parental treatment, possess them in an aggravated form.

While the normal person can resolve these conflicts by integrating the three orientations, since they are not mutually exclusive, the neurotic person, because of greater basic anxiety, must utilize irrational and artificial solutions. He or she consciously recognizes only one of the trends and denies or represses the other two. Or the person creates an idealized self image in which the contradictory trends presumably disappear, although actually they do not. In a later book (1950), Horney has a great deal more to say about the unfortunate consequences that flow from the development of an unrealistic conception of the self and from attempts to live up to this idealized picture. The search for glory, feelings of self-contempt, morbid dependency upon other people, and self-abasement are some of the unhealthy and destructive results that grow out of an idealized self. A third solution employed by the neurotic person for inner conflicts is to externalize them. The person says, in effect, "I don't want to exploit other people, they want to exploit me." This solution creates conflicts between the person and the outside world.

All of these conflicts are avoidable or resolvable if the child is raised in a home where there is security, trust, love, respect, tolerance, and warmth. That is, Horney, unlike Freud and Jung, does not feel that conflict is built into the nature of humans and is therefore inevitable. Conflict arises out of social conditions. "The person who is likely to become neurotic is one who has experienced the culturally determined difficulties in an accentuated form, mostly through the medium of childhood experience" (1937, p. 290).

HARRY STACK SULLIVAN

Harry Stack Sullivan was the creator of a new viewpoint that is known as the *interpersonal theory of psychiatry*. Its major tenet as it relates to a theory of personality is that personality is "the relatively enduring pattern of recurrent interpersonal situations which characterize a human life" (1953, p. 111). Personality is a hypothetical entity that cannot be isolated from interpersonal situations, and interpersonal behavior is all that can be observed as personality. Consequently, it is vacuous, Sullivan believes, to speak of the individual as the object of study because the individual does not and cannot exist apart from his or her relations with other people. From the first day of life, the baby is a part of an in-

Harry Stack Sullivan

terpersonal situation, and throughout the rest of its life it remains a member of a social field. Even a hermit who has resigned from society carries with him into the wilderness memories of former personal relationships that continue to influence his thinking and acting.

Although Sullivan does not deny the importance of heredity and maturation in forming and shaping the organism, he feels that that which is distinctly human is the product of social interactions. Moreover, the interpersonal experiences of a person may and do alter his or her purely physiological functioning, so that even the organism loses its status as a biological entity and becomes a social organism with its own socialized ways of breathing, digesting, eliminating, circulating, and so forth.

For Sullivan, the science of psychiatry is allied with social psychology, and his theory of personality bears the imprint of his strong preference for social psychological concepts and variables. He writes,

> The general science of psychiatry seems to me to cover much the same field as that which is studied by social psychology, because scientific psychiatry has to be defined as the study of interpersonal relations, and this in the end calls for the use of the kind of conceptual framework that we now call *field theory*. From such a standpoint, personality is taken to be hypothetical. That which can be studied is the pattern of processes which characterize the interaction of personalities in particular recurrent situations or fields which "include" the observer (1950, p. 92).

Harry Stack Sullivan was born on a farm near Norwich, New York, on February 21, 1892, and died on January 14, 1949, in Paris, France, on his way home from a meeting of the executive board of the World Federation for Mental Health in Amsterdam. He received his medical degree from the Chicago College of Medicine and Surgery in 1917, and served with the armed forces during World War I. Following the war he was a medical officer of the Federal Board for Vocational Education and then became an officer with the Public Health Service. In 1922 Sullivan went to Saint Elizabeth's Hospital in Washington, D.C., where he came under the influence of William Alanson White, a leader in American neuropsychiatry. From 1923 until the early thirties he was associated with the Medical School of the University of Maryland and with the Sheppard and Enoch Pratt Hospital in Towson, Maryland. It was during this period of his life that Sullivan conducted investigations of schizophrenia that established his reputation as a clinician. He left Maryland to open an office on Park Avenue in New York City for the express purpose of studying the obsessional process in office patients. At this time he began his formal analytic training with Clara Thompson, a student of Sandor Ferenczi. This was not Sullivan's first exposure to psychoanalysis. He had about 75 hours of analysis while he was still a medical student. In 1933 he became president of the William Alanson White Foundation, serving in that office until 1943. In 1936, he helped found and became director of the Washington School of Psychiatry, which is the training institution of the foundation. The journal *Psychiatry* began publication in 1938 to promote Sullivan's theory of interpersonal relations. He was its coeditor and then editor until his death. Sullivan served as consultant for the Selective Service System in 1940–1941; he was a participant during 1948 in the UNESCO Tensions Project established by the United Nations to study tensions affecting international understanding; and he was appointed a member of the international preparatory commission for the International Congress of Mental Health in the same year. Sullivan was a scientific statesman as well as a prominent spokesman for psychiatry, the leader of an important school for training psychiatrists, a remarkable therapist, an intrepid theorist, and a productive medical scientist. By his vivid personality and original thinking, he attracted a number of people who became his disciples, students, colleagues, and friends.

Aside from William Alanson White, the chief influences on Sullivan's intellectual development were Freud, Adolph Meyer, and the Chicago School of Sociology which consisted of George Herbert Mead, W. I. Thomas, Edward Sapir, Robert E. Park, E. W. Burgess, Charles E. Merriam, William Healy, and Harold Lasswell. Sullivan felt particularly close to Edward Sapir who was one of the pioneers in advocating a closer working relationship between anthropology, sociology, and psychoanalysis. Sullivan began to formulate his theory of interpersonal relations in 1929 and had consolidated his thinking by the mid-1930s.

During his lifetime Sullivan published only one book setting forth his theory (1947). However, he kept detailed notebooks and many of his lectures to the students of the Washington School of Psychiatry were recorded. These notebooks and recordings, as well as other unpublished material, have been turned over to the William Alanson White Psychiatric Foundation. Five books based upon the Sullivan material have been published, the first three with introductions and commentaries by Helen Swick Perry and Mary Gavell, the last two by Mrs. Perry alone. *The interpersonal theory of psychiatry* (1953) consists mainly of a series of lectures given by Sullivan in the winter of 1946–1947 and represents the most complete account of his theory of interpersonal relations. *The psychiatric interview* (1954) is based upon two lecture series that Sullivan gave in 1944 and 1945, and *Clinical studies in psychiatry* (1956) is drawn from lectures given in 1943. Sullivan's papers on schizophrenia, most of which date back to the time he was associated with the Sheppard and Enoch Pratt Hospital, have been brought together and published under the title *Schizophrenia as a human process* (1962). The last volume that has appeared is *The fusion of psychiatry and social science* (1964). The first and last volumes in this series of five are the most pertinent for gaining an understanding of Sullivan's social-psychological theory of personality.

Patrick Mullahy, a philosopher and disciple of Sullivan, has edited several books dealing with the theory of interpersonal relations. One of these, *A study of interpersonal relations* (1949), contains a group of papers by people associated with the Washington School and the William Alanson White Institute in New York City. All of the articles were originally printed in *Psychiatry,* including three by Sullivan. Another book entitled *The contributions of Harry Stack Sullivan* (1952) consists of a group of papers presented at a memorial symposium by representatives of various disciplines, including psychiatry, psychology, and sociology. This book contains a succinct account of interpersonal theory by Mullahy and a complete bibliography of Sullivan's writings through 1951. Digests of Sullivan's views also appear in three other books by Mullahy (1948, 1970, 1973). Sullivan's interpersonal theory has been treated at length by Dorothy Blitsten (1953) and his live and work by Chapman (1976).

THE STRUCTURE OF PERSONALITY

Sullivan insists repeatedly that personality is a purely hypothetical entity, "an illusion," which cannot be observed or studied apart from interpersonal situations. The unit of study is the interpersonal situation and not the person. The organization of personality consists of interpersonal events rather than intrapsychic ones. Personality only manifests itself when the person is behaving in relation to one or more other individuals. These people do not need to be present; in fact they can even be illusory or nonexistent figures. A person may have a relationship with a folk hero like Paul Bunyan or a fictional character like Anna Karenina or with ancestors or with as yet unborn descendants. "Psychiatry is the study of phenomena that occur in interpersonal situations, in configurations made up of two or more people all but one of whom may be more or less completely illusory" (1964, p. 33). Perceiving, remembering, thinking, imagining, and all of the other psychological processes are interpersonal in character. Even nocturnal dreams are interpersonal, since they usually reflect the dreamer's relationships with other people.

Although Sullivan grants personality only hypothetical status, nonetheless he asserts that it is a dynamic center of various processes that occur in a series of interpersonal fields. Moreover, he gives substantive status to some of these processes by identifying and naming them and by conceptualizing some of their properties. The principal ones are *dynamisms, personifications,* and *cognitive processes.*

Dynamisms   A dynamism is the smallest unit that can be employed in the study of the individual. It is defined as "the relatively enduring pattern of energy transformations, which recurrently characterize the organism in its duration as a living organism" (1953, p. 103). An energy transformation is any form of behavior. It may be overt and public like talking, or covert and private like thinking and fantasying. Because a dynamism is a pattern of behavior that endures and recurs, it is about the same thing as a habit. Sullivan's definition of pattern is quaintly phrased; he says it is "an envelope of insignificant particular differences" (1953, p. 104). This means that a new feature may be added to a pattern without changing the pattern just as long as it is not significantly different from the other contents of the envelope. If it is significantly different it changes the pattern into a new pattern. For example, two apples may be quite different in appearance and yet be identified as apples because their differences are not important. However, an apple and a banana are different in significant respects and consequently form two different patterns.

The dynamisms that are distinctively human in character are those that characterize one's interpersonal relations. For example, one may behave in a habitually hostile way toward a certain person or group of persons, which is an expression of a dynamism of malevolence. A man who tends to seek out lascivious relationships with women displays a dynamism of lust. A child who is afraid of strangers has a dynamism of fear. Any habitual reaction towards one or more persons, whether it be in the form of a feeling, an attitude, or an overt action, constitutes a dynamism. All people have the same basic dynamisms but the mode of expression of a dynamism varies in accordance with the situation and the life experience of the individual.

A dynamism usually employs a particular zone of the body such as the mouth, the hands, the anus, and the genitals by means of which it interacts with the environment. A zone consists of a receptor apparatus for receiving stimuli, an effector apparatus for performing action, and a connecting apparatus called *eductors* in the central nervous system that connects the receptor mechanism with the effector mechanism. Thus, when the nipple is brought to the baby's mouth it stimulates the sensitive membrane of the lips which discharges impulses along nerve pathways to the motor organs of the mouth which produced sucking movements.

Most dynamisms serve the purpose of satisfying the basic needs of the organism. However, there is an important dynamism that develops as a result of anxiety. This is called the dynamism of the self or the self-system.

THE SELF-SYSTEM. Anxiety is a product of interpersonal relations, being transmitted originally from the mother to the infant and later in life by threats to one's security. To avoid or minimize actual or potential anxiety, people adopt various types of protective measures and supervisory controls over their behavior. One learns, for example, that one can avoid punishment by conforming to parents' wishes. These security measures form the self-system that sanctions certain forms of behavior (the good-me self) and forbids other forms (the bad-me self).

The self-system as the guardian of one's security tends to become isolated from the rest of the personality; it excludes information that is incongruous with its present organization and fails thereby to profit from experience. Since the self guards the person from anxiety, it is held in high esteem and is protected from criticism. As the self-system grows in complexity and independence, it prevents the person from making objective judgments of his or her own behavior and it glosses over obvious contradictions between what the person really is and what the self-system says he or she is. In general, the more experiences people have with anxiety, the more inflated their self-system becomes and the more it becomes dissociated from the rest of the personality. Although the self-system serves the useful purpose of reducing anxiety, it interferes with one's ability to live constructively with others.

Sullivan believes that the self-system is a product of the irrational aspects of society. By this he means that the young child is made to feel anxious for reasons that would not exist in a more rational society; it is forced to adopt unnatural and unrealistic ways of dealing with its anxiety. Although Sullivan recognizes that the development of a self-system is absolutely necessary for avoiding anxiety in modern society, and perhaps in any kind of society that humans are capable of fashioning, he also acknowledges that the self-system as we know it today is "the principal stumbling block to favorable changes in personality" (1953, p. 169). Perhaps with tongue-in-cheek, he wrote, "The self is the content of consciousness at all times when one is thoroughly comfortable about one's self respect, the prestige that one enjoys among one's fellows, and the respect and deference which they pay one" (1964, p. 217).

A personification is an image that an individual has of him or herself or of another person. It is a complex of feelings, attitudes, and conceptions that grows out of experiences with need-satisfaction and anxiety.   *Personifications*

For example, the baby develops a personfication of a good mother by being nursed and cared for by her. Any interpersonal relationship that involves satisfaction tends to build up a favorable picture of the satisfying agent. On the other hand, the baby's personification of a bad mother results from experiences with her that evoke anxiety. The anxious mother becomes personified as the bad mother. Ultimately, these two personifications of the mother along with any others that may be formed, such as the seductive mother or the overprotective mother, fuse together to form a complex personification.

These pictures that we carry around in our heads are rarely accurate descriptions of the people to whom they refer. They are formed in the first place in order to cope with people in fairly isolated interpersonal situations, but once formed they usually persist and influence our attitudes toward other people. Thus, a person who personifies his or her father as a mean and dictatorial man may project this same personification onto other older men, for example, teachers, police officers, and employers. Consequently, something that serves an anxiety-reducing function in early life may interfere with one's interpersonal relations later in life. These anxiety-fraught pictures distort one's conceptions of currently significant people. Personifications of the self such as the good-me and the bad-me follow the same principles as personifications of others. The good-me personification results from interpersonal experiences that are rewarding in character, the bad-me personification from anxiety-arousing situations. And like personifications of other people, these self-personifications tend to stand in the way of objective self-evaluation.

Personifications that are shared by a number of people are called *stereotypes*. These are consensually validated conceptions, that is, ideas that have wide acceptance among the members of a society and are handed down from generation to generation. Examples of common stereotypes in our culture are the absent-minded professor, the unconventional artist, and the hard-headed business executive.

Cognitive Processes   Sullivan's unique contribution regarding the place of cognition in the affairs of personality is his threefold classification of experience. Experience, he says, occurs in three modes; these are *prototaxic, parataxic,* and *syntaxic*. Prototaxic experience "may be regarded as the discrete series of momentary states of the sensitive organism" (1953, p. 29). This type of experience is similar to what James called the "stream of consciousness," the raw sensations, images, and feelings that flow through the mind of a sensate being. They have no necessary connections among themselves and possess no meaning for the experiencing person. The prototaxic mode of experience is found in its purest form during the early months of life and is the necessary precondition for the appearance of the other two modes.

The parataxic mode of thinking consists of seeing causal relationship between events that occur at about the same time but which are not logically related. The eminent Czech writer, Franz Kafka, portrays an interesting case of parataxic thinking in one of his short stories. A dog who lived in a kennel surrounded by a high fence was urinating one day when a bone was thrown over the fence. The dog thought, "My urinating made that bone appear." Thereafter whenever he wanted something to eat he lifted his leg. Sullivan believes that much of our thinking does not advance beyond the level of parataxis; that we see causal connections between experiences that have nothing to do with one another. All superstitions, for instance, are examples of parataxic thinking.

The third and highest mode of thinking is the syntaxic, which consists of consensually validated symbol activity, especially of a verbal nature. A consensually validated symbol is one which has been agreed upon by a group of people as having a standard meaning. Words and numbers are the best examples of such symbols. The syntaxic mode produces logical order among experiences and enables people to communicate with one another.

In addition to this formulation of the modes of experience, Sullivan emphasizes the importance of foresight in cognitive functioning. "Man, the person, lives with his past, the present and the neighboring future all clearly relevant in explaining his thought and action" (1950, p. 84). Foresight depends upon one's memory of the past and interpretation of the present.

Although dynamisms, personifications, and cognitive processes do not complete the list of the constituents of personality, they are the chief distinguishing structural features of Sullivan's system.

THE DYNAMICS OF PERSONALITY

Sullivan, in common with many other personality theorists, conceives of personality as an energy system whose chief work consists of activities that will reduce tension. Sullivan says there is no need to add the term "mental" to either energy or tension since he uses them in exactly the same sense as they are used in physics.

Tension

Sullivan begins with the familiar conception of the organism as a tension system that theoretically can vary between the limits of absolute relaxation, or euphoria as Sullivan prefers to call it, and absolute tension as exemplified by extreme terror. There are two main sources of tension: (1) tensions that arise from the needs of the organism, and (2) tensions that result from an anxiety. Needs are connected with the physiochemical requirements of life; they are such conditions as lack of food or water or oxygen that produce a disequilibrium in the economy of the organism. Needs may be general in character, such as hunger, or they may be more specifically related to a zone of the body, such as the infant's need to suck. Needs arrange themselves in a hierarchical order; those lower down on the ladder must be satisfied before those higher on the ladder can be accommodated. One result of need reduction is an experience of satisfaction. "Tensions can be regarded as needs for particular energy transformations that will dissipate the tension, often with an accompanying change of 'mental' state, a change of awareness, to which we can apply the general term, *satisfaction*" (1950, p. 85). The typical consequence of prolonged failure to satisfy the needs is a feeling of apathy that produces a general lowering of the tensions.

Anxiety is the experience of tension that results from real or imaginary threats to one's security. In large amounts, it reduces the efficiency of the individuals in satisfying their needs, disturbs interpersonal relations, and produces confusion in thinking. Anxiety varies in intensity depending upon the seriousness of the threat and the effectiveness of the security operations that the persons have at their command. Severe anxiety is like a blow on the head; it conveys no information to the person but instead produces utter confusion and even amnesia. Less severe forms of anxiety can be informative. In fact, Sullivan believes that anxiety is the first great educative influence in living. Anxiety is transmitted to the infant by the "mothering one" who is herself expressing anxiety in her looks, tone of voice, and general demeanor. Sullivan admits that he does not know how this transmission takes place, although it is probably accomplished by some kind of empathic process whose nature is obscure. As a consequence of this mother-transmitted anxiety, other objects in the near surroundings become freighted with anxiety by the operation of the parataxic mode of associating contiguous experiences. The mother's nipple, for example, is changed into a bad nipple that produces avoidance reactions in the baby. The infant learns to veer away from activities and objects that increase anxiety. When the baby cannot escape anxiety, it tends to fall asleep. This dynamism of somnolent detachment, as Sullivan calls it, is the counterpart of apathy, which is the dynamism aroused by unsatisfied needs. In fact, these two dynamisms cannot be objectively differentiated. Sullivan says that one of the great tasks of psychology is to discover the basic vulnerabilities to anxiety in interpersonal relations rather than to try to deal with the symptoms resulting from anxiety.

Energy is transformed by performing work. Work may be overt actions involving the striped muscles of the body or it may be mental such as perceiving, remembering, and thinking. These overt or covert activities have as their goal the relief of tension. They are to a great extent conditioned by the society in which the person is raised. "What anyone can discover by investigating his past is that patterns of tensions and energy transformations which make up his living are to a truly astonishing extent matters of his education for living in a particular society" (1950, p. 83).

Sullivan does not believe that instincts are important sources of human motivation nor does he accept the libido theory of Freud. An individual learns to behave in a particular way as a result of interactions with people, and not because he or she possesses innate imperatives for certain kinds of action.

Sullivan was very assiduous in spelling out the sequence of interpersonal situations to which the person is exposed in passing from infancy to adulthood, and the ways in which these situations contribute to the formation of personality. More than any other personality theorist, with the possible exceptions of Freud and Erikson, Sullivan viewed personality from the perspective of definite stages of development. Whereas Freud held the position that development is largely an unfolding of the sex instinct, Sullivan argued persuasively for a more social-psychological view of personality growth, one in which the unique contributions of human relationships would be accorded their proper due. Although Sullivan did not reject biological factors as conditioners of the growth of personality, he did subordinate them to the social determiners of psychological development. Moreover, he was of the opinion that sometimes these social influences run counter to the biological needs of the person and have detrimental effects upon his personality. Sullivan was not one to shy away from recognizing the deleterious influences of society. In fact, Sullivan, like other social-psychological theorists, was a sharp, incisive critic of contemporary society.

Sullivan delineates six stages in the development of personality prior to the final stage of maturity. These six stages are typical for Western European cultures and may be different in other societies. They are (1) infancy, (2) childhood, (3) the juvenile era, (4) preadolescence, (5) early adolescence, and (6) late adolescence.

The period of infancy extends from birth to the appearance of articulate speech. It is the period in which the oral zone is the primary zone of interaction between the baby and its environment. Nursing provides the baby with its first interpersonal experience. The feature of the environment that stands out during infancy is the object that supplies food to the hungry baby, either the nipple of the mother's breast or the nipple of the bottle. The baby develops various conceptions of the nipple depending upon the kinds of experiences it has with it. These are: (1) the good nipple that is the signal for nursing and a sign that satisfaction is forthcoming, (2) the good but unsatisfactory nipple because the baby is not hungry, (3) the wrong nipple because it does not give milk and is a signal for rejection and subsequent search for another nipple, and (4) the bad nipple of the anxious mother, which is a signal for avoidance.

Other characteristic features of the infantile stage are (1) the appearance of the dynamisms of apathy and somnolent detachment, (2) the transition from a prototaxic to a parataxic mode of cognition, (3) the organization of personifications such as the bad, anxious, rejecting, frustrating mother and the good, relaxed, accepting, satisfying mother, (4) the organization of experience through learning and the emergence of the rudiments of the self-system, (5) the differentiation of the baby's own body so that the baby learns to satisfy its tensions independently of the mothering one, for example, by thumbsucking, and (6) the learning of coordinated movements involving hand and eye, hand and mouth, and ear and voice.

The transition from infancy to childhood is made possible by the learning of language and the organization of experience in the syntaxic mode. Childhood extends from the emergence of articulate speech to the appearance of the need for playmates. The development of language permits, among other things, the fusion of different personifications, for instance, the good and bad mother, and the integration of the self-system into a more coherent structure. The self-system begins to develop the conception of gender: the little boy identifies with the masculine role as prescribed by society, the little girl with the feminine role. The growth of symbolic ability enables the child to play at being a grownup—Sullivan calls these as-if performances *dramatizations*—and to become concerned with various activities both overt and covert that serve the purpose of warding off punishment and anxiety—Sullivan calls these *preoccupations*.

One dramatic event of childhood is the *malevolent transformation*, the feeling that one lives among enemies. This feeling, if it becomes strong enough, makes it impossible for the child to respond positively to the affectionate advances of other people. The malevolent transformation distorts the child's interpersonal relations and causes the child to isolate itself. It says, in effect, "Once upon a time everything was lovely, but that was before I had to deal with people." The malevolent transformation is caused by painful and anxious experiences with people, and may lead to a regression to the less threatening stage of infancy.

Sublimation, which Sullivan defines as "the unwitting substitution for a behavior pattern which encounters anxiety or collides with the self-system, of a socially more acceptable activity pattern which satisfies parts of the motivational system that caused trouble" (1953, p. 193), appears during childhood. The excess of tension that is not discharged by sublimation is expended in symbolic performances, for instance, in nocturnal dreams.

The juvenile stage extends throughout most of the grammar-school years. It is the period for becoming social, for acquiring experiences of social subordination to authority figures outside of the family, for becoming competitive and cooperative, for learning the meaning of ostracism, disparagement, and group feeling. The juvenile learns to be inattentive to external circumstances that do not interest him or her, to supervise behavior by internal controls, to form stereotypes in attitudes, to develop new and more effective modes of sublimation, and to distinguish more clearly between fantasy and reality.

One great event of this period is the emergence of a conception of orientation in living.

One is oriented in living to the extent to which one has formulated, or can easily be led to formulate (or has insight into), data of the following types: the integrating tendencies (needs) which customarily characterize one's interpersonal relations; the circumstances appropriate to their satisfaction and relatively anxiety-free discharge; and the more or less remote goals for the approximation of which one will forego intercurrent opportunities for satisfaction or the enhancement of one's prestige (1953, p. 243).

The relatively brief period of preadolescence is marked by the need for an intimate relationship with a peer of the same sex, a chum in whom one can confide and with whom one can collaborate in meeting the tasks and solving the problems of life. This is an extremely important period because it marks the beginning of genuine human relationships with other people. In earlier periods, the interpersonal situation is characterized by the dependence of the child upon an older person. During preadolescence, the child begins to form peer relationships in which there are equality, mutuality, and reciprocity between the members. Without an intimate companion, the preadolescent becomes the victim of a desperate loneliness.

The main problem of the period of early adolescence is the development of a pattern of heterosexual activity. The physiological changes of puberty are experienced by the youth as feelings of lust; out of these feelings the lust dynamism emerges and begins to assert itself in the personality. The lust dynamism involves primarily the genital zone, but other zones of interaction such as the mouth and the hands also participate in sexual behavior. There is a separation of erotic need from the need for intimacy; the erotic need takes as its object a member of the opposite sex while the need for intimacy remains fixated upon a member of the same sex. If these two needs do not become divorced, the young person displays a homosexual rather than a heterosexual orientation. Sullivan points out that many of the conflicts of adolescence arise out of the opposing needs for sexual gratification, security, and intimacy. Early adolescence persists until the person has found some stable pattern of performances that satisfies the person's genital drives.

"Late adolescence extends from the patterning of preferred genital activity through unnumbered educative and eductive steps to the establishment of a fully human or mature repertory of interpersonal relations as permitted by available opportunity, personal and cultural" (1953, p. 297). In other words, the period of late adolescence constitutes a rather prolonged initiation into the privileges, duties, satisfactions, and responsibilities of social living and citizenship. The full complement of interpersonal relations gradually takes form and there is a growth of experience in the syntaxic mode that permits a widening of the symbolic horizons. The self-system becomes stabilized, more effective sublimations of tensions are learned, and stronger security measures against anxiety are instituted.

When the individual has ascended all of these steps and reached the final stage of adulthood, he or she has been transformed largely by means of their interpersonal relations from an animal organism into a human person. One is not an animal, coated by civilization and humanity, but an animal that has been so drastically altered that one is no longer an animal but a human being—or, if one prefers, a human animal.

Determiners of Development   Although Sullivan firmly rejects any hard and fast instinct doctrine, he does acknowledge the importance of heredity in providing certain capacities, chief among which are the capacities for receiving and elaborating experiences. He also accepts the principle that training cannot be effective before maturation has laid the structural groundwork. Thus, the child cannot learn to walk until the muscles and bony structure have reached a level of growth that will support it in an upright position. Heredity and maturation provide the biological substratum for the development of personality, that is, the capacities and predispositions and inclinations, but the culture operating through a system of interpersonal relations makes manifest the abilities and the actual performances (energy transformations) by which the person reaches the goal of tension reduction and need–satisfaction.

The first educative influence is that of anxiety that forces the young organism to discriminate between increasing and decreasing tension and to guide its activity in the direction of the latter. The second great educational force is that of trial and success. Success, as many psychologists have pointed out, tends to stamp in the activity that has led to gratification. Success may be equated with the earning of rewards—a mother's smile or a father's praise; failure with punishments—a mother's forbidding look or a father's words of disapproval. One may also learn by imitation and by inference; for the latter type of learning Sullivan adopts the name proposed by Charles Spearman: eduction of relations.

Sullivan does not believe that personality is set at an early age. It may change at any time as new interpersonal situations arise because the human organism is extremely plastic and malleable. Although the forward thrust of learning and development predominates, regressions can and do occur when pain, anxiety, and failure become intolerable.

Harry Stack Sullivan, in common with other psychiatrists, acquired his empirical knowledge of personality by working with patients suffering from various types of personality disorders but chiefly with schizophrenics and obsessional cases. (A good short account of Sullivan's use of case material for formulating ideas about personality may be found in his article *The data of psychiatry,* 1964, pp. 32–55.) As a young psychiatrist, Sullivan discovered that the method of free association did not work satisfactorily with schizophrenics because it aroused too much anxiety. Other methods were tried but these also proved to provoke anxiety that interfered with the communication process between patient and therapist. Consequently, Sullivan became interested in studying the forces that impede and facilitate communication between two people. In so doing, he found that the psychiatrist was much more than an observer; he or she was also a vital participant in an interpersonal situation. The psychiatrist had his or her own apprehensions, such a professional competence and personal problems, to deal with. As a result of this discovery Sullivan developed his conception of the therapist as a *participant observer*.

CHARACTERISTIC RESEARCH AND RESEARCH METHODS

The theory of interpersonal relations lays great stress on the method of participant observation, and relegates data obtained by other methods to at most a secondary importance. This in turn implies that skill in the face to face, or person to person *psychiatric interview* is of fundamental importance (1950, p. 122).

In another place, he wrote, "The crying need is for observers who are growing observant of their observing" (1964, p. 27).

The Interview   The psychiatric interview is Sullivan's term for the type of interpersonal, face to face situation that takes place between the patient and the therapist. There may be only one interview or there may be a sequence of interviews with a patient extending over a long period of time. Sullivan defines the interview as "a system, or series of systems, of *interpersonal processes,* arising from participant observation in which the interviewer derives certain conclusions about the interviewee" (1954, p. 128). How the interview is conducted and the ways in which the interviewer reaches conclusions regarding the patient form the subject matter of Sullivan's book, *The psychiatric interview* (1954).

Sullivan divides the interview into four stages: (1) the formal inception, (2) reconnaissance, (3) detailed inquiry, and (4) the termination.

The interview is primarily a vocal communication between two people. Not only what the person says but how he or she says it—intonations, rate of speech, and other expressive behavior—are the chief sources of information for the interviewer. The interviewer should be alert to subtle changes in the patient's vocalizations (e.g., changes in volume) because these clues often reveal vital evidence regarding the patient's focal problems and attitudinal changes towards the therapist. In the inception, the interviewer should avoid asking too many questions but should maintain an attitude of quiet observation. The interviewer should try to determine the reasons for the patient's coming and something about the nature of the patient's problems.

Sullivan is very explicit about the role of the therapist in the interview situation. Therapists should never forget that they are earning their living as experts in the area of interpersonal relations, and that the patient has a right to expect to learn something that will benefit him or her. The patient should feel this from the very first interview, and it should be continually reinforced throughout the course of treatment. Only by having such an attitude will the patient divulge information from which the interviewer can reach the proper conclusions regarding the patterns of living that are causing trouble for the patient. Obviously, psychiatrists should not use their expert knowledge to obtain personal satisfaction or to enhance their prestige at the expense of the patient. The interviewer is not a friend or enemy, a parent or lover, a boss or employee, although the patient may cast the person in one or more of these roles as a result of distorted parataxic thinking; the interviewer is an expert in interpersonal relations.

The period of reconnaissance centers about finding out who the patient is. The interviewer does this by means of an intensive interrogatory into the past, present, and future of the patient. These facts about the patient's life fall under the heading of personal data or biographical information. Sullivan does not advocate a hard-and-fast, structured type of questioning that adheres to a standard list of questions. On the other hand, Sullivan insists that the interviewer should not let the patient talk about irrelevant and trivial matters. The patient should learn that the interview is serious business and that there should be no fooling around. Nor should the interviewer ordinarily make notes of what the patient says at any time during the course of treatment because note-taking is too distracting and tends to inhibit the communication process.

Sullivan does not believe that one should start with any formal prescription to the effect "say everything that comes into your mind." Instead, the therapist should take advantage of the patient's memory lapses during the interrogatory to teach him or her how to free-associate. In this way, the patient not only learns how to free-associate without becoming alarmed by this unfamiliar mode of discourse but also experiences the usefulness of the free-association technique before being given any formal explanation of its purpose.

By the end of the first two stages of the interview process the psychiatrist should have formed a number of tentative hypotheses regarding the patient's problems and their origins. During the period of detailed inquiry, the psychiatrist attempts to ascertain which of several hypotheses is the correct one. He or she does this by listening and by asking questions. Sullivan suggests a number of areas that should be inquired into—such matters as toilet training, attitude toward the body, eating habits, ambition, and sexual activities—but here again he does not insist upon any formal prospectus that should be rigidly followed.

As long as everything runs smoothly the interviewer is not likely to learn anything about the vicissitudes of interviewing, chief of which is the impact of the interviewer's attitudes upon the patient's capacity for communication. But when the communication process deteriorates, the interviewer is forced to ask him or her self, "What did I say or do which caused the patient to become anxious?" There is always a good deal of reciprocity between the two parties—Sullivan's term for it is *reciprocal emotion*—and each is continually reflecting the feelings of the other. It is incumbent upon therapists to recognize and to control their own attitudes in the interest of maximum communication. In other words, they should never forget their role as an expert participant observer. A series of interviews is brought to termination by the interviewer making a final statement of what he or she has learned, by prescribing a course for the patient to follow, and by assessing for the patient the probable effects of the prescription upon his or her life.

It is quite apparent from reading Sullivan's sage remarks on interviewing that he considers it to be an immense challenge to the accuracy of observation of the participant observer. The reader may be interested in contrasting the type of interviewing advocated by Sullivan with the wide variety of interviewing procedures discussed by the Maccobys (1954) and by Cannell and Kahn (1968), and with the techniques of clinical interviewing set forth in the book, *The clinical interview* (1955), edited by Felix Deutsch and William Murphy.

Research on Schizophrenia   Sullivan's principal research contribution in psychopathology consists of a series of articles on the etiology, dynamics, and treatment of schizophrenia. These studies were conducted for the most part during his period of association with the Sheppard and Enoch Pratt Hospital in Maryland and were published in psychiatric journals during the years 1924 to 1931. They reveal Sullivan's great talents for making contact with and understanding the mind of the psychotic. Empathy was a highly developed trait in Sullivan's personality, and he used it to excellent advantage in studying and treating the victims of schizophrenia. For Sullivan, these victims are not hopeless cases to be shut away in the back wards of mental institutions; they can be treated successfully if the psychiatrist is willing to be patient, understanding, and observant.

While Sullivan was at Sheppard and Enoch Pratt Hospital he established a special ward for patients. It consisted of a suite of two bedrooms and a sitting room for six male schizophrenics. This ward was isolated from the rest of the hospital and was staffed by six male attendants who were handpicked and trained by Sullivan. He made it a practice of having an attendant in the room with him while he was interviewing a patient, because he found it was reassuring to the patient. No female nurses—in fact, no women—were allowed in the ward. Sullivan believed in the effectiveness of the homogeneous ward consisting of patients of the same sex, the same age group, and the same psychiatric problem.

Sullivan was also instrumental in stimulating other psychiatrists and social scientists to carry on research related to interpersonal theory. Many of these studies are reported in the journal *Psychiatry,* which was founded largely to promote and advance Sullivan's ideas. Three books that owe a great deal to Sullivan may be mentioned here. In *Communication, the social matrix of psychiatry* (1951), Ruesch and Bateson apply Sullivan's concepts to problems of human relations and to the interrelations between culture and personality. Frieda Fromm-Reichmann in her influential book, *Principles of intensive psychotherapy* (1950), has elaborated many of Sullivan's ideas regarding the therapeutic process. The study of a mental hospital by Stanton and Schwartz (1954) depicts very clearly the kinds of interpersonal situations that exist in an institution and the effect of these situations upon the patients and personnel alike.

Sullivan's role as a political psychiatrist was also evident in some of his research activities. He believed that one had "to serve in order to study." He did research on southern blacks with Charles S. Johnson and on Washington blacks with E. Franklin Frazier (Sullivan, 1964). His work during the war consisted of setting up procedures for screening draftees, of building morale and of developing effective leadership. And we have already noted his intense concern with working for a world free of tensions and conflicts.

Of the four theorists presented in this chapter, Sullivan's interpersonal theory has probably been the greatest stimulus to research. One reason for this is that Sullivan employed a more objective language in describing his theory, a language that helped to span the gap between theory and observation. Sullivan kept his conceptual constructions quite closely tied to empirical observation, with the result that he seemed to be describing at close quarters the behavior of real people. In spite of the abstractness of his thought, he did not become so abstruse as to lose touch with concrete—one might almost say everyday—conduct of individuals. Interpersonal theory is a down-to-earth proposition mill that invites and encourages empirical testing.

CURRENT STATUS AND EVALUATION

The four theories presented in this chapter belong together because they all emphasize the influence of social variables in shaping personality. All of them, in one way or another, constitute a reaction against the instinctivist position of Freudian psychoanalysis, yet each of the theorists acknowledges their indebtedness to the seminal thinking of Freud. They have all stood on Freud's shoulders, and have added their own cubits to his towering height. They have invested personality with social dimensions equal if not superior in importance to the biological dimensions provided by Freud and Jung. Moreover, these theories have helped to place psychology in the sphere of the social sciences.

In spite of the common ground that they occupy, each theory stresses somewhat different clusters of social variables. Erich Fromm devotes most of his attention to describing the ways in which the structure and dynamics of a particular society mold its members so that their social character fits the common values and needs of that society. Karen Horney, although she recognizes the influence of the social context in which a person lives, dwells more upon the intimate factors within the family setting that shape personality. In this respect, Sullivan's interpersonal theory resembles Horney's views more than it does Fromm's. For Sullivan the human relationships of infancy, childhood, and adolescence are of paramount concern, and he is most eloquent and persuasive when he is describing the nexus between the "mothering one" and the baby. Adler, on the other hand, roams widely throughout society looking for factors that are relevant to personality and finds them everywhere.

Although all four theories strenuously oppose Freud's instinct doctrine and the fixity of human nature, none of the four adopts the radical environmentalist position that an individual's personality is created solely by the conditions of the society into which he or she is born. Each theory, in its own way, agrees that there is such a thing as human nature that the baby brings with it, largely in the form of fairly general predispositions or potentialities rather than as specific needs and traits. These generalized potentialities as exemplified by Adler's social interest and Fromm's need for transcendence are actualized in concrete ways by means of the formal and informal educative agencies of the society. Under ideal conditions, these theories agree, the individual and society are interdependent; the person serves to further the aims of the society and society in turn helps the person to attain his or her goals. In short, the stand adopted by these four theorists is neither exclusively social or sociocentric nor exclusively psychological or psychocentric; it is truly social-psychological in character.

Furthermore, each theory not only asserts that human nature is plastic and malleable but also that society is equally plastic and malleable. If a particular society does not fulfill the demands of human nature it can be changed by humans. In other words, humans create the kind of society they think will benefit them the most. Obviously, mistakes are made in developing a society and once these errors have become crystallized in the form of social institutions and customs it may be difficult to change them. Yet each theorist was optimistic regarding the possibility of change, and each in his or her own way tried to bring about fundamental changes in the structure of society. Adler supported social democracy, pressed for better schools, started child guidance centers, urged reforms in the treatment of criminals, and lectured widely on social problems and their cures. Fromm and Horney through their writings and talks have pointed the way to a better society. Fromm, in particular, has spelled out some of the basic reforms that need to be made to achieve a sane society. Sullivan was actively engaged in trying to bring about social amelioration through the medium of international cooperation at the time of his death. All four of them in their professional capacities as psychotherapists had extensive experiences with the casualties of an imperfect social order; consequently, they spoke from personal knowledge and practical experience in their roles as critics and reformers.

Another assumption each theory makes is that anxiety is socially produced. Humans are not by nature "the anxious animal." They are made anxious by the conditions under which they live—by the specter of unemployment, by intolerance and injustice, by threat of war, by hostile parents. Remove these conditions, say our theorists, and the wellsprings from which anxiety gushes forth will dry up. Nor are humans by nature destructive as Freud believed. They may become destructive when their basic needs are frustrated, but even under conditions of frustration other avenues such as submission or withdrawal may be taken.

All of the theories with the exception of Sullivan's also underscore the concepts of the unique individual and the creative self. In spite of attempts by society to regiment people, each person manages to retain some degree of creative individuality. Indeed, it is by virtue of a person's inherent creative powers that he or she is able to effect changes in society. People create different kinds of societies on different parts of the globe, and at different times in history, in part, because people are different. Humans are not only creative; they are also self-conscious. They know what they want and strive consciously to reach their goals. The idea of unconscious motivation is not accorded much weight by these social-psychological theorists.

In general, the theories developed by Adler, Fromm, Horney, and Sullivan enlarged the scope of Freudian psychology by providing room for the social determinants of personality. A number of critics, however, have disparaged the originality of these social-psychological theories. They say that such theories merely elaborate upon one aspect of classical psychoanalysis, namely, the ego and its defenses. Freud saw clearly that personality traits often represented the person's habitual defenses or strategies against inner and outer threats to the ego. The needs, trends, styles, orientations, personifications, dynamisms, and so forth, in the theories treated in this chapter are accommodated in Freudian theory under the heading of ego-defenses. Therefore, these critics conclude, nothing new has been added to Freud, and a great deal has been subtracted. By reducing personality to the single system of the ego, the social-psychological theorist has cut the personality off from the vital springs of human behavior, springs that have their ultimate sources in the evolution of humans as a species. By enlarging upon the social character of human personality, they have alienated humans from their great biological heritage.

A criticism sometimes voiced against the conception of humans evolved by Adler, Fromm, and Karen Horney (it does not apply to Sullivan) is that it is too sugar-coated and idealistic. In a world that has been torn apart by two great wars and the threat of a third one, not to mention the many other forms of violence and irrationality that people display, the picture of a rational, self-conscious, socialized individual strikes one as being singularly inappropriate and invalid. One can, of course, blame society and not humans for this deplorable state of affairs, and this is what these theorists do. But then they say, or at least imply, that rational humans created the kind of social arrangements that are responsible for human irrationality and unhappiness. This is the great paradox of these theories. If people are so self-conscious, so rational, and so social, why have they evolved so many imperfect social systems?

It has been pointed out by a philosopher, Isaac Franck (1966), that the conception of the person presented by Fromm and other social and humanistic psychologists is less a product of research and more a result of their normative preconceptions. They are moralists and not scientists. Franck insists that human propensities and traits are ethically neutral and therefore ethical prescriptions cannot be deduced from factual statements about humans. It would be difficult, however, to find any personality theorist from Freud to Fromm who does not openly or covertly make moralistic and ethical judgments about the harmful effects of the social environment upon humans. And many of them do prescribe remedies. Participant–observers are not likely to remain neutral, however scientific they may be.

Another less devastating criticism, but one that carries more weight with psychologists as distinguished from psychoanalysts, is the failure of these social-psychological theories to specify the precise means by which a society molds its members. How does a person acquire social character? How does one learn to be a member of society? This evident neglect of the learning process in theories that depend so heavily upon the concept of learning to account for the ways in which personality is formed is considered to be a major omission. Is it enough just to be exposed to a condition of society in order for that condition to affect the personality? Is there a mechanical stamping in of socially approved behavior and an equally mechanical stamping out of socially disapproved behavior? Or does the person react with insight and foresight to the social milieu, selecting those features that he or she thinks will produce a better organization of personality and rejecting other features that he or she feels are inconsistent with their self-organization? For the most part these theories stand silent on the nature of the learning process, in spite of the fact that learning has been a central topic in American psychology for a good many years.

Although these social-psychological theories have not stimulated a great deal of research in comparison with some other theories, they have served to foster an intellectual climate in which social-psychological research could flourish and has done so. Social psychology is no longer the stepchild of psychology. It is a large and exceedingly active component part in the science of psychology. Adler, Fromm, Karen Horney, and Sullivan are not solely responsible for the rise of social psychology, but their influence has been considerable. Each of them has contributed in no small measure to the picture of humans as social beings. This is their great value in the contemporary scene.

BIBLIOGRAPHY
PRIMARY SOURCES

Adler, A. *The practice and theory of individual psychology*. New York: Harcourt, Brace & World, 1927.

Ansbacher, H. L., and R. R. (Eds.). *The Individual-Psychology of Alfred Adler*. New York: Basic Books, 1956.

Ansbacher, H. L., and R. R. (Eds.) *Superiority and social interest by Alfred Adler*. Evanston, Ill.: Northwestern Univ. Press, 1964.

Fromm, E. *Escape from freedom*. New York: Rinehart, 1941.

Fromm, E. *Man for himself*. New York: Rinehart, 1947.

Fromm, E. *The heart of man*. New York: Harper and Row, 1964.

Fromm, E. *The revolution of hope*. New York: Harper and Row, 1968.

Fromm, E. *The sane society*. New York: Rinehart, 1955.

Horney, K. *Neurotic personality of our times*. New York: Norton, 1937.

Horney, K. *New ways in psychoanalysis*. New York: Norton, 1939.

Horney, K. *Self-analysis*. New York: Norton, 1942.

Horney, K. *Our inner conflicts*. New York: Norton, 1945.

Horney, K. *Neurosis and human growth*. New York: Norton, 1950.

Sullivan, H. S. *The interpersonal theory of psychiatry*. New York: Norton, 1953.

Sullivan, H. S. *The fusion of psychiatry and social science*. New York: Norton, 1964.

REFERENCES

Adler, A. *Study of organ inferiority and its psychical compensation*. New York: Nervous and Mental Diseases Publishing Co., 1917.

Adler, A. *Practice and theory of individual psychology*. New York: Harcourt, Brace & World, 1927.

Adler, A. *The science of living*. New York: Greenberg, 1929a.

Adler, A. *Problems of neurosis*. London: Kegan Paul, 1929b.

Adler, A. Individual Psychology. In C. Murchison (Ed.). *Psychologies of 1930.* Worcester, Mass.: Clark Univ. Press, 1930, pp. 395–405.

Adler, A. *What life should mean to you.* Boston: Little, Brown, 1931.

Adler, A. The fundamental views of Individual Psychology. *Int. J. Indiv. Psychol.,* 1935, **1,** 5–8.

Adler, A. *Social interest.* New York: Putnam, 1939.

Ansbacher, H. L., and R. R. (Eds.). *The Individual-Psychology of Alfred Adler.* New York: Basic Books, 1956.

Ansbacher, H. L., and R. R. (Eds.). *Superiority and social interest by Alfred Adler.* Evanston, Ill.: Northwestern Univ. Press, 1964.

Blitsten, D. R. *The social theories of Harry Stack Sullivan.* New York: The William-Frederick Press, 1953.

Bottome, P. *Alfred Adler; a biography.* New York: Putnam, 1939.

Cannell, C. F., and Kahn, R. L. Interviewing. In G. Lindzey and E. Aronson (Eds.). *Handbook of social psychology.* Vol. 2. Reading, Mass.: Addison-Wesley, 1968, pp. 526–595.

Chapman, A. H. *Harry Stack Sullivan: his life and his work.* New York: Putnam, 1976.

Colby, K. M. On the disagreement between Freud and Adler. *Amer. Imago,* 1951, **8,** 229–238.

Deutsch, F., and Murphy, W. F. *The clinical interview.* New York: International Universities Press, 1955.

Franck, I. The concept of human nature: a philosophical analysis of the concept of human nature in the writings of G. W. Allport, S. E. Asch, Erich Fromm, A. H. Maslow, and C. R. Rogers. Unpublished doctoral dissertation, Univ. of Maryland, 1966.

Fromm, E. *Escape from freedom.* New York: Rinehart, 1941.

Fromm, E. *Man for himself.* New York: Rinehart, 1947.

Fromm, E. *The sane society.* New York: Rinehart, 1955.

Fromm, E. *Sigmund Freud's mission.* New York: Harper, 1959.

Fromm, E. *Marx's concept of man.* New York: Ungar, 1961.

Fromm, E. *Beyond the chains of illusion.* New York: Simon and Schuster, 1962.

Fromm, E. *The heart of man.* New York: Harper and Row, 1964.

Fromm, E. *The revolution of hope.* New York: Harper and Row, 1968.

Fromm, E., and Maccoby, M. *Social character in a Mexican village.* Englewood Cliffs, N.J.: Prentice-Hall, 1970.

Fromm-Reichmann, F. *Principles of intensive psychotherapy.* Chicago: Univ. of Chicago Press, 1950.

Furtmüller, C. Alfred Adler: a biographical essay. In H. L. and R. R. Ansbacher (Eds.). *Superiority and social interest by Alfred Adler.* Evanston, Ill.: Northwestern Univ. Press, 1964, pp. 311–393.

Horney, K. *Neurotic personality of our times*. New York: Norton, 1937.

Horney, K. *New ways in psychoanalysis*. New York: Norton, 1939.

Horney, K. *Self-analysis*. New York: Norton, 1942.

Horney, K. *Our inner conflicts*. New York: Norton, 1945.

Horney, K. *Neurosis and human growth*. New York: Norton, 1950.

Horney, K. *Feminine psychology*. New York: Norton, 1967.

James, W. T. Karen Horney and Erich Fromm in relation to Alfred Adler. *Indiv. Psychol. Bull.,* 1947, **6,** 105–116.

Jones, E. *The life and work of Sigmund Freud*. Vol. 2. New York: Basic Books, 1955.

Jones, H. E. Order of birth in relation to the development of the child. In C. Murchison (Ed.). *Handbook of child psychology*. Worcester, Mass.: Clark Univ. Press, 1931, 204–241.

Maccoby, E. E., and Maccoby, N. The interview: a tool of social science. In G. Lindzey (Ed.). *Handbook of social psychology*. Vol. 1. Cambridge: Addison-Wesley, 1954, 449–487.

Martin, A. R. Karen Horney's theory in today's world. *Amer. J. Psychoanal.,* 1975, **35,** 297–302.

Mosak, H. H. Early recollections as a projective technique. *J. Projective Techniques,* 1958, **22,** 302–311.

Mullahy, P. *Oedipus—myth and complex*. New York: Hermitage House, 1948.

Mullahy, P. (Ed.). *A study of interpersonal relations*. New York: Hermitage House, 1949.

Mullahy, P. (Ed.). *The contributions of Harry Stack Sullivan*. New York: Hermitage House, 1952.

Mullahy, P. *Psychoanalysis and interpersonal psychiatry: the contributions of Harry Stack Sullivan*. New York: Science House, 1970.

Mullahy, P. *The beginnings of modern American psychiatry: the ideas of Harry Stack Sullivan*. Boston: Houghton Mifflin, 1973.

Munroe, R. *Schools of psychoanalytic thought*. New York: Dryden Press, 1955.

Orgler, H. *Alfred Adler: the man and his work*. New York: Liveright, 1963.

Ruesch, J., and Bateson, G. *Communication, the social matrix of psychiatry*. New York: Norton, 1951.

Schaar, J. H. *Escape from authority: the perspectives of Erich Fromm*. New York: Basic Books, 1961.

Schachter, S. *The psychology of affiliation*. Stanford, Calif.: Stanford Univ. Press, 1959.

Sperber, M. *Masks of loneliness: Alfred Adler in perspective*. New York: Macmillan, 1974.

Stanton, A. H., and Schwartz, M. S. *The mental hospital*. New York: Basic Books, 1954.

Sullivan, H. S. *Conceptions of modern psychiatry*. Washington, D.C.: William Alanson White Psychiatric Foundation, 1947.

Sullivan, H. S. Tensions interpersonal and international: a psychiatrist's view. In H. Cantril (Ed.). *Tensions that cause war*. Urbana, Ill.: Univ. of Illinois Press, 1950, 79–138.

Sullivan, H. S. *The interpersonal theory of psychiatry*. New York: Norton, 1953.

Sullivan, H. S. *The psychiatric interview*. New York: Norton, 1954.

Sullivan, H. S. *Clinical studies in psychiatry*. New York: Norton, 1956.

Sullivan, H. S. *Schizophrenia as a human process*. New York: Norton, 1962.

Sullivan, H. S. *The fusion of psychiatry and social science*. New York: Norton, 1964.

Vaihinger, H. *The philosophy of "as if."* New York: Harcourt, Brace, & World, 1925.

Vockell, E. L., Felker, D. W., and Miley, C. H. Birth order literature 1967–1972. *J. ind. Psychol.*, 1973, **29,** 39–53.

MURRAY'S PERSONOLOGY 6

Unique among personality theorists is the sophistication in biological science, clinical practice, and academic psychology that Henry A. Murray brings to his theoretical efforts. As a rich integrative force for these diverse talents Murray possesses a brilliant writing style nurtured by a deep and enduring interest in literature and the humanities. The theory that has evolved from these sources shows a considerable respect for the determinant importance of biological factors, a full appreciation for the individual complexity of the human organism, and an interest in representing behavior in such a manner that controlled investigation is a natural outcome of these formulations.

The focus of this theory is upon individuals in all their complexity and this point of view is highlighted by the term "personology," which was introduced by Murray (1938) as a label for his own efforts and those of others who were primarily concerned with a full understanding of the individual case. He has emphasized consistently the organic quality of behavior, indicating that a single segment of behavior is not to be understood in isolation from the rest of the functioning person. In contrast to many other theorists who share this belief, Murray is perfectly willing to engage in the abstraction necessary to permit various kinds of specialized study—always insisting that the task of reconstruction must be engaged in after analysis is completed. A further contrast to some holistic theorists is his "field" orientation: his insistence that the environmental context of behavior must be thoroughly understood and analyzed before an adequate account of individual behavior is possible. Not only has Murray placed general emphasis upon the importance of environmental determinants but, more distinctively, he has developed an elaborate set of concepts designed to represent these environmental forces.

The past or history of the individual is fully as important in Murray's view as the present individual and his or her environment. His theory shares with psychoanalysis the assumption that events taking place in infancy and childhood are crucial determinants of adult behavior. A further similarity between this position and psychoanalysis lies in the considerable importance attributed to unconscious motivation and the deep interest displayed in the subjective or free, verbal report of the individual, including imaginative productions.

In many ways the most distinctive feature of this theory is its highly differentiated and carefully specified treatment of motivation. Murray's scheme of motivational concepts has seen wide usage and has been of great influence. A further unusual feature of the theory is the consistent emphasis upon the coexisting and functionally linked physiological processes that accompany all psychological processes. His concept of "regnancy," which we shall discuss later, serves to keep the theorist continuously oriented toward the brain as the locus of personality and all its component parts. Murray has often emphasized the importance of detailed description as a necessary prelude to complicated theoretical formulation and investigation. Consistent with this point of view is his deep interest in taxonomy and the exhaustive classifications that he has established for many aspects of behavior.

Murray has made serious efforts to effect a compromise between the often conflicting demands of clinical complexity and investigative economy. He has devised means of representing, at least in part, the tremendous diversity of human behavior; and at the same time he has focused upon the task of constructing operations for assessing variables that occupy a central role in this theoretical scheme. This twofold emphasis has led naturally to narrowing the gap between clinical practice and the psychological laboratory.

We have now seen the broad outlines of Murray's personology, but what of the man who constructed this theory? Henry Murray was born in New York City on May 13, 1893, and received his education at Groton School and Harvard College, securing his A.B. in 1915 with a major in history. Following graduation from Harvard he enrolled in the Columbia College of Physicians and Surgeons where he graduated at the head of his class in 1919. In 1920 he received an M.A. in biology from Columbia and served briefly as an instructor in physiology at Harvard University following which he served a two-

Henry Murray

year surgical interneship at Presbyterian Hospital in New York. He then joined the staff of the Rockefeller Institute for Medical Research in New York City where as an assistant he carried on embryological research for two years. Following this came a period of study at Cambridge University where he conducted biochemical research that led to his securing a Ph.D. in biochemistry from Cambridge in 1927. It was during this interval of European study that he became interested in psychology, an interest that was confirmed by a visit to Carl Jung in Zurich, "the first full-blooded, spherical . . . intelligence I had ever met."

We talked for hours, sailing down the lake and smoking before the hearth of his Faustian retreat. 'The great floodgates of the wonder-world swung open,' and I saw things that my philosophy had never dreamt of. Within a month a score of bi-horned problems were resolved, and I went off decided on depth psychology. I had *experienced* the unconscious, something not to be drawn out of books (Murray, 1940, p. 153).

Thus, deeply interested in psychology Murray returned to this country and the Rockefeller Institute where he remained for one year as an associate before accepting in 1927 an invitation to come to Harvard University as an instructor in psychology. This unconventional choice of an unusual man, untrained in academic psychology, by a distinguished, academic department was arranged by Morton Prince who had just founded the Harvard Psychological Clinic. The clinic was endowed with the explicit provision that it be devoted to the study and teaching of abnormal and dynamic psychology and Prince, searching for a young and promising scholar to guide the future of the clinic, selected Murray. In 1928 Murray was made an assistant professor and director of the Psychological Clinic, and in 1937 he was made an associate professor. He was one of the founding members of the Boston Psychoanalytic Society and by 1935 had completed his training in psychoanalysis under Franz Alexander and Hans Sachs. A fascinating account of his training analysis and his attitudes toward psychoanalysis is contained in a symposium concerning psychologists and psychoanalysis (Murray, 1940).

During the roughly fifteen years that transpired before war interrupted, the Harvard Psychological Clinic, under the intellectual and spiritual leadership of Henry Murray, was the scene of an intensely creative theoretical and empirical enterprise. Murray gathered about him a group of able young students whose joint efforts to formulate and investigate the human personality were exceedingly fruitful. The *Explorations in personality* volume (1938) contains a partial record of the generativeness of this era but the most important outcomes were carried away in the form of values, conceptions, and intentions by individuals such as Donald W. MacKinnon, Saul Rosenzweig, R. Nevitt Sanford, Silvan S. Tomkins, and Robert W. White. Here at the Clinic for the first time psychoanalytic theory was given a serious academic audience and earnest efforts were made to devise means of translating the brilliant clinical insights of Freud into experimental operations that would permit some degree of empirical confirmation or rejection. Not only did Murray create a sense of excitement and imminent discovery among his own students but the Clinic also opened its doors to mature scholars from a variety of fields (Erik Homburger Erikson, Cora DuBois, Walter Dyk, H. Scudder McKeel) so that there was a marked interdisciplinary aura to the enterprise.

In 1943 this era came to a close as Murray left Harvard to join the Army Medical Corps where as a major, and subsequently lieutenant colonel, he established and directed an assessment service for the Office of Strategic Services. His organization was given the difficult task of screening candidates for complex, secret, and dangerous missions. The activities of this group have been summarized in *Assessment of men* (1948). His work with the Army led to his being awarded the Legion of Merit in 1946. In 1947 he returned to Harvard on a part-time basis as a lecturer on clinical psychology in the newly formed Department of Social Relations and in 1950 he was appointed professor of clinical psychology. He established the Psychological Clinic Annex at Harvard University in 1949 where he and a few colleagues and graduate students conducted studies of personality including the collection of 88 copious case histories. Murray became emeritus professor in 1962. He has been awarded the Distinguished Scientific Contribution Award of the American Psychological Association as well as the Gold Medal Award of the American Psychological Foundation for a lifetime of contribution to the field.

In addition to revising and expanding his theoretical views, Murray turned his attention to some of the broader problems of contemporary life, including abolition of war and the creation of a world state (Murray, 1960a, 1961, 1962b). Murray is an ardent champion of the power of creative imagination tempered by reason for solving any problem besetting humans. He has been sharply critical of psychology for projecting a negative image of humans and for its "malignant narcissism." Murray stands firmly for a humanistic, optimistic psychology.

Murray's medical and biological research and training have contributed to the deep respect he has consistently shown for the importance of physical and biological factors in behavior. His experience in medical diagnosis has had an obvious outcome in his belief that personality should ideally be assessed by a team of specialists and that in this assessment the subject's statement about him or her self should be given serious audience. His interest in the taxonomy or classification of behavior, as well as his conviction that the careful study of individual cases is an essential to future psychological progress, are also highly congruent with his medical background. His detailed awareness of mythology (1960b) and of the great literary creations of our own and past eras, and particularly his expert knowledge of Melville and his works, have provided him with an inexhaustible source of ideas concerning humans and their potentialities for good and evil. The exquisite mind of Alfred North Whitehead provided a model of logical and synthetic thought, while the truculent but brilliant Lawrence J. Henderson served as a model of rigor and critical orientation. His debt to these men and to numerous others, including several generations of students, is amply acknowledged in four very personal documents (1940, 1959, 1967, 1968a) and in a volume of essays written in honor of Murray (White, 1963). From such a complex lineage it is no wonder that the evolved product is an elaborate and many-sided structure.

It is clear to all who have known him that Henry Murray's talent and devotion to the study of the human personality are only partially revealed in his published works. His casual remarks and free-ranging speculations concerning an endless variety of topics, which were so integral a part of lunches at the Psychological Clinic, have provided fruitful research ideas for dozens of his students and colleagues. Unfortunately, not all of these messages fell on fertile ground and one can only regret that the spoken word has not been preserved to enrich the written record. Murray's tendency to reveal only occasional fruits of his intellect is clearly demonstrated in the publications that have stemmed from his twenty-five years of intensive study of Herman Melville. These years of dedicated scholarship have earned him a reputation among students of Melville without parallel and yet he has thus far published only two papers dealing with this engrossing writer. One is a brilliant analysis of the psychological meaning of *Moby Dick* (Murray, 1951c), and the other an introduction to and penetrating analysis of *Pierre* (Murray, 1949a), one of Melville's most intriguing and baffling novels.

Granted the inadequacy of the written record, we find that Murray's psychological theorizing and research are best represented in *Explorations in personality* (1938), which summarizes the thought and research of the Psychological Clinic staff at the end of its first decade of existence. A partial record of some of the subsequent research is contained in *A clinical study of sentiments* (1945), which was written with his long-time collaborator Christiana Morgan, and in *Studies of stressful interpersonal disputations* (1963). The major changes that his theoretical convictions have undergone during the subsequent years are best represented in a chapter written jointly with Clyde Kluckhohn (1953), a chapter published in *Toward a general theory of action* (1951a), an article published in *Dialectica* (1951b), a talk he gave at Syracuse University (1958), a chapter written for *Psychology: a study of a science* (1959), and an article written for the *International encyclopedia of the social sciences* (1968b). The *Manual of Thematic Apperception Test* (1943) serves as the best introduction to this personality instrument, devised jointly with Christiana Morgan (Morgan and Murray, 1935), which has become one of the most important and widely used empirical tools of the clinician and personality investigator. The great sensitivity and ingenuity that Murray has shown in developing means of appraising and analyzing human capacities and directional tendencies are vividly revealed in *Assessment of men* (1948).

THE STRUCTURE OF PERSONALITY

The nature of personality and its acquisitions and attainments have occupied a considerable portion of Murray's theoretical attention. His views on the structure of personality have been heavily influenced by psychoanalytic theory and yet in many respects thay are strikingly differentiated from an orthodox Freudian view. Murray is somewhat wary of the word "structure" because of its connotations of permanence, regularity, and lawfulness. He recognizes that personality is usually in a state of flux. Here we shall consider Murray's definition of personality and the concepts he has elaborated in the attempt to represent the nature of personality.

Definition of Personality

Although Murray has proposed many definitions of personality at different times, the main components of these definitions may be summarized as follows.

1. An individual's personality is an abstraction formulated by the theorist and not merely a description of the individual's behavior.

2. An individual's personality refers to a series of events that ideally span the person's lifetime. "The history of the personality *is* the personality."

3. A definition of personality should reflect the enduring and recurring elements of behavior as well as the novel and unique.

4. Personality is the organizing or governing agent of the individual. Its functions are to integrate the conflicts and constraints to which the individual is exposed, to satisfy the individual's needs, and to make plans for the attainment of future goals.

5. Personality is located in the brain. "No brain, no personality."

Thus, Murray's attempts at a definition of personality make clear that he is strongly oriented toward a view that gives adequate weight to the history of the organism, to the organizing function of personality, to the recurrent and novel features of the individual's behavior, to the abstract or conceptual nature of personality, and to the physiological processes underlying the psychological.

Proceedings and   The basic data of the psychologist are proceedings, which are subject-
Serials   object interactions, or subject–subject interactions, of sufficient duration to include the significant elements of any given behavioral sequence. In Murray's words:

> . . . proceedings are the things which we observe, and try to represent with models, and to explain, the things which we attempt to predict, the facts against which we test the adequacy of our formulations (Murray, 1951b, pp. 269–270).

Although in certain settings it is possible to define a proceeding exactly, for example, a verbal response and its reply, it is usually possible to provide only a very general definition. In this spirit Murray suggests that, "Ideally, the duration of a proceeding is determined by (1) the initiation, and by (2) the completion, of a dynamically significant pattern of behavior . . ." (Murray, 1951b, p. 269).

This conception of the basic unit of the psychologist as consisting of proceedings reflects Murray's conviction that behavior is inextricably caught in a time dimension. Thus, the proceeding is a compromise between the practical limitations imposed by the intellect and techniques of the investigator and the empirical given that behavior exists in a time dimension. Murray suggests that proceedings can be classified in terms of whether they are *internal* (daydreaming, problem-solving, planning in solitude) or *external* (interacting with persons or objects in the environment). External proceedings have two aspects: a subjective *experiential* aspect and an objective *behavioral* aspect.

For many purposes the representation of behavior in terms of proceedings is perfectly adequate. However, under some circumstances it is necessary to include in a single unit or formulation behavior taking place over a longer period of time. This longer functional unit of behavior is referred to as a *serial*.

. . . a directionally organized intermittent succession of proceedings may be called a *serial*. Thus, a serial (such as friendship, a marriage, a career in business) is a relatively long functional unit which can be formulated only roughly. One must obtain records of critical proceedings along its course and note such indices of development as changes of disposition, increase of knowledge, increase of ability, improvement in the quality of the work accomplished, and so forth. No one proceeding in the serial can be understood without reference to those which have led up to it and without reference to the actor's aims and expectations, his design for the future (Murray, 1951b, p. 272).

Thus, representation of behavior in terms of serials is made necessary because certain proceedings are so intimately related to one another that it is impossible to study them separately without destroying their full meaning.

A very important function for the individual is served by *serial programs,* which are orderly arrangements of subgoals that stretch into the future perhaps for months or years and which, if all goes well, will lead eventually to some desired end state. Thus, the individual aspires to the goal of becoming a medical doctor but intervening between the present situation and this goal are years of study and special training. If he or she develops a set of subgoals, each of which plays a part in bringing the person closer to their medical degree, this would be referred to as a serial program.

Serial Programs and Schedules

Likewise of importance are *schedules* that represent devices for reducing conflict among competing needs and goal objects by arranging for expression of these tendencies at different times. By means of a schedule the individual may give a maximum of expression to his or her various aims. If one is efficient at constructing schedules one can greatly diminish the quantity and intensity of one's conflicts.

Murray has recently subsumed serial programs and schedules under the term *ordination,* which includes the process of plan-making as well as the outcome of the process—an established program or schedule. According to Murray's present views, ordination is a higher mental process on the same level as cognition. The aim of cognition is a complete conceptual understanding of the environment, but once the external situation has been sufficiently understood, the process of ordination asserts itself in order to arrange policymaking and planning of strategy and tactics.

In contrast to many personality psychologists, Murray has shown a consistent interest in ability and achievement and considers these qualities an important part of the personality. These components of the individual serve a central function in mediating between dispositions to

Abilities and Achievements

action and the end results toward which these dispositions are oriented. In virtually all of his personality research subjects have been appraised in terms of a variety of different areas of ability and achievement: physical, mechanical, leadership, social, economic, erotic, and intellectual.

Even if we accept personality as an everchanging phenomenon, there are still certain stabilities or structures that appear over time and are crucial to understanding behavior. In representing these mental structures, Murray borrows the terms ego, id, and superego from psychoanalysis but introduces certain distinctive elements in his development of these concepts.

Murray agrees with Freud in conceiving of the *id* as the repository of primitive and unacceptable impulses. Here is the origin of energy, the source of all innate motives, the unseeing and unsocialized self. More than this, insists Murray, the id includes impulses that are acceptable to the self and society. Not only does the id contain impulses toward both good and evil but the strength of these tendencies varies between individuals. Thus, the task facing different individuals in controlling or directing their id tendencies is by no means of equal difficulty.

Further, the *ego* is not solely an inhibitor and repressor. Not only must the ego hold back or repress certain impulses or motives but more importantly it must arrange, schedule, and control the manner in which other motives are to appear. The ego, consistent with psychoanalytic theory, is viewed as the central organizer or integrator of behavior. Part of this organization, however, is intended to facilitate or promote the expression of certain id impulses. The strength and effectiveness of the ego is an important determinant of the individual's adjustment.

The *superego* in Murray's theory, as in Freud's, is considered to be a cultural implant. It is an internalized subsystem that acts within the individual to regulate behavior in much the same manner that agents outside the individual once acted. These agents, typically the parents but also one's peers, teachers, public personalities, and fictional characters, act as representatives of the culture so that internalizing their prescriptions represents a move in the direction of internalizing cultural prescriptions.

Intimately related to the superego is the *ego-ideal,* which consists of an idealized picture of the self—an aspired self, or a set of personal ambitions toward which the individual strives. The ego-ideal may be entirely divorced from the superego, as in the case of the individual who aspires to be a master criminal, or it may be closely related, so that the individual moves toward personal ambitions in a manner conforming exactly with the sanctions of society. If the superego is dominant and the ego-ideal is suppressed, the person may attempt to serve "God's will" or the "welfare of the society" at the expense of giving up all personal ambition.

It is important to note that Murray's conception of the superego and ego-ideal provides more latitude for alteration and development in the years subsequent to childhood than does the orthodox psychoanalytic view. In normal development the relation between these three institutions changes so that where once the id ruled supreme, the superego and eventually the ego come to have determinant roles. In the happiest of instances a benign superego and a strong and ingenious ego combine to permit adequate expression of id impulses under circumstances that are culturally approved.

In a later revision of his theory, Murray (1959) has stressed the more positive establishments of the personality. There are, he believes, formative and constructive processes that are not just useful for survival or as defenses against anxiety but that have their own energies, goals, and fulfillments. A person *needs* to be creative and imaginative, to compose and construct if he or she is to remain psychologically healthy. Creative imagination may, in fact, be the strongest feature of a personality, and the one that is often given the least opportunity to express itself.

THE DYNAMICS OF PERSONALITY

It is in the representation of human striving, seeking, desiring, wishing, and willing that Murray's contributions to psychological theory have been most distinctive. One might fairly say that his position is primarily a motivational psychology. This focusing upon the motivational process is perfectly congruent with Murray's conviction that the study of a person's directional tendencies holds the key to understanding human behavior. ". . . the most important thing to discover about an individual . . . is the superordinate *directionality* (or directionalities) of his activities, whether mental, verbal, or physical" (Murray, 1951b, p. 276). Murray's interest in directionality has led to the most complex and carefully delineated system of motivational constructs that can be found on the contemporary psychological scene. His taxonomic interests are clearly revealed here in the patient and absorbed classifying of the elements of human behavior in terms of their underlying determinants or motives.

Murray is certainly not the first person to place heavy emphasis upon the importance of motivational analysis. However, his formulations possess several distinctive elements. While the prevailing tides in psychology have flowed in the direction of simplicity and a small number of concepts, Murray has insisted that an adequate understanding of human motivation must rest upon a system that employs a sufficiently large number of variables to reflect, at least partially, the tremendous complexity of human motives in the raw. He also has made serious efforts to provide empirical definitions for his variables that, if imperfect, at least far exceed the operational effectiveness of most of the preceding schemes in the field of human motivation. The result of these efforts is a set of concepts that makes a bold attempt to bridge the gap between clinical description and the demands of empirical research.

In considering Murray's theory of motivation we shall start with a discussion of the *need* concept, which from the beginning has been the focus of his conceptual efforts, and follow this with a discussion of such related concepts as *press, tension reduction, thema, need integrate, unity-thema,* and *regnancy.* Finally we shall turn to his related *value* and *vector* concepts that represent a more recent turn in his theorizing.

Need   Although the concept of need has been widely used in psychology, no other theorist has subjected the concept to so careful an analysis nor provided such a complete taxonomy of needs as has Murray. The detail of Murray's analysis of this concept is suggested by his definition:

> A need is a construct (a convenient fiction or hypothetical concept) which stands for a force . . . in the brain region, a force which organizes perception, apperception, intellection, conation and action in such a way as to transform in a certain direction an existing, unsatisfying situation. A need is sometimes provoked directly by internal processes of a certain kind . . . but, more frequently (when in a state of readiness) by the occurrence of one of a few commonly effective press [environmental forces]. . . . Thus, it manifests itself by leading the organism to search for or to avoid encountering or, when encountered, to attend and respond to certain kinds of press. . . . Each need is characteristically accompanied by a particular feeling or emotion and tends to use certain modes . . . to further its trend. It may be weak or intense, momentary or enduring. But usually it persists and gives rise to a certain course of overt behavior (or fantasy), which . . . changes the initiating circumstance in such a way as to bring about an end situation which stills (appeases or satisfies) the organism (Murray, 1938, pp. 123–124).

We find from this definition that the concept of need, as was true for the concept of personality, is granted an abstract or hypothetical status but is nevertheless linked to underlying physiological processes in the brain. It is also conceived that needs may be either internally aroused or set into action as a result of external stimulation. In either case the need produces activity on the part of the organism and maintains this activity until the organism-environment situation has been altered so as to reduce the need. Some needs are accompanied by particular emotions or feelings, and they are frequently associated with particular instrumental acts that are effective in producing the desired end state.

Murray states that the existence of a need can be inferred on the basis of: (1) the effect or end result of the behavior, (2) the particular pattern or mode of behavior involved, (3) the selective attention and response to a particular class of stimulus objects, (4) the expression of a particular emotion or affect, and (5) the expression of satisfaction when a particular effect is achieved or disappointment when the effect is not achieved (1938, p. 124). Subjective reports regarding feelings, intentions, and goals provide additional criteria. Given the general definition and the above criteria for inferring or classifying needs, Murray, following the intensive study of a small number of subjects, arrived at a tentative list of twenty needs. Although this list has been subjected to considerable modification and elaboration the original twenty needs remain highly representative. These variables were presented in *Explorations in personality* (1938) with an outline of pertinent facts concerning each need, including questionnaire items for measuring the need, accompanying emotions, and illustrations of the need. The twenty needs are briefly listed and defined in Table 6-1.

TYPES OF NEEDS. Thus far, we have seen how Murray defines need, we have examined the criteria he provides for their identification, and we have seen a typical list of needs. In addition to this it is important to consider the basis for distinguishing between different types of needs. First of all, there is the distinction between primary and secondary needs. The primary or *viscerogenic needs* are linked to characteristic organic events and typically refer to physical satisfactions. Illustrative of these are the needs for air, water, food, sex, lactation, urination, and defecation. The secondary or *psychogenic needs* are presumably derived from the primary needs and are characterized by a lack of focal connection with any specific organic processes or physical satisfactions. Illustrative of these are the needs for acquisition, construction, achievement, recognition, exhibition, dominance, autonomy, and deference.

Second, we have the distinction between *overt needs* and *covert needs,* that is, manifest needs and latent needs. Here we are differentiating between those needs that are permitted more or less direct and immediate expression and those that are generally restrained, inhibited, or repressed. One might say that overt needs typically express themselves in motor behavior while covert needs usually belong to the world of fantasy or dreams. The existence of covert needs is in large part the outcome of the development of internalized structures (superego) that

TABLE 6-1	Need	Brief definition
Illustrative list of Murray's needs [a]	Abasement	To submit passively to external force. To accept injury, blame, criticism, punishment. To surrender. To become resigned to fate. To admit inferiority, error, wrongdoing, or defeat. To confess and atone. To blame, belittle, or mutilate the self. To seek and enjoy pain, punishment, illness, and misfortune.
	Achievement	To accomplish something difficult. To master, manipulate, or organize physical objects, human beings, or ideas. To do this as rapidly and as independently as possible. To overcome obstacles and attain a high standard. To excel oneself. To rival and surpass others. To increase self-regard by the successful exercise of talent.
	Affiliation	To draw near and enjoyably cooperate or reciprocate with an allied other (an other who resembles the subject or who likes the subject). To please and win affection of a cathected object. To adhere and remain loyal to a friend.
	Aggression	To overcome opposition forcefully. To fight. To revenge an injury. To attack, injure, or kill another. To oppose forcefully or punish another.
	Autonomy	To get free, shake off restraint, break out of confinement. To resist coercion and restriction. To avoid or quit activities prescribed by domineering authorities. To be independent and free to act according to impulse. To be unattached, irresponsible. To defy convention.
	Counteraction	To master or make up for a failure by restriving. To obliterate a humiliation by resumed action. To overcome weaknesses, to repress fear. To efface a dishonor by action. To search for obstacles and difficulties to overcome. To maintain self-respect and pride on a high level.
	Defendance	To defend the self against assault, criticism, and blame. To conceal or justify a misdeed, failure, or humiliation. To vindicate the ego.
	Deference	To admire and support a superior. To praise, honor, or eulogize. To yield eagerly to the influence of an allied other. To emulate an exemplar. To conform to custom.
	Dominance	To control one's human environment. To influence or direct the behavior of others by suggestion, seduction, persuasion, or command. To dissuade, restrain, or prohibit.
	Exhibition	To make an impression. To be seen and heard. To excite, amaze, fascinate, entertain, shock, intrigue, amuse, or entice others.
	Harmavoidance	To avoid pain, physical injury, illness, and death. To escape from a dangerous situation. To take precautionary measures.
	Infavoidance	To avoid humiliation. To quit embarrassing situations or to avoid conditions that may lead to belittlement: the scorn, derision, or indifference of others. To refrain from action because of the fear of failure.
	Nurturance	To give sympathy and gratify the needs of a helpless object: an infant or any object that is weak, disabled, tired, inexpe-

Need	Brief definition
	rienced, infirm, defeated, humiliated, lonely, dejected, sick, mentally confused. To assist an object in danger. To feed, help, support, console, protect, comfort, nurse, heal.
Order	To put things in order. To achieve cleanliness, arrangement, organization, balance, neatness, tidiness, and precision.
Play	To act for "fun" without further purpose. To like to laugh and make jokes. To seek enjoyable relaxation of stress. To participate in games, sports, dancing, drinking parties, cards.
Rejection	To separate oneself from a negatively cathected object. To exclude, abandon, expel, or remain indifferent to an inferior object. To snub or jilt an object.
Sentience	To seek and enjoy sensuous impressions.
Sex	To form and further an erotic relationship. To have sexual intercourse.
Succorance	To have one's needs gratified by the sympathetic aid of an allied object. To be nursed, supported, sustained, surrounded, protected, loved, advised, guided, indulged, forgiven, consoled. To remain close to a devoted protector. To always have a supporter.
Understanding	To ask or answer general questions. To be interested in theory. To speculate, formulate, analyze, and generalize.

[a] Adapted from Murray (1938), pp. 152–226.

define proper or acceptable conduct. Certain needs cannot be given free expression without violating the conventions or standards that have been taken over from society by means of the parents and these needs often operate at a covert level.

Third, there are *focal needs* and *diffuse needs*. Some needs are closely linked to limited classes of environmental objects whereas others are so generalized as to be applicable in almost any environmental setting. Murray points out that unless there is some unusual fixation a need is always subject to change in the objects toward which it is directed and the manner in which these are approached. That is, the sphere of environmental events to which the need is relevant may be broadened or narrowed and the instrumental acts linked to the need may be increased or decreased. If the need is firmly attached to an unsuitable object this is called a *fixation* and is customarily considered pathological. However, as Murray indicates, the inability of the need to show any enduring object preference, jumping from object to object, may be just as pathological as a fixation.

Fourth, there are *proactive needs* and *reactive needs*. The proactive need is one that is largely determined from within, one that becomes "spontaneously kinetic" as the result of something in the person rather than something in the environment. Reactive needs on the other hand are activated as a result of, or in response to, some environmental event. The distinction here is largely that between a response elicited by appropriate stimulation and a response produced in the absence of any important stimulus variation. Murray uses these concepts also to describe interaction between two or more persons where usually one individual can be identified as the *proactor* (initiates the interaction, asks the questions, in general provides the stimulus to which the other must respond) and another individual can be identified as the *reactor* (reacts to the stimuli provided by the proactor).

Fifth, there is the distinction between *process activity, modal needs,* and *effect needs*. American psychologists with their conventional emphasis upon function and utility have consistently emphasized effect needs—needs that lead to some desired state or end result. Murray, however, has insisted upon the equal importance of process activity and modal needs—tendencies to perform certain acts for the sake of the performance itself. The random, uncoordinated, nonfunctional operation of various processes (vision, hearing, thought, speech, and so forth) that occurs from birth on is called process activity. This is "sheer function pleasure," doing for the sake of doing. Modal needs, on the other hand, involve doing something with a certain degree of excellence or quality. It is still the activity that is sought and enjoyed but it is now rewarding only when it is performed with a certain degree of perfection.

INTERRELATION OF NEEDS. It is evident that needs do not operate in complete isolation from each other and the nature of this interaction or mutual influence is of crucial theoretical importance. Murray accepts the fact that there exists a hierarchy of needs with certain tendencies taking precedence over others. The concept of *prepotency* is used to refer to needs that "become regnant with the greatest urgency if they are not satisfied" (Murray, 1951a, p. 452). Thus, in situations where two or more needs are aroused simultaneously and motivate incompatible responses, it is the prepotent need (such as pain, hunger, thirst) that ordinarily will be translated into action as prepotent needs cannot be postponed. A minimal satisfaction of such needs is necessary before other needs can operate. In his investigation of personality Murray has habitually employed a set of concepts to represent *conflict* involving important needs. Thus, it is customary in his research to secure estimates for each subject of the intensity of conflict in certain key areas, for example, autonomy versus compliance, achievement versus pleasure.

Under certain circumstances multiple needs may be gratified by a single course of action. In instances where the outcome of different needs is behaviorally the same Murray speaks of *fusion* of needs. Another important kind of relation among needs is referred to by the concept of *subsidiation*. A subsidiary need is one that operates in the service of another; for instance, the individual may show aggressive needs but these may be serving only to facilitate acquisitive needs. In any instance where the operation of one need is merely instrumental to the gratification of another we speak of the first need as subsidiary to the second. Tracing chains of subsidiation can be of great value in revealing the dominant or root motives of the individual.

We have now examined the manner in which Murray chooses to represent motivation of the individual. However, these personal motivations are intimately linked with events taking place outside of the individual and it remains for us to scrutinize the manner in which Murray proposes to represent these significant environmental happenings.

Just as the concept of "need" represents the significant determinants of behavior within the person so the concept of "press" represents the effective or significant determinants of behavior in the environment. In simplest terms a press is a property or attribute of an environmental object or person that facilitates or impedes the efforts of the individual to reach a given goal. Press are linked to persons or objects that have direct implications for the efforts of the individual to satisfy their need strivings. "The *press* of an object is what it can *do to the subject* or *for the subject*—the power that it has to affect the well-being of the subject in one way or another" (1938, p. 121). By representing the environment in terms of press the investigator hopes to extract and classify the significant portions of the world in which the individual lives. Clearly we know a great deal more about what an individual is likely to do if we have a picture not only of their motives or directional tendencies but also a picture of the way in which the person views or interprets their environment. It is this later function that the press concepts are designed to fulfill.

Murray has developed various lists of press for particular purposes. Representative of these is the classification contained in Table 6-2, which was designed to represent significant childhood events or influences. In practice these press are not only identified as operating in a given individual's experience but they are also assigned a quantitative rating to indicate their strength or importance in the individual's life.

It is important to distinguish between the significance of environmental objects as they are perceived or interpreted by the individual (*beta press*) and the properties of those environmental objects as they

Press

TABLE 6-2
Abbreviated list of press[a]

1. Family Insupport
   Cultural Discord
   Family Discord
   Capricious Discipline
   Parental Separation
   Absence of Parent: Father, Mother

   Parental Illness: Father, Mother
   Death of Parent: Father, Mother
   Inferior Parent: Father, Mother

   Dissimilar Parent: Father, Mother
   Poverty
   Unsettled Home
2. Danger or Misfortune

   Physical Insupport, Height
   Water
   Aloneness, Darkness
   Inclement Weather, Lightning
   Fire

   Accident
   Animal
3. Lack or Loss
   of Nourishment
   of Possessions
   of Companionship
   of Variety

4. Retention, Withholding Objects
5. Rejection, Unconcern, and Scorn
6. Rival, Competing Contemporary
7. Birth of Sibling
8. Aggression
   Maltreatment by Elder Male,
     Elder Female
   Maltreatment by Contemporaries
   Quarrelsome Contemporaries
9. Dominance, Coercion, and Pro-
   hibition
   Discipline
   Religious Training
10. Nurturance, Indulgence
11. Succorance, Demands for Ten-
    derness
12. Deference, Praise, Recognition
13. Affiliation, Friendships
14. Sex
    Exposure
    Seduction; Homosexual, Hetero-
      sexual
    Parental Intercourse
15. Deception or Betrayal
16. Inferiority
    Physical
    Social
    Intellectual

[a] Adapted from Murray (1938), pp. 291–292.

exist in reality or as objective inquiry discloses them (*alpha press*). The individual's behavior is most closely correlated with the beta press but it is nevertheless important to discover situations in which there is a wide discrepancy between the beta press to which the individual is reacting and the alpha press which actually exist.

Tension Reduction   We have already seen that Murray conceives of the individual as set into action by a complex set of motives. Further, he grants that when a need is aroused the individual is in a state of tension, and satisfaction of the need involves reduction of the tension. Finally, the organism will learn to attend to objects and perform acts that it has found in the past to be associated with tension reduction.

Although this conventional formulation meets with Murray's approval he contends that it is an incomplete picture. Not only does the individual learn to respond in such a manner as to reduce tension and thus experience satisfaction but also he learns to respond in such a manner as to develop tension so that it can later be reduced, thereby enhancing the amount of pleasure. An example of increasing tension in order to derive greater satisfaction from the activity is that of engaging in foreplay prior to sexual consummation.

One should note that this formulation applies only to effect needs. In process activity and modal needs the satisfaction is intrinsic to the activity and may be just as intense at the beginning or middle as at the end.

Murray accepts the proposition that man acts in such a way as to *intend* the increase of satisfaction and decrease of tension. However, this is only an intention or belief on the actor's part and it does not always turn out that the act that the person believes will reduce tension, and lead to satisfaction, is successful in attaining this goal. Moreover, humans are not motivated to increase satisfaction *in general;* it is always a specific tension relevant to a particular need they are attempting to reduce. Satisfaction is thus largely an outcome or result of need states and their behavioral consequences.

Thema

A thema is simply a molar and interactive behavioral unit. It includes the instigating situation (press) and the need that is operating. Thus, it deals with the interaction between needs and press and permits a more global and less segmental view of behavior. By means of this concept the theorist can represent the situations that instigate or lead to the operation of particular needs, as well as the outcome or resultants of the operation of these needs.

Themas vary from simple formulations of a single subject-object interaction to more general and cruder formulations of longer transactions, and include formulations that represent the combination of a number of simple themas (*serial themas*). The thema as an analytic unit is a natural outcome of Murray's conviction that interpersonal relations should be formulated as a *dyadic unit.* That is, the theorist must represent not only the subject who is the focus of interest but must also represent fully the nature of the person with whom the subject is interacting. The theorist must show an equal concern for the details of both subject and object to predict concrete social interactions between two people.

Need Integrate

Although needs are not necessarily linked to specific objects in the environment, it often happens that with experience the individual comes to associate particular objects with certain needs. Likewise particular modes of response, or means of approaching or avoiding these objects, may be acquired and associated with the need. When this integration of the need and the image or thought of the environmental object, as well as instrumental acts, has taken place, Murray speaks of a *need integrate*. A need integrate is a well-established "thematic diposition"—a need for a certain kind of interaction with a certain kind of person or object. Under circumstances where a need integrate exists the arousal of the need will ordinarily lead the person to seek in an appropriate way the environmental object corresponding to the image that was a part of the need integrate.

Unity-Thema   The unity-thema is essentially the single pattern of related needs and press, derived from infantile experience, that gives meaning and coherence to the largest portion of the individual's behavior. It operates largely as an unconscious force. It is not always possible to discover a unity-thema, although one can usually arrive at a developmental formulation that sheds light upon all or most of the individual's behavior and without which it would not be possible to bring much order to behavior. Murray refers to a person's unity-thema as the "key to his unique nature" and suggests:

> A *unity-thema* is a compound of interrelated—collaborating or conflicting—dominant needs that are linked to press to which the individual was exposed on one or more particular occasions, gratifying or traumatic, in early childhood. The thema may stand for a primary infantile experience or a subsequent reaction formation to that experience. But, whatever its nature and genesis, it repeats itself in many forms during later life (1938, pp. 604–605).

Regnant Processes   A regnant process is the physiological accompaniment of a dominant psychological process. We have already seen in Murray's definition of personality, as well as in our discussion of the need concept, that he places great emphasis upon the importance of the physiological or neurological processes that underlie the phenomena of interest to the psychologist. This clear intention of locating or referring all psychological processes to brain function led to the development of a specific concept (regnancy) designed to keep this brain-personality identity in the forefront of the theorist's attention. In defining this concept Murray suggests:

> It may prove convenient to refer to the mutually dependent processes that constitute dominant configurations in the brain as *regnant* processes; and, further, to designate the totality of such processes occurring during a single moment (a unitary temporal segment of brain processes) as a *regnancy*. . . . To a certain extent the regnant need dominates the organism (1938, p. 45).

Murray also makes clear that all conscious processes are regnant but that not all regnant processes are conscious. Thus, consciousness is just one property of a dominant psychological process, and this may or may not be present in a given instance.

One of the shortcomings of the concepts of need and press as they have been elaborated above is the fact that they do not show sufficient respect for the embeddedness of behavior, for the extent to which given needs are linked with specific press and other needs. Murray has made efforts to represent more adequately this interaction among the determinants of behavior. He reasons that needs always operate in the service of some value, or with the intent of bringing about some end state and, therefore, this value should be made a part of the analysis of motives:

Vector-Value Scheme

Since observation and experience testify to the fact that aggression, as well as every other kind of action, has an effect (function) which can be best defined in terms of some valued entity (its construction, conservation, expression, or reproduction), the naming of the valued entity in conjunction with the named activity should contribute a good deal to our understanding of the dynamics of behavior (1951b, p. 288).

In this scheme Murray proposes that behavioral tendencies be represented in terms of vectors that represent broad "physical or psychological directions of activity." The values that the vectors serve are represented by a series of value concepts. Although the scheme is not completely worked out Murray has provided tentative lists of values and vectors. The vectors consist of rejection, reception, acquisition, construction, conservation, expression, transmission, expulsion, destruction, defendance, and avoidance. The values consist of body (physical well-being), property (useful objects, wealth), authority (decision-making power), affiliation (interpersonal affection), knowledge (facts and theories, science, history), aesthetic form (beauty, art), and ideology (system of values, philosophy, religion). In practice it is intended that these vectors and values be arranged in a matrix of intersecting rows and columns so that each cell in the matrix will represent behavior that corresponds to a particular vector in the service of a particular value.

We have examined the elaborate set of concepts developed by Murray to represent the dispositions or striving of the individual and we have also viewed the concepts with which he proposes to represent significant environmental events. Thus, it is now possible to represent the individual at any point in time as a complex integrate of needs and

THE
DEVELOPMENT
OF PERSONALITY

press or vectors and values, as well as personality structures, abilities, achievements, and sentiments. However, we have also learned that the "history of the organism is the organism," and this clearly indicates that representing the individual at a single point in time is not sufficient. The longitudinal study of the individual is a matter of prime importance and Murray has a good deal to say about the path of psychological development.

The variables we have already considered can, of course, be applied at any point in development. In addition to these concepts, however, Murray has elaborated and refined the psychoanalytic conception of "complex" so as to represent a particularly important set of early childhood experiences. Although Murray's treatment of development is heavily flavored by psychoanalytic theorizing, he introduces novel dimensions into his use of these conceptions and has been particularly inventive in devising means of measuring some of the important variables.

In discussing development we shall begin with a consideration of the infantile complexes and follow this with a brief summary of Murray's position in regard to several theoretical issues including genetic-maturational determinants, learning, sociocultural determinants, uniqueness of the individual, the role of unconscious factors, and the socialization process.

Infantile Complexes   If we accept the fact that events taking place early in the individual's life are of unusual importance as determinants of adult behavior we find an empirical dilemma posed by the fact that these events take place, for the most part, prior to the development of language. Consequently, the usual methods of appraisal or measurement are inappropriate and the investigator must depend upon external observation of the child and vague reconstructions which the individual can make after language has developed. Utilization of these two sources of data has led to the isolation of certain areas of experience as possessing particular importance for the development of the child and subsequently the adult. Murray suggests that these are:

. . . five highly enjoyable conditions or activities, each of which is terminated, frustrated or limited (at some point in development) by external forces: (1) the secure, passive and dependent existence within the womb (rudely interrupted by the painful experience of birth); (2) the sensuous enjoyment of sucking good nourishment from the mother's breast (or from a bottle) while lying safely and dependently in her arms (brought to a halt by weaning); (3) the free enjoyment of the pleasurable sensations accompanying defecation (restricted by toilet training); (4) the pleasant sense impressions accompanying urination . . . ; and (5) the thrilling excitations that arise from genital friction (prohibited by threats of punishment) (1938, pp. 361–362).

All of these areas have been indicated by the psychoanalyst as posing special problems for the growing child. Murray's contributions here represent an elaboration and clarification of the orthodox Freudian views.

In cases where the effects of these infantile experiences upon later behavior are clear and extensive we speak of a *complex*. Actually it is presumed that all individuals have "complexes" of varying severity and it is only in extreme cases that this implies abnormality. In Murray's terms a complex is "An enduring integrate (derived from one of the above-mentioned enjoyed conditions) that determines (unconsciously) the course of later development . . ." (1938, p. 363).

Murray defines and provides rough specification for the measurement of five complexes: claustral, oral, anal, urethral, and castration. Each represents the outcome of happenings involving one of the five areas of pleasurable experience outlined above.

The *claustral complexes* represent residuals of the uterine or prenatal experience of the individual. This area of experience has been dealt with by analysts including Freud and Rank. Murray brought together and systematized these ideas, elaborated upon them, and added a suitable label. He suggests that under this general heading there are three specific types of complex:

. . . 1) a complex constellated about the wish to reinstate the conditions similar to those prevailing before birth; 2) a complex that centres about the anxiety of insupport and helplessness, and 3) a complex that is anxiously directed against suffocation and confinement (1938, p. 363).

Having provided a general specification of the complexes, Murray proceeds to provide detailed symptoms or criteria in terms of which each of the three types of claustral complex may be identified. The *simple claustral complex* (reinstatement of uterine conditions) is characterized by: cathexis for claustra (womblike enclosures), nurturant or motherly objects, death, the past, and resistance to change, needs for passivity, harmavoidance, seclusion, and succorance. Thus, the overall picture is of a passive, dependent person who is oriented toward the past and generally resistant to novelty or change. The *fear of insupport complex* manifests itself in fear of open spaces, falling, drowning, earthquake, fire, and family insupport. The *egression complex* is concerned with escaping or departing and displays itself in cathexis for open spaces and fresh air, need to move and travel, cathexis for change, claustrophobia, and a strong need for autonomy. Thus, the individual who displays this complex is in most respects the opposite of the person displaying the simple claustral complex.

The oral complexes represent derivatives of early feeding experiences and again we find that Murray has proposed three specific subcomplexes, all of which involve the mouth but each of which implies a distinctive kind of activity. The *oral succorance* complex involves oral activity in combination with passive and dependent tendencies. The existence of this complex can be inferred from oral automatisms such as sucking; cathexis for oral objects such as the nipple, breast, or thumb; compulsive eating and drinking; need for passivity and succorance; cathexis for words, nurturant objects; and inhibited aggressive needs. The *oral aggression complex* combines oral activity with aggression and is manifested in oral automatisms such as biting; cathexis for solid oral objects (meat, bones); strong aggressive needs; ambivalence toward authority figures; projection of oral aggression (seeing the environment as full of biting aggressive objects); need for harmavoidance; phobia for biting objects; and stuttering. The *oral rejection complex* involves spitting out and disgust over oral activities and objects. More specifically it is revealed in a negative cathexis for certain foods, low need for food, fear of oral infection or injury, need to reject, need for seclusion and autonomy, and dislike for nurturant objects.

The *anal complexes* are derived from events associated with the act of defecating and bowel training. Murray suggests, following Freud and Abraham, that there are two specific complexes here, one concerned primarily with the tendency to expel and the other with the tendency to retain. The *anal rejection complex* includes diarrhea and cathexis for feces and further involves need for aggression, particularly involving disorder and dirtying or smearing; anal theory of birth, need for autonomy, anal sexuality. The *anal retention complex* involves an underlying cathexis for feces but this is concealed behind an apparent disgust, prudishness, and negative reaction to defecation. This complex also is associated with the anal theory of birth and anal sexuality as well as the need for autonomy, although in this instance the autonomy is displayed through resistance to suggestion rather than seeking for independence or freedom. There is a strong need for order and cleanliness, and also a need to retain possessions. This complex, of course, restates the famous Freudian trilogy of "parsimony, cleanliness, and obstinacy" that were suggested as typifying the "anal character."

Originally Murray (1938) considered the *urethral complex* of rather minor importance. He indicated initially that the complex involved bedwetting, urethral soiling, and urethral erotism. Postwar research has convinced him of the central importance for many individuals of this area of experience, and he has since provided a further description of the complex as well as a series of empirical devices for assessing it, although as yet this material has not been published. He has also suggested that the syndrome be called the *Icarus complex* after the mythological figure who flew too near the sun against his father's advice, with the result that his artificial wings melted and he plunged to his death. A detailed case history of an *American Icarus* has been published (Murray, 1955). In his recent formulations he has indicated that the individual who is an Icarian typically displays such qualities as cathexis for fire, a history of enuresis, a craving for immortality, strong narcissism, and a lofty ambition that dissolves in the face of failure.

The *castration complex* is also given less attention in Murray's early writing than the first three complexes. He suggests that the complex should be given a more limited meaning or significance than that commonly assigned to it by the psychoanalysts:

To us it seems better to confine the term castration complex to its literal meaning; anxiety evoked by the fantasy that the penis might be cut off. This complex occurs often enough, but it does not seem possible that it is the root of all neurotic anxiety. It usually comes as a resultant of the fantasies associated with infantile masturbation (1938, p. 385).

Any one of these complexes may persist throughout a person's life in the form of character traits, that is, characteristic ways of behaving.

In a recent formulation of his views, Murray (1968b) ascribes an important role to genetic and maturational factors in the development of personality. He conceives of genetic-maturational processes as being responsible for programming a succession of eras throughout an individual's life. During the first era—that of childhood, adolescence, and young adulthood—new structural compositions emerge and multiply. The middle years are marked by conservative recompositions of the already emerged structures and functions. In the final era, senescence, the capacity for forming new compositions and recompositions decreases and the atrophy of existing forms and functions increases. Within each period, there are numerous smaller programs of behavioral and experiential events that run off under the guidance of genetically controlled maturational processes.

Murray attributes these developments to metabolic processes. In the first era, anabolism outdistances catabolism; in the second, the two are about equal; and in the third, catabolism is greater than anabolism. Murray favors a metabolic model because "it conforms with a concep-

Genetic-Maturational Determinants

tion of reality that is *not* expressible in terms of spatial structures of matter as such but in terms of the interdependent, operating properties of matter—that is, in terms of process, time, and energy" (1968b, p. 9). Moreover, it is a model that provides for progression, creativity, and self-actualization, which are not accounted for by a purely psychoanalytic formulation.

Learning   Genetic factors cannot be overlooked in discussing learning since Murray believes they are responsible for the presence of pleasure (hedonic) and displeasure (anhedonic) centers in the brain. Learning consists of discovering what generates pleasure and what generates distress for the individual. These hedonic and anhedonic generators may be classified in several ways. They may be *retrospective* (memories of past experiences that were delightful or distressful), *spective* (current experiences), or *prospective* (anticipations of future pleasures or pains). Current generators may be classified according to whether they are located predominantly in the person, in the environment, or in an interpersonal transaction. These generators may be further subdivided. For example, generators in the person may be located in the body, in some emotional center of the brain, in some type of psychological process, or in the judgments of conscience.

Murray specifically rejects the concept of habit as being of primary importance in personality development. Instead of being a creature of habit, the individual is continually looking for new ways to express him or her self, eager for new forms of stimulation, new ventures, and new accomplishments, and capable of being transformed by spiritual insights (Murray, 1968b, p. 12).

Sociocultural Determinants   Murray, in marked contrast to most theorists who have drawn heavily from psychoanalytic theory, has deliberately assigned a major role in development to environmental factors. We have already seen that in distinction to most students of motivation he has developed an elaborate set of concepts (press) designed to represent the environment of the individual. He has done so partly on the basis of Darwin's theory that the group more than the individual is the evolutionary unit. Survival of the fittest applies to rival groups. Accordingly, Murray writes, "This theory of group evolution helps us to understand why man is a social . . . creature, and why as a social creature he is both humane and brutal" (1959, p. 46). Further, he has made frequent reference to the fact that the path of development cannot be adequately understood without a full picture of the social setting in which the process evolves. Consistently, his concepts of "proceeding" and "thema" imply an interactionist belief—a conviction that full understanding of behavior will follow only when both subject and object are adequately represented. All of these considerations make clear that Murray accepts and accentuates the importance of a "field" view of behavior.

In spite of his attention to general categories of analysis Murray has always taken the essential uniqueness of each person, and even of each behavioral event, as self-evident facts. His respect for naturalistic observation and his creative and intuitive literary talents make it easy for him to grasp and express compellingly the individuality and elusive complexity of each subject or event. In his words:

Uniqueness

Every proceeding leaves behind it some trace of its occurrence—a new fact, the germ of an idea, a re-evaluation of something, a more affectionate attachment to some person, a slight improvement of skill, a renewal of hope, another reason for despondency. Thus, slowly, by scarcely perceptible gradations—though sometimes suddenly by a leap forward or a slide backward—the person changes from day to day. Since his familiar associates also change, it can be said that every time he meets with one of them, both are different. In short, every proceeding is in some respects unique (Murray and Kluckhohn, 1953, p. 10).

Among academic psychologists Murray was one of the first to accept the insidious and pervasive role of unconscious determinants of behavior (Murray, 1936). As we have observed, in his first major theoretical statement (1938) he made clear that not all regnant processes have conscious correlates and, naturally enough, those that do not, determine behavior without the individual's awareness. Not only is the individual unaware of certain tendencies that influence behavior but, more important, some of these tendencies are actively defended against or warded off from consciousness. Thus, Murray not only accepts the role of unconscious determinants of behavior but also recognizes the operation of the Freudian mechanisms of repression and resistance.

Unconscious Processes

Murray has suggested that the human personality is a compromise between the individual's own impulses and the demands and interests of other people. These demands of other people are represented collectively by the institutions and cultural patterns to which the individual is exposed, and the process whereby his or her own impulses are compromised by these forces is referred to as the socialization process. Conflicts between the individual and the approved patterns of the social milieu are customarily solved by means of the individual conforming to the group patterns in some manner. Only occasionally and in unusual individuals is it possible for the person to bring about a change in the cultural patterns that will ease the conflict with his or her

The Socialization Process

own impulses. For the most part it is the personality that is more malleable and therefore the conflict is usually reduced by altering the person.

An essential element in achieving the goals of socialization is the development of an adequate superego. As we have already seen, by internalizing aspects of the authority figures to whom one has been exposed, the person develops an internal structure that serves to reward and punish one when one is behaving appropriately or inappropriately in terms of the culture pattern as interpreted by these authority figures. This implies that the parents, as the most important authority figures, are the chief agents of the socialization process. The effectiveness of the parents in rewarding approved and punishing disapproved patterns of behavior will largely determine the success of this developmental process. An important component of the parents' role as socializer is the effectiveness with which they develop a mutually affectionate relationship with the child so that mere approval or disapproval can serve as significant motivating conditions in controlling the child's behavior.

Socialization is not without its negative qualities. An individual can be oversocialized, and conceivably an entire society may be exposed to socialization processes that are debilitating rather than preparatory for a fruitful life. As Murray suggests, a human is fundamentally an animal and to the extent that socialization denies this fundamental, biological nature it may destroy the creative spontaneity and vigor essential to the most important kinds of human advances.

CHARACTERISTIC
RESEARCH AND
RESEARCH
METHODS

We have already pointed out that Murray's research has been distinguished primarily by its originality and this very fact makes it singularly difficult to characterize in a representative fashion the investigations he has inspired and conducted. Before turning to the difficult task of selecting representative investigations to summarize, let us examine very briefly several distinctive qualities of Murray's general approach to personality research. The interested reader will find several papers in which Murray has outlined his conception of how personality research should be pursued (Murray, 1947, 1949b, 1963).

*Intensive Study of
Small Numbers of
Normal Subjects*

The large-scale study of human behavior, in which findings consist of group tendencies or over-all relations that may characterize very poorly any single individual within the group, represents a limited avenue to understanding human behavior. Murray is convinced, with the wisdom of the naturalist and clinician, that an adequate understanding of behavior must follow a complete and detailed study of individual subjects. Just as case study has provided indispensable assistance in the growth and development of medical science, so the future of psychology is linked to the willingness of investigators to take the time and effort to understand thoroughly individual cases. Group relations are important only when accompanied by a careful inquiry into the deviations within the group, and conditions that cause or accompany these deviations. To report a finding that characterizes 80 percent of a specified group is of little value unless some explanation can be provided for the failure of the other 20 percent to fit into this pattern. Murray's consistent emphasis on this point is one of his principal contributions to research methods.

If we are interested in the individual subject and also concerned with reasons for subjects representing exceptions to general relationships, it is clear that we must secure a very large amount of information concerning each subject. Thus, it is inevitable that Murray's position should lead him to the intensive study of his subjects and this, of course, has the natural result of reducing the number of subjects who can be studied at any one time and the total number of studies that can be carried out by any one investigator in a given number of years.

A further distinctive quality of his research has been its emphasis upon the study of *normal individuals in natural settings.* In general, the intensive study of individual cases has been reserved for the clinical setting where the pathology of the patients has made them a subject of particular interest or else the demands of diagnostic or therapeutic expediency have necessitated extensive information. Thus, Murray's choice of the normal subject as the focus of his research provided a natural complement to the case histories available from psychiatric settings.

Murray (1958) believes that the ultimate concern of the personologist is to explain and predict the individual's *activities in everyday life.* For that reason, he or she should not be content to limit their predictions to the subculture of the laboratory nor to try to understand the individual merely by validating one test against the other.

He was also one of the pioneers in *interdisciplinary co-operation in personality research.* The Harvard Psychological Clinic staff habitually included representatives of psychiatry, psychology, anthropology, and other disciplines, in an era when this was anything but commonplace.

Murray has placed great emphasis upon the importance of the observer or the psychologist as an instrument in psychological research. Although we may use rating scales, category sets, or psychological tests to appraise personality, still, at the base of all these instruments is the sensitive observation of the investigator or clinician. Because of the root status of the observer Murray is convinced that

The Diagnostic Council

more attention should be paid to his or her frailties and more serious efforts directed at improving their powers of observation. These considerations have led him to refer to the psychologist as the most important "instrument of precision" in psychological research.

One evident means of placing checks upon, and improving the quality of, observation is to have multiple observers all examining the same data from a different perspective. Thus, using a number of investigators to study the same individual, or individuals, offers unique rewards in the form of canceling out limitations posed by the biases of particular observers or the limitations offered by specialized sets of data. Not only is the end result of such group observation presumably superior to individual observation but the members of the group should sharpen and improve their powers of observation as a result of the corrective function of the observations of others.

These considerations led Murray to devise the *diagnostic council* that involves many observers all studying the same subjects from different points of view, and with the opportunity for a final discussion and synthesis of the information secured from these different vantage points. After a period of individual observation during which each investigator studies the subjects through his or her own specialized techniques there is a conference for each subject. At this time every investigator presents their data and their interpretation with a full opportunity for the observations and interpretations of other observers to support or suggest modifications in the report. A single investigator has primary responsibility for assembling and presenting the synthesis of each case but each member of the council is given an unlimited opportunity for contributing to this final product.

Instruments of Personality Measurement

Among contemporary psychologists there is no one who has made more significant contributions to personality assessment than Murray. He has devised a large number of ingenious devices for the measurement of personality, only a small number of which have been systematically exploited. The volumes, *Explorations in personality* and *Assessment of men,* provide ample illustration of the ingenuity and diversity of the instruments which he has devised or been influential in developing. One of these, the *Thematic Apperception Test,* has become, next to the *Rorschach Test,* the most widely used projective technique in current use (Lindzey, 1961; Murstein, 1963; Zubin, Eron, and Schumer, 1965).

Almost all of Murray's instruments have been congruent with his fundamental conviction that an ultimate understanding of human behavior will derive not from the study of lower organisms or the study of humans under highly restricted conditions but rather from the complex study of individual behavior. That is, Murray has argued for the collection of rich and multiform data that can be expected to reflect a wide range of behavioral tendencies and capacities. He is convinced that one of the natural advantages of the psychologist is the fact that he or she deals with a talking organism and that this should be capitalized upon fully. In contrast to the biologist, the zoologist, or the physicist, the psychologist deals with a subject who can tell a great deal about internal processes that operate, about external events that are attended to, about the major determinants of behavior. It is true that these reports must be assessed carefully, and that they cannot always be taken at their face value, but nevertheless they represent a crucial beginning in the attempt to unravel the secrets of human behavior.

Given this interest in subjectivity it is quite natural that Murray should have pioneered in developing personality instruments that explore the full mental content of the subject. His instruments typically do not limit the response alternatives of the subject by means of predetermined categories but rather they permit and encourage a full and subjective exposition on the part of the subject. Imagination and fantasy are permitted full participation by these techniques. They provide the investigator with a fullness of data that is at the same time richly promising and complexly discouraging.

CURRENT STATUS AND EVALUATION

We have already seen that Murray's theoretical conceptions undergo a constant process of re-examination and modification. Even in the face of this constant flux, however, certain elements stand firm. At no time has his deep interest in the motivational process wavered nor has he shown any inclination to desert his descriptive and taxonomic activities. Similarly, his theory has always emphasized the importance of unconscious sources of motivation and has throughout stressed the relation of psychological process to brain process.

Murray's formulations have been found useful not only by his students but also by many other investigators and clinicians interested in studying personality. His concepts of need and press have had a wide usage, particularly among clinicians and investigators who have used the Thematic Apperception Test. Few persons who have been concerned with the details of classifying human behavior have failed to gain something from the several important classifications that Murray has proposed. As we have indicated, his influence upon the current methods or procedures for assessing personality has been profound. Both in the development of specific instruments and in the presentation of a point of view his work has had a great deal to do with contemporary developments in this area. Fully as important as these substantive contributions has been Murray's capacity to intrigue, excite, and inspire his students and colleagues. The enthusiasm and conviction with which he has imbued his students is undoubtedly responsible to a considerable extent for the fact that they have played such an important role in the development of personality research.

Which of the features of his theoretical position have been of most influence? Perhaps the most distinctive component in Murray's position, as suggested earlier, is the careful and sensitive treatment of the motivational process. There has been a strong tendency on the part of recent personality theorists to deal with motivation through one of two rather simple paths. The first path assigns all behavior to a remarkably small number of cardinal motives so that everything can be viewed as stemming from these master motives. The second path assumes that the number of motives is legion and that each individual is driven by motives that are so complex and so uniquely different from those of other individuals that it is not possible to specify motives that can be usefully applied to more than one person. This alternative denies the utility of any attempt at a general classification of motives. Murray's position is clearly between these easy extremes. He grants the complexity of human motivation and firmly avers his conviction that the process cannot be represented adequately in terms of two, three, four, or five general motives. However, he insists that there are motives of sufficient generality so that they can be used fruitfully to represent the behavior of all or most individuals within specified groups. Thus, he faces realistically the task of developing a set of constructs that will do justice to the complexity of human behavior, but at the same time will be carefully specified so that they can be used repeatedly by different investigators. The result, as we have seen, is a classification of motives that is probably more widely useful than any other comparable classification. One need only look at the massive amount of research concerned with need affiliation and need achievement (for example, Atkinson, 1958) to gain an impression of the impact of Murray upon research in the area of human motivation.

Murray's theory and his research have played a crucial role in promoting a more serious interest in psychoanalytic theory on the part of academic psychologists. In the era when Murray first came to the Harvard Psychological Clinic psychoanalysis was largely an alien and a trespasser within the domain of psychology. The subsequent years have found Freud firmly ensconced as one of the intellectual giants of our field, and this shift is in no small part attributable to the importance of Murray's example.

As we have seen, his theory possesses the unique feature of a simultaneous emphasis upon the importance of the past of the organism and the present context within which behavior takes place. In a psychological world where most theorists have self-consciously developed a preoccupation with the contemporary field, or else have turned to the past of the organism as the sole key to understanding behavior, it is decidedly healthy to have one position where both of these classes of determinants are given their due. His interest in the field or environment within which behavior takes place led to the distinctive system of press concepts that permits the investigator to represent the perceived environment as well as the objective environment. It is one thing to speak generally of the importance of the environment and quite another thing to undertake the grim and exacting task of specifying categories in terms of which the significant aspects of the environment can be represented. Murray is one of a remarkably small number of theorists who have undertaken this task.

The negative aspects of Murray's theory are in many respects the mirror image of the positive. To a considerable extent the main criticisms of the theory are closely related to the originality, the incorporativeness, and the complexity of the theory. We have already agreed that the most serious allegation that can be leveled against any theory is the charge that it does not lead to research. The critic may maintain that in Murray's system there is definitely a set of concepts, and a related set of empirical definitions, but that there is *no* set of explicitly stated psychological assumptions linked to these concepts in such a manner as to produce testable consequences.

In defense of the theory it must be admitted that its assumptions and concepts do provide a general point of view concerning behavior that clearly has a lot to do with the specific manner in which particular research problems are approached. Further, the defined variables are applicable to most or many such problems. One may claim with considerable justice that these functions are about all that most personality theories are equipped to do at present.

Some critics have felt that the theory is so broadly incorporative as to lose the power or vigor that would attach to a more limited and specialized point of view. Thus, the very qualities that make the theory complex and at the same time protect it against many of the usual criticisms that are raised against personality theories might combine to reduce the effectiveness of the theory is a compelling point of view. It is as though the theory says so much that no single thing is said with a salience and conviction that makes it stand out from the rest of the theory, or that makes the theory itself stand out from others.

In spite of the breadth and diversity of Murray's theoretical formulations it is clear that he has devoted more of his attention to the motivational process than he has to the learning process. This has led some critics to believe that Murray's theory suffers from an inability to account for the manner in which motives become transformed and develop. Although his classification of motives is uniquely useful, and his methods for measuring motivation of central importance, he has relatively little to say concerning the exact process whereby these motives develop.

Murray's patience and skill as a taxonomist have led him to create so many fine distinctions and detailed classifications that some observers feel he has been unnecessarily complex in his approach to the study of behavior. It is certainly true that the number of different categories he has developed, coupled with his tendency to change or modify these frequently, and his further tendency to introduce new terms for describing these concepts produce considerable confusion in the casual reader. While one may maintain that the task of a taxonomist is to represent reality accurately and not necessarily to make the reader happy, it must be admitted that many of Murray's variables have not seen extensive and prolonged application to empirical data.

In general Murray's writings and his research are not fashionable within the existing psychological world. There is too much of the poet and too little of the positivist in his make-up. He is at home with his imagination, he is willing to speculate freely about issues that offer no immediate possibility for empirical translation, and he is willing to make his unbridled speculations public. None of these are qualities that lead to immediate acceptance on the part of the professionals who are still sensitive concerning their suspended position between the natural sciences and the humanities. There is a strong tendency for the experimentalist to dismiss as mere subjectivity the problems and issues raised by his contemporaries who do not choose to be bound by manipulable method and technique. Thus, understandably, many investigators have considered Murray's writings irreverent in the respect they show for experimental technique and distressing in the complex considerations which they introduce as necessary for an adequate understanding of human behavior.

In any final appraisal of Murray's contributions one must combine the theory, the man, and his research. There can be no doubt that this combination has introduced a note of vivid originality into an area of research sorely in need of such qualities. In the long run one of the great enemies of empirical and theoretical progress is the fixation upon stable but trivial events, and there has been no more ruthless critic of trivial investigation and formulation in personality research than Henry Murray.

Murray, H. A. (and collaborators). *Explorations in personality*. New York: Oxford, 1938.

Murray, H. A. Some basic psychological assumptions and conceptions. *Dialectica,* 1951b, **5,** 266–292.

Murray, H. A. Preparations for the scaffold of a comprehensive system. In S. Koch (Ed.). *Psychology: a study of a science,* vol. 3. New York: McGraw-Hill, 1959, pp. 7–54.

Murray, H. A. Studies of stressful interpersonal disputations. *Amer. Psychologist,* 1963, **18,** 28–36.

Murray, H. A. Components of an evolving personological system. In D. L. Sills (Ed.). *International encyclopedia of the social sciences.* New York: Macmillan and Free Press, 1968b, **12,** 5–13.

Murray, H. A. and Kluckhohn, C. Outline of a conception of personality. In C. Kluckhohn, H. A. Murray, and D. Schneider (Eds.). *Personality in nature, society, and culture.* 2nd Ed. New York: Knopf. 1953, pp. 3–52.

Atkinson, J. W. (Ed.). *Motives in fantasy, action, and society.* Princeton: Van Nostrand, 1958.

Lindzey, G. *Projective techniques and cross-cultural research.* New York: Appleton-Century-Crofts, 1961.

Morgan, C. D., and Murray, H. A. A method for investigating fantasies. *Arch. Neurol. Psychiat.,* 1935, **34,** 289–306.

Murray, H. A. The effect of fear upon estimates of the maliciousness of other personalities. *J. Soc. Psychol.,* 1933, **4,** 310–329.

Murray, H. A. Basic concepts for a psychology of personality. *J. Gen. Psychol.* 1936, **15,** 241–268.

Murray, H. A. (and collaborators). *Explorations in personality.* New York: Oxford, 1938.

Murray, H. A. What should psychologists do about psychoanalysis? *J. Abnorm. Soc. Psychol.,* 1940, **35,** 150–175.

Murray, H. A. *Manual of Thematic Apperception Test.* Cambridge, Mass.: Harvard Univ. Press, 1943.

Murray, H. A. Problems in clinical research: round table. *Amer. J. Ortho-Psychiat.,* 1947, **17,** 203–210.

Murray, H. A. Introduction. In H. Melville. *Pierre, or the ambiguities.* New York: Farrar Straus, 1949a, pp. xiii–ciii.

Murray, H. A. Research planning: a few proposals. In S. S. Sargent (Ed.). *Culture and personality.* New York: Viking Fund, 1949b, pp. 195–212.

Murray, H. A. Toward a classification of interaction. In T. Parsons and E. A. Shils (Eds.). *Toward a general theory of action.* Cambridge: Harvard Univ. Press, 1951a, pp. 434–464.

Murray, H. A. Some basic psychological assumptions and conceptions. *Dialectica,* 1951b, **5,** 266–292.

Murray, H. A. *In Nomine Diaboli, New Eng. Quart.*, 1951c, **24,** 435–452. (*Princeton Univ. Library Chronicle*, 1952, **13,** 47–62.)

Murray, H. A. American Icarus. In A. Burton and R. E. Harris (Eds.). *Clinical studies in personality.* Vol. 2. New York: Harper, 1955, pp. 615–641.

Murray, H. A. Drive, time, strategy, measurement, and our way of life. In G. Lindzey (Ed.). *Assessment of human motives.* New York: Holt, Rinehart and Winston, 1958, pp. 183–196.

Murray, H. A. Preparations for the scaffold of a comprehensive system. In S. Koch (Ed.). *Psychology: a study of a science,* vol. 3. New York: McGraw-Hill, 1959, pp. 7–54.

Murray, H. A. Two versions of man. In H. Shapley (Ed.). *Science ponders religion.* New York: Appleton-Century-Crofts, 1960a, pp. 147–181.

Murray, H. A. The possible nature of a "mythology" to come. In H. A. Murray (Ed.). *Myth and mythmaking.* New York: George Braziller, 1960b.

Murray, H. A. Unprecedented evolutions. *Daedalus,* 1961, **90,** 547–570.

Murray, H. A. The personality and career of Satan. *J. Soc. Issues,* 1962a, **28,** 36–54.

Murray, H. A. Prospect for psychology. *Science,* 1962b, **136,** 483–488.

Murray, H. A. Studies of stressful interpersonal disputations. *Amer. Psychologist,* 1963, **18,** 28–36.

Murray, H. A. Autobiography. In E. G. Boring and G. Lindzey (Eds.). *A history of psychology in autobiography,* vol. V. New York: Appleton-Century-Crofts, 1967, pp. 283–310.

Murray, H. A. A conversation with Mary Harrington Hall. *Psychology Today,* 1968a, **2,** 56–63.

Murray, H. A. Components of an evolving personological system. In D. L. Sills (Eds.). *International Encyclopedia of the Social Sciences.* New York: Macmillan and Free Press, 1968b, **12,** 5–13.

Murray, H. A., and Kluckhohn, C. Outline of a conception of personality. In C. Kluckhohn, H. A. Murray, and D. Schneider (Eds.). *Personality in nature, society, and culture.* 2nd Ed. New York: Knopf, 1953, pp. 3–52.

Murray, H. A., and Morgan, C. D. A clinical study of sentiments. *Genet. Psychol. Monogr.,* 1945, **32,** 3–311.

Murstein, B. I. *Theory and research in projection techniques.* New York: Wiley, 1963.

Office of Strategic Services Assessment Staff. *Assessment of Men.* New York: Rinehart, 1948.

White, R. W. (Ed.). *The study of lives.* New York: Atherton, 1963.

Wolf, R., and Murray, H. A. An experiment in judging personalities. *J. Psychol.,* 1937, **3,** 345–365.

Zubin, J., Eron, L. D., and Schumer, F. *An experimental approach to projective techniques.* New York: Wiley, 1965.

ORGANISMIC THEORY　　　7

Ever since Descartes in the seventeenth century split the individual into two separate yet interacting entities, body and mind, and Wundt in the nineteenth century, subscribing to the tradition of British associationism, atomized the mind by reducing it to the elementary particles of sensations, feelings, and images, there have been recurrent attempts to put the mind and the body back together and to treat the organism as a unified, organized whole. One notable attempt that has attracted a large following within recent years is known as the organismic or holistic viewpoint. This viewpoint has found expression in the psychobiology of Adolf Meyer (Meyer, 1948; Rennie, 1943), in the medical orientation called psychosomatics (Dunbar, 1954), and in the fundamental work of Coghill on the development of the nervous system in relation to behavior (1929). The most important medical forerunners of the organismic concept are Hughlings Jackson, the pre-eminent English neurologist (1931) and Claude Bernard, the famous French physiologist (1866). Jan Smuts, the South African statesman and soldier, is recognized as the leading philosophical proponent of organismic theory and his notable book *Holism and evolution* (1926) has been very influential. General Smuts coined the word *holism* from the Greek root *holos* meaning complete, whole, entire. In psychology, organismic theory has been expounded by J. R. Kantor (1924, 1933, 1947), R. H. Wheeler (1940), Heinz Werner (1948), Gardner Murphy (1947), and Carl Rogers (see Chapter 8). Organismic theory drew nourishment from John Dewey's epoch-making article, *The reflex arc concept in psychology* (1896). Aristotle, Goethe, Spinoza, and William James have been mentioned as providing the seedbed from which organismic theory germinated. Although not all of these authors presented full-fledged organismic theories, their concepts are pointed in that direction.

Closely related to the organismic point of view is the Gestalt movement initiated by Wertheimer, Koffka, and Köhler, who in the years just prior to World War I led a revolt against the type of mental analysis then being performed by Wundt and his followers. This movement stood for a new kind of analysis of conscious experience. Starting with the perceptual field as a whole, they proceeded to differentiate it into figure and background and then studied the properties of each of these components and their mutual influences. In the area of learning, they replaced the doctrine of association with the concept of insight. A person learns a task as a meaningful whole rather than in a piecemeal fashion. Although Gestalt psychology has had a tremendous influence upon modern thought and is certainly congenial to organismic theory, it cannot be regarded, strictly speaking, as an organismic psychology. The reason for this is that Gestalt psychology as developed by Wertheimer, Koffka, and Köhler has tended to restrict its attention to the phenomena of conscious awareness and has said very little about the organism or personality as a whole. Organismic theory has borrowed many of its concepts from Gestalt psychology, and the two viewpoints are on the friendliest terms. Organismic psychology may be regarded as the extension of Gestalt principles to the organism as a whole.

The leading exponent of organismic theory was Kurt Goldstein, the eminent neuropsychiatrist. Largely as a result of his observations and investigations of brain-injured soldiers during World War I, and his earlier studies of speech disturbances, Goldstein came to the conclusion that any particular symptom displayed by a patient could not be understood solely as the product of a particular organic lesion or disease but had to be considered as a manifestation of the total organism. The organism always behaves as a unified whole and not as a series of differentiated parts. Mind and body are not separate entities, nor does the mind consist of independent faculties or elements and the body of independent organs and processes. The organism is a single unity. What happens in a part affects the whole. The psychologist studies the organism from one perspective, the physiologist from another. However, both disciplines need to operate within the framework of organismic theory because any event, be it psychological or physiological, always occurs within the context of the total organism unless it has become artificially isolated from this context. The laws of the whole govern the functioning of the differentiated parts of the whole. Consequently, it is necessary to discover the laws by which the whole organism functions in order to understand the functioning of any member component. This is the basic tenet of organismic theory.

The principal features of organismic theory as they pertain to the psychology of the person may be summarized as follows.

1. Organismic theory emphasizes the unity, integration, consistency, and coherence of the normal personality. Organization is the natural state of the organism; disorganization is pathological and is usually brought about by the impact of an oppressive or threatening environment, or by intraorganic anomalies.

2. Organismic theory starts with the organism as an organized system and proceeds to analyze it by differentiating the whole into its constituent members. A member is never abstracted from the whole to which it belongs and studied as an isolated entity; it is always considered to have membership character in the total organism. Organismic theorists believe that it is impossible to understand the whole by directly studying isolated parts and segments because the whole functions according to laws that cannot be found in the parts. The atomistic viewpoint is felt to be particularly cumbersome because after the organism has been reduced to its elements it is then necessary to postulate an "organizer" that integrates the elements into an organized whole. Organismic theory does not require an "organizer" because organization is built into the system from the beginning and the integrity of the organism is not permitted to be lost or destroyed by analysis.

3. Organismic theory assumes that the individual is motivated by one sovereign drive rather than by a plurality of drives. Goldstein's name for this sovereign motive is *self-actualization* or *self-realization,* which means that humans strive continuously to realize their inherent potentialities by whatever avenues are open. This singleness of purpose gives direction and unity to one's life.

4. Although organismic theory does not regard the individual as a closed system, it tends to minimize the primary and directive influence of the external environment on normal development and to stress the inherent potentialities of the organism for growth. The organism selects the features of the environment to which it will react and—except in rare and abnormal circumstances—the environment cannot force the individual to behave in a manner that is foreign to his or her nature. If the organism cannot control the environment it will try to adapt itself to it. In general, organismic theory feels that the potentialities of the organism, if allowed to unfold in an orderly way by an appropriate environment, will produce a healthy, integrated personality, although malignant environmental forces may at any time destroy or cripple the person. There is nothing inherently "bad" in the organism; it is made "bad" by an inadequate environment. On this point, organismic theory has much in common with the views of the French philosopher, Jean Jacques Rousseau, who believed that natural human beings are good but that they can be and often are perverted by an environment that denies them the opportunity to act and develop in accordance with their nature.

5. Organismic theory frequently makes use of the principles of Gestalt psychology but it feels that the preoccupations of the Gestaltists with isolated functions of the organism such as perception and learning provide too narrow a base for understanding the total organism. Organismic theory has broadened the base by including within its scope everything that the organism is and does. Although there is much in organismic theory to remind one of Lewin, nevertheless Lewin's topology is strictly psychological in character and does not include the whole biological organism.

6. Organismic theory feels that there is more to be learned from a comprehensive study of one person than from an extensive investigation of an isolated psychological function abstracted from many individuals. For this reason, organismic theory has tended to be more popular with clinical psychologists who are concerned with the total person than it has been with experimental psychologists who are primarily interested in separate processes or functions, like perception and learning.

In the present chapter, we shall present first an account of organismic theory as developed by Kurt Goldstein and some typical examples of the research his theory has led to. We shall then consider two other formulations of organismic theory, one by Andras Angyal, the other by Abraham Maslow.

KURT GOLDSTEIN

Kurt Goldstein received his training in neurology and psychiatry in Germany and rose to a position of eminence as a medical scientist and professor before migrating to the United States in 1935 after the Nazis came to power. He was born in Upper Silesia, then a part of

Germany but now a part of Poland, November 6, 1878, and earned a medical degree at the University of Breslau, Lower Silesia, in 1903. He served an apprenticeship with several outstanding medical scientists for several years prior to accepting a teaching and research position at the Psychiatric Hospital in Koenigsberg. During his eight years in this post he did a great deal of research and wrote numerous

Kurt Goldstein

papers that established his reputation and led to his appointment at the age of thirty-six as professor of neurology and psychiatry and director of the Neurological Institute of the University of Frankfurt. During World War I, he became director of the Military Hospital for Brain-Injured Soldiers and was instrumental in establishing an institute for research on the aftereffects of brain injuries. It was in this institute that Goldstein made the fundamental studies that laid the basis for his organismic viewpoint (Gelb and Goldstein, 1920). In 1930 he went to the University of Berlin as professor of neurology and psychiatry and also served as director of the Department of Neurology and Psychiatry at Moabit Hospital. When Hitler took over Germany, Goldstein was jailed and then released on the condition that he leave the country. He went to Amsterdam where he completed his most important book, *Der aufbau des organismus,* which was translated into English under the title, *The organism* (1939). Coming to the United States in 1935 he worked for a year at the New York Psychiatric Institute, following which he became chief of the Laboratory of Neurophysiology at Montefiore Hospital, New York City, and clinical professor of neurology at the College of Physicians and Surgeons of Columbia University. During this period he lectured on psychopathology in the Department of Psychology at Columbia and was invited to give the William James lectures at Harvard University, which were published under the title *Human nature in the light of psychopathology* (1940). During the war years he was clinical professor of neurology at Tufts Medical School in Boston and published a book on the aftereffects of brain injuries in war (1942). In 1945 he returned to New York City to engage in the private practice of neuropsychiatry and psychotherapy. He became associated with Columbia University and the New School for Social Research, and was guest professor at Brandeis University commuting weekly to Waltham. There he was associated with two other holistic theorists, Andras Angyal and Abraham Maslow. His last book was on language and language disturbances (1948), an area in which he had done research throughout his professional life. In his later years, Goldstein become more closely identified with phenomenology and existential psychology. He died in New York City September 19, 1965, at the age of 86. His autobiography (1967) appeared posthumously. A memorial volume (Simmel, 1968) contains a complete bibliography of Goldstein's writings.

THE STRUCTURE OF THE ORGANISM

The organism consists of differentiated members that are articulated together; these members do not become detached and isolated from one another except under abnormal or artificial conditions, for example, strong anxiety. The primary organization of organismic functioning is that of figure and ground. A figure is any process that emerges and stands out against a background. In terms of perception, it is that which occupies the center of attentive awareness. When, for instance, a person is looking at an object in a room, the perception of the object becomes a figure against the background of the rest of the room. In terms of action, the figure is the principal, ongoing activity of the organism. When one is reading a book, the reading is the figure that stands out from such other activities as twisting one's hair, chewing one's pencil, hearing the rumble of voices in the next room, and breathing. A figure has a definite boundary or contour that encloses it and separates it from the surroundings. The background is continuous; it not only surrounds the figure but extends behind it. It is like a carpet on which an object has been placed or the sky against which an airplane is seen. A member part of the organism may stand out as figure against the background of the whole organism and still retain its membership in the structure of the total organism.

What causes a figure to emerge from the background of the total organism? It is determined by the task that the nature of the organism at the time requires. Thus, when a hungry organism is confronted by the task of getting food, any process that will aid in perfoming the task becomes elevated as a figure. It may be a memory of where food has been found in the past, a perception of food objects in the environment, or an activity that will produce food. However, if the organism should change, for example, when a hungry person becomes frightened, a new process will emerge as figure appropriate to the task of dealing with the fear. New figures emerge as the tasks of the organism change.

Goldstein distinguishes between natural figures that are functionally embedded in a background consisting of the totality of the organism and unnatural figures that have become isolated from the total organism and whose background is also an isolated part of the organism. These unnatural figures are produced by traumatic events and by repetitive drill under conditions that are meaningless to the person. Goldstein believes that many psychological experiments that are designed to study isolated stimulus-response connections bear little or no relation to the natural behavior of the organism and so provide little useful knowedge of the laws by which the organism functions.

By what criteria can a natural, embedded figure be distinguished from an unnatural, isolated one? Goldstein says that the figure is a natural one if it represents a preference on the part of the person and if the behavior that is called forth is orderly, flexible, and appropriate to the situation. It is an unnatural one if it represents a task that is imposed upon the person and if the resulting behavior is rigid and mechanical. A person in a deep hypnotic trance who performs various actions at the suggestion of the hypnotist often behaves unnaturally because behavior is cut off by the dissociated state of hypnosis from their normal personality. They do not represent the person's preferences but those of the hypnotist, and they are often completely inappropriate to the situation. The subject is an automaton rather than a person. A young child who has been taught the words of a song and sings them without knowing what he or she is singing exemplifies the kind of automatic behavior that Goldstein characterizes as being an unnatural figure.

Although Goldstein emphasizes the flexible and plastic nature of natural processes as against the rigid character of unnatural processes, he recognizes that preferred activities may remain fairly constant throughout life without losing their intimate relationship to the whole organism. Traits and habits do not necessarily become precipitated out and lose touch with the total matrix in which they are embedded. In fact, Goldstein attributes many constancies to the organism such as sensory thresholds, motor performances, intellectual characteristics, emotional factors, and the like. These constants are inborn and operate as selective agents for behavior. However, the constants are also shaped and molded by experience and training to a certain extent so that their concrete manifestations always bear the imprint of the culture in which the person has been raised.

Although Goldstein does not have much to say regarding the structure of the organism aside from differentiating between figure and ground, he does point out that there are three different kinds of behavior. These are the *performances* that are voluntary, consciously experienced activities, *attitudes* that are feelings, moods, and other inner experiences, and *processes* that are bodily functions that can be experienced only indirectly (1939, pp. 307 ff.).

Another structural distinction that Goldstein makes great use of is that between concrete and abstract behavior. Concrete behavior consists of reacting to a stimulus in a fairly automatic or direct manner while abstract behavior consists of action upon the stimulus by the organism. For example, in concrete behavior one perceives the stimulus configuration and reacts to it as it appears at the moment whereas in abstract behavior the person thinks about the stimulus pattern, what it means, its relation to other configurations, how it can be used, and what its conceptual properties are. The difference between concrete and abstract behavior is the difference between a direct reaction to a stimulus and reacting to it after thinking about the stimulus. These two kinds of behavior depend upon contrasting attitudes toward the world, which will be discussed in the section on Characteristic Research and Research Methods.

The main dynamic concepts presented by Goldstein are (1) the equalization process or the centering of the organism, (2) self-actualization or self-realization, and (3) "coming to terms" with the environment.

Equalization

Goldstein postulates an available energy supply that is fairly constant and that tends to be evenly distributed throughout the organism. This constant, evenly distributed energy represents the "average" state of tension in the organism, and it is to this average state that the organism always returns or tries to return following a stimulus that changes the tension. This return to the "average" state is the *equalization process*. For example, one hears a sound coming from the right and turns one's head in that direction. The turning of the head equalizes the distribution of energy in the system that has been unbalanced by the sound. Eating when hungry, resting when tired, and stretching when cramped are other familiar examples of the equalization process.

The goal of a normal, healthy person is not simply to discharge tension but to equalize it. The level at which tension becomes balanced represents a centering of the organism. This center is one that enables the organism to perform most effectively its work of coping with the environment and of actualizing itself in further activities according to its nature. Full centering or complete balance is an ideal holistic state and is probably rarely achieved.

The principle of equalization explains the consistency, coherence, and orderliness of behavior in spite of disturbing stimuli. Goldstein does not believe that the sources of disturbance are primarily intraorganic except under abnormal and catastrophic circumstances that produce isolation and inner conflict. In an adequate environment, the organism will always remain more or less in balance. Energy redistributions and imbalance of the system result from environmental interferences and sometimes from inner conflict. As a result of maturation and experience, the person develops preferred ways of behaving that keep the interferences and conflicts to a minimum and preserve the balance of the organism. An individual's life becomes more centered and less subject to the fortuitous changes of the inner and outer world as he or she grows older.

Self-Actualization

This is Goldstein's master motive; in fact, it is the only motive that the organism possesses. What appear to be different drives such as hunger, sex, power, achievement, and curiosity are merely manifestations of the sovereign purpose of life, to actualize oneself. When people are hungry they actualize themselves by eating; when they crave power they actualize themselves by obtaining power. The satisfaction of any particular need is in the foreground when it is a prerequisite for the self-realization of the total organism. Self-actualization is the creative trend of human nature. It is the organic principle by which the organism becomes more fully developed and more complete. The ignorant person who desires knowledge feels an inner emptiness; he or she has a sense of their own incompleteness. By reading and studying, their desire for knowledge is fulfilled and the emptiness disappears. A new person has been created, thereby, one in whom learning has taken the place of ignorance. Their desire has become an actuality. Any need is a deficit state that motivates the person to replenish the deficit. It is like a hole that demands to be filled in. This replenishment or fulfillment of a need is what is meant by self-actualization or self-realization.

Although self-actualization is a universal phenomenon in nature, the specific ends toward which people strive vary from person to person. This is so because people have different innate potentialities that shape their ends and direct the lines of their individual development and growth as well as different environments and cultures to which they must adjust and from which they must secure the necessary supplies for growth.

How can an individual's potentialities be determined? Goldstein says that this can best be done by finding out what the person prefers and what he or she does best. Their preferences correspond to their potentialities. This means that if we are to know what people are trying to actualize we must familiarize ourselves with what they like to do and what they have a gift for doing. The baseball player is actualizing those potentialities that are developed by playing baseball, the lawyer those potentialities that are realized by the practice of law.

In general, Goldstein stresses conscious motivation over unconscious motivation. The unconscious, in his eyes, is the background into which conscious material recedes when it is no longer useful for self-realization in a definite situation and from which it emerges when it again becomes suitable and appropriate for self-realization. "All the peculiarities which Freud enumerates as characteristic for the unconscious, correspond completely to the changes which normal behavior undergoes through isolation by disease" (1939, p. 323).

"Coming to Terms"
with the Environment
Although Goldstein as an organismic theorist emphasizes the inner determinants of behavior and the principle that the organism finds the environment that is most appropriate for self-actualization, he does not adopt the extreme position that the organism is immune to the events in the external world. He recognizes the importance of the objective world both as a source of disturbance with which the individ-

ual must cope and as a source of supplies by means of which the organism fulfills its destiny. That is, the environment intrudes upon the organism by stimulating or overstimulating it so that the organic equilibrium is upset, while on the other hand the upset organism searches in the environment for what it needs to equalize the inner tension. In other words, there is an interaction between the organism and the environment.

The person has to come to terms with the environment both because it affords the means by which self-actualization can be achieved and because it contains obstructions in the form of threats and pressures that hinder self-realization. Sometimes the threat from the environment may be so great that the individual's behavior becomes frozen by anxiety and he or she is unable to make any progress toward the goal. At other times, self-actualization may be hampered because the environment lacks those objects and conditions that are necessary for actualization.

Goldstein tells us that a normal, healthy organism is one "in which the tendency towards self-actualization is acting from within, and overcomes the disturbance arising from the clash with the world, not out of anxiety but out of the joy of conquest" (1939, p. 305). This moving statement suggests that coming to terms with the environment consists primarily of mastering it. If this cannot be done, then the person has to accept the difficulties and adjust as best as possible to the realities of the outer world. If the discrepancy between the organism's goals and the realities of the environment is too great, the organism either breaks down or has to give up some of its aims and try to actualize itself on a lower level of existence.

Goldstein has provided a concise summary of his views regarding the organization and dynamics of the organism in the following passage.

There is a continuous alteration as to which "part" of the organism stands in the foreground . . . and which in the background. The foreground is determined by the task which the organism has to fulfill at any given moment, i.e. by the situation in which the organism happens to find itself, and by the demands with which it has to cope.

The tasks are determined by the "nature" of the organism, its "essence," which is brought into actualization through environmental changes that act upon it. The expressions of this actualization are the performances of the organism. Through them the organism can deal with the respective environmental demands and actualize itself. The possibility of asserting itself in the world, while preserving its character, hinges upon a specific kind of "coming to terms" of the organism with its environment. This has to take place in such a fashion that each change of the organism, caused by environmental stimuli, *is equalized after a definite time,* so that the organism regains that "average" state which corresponds to its nature, which is "adequate" to it. *Only when this is the case is it possible that the same environmental events can produce the same changes,* can lead to the same effects and to the same experiences. Only under this condition can the organism maintain its constancy and identity. If this equalization towards the average or adequate state did not occur, then the same environmental events would produce diverse changes in the organism. Thereby, the environment would lose its constancy for the organism, and would alter continually. An ordered course of performances would be impossible. The organism would be in a continual state of disquiet, would be endangered in its existence, and *actually would be continuously* "another" organism. This, however, is actually not the case. On the contrary we can observe that the performances of the organism show a *relatively great constancy,* with fluctuations around a constant mean. If this relative constancy did not exist it would not even be possible to recognize an organism as such; we could not even *talk of a specific organism* (1939, pp. 111–112).

<table>
<tr><td>THE
DEVELOPMENT
OF THE
ORGANISM</td><td>Although the concept of self-actualization suggests that there are patterns or stages of development through which the person progresses, Goldstein does not have much to say concerning the course of growth, except for some generalities to the effect that behavior becomes more even and orderly and more fitted to the environment as</td></tr>
</table>

the person grows older. Goldstein hints that there are tasks peculiar to certain age levels but he does not specify what these tasks are or whether they are the same for all individuals. The importance of heredity is also implied but its relative contribution is not made explicit. Nor does Goldstein present a theory of learning. He does talk about the "reorganization" of old patterns into new and more effective patterns, the "repression of attitudes and urges that are in opposition to the development of the *whole* personality," the acquisition of preferred ways of behaving, the emergence of figure from background, the fixation of patterns of behavior by traumatic stimuli or by repetitive practice with isolated stimuli, adjustmental shifts, and substitute formations, but these notions are not brought together into a systematic theory of learning. They are most congenial to a Gestalt theory of learning.

Goldstein does say that if a child is exposed to situations with which it can cope, it will develop normally through maturation and training. As new problems arise it will form new patterns to deal with them. Reactions no longer useful for the goal of self-actualization will drop out. However, if the conditions of the environment are too arduous for the child's capacities, it will develop reactions inconsistent with the principle of self-actualization. In this case, the process tends to become isolated from the person's pattern of life. Isolation of a process is the primary condition for the development of pathological states. For example, humans are neither aggressive nor submissive by nature, but in order to fulfill their nature they sometimes have to be aggressive and at other times submissive, depending upon circumstances. However, should a strong, fixated habit of either aggression or submission be formed it will tend to have a disruptive influence upon personality by asserting itself at inappropriate times and in ways that are contrary to the interests of the whole person.

As an investigator trained in medicine and practicing the medical specialty of neuropsychiatry, Kurt Goldstein spent his long productive life studying symptoms and behavior patterns not as isolated events but as reactions that are embedded in and are expressions of the total organism. For Goldstein, a symptom is not simply a manifestation of changes in a specific function or structure of the organism; it is also to be considered as a form of adjustment made by the sick or defective person. In his study of the aphasias or language disturbances, for example, he rejects the theory that aphasia is the result of a lesion in a particular area of the brain and maintains instead that since *"language is a means of the individual to come to terms with the outer world and to realize himself"* (1948, p. 23) *"it follows that every individual speech-performance is understandable only from the aspect of its relation to the function of the total organism in its endeavor to realize itself as much as possible in the given situation"* (1948, p. 21).

CHARACTERISTIC RESEARCH AND RESEARCH METHODS

Beginning with his observations on soldiers who had received head wounds during the First World War, Goldstein has conducted numerous investigations on the effects of injury to the brain. These studies, most of which were published in Germany, have been brought together and summarized in his book *After-effects of brain injuries in war* (1942). This book is based on the observations of nearly two thousand patients, some of whom were seen more or less continuously for ten years, and it gives an account of the neurological and psychological symptoms of patients suffering from brain damage, methods of testing psychological functions, and the treatment of this type of patient. Throughout this book, as well as in his other published writings, Goldstein maintains a consistent organismic point of view, which illuminates and explains the behavior of brain-injured patients. For example, one marked feature of the behavior of these patients is their orderliness and neatness. They spend a great deal of time keeping their possessions in order and seeing that everything is ship-

Studies of Brain-injured Cases

shape. They are very good hospital patients because they quickly adapt themselves to routine activities and readily become absorbed in housekeeping tasks. Goldstein found that this behavior was a symptom resulting from their defect. By devoting their full attention to routine tasks, the patients were able to avoid the unusual and unexpected situation. Such situations may have catastrophic effects on the behavior of the patient. In other words, their routine orderliness is an expression of the struggle of the changed personality to cope with the defect by avoiding situations that can no longer be mastered or adjusted to. Indeed, much of the behavior of brain-injured persons is compensatory in character and permits them to come to terms with the world in the best possible way under the given circumstances.

Goldstein observes that the organism is very resilient and quickly adapts itself to any localized damage as long as the person feels that he or she can come to terms with their environment and is not thrown off balance by undue pressures from the external world. One patient was not able to recognize visually even the simplest form, yet he learned to read. He could differentiate between light and dark so that by following or tracing the border between the dark spots of the letters and the light area of the background, he could make out the words and read them. The motor images produced by the kinesthetic tracing of the dark spots took the place of visual images. This substitution was made unconsciously and the patient was not aware of how he did it. In this case, as in so many others, motivation plays an important role. A patient will make an effort to realize himself as much as possible in the environment if there is some incentive for doing so.

The organismic viewpoint regarding symptoms has practical implications as well as theoretical ones. In testing a brain-injured patient, for example, it is essential to employ tests and to administer them in such a way as to reveal the modifications in abilities that are the direct result of the damage and to distinguish these symptoms from those that arise as secondary reactions to the defect. One important reason for making this distinction is that the kind of training and therapy that is employed depends upon knowing what symptoms can be more or less directly remedied and what symptoms have to be altered by working on the personality as a whole. In the one case, a visual defect may be improved by specific training in the visual function; in the other case, an apparent visual defect may be removed by methods that increase the self-confidence of the patient.

The careful analysis of the meaning of a symptom also requires an intensive study of all aspects of the person's functioning. It is not enough ordinarily to give a patient a battery of tests that yield a set of numerical scores or pluses and minuses. The examiner must be alert to qualitative features of the patient's performance as well and pay heed to even the slightest clues that may shed light upon behavior. He or she must not depend entirely upon diagnostic tests, useful as these may be, for understanding the patient. The examiner must also observe patients in their daily life under more or less natural conditions, for the patients' success and failure in meeting the common problems of daily existence are the ultimate tests of their abilities. Goldstein favors the intensive study of a single case over a fairly long period of time.

The intensive study of one person is exemplified by a case of a brain-damaged, middle-aged man observed by Goldstein and his colleagues (Hanfmann, Rickers-Ovsiankina, and Goldstein, 1944) over a period of years. This man lived in an institution and his daily behavior in this setting as well as his performance in standardized test and interview situations were observed and recorded. He could find his way around the hospital quite well but this ability depended upon his recognition of fairly concrete objects rather than upon any generalized frames of reference. For example, he recognized the testing room because unlike the other rooms it had three windows in it. However, he had to open a number of doors before he found the correct one because he had no spatial orientation that would tell him where the room with the three windows was located. He learned to follow other patients to the shop where he worked and to the dining hall but if he got separated from them he became lost. He could recognize his own bedroom because he had tied a string to the bedpost. Someone watching him might think that he was fairly well oriented in space and time but a closer familiarity with his conduct would show otherwise.

Single Case Studies

He was usually sociable and friendly when he was with people but he did not form any kind of permanent attachment to another person. The reason for this was that he could not remember or recognize the same person from one day to the next. Only by a careful analysis of his total behavior was it revealed that his inability to form stable relations with others and be a permanent part of a group was due to a lack of recognition of characteristics that could be remembered rather than a distaste for social relations or a desire not to become involved intimately with another person.

He had great trouble listening to someone read or tell a story, not because he was distractible or because he lacked comprehension but because he could not distinguish between reality and fiction. If the story started out "Once there was a little boy," he began looking around for the boy and when he could not find him he became quite agitated. Everything that he experienced was regarded as existing here and now. Not only did he fail to differentiate between fact and fiction but he also could not understand what was meant by past, present, and future.

Once he was shown a picture of an animal and was asked to identify it. When he could not decide whether it was a dog or a horse, he spoke directly to the picture, saying "Are you a dog?" When the picture did not reply he became very angry. When he was given a mirror he looked behind it for the person he saw in the mirror and became excited when he did not find a person there. The casual observer might think that this patient was highly excitable and emotionally unstable from watching his behavior in various situations, when actually he was a fairly mild man whose excitement was brought on by threatening conditions of an environment that to a normal person would not have been threatening at all. When one does not possess any stable, dependable frames of reference regarding space and time, fact and fiction, object and subject, the world is bound to be an unpredictable and highly frustrating place.

Although he could not understand the principle of a mirror when it alone was shown to him, he behaved in an appropriate manner when he was given a comb along with a mirror. He took the comb, looked in the mirror, and combed his hair in quite a natural manner. This behavior showed that he had no abstract concept of a mirror as such but he did know how to use it for performing a concrete task. Another example of this same type of behavior was his failure to distinguish between a ball and an egg until he had discovered by trying them out that the ball was throwable whereas the egg was breakable and edible. He had no abstract concept of an egg and a ball. In fact, his capacity for abstract behavior was almost totally lacking, and it was this impairment of the abstract attitude that accounted for so much of his unusual behavior.

Another case studied intensively by the method of organismic theory was that of an eleven-year-old boy, a so-called "idiot savant" (Scheerer, Rothman, and Goldstein, 1945). In spite of his serious intellectual deficiency in some respects this boy could perform amazing feats of computation. Given the date of one's birthday he could rapidly tell what day of the week it fell on for any specified year. He was also regarded as a musical genius because he could reproduce any piece he heard on the piano. Actually however, a more careful analysis of his behavior revealed that his lightning calculations and his musical performances were merely mechanical reproductions. There was nothing creative about them. Given the native endowment of counting and playing by ear, he concentrated all of his energy in actualizing these two potentialities. He learned as a very young child that these were satisfying ways for coming to terms with the world and so they became his preferred performances. He had practically no ability for dealing with symbols, concepts, words, shapes, and other abstractions. His social relationships were virtually nonexistent although he had learned to say polite things in a robot fashion. His deficiencies all stemmed from a defect of the abstract attitude. The authors make the point that the "concept of abstract attitude should serve as a methodological frame of reference . . . for understanding of these symptoms from a unitary point of view" (p. 29).

Abstract Versus
Concrete Behavior

Goldstein's most important psychological studies have been made on abstract and concrete behavior. He and his associates have developed a number of tests for diagnosing the amount of impairment of the abstract attitude (Goldstein and Scheerer, 1941, 1953). These tests are widely used in clinical practice, especially for assessing the presence and amount of brain damage. Goldstein strongly urges the examiner who uses these tests not to be restricted to the mechanical adding up of passes and failures but to take note of the qualitative aspects of the patient's behavior during testing as well. Goldstein feels that these qualitative features may be even more enlightening than the numerical scores earned by the patient.

A detailed analysis of impairment of the abstract attitude produced by injury to the frontal lobes reveals the following deficiencies. (1) Patients are unable to separate the outer world from inner experience. For example, brain-injured patients cannot be induced to repeat the sentence "The sun is shining" when it is actually raining outside. (2) They cannot assume a set to do something willfully and consciously. When asked to set the hands of a clock to a certain hour, they cannot do it although they can recognize what time it is when presented with a clock. (3) They have no sense of spatial relations. They can point correctly to the source of a sound but cannot say what direction it is coming from. (4) They cannot shift from one task to another. When asked to call out a series of numbers starting with one they can do so, but when asked to start with a number other than one they are lost. (5) They are unable to hold a discrimination in mind for any length of time. For example, when instructed to cross out a particular letter in a printed passage they begin correctly but soon shift to crossing out every letter. (6) They lack the ability to react to an organized whole, to break the whole up into parts, and to synthesize them again. This defect prevents them from telling any sort of organized story to a picture. They can only enumerate the individual items in a picture. (7)

They cannot abstract the common properties of a series of objects or form any part–whole relationships. This means that they are unable to understand an analogy like "shoe is to foot as what is to hand?" (8) The brain-injured person is unable to plan ahead, to take into account the probability of something happening in the future, or to think in symbolic terms. He or she may be able to find their way around in a fixed environment but cannot draw a map or give a verbal account of how they got from one place to another.

A defect in the abstract attitude produces changes in the personality as a whole and cuts across all forms of behavior. The abstract attitude is not a synthesis of lower mental functions but represents an entirely new mental set in which the factor of conscious will is one of its most essential features. Lacking this attitude, the person is qualitatively different from the normal person.

Goldstein's empirical studies of abstract and concrete behavior illustrate the organismic dictum that whatever happens in one part of the organism affects the whole organism. In the case of a severe injury to the frontal lobes the effects are particularly massive. Injuries to other tissues or organs may be less dramatic and less obvious in their effects on the whole person, but whatever happens, happens to and affects the whole person. (For a careful, critical analysis of Goldstein's concepts of abstract and concrete behavior see Pikas, 1966.)

In this brief survey of Goldstein's research activities we have not been able to do justice to the richness of his empirical data; nor has it been possible to convey to the reader the full measure of his insights into the reasons for human conduct. We have merely tried to give some idea of the type of research strategy employed by a representative organismic theorist. This strategy may be summarized in the following set of directions to the investigator who wishes to conduct research in the organismic manner. (1) Study the whole person. (2) Make intensive studies of individual cases using tests, interviews, and observations under natural conditions. Do not depend upon just one type of evidence. (3) Try to understand the behavior of the person in terms of such system principles as self-actualization, coming to terms with the environment, abstract versus concrete attitudes rather than as specific responses to specific stimuli. (4) Use both qualitative and quantitative methods in the collection and analysis of the data. (5) Do not employ experimental controls and standardized conditions that destroy the integrity of the organism and make the behavior unnatural and artificial. (6) Always bear in mind that the organism is a complex structure and its behavior is the resultant of a vast network of determiners.

ANDRAS ANGYAL

Angyal, like Goldstein, feels that there is a need for a new science that will not be primarily psychological, sociological, or physiological in character but which will embrace the person as a whole. Unlike Goldstein, however, Angyal insists that it is impossible to differentiate the organism from the environment because they interpenetrate one another in such a complex manner that any attempt to unravel them tends to destroy the natural unity of the whole and to create an artificial distinction between organism and environment.

Andras Angyal is known primarily to psychologists for his important book, *Foundations for a science of personality* (1941). He was born in Hungary in 1902. Educated at the University of Vienna where he was awarded a Ph.D. in 1927 and at the University of Turin where he received an M.D. in 1932, Angyal came to the United States in 1932

Andras Angyal

as a Rockefeller fellow in the Department of Anthropology of Yale University. For a number of years he was engaged in research at Worcester State Hospital, Massachusetts, serving as Director of Research from 1937 to 1945. He left this post to enter private practice as a psychiatrist in Boston. In 1953 Angyal assumed the post of Psychiatric Consultant of the Counseling Center of Brandeis University. He died in 1960. Angyal's views on psychopathology and psychotherapy were posthumously published in a book, *Neurosis and treatment: A holistic theory* (1965) edited by two of his Brandeis associates, Eugenia Hanfmann and Richard Jones. (For biographical material on Angyal see Hanfmann, 1968.)

THE STRUCTURE OF THE BIOSPHERE

Angyal has coined a new term, the *biosphere,* to convey his conception of a holistic entity that includes both the individual and the environment "not as interacting parts, not as constituents which have independent existence, but as aspects of a single reality which can be separated only by abstraction" (1941, p. 100). The biosphere does not refer exclusively to somatic processes as the name suggests but includes the psychological and social as well. The psychological domain consists of the symbolic functions of the organism—that is, perceiving, thinking, remembering, imagining, and the like; the social domain consists of the individual's interactions with society.

Although the biosphere is an indivisible whole, it possesses an organization that consists of systems structurally articulated with one another. It is the task of the organismic scientist to identify those lines of demarcation within the biosphere that are prescribed by the natural structure of the whole itself. These lines of division constitute the real holistic units of the biosphere.

The largest and most basic division that can be made in the biosphere is that between the organism, which is called the *subject,* and the environment, which is called the *object.* The organism constitutes one pole of the biosphere and the environment constitutes the other pole, and the whole dynamics of life consists of the interactions between these two poles. Angyal maintains that neither organismic processes nor environmental events alone reflect reality but rather that *biospheric occurrences,* which are bipolar in character, are the reality with which the biological and social scientist must deal. "Instead of studying the 'organism' and the 'environment' and their interaction, we propose to study life as a unitary whole and endeavor to describe the organization and dynamics of the biosphere" (1941, pp. 100–101).

Angyal acknowledges that it is possible to distinguish between processes that fall more under the domination of organismic government from those that are more environmentally governed, although processes can never be exclusively one or the other. They are always biospheric.

The holistic units of the biosphere are called *systems*. Angyal prefers system analysis to the more usual type of relationship analysis that is employed in psychology for the following reasons.

1. A system may include as many members as are necessary to explain a given phenomenon whereas a relationship involves only two members. Angyal feels that the reduction of a complex structure like that of the biosphere to pairs of related members tends to destroy its natural coherence and unity and oversimplify the kinds of connections that exist in the biosphere.

2. The components of a system are connected with one another by virtue of their respective positions in the system whereas the members of a relationship are connected by virtue of possessing some common property such as color or form. Two red objects are related to one another by their redness, but the parts of a machine are organized in terms of their respective positions in the whole machine. Angyal feels that position is more important than attribute for organismic analysis. In a power system, such as a government or other institution, the position of each person in the system is far more important than any specific relationship that a person may possess with other members of the system.

3. The members of a system need have no direct connection with one another but the two members of a relationship must be directly connected. This necessity for direct connection limits the kind of analysis that can be made using relations. For instance, two citizens of the same country may have absolutely no direct relation to one another yet as holistic units living within the same political region they are governed by the same laws and customs.

For these reasons Angyal believes that systems, not relations, are the true holistic units of the biosphere. In a paper on the holistic approach in psychiatry (1948) Angyal states that system analysis consists of two steps: (1) the location of the context in which a given phenomenon belongs, and (2) the determination of its position in this context. When these two steps are taken, the phenomenon is said to be properly defined and fully explained. (For a further discussion of the theory of systems in biology and psychology see Bertalanffy, 1950a, 1950b, 1962; Krech, 1950.)

One important property of a system is its rigidity or plasticity. In a rigid system the parts have fixed positions and are relatively immovable whereas in a plastic system the parts are more flexible and can shift about to form new constellations within the system. As might be expected, events produced by a rigid system are highly standardized and uniform whereas those produced by a plastic system have a broad range of functional variations. The processes that go on in a rigid system are likely to be quite localized happenings which have little impact upon surrounding systems; those of a plastic system tend to spread into neighboring systems. Rigid systems tend to be associated with a high degree of environmental stability and plastic systems with a low degree of environmental stability. The operations of a rigid system run off more automatically and with less conscious control than those of a plastic system. Both kinds of systems are found in the biosphere in varying degrees. Sensory-neuromuscular functions, for example, tend to be fairly plastic and visceral functions tend to be fairly rigid.

A system consists of parts that are either fully differentiated or still embedded in the whole in an undifferentiated state. Differentiation of parts within the whole occurs when a complex operation requires a division of labor among the parts of the system. In a highly differentiated whole the parts are more individualized and possess greater relative autonomy. Since this state of affairs tends to produce disunity and disintegration in the system and will eventually destroy the system if allowed to go unchecked, there has to be a counterbalancing principle. This principle that is integrative in nature coordinates the differentiated part functions under the general system principle of *self-expansion*. A system expands by successive stages of differentiation and integration, although the tendency of any system is to be conservative with respect to differentiation and to permit it only when it is absolutely essential.

A part of a whole has to have two characteristics; it must be relatively complete in itself and it has to occupy a position in a system that does not require the mediation of intermediary systems for its maintenance. In other words, it has to be relatively autonomous and independent without becoming isolated from the system.

The Dimensions of Personality Structure

There are three main dimensions within the biosphere. These are called vertical, progressive, and transverse. The *vertical* dimension extends from overt behavior at the surface of the biosphere down into the central core of the biosphere. Occurrences that lie near the surface are the concrete or behavioral expressions of deeper processes. An act of aggression, for example, is the expression of an underlying attitude of hostility and this attitude in turn can be traced to even deeper lying and more generalized attitudes. Surface behavior changes more easily than do the deeper processes. The goal of surface behavior is to create a biospheric condition that represents the satisfaction of a need in the core of personality. As a rule, gratification cannot be achieved with one behavior act; rather a succession of acts is required. A series of acts that brings the person closer and closer to a final goal constitutes the *progressive* dimension. The points along this dimension are defined in terms of the distance from the goal. The *transverse* dimension consists of the coordination of discrete acts into a larger, better integrated, and more effective behavior unit. Accordingly, any behavior act can be described as an expression of underlying processes, as a phase in a means-end organization, and as a coordination of discrete acts. For example, the taking of an examination that represents an overt activity on the surface of the biosphere fulfills the deeper need to prove one's intellectual adequacy. At the same time, it is a step along the progressive dimension toward the ultimate goal of becoming a fully educated person. It also represents the coordination of many discrete facts that have been learned during the course of study.

The Symbolic Self

Angyal observes that humans are capable of developing ideas about themselves as organisms because many of their organic processes become conscious. The sum total of these self-conceptions constitutes the symbolic self. However, Angyal warns us that the symbolic self is not always a reliable representation of the organism, that what a person thinks about himself or herself rarely yields a true picture of reality. Consequently, if behavior is governed by the symbolic self, that is, if people behave according to the image they have of themselves, their behavior may not be appropriate to the real needs of the organism. "The relative segregation of the symbolic self within the organism is perhaps the most vulnerable point of the human personality organization" (1941, p. 121), because the symbolic self may falsify and distort the reality of the biosphere.

THE DYNAMICS OF THE BIOSPHERE

The energy of the biosphere is supplied by the tensions that arise between the environmental pole and the organismic pole. These tensions arise because the environment pulls in one direction and the organism in another. These opposite directional trends of the organism and the environment within the biosphere are called *autonomy* and *homonomy* respectively. The trend toward autonomy consists of the expansion of the organism by assimilating and mastering the environment. It is analogous to an egoistic drive in which the person strives to satisfy cravings and advance interests by bending the environment to their needs. The trend toward autonomy is expressed through a number of specific channels, for instance, the desire for superiority, for acquisition, for exploration, and for achievement. The trend toward homonomy motivates the person to fit him or her self to the environment and to share and participate in something that is larger than the individual self. One submerges one's individuality by forming a harmonious union with the social group, with nature, or with a supernatural, omnipotent being. Homonomy expresses itself through such specific motives as the desire for love, interpersonal relation, and esthetic experiences, love of nature, religious sentiments, and patriotism. Angyal says that in a general sense "the whole concept of homonomy could be equated with love" (1965, p. 16).

In another presentation of his views, Angyal (1951, 1952) has called these directional trends of the biosphere, self-determination versus self-surrender.

Although autonomy or self-determination and homonomy or self-surrender may appear to be opposed to one another, they are really two phases of a more inclusive trend of the biosphere, that of *self-expansion*. The person is an open system with an input phase and an output phase. The input phase consists of assimilating the environment, which is the basis for autonomy, and the output phase consists of productivity, which is the basis for homonomy. Both phases are necessary for the full development of the individual. The person develops him or her self by incorporating things from the environment and expands the environment by making personal contributions to it. One both takes and gives and in so doing expands the whole biosphere that, it will be remembered, includes both the organism and the environment. The trends toward increased autonomy and increased homonomy, that is, toward self-expansion, constitute the chief system principle of the biosphere.

THE DEVELOPMENT OF PERSONALITY

Angyal views personality as an extended "temporal Gestalt" or pattern in which past, present, and future are firmly embedded. Personality is an organized process extending through time. The past is not immutable; it changes as a past event acquires a new positional value in the biosphere. An experience that was terrifying when it occurred in childhood may be remembered later as merely a ludicrous incident. Consequently, the influence of the past on the present is continuously changing. The future is always active in the present as a potentiality or disposition. It, too, can change as the biosphere undergoes reorganization. New hopes supplant old ones as a person grows older.

The course of life is not merely a sequence of episodes in which tensions arise and are resolved; it also possesses an intrinsic design or purpose. For Angyal, this central design of life is the desire to shape one's existence into a meaningful, fully expanded whole that will give perfect coherence and unity to one's life. Development consists of forming a strong, extended, integrated pattern.

Angyal (1965) observes, however, that instead of just one pattern of personality developing there are actually two. One pattern is healthy, the other is neurotic. The former is based on feelings of confidence that one can realize one's autonomous and homonomous strivings; the latter grows out of isolation, feelings of helplessness, being unloved, and doubts about one's abilities to master the environment. These two patterns exist in everyone but one is usually dominant over the other. Moreover, one pattern can be replaced by the other very suddenly since it is not the elements that change but the guiding system principle of health or neurosis.

Health and neurosis are to be thought of as two organized processes, two dynamic Gestalts organizing the same material, so that each item has a position within two different patterns. There can be shifts between the two, lasting or short lived, in either direction, but at any given moment the person is either healthy or neurotic depending on which system is dominant (1965, p. 103).

Angyal likens this dual organization of personality to an ambiguous figure that may be seen in either of two ways. The elements of the figure remain the same but what is seen changes. This theory of universal ambiguity, as Angyal calls it, has far-reaching implications for the treatment of neurotic people. "It precludes the conception of neurosis as a rotten part of a healthy apple, or a limited segregated growth within the person, a plant that can be pulled out by the roots without disturbing or changing the rest of the personality. The neurotic person is neurotic throughout, in every area of his life, in all the crannies and crevices of his existence" (1965, pp. 103–104).

Development proceeds along the three dimensions of personality. In the depth dimension, the person grows from a median position on the scale outward as well as inward. He or she develops deeper, more profound needs as well as more elaborate behavior patterns by which to satisfy the needs. In the progressive dimension, development means increased efficiency and productivity. He or she gets to their goals more directly and with less wasted motion. In the transverse dimension, growth results in better coordination and a greater versatility of behavior. Harmonious growth in all three dimensions enriches and expands the personality.

The span of life is divided into phases in which each phase forms a relatively autonomous part of the whole temporal pattern. A phase is defined by a particular problem of life that furnishes the theme for that period and gives to it its specific meaning. Thus, the theme of the first phase of life centers around eating and sleeping. Later, the opportunities and relevancies of the environment are discovered. During the early part of this phase the child does not recognize the independent nature of the environment and deals with it in an arbitrary and unrealistic manner. It tries to force the environment to be what it wants it to be. The limitations of this approach are soon realized, however, and the child gradually learns to accommodate itself to the objective properties of the environment. The uniformities of development throughout the successive phases are due to maturational sequences and to cultural standardization. However, it is impossible to predict with complete accuracy the course of a person's life because the influence of the environment cannot always be known beforehand. Environmental events are pretty much independent of and beyond the control and foresight of the person; they are fortuitous and unpredictable. Predictions may be made on the basis of the laws of personality development but such predictions are merely approximate. One can predict with reasonable accuracy that a young person will eventually enter some vocation, but to foretell exactly what vocation it will be involves considerable guesswork. However, as a person grows older, he or she becomes more rigid and set in their ways and less open to influences from the environment, so that their behavior is easier to foretell.

Although Angyal acknowledges that regression can and does occur, he feels, like Jung, that regression often serves the forward-going tendency of personality growth. That is, an individual may learn something from regression that enables him or her to return to their present problems and wrestle more effectively with them.

Angyal also believes that the symbolic functions of the organism, for example, thinking, develop with age and that "the center of gravity of life shifts more and more toward the psychological realm" (1941, p. 77). As people grow older they tend to satisfy more and more of their needs by means of instrumental psychological processes. That is, they spend more time thinking and less time acting.

Angyal does not espouse or enunciate any theory of learning. He is content to use such terms as differentiation, reorganization, shifting, and the like, most of which are borrowed from the vocabulary of Gestalt psychology.

ABRAHAM MASLOW

Abraham Maslow in his numerous writings [see especially *Motivation and personality* (1954, revised edition, 1970), *Toward a psychology of being* (1968a), and *The farther reaches of human nature* (1971)] espoused a holistic-dynamic point of view that has much in common with those of Goldstein and Angyal, who were colleagues of his at Brandeis University. Maslow considered that his position fell within the broad province of humanistic psychology—which he characterized as a "third force" in American psychology, the other two being behaviorism and psychoanalysis.

Maslow was born in Brooklyn, New York, on April 1, 1908. All of his degrees were earned at the University of Wisconsin where he did research on primate behavior. For fourteen years (1937–1951) he was on the faculty of Brooklyn College. In 1951, Maslow went to Brandeis University where he remained until 1969 when he became resident fellow of the Laughlin Foundation in Menlo Park, California. Maslow suffered a fatal heart attack on June 8, 1970.

Since his death a number of books about his life and work have appeared. Among these are a memorial volume containing eulogies, some unpublished notes by Maslow, and a complete bibliography of his writings (B. G. Maslow, 1972) and an intellectual portrait by a close associate (Lowry, 1973a). Lowry (1973b) has also brought together in one volume the germinal papers by Maslow. Other books on Maslow have been written by Goble (1970) and Wilson (1972).

We shall single out for discussion some of the distinctive features of Maslow's views regarding personality. It is important to bear in mind that Maslow, unlike Goldstein and Angyal who based their views on the study of brain damaged and mentally disturbed persons, draws upon his investigations of healthy and creative persons to arrive at certain formulations regarding personality.

Maslow upbraids psychology for its "pessimistic, negative and limited conception" of humans. He feels that psychology has dwelled more upon human frailties than it has upon human strengths; that it has thoroughly explored the sins while neglecting the virtues. Psychology has seen life in terms of an individual making desperate attempts to avoid pain rather than in taking active steps to gain pleasure and happiness. Where is the psychology, Maslow asks, that takes account of gaiety, exuberance, love, and well-being to the same extent that it deals with misery, conflict, shame, and hostility? Psychology "has voluntarily restricted itself to only half of its rightful jurisdiction, and that the darker, meaner half." Maslow has undertaken to supply the other half of the picture, the brigher, better half, and to give a portrait of the whole person.

He writes as follows.

Now let me try to present briefly and at first dogmatically the essence of this newly developing conception of the psychiatrically healthy man. First of all and most important of all is the strong belief that man has an essential nature of his own, some skeleton of psychological structure that may be treated and discussed analogously with his physical structure, that he has needs, capacities and tendencies that are genetically based, some of which are characteristic of the whole human species, cutting across all cultural lines, and some of which are unique to the individual. These needs are on their face good or neutral rather than evil. Second, there is involved the conception that full healthy and normal and desirable development consists in actualizing this nature, in fulfilling these potentialities, and in developing into maturity along the lines that this hidden, covert, dimly seen essential nature dictates, growing from within rather than being shaped from without. Third, it is now seen clearly that psychopathology in general results from the denial or the frustration or the twisting of man's essential nature. By this conception what is good? Anything that conduces to this desirable development in the direction of actualization of the inner nature of man. What is bad or abnormal? Anything that frustrates or blocks or denies the essential nature of man. What is psychopathological? Anything that disturbs or frustrates or twists the course of self-actualization. What is psychotherapy, or for that matter any therapy of any kind? Any means of any kind that helps to restore the person to the path of self-actualization and of development along the lines that his inner nature dictates (1954, pp. 340–341).

In a further statement of his basic assumptions, Maslow has added this important one:

This inner nature is not strong and overpowering and unmistakable like the instincts of animals. It is weak and delicate and subtle and easily overcome by habit, cultural pressure, and wrong attitudes toward it. Even though weak, it rarely disappears in the normal person—perhaps not even in the sick person. Even though denied, it persists underground forever pressing for actualization (1968a, p. 4).

Further, Maslow writes "All the evidence that we have (mostly clinical evidence, but already some other kinds of research evidence) indicates that it is reasonable to assume in practically every human being, and certainly in almost every newborn baby, that there is an active will toward health, an impulse towards growth, or towards the actualization of human potentialities" (1967b).

In these eloquent and representative passages, Maslow has made a number of striking assumptions regarding the nature of humans. People have an inborn nature that is essentially good or at least neutral. It is not inherently evil. This is a novel conception since many theorists assume that some of the instincts are bad or antisocial and must be tamed by training and socialization.

As personality unfolds through maturation in a benign environment and by active efforts on the part of the person to realize their nature, the creative powers of humans manifest themselves ever more clearly. When humans are miserable or neurotic, it is because the environment has made them so through ignorance and social pathology, or because they have distorted their thinking. Maslow also feels that many people are afraid of and draw back from becoming fully human (self-actualized). Destructiveness and violence, for example, are not indigenous to humans. They become destructive when their inner nature is twisted or denied or frustrated. Maslow (1968b) distinguishes between pathological violence and healthy aggression that contends against injustice, prejudice, and other social ills.

Maslow (1967a) has propounded a theory of human motivation that differentiates between basic needs and metaneeds. The basic needs are those of hunger, affection, security, self-esteem, and the like. Metaneeds are those of justice, goodness, beauty, order, unity, and so forth. The basic needs are deficiency needs whereas the metaneeds are growth needs. The basic needs are prepotent over the metaneeds in most cases and are arranged in a hierarchical order. The metaneeds have no hierarchy—they are equally potent—and can be fairly easily substituted for one another. The metaneeds are as instinctive or inherent in humans as the basic needs are, and when they are not fulfilled the person may become sick. These metapathologies consist of such states as alienation, anguish, apathy, and cynicism.

Maslow believes that if psychologists study crippled, stunted, neurotic people exclusively they are bound to produce a crippled psychology. In order to develop a more complete and comprehensive science of the human person it is also incumbent upon psychologists to study people who have realized their potentialities to the fullest. Maslow has done just this; he has made an intensive and far-reaching investigation of a group of self-actualizing people. They are rare birds as Maslow found when he was securing his group. After finding suitable subjects, some of whom were historical personages, such as Lincoln, Jefferson, Walt Whitman, Thoreau, and Beethoven, while others were living at the time they were studied, like Eleanor Roosevelt, Einstein, and friends and acquaintances of the investigator, they were investigated clinically to discover what characteristics distinguished them from the ordinary run of people. These turned out to be their distinguishing features: (1) They are realistically oriented. (2) They accept themselves, other people, and the natural world for what they are. (3) They have a great deal of spontaneity. (4) They are problem-centered rather than self-centered. (5) They have an air of detachment and a need for privacy. (6) They are autonomous and independent. (7) Their appreciation of people and things is fresh rather than stereotyped. (8) Most of them have had profound mystical or spiritual experiences although not necessarily religious in character.

(9) They identify with mankind. (10) Their intimate relationships with a few specially loved people tend to be profound and deeply emotional rather than superficial. (11) Their values and attitudes are democratic. (12) They do not confuse means with ends. (13) Their sense of humor is philosophical rather than hostile. (14) They have a great fund of creativeness. (15) They resist conformity to the culture. (16) They transcend the environment rather than just coping with it.

Maslow has also investigated the nature of what he calls "peak experiences." Reports were obtained in answer to the request to think of the most wonderful experiences in one's life. It was found that persons undergoing peak experiences feel more integrated, more at one with the world, more their own boss, more spontaneous, less aware of space and time, more perceptive and so on (1968a, Chapters 6 and 7).

Maslow (1966) has been critical of science. He feels that classical mechanistic science as represented by behaviorism is not suitable for studying the whole person. He advocates a humanistic science not as an alternative to mechanistic science but as a complement to it. Such a humanistic science would deal with questions of value, individuality, consciousness, purpose, ethics and "the higher reaches of human nature."

It appears that Maslow's unique contribution to the organismic viewpoint lies in his preoccupation with healthy people rather than sick ones, and his feeling that studies of these two groups generate different types of theory. Both Goldstein and Angyal, as medical specialists and psychotherapists, have come into contact with defective and disorganized people, yet in spite of this biased sample each has fashioned a theory that embraces the whole organism, and one that applies to the sick as well as to the healthy. Maslow has chosen the more direct course of studying healthy people whose wholeness and unity of personality are readily apparent. As self-actualizers, these people whom Maslow has observed are the embodiment of organismic theory.

CURRENT STATUS AND EVALUATION

Organismic theory as a reaction against mind-body dualism, faculty psychology, and stimulus-response behaviorism has been immensely successful. Who is there in psychology today who is not a proponent of the main tenets of organismic theory that the whole is something other than the sum of its parts, that what happens to a part happens to the whole, and that there are no separate compartments within the organism? What psychologist believes that there is a mind that is separate from the body, a mind that obeys laws different from those pertaining to the body? Who believes that there are isolated events, insulated processes, detached functions? Very few if any psychologists subscribe any longer to an atomistic viewpoint. We are all organismic psychologists whatever else we may be.

In this sense, organismic theory is more of an attitude or orientation or frame of reference than it is a systematic behavior theory. It says, in effect, that since everything is related to the whole, true understanding results from the correct placing of a phenomenon within the context of the total system. It directs the investigator to take into account a web of variables rather than pairs of variables, to consider the event that he or she is studying as a component of a system rather than as an isolated happening. To understand the laws by which the total system operates *is* in fact the ultimate concern of scientists; it is the ideal toward which they constantly strive. The organismic viewpoint as applied within the province of human psychology asserts that the total person is the natural unit of study. Since the normal, healthy human being, or any other organism for that matter, always functions as an organized whole, the person should be studied as an organized whole. While recognizing that present techniques of research and quantitative analysis may not permit the psychological investigator to realize the organismic goal of studying the whole person, it urges psychology to find the means for doing so. If quantitative methods are not available then qualitative methods should be used. Meanwhile, psychology should address itself to the task of developing methods that will bring it closer to the organismic goal of understanding the whole person. Organismic theory in this sense is much more of a set of directives than it is a system of facts, principles, and laws.

There is not one official organismic theory of personality; there are many. An organismic theory of personality is defined by the attitude of the theorist, not by the contents of the model of personality that is constructed. If the theory focuses upon the whole organism as a unified system rather than upon separate traits or drives or habits then the theory may be called an organismic one. Goldstein, Angyal, Maslow, Allport, Murray, Rogers, Freud, Jung, and virtually all other contemporary personality theorists adopt an organismic orientation yet there are radical differences among these theories. What Goldstein finds in the organism is not precisely what Allport or Freud finds there, although all three may be classified properly as organismic in their general orientation.

There is little to find fault with in the organismic approach because it is so universally accepted. One can, however, evaluate a *particular* organismic theory such as Goldstein's or Angyal's. Perhaps the most serious charge that has been made against Goldstein's version of organismic theory is that it is not sufficiently holistic. Goldstein treats the organism as a segregated unit that is set apart from the rest of the world. The skin is the boundary between the organism and the world; exchanges take place across the boundary but the organism and the environment are treated as separate realms. A thoroughgoing holistic approach would make no such arbitrary division between what takes place within the skin and what takes place outside of it. The organism should be regarded as a differentiated component of a larger system, a system that includes the whole universe. Goldstein, while acknowledging the truth of this criticism, would reply that the whole universe is much too large a chunk for any scientist to study. The holistic theorist has to be realistic about what can and what cannot be taken into account. It is conceivable that events in outer space affect our behavior but we just do not possess the means of including such events within our scientific ken. Tennyson's flower in the crannied wall, could he but know it "all and all, I should know what God and man is" is a moving poetic truth, but it is scarcely an attainable goal. Although everything is related to everything else, Goldstein believes that many of the strands making up the total cosmic web are so distantly connected with one another that they can be ignored without doing any serious injustice to our understanding of personality.

Where is one to draw the line, however, and say "Beyond this boundary the effects are virtually zero"? If everything is a component in the grand scheme of nature, how can it be known without making a test what is and what is not relevant? The answer obviously is that it cannot be known. W. A. Hunt (1940) in reviewing *The organism* calls this the organismic paradox. The organismic theorist denies the validity of partitive concepts yet is forced to use them. If Goldstein is justified in treating a part, the organism, as a segregated whole, then why is another psychologist not justified in considering learning or perception or emotion as holistic processes? Angyal's biosphere is one attempt to broaden the holistic base of organismic theory. According to this conception, the organism and the environment are poles of a larger system. If by environment Angyal means everything in the universe other than the organism, then the total biospheric system is identical with the universe, and the paradox is resolved.

That the question of deciding where to draw the limits of one's system is not an academic one is indicated by the diverse hypotheses that have been put forward to explain human conduct. For example, serious attempts have been made to show that the course of the stars influences human behavior, that remote historical and prehistorical happenings as well as future events have a bearing upon present behavior. If clairvoyance and mental telepathy should prove to be true—and there are many today who believe that they are authentic phenomena—the limits of the holistic system to which a person belongs would be greatly extended. In the light of these considerations Goldstein's critics may well ask: Why stop at the skin, or even at the boundary of the near environment?

A number of more or less specific criticisms have been raised regarding Goldstein's theory. He has been criticized for not distinguishing sufficiently between what is inherent in the organism and what has been put there by the culture. Kattsoff (1942), for example, has raised this question. Goldstein's concept of self-actualization has been regarded as being too general in character to be useful for making specific predictions. Skinner (1940) considers self-actualization a metaphysical concept because it cannot be put to an experimental test. Some psychologists object to Goldstein's apparent disregard of statistical analysis in favor of a qualitative approach in his role as an investigator. These psychologists feel that qualitative analysis is highly subjective and that it is difficult to repeat an investigation when it is couched in purely qualitative terms. Other psychologists do not see eye to eye with Goldstein's strictures regarding the use of psychological tests. They feel that tests should be administered and scored in a standardized manner and that they should not be changed to meet the needs of the individual case. Goldstein has been criticized for placing too much emphasis upon maturation and not enough upon learning, and for exaggerating the importance of the abstract attitude in psychological functioning. Finally, there have been objections to trying to understand the normal personality by studying brain-injured patients. In spite of these specific criticisms, the prevailing attitude among psychologists toward the theoretical formulations of Goldstein is a highly favorable one. In conjunction with the holistic psychologies of the Gestaltists, of Lewin, and of Tolman, Goldstein's views have had great influence upon contemporary psychology and his significance as a theorist can hardly be overestimated.

When we come to evaluate Angyal's work our task is more difficult than is the case with Goldstein. Angyal's volume, Foundations for a science of personality (1941), received little critical notice when it was published and there has been little public response to his views during the last fifteen years. This is surprising not only because it is a very provocative and in many respects a highly original piece of theoretical reasoning but also because Angyal made a serious effort to formulate a theory of personality, something that Goldstein never essayed. The reason for this neglect may be due to Angyal's failure to heel in his theoretical speculations in the fertile soil of clinical observations and experimental investigations. Although Angyal has published a number of research papers, they do not seem to have much connection with his systematic position. Goldstein, on the other hand, has rich data from the clinic and the laboratory with which to support and illustrate his general theory. Whatever the reason may be for psychology's failure to react to Angyal's book, the fact remains that it has not received the critical attention that it merits.

It remains to be seen whether Angyal's posthumously published book, *Neurosis and treatment,* will have any more impact on the psychological community than the first volume did. *Neurosis and treatment* was written after Angyal had been engaged in clinical activities for a number of years, and the abstruse concepts of the earlier volume are illuminated by case material in the new one. Moreover, Angyal now has some articulate promulgators of his views, among them being Eugenia Hanfmann, Richard Jones, and Abraham Maslow. Maddi (1968), in his comparative analysis of personality theories, devotes considerable space to a consideration of Angyal's views. Whether the theory has relevance for areas other than psychotherapy is something that only the future can tell. It has not generated any personality research in its own right although it may have had subterranean influences on some investigators.

The concept of a biosphere that includes both the organism and its environment is not entirely successful in solving the problem of how to bring the person and the world into some kind of holistic union. In reading Angyal one is puzzled by his tendency to treat the two not as poles of a single globe but as distinctive entities that interact with one another. In spite of his concept of an all-inclusive biosphere, Angyal writes as though it were still a matter of an organism versus an environment. The environment does things to the person and the person does things to the environment; they do not seem to behave as components of a single system. Whereas Lewin gets himself trapped in a purely psychological world, Angyal seems to be lost in the whole universe. Whenever Angyal discusses concrete problems dealing with personality organization, dynamics, and development, he has to put aside the notion of a cosmic whole and deal with the organism and the environment as separate but interdependent and interacting systems.

Maslow's version of organismic theory may turn out to be more influential than any of the others. Maslow was an indefatigable and articulate writer and lecturer. Moreover, he became one of the leaders of humanistic psychology that appeals to many psychologists. In reading Maslow it is sometimes difficult to draw the line between the inspirational and the scientific. Some critics believe that humanistic psychology is more of a secular replacement for religion than it is a scientific psychology. Others feel that the contributions of the humanists to the empirical foundations of psychology have not been commensurate with their speculative writings. Some psychologists accuse the humanists of accepting as true that which is still hypothetical, of confusing theory with ideology, and of substituting rhetoric for research. In spite of these criticisms of the sort of psychology that Maslow stands for, there are a large number of psychologists who are attracted to this viewpoint because it tries to deal with vital and contemporary human concerns.

In conclusion it may be said that organismic theory for all of its weaknesses has tried to right the wrong committed by Descartes three hundred years ago. It has conscientiously insisted that the organism is not a dual system of mind and body, each with its own motors of driving principles, but that it is a single entity consisting of many part-functions. For promulgating and promoting this cardinal conception, the organismic point of view richly deserves the esteem in which it is held.

BIBLIOGRAPHY
PRIMARY SOURCES

Angyal, A. *Foundations for a science of personality*. New York: Commonwealth Fund, 1941.

Angyal, A. *Neurosis and treatment: a holistic theory*. New York: Wiley, 1965.

Goldstein, K. The organism. New York: American Book Co., 1939.

Goldstein, K. *Human nature in the light of psychopathology*. Cambridge: Harvard Univ. Press, 1940.

Maslow, A. H. *Motivation and personality*. New York: Harper, 1954, 2nd ed., 1970.

Maslow, A. H. *Toward a psychology of being*. (2nd ed.) Princeton: Van Nostrand, 1968a.

Maslow, A. H. *The farther reaches of human nature*. New York: Viking Press, 1971.

REFERENCES

Angyal, A. *Foundations for a science of personality*. New York: Commonwealth Fund, 1941.

Angyal, A. The holistic approach in psychiatry. *Amer. J. Psychiat.*, 1948, **105**, 178–182.

Angyal, A. A theoretical model for personality studies. *J. Pers.*, 1951, **20**, 131–142. (Reprinted in D. Krech and G. S. Klein (Eds.). *Theoretical models and personality theory*. Durham, N.C.: Duke Univ. Press, 1952, 131–142.)

Angyal, A. *Neurosis and treatment: a holistic theory*. New York: Wiley, 1965.

Bernard, C. *An introduction to the study of experimental medicine*. New York: Dover, 1957. (First published in 1866.)

Bertalanffy, L. von. An outline of general system theory. *Brit. J. Phil. Sci.*, 1950a, **1**, 134–165.

Bertalanffy, L. von. The theory of open systems in physics and biology. *Science*, 1950b, **111**, 23–29.

Bertalanffy, L. von. General system theory. *General Systems: Yearbook of the Society for General Systems Research,* 1962, **7,** 1–20.

Coghill, G. E. *Anatomy and the problem of behavior.* London: Cambridge Univ. Press, 1929.

Dewey, J. The reflex arc concept in psychology. *Psychol. Rev.,* 1896, **3,** 357–370.

Dunbar, H. Flanders. *Emotions and bodily changes.* (4th ed.) New York: Columbia Univ. Press, 1954.

Gelb, A., and Goldstein, K. *Psychologische Analysen hirnpathologischer Faelle.* Leipzig: Barth, 1920. (Partially translated in W. D. Ellis (Ed.). *Source book of Gestalt psychology.* New York: Harcourt, 1938, selections 26–30.)

Goble, F. G. *The third force: the psychology of Abraham Maslow.* New York: Grossman, 1970.

Goldstein, K. *The organism.* New York: American Book Co., 1939.

Goldstein, K. *Human nature in the light of psychopathology.* Cambridge: Harvard Univ. Press, 1940.

Goldstein, K. *After-effects of brain injuries in war.* New York: Grune and Stratton, 1942.

Goldstein, K. *Language and language disturbances.* New York: Grune and Stratton, 1948.

Goldstein, K. Autobiography. In E. G. Boring and G. Lindzey (Eds.). *A history of psychology in autobiography.* Vol. 5. New York: Appleton-Century-Crofts, 1967, pp. 147–166.

Goldstein, K., and Scheerer, M. Abstract and concrete behavior: an experimental study with special tests. *Psychol. Monogr.,* 1941, **53** (2).

Goldstein, K., and Scheerer, M. Tests of abstract and concrete thinking. A. Tests of abstract and concrete behavior. In A. Weider (Ed.). *Contributions toward medical psychology.* New York: Ronald Press, 1953.

Hanfmann, E. Andras Angyal. In D. L. Sills (Ed.). *International encyclopedia of the social sciences.* New York: Macmillan and Free Press, 1968, 302–304.

Hanfmann, E. Rickers-Ovsiankina, M., and Goldstein, K. Case Lanuti: extreme concretization of behavior due to damage of the brain cortex. *Psychol. Monogr.,* 1944, **57** (4).

Hunt, W. A. Review of K. Goldstein's *The organism. Psychol. Bull.,* 1940, **37,** 637–639.

Jackson, J. H. *Selected writings of John Hughlings Jackson.* J. Taylor (Ed.). London: Hodder and Stoughton, 1931.

Kantor, J. R. *Principles of psychology.* 2 vols. New York: Knopf, 1924.

Kantor, J. R. *A survey of the science of psychology.* Bloomington, Ind.: Principia Press, 1933.

Kantor, J. R. *Problems of physiological psychology.* Bloomington, Ind.: Principia Press, 1947.

Katsoff, L. O. Review of K. Goldstein's *Human nature in the light of psychopathology. J. Gen. Psychol.,* 1942, **26,** 187–194.

Krech, D. Dynamic systems as open neurological systems. *Psychol. Rev.*, 1950, **57,** 345–361.

Lowry, R. J. *A. H. Maslow: an intellectual portrait.* Monterey, Calif.: Brooks/Cole, 1973a.

Lowry, R. J. *Dominance, self-esteem, self-actualization: germinal papers of A. H. Maslow.* Monterey, Calif.: Brooks/Cole, 1973b.

Maddi, S. R. *Personality theories: a comparative analysis.* Homewood, Ill.: Dorsey Press, 1968.

Maslow, A. H. *Motivation and personality.* New York: Harper, 1954, 2nd ed., 1970.

Maslow, A. H. *The psychology of science.* New York: Harper and Row, 1966.

Maslow, A. H. A theory of metamotivation: the biological rooting of the value life. *J. Humanistic Psychol.*, 1967a, **7,** 93–127.

Maslow, A. H. Neurosis as a failure of personal growth. *Humanitas,* 1967b, **3,** 153–170.

Maslow, A. H. *Toward a psychology of being.* (2nd. ed.) Princeton: Van Nostrand, 1968a.

Maslow, A. H. Toward the study of violence. In L. Ng (Ed.). *Alternatives to violence.* New York: Time-Life Books, 1968b, 34–37.

Maslow, A. H. *The farther reaches of human nature.* New York: Viking Press, 1971.

Maslow, B. G. (Ed.). *Abraham H. Maslow: a memorial volume.* Monterey, Calif.: Brooks/Cole, 1972.

Meyer, A. *The commonsense psychiatry of Dr. Adolf Meyer.* A Lief (Ed.). New York: McGraw-Hill, 1948.

Murphy, G. *Personality: a biosocial approach to origins and structure.* New York: Harper, 1947.

Pikas, A. *Abstraction and concept formation.* Cambridge: Harvard Univ. Press, 1966.

Rennie, T. A. C. Adolf Meyer and psychobiology; the man, his methodology and its relation to therapy. *Pap. Amer. Congr. Gen. Semant.*, 1943, **2,** 156–165.

Scheerer, M., Rothman, E., and Goldstein, K. A case of "idiot savant": An experimental study of personality organization. *Psychol. Monogr.*, 1945, **58** (4).

Simmel, M. L. (Ed.). *The reach of the mind: essays in memory of Kurt Goldstein.* New York: Springer, 1968.

Skinner, B. F. Review of K. Goldstein's *The organism. J. Abnorm. Soc. Psychol.*, 1940, **35,** 462–465.

Smuts, J. C. *Holism and evolution.* New York: Macmillan, 1926.

Werner, H. *Comparative psychology of mental development.* Rev. ed. Chicago: Follett, 1948.

Wheeler, R. H. *The science of psychology.* (2nd ed.) New York: Crowell, 1940.

Wilson, C. *New pathways in psychology: Maslow and the post-Freudian revolution.* New York: Taplinger, 1972.

ROGERS' PERSON-CENTERED THEORY

8

The theory to be discussed in this chapter is, properly speaking, another member of the family of organismic theories discussed in the preceding chapter. Because of its importance and influence, however, the viewpoint developed by Carl Rogers deserves separate treatment.

In previous editions, we called Rogers' viewpoint "self theory" but that no longer seems to us to characterize accurately Rogers' position. It is clear from his recent writings that the emphasis should fall on the organism, not the self. Indeed the self or self-concept, as we shall see, is apt to be a distorted picture of the person's authentic nature.

Rogers also identifies himself with the humanistic orientation in contemporary psychology. Humanistic psychology opposes what it regards as the bleak pessimism and despair inherent in the psychoanalytic view of humans on the one hand, and the robot conception of humans portrayed in behaviorism on the other hand. Humanistic psychology is more hopeful and optimistic about humans. It believes that the person, any person, contains within him or herself the potentialities for healthy and creative growth. The failure to realize these potentialities is due to the constricting and distorting influences of parental training, education, and other social pressures. These harmful effects can be overcome, however, if the individual is willing to accept the responsibility for his or her own life. If this responsibility is accepted, Rogers believes, we shall soon see—barring the rise of world-wide repression and enslavement—the emergence of a new person "highly aware, self-directing, an explorer of inner, perhaps more than outer, space, scornful of the conformity of institutions and the dogma of authority" (Rogers, 1974).

Rogers' theory also has something in common with existential psychology (see Chapter 9). It is basically phenomenological, that is, Rogers places a strong emphasis on the experiences of the person, their feelings and values, and all that is summed up by the expression "inner life."

Rogers' theory of personality, like those of Freud, Jung, Adler, Sullivan, and Horney, grew out of his experiences in working with individuals in the therapeutic relationship. The major stimulus to his psychological thinking, he acknowledges, is "the continuing clinical experience with individuals who perceive themselves, or are perceived by others to be, in need of personal help. Since 1928, for a period now approaching thirty years, I have spent probably an average of 15 to 20 hours per week, except during vacation periods, in endeavoring to understand and be of therapeutic help to these individuals. . . . From these hours, and from my relationships with these people, I have drawn most of whatever insight I possess into the meaning of therapy, the dynamics of interpersonal relationships, and the structure and functioning of personality" (1959, p. 188).

In the eyes of the psychological world, Carl Rogers is identified with a method of psychotherapy that he originated and developed. This type of therapy is called nondirective or client-centered. In the words of its originator, successful client-centered therapy conducted under optimal conditions

. . . would mean that the therapist has been able to enter into an intensely personal and subjective relationship with this client—relating not as a scientist to an object of study, not as a physician expecting to diagnose and cure,—but as a person to a person. It would mean that the therapist feels this client to be a person of unconditional self-worth; of value no matter what his condition, his behavior or his feelings. It would mean that the therapist is genuine, not hiding behind a defensive facade, but meeting the client with the feelings the therapist is experiencing. It would mean that the therapist is able to let himself go in understanding this client; that no inner barriers keep him from sensing what it feels like to be the client at each moment of the relationship; and that he can convey something of his empathic understanding to the client. It means that the therapist has been comfortable in entering this relationship fully, without knowing cognitively where it will lead, satisfied with providing a climate which will permit the client the utmost freedom to be himself.

For the client, this optimal therapy would mean an exploration of increasingly strange and unknown and dangerous feelings in himself, the exploration proving possible only because he is gradually realizing that he is accepted unconditionally. Thus he becomes acquainted with elements of his experience which have in the past been denied to awareness as too threatening, too damaging, to the structure of the self. He finds himself experiencing these feelings fully, completely, in the relationship, so that for the moment he *is* his fear, or his anger, or his tenderness, or his strength. And as he lives these widely varied feelings, in all their degrees of intensity, he discovers that he has experienced *himself,* that he *is* all these feelings. He finds his behavior changing in constructive fashion in accordance with his newly experienced self. He approaches the realization that he no longer needs to fear what experience may hold, but can welcome it freely as a part of his changing and developing self (1961, p. 185).

From these experiences, Rogers initially developed a theory of therapy and personality change. The principal feature of this conceptualization of the therapeutic process is that when clients perceive that the therapist has unconditional positive regard for them and an empathic understanding of their internal frame of reference, then a process of change is set in motion. During this process, clients become increasingly more aware of their true feelings and experiences and their self-concept becomes more congruent with the total experiences of the organism (1959, pp. 212–221).

If complete congruence should be achieved, the client would then be a fully functioning person. Rogers has set forth what it means to be such a person (1959, pp. 234–235; 1961, pp. 183–196). It includes such characteristics as openness to experience, absence of defensiveness, accurate awareness, unconditional self-regard, and harmonious relations with others.

In recent years, Rogers has come to view the therapeutic process as one instance of all interpersonal relationships and communications. This led him to formulate a general theory of interpersonal relationship (1959, pp. 235–240; 1961, pp. 338–346). The main postulate of the theory is stated by Rogers as follows:

Assuming (a) a minimal willingness on the part of two people to be in contact; (b) an ability and minimal willingness on the part of each to receive communication from the other; and (c) assuming the contact to continue over a period of time; then the following relationship is hypothesized to hold true.

The greater the congruence of experience, awareness and communication on the part of one individual, the more the ensuing relationship will involve a tendency toward reciprocal communication with a quality of increasing congruence; a tendency toward more mutually accurate understanding of the communications; improved psychological adjustment and functioning in both parties; mutual satisfaction in the relationship (1961, p. 344).

It will be noted that only one of the persons in the relationship needs to feel congruence for changes to occur in the other person.

The foregoing theories have been applied by Rogers to family life (1972), to education and learning (1969), to encounter groups (1970), and to group tension and conflict (1977).

Nondirective therapy has enjoyed considerable popularity among psychological counselors partly because it is tied historically to psychology rather than to medicine. It is said to be fairly easy to learn and requires little or no knowledge of personality diagnosis and dynamics to use it. Moreover, the course of treatment is relatively brief compared, for example, to psychoanalysis, and some clients are said to be benefited after a few therapy sessions.

However, psychotherapy is not our concern in this book, and we have mentioned it only because Rogers' theory of personality has evolved out of his experiences as a client-centered therapist. His therapeutic observations have provided Rogers with a "precious vein of observational material of unusual value for the study of personality" (1947, p. 358). The formulation of a personality theory has helped also to illuminate and elucidate Rogers' therapeutic practices.

Carl Rogers was born in Oak Park, Illinois, January 8, 1902, "the middle child in a large, closeknit family, where hard work and a highly conservative (almost fundamentalist) Protestant Christianity

Carl Rogers

were about equally revered" (1959, p. 186). When Carl was twelve years old, his family moved to a farm and he became interested in scientific agriculture. This interest in science carried over to college where during his first years he was fond of the physical and biological sciences. After his graduation from the University of Wisconsin in 1924, he attended Union Theological Seminary in New York City where he became exposed to a liberal, philosophical viewpoint regarding religion. Transferring to Teachers College of Columbia University, he fell under the philosophical influence of John Dewey and was introduced to clinical psychology by Leta Hollingworth. He was awarded the master's degree in 1928 and the doctorate in 1931 by Columbia. His first practical experience in clinical psychology and psychotherapy was obtained as an interne at the Institute for Child Guidance, which had a strongly Freudian orientation. Rogers observes that "the sharp incompatibility of the highly speculative Freudian thinking of the Institute with the highly statistical and Thorndikean views at Teachers College was keenly felt" (1959, p. 186).

After receiving his doctor's degree in psychology, Rogers joined the staff of the Rochester Guidance Center and later became its director.

The staff was eclectic, of diverse background, and our frequent and continuing discussion of treatment methods was based on our practical everyday working experience with the children, adolescents and adults who were our clients. It was the beginning of an effort, which has had meaning for me ever since, to discover the order which exists in our experience of working with people. The volume on the *Clinical Treatment of the Problem Child* (1939) was one outcome of this effort (1959), pp. 186–187).

During this period, Rogers was influenced by Otto Rank, the psychoanalyst, who had by that time broken away from the orthodox teachings of Freud.

In 1940, Rogers accepted an invitation to become professor of psychology at Ohio State University. This shift from a clinical setting to an academic environment proved to be a sharp one for Rogers. Under the stimulus provided by intellectually curious and critical graduate students, Rogers felt impelled to make his views on psychotherapy more explicit, which he did in his book *Counseling and psychotherapy* (1942). In 1945 Rogers went to the University of Chicago as professor of psychology and executive secretary of the Counseling Center where he elaborated his client-centered method of psychotherapy, formulated a theory of personality, and conducted research on psychotherapy (Rogers, 1951; Rogers and Dymond, 1954). From 1957 to 1963, Rogers was professor of psychology and psychiatry at the University of Wisconsin. During those years, he headed a research group that made an intensive, controlled study of psychotherapy with schizophrenic patients in a mental hospital (Rogers, 1967a). Since 1964, he has been associated with the Center for Studies of the Person in La Jolla, California. Rogers has had bestowed upon him by his fellow psychologists numerous honors including the presidency of the American Psychological Association and its Distinguished Scientific Contribution Award and its Distinguished Professional Contribution Award. Rogers' autobiography appears in Volume 5 of the *History of psychology in autobiography* (1967b).

We turn now to consider Rogers' theory of personality. This theory was originally presented in *Client-centered therapy* (1951), elaborated and formalized in a chapter written for *Psychology: a study of a science* (1959), and more informally described in *On becoming a person* (1961) and *Carl Rogers on personal power* (1977). This last volume is a useful overview of Rogers' activities and observations in recent years. Rogers' conception of the way in which theorizing should proceed is graphically revealed in the following statement:

I came to the conclusion which others have reached before, that in a new field perhaps what is needed first is to steep oneself in the *events,* to approach the phenomena with as few preconceptions as possible, to take a naturalist's observational, descriptive approach to those events, and to draw forth those low-level inferences which seem most native to the material itself (1961, p. 128).

THE STRUCTURE
OF PERSONALITY

Although Rogers does not appear to emphasize structural constructs, preferring to devote his attention to change and development of personality, there are two such constructs that are of fundamental importance to his theory and may even be regarded as the footing upon which the whole theory rests. These are the *organism* and the *self*.

The Organism

The organism, psychologically conceived, is the locus of all experience. Experience includes everything potentially available to awareness that is going on within the organism at any given moment. This totality of experience constitutes the *phenomenal field*. The phenomenal field is the individual's frame of reference that can only be known to the person. "It can never be known to another except through empathic inference and then can never be perfectly known" (Rogers, 1959, p. 210). How the individual behaves depends upon the phenomenal field (subjective reality) and not upon the stimulating conditions (external reality).

The phenomenal field, it should be noted, is not identical with the field of consciousness. "Consciousness (or awareness) is the symbolization of some of our experience" (Rogers, 1959, p. 198). Thus, the phenomenal field at any given moment is made up of conscious (symbolized) and unconscious (unsymbolized) experiences. The organism may, however, discriminate and react to an experience that is not symbolized. Following McCleary and Lazarus (1949), Rogers calls this *subception*.

Experience may not be correctly symbolized in which case the person will behave inappropriately. However, a person tends to check their symbolized experiences against the world as it is. This testing of reality provides one with dependable knowledge of the world so that one is able to behave realistically. However, some perceptions remain untested or are inadequately tested, and these untested experiences may cause one to behave unrealistically and even to one's own detriment. Although Rogers does not deal with the issue of a "true" reality, it is apparent that people must have some conception of an external or impersonal standard of reality, for otherwise they could not perform the act of testing an inner picture of reality against an "objective" one. The question then arises as to how people can differentiate between a subjective image that is not a correct representation of reality and one that is. What enables people to separate fact from fiction in their subjective world? This is the great paradox of phenomenology.

Rogers resolves the paradox by leaving the conceptual framework of pure phenomenology. What a person experiences or thinks is actually not reality for the person; it is merely a tentative hypothesis about reality, a hypothesis that may or may not be true. The person suspends judgment until he or she puts the hypothesis to a test. What is this test? It consists of checking the correctness of the information received and upon which the person's hypothesis is based with other sources of information. For example, a person who wishes to salt his food is confronted with two identical shakers, one of which contains salt, the other pepper. The person believes that the shaker with the larger holes contains salt, but not being dead sure shakes a little of the contents on the back of the hand. If the particles are white rather than black the person feels reasonably sure that it is salt. A very cautious person may even then put a little to the lips because it might be white pepper instead of salt. What we have here is a testing of one's ideas against a variety of sensory data. The test consists of checking less certain information against more direct knowledge. In the case of salt, the final test is its taste; a particular kind of sensation defines it as salt.

Of course, the foregoing example describes an ideal condition. In many cases, a person accepts their experiences as faithful representations of reality and fails to treat them as hypotheses about reality. As a consequence, the person often ends up with a lot of misconceptions about him or her self and about the external world. "The whole person," Rogers writes recently, "is one who is completely open to the data from internal experiencing and the data from experiencing of the external world" (1977, p. 250).

The Self   A portion of the phenomenal field gradually becomes differentiated. This is the self. Self or self-concept denotes

> the organized, consistent conceptual gestalt composed of perceptions of the characteristics of the 'I' or 'me' and the perceptions of the relationships of the 'I' or 'me' to others and to various aspects of life, together with the values attached to these perceptions. It is a gestalt which is available to awareness though not necessarily in awareness. It is a fluid and changing gestalt, a process, but at any given moment it is a specific entity (Rogers, 1959, p. 200).

The self is, of course, one of the central constructs in Rogers' theory, and he has given an interesting account of how this came about.

> Speaking personally, I began my work with the settled notion that the 'self' was a vague, ambiguous, scientifically meaningless term which had gone out of the psychologist's vocabulary with the departure of the introspectionists. Consequently I was slow in recognizing that when clients were given the opportunity to express their problems and their attitudes in their own terms, without any guidance or interpretation, they tended to talk in terms of the self. . . . It seemed clear . . . that the self was an important element in the experience of the client, and that in some odd sense his goal was to become his 'real self' (1959, pp. 200–201).

In addition to the self as it is (the self structure), there is an *ideal self* which is what the person would like to be.

Organism and Self: The basic significance of the structural concepts, organism and self,
Congruence and   for Rogers' theory becomes clear in his discussion of congruence and
Incongruence   incongruence between the self as perceived and the actual experience of the organism (1959, pp. 203, 205–206). When the symbolized experiences that constitute the self faithfully mirror the experiences of the organism, the person is said to be adjusted, mature, and fully functioning. Such a person accepts the entire range of organismic experience without threat or anxiety. He or she is able to think realistically. Incongruence between self and organism makes individuals feel threatened and anxious. They behave defensively and their thinking becomes constricted and rigid.

Implicit in Rogers' theory are two other manifestations of congruence–incongruence. One is the congruence or lack of it between subjective reality (the phenomenal field) and external reality (the world as it is). The other is the degree of correspondence between the self and ideal self. If the discrepancy between self and ideal self is large, the person is dissatisfied and maladjusted.

How incongruence develops and how self and organism can be made more congruent are Rogers' chief concerns, and it is to the illumination of these vital questions that he has devoted so much of his professional life. How he deals with these questions will be discussed in the section on the development of personality. (For another version of the structural constructs of Rogers' theory see Krause, 1964.)

"The organism has one basic tendency and striving—to actualize, maintain, and enhance the experiencing organism" (1951, p. 487). This actualizing tendency is selective, paying attention only to those aspects of the environment that promise to move the person constructively in the direction of fulfillment and wholeness. On the one hand, there is a single motivating force, the self-actualizing drive; on the other hand, there is a single goal of life, to become self-actualized or a whole person.

THE DYNAMICS OF PERSONALITY

The organism actualizes itself along the lines laid down by heredity. It becomes more differentiated, more expanded, more autonomous, and more socialized as it matures. This basic tendency of growth—to actualize and expand oneself—is seen to best advantage when an individual is observed over a long period of time. There is a forward movement in the life of every person; it is this ongoing tendency that is the only force that the therapist can really rely upon to effect an improvement in the client.

Rogers adds a new feature to the concept of growth when he observes that the forward-moving tendency can only operate when the choices are *clearly perceived* and *adequately symbolized*. A person cannot actualize him or her self unless they are able to discriminate between progressive and regressive ways of behaving. There is no inner voice that tells one which is the path of progress, no organismic necessity that thrusts one forward. People have to know before they can choose but when they do know they always choose to grow rather than to regress.

"Behavior is basically the goal-directed attempt of the organism to satisfy its needs as experienced, in the field as perceived" (1951, p. 491). This proposition, referring as it does to plural "needs," does not contradict the notion of a single motive. Although there are many needs, each of them is subservient to the basic tendency of the organism to maintain and enhance itself.

Rogers remains faithful to his phenomenological position by employing the qualifying phrases "as experienced" and "as perceived." However, in discussing this proposition, Rogers admits that needs may evoke appropriate behavior even though the needs are not consciously experienced (adequately symbolized). In fact recently Rogers (1977) has played down the role of consciousness or self-consciousness in the functioning of the healthy individual. He writes, "In the person who is functioning well, awareness tends to be a reflexive thing, rather than a sharp spotlight of focused attention. Perhaps it is more accurate to say that in such a person awareness is simply a reflection of something of the flow of the organism at that moment. It is only when the functioning is disrupted that a sharply self-conscious awareness arises" (pp. 244–245).

In 1959, Rogers introduced a distinction between the actualizing tendency of the organism and a self-actualizing tendency.

Following the development of the self-structure, this general tendency toward actualization expresses itself also in the actualizing of that portion of the experience of the organism which is symbolized in the self. If the self and the total experience of the organism are relatively congruent, then the actualizing tendency remains relatively unified. If self and experience are incongruent, then the general tendency to actualize the organism may work at cross purposes with the subsystem of that motive, the tendency to actualize the self (1959, pp. 196–197).

Despite the monistic character of Rogers' motivational theory, he has singled out for special attention two needs: the need for positive regard and the need for self-regard. Both are learned needs. The former develops in infancy as a consequence of the baby's being loved and cared for, the latter is established by virtue of the baby's receiving positive regard from others (1959, pp. 223–224). These two needs, as we shall see in the next section, may also work at cross purposes with the actualizing tendency by distorting the experiences of the organism.

THE DEVELOPMENT OF PERSONALITY   Organism and self, although they possess the inherent tendency to actualize themselves, are subject to strong influences from the environment and especially from the social environment. Rogers, unlike such other clinic-rooted theorists as Freud, Sullivan, and Erikson, does not provide a time table of significant stages through which a person passes in traveling from infancy to maturity. Instead he focuses upon the ways in which evaluations of an individual by others, particularly during childhood, tend to favor distancing between experiences of the organism and experiences of the self.

If these evaluations were exclusively positive in sign (what Rogers calls unconditional positive regard), then no distancing or incongruity between organism and self would occur. Rogers says, "If an individual should *experience* only *unconditional positive regard,* then no *conditions of worth* would develop, *self-regard* would be unconditional, the needs for *positive regard* and *self-regard* would never be at variance with *organismic evaluation,* and the individual would continue to be *psychologically adjusted,* and would be fully functioning" (1959, p. 224).

But because evaluations of the child's behavior by its parents and others are sometimes positive and sometimes negative, the child learns to differentiate between actions and feelings that are worthy (approved) and those that are unworthy (disapproved). Unworthy experiences tend to become excluded from the self-concept even though they are organismically valid. This results in a self-concept out of line with organismic experience. The child tries to be what others want it to be instead of trying to be what it really is. Rogers says, "He values an experience positively or negatively solely because of these conditions of worth which he has taken over from others, not because the experience enhances or fails to enhance his organism" (1959, p. 209).

This is what happens in the following case. A boy has a self-picture of being a good boy, and of being loved by his parents but he also enjoys tormenting his little sister for which he is punished. As a result of this punishment he is called upon to revise his self-image and his values in one of the following ways: (a) "I am a bad boy," (b) "My parents don't like me," (c) "I don't like to tease my sister." Each of these self-attitudes may contain a distortion of the truth. Let us suppose that he adopts the attitude "I don't like to tease my sister," thereby denying his real feelings. Denial does not mean that the feelings cease to exist; they will still influence his behavior in various ways even though they are not conscious. A conflict will then exist between the introjected and spurious conscious values and the genuine unconscious ones. If more and more of the "true" values of a person are replaced by values taken over or borrowed from others, yet which are perceived as being one's own, the self will become a house divided against itself. Such a person will feel tense, uncomfortable, and out of sorts. He or she will feel as if they do not really know what they are and what they want.

Gradually, then, throughout childhood the self-concept becomes more and more distorted due to evaluations by others. Consequently, an organismic experience that is at variance with this distorted self-concept is felt as a threat and evokes anxiety. In order to protect the integrity of the self-concept, these threatening experiences are denied symbolization or are given a distorted symbolization.

Denying an experience is not the same thing as ignoring it. Denial means falsifying reality either by saying it does not exist or by perceiving it in a distorted way. People may deny their aggressive feelings because they are inconsistent with the picture they have of themselves as peaceful and friendly. In such case, the denied feelings may be allowed to express themselves by means of a distorted symbolization, for example, by projecting them onto other people. Rogers points out that people will often stoutly maintain and enhance a self-picture that is completely at variance with reality. The person who feels that he or she is worthless will exclude from awareness evidence that contradicts this picture or will reinterpret the evidence to make it congruent with their sense of worthlessness. For example, if they receive a promotion in their work they will say that "the boss felt sorry for me" or "I don't deserve it." Some people may even do poorly in the new position to prove to themselves and to the world that they are no good.

How can one deny a threat to the self-picture without first being aware of the threat? Rogers says that there are levels of discrimination below the level of conscious recognition, and that the threatening object may be unconsciously perceived or "subcepted" before it is perceived. The threatening object or situation, for example, may produce visceral reactions such as a pounding heart, which are consciously experienced as sensations of anxiety, without the person being able to identify the cause of the disturbance. Feelings of anxiety evoke the mechanism of denial that prevent the threatening experience from becoming conscious.

Not only does the breach between self and organism result in defensiveness and distortion, but it also affects a person's relations with other people. People who are defensive are inclined to feel hostile toward other people whose behavior. in their eyes, represents their own denied feelings.

How can this breach between self and organism, and between self and others be healed? Rogers proposes the three following propositions.

"Under certain conditions, involving primarily complete absence of any threat to the self-structure, experiences which are inconsistent with it may be perceived, and examined, and the structure of self revised to assimilate and include such experiences" (1951; p. 517).

In client-centered therapy the person finds him or her self in a nonthreatening situation because the counselor is completely accepting of everything the client says. This warm accepting attitude on the part of the counselor encourages clients to explore their unconscious feelings and to bring them into awareness. Slowly and tentatively they explore the unsymbolized feelings that threaten their security. In the safety of the therapeutic relationship these hitherto threatening feelings can now be assimilated into the self-structure. The assimilation may require rather drastic reorganization in the self-concept of the client in order to bring it into line with the reality of organismic experience. "He will *be,* in more unified fashion, what he organismically *is,* and this seems to be the essence of therapy" (1955, p. 269). Rogers admits that some people may be able to accomplish this process without undergoing therapy.

An important social benefit gained from the acceptance and assimilation of experiences that have been denied symbolization is that the person becomes more understanding and accepting of other people. This idea is presented in the next proposition.

"When the individual perceives and accepts into one consistent and integrated system all his sensory and visceral experiences, then he is necessarily more understanding of others and is more accepting of others as separate individuals" (1951, p. 520). When a person feels threatened by sexual impulses he or she may tend to criticize others whom they perceive as behaving in sexual ways. On the other hand, if one accepts one's own sexual and hostile feelings one will be more tolerant of their expression by others. Consequently social relationships will improve and the incidence of social conflict will decrease. Rogers believes that the social implications of this proposition "are such as to stretch the imagination" (p. 522). It may even contain the key to the eventual abolition of international strife.

In his last proposition, Rogers points out how important it is for wholesome adjustment to maintain a continuous examination of one's values.

"As the individual perceives and accepts into his self-structure more of his organic experiences, he finds that he is replacing his present value system—based so largely upon introjections which have been distortedly symbolized—with a continuing valuing process" (1951, p. 522). The emphasis falls upon the two words, *system* and *process.* A system carries the connotation of something that is fixed and static, whereas a process signifies that something is taking place. For healthy, integrated adjustment one must constantly be evaluating experiences to see whether they require a change in the value structure. Any fixed set of values will tend to prevent the person from reacting effectively to new experiences. One must be flexible to adjust appropriately to the changing conditions of life.

In this connection Rogers raises the question as to whether a continuing process of evaluating one's experiences in purely personal terms may not lead to social anarchy. He believes not. All people have "basically the same needs, including the need for acceptance by others" (p. 524). Consequently their values will possess a "high degree of commonality" (p. 524).

In concluding this account of the principal features of Rogers' theory the reader might wonder why it is called "person–centered" and not "organismic-centered." The answer is quite simple. In a fully functioning individual the person *is* the organism. In other words, it does not make any difference which it is called. Person is preferred because it has more of a psychological connotation. The person is the *experiencing* organism. Person and self are also the same when the self is completely congruent with the organism. It all comes down to this: The organism, a living, growing, holistic system, is the basic psychological reality. Any deviation from this reality threatens the integrity of the person.

CHARACTERISTIC RESEARCH AND RESEARCH METHODS

Rogers has been a pioneer investigator in the area of counseling and psychotherapy, and deserves a great deal of credit for stimulating and conducting research into the nature of the processes that occur during clinical treatment. Well-controlled studies of psychotherapy are exceedingly difficult to design and carry out because of the subtle and private nature of the psychotherapeutic setting. Therapists have been reluctant to subordinate the welfare of the patient to the needs of research by permitting any invasion of the privacy of the treatment room. Rogers, however, has shown that the electrical recording of therapy sessions, with the permission of the patient, is not injurious to the course of treatment. In fact, both patient and therapist soon ignore the presence of the microphone and behave quite naturally. The accumulation of a set of exact transcriptions of therapy sessions by Rogers and his associates has made it possible to study the course of treatment objectively and quantitatively. Largely through his efforts, we are beginning to learn something about the processes of psychotherapy. (See, for example, Rogers, 1967a; Rogers and Dymond, 1954; Seeman and Raskin, 1953; Cartwright and Lerner, 1963; and for a critical review, Wylie, 1978.)

Although the empirical studies undertaken by Rogers and his associates have been aimed primarily at understanding and elucidating the nature of psychotherapy and evaluating its results, many of their findings bear directly upon the theory of personality developed by Raimy (1943) and Rogers. In fact, Rogers' systematic formulation of his theory was dictated by the research findings; it was not a preconceived viewpoint that determined the nature and direction either of the therapy or of the research. On this point, Rogers says, "The self has for many years been an unpopular concept in psychology, and those doing therapeutic work from a client-centered orientation certainly had no initial leanings toward using the self as an explanatory concept" (1951, p. 136).

Since the formulation of his personality theory Rogers has enlarged his therapy research program to include tests of inferences from this theory.

Many of Rogers' ideas about personality have been explicated by a qualitative, pointing-to procedure that consists of demonstrating by extracts from the record of the client's verbalizations what his or her self-picture is and what changes occur in it during therapy. The literature on nondirective or client-centered therapy is filled with examples of this type (Rogers, 1942, 1948, 1951, 1961, pp. 73–106, 1967a, pp. 401–418; Rogers and Dymond, 1954; Rogers and Wallen, 1946; Muench and Rogers, 1946; Snyder *et al.,* 1947). Rogers himself seems to have a preference for this mode of presenting his ideas, although, of course, he does not regard excerpts from case records as proof of the validity of his personality theory. They are used more for the purpose of acquainting the reader with typical phenomena that occur during therapy sessions and to point out the kinds of experiences that are in need of explanation.

Qualitative Studies

This research method consists of formulating a set of categories by means of which the verbalizations of a client can be classified and counted. In a pioneer study, Porter (1943) laid the groundwork for much of the later work on the categorization of the recorded content of counseling interviews by showing that this method of analysis yields reliable results. In another early study by a Rogers' student (Raimy, 1948), an analysis of the characteristic changes in self-references during therapy was undertaken. For this purpose, Raimy used the following categories: positive or approving self-reference, negative or disapproving self-reference, ambivalent self-reference, ambiguous self-reference, references to external objects and persons, and questions. The transcribed records of fourteen cases who had had from two to twenty-one interviews were itemized and sorted into the foregoing six classes, and the number in each category at successive stages of counseling was counted. It was found that at the start of therapy the clients gave a preponderance of disapproving or ambivalent self-references, and that as counseling progressed fluctuations in self-approval occurred with mounting ambivalence. At the

Content Analysis

conclusion of counseling those clients who were judged to be improved were making a preponderant number of self-approving statements while those who had not improved were still being ambivalent and disapproving of themselves. Other investigators (Snyder, 1945; Lipkin, 1948; Seeman, 1949) have obtained substantially the same results.

In another group of studies employing content analysis an attempt was made to test the proposition that as a people become more accepting of themselves they also become more accepting of other people. Categories of positive, negative, and ambivalent feelings toward self and others were formulated and applied to cases in therapy. In one study (Seeman, 1949), the number of positive self-references increased and the number of negative self-references decreased during therapy without any concomitant change in the feelings toward others. Another investigator (Stock, 1949), using a similar method of content analysis, could find no evidence that changes in self-feeling occur prior to and produce changes in feelings toward others. In a third investigation (Sheerer, 1949), some positive support for the proposition was obtained although the changes in attitudes toward others were neither as marked nor as regular as the increases in the acceptance of self. An investigation of the proposition by Gordon and Cartwright (1954) in which various tests and scales were employed in place of content analysis failed to support the hypothesis that increasing acceptance of self leads to an increasing acceptance of others.

It is of interest, however, that there is a fairly significant correlation, .51 in Sheerer's study and .66 in Stock's study, between conceptions of self and conceptions of others. This means that if an individual thinks well of him or her self they are likely to think well of others, and that if they disapprove of themselves they are likely to disapprove of others. Correlations of about the same magnitude have been found by Phillips (1951) in an investigation of self-feelings and feelings toward others of various groups of people not in therapy.

Medinnus and Curtis (1963), observing that the majority of studies of self-acceptance and acceptance of others used as subjects persons receiving therapy or college students, performed an investigation with normal mothers. Mothers who accepted themselves were more likely to accept their children than were nonaccepting mothers. After surveying a number of studies, Wylie (1961, 1978) concludes that the available evidence generally supports the hypothesis that self-acceptance is associated with acceptance of others, although she feels that most of the studies are so seriously flawed as to render the findings equivocal.

One of Rogers' and his collaborators' principal contributions in recent years to the investigation of psychotherapy is the measurement of process and change during therapy by the use of rating scales. Although not ruling out the importance of assessing the outcome of therapy, Rogers feels more is to be learned about therapeutic effectiveness by studying the attitudes and behavior of the therapist in relation to changes in the client. For this purpose, two types of rating scales have been developed: those which measure the therapist's attitudes and those which measure change in the client. An example of the former is the following congruence scale developed by Kiesler (Rogers, 1967a, pp. 581–584).

Stage 1. There is clear evidence of a discrepancy between the therapist's experiencing of the client and the current communication.
Stage 2. The therapist communicates information to the client in response to the client's questioning, but the response has a phony, deceptive, or "half-truth" quality.
Stage 3. The therapist does not contradict his or her feelings about the client, but neither does he or she communicate their exact feelings toward the client.
Stage 4. The therapist communicates information to the client, either spontaneously or in response to the client's questioning rather than withholding it for personal or professional reasons.
Stage 5. The therapist communicates openly and freely his or her feelings, both positive and negative, about the client at a given moment—without traces of defensiveness, or retreat into professionalism.

An example of a scale for measuring therapeutic process is one developed by Gendlin (Rogers, 1967a, pp. 603–611) for assessing the quality of the relationship.

Stage 1. Refusal of a relationship.
Stage 2. Physical acceptance of a relationship without overt acceptance.
Stage 3. Partial acceptance of relationship quality or intermittent parallel relationship quality.
Stage 4. Parallel and together, the relationship as a context of therapy.
Stage 5. The relationship as specific therapy, rather than only as general context for therapy.
Stage 6. The relationship is ready to be a permanent reality and therefore could be approaching termination.

Rating Scales

The most ambitious use of these scales to date was in a study of psychotherapy with schizophrenics (Rogers, 1967a). Although Rogers and his associates were interested in finding out whether client-centered therapy would work with state hospital patients, it was primarily a study of therapeutic relationships and not of schizophrenia. Rating scales were filled out by the therapists, patients, and judges who had no information about the cases other than excerpts from the transcripts of therapy sessions. The findings are much too extensive to be summarized here. Several of the more important ones may be noted, however.

The rating scales proved to have satisfactory reliability except for the one that measured unconditional positive regard. Independent judges were able to make reliable ratings after reading a fairly short series of excerpts from the whole therapy transcription. There was a negative correlation between the therapist's evaluation of the therapeutic relationship and either the patient's own evaluation or that of an unbiased rater. Rogers comments on this unexpected result:

It is a sobering finding that our therapists—competent and conscientious as they were—had over-optimistic and, in some cases, seriously invalid perceptions of the relationships in which they were involved. The patient, for all his psychosis, or the bright young college student with no knowledge of therapy, turned out to have more useful (and probably more accurate) perceptions of the relationship (1967a, p. 92).

There was generally little process movement (improvement) during therapy with this group of eight chronic and eight acute schizophrenics.

Q-Technique Studies   The appearance of the English psychologist William Stephenson at the University of Chicago proved to be a great boon to Rogers and his associates. The methods of research that he has developed are uniquely adapted for investigating the self-concept by the single case method. These methods are referred to be Stephenson as Q-technique.

There is a difference between Stephenson's Q-technique and the logical basis upon which it rests that Stephenson calls Q-methodology. Logical hypotheses are derived from theory by Q-methodology and these hypotheses may then be tested by Q-technique. However, the investigator may employ Q-technique without using Q-methodology. This is what Rogers and his associates have done. The difference between the type of research fostered by Stephenson and that done under the influence of Rogers is brought out clearly by comparing the studies of Nunnally (1955), a student of Stephenson's, with those of Butler and Haigh (1954), students of Rogers. Both of them investigated the changes in self-conceptions before and after therapy. Nunnally used Q-methodology in designing his experiment and the full complement of Q-techniques, including factor analysis, whereas Butler and Haigh used only the Q-sorting device and intrapersonal correlations. Moreover, Nunnally employed a single case, as Stephenson recommends, and Butler and Haigh employed a number of cases.

What is Q-technique? Essentially, it is a method of studying systematically the notions of a person about him or her self, although it can be used for other purposes as well. The person is given a packet of statements and is asked to sort them into a prearranged distribution along a continuum from those most characteristic of the person doing the sorting to those least characteristic of the person. The distribution approximates a normal distribution and is exactly the same for all subjects in a given experiment. This constant feature expedites the statistical handling of the results since all sortings are forced into a distribution whose mean and standard deviation are the same.

Sortings may be made not only for how people see themselves at the present time but also for how they would like to be, called the *ideal* sort, how they were at the age of fifteen, how their mothers see them, and so on. There may be as many different sortings or variates, as they are named, as the investigator chooses to use. Bowdlear (1955), for example, used twenty-five sortings in his study of an epileptic patient undergoing psychotherapy. The results of such a multivariate design may be analyzed by correlational methods, factor analysis, and analysis of variance.

The items for a Q-sort may be made up in various ways. They may be formulated so as to conform to a particular theory of personality of which many examples are given in Stephenson's book (1953) or they may be selected from a population of items obtained from therapeutic protocols, self-descriptions, personality inventories, and the like.

In order to illustrate the way in which Rogers and his associates have used Q-technique let us consider the study performed by Butler and Haigh (1954). These investigators set out to test the assumption that people who come for counseling are dissatisfied with themselves and that following successful counseling their dissatisfaction will be reduced. The Q-sort items for this study were chosen at random from a number of therapeutic protocols. They consisted of such items as "I am a submissive person," "I am a hard worker," "I am likable," and "I am an impulsive person." Prior to the beginning of counseling each client was asked to sort the statements in two ways, according to the following instructions:

Self-sort. Sort these cards to describe yourself as you see yourself today, from those that are least like you to those that are most like you.

Ideal-sort. Now sort these cards to describe your ideal person—the person you would most like within yourself to be.

The distributions of these two sortings were then correlated for each person. The average correlation between self-sort and ideal-sort for the group of subjects was zero, which shows that there is no congruence between the way people see themselves and the way they would like to be. A control group of subjects who were matched with the client group but who were not interested in being counseled made the same two sortings. The average correlation for this group between self-sort and ideal-sort was .58, which proves that a non-treatment group is much better satisfied with itself than a group seeking therapy is. Following the completion of the counseling (there were an average of thirty-one sessions per client), the clients were again asked to make a self-sort and an ideal-sort. The average correlation between the two sorts turned out to be .34, a significant increase over what it had been prior to counseling although still short of the control group correlation. The control group was also retested after an interval of time equivalent to that for the client group and their average self-ideal correlation had not changed. Another group that had sought therapy but who were asked to wait sixty days before starting treatment showed no change in their self-ideal correlations during the waiting period.

As a check upon the permanence of the change that had taken place in the client's self-esteem during therapy, a follow-up study was made of the clients from six months to one year after therapy had been terminated. The average correlation between self-sort and ideal-sort was about the same as it had been at the close of counseling, .31 versus .34. The investigators conclude that self-esteem, which they define as the congruence between self- and ideal-sorts, increases as a direct result of client-centered counseling. It may occur to the reader that the increase in the average correlation from zero to .34 could have been the result of a change of the self-concept in the direction of the ideal, or of a change in the ideal in the direction of the self-concept, or of changes in both directions. In another study (Rudikoff, 1954), it was found that the ideal was somewhat lowered in the direction of the self-image during therapy, which suggests that both kinds of changes do occur.

It is of interest to note a few of the changes in individual correlations that occur between precounseling, postcounseling, and follow-up. Some of the correlations start out fairly low, increase markedly during therapy, and remain that way during the follow-up period. The following person, identified as Oak, exemplifies this pattern.

	Precounseling	Postcounseling	Follow-up
Oak	.21	.69	.71

Others remain low throughout as Baac's do.

	Precounseling	Postcounseling	Follow-up
Baac	−.31	.04	−.19

Still others start out low, increase following counseling, and then regress during the follow-up period.

	Precounseling	Postcounseling	Follow-up
Beel	.28	.52	−.04

For another type of person, the correlation starts out low, increases during therapy, and continues to increase after therapy has been concluded.

	Precounseling	Postcounseling	Follow-up
Bett	−.37	.39	.61

One might think that these different patterns of changes would be related to the amount of improvement shown during therapy. This is not the case. When the subjects were divided into an improved group and a nonimproved group, as judged by counselors and from projective test protocols, the two groups did not differ in respect to their self-ideal correlations at the termination of counseling, although at the time of the follow-up administration of the Q-sorts there was a tendency for the improved group to have somewhat higher correlations.

Butler and Haigh explain this failure to find a relationship between increased self-ideal correlations and improvement in terms of what they call "defensive sortings." A defensive sorting is one in which people give a distorted picture of themselves so that it appears as if they are well-adjusted when actually they are not. For example, in another study the highest self-ideal correlation that was found, an extremely high .90, was secured by a person who was clearly pathological.

The question of defensiveness has received considerable attention from Rogers and his associates because it raises some serious problems regarding the validity of self-reports. Is it true, for example, that when one says one is satisfied with oneself one really is? Does the internal frame of reference give an accurate picture of personality? Haigh (1949) has made special studies of defensive behavior and finds that it may assume many forms, including denial, withdrawal, justification, rationalization, projection, and hostility. During client-centered therapy some clients show a decrease in defensiveness whereas others show an increase. However, Haigh tends to minimize the importance of defensive behavior. He assumes that most of it consists of intentional deception on the part of the client to save face. This view is in marked contrast to the psychoanalytic theory of defense mechanisms that assumes that they operate unconsciously.

A study undertaken by Friedman (1955) sheds some further light upon the problem of defensiveness. Three groups of white males classified as normal, psychoneurotic, and paranoid schizophrenic made self and ideal Q-sorts. The median correlation for the sixteen normal subjects was .63, for the sixteen neurotic subjects .03, and for the sixteen psychotic patients .43. In other words, the psychotic patients displayed considerably more self-esteem than did the neurotics and not a great deal less than the normal subjects. Friedman concludes that "to employ a high correlation between the self and ideal-self conceptions as a sole criterion of adjustment, however, would lead to the categorization of many maladjusted people, particularly paranoid schizophrenics, as adjusted" (p. 73).

Friedman's finding, that paranoid schizophrenics show almost as much congruence in their self-ideal-sorts as normal subjects do, has been confirmed by Havener and Izard (1962). In a study of adolescent girls with behavior problems, Cole, Oetting, and Hinkle (1967) discovered that some of the subjects rated the self *higher* than the ideal-self. This would appear to be another indication of defensive sorting.

Another study in which a measure of defensiveness was correlated with self-attitudes and the assessment of personality by outside observers was conducted by Chodorkoff (1954). Chodorkoff secured self-reports from thirty college students by having them sort 125 items into thirteen piles from most characteristic to least characteristic. Four judges who had access to biographical information, Rorschach protocols and a summary of Rorschach scores, word association test data, and Thematic Apperception Test (TAT) protocols made a Q-sort for each subject using the same 125 items. A measure of perceptual defense was obtained by exposing threatening and neutral words beginning with a subliminal exposure speed and increasing it gradually until the subject was able to recognize all of the words.

Measures of perceptual defense were computed by finding the difference between the recognition thresholds for the neutral words and the thresholds for the threatening words.

Chodorkoff was interested in testing the following hypotheses: (1) the greater the agreement between the person's self-description and description of the person by others, the less perceptual defense he or she will manifest, (2) the greater the agreement between the person's self-description and an appraisal made by judges, the more adequate will be the individual's personal adjustment, and (3) the more adequate the personal adjustment, the less perceptual defense the person will show. Two measures of adjustment were employed: (1) the Munroe Inspection Rorschach check list and (2) the ratings made by judges on eleven adjustment scales.

The results confirmed all of the hypotheses. The higher the agreement between self-descriptions and descriptions by others, the less perceptual defense there is and the better is the personal adjustment. The better adjusted subjects also displayed less perceptual defense.

These studies indicate that defensiveness is an important variable in the self-judgments of people, and that self-reports cannot be relied upon to give the same picture of personality as are obtained from outside judges.

Another variable that affects self-ratings is social desirability (Milgram and Helper, 1961). A trait that is regarded as desirable is given a higher self-rating than one regarded as undesirable. This factor of social desirability influences the discrepancy between self- and ideal-self-ratings. For example, in a study of child molesters, Frisbie, Vanasek, and Dingman (1967) found that trait terms that were evaluative in character showed no discrepancy between self- and ideal-ratings whereas purely descriptive nonevaluative terms produced large discrepancies.

A critical and comprehensive survey of self-ideal Q-sort studies has been made by Wylie (1974, pp. 128–149).

Experimental Studies of the Self-Concept

Current interest in the self-concept has transcended its original locus in the therapy situation and has become a subject for investigation under laboratory conditions. Moreover, testable hypotheses regarding the self-concept are now being derived from theories other than Rogers'. For example, Pilisuk (1962) predicted on the basis of Heider's theory of cognitive balance that subjects who were adversely criticized for their performance on a task would not change their self-evaluations. This prediction was confirmed. Subjects used a varriety of rationalizations to sustain a favorable self-image in the face of criticism.

That the self-concept can be changed under certain conditions is brought out by other studies. Proceeding from Festinger's dissonance theory, Bergin (1962) performed the following experiment. Subjects first made self-ratings of their masculinity. They were then informed that their masculinity was viewed by others in a way that was discrepant with their self-evaluations. When the discrepant communication was a highly credible one, the subjects changed their self-ratings to make them more consonant with the opinion of others. When the communicated opinion could be discredited their self-evaluations did not change substantially.

Numerous other studies of this type will be found reviewed by Wylie (1961, 1968, 1974, 1978) and London and Rosehan (1964, pp. 474–479).

Other Empirical Approaches

Although qualitative descriptions, content analysis of therapeutic protocols, and the use of Q-technique constitute the principal empirical approaches of Rogers and his associates to the study of personality, they have also employed a number of other methods. These methods consist of approaching the person from an external frame of reference. Such standard tests as the Rorschach (Muench, 1947; Carr, 1949; Haimowitz, 1950; Mosak, 1950; Haimowitz and Haimowitz, 1952; Rogers, 1967a), the TAT (Dymond, 1954; Grummon and John, 1954; Rogers, 1967a), the Minnesota Multiphasic (Mosak, 1950; Rogers, 1967a), the Bell Adjustment Inventory (Muench, 1947; Mosak, 1950), and the Kent-Rosanoff Word Association Test (Muench, 1947) have been used with clients in therapy. One of Rogers' students has also used physiological indices for measuring tension and emotion (Thetford, 1949, 1952).

CURRENT STATUS AND EVALUATION

Although Rogers continues to write and to promulgate his views for professionals and for the public at large, the mainlines of his thinking appear to have become consolidated. There has been no major change in his theoretical viewpoint since 1959 although he has become more forceful in presenting his views, more assured of their essential validity, more aware of their applicability to helping to solve the problems of the modern world, and more convinced that mankind has a hopeful future (Rogers, 1977). Client-centered therapy is an established and widely used method of treatment. Person-centered theory as formulated by Rogers has become a formidable stimulus for investigative activities. Research on the person has grown from a tiny trickle in the 1940s to a broad stream in the 1960s and 1970s. Not all of the empirical findings are favorable to Rogers' theory nor can all research on the self be attributed directly to Rogers. Nevertheless, no one has been more influential in providing an intellectual tradition in which research on the self might flourish. His dictum that "the best vantage point for understanding behavior is from the internal frame of reference of the individual himself" has been a rallying point for many psychologists. His passionate regard for humanistic values in psychological research as presented in so many of his writings and in his famous debate with B. F. Skinner (Rogers, 1956) has helped to polarize the thinking of psychologists. His optimism, his implicit faith in the inherent goodness of humans, and his steadfast belief that troubled people can be helped are attitudes that have attracted many people who consider behaviorism too cold and psychoanalysis too pessimistic. That there is a "third force" in psychology as viable as behaviorism and psychoanalysis are, is due in very large part to Carl Rogers.

It has already been noted that Rogers' theoretical views, like those of Freud, Jung, Adler, Horney, and Sullivan, grew out of his experiences in working with emotionally disturbed persons. There is, however, one very significant difference between Rogers and these other clinic-based theorists. From 1940 when Rogers accepted an appointment as professor of psychology at Ohio State University, his primary identification has been with academic psychology. It is no secret that advancement in the university setting and professional prestige are largely determined by one's research productivity and the research activities of one's students. Moreover, the academic psychologist has to face up to the exacting critical scrutiny of his or her colleagues. That Rogers has met these tests with great success is attested to by the quantity and quality of his publications, by the number of students he has had, and by the honors which his fellow psychologists have accorded him. He was one of the first three psychologists chosen to receive a Distinguished Scientific Contribution Award from the American Psychological Association in 1956. On the other hand, despite his association with the academic process for many years, Rogers has not been very happy with this involvement and has been sharply critical of traditional university structures. He views himself as having gone his own way uninfluenced, as far as possible, by the pressures and politics of academic departments.

The chief criticism that many psychologists make of Rogers' theory is that it is based upon a naive type of phenomenology. (See, for example, Smith, 1950.) There is abundant evidence to show that factors unavailable to consciousness motivate behavior, and that what a person says of him or herself is distorted by defenses and deceptions of various kinds. Self-reports are notoriously lacking in reliability, not only because people may intend to deceive their listeners, but also because they do not know the whole truth about themselves. Rogers has been criticized for ignoring the unconscious whose potency for controlling human conduct has been attested to by psychoanalytic investigations over a period of eight decades. Rogers believes there is no need to probe, to interpret, to carry on extensive and intricate analyses of dreams, or to excavate layer after layer of psychic strata—because the person is revealed in what the person says about himself.

The criticism of naivete´ cannot be urged too strongly against Rogers, however. Explicitly recognized in Rogers' theory is the concept of an organism that has many experiences of which the person is not aware. Some of these unsymbolized experiences are denied entrance to consciousness because they are inconsistent with the self-image. If this is not repression, in the psychoanalytic sense, then the distinction between it and repression is so slight as to be negligible. The principal difference between Rogers and psychoanalysis lies in Rogers' conviction that repression can be prevented in the first place by the parents giving unconditional positive regard to the child. Or if the damage has been done, it can be corrected later by therapeutic intervention in which the therapist prizes the client. When given unconditional positive regard, the client eventually discovers his or her real self. This real self is then one that is completely congruent with the experiencing organism. Psychoanalysts would object that unconditional positive regard, even if it could be consistently maintained by the therapist, would not be sufficient to overcome repression in the patient. Analysis and interpretation of what the patient is thinking and feeling, of dreams, and of the transference are necessary to penetrate the defenses and make conscious that which is unconscious. Even under the most favorable therapeutic conditions, a portion of one's experiences still remains unconscious.

Recently, Rogers (1977) has modified his view of the unconscious. He now feels that unconscious organismic processes do in fact, and should, guide much of our behavior. These processes are not antisocial and impulsive in the Freudian sense; they are dependable guides for achieving personal fulfillment and for developing warm interpersonal relations. Rogers seems to be saying "Trust your unconscious."

Rogers is not unmindful of the adverse criticisms his theory has received, especially from psychoanalytically oriented psychologists. He recognizes the dilemma that defensive behavior places person-centered theory in. "Some would have us resolve it by throwing overboard any attempt to make objective measurements of the phenomenal field" (Rogers and Dymond, 1954, p. 430). However, Rogers is not ready yet to jettison a viewpoint that in his opinion has been so tremendously fruitful. "Consequently, we prefer to live with this dilemma until we understand it more deeply and perhaps can develop more sensitive theories as well as better instruments to deal with it" (Rogers and Dymond, 1954, p 431). Yet, he does not seem to be satisfied with this conclusion, either, because a few pages later he raises this question regarding the quest for the "real" personality.

Is it possible that in place of this hypothetical single reality we shall have to substitute a recognition that there are various perceptual vantage points from which to view the person, one of these being from within the consciousness of the person himself? Certainly our evidence would suggest the lawfulness and internal order within each of these perceptual views. There is also a suggestion of significant and perhaps predictable relationships between these perceptual systems. But whether there is *a* reality with which the science of personality may deal remains a question (Rogers and Dymond, 1954, p. 433).

By "perceptual vantage points" Rogers means various ways of observing and describing behavior. One can, for example, study the person's responses in a standard test situation such as that provided by the Rorschach method, by the TAT, and by the Minnesota Multiphasic Test. One can also measure the physiological changes that accompany increased tension and emotion. Or one can observe another person's behavior in a natural life situation. Rogers in his role as a scientific investigator has not hesitated to employ these and other methods. He has by no means limited his observations to those of phenomenal self-reports, although such reports are favored by his theory.

Another criticism focuses on Rogers' failure to describe the nature of the organism. If the organism is the basic psychological reality what are the characteristics of this reality? What precisely are the potentialities residing within the organism that are to be actualized? Other theorists have postulated such elements as life and death instincts (Freud), archetypes (Jung), needs (Murray, Lewin, Fromm, and Maslow), drives (Miller and Dollard), and traits (Allport and Cattell), but Rogers does not postulate anything other than the very general actualizing tendency.

Rogers might answer this type of criticism by saying that as a phenomenologist he is interested only in the experiences flowing from the organism and the person's openness to these experiences, and not in the organism itself. It is, of course, a theorist's prerogative to place a theory within a frame and to ignore what lies outside the frame because it is considered to be either unimportant or irrelevant. All theorists exercise this right.

Whatever the future of Rogers' theory may be it has served well the purpose of making the self an object of empirical investigation. Many psychologists have given theoretical status to the self, but it is to Rogers' credit that his formulations regarding the phenomenal self have led directly to the making of predictions and to investigative activities. Heuristically, his theory has been an extremely potent and pervasive force in contemporary psychology.

BIBLIOGRAPHY
PRIMARY SOURCES

Rogers, C. R. *Client-centered therapy; its current practice, implications, and theory.* Boston: Houghton Mifflin, 1951.

Rogers, C. R. A theory of therapy, personality, and interpersonal relationships, as developed in the client-centered framework. In S. Koch (Ed.). *Psychology: a study of a science.* Vol. 3. New York: McGraw-Hill, 1959, 184–256.

Rogers, C. R. *On becoming a person.* Boston: Houghton Mifflin, 1961.

Rogers, C. R. *Carl Rogers on personal power.* New York: Delacorte Press, 1977.

REFERENCES

Bergin, A. E. The effect of dissonant persuasive communications upon changes in a self-referring attitude. *J. Personality,* 1962, **30,** 423–438.

Bowdlear, C. Dynamics of idiopathic epilepsy as studied in one case. Unpublished doctor's dissertation, Western Reserve Univ., 1955.

Butler, J. M., and Haigh, G. V. Changes in the relation between self-concepts and ideal concepts consequent upon client-centered counseling. In C. R. Rogers and Rosalind F. Dymond (eds.) *Psychotherapy and personality change; co-ordinated studies in the client-centered approach.* Chicago: Univ. of Chicago Press, 1954, 55–76.

Carr, A. C. An evaluation of nine nondirective psychotherapy cases by means of the Rorschach. *J. Consult. Psychol.,* 1949, 13, 196–205.

Cartwright, R. D., and Lerner, B. Empathy, need to change, and improvement with psychotherapy. *J. Consult. Psychol.,* 1963, **27,** 138–144.

Chodorkoff, B. Self-perception, perceptual defense, and adjustment. *J. Abnorm. Soc. Psychol.,* 1954,**49,** 508–512.

Cole, C. W., Oetting, E. R., and Hinkle, J. E. Non-linearity of self-concept discrepancy: the value dimension. *Psychol. Rep.,* 1967, **21,** 58–60.

Dymond, R. F. Adjustment changes over therapy from Thematic Apperception Test ratings. In C. R. Rogers and Rosalind F. Dymond (Eds.). *Psychotherapy and personality change: co-ordinated studies in the client-centered approach.* Chicago: Univ. of Chicago Press, 1954, 109–120.

Friedman, I. Phenomenal, ideal and projected conceptions of self. *J. Abnorm. Soc. Psychol.,* 1955, **51,** 611–615.

Frisbie, L. V., Vanasek, F. J., and Dingman, H. F. The self and the ideal self: methodological study of pedophiles. *Psychol. Rep.,* 1967, **20,** 699–706.

Gordon, T., and Cartwright, D. The effect of psychotherapy upon certain attitudes toward others. In C. R. Rogers and Rosalind F. Dymond (Eds.). *Psychotherapy and personality change; co-ordinated studies in the client-centered approach.* Chicago: Univ. of Chicago Press, 1954, 167–195.

Grummon, D. L, and John, E. S. Changes over client-centered therapy evaluated on psychoanalytically based Thematic Apperception Test scales. In C. R. Rogers and Rosalind F. Dymond (Eds.). *Psychotherapy and personality change; co-ordinated studies in the client-centered approach.* Chicago: Univ. of Chicago Press, 1954, 121–144.

Haigh, G. Defensive behavior in client-centered therapy. *J. Consult. Psychol.,* 1949, **13,** 181–189.

Haimowitz, N. R. An investigation into some personality changes occurring in individuals undergoing client-centered therapy. Unpublished doctor's dissertation, Univ. of Chicago, 1950.

Haimowitz, N. R., and Haimowitz, M. L. Personality changes in client-centered therapy. In W. Wolff and J. A. Precker (Eds.). Success in psychotherapy. *Pers. Monogr.,* 1952, **3,** 63–93.

Havener, P. H. and Izard, C. E. Unrealistic self-enhancement in paranoid schizophrenics. *J. Consult. Psychol.,* 1962, **26,** 65–68.

Krause, M. S. An analysis of Carl R. Rogers' theory of personality. *Genetic Psychol. Monog.,* 1964, **69,** 49–99.

Lipkin, S. The client evaluates nondirective psychotherapy. *J. Consult. Psychol.,* 1948, **12,** 137–146.

London, P., and Rosehan, D. Personality dynamics. In P. R. Farnsworth (Ed.). *Annual Review of Psychology,* Palo Alto, Calif.: Annual Reviews, Vol. 15, 1964, 447–492.

McCleary, R. A., and Lazarus, R. S. Autonomic discrimination without awareness. *J. Pers.,* 1949, **18,** 171–179.

Medinnus, G. R., and Curtis, F. J. The relation between maternal self-acceptance and child acceptance. *J. Consult. Psychol.,* 1963, **27,** 542–544.

Milgram, N. A., and Helper, M. M. The social desirability set in individual and grouped self-ratings. *J. Consult. Psychol.,* 1961, **25,** 91.

Mosak, H. Evaluation in psychotherapy: a study of some current measures. Unpublished doctor's dissertation, Univ. of Chicago, 1950.

Muench, G. A. An evaluation of non-directive psychotherapy by means of the Rorschach and other tests. *Appl. Psychol. Monogr.,* 1947, no. 13.

Muench, G. A., and Rogers, C. R. Counseling of emotional blocking in an aviator. *J. Abnorm. Soc. Psychol.,* 1946, **41,** 207–215.

Nunnally, J. C. An investigation of some propositions of self-conception: the case of Miss Sun. *J. Abnorm. Soc. Psychol.,* 1955, **50,** 87–92.

Phillips, E. L. Attitudes toward self and others: a brief questionnaire report. *J. Consult. Psychol.,* 1951, **15,** 79–81.

Pilisuk, M. Cognitive balance and self-relevant attitudes. *J. Abnorm. Soc. Psychol.,* 1962, **65,** 95–103.

Porter, E. H., Jr. The development and evaluation of a measure of counseling interview procedures. *Educ. Psychol. Measmt.,* 1943, **3,** 105–126, 215–238.

Raimy, V. C. The self-concept as a factor in counseling and personality organization. Unpublished doctor's dissertation, Ohio State Univ., 1943.

Raimy, V. C. Self-reference in counseling interviews. *J. Consult. Psychol.,* 1948, **12,** 153–163.

Rogers, C. R. *The clinical treatment of the problem child.* Boston: Houghton Mifflin, 1939.

Rogers, C. R. *Counseling and psychotherapy; newer concepts in practice.* Boston: Houghton Mifflin, 1942.

Rogers, C. R. Some observations on the organization of personality. *Amer. Psychologist,* 1947, **2,** 358–368.

Rogers, C. R. *Dealing with social tensions: a presentation of client-centered counseling as a means of handling interpersonal conflict.* New York: Hinds, 1948.

Rogers, C. R. *Client-centered therapy; its current practice, implications, and theory.* Boston: Houghton Mifflin, 1951.

Rogers, C. R. Persons or science? A philosophical question. *Amer. Psychologist,* 1955, **10,** 267–278.

Rogers, C. R. Some issues concerning the control of human behavior. (Symposium with B. F. Skinner.) *Science,* 1956, **124,** 1057–1066.

Rogers, C. R. A theory of therapy, personality, and interpersonal relationships, as developed in the client–centered framework. In S. Koch (Ed.). *Psychology: a study of a science.* Vol. 3. New York: McGraw-Hill, 1959, 184–256.

Rogers, C. R. *On becoming a person.* Boston: Houghton Mifflin, 1961.

Rogers, C. R. (Ed.). *The therapeutic relationship and its impact: a study of psychotherapy with schizophrenics.* Madison, Wisc.: Univ. of Wisconsin Press, 1967a.

Rogers, C. R. Autobiography. In E. G. Boring and G. Lindzey (Eds.). *A History of psychology in autobiography.* Vol. 5. New York: Appleton-Century-Crofts, 1967b, 341–384.

Rogers, C. R. *Freedom to learn: a view of what education might become.* Columbus, Ohio: Merrill, 1969.

Rogers, C. R. *Carl Rogers on encounter groups.* New York: Harper and Row, 1970.

Rogers, C. R. *Becoming partners: marriage and its alternatives.* New York: Delacorte Press, 1972.

Rogers, C. R. In retrospect: Forty-six years. *Amer. Psychologist,* 1974, **29,** 115–123.

Rogers, C. R. *Carl Rogers on personal power.* New York: Delacorte Press, 1977.

Rogers, C. R., and Dymond, R. F. (Eds.). *Psychotherapy and personality change; co-ordinated studies in the client-centered approach.* Chicago: Univ. of Chicago Press, 1954.

Rogers, C. R., and Wallen, J. L. *Counseling with returned servicemen.* New York: McGraw-Hill, 1946.

Rudikoff, E. C. A comparative study of the changes in the concepts of the self, the ordinary person, and the ideal in eight cases. In C. R. Rogers and Rosalind F.

Dymond (Eds.). *Psychotherapy and personality change; co-ordinated studies in the client-centered approach.* Chicago: Univ. of Chicago Press, 1954, 85–98.

Seeman, J. A study of the process of non-directive therapy. *J. Consul. Psychol.,* 1949, **13,** 157–168.

Seeman, J., and Raskin, N. J. Research perspectives in client-centered therapy. In O. H. Mowrer (Ed.). *Psychotherapy.* New York: Ronald Press, 1953, 205–234.

Sheerer, E. T. An analysis of the relationship between acceptance of and respect for self and acceptance of and respect for others in ten counseling cases. *J. Consult. Psychol.,* 1949, **13,** 169–175.

Smith, M. B. The phenomenological approach in personality theory: some critical remarks, *J. Abnorm. Soc. Psychol.,* 1950, **45,** 516–522.

Snyder, W. U. An investigation of the nature of nondirective psychotherapy. *J. Gen. Psychol.,* 1945, 33, 193–223.

Snyder, W. U., *et al. Casebook of nondirective counseling.* Boston: Houghton Mifflin, 1947.

Stephenson, W. *The study of behavior.* Chicago: Univ. of Chicago Press, 1953.

Stock, Dorothy. An investigation into the interrelations between self-concept and feelings directed toward other persons and groups. *J. Consult. Psychol.,* 1949, **13,** 176–180.

Suinn, R. M. The relationship between self-acceptance and acceptance of others: a learning theory analysis. *J. Abnorm. Soc. Psychol.,* 1961, **63,** 37–42.

Thetford, W. N. The measurement of physiological responses to frustration before and after nondirective psychotherapy. Unpublished doctor's dissertation, Univ. of Chicago, 1949.

Thetford, W. N. An objective measurement of frustration tolerance in evaluating psychotherapy. In W. Wolff and J. A. Precker (Eds.). *Success in psychotherapy, Pers. Monogr.,* 1952, **3,** 26–62.

Wolff, W. Involuntary self-expression in gait and other movements: an experimental study. *Character & Pers.,* 1935, **3,** 327–344.

Wylie, R. C. *The self concept: a critical survey of pertinent research literature.* Lincoln, Neb.: Univ. of Nebraska Press, 1961.

Wylie, R. C. The present status of self theory. In E. F. Borgatta and W. W. Lambert (Eds.). *Handbook of personality theory and research.* Chicago: Rand McNally, 1968, 728–787.

Wylie, R. C. *The self-concept.* Lincoln: Univ. of Nebraska Press. Vol. 1, *A review of methodological considerations and measuring instruments,* 1974. Vol. 2, *Theory and research on selected topics,* 1978.

EXISTENTIAL PSYCHOLOGY

9

In the years immediately after the end of World War II a popular movement known as *existentialism* rose to prominence in Europe and quickly spread to the United States. The movement was born out of the French resistance to the German occupation, and its two most articulate spokesmen were Jean Paul Sartre and Albert Camus. Sartre was a brilliant graduate of the Sorbonne who was to become a distinguished philosopher, writer, and political journalist. Camus, a native of Algeria, became famous as a novelist and essayist. Both men were awarded the Nobel Prize in literature although Sartre refused to accept the award. Camus' life was tragically ended in an automobile accident when he was forty-six years old.

As often happens with *avant garde* movements that are taken up by a heterogeneous assortment of people—artists, writers, intellectuals, clergy, university students, sophisticates, dissidents, and rebels of various kinds—existentialism came to stand for many different things. Camus even denied that he was an existentialist. In view of the popular base of existentialism, its clichés and slogans, and its many schisms, it might have spent itself in a few years as many other intellectual fads have done. The fact that it did not suffer this fate but actually emerged as a potent force in modern thought, including psychology and psychiatry, can be attributed to the discovery that existentialism had a sturdy tradition with very impressive ancestors as well as solid contemporary proponents in addition to

Sartre. Its most notable ancestral figure was the Danish eccentric, Soren Kierkegaard (1813–1855). This tortured soul was a prolific, impassioned polemic writer whose books now constitute a sort of sacred writing for existentialism. A long list of other famous names including those of Nietzsche, Dostoevsky, and Bergson were added to the genealogy of existentialism. Among moderns, Berdyaev, Buber, Heidegger, Jaspers, Kafka, Marcel, Merleau-Ponty, and Tillich have been identified with the existentialist movement. (An excellent introduction to existentialism is William Barret's book *Irrational man*, 1962.)

For our purposes, the name of Martin Heidegger (1889–1976), the German philosopher, has the greatest pertinence. He and Karl Jaspers (1883–1969) are considered by Barrett to be the creators of existential philosophy in this century. More important, Heidegger is the bridge to the psychologists and psychiatrists whose views of humans we shall concentrate on in this chapter. The central idea in Heidegger's ontology (ontology is that branch of philosophy dealing with being or existence) is that an individual is a being-in-the-world. He or she does not exist as a self or a subject in relation to an external world; nor is a person a thing or object or body interacting with other things that make up the world. Humans have their existence by being-in-the-world, and the world has its existence because there is a Being to disclose it. Being and world are one. Barrett calls Heidegger's ontology a Field Theory of Being. Heidegger's philosophy of existence is set forth in his book *Being and time* (1962), which is regarded as one of the most influential books, as well as one of the most difficult, in modern philosophy.

Heidegger was also a phenomenologist, and phenomenology has played an important role in the history of psychology. Heidegger was a student of Edmund Husserl (1859–1938), the founder of modern phenomenology, and Husserl in turn was a student of Carl Stumpf, one of the leaders of the "new" experimental psychology that emerged in Germany during the last half of the nineteenth century. Köhler and Koffka, who along with Wertheimer founded Gestalt psychology, were also students of Stumpf and adopted phenomenology as a method of analyzing psychological phenomena. We point out these historical facts to emphasize the common antecedents of psychology, phenomenology, and existentialism.

Phenomenology is the description of the data (literally the "givens") of immediate experience. It seeks to understand rather than to explain phenomena. Van Kaam (1966) defines it "as a method in psychology [that] seeks to disclose and elucidate the phenomena of behavior as they manifest themselves in their perceived immediacy"

(p. 15). Phenomenology is sometimes regarded as a method that is ancillary to every science, since a science begins by observing what is in immediate experience (Boring, 1950, p. 18). This idea of phenomenology is beautifully expressed in the opening paragraph of Köhler's *Gestalt psychology* (1947).

There seems to be a single starting point for psychology, exactly as for all the other sciences: the world as we find it, naively and uncritically. The naiveté may be lost as we proceed. Problems may be found which were at first compeletely hidden from our eyes. For their solution it may be necessary to devise concepts which seem to have little contact with direct primary experience. Nevertheless, the whole development must begin with a naive picture of the world. This origin is necessary because there is no other basis from which a science can arise. In my case, which may be taken as reprsentative of many others, that naive picture consists, at this moment, of a blue lake with dark forests around it, a big, gray rock, hard and cool, which I have chosen as a seat, a paper on which I write, a faint noise of the wind which hardly moves the trees, and a strong odor characteristic of boats and fishing. But there is more in this world: somehow I now behold, though it does not become fused with the blue lake of the present, another lake of a milder blue, at which I found myself, some years ago, looking from its shore in Illinois. I am perfectly accustomed to beholding thousands of views of this kind which arise when I am alone. And there is still more in this world: for instance, my hand and fingers as they lightly move across the paper. Now, when I stop writing and look around again, there also is a feeling of health and vigor. But in the next moment I feel something like a dark pressure somewhere in my interior which tends to develop into a feeling of being hunted—I have promised to have this manuscript ready within a few months (pp. 3–4).

One of the most articulate and sophisticated contemporary phenomenologists is Erwin Straus (1963, 1966). For a concise, scholarly discussion of phenomenology by one of its chief psychological proponents in the United States, see MacLeod (1964).

Phenomenology, as represented in the works of the Gestalt psychologists and of Erwin Straus, has been employed primarily for investigating the phenomena of such psychological processes as perceiving, learning, remembering, thinking, and feeling, but has not been used in personality studies. Existential psychology, on the other hand, has used phenomenology for elucidating those phenomena that are often regarded as belonging to the sphere of personality. *Existential psychology may be defined as an empirical science of human existence that employs the method of phenomenological analysis.*

In this chapter we shall deal primarily with existential psychology as set forth in the writings of the Swiss psychiatrists, Ludwig Binswanger and Medard Boss, for a variety of reasons. They remain very close to the fountainhead of European existential thought and their identification with existentialism is of long standing. Their translation of Heidegger's ontology of abstract Beingness to the study of individual beings is carefully worked out, often in collaboration with Heidegger himself. (That part of southern Germany where Heidegger lived is adjacent to Switzerland.) As practicing psychiatrists they have accumulated a wealth of emprical material from the analysis of patients. Finally, both men write clearly and vividly about abstruse matters and many of their writings are available in English translation.

There are a number of American existential psychologists, but they derive their views largely from Binswanger and other European psychologists and psychiatrists. Rollo May is one of the most ardent American exponents of existentialism and his introductory chapters in the book, *Existence* (edited by May, Angel, and Ellenberger, 1958) and his book *Existential psychology* (second edition, 1969) have been a principal source of information about existentialism for American psychologists. Adrian Van Kaam, professor of psychology at Duquesne University, is a prolific writer on phenomenology and existentialism. He has the advantage of having been trained in existential thought and phenomenology in European universities as well as in the United States. His book, *Existential foundations of psychology* (1966), is a comprehensive treatment of the subject. Another prominent American existential psychologist is James Bugental (1965). Some of the other theorists treated in the present book who have been influenced to varying degrees by existentialism are Allport, Angyal, Fromm, Goldstein, Lewin, Maslow, and Rogers.

Ludwig Binswanger was born in Kreuzlingen, Switzerland April 13, 1881, and took his medical degree at the University of Zurich in 1907. He studied under Eugen Bleuler, a leading Swiss psychiatrist, and with Jung. He was one of the first Swiss followers of Freud, and maintained a friendship with him throughout their lives. (For an account of this close relationship, see Binswanger, 1957.) Binswanger succeeded his father (and his grandfather before him) as chief medical director of the Bellevue sanatorium in Kreuzlingen. He died in 1966.

In the early 1920s, Binswanger became one of the first proponents of the application of phenomenology to psychiatry. Ten years later he became an existential analyst. Binswanger defines existential analysis as a phenomenological analysis of actual human existence. Its aim is the reconstruction of the inner world of experience. His system is expounded in his major work, *Grundformen und Erkenntnis menschlichen Daseins* (1943, revised edition, 1953), which has not been translated into English. Sources for the English reader are three chapters by

Ludwig Binswanger

Binswanger (1958a, 1958b, 1958c) in the book *Existence,* edited by May, Angel, and Ellenberger, and *Being-in-the-world: selected papers of Ludwig Binswanger* (1963). This later book contains a long critical introduction by the editor and translator, Jacob Needleman (1963).

Although Binswanger's main influence was Heidegger, he also incorporated in his viewpoint ideas derived from Martin Buber (1958).

Medard Boss was born in St. Gallen, Switzerland, on October 4, 1903. When he was two years old, his parents moved to Zurich, where Boss has resided ever since. After trying unsuccessfully to be-

Medard Boss

come an artist, Boss decided to study medicine. He received his medical degree from the University of Zurich in 1928. Prior to obtaining
the degree, he studied in Paris and Vienna and was analyzed by Sigmund Freud. From 1928 to 1932, Boss was assistant to Eugen Bleuler, the famous director of the Burgholzli psychiatric hospital in
Zurich. Thereafter, for two years, Boss underwent further psychoanalytic training in London and Germany with such prominent psychoanalysts as Ernest Jones, Karen Horney, Otto Fenichel, Hanns Sachs,
and Wilhelm Reich. While in Germany he also worked with Kurt
Goldstein. After this excellent preparation, Boss went into private
practice as a psychoanalyst at the age of 32. About this time, he and
several other psychotherapists began a series of monthly meetings at
the home of Carl Jung.

The year 1946 was a turning point in Boss's intellectual life. It was
then that he became personally acquainted with Martin Heidegger.
As a result of their close association Boss generated an existential
form of psychology and psychotherapy that he called *Daseinsanalysis*.
Dasein is a German word that has been translated into English by the
hyphenated expression "being-in-the-world." (The names existential psychology and *Daseinsanalysis* are used interchangeably
in this chapter.)

Boss's outlook was also greatly influenced by his encounter with
the wisdom of India in two trips he made there in 1956 and 1958. He
describes his experiences in a book *A psychiatrist discovers India* (1965).

For a number of years, Boss was president of the International Federation for Medical Psychotherapy and is now its honorary president.
From 1954 until his retirement in 1973 he was professor of psychotherapy at the University of Zurich. He is president of the Daseins-
analytic Institute for Psychotherapy and Psychosomatics in Zurich.
Boss was the recipient of the "Great Therapist Award" given by the
American Psychiatric Association in 1971.

Boss has written a number of books some of which have been
translated into English. For a more complete understanding of Boss's
viewpoint the following books are recommended: *The analysis of
dreams* (1958), *Psychoanalysis and Daseinsanalysis* (1963), *Existential
foundations of medicine and psychology* (1977), and *"I dreamt last night
. . ."* (1978). The *Existential foundations of medicine and psychology* contains the most mature statement of Boss's position.

What does existential psychology, as represented in the writings of
Binswanger and Boss, react against in other psychological systems,
and what does it stand for? First and most important, it objects to carrying over the concept of *causality* from the natural sciences into psychology. There are no cause–effect relationships in human existence.

At most, there are only sequences of behaviors, but it is impermissible to derive causality from sequence. Something that happens to a child is not the cause of its later behavior as an adult. Both events may have the same existential meaning but that does not signify that Event A caused Event B. In short, existential psychology by rejecting causality also rejects positivism, determinism, and materialism. It asserts that psychology is not like any of the other sciences and should not model itself after them. It requires its own method—phenomenology—and its own concepts—being-in-the-world, modes of existence, freedom, responsibility, becoming, transcendence, spatiality, temporality and many others, all derived from Heidegger's ontology.

The existential psychologist replaces the concept of causality by the concept of motivation. Motivation always presupposes an understanding (or misunderstanding) of the relation between cause and effect. Boss uses the example of a window being closed by the wind and by a person to illustrate the difference between cause and motive. The wind *causes* the window to shut, but a person is *motivated* to close the window because he or she knows when the window is closed rain cannot come in or the noise from the street will be muted or the room will be less drafty. One may say that the pressure exerted by the person's arm on the window *caused* it to close—which would be true, but would omit the whole motivational and cognitive context of which the final act is merely a completion. Even the act of applying pressure itself requires an understanding of where to place one's hand, what it means to pull or push on something, and the like. Consequently, causality has little or no relevance for human behavior. Motivation and understanding are the operative principles in an existential analysis of behavior.

Closely related to this first objection is the firm opposition of existential psychology to the *dualism* of subject (mind) and object (body, environment, or matter). It is this split, attributed to Descartes, that results in explaining man's experience and behavior in terms of environmental stimuli or bodily states. "Man thinks, not the brain" (Straus, 1963). Existential psychology stands for the unity of the individual-in-the-world. Any view that destroys this unity is a falsification and fragmentation of human existence.

Existential psychology also denies that something lies behind phenomena that explains them or causes their appearance. Explanations of human existence in terms of a self, or an unconscious, psychic or physical energy, or forces such as instincts, brain waves, drives, and archetypes are ruled out. Phenomena are what they are in all of their immediacy; they are not a façade or a derivative of something else. It is, or should be, the business of psychology to describe phenomena as carefully and as fully as possible. Phenomenological description or explication, not causal explanation or proof, is the aim of psychological science.

Existential psychology is suspicious of theory because theory—any theory—implies that something that cannot be seen is producing that which is visible. For the phenomenologist, only that which can be seen or otherwise experienced is real. Truth is not arrived at by an intellectual exercise; it is revealed or disclosed in the phenomena themselves. Moreover, theory, or any preconception, acts as a blinder for apprehending the revealed truth of experience. This truth can only be attained by a person who is completely open to the world. See what there is to see without any hypotheses or prejudgments is the existential psychologist's prescription for studying behavior.

. . . Heidegger places in the psychiatrist's hands a key by means of which he can, free of the prejudice of any scientific *theory,* ascertain and describe the *phenomena* he investigates in their full phenomenal content and intrinsic context (Binswanger, 1963, p. 206).

Binswanger and Boss have succeeded in divesting themselves of the whole complex apparatus of Freudian and Jungian theory, despite the fact that they were trained in psychoanalysis and practiced it for many years. One gains the impression from reading their works that this divestment was a very freeing experience for them.

Dissection is not countenanced because it reduces humans to a heap of fragments that defy, as much as Humpty Dumpty did, resynthesis. The aim of existential psychology, as stated by Boss, is to make the articulated structure of the human being transparent. "Articulation is possible only in the context of a whole that has been left intact; all articulation as such derives from wholeness" (Boss, 1963, p. 285).

Finally, existential psychology adamantly opposes regarding an individual as a thing like a stone or a tree. Not only does such a view prevent the psychologist from understanding humans in the full light of their existence-in-the-world, but it also results in the dehumanization of people. Existential psychology enters the arena of social criticism when it polemicizes against the estrangement, alienation, and fragmentation of humans by technology, bureaucracy, and mechanization. When people are treated as things and come to regard themselves as things that can be managed, controlled, shaped, and exploited, they are prevented from living in a truly human manner. A person is free, and he or she alone is responsible for their existence. Freedom, as Boss points out, is not something humans *have,* it is something they *are*. It is this tenet of existential psychology that makes it appealing to the humanistic movement in American psychology.

It would be wrong to conclude, however, that existential psychology is primarily optimistic or hopeful about humans. One does not need to read far in Kierkegaard, Nietzsche, Heidegger, Sartre, Binswanger, or Boss to realize that this is far from being the case. Existential psychology is as concerned with death as it is with life. Nothingness yawns always at one's feet. Dread looms as large as love does in the existentialists' writings. There can be no light without shadows. A psychology that makes guilt inborn and an inescapable feature of existence does not offer much solace. "I am free" means at the same time "I am completely responsible for my existence." The implications of the freedom-responsibility nexus are spelled out in Erich Fromm's *Escape from freedom* (1941). Becoming a human being is a tough project and few achieve it. Much of this bleakness has been excised or played down in some of the American offshoots of existential psychology.

We now consider some of the basic concepts of existential psychology (*Daseinsanalysis*) as formulated by Binswanger and Boss.

STRUCTURE OF EXISTENCE
Being-in-the-World (Dasein)

This is the fundamental concept of existential psychology. All the structure of human existence is based on this concept. Being-in-the-world, or *Dasein, is* human existence. *Dasein* is not a property or attribute of a person, nor a part of their being like Freud's ego or Jung's anima; it is the whole of human existence. Thus, when Boss uses the term *Daseinsanalysis* he means the careful elucidation of the specific nature of human existence or being-in-the-world. *Dasein* is a German word used by Heidegger and contrasts with *Vorhandsein,* which characterizes the existence of nonhuman things. Literally translated, *Dasein* means "to be" (*sein*) "there" (*da*). But this literal translation does injustice to the actual meaning Heidegger had in mind. The meaningful translation is "to be *the* there." "*The* there" is definitely not the world as an external terrain. It is the luminating, understanding world-openness—a state of being in the world in which an individual's whole existence that is and has to be can appear and *become* present and *be present*.

One is *there* expresses the primary immediacy and inevitability of the existential condition. Humans have no existence apart from the world, and the world has no existence apart from humans. As Boss reiterates, "Man discloses [elucidates] the world." People are "the luminated realm into which all that is to be may actually shine forth, emerge, and appear as a phenomenon, i.e., as that which shows itself" (1963, p. 70). A phenomenon is a "shining forth" of immediate reality. Nothing lies behind phenomena; they are not the visible manifestations of an ultimate reality. They *are* reality. Consequently, in existential or *Dasein* analysis, one tries to see what is in one's experience and to describe it as accurately as language permits. This is a very difficult concept for Westerners to comprehend or accept since they have been conditioned by the scientific view of the world to look for concealed or invisible meanings and causes. A person does not confer meaning on objects; they reveal their meanings to the person when he or she is open to receive them. The basic characteristic of *Dasein* is its openness to perceiving and responding to what is there in its presence. Boss speaks of humans *dwelling* in the world to emphasize the inseparable unity of being-in-the-world.

Being-in-the-world heals the split between subject and object and restores the oneness of humans and the world. It is necessary to emphasize that this view does not state that humans are related to or interact with the world. This would suggest that people and environment are two separate things. Nor are there two poles, human and world, as in Angyal's biosphere. Part of the difficulty in rendering this concept is due to differences between German and English. In German, new concepts can be expressed by combining words as *da* and *sein*. In English this is accomplished by the less satisfactory method of employing hyphens to connect words, for example, being-in-the-world. Hyphens do not entirely eliminate the suggestion of separateness. Moreover, hyphenated expressions appear pedantic and contrived. (It is ironical that Boss in his recent writings has taken to hyphenating *Da-sein,* probably to emphasize that *Da* means "*the* there" and not simply "there.")

The world in which humans have their existence comprises three regions: (1) the biological or physical surroundings or landscape (*Umwelt*), (2) the human environment (*Mitwelt*), and (3) the person him or her self including the body (*Eigenwelt*). In order to clarify the meaning of these three world-regions and the use that is made of them in existential analysis, we cannot do better than to quote a long passage from Binswanger's *Case of Ellen West* (1958c). Ellen was a young woman who had been in and out of medical and psychiatric treatment for most of her adult life. She was finally referred to Binswanger's sanatorium where she spent the last months of her life. She committed suicide three days after being discharged from the sanatorium. Ellen's most marked symptom was an eating compulsion. Here is Binswanger's summary of Ellen's modes of being in the three world-regions. It is based upon past medical and psychiatric records, Binswanger's personal observations and interviews, and Ellen's own writings consisting of poems, letters, diaries, and a circumstantial account of the history of her neurosis.

If, then, we attempt to summarize once more the individual features and phenomenal forms of [Ellen's] mode of being-in-the-world within the various world-regions . . . we shall again do best to start out from the landscape-world [*Umwelt*]: the being-limited and being-oppressed showed itself here as darkening, darkness, night, cold, ebb-tide; the boundaries or limits as moist fog-walls or clouds, the emptiness as the Uncanny, the longing for freedom (from the world) as ascending into the air, the self as a hushed bird. Within the world of *vegetation,* the being-restricted and being-oppressed showed itself as wilting, the barriers as suffocating air, the emptiness as weeds, the longing for freedom as urge to grow, the self as withered plant. Within the world of things we found the being-restricted in the hole, cellar, tomb; the barriers in walls, masonry, fetters, nets; the longing for freedom in the vessel of fertility, the self in the discarded husk. Within the *animal* world, the being-restricted is seen as being-holed-in, the barriers as earth or black night, the self as worm no longer capable of any longing for freedom, the emptiness as merely vegetating. Within the *Mitwelt* being-restricted is seen as being subjugated, oppressed, impaired and pursued; the emptiness as lack of peace, indifference, joyless submission, seclusion, loneliness; the barriers as fetters, or adders of the everyday, or suffocating air; the hole itself as the little world (of the everyday); the longing for freedom as urge for independence, defiance, insurrection, revolt; the self as rebel, nihilist, later as cowardly compromiser. Within the *Eigenwelt* as thought-world, we recognized being-restricted in cowardice, indulgence, giving up of high-flown plans; the barriers in accusing, jeering ghosts or specters encircling and invading from all sides, the emptiness in being-ruled by one single idea, even as Nothingness; the self in the timid earthworm, the frozen heart, the longing for freedom as desperation. Finally, within the *Eigenwelt* as body-world, we found the being-restricted or oppressed in being fat, the barriers or walls in the layer of fat against which the existence beats its fists as against walls, the emptiness in being dull, stupid, old, ugly, and even being dead, the longing for freedom in wanting-to-be-thin, the self as a mere tube for material filling-up and re-emptying (1958c, pp. 328–329).

The reader will observe in this selection a style of writing that is characteristic of phenomenological analysis. There is an absence of technical terminology except for the German words, *Umwelt, Mitwelt,* and *Eigenwelt* but these only appear to be technical to English readers because they are foreign words. One notes, also, the use of a very evocative, even poetic vocabulary. Such imagery seems to be a far cry from the sober, mundane, and even abrasive vocabulary usually employed in scientific exposition. One must bear in mind, however, that existentialism has always had strong ties with literature, and that one of its ancestors, Nietzsche, was as much a poet as he was a philosopher. Indeed, great literature has always been and, in fact, has to be existential since it deals with being-in-the-world. Literature *is* psychology, the difference being that literature is fictional whereas psychology is or should be factual. This difference is a trivial one, however.

Moreover, Boss insists that what science regards as being a respectable scientific vocabulary is a usurpation of the word "scientific." One should use words that best describe the phenomena and not be bound by an authoritarian tradition. New scientific outlooks usually require a wholly new vocabulary. It is not surprising, therefore, that much of the existential writing sounds strange and esoteric to those brought up in the scientific world-view of the nineteenth century. Like new forms of music or art, the dissonance created by the existential vocabulary will gradually be reduced and disappear.

Existential analysis approaches human existence with no other consideration than that humans are in the world, have a world, and long to get beyond the world (Binswanger). By being-beyond-the-world Binswanger does not mean otherworldliness (Heaven), but expresses the manifold possibilities humans have for transcending the world in which they sojourn and for entering a new world. They can, indeed they long to, realize the full possibilities of their being (Nietzsche's overcoming). For it is only by actualizing their potentialities that they can live an authentic life. When they deny or restrict the full possibilities of their existence, or permit themselves to be dominated by others or by their environment, then they are living an inauthentic existence. Humans are free to choose either kind of life.

Being-Beyond-the-World (Human Possibilities)

Boss states quite flatly that existence consists of nothing but our possibilities of relating to what we encounter. "In reality," Boss writes, "man exists always and only as the myriad of possibilities for relating and disclosing the living beings and things he encounters" (1963, p. 183). Moreover,

man must responsibly take over all his possibilities for world-disclosing relationships, so that whatever may show itself in the light of these relationships can come forth into its being to the best possible extent. In other words, man is to accept all his life-possibilities, he is to appropriate and assemble them to a free authentic own self no longer caught in the narrowed-down mentality of an anonymous, inauthentic 'everybody.' Man's freedom consists in becoming ready for accepting and letting be all that is. . . . (1963, p. 48).

In order to illustrate what it means for humans to refuse to exercise their freedom to realize the possibilities of their existence, Boss (1963) presents the example of a person suffering from melancholia.

It is always the whole existence of the melancholic patient which has failed to take over openly and responsibly all those possibilities of relating to the world which actually would constitute his own genuine self. Consequently, such an existence has no independent standing of its own but continuously falls prey to the demands, wishes, and expectations of others. Such patients try to live up to those foreign expectations as best they can, in order not to lose the protection and love of their surroundings. But the longer these patients allow others to govern their ways of feeling, acting, and perceiving, the more deeply indebted they become in regard to their fundamental task in life, which is to appropriate and carry out, independently and responsibly, all their authentic possibilities of relating to that which they encounter. Hence the terrible guilt feelings of the melancholic. His incessant self-accusations derive from his existential guilt. The severity of his symptoms varies according to the degree in which he fails to exist as the world-openness in whose light everything encountered can unfold and shine forth in its full meaning and content (pp. 209–210).

In his recent book *Existential foundations of medicine and psychology* (1977), Boss says all pathological symptoms, whether physical or psychological, are to be viewed as encroachments on and impairments of the free, open fulfillment of human existence.

Ground of Existence   Are there no limitations to what humans can freely become? One limitation is the ground of existence into which people are "thrown." The conditions of this "throwness," that is, how humans find themselves in the world that is their ground, constitute their destiny. They have to live out this destiny to achieve an authentic life. If one is born a female the ground of her existence will not be the same as that of a male. The fact of being a woman defines, in part, the possibilities of her existence. If she rejects these possibilities, and tries, for instance, to become a man or masculine then she will have chosen an inauthentic mode of being-in-the-world. The punishment for inauthenticity are feelings of guilt. An authentic existence is designed by recognizing the ground of one's existence; an inauthentic existence results from shutting oneself off from one's ground. "The more stubbornly the human being opposes his being-thrown into his existence . . . the more strongly this throwness gains in influence" (Binswanger, 1958c, p. 340). This results in existential weakness by which is meant "that a person does not stand autonomously in his world, that he blocks himself off from the ground of his existence, that he does not take his existence upon himself but trusts himself to alien powers, that he makes alien powers 'responsible' for his fate instead of himself" (Binswanger, 1963, p. 290).

Throwness is also used in the sense of being imposed upon by the world to the extent that people are alienated from themselves. They have succumbed to an alien power. An extreme case of this is the addict whose existence is ruled by narcotics, alcohol, gambling or sex, to name only a few of the many compulsions to which humans are susceptible. In spite of the limiting features of throwness and ground there are still many possibilities over which choice can be exercised.

World-Design

World-design is Binswanger's term for the all-encompassing pattern of an individual's mode of being-in-the-world. A person's world-design determines how he or she will react in specific situations and what kinds of character traits and symptoms they will develop. It makes an imprint on everything the person does. The borders of the design may be narrow and constricted or they may be broad and expansive.

Binswanger gives examples of some narrowly conceived world-design that he has found in his patients. One patient's design was constructed around the need for continuity. Any disruption of continuity—a gap, tearing, or separating—produced great anxiety. One time she fainted when the heel of her shoe fell off. Separation from the mother also evoked anxiety because it broke the continuity of the relationship. Holding onto mother meant holding onto the world; losing her meant falling into the dreadful abyss of Nothingness. Parenthetically, it may be pointed out here and will be elaborated later that the anxiety resulting from losing a heel is not considered by Binswanger to be a symbolic representation of separation from mother. They are both ways—the same way—of relating to the world and one is not a derivative or displacement or cause of the other.

Another patient who had been an active business executive became inactive, dull, and listless. His world-design as a business executive was based on push, pressure, threat, and general world-disharmony. His mode of being-in-the-world was that of bumping up against things and being bumped into. He viewed his fellow humans as being disrespectful, contemptuous, and threatening. When he tried to control his anxiety by keeping his distance from the world, his efforts resulted in exhaustion.

The design for a third patient consisted of the categories of familiarity and strangeness. His existence was constantly being endangered by impersonal hostile powers. He defended himself against these nameless fears by personalizing them as feelings of persecution.

Binswanger observes that when the world-design is dominated by a few categories, threat is more imminent than when the world-design is more varied. In the latter case, if a person is threatened in one region, other regions can emerge and offer him or her a safe foothold. In many instances, a person may have more than one world-design.

Boss does not speak of different world-designs but he does speak of existence in terms of being open or closed, disclosed or concealed, light or dark, expanded or constricted. For example, one's whole existence can become absorbed into a compulsion, such as eating or hoarding. A psychological or somatic condition can be a limiting factor by impeding "the carrying out of one or another of the possible world-relationships which a human existence consists of" (Boss, 1963, p. 228).

Modes of Being-in-the-World

There are many different modes of being-in-the-world. Each mode is a way by which *Dasein* understands, interprets, and expresses itself. Binswanger, for example, speaks of the *dual mode* achieved by two people in love. "I" and "Thou" become "We." This is the authentic mode of being human. A *plural mode* is described by Binswanger as being a world of formal relations, competition, and struggle. An individual who lives to himself has chosen a *singular mode* of existence, whereas one who buries herself in a crowd has chosen the *mode of anonymity*. Normally, a person has not one mode of existence but many. "The task of a science of man [existentialists call this science *anthropology*] is to understand the totality of man's experience of himself in *all* his modes of existence" (Binswanger, 1963, p. 173).

Existentials

Boss does not speak of modes of being-in-the-world in the same sense that Binswanger does. Instead, he prefers to speak of those characteristics that are inherent in every human existence. These inherent characteristics are called *existentials*. Among the more important ones discussed by Boss are spatiality, temporality, bodyhood, existence in a shared world, and mood or attunement. Let us consider each of these in turn.

SPATIALITY OF EXISTENCE. Spatiality, in existential terms, is not to be confused with physical space. Existentially, my friend a thousand miles away may be much closer to me at this moment than my next-door neighbor is. Openness and clearness constitute the true nature of spatiality in the human world. I am more open to my distant friend and he is clearer to me than my neighbor is.

TEMPORALITY OF EXISTENCE. Temporality is not clock or calendar time. Nor is it an endless series of nowpoints as in physics. Time is always there in the world to be used or consumed as one wishes. Time is always having time *for* (or *not* having time for) doing something. This "time *for*" is its chief significance for human being. Time can be expanded when one says, for example, "I am going to spend next year going around the world" or it can be contracted when one says, for example, "I have only a minute to spare." Human time also has the characteristic of being *datable*. We use such words as "now," "formerly," and "when" to indicate present, past, and future time. (We shall have more to say about past, present, and future in the Development section.)

BODYHOOD. Bodyhood is defined as the bodily sphere of the fulfillment of human existence. Bodyhood is not limited to what lies within the skin; it extends as far as one's relationships to the world. Boss speaks of a *bodying forth* of the ways of being-in-the-world. He uses the example of pointing at something. My bodily existence does not end at the tip of my finger. It extends (body forths) as far as the object pointed to, and even further to all the phenomena of the world in which I am then dwelling. The boundaries of my bodyhood coincide with those of my openness to the world.

HUMAN EXISTENCE IN A SHARED WORLD. Existential psychology has sometimes been accused of being solipsistic, of viewing each individual living encased in his or her own private world and not knowing anything about the world in which another person may live. Boss denies the validity of this accusation. Human beings always *coexist* or dwell together in the same world. Their mutual openness to the world permits the same phenomena to shine forth in the same meaningful ways to all human beings. Human existence is never private, except in certain pathological conditions; it is always a sharing of the world with each other.

MOOD OR ATTUNEMENT. This is an extremely important existential because it explains why our openness to the world expands and contracts and why it illuminates different phenomena from time to time. What one perceives and responds to depends upon one's mood at that moment. If a person is anxious, their *Dasein* will be attuned to threats and dangers. If one is happy, one's existence will be attuned to a world of felicitous relationships and meanings. If a mood changes suddenly from hope to despair, the clearness of the world will darken and its openness will contract. The human mode of dwelling in the world is constantly attuned to one mood or another. Moods themselves are existentials; they are potentialities inherent in every human existence.

DYNAMICS AND
DEVELOPMENT
OF EXISTENCE
Dynamics

Since existential psychology rejects the concept on causality, the dualism of mind and body, and the separation of the person from his or her environment, its conception of dynamics is not the usual one. It does not conceive of behavior resulting from external stimulation and internal bodily conditions. An individual is neither the pawn of the environment nor the creature of instincts, needs, and drives. Instead, he or she has the freedom to choose, and he or she alone is responsible for their own existence. Humans can transcend both their physical environment and their physical bodies if they choose. Whatever they do it is their choice. People themselves determine what they will be and do.

Why then if humans are free to choose do they so often suffer from anxiety, alienation, boredom, compulsions, phobias, delusions, and a host of other disabling disorders? There are two answers to this question. The first and most obvious one is that freedom to choose does not insure that the choices will be wise ones. Humans can realize their possibilities or can turn their backs on them. In existential language one can choose to live authentically or one can choose to live inauthentically. There is no less freedom in the one choice than in the other although, of course, the consequences are radically different.

If humans are to choose wisely it is necessary for them to be aware of the possibilities of their existence. This means that they must remain open at times in order for the possibilities to disclose themselves. Openness is the precondition for disclosure, and its opposite, closedness, is the ground for concealment. Boss writes, *"Daseinsanalysis* never loses sight of primary awareness of Beingness and of the fact that man's existence is claimed to serve as the luminated realm into which that is to be may actually shine forth, emerge, and appear as a phenomenon, i.e., as that which shows itself" (1963, p. 80).

Are there unlimited possibilities? Can people be anything they want to be? No, because there is always the ground of existence—the throwness into the world—to reckon with. This ground places definite limits on what a person may become. Moreover, there is the influence of the parental environment as well as later environments that reduce or expand the fulfillment of the innate possibilities of being. Boss, for example, recognizes this when he says, "A parent-child relationship whose openness is sufficiently in accord with all of the child's genuine nature is the only realm into which his possibilities of existing can come forth in a healthy way" (1963, p. 207).

The other answer to the question of why people suffer if they really are free beings is even more drastic. Humans, after all, can transcend the wounds of childhood and later insults to their existence.

(See, for example, Viktor Frankl's *The doctor and the soul,* 1969, for an account of how some inmates of concentration camps transcended the horrors of their existence.) They can metamorphosize themselves from an existentially sick person into an existentially well person. There is always the possibility of changing one's existence, of disclosing and unfolding a whole new world.

But one thing humans can never transcend is their guilt. Guilt is an *existential,* that is, a fundamental characteristic of *Dasein.* Boss states this great dilemma that faces every person in the following words.

. . . man is *primarily* guilty. His primary guilt starts at birth. For it is then he begins to be in debt to his *Dasein,* insofar as carrying out all the possibilities for living of which he is capable is concerned. Throughout his life, man remains guilty in this sense, i.e., indebted to all the requests that his future keeps in store for him until he breathes his last . . . every act, every decision, every choice, involves the rejection of all the other possibilities which also belong to a human being at a given moment. . . . Man's existential guilt consists in his failing to carry out the mandate to fulfill all his possibilities (1963, p. 270).

Examples of this primary and inescapable guilt abound in literature and case studies. Joseph K. in Kafka's *The trial* tried to exonerate himself but to no avail, and finally went willingly to his death as his ultimate exoneration or escape. Tolstoy's Ivan Ilyich also found in death the answer to an unfulfilled (guilty) life. Binswanger's patient, Ellen West, began to live relatively free of existential guilt when she had seriously resolved to end her life.

Something else that no person can avoid is dread—the dread of Nothingness or what Barrett calls "the dreadful and total contingency of human existence" (1962, p. 65). Nothingness is a presence within Being of non-Being (Heidegger). It is always there, fearful, uncanny, and beckoning. To fall into Nothingness means to lose one's being, to become nothing. Death is the absolute Nothingness but there are other less absolute ways by which non-Being can invade Being— alienation and isolation from the world, for example. The extent to which the possibilities of existence fall short of fulfillment is the extent to which non-Being has taken over Being.

Dynamics abound in existential writings despite existentialism's disavowal. For example, when people are hungry their mode of being-in-the-world is quite different than when they are sexually aroused. The body is, after all, a part of the *Eigenwelt,* and its demands cannot be ignored. In other words, the possibilities of existence include such things as bodily states and conditions as well as the limiting or expanding possibilities of the world. But these bodily states are never conceptualized as drives, for to do so would mean that something lies behind being-in-the-world—and this is repugnant to existentialists. Boss, as we have seen, classifies under *moods* such things as hunger, fatigue, and sex. Moods do not have dynamic properties, however, in the sense of causing behavior. Rather they determine the scale and attunement of world-openness of an individual at a given moment. Moods are responsible for the disclosed meanings and motivations of the encountered things. The mood of hunger, for instance, luminates a world of food and possible actions in this food-disclosed world.

Development   Genetic explanations, such as early experiences causing later behavior, are also disavowed by existential psychologists; nor do they emphasize in their writings any succession of developmental events that characterize the growing individual. On the other hand, they do insist that an individual's whole existence is a historical event. Boss, for example, states that *"Dasein*'s whole history is inherent and present at any given moment." This history does not consist of stages but different modes of existence. The infant's mode of existence is different from that of the child's, and the child's is different from that of the adolescent's, but these modes of existence have not been spelled out yet.

Genetic understanding, Boss says, can only come to the fore *after* one understands the present phenomena in their own right. When one has reached this understanding, genetic explanations seem tautological since they add nothing new to what is already known. A person may act today as he or she did yesterday—or in childhood—because they perceive that the present encounter has the same meaning as a past one. Then and only then can one be said to have been *motivated* by the past, but even this motivation is predicated by the present being-in-the-world. We eat today not because we ate yesterday but because our present mood and attunement to the world luminates it in a particular way. It is true we may remember what we did yesterday and repeat yesterday's acts today, but the repetition is due to the meaning the act has for us *now*. In other words, *habit* is not used as an explanatory principle in existential psychology.

Boss points out that dwelling in the world always means dwelling in a past, present, and future simultaneously. When we recall something from the past it means our existence here and now is open to the past. We do not exist in the past, the past exists in us. Similarly, when we look forward to something in the future, our *Dasein* is open at the moment to the future. The temporality of existence expands or contracts to include more or less of the past and future. We recognize this essential feature of existence when we say of a person "He's living in the past" or "She's living just for the moment." Ideally, *Dasein* should be open to all of one's past and all of one's future as well as all of one's present.

The most important existential developmental concept is that of *becoming*. Existence is never static; it is always in the process of becoming something new, of transcending itself. The goal is to become completely human, that is, to fulfill all the possibilities of *Dasein*. Of course, this is an endless and hopeless project because the choice of one possibility always means the rejection of all other possibilities.

Granted the difficult situation, nevertheless it is one's responsibility as a free person to realize as many of the possibilities of being-in-the-world as one can. To refuse to become is to lock oneself in a constricted and darkened room. This is what people overcome by phobias, compulsions, delusions, and other neurotic and psychotic symptoms have done. They have refused to grow. However, most people do make some progress in actualizing their possibilities, which means that the adult is typically more actualized that the child. Becoming implies direction and continuity but the direction can change and the continuity can be broken.

Becoming of person and becoming of world are always related; they are a co-becoming (Straus). This is necessarily so because a person is in-the-world. He or she discloses the possibilities of their existence through the world, and the world in turn is disclosed by the person who is in it. As one grows and expands, the other must perforce also grow and expand. By the same token, if one is stunted the other will also be stunted. Historical events are expressions of the various possibilities of human existence.

That life, or at least human existence as being-in-*this*-world, ends in death is a fact known to everyone. Boss points out that this knowledge of death leaves humans no choice but to live in some sort of permanent relationship to death. Human existence might be called, from this vantage point, a "being-unto-death." Mortality, Boss says, is an *existential*, "the most thoroughly pervasive and peculiarly human trait of all." Consequently, inescapable termination of being-in-the-world confers upon humans the responsibility for making the most of every moment of their existence and for fulfilling their existence. Existential psychology was the first viewpoint to concern itself with the implications of mortality and doubtless provided the main stimulus for the recent spate of books on death and dying.

CHARACTERISTIC
RESEARCH AND
RESEARCH
METHODS
*Phenomenological
Analysis*

Existential psychology employs the phenomenological method for conducting investigations of human existence. This method consists of describing or explicating experience in the language of experience. The language of experience is concrete rather than abstract; its vocabulary is made up of commonplace, everyday words and not technical terms or neologisms. Phenomenological analysis is not to be confused with the classical method of introspection used by early experimental psychologists to investigate the elements of consciousness. Phenomenologists do not look for elements; they attempt to describe and understand experience as it immediately appears in awareness. Van Kaam (1966) writes, for example, ". . . experiences such as responsibility, dread, anxiety, despair, freedom, love, wonder or decision cannot be measured or experimented with. . . . They are simply there and can only be explicated in their givenness" (p. 187).

Here is an example of that "givenness" of experience. It is the beautiful opening paragraph of the second volume of Oswald Spengler's *Decline of the West* (1932).

Regard the flowers at eventide as, one after the other, they close in the setting sun. Strange is the feeling that then presses in upon you—a feeling of enigmatic fear in the presence of this blind dreamlike earth-bound existence. The dumb forest, the silent meadows, this bush, that twig, do not stir themselves, it is the wind that plays with them. Only the little gnat is free—he dances still in the evening light, he moves whither he will (p. 3).

Although a phenomenological report may be given by a subject in an investigation or by a patient in psychotherapy, the usual procedure is for the investigator to make a phenomenological analysis of the subject's or patient's verbal reports and observed behavior. That is, a distinction is made between the reports of an untrained, naive subject and those of a trained, experienced phenomenologist. The question arises as to the validity of the phenomenological analysis of experience. When, for example, Boss analyzes a dream phenomenologically or Binswanger explicates a character trait (see below) how much confidence can be placed in their descriptions? Would the descriptions by two phenomenologists of the same phenomenon agree?

Van Kaam (1966, pp. 216–269) discusses the various methods of validating phenomenological explications. The first such method is *intrasubjective validation*. The investigator performs a number of explications of the same behavior in a variety of situations, and if there is consistency among the descriptions this confirms the validity of the explications. This is the method most often used in existential case studies.

A variant of the intrasubjective method is to gather spontaneous descriptions of a given phenomenon from untrained subjects. The phenomenologist then takes these descriptions and identifies the basic structure that appears in various manifestations of behavior of the same kind. Van Kaam (1966, Chapter 10) used this method to secure data for his doctoral dissertation. The phenomenon to be explicated was the experience of "being understood."

A large number of high school and college students were asked to recall situations in which they felt they were being understood by somebody and to describe how they felt in each of the situations. These descriptions were then listed, omitting duplicates. The resulting 157 descriptions were examined to see whether each description met the criterion of being a "necessary and sufficient constituent of the experience of really feeling understood." If it did not, it was eliminated from further consideration. Items were also eliminated when it was not possible to abstract and label the experience without violating the formulation made by the subject. These two reductive strategies left a pool of experiences that could be accommodated under the following nine headings.

Constituents of the experience of "Really Feeling Understood"	Percentages expressing the constituents
Perceiving signs of understanding from person	87
Perceiving that a person co-experiences what things mean to subject	91
Perceiving that the person accepts the subject	86
Feeling satisfaction	99
Feeling initially relief	93
Feeling initially relief from experiential loneliness	89
Feeling safe in the relationship with the person understanding	91
Feeling safe experiential communion with the person understanding	86
Feeling safe experiential communion with that which the person understanding is perceived to represent	64

Van Kaam summarizes the experience of "really feeling understood" in the following words: "[It] is a perceptual-emotional Gestalt:/A subject, perceiving/that a person/co-experiences/what things mean to the subject/and accepts him/feels, initially, relief from existential loneliness/and gradually, safe experiential communion/with that person/and with that which the subject perceives this person to represent" (pp. 325–326).

A second method, *intersubjective validation,* consists of having several trained phenomenologists independently describe the same phenomenon and then compare the results.

Validity may be determined *experimentally* by testing hypotheses deduced from phenomenological analysis. For example, the generalization is made that humans always maintain some kind of dialogue with their environment. The prediction deduced from this statement is that if a person is deprived of sensory stimulation, he or she will maintain the dialogue by imagination, fantasy, and hallucination. This prediction has been experimentally confirmed by the results of sensory deprivation studies. Van Kaam points out that experimental validation is indirect because it does not verify the phenomenological description itself.

Some explications are self-evident and do not require validation. No validation is required for the description "He is experiencing embarrassment" when one observes a person blushing.

There is another type of face validity that Van Kaam calls "existential." These are descriptions that are confirmed by the very nature of existence itself. It is self-evident, for example that humans have some degree of freedom in making choices. Should a determinist or mechanist take issue with this statement and try to persuade the existential psychologist it is not true, their attempts to persuade would themselves confirm the proposition they were attempting to negate. For if humans were not free to change their mind, there would be no sense in trying to persuade them to. Only free people can be converted, says Van Kaam. (The determinist might argue that the arguments themselves are the determining factors in changing a person's mind and not the person's freedom to do so.)

Daseinsanalysis Versus Psychoanalysis
Since both Binswanger and Boss were identified with psychoanalysis before they became existential psychiatrists, the inferences they draw from their phenomenologically oriented investigations are frequently compared with inferences that might be drawn by psychoanalysis. We have selected two examples from the writings of Binswanger to illustrate this contrast. One example deals with anal eroticism, the other with the character trait of miserliness.

ANAL EROTICISM. We quote verbatim to perserve the distinctive language of existential psychology.

The main feature of anal-eroticism is tenaciously keeping-to-oneself or not-giving-away. It is a very important insight of psychoanalysis, with which existential analysis completely agrees, that such a basic trait is not tied to the mind-body distinction, but transcends it. But there the agreement stops. . . . existential analysis asks first of all what world-design is basic to anality. In regard to the case of Ellen West the answer is particularly easy: in this world-design the multiplicity and multiformity of the world are reduced to the forms of the hole. The form of being in such a world is that of being confined or oppressed; the self which designs such a world is an 'empty' self, concerned only with the filling of the emptiness. Consequently a decided anality is concurrent with a decided orality, with a greed for 'incorporating'. But since this expression (as psychoanalysis has quite correctly observed) is not restricted to the bodily sphere, we prefer to speak of appropriating, but in the sense of mere filling up. The 'category' which dominates equally this world-design, the being-in-it and the self which designs it, is only and solely that of emptiness and fullness, of being-empty and being-full, of the starving and satiated self. The basic trait of such an exis-tence-form is greed, the throwing-oneself-upon (food). This existential movement has, as we have seen, the temporal character of suddenness, the spatial one of near-ness. The world in which such an existence 'moves' is temporally oriented to the mere Now of the filling-up possibility and the mere Here of the stuffing; such a world is lightless and colorless (gloomy), monotonous and monomorphous, in a word, joyless or dreary. To this emptied world corresponds—and is indeed prere-quisite to it—the existentially empty self, the existential emptiness and the corres-ponding existential pressure. . . . Where the world is nothing more than a hole, the self too is (bodily as well as mentally) only a hole; after all, world and self are recip-rocal determinants (in accordance with the principle which cannot be repeated often enough, that the individuality is what its world is, in the sense of its own world) (Binswanger, 1958c, pp. 317–318).

MISERLINESS. The miser is primarily interested in filling containers with money. Hoarding and stinginess are merely consequences of the filling orientation, for if the miser were to spend or give away his or her money the containers would be empty and the miser's anxiety would return. Filling is the common denominator for retention of feces and retention of money; the former does not cause the latter as the psychoanalysts maintain.

The prevalence of filling up and its worldly correlate, the cavity, point to something 'Moloch'-like [a reference to the hollow idol of that name] in such a world existence. This, naturally, carries with it (according to the unitary structure of being-in-the-world) also a certain Moloch-like form of the self-world, and in this case particularly of the body-world and of body-consciousness, as rightly emphasized by psychoana-lysis (Binswanger, 1958a, p. 211).

Binswanger goes on to say that misers are also stingy with their time since their temporality is spatialized in a Moloch-like sense. Time is constantly being saved, accumulated, and guarded against those who would steal it.

Containers are designed not only to be filled but also to hide their contents from others. The miser "squats" on his money. There are also the pleasures of secret viewing, handling, and counting. The lust for sparkling gold is "the only spark of life and love which is left to the miser" (Binswanger, 1958a, p. 211).

An Existential Case Study: Ilse

Binswanger's most famous case study, which is available in English translation, is *Ellen West* (1958c). Excerpts from this study have been used in the present chapter to illustrate various concepts of existential psychology but it is much too long and complex to digest here. The reader who is interested in learning how an existential psychotherapist works in making a phenomenological analysis of a patient's behavior and how he uses the findings of such an analysis to formulate the patient's existence or modes of being-in-the-world should read *Ellen West* in its entirety.

For practical reasons, we have chosen to discuss one of Binswanger's shorter case studies, *Insanity as life-historical phenomenon and as mental disease: the case of Ilse* (1958b). Ilse, a married woman in her late thirties, became a patient in Binswanger's sanatorium when she developed various types of delusions. Her delusional behavior appeared several months after she had performed a very dramatic and painful act. She plunged her right hand into the hot coals of a stove, then held the badly burned hand out to her father, and said, "Look, this is to show you how much I love you." Ostensibly, Ilse burned herself in a supreme effort to change the father's harsh and tyrannical treatment of the mother. The father's behavior did change for a few months but then he returned to his old ways. Ilse reacted to this by lapsing into insanity from which she recovered following treatment.

Ilse's life-history contained only one key theme—the father theme—around which her whole existence rotated. The oppressiveness of this theme finally became intolerable and she tried to free herself from it by an extreme act. It did not work, however, with the result that Ilse's existence became even more dominated by the father "complex."

This theme now no longer worries about limitations but sweeps the whole existence along with it, perceiving only itself and living only for itself. It forces the person [Ilse] whom it rules to meet the 'father' all over the world of fellow men, (*Mitwelt*) and to struggle with it in love and hatred, fight and surrender, and again and again in conflict. . . . Just as the father's harshness and coldness, inaccessibility to love and sacrifice, turned into a tortuous riddle for Ilse, so the entire environment now becomes an enigmatic power; at one time it is a loving You, one to which she would like to surrender not just her hand but herself altogether; at another time it is a harsh, loveless, inaccessible world which scoffs at her love, derides and humiliates her, wounds her honor. Her entire existence is now limited to the motions and unrest of being attracted and being rejected. But with the pluralization of the You, with the theme extended all over her existence without limit, and with the loss of the original thematic goal, the father, no solution of the problem is possible any longer (1958b, p. 224).

Hence, the insanity.

Regarding the specific nature of the sacrifice, the burning of her hand, Binswanger observes that it means different things to Ilse. On the surface, it was done for her mother's benefit. But it was also an act of purification (since fire purifies) and atonement for her "red hot" love for the father. She tries to burn out of herself the "inner fire" that threatens to consume her. One fights fire with fire. But it also signifies an attempt to melt the "ice-cold" heart of her father in the fire of her own love for him. The sacrifice was in vain. Not only did it fail to change her father, it also failed to purify Ilse. In order to be successful, a sacrifice has to result in a union between the sacrificer and the one for whom the sacrifice is made. Ilse wanted to purify herself and her father so that a new union between them might be founded. ". . . through the failure of the union, of unity with the father on the level of a pure We, the self-purification became meaningless" (1958b, p. 220).

The consequence of this failure is that Ilse "pluralizes" the father theme to all men; hence her delusions of self-reference, of love, and of persecution. She is attracted to and repulsed by men with all the guilt feelings and hatred such a conflict entails.

Binswanger admonishes the reader not to, "in the manner of psychoanalysis, see in this history merely a history of the libido, of its fixation onto the father, its forced withdrawal from father, and its eventual transference to the world-around" (1958b, p. 225). A person's history rests upon its attitude toward its "ground." Having a father and a mother is part of the ground of most people's existence.

But that Ilse got just that father and that mother was her destiny, received as a heritage and as a task; how to bear up under this destiny was the problem of her existence. Hence, in her 'father complex' were destiny *and* freedom at work (1958b, p. 225).

The unique features of existential psychology are brought out very clearly in their treatment of dreams. Both Boss (1958) and Binswanger (1963) have written on dreams but we will restrict our attention to Boss's studies because they are much more extensive. In an

Daseinsanalysis of Dreams

early investigation of dreams before he had become an existential psychologist, Boss (1938) showed how the dreams of schizophrenic patients became more open (less disguised and symbolized) as the schizophrenic condition worsened and became more symbolic as the condition improved. A female schizophrenic during the early stages of the disease dreamed of a cow getting stuck in the mud and later when she had become much worse, she dreamed of pushing her mother into a pile of manure.

As an existentialist Boss now rejects the concept of symbolism as well as all the other Freudian mechanisms and interpretations. A dream is another mode of being-in-the-world. The contents of a dream must be accepted as things with their own full meaning and content, just as they are felt to be within the experience of the dreamer. Dreaming and waking are not entirely different spheres of existence. In fact, a person's mode of existence as portrayed in their dreams often duplicates their mode of existence in waking life. This is illustrated by a very dramatic series of 823 dreams reported by a patient during three years of therapy (Boss, 1958, pp. 113–117).

The patient, an engineer in his forties, came to therapy because of depression and sexual impotence. During the first six and a half months of treatment, he dreamed exclusively of machinery and other material objects. No living plants, animals, or persons ever appeared in his dreams. At the end of this first period, he began to dream about plants, trees, and flowers. Four months later, insects which were usually dangerous and harmful came into his dreams frequently. These were succeeded by toads, frogs, and snakes. The first mammal he dreamed about was a mouse, then a rabbit, and a wild pig. Pigs became a favorite dream animal, but finally their place was taken by lions and horses. The first dream of a human being took place two years after beginning therapy. It was a dream of an unconscious woman. Six months later he dreamed he was dancing with a woman who was very passionate and with whom he fell deeply in love.

Changes in the contents of this patient's dreams paralleled changes in his waking experience and behavior. The depressing meaninglessness of his life had already begun to disappear at the time he began to dream of plants. His sexual potency returned to full strength when lions and horses were admitted into his dreams. When he began therapy his mode of existence was that of a machinelike robot. There was no awareness of the full reality of existence, of his being-in-the-world with plants, animals, people, or even his wife. Instead of disclosing and luminating the full rich world of existence, his *Dasein* was constricted, mutilated, and concealing.

One might ask why, if dreams and waking life are so homologous, it is necessary to take account of dreams? The answer is that the dreaming *Dasein* often beings to light realms of the human world of which the dreamer is not aware in waking life. In a recent book on dreams, Boss (1978) has set forth three basic questions that should be asked about a dream: (1) What is the dreamer's *Dasein* open to during the dream; that is, what phenomena (people, animals, and objects) appear in the dream? (2) How do the phenomena affect the dreamer? Is he or she frightened? angry? happy? sad? indifferent? (3) How does the dreamer respond to the phenomena in the dream? Does he or she run from them? attack them? embrace them? Answers to these questions provide a basis for an existential analysis of a dream.

Boss, as we have said, rejects the whole panoply of wishes, mechanisms, archetypes, compensations, and disguises that psychoanalysts use in interpreting dreams. His reasons for doing so are illustrated in his analysis of one detail in a dream recounted by a mentally and physically healthy young married woman.

The dream begins with her sitting at the dinner table with her husband and children in a peaceful mood. She is attracted by the food and greedily takes one bite after another because "I was very hungry." Since she had been hungry when she retired for the night this dreaming of eating would be interpreted as simple wish fulfillment according to Freudian theory. Boss objects to this interpretation because the dreamer did not feel any wish to eat. "Our dreamer is supplied with food from the very start of her dream and does not need to wish it but only to eat it" (1958, p. 84). Nor can it be accounted for by an oral drive or an instinct because the immediate experience of the dreamer was neither that of a drive or an instinct. To interpret behavior whether in dreams or in waking life as the result of drives and instincts is to envisage humans driven by internal and external forces like any other object, an envisagement that existential psychology rejects.

Existentially, what hunger does is to reveal a world of eatable things. "Both the active eating in the dream as well as the desire for food beforehand in waking life spring from one and the same source: they are only two different forms of activity of an existence attuned to hunger" (1958, p. 85).

Although Boss dispenses with symbolism, he does say that an object appearing in a dream may have many different meanings and frames of reference for the dreamer. In order to bring out the various meanings of a dream object, the analyst does not ask the dreamer to free associate to the object (Freud) or to amplify it (Jung). Instead the existential analyst asks questions of the dreamer. The answers to these questions will enable the analyst—more importantly the dreamer if he or she is in therapy—to see more clearly and openly the meaning of a dream in relation to the patient's waking life existence. Herein lies the value of dream analysis for psychotherapy. Patients gain valuable insights into their ways of being-in-the-world. They are then free to use these insights to build a more healthy *Dasein*. Boss acknowledges that these insights do not come easily to patients so that the analyst has stubbornly to persist in asking the same questions over and over again to successive dreams.

Boss's treatment of symbolism is exemplified by an experiment he performed on five women. He hypnotized each woman, in turn, and suggested she would dream about a man well known to her, who loved her, and who approached her nude with sexual intentions. Three of the women who had healthy attitudes toward sex had pleasant, openly erotic dreams. One of the other two who was a neurotic spinster and who feared sex had a dream of being attacked by a coarse man in uniform carrying a pistol. Boss says that neither the uniform nor the gun should be regarded as symbols. The uniform expresses the dreamer's narrow, hidden, anxious mode of existence rather than acting as a disguise for the body. The pistol is not the phallus in disguise but expresses the dreamer's feelings of threat and danger. It was her overpowering anxiety that disclosed a gun because in waking life she was afraid of guns. Dreams are revelations of existence and not concealments. Their existential meaning is made manifest and is not to be found in some hypothetical behind-the-scenes latent content and dream work. "Dream phenomena are therefore always just what they are as they shine forth; they are an *un*covering, and *un*veiling and never a covering up or a veiling of psychic content" (1958, p. 262).

CURRENT STATUS AND EVALUATION

Existential psychology, like psychoanalysis, was nurtured in Europe by medical practitioners and was exported to the United States. Unlike psychoanalysis, however, existential psychology did not have to undergo many years of academic rejection and harsh criticism by American psychologists before being accepted or at least tolerated. It had an almost immediate impact on the thinking and practices of a number of psychologists and has been one of the chief influences in bringing about the emergence of new viewpoints and techniques, especially in the areas of counseling and psychotherapy. Part of the difference in the response to psychoanalysis and existential psychology can be traced to the changing complexion of psychology between 1910 and 1950. In 1910, psychology was made up almost entirely of university-based psychologists whose activities were purely scientific and theoretical. By 1950, a large number of psychologists were involved in applied psychology and were finding, to their dismay, that much of what they had learned in graduate school was not very relevant or applicable in their jobs. They began to look for more relevant viewpoints and knowledge, and they believed they found them in psychoanalysis and existential psychology.

Then, too, by 1950, many American psychologists felt that psychology had become straight-jacketed by behaviorism, and thereby had lost sight of the person and human values. Existentialism was seen by these dissidents as offering a basis for a humanistically oriented psychology.

Existential psychology resembles psychoanalysis in another respect; it was founded by psychiatrists as a number of the other theories of personality treated in this book were. Working intensively with people in a therapeutic setting seems to favor the development of broad conceptions of humans. Unlike psychoanalysis, however, which was based firmly upon the unyielding positivism of nineteenth century science, existential psychology grew out of philosophy and has continued to maintain close relations with its philosophical roots. With respect to the two orientations—science versus philosophy—psychoanalysis is closer to behaviorism, and existential psychology is closer to Gestalt psychology.

That European existential psychology has been acclaimed by many American psychologists and that its influence is a growing one cannot be denied. It has not escaped criticism, however.

One criticism stems from the fact that American psychology fought hard to free itself from the domination of philosophy. Having largely succeeded in obtaining its independence, many psychologists strongly resist any new alliance with philosophy, particularly the kind of philosophy that openly acknowledges its distaste for positivism and determinism. For at least seventy years American psychology has tried to become a "respectable" science. Hypothesis testing by carefully designed experiments performed under controlled conditions and sophisticated statistical treatment of the data have been inculcated in the thinking of virtually every recent graduate student in psychology. For years psychoanalysis was considered to be unscientific and its acceptance by academic psychologists—or some psychologists—only came about when its hypotheses began to be tested under controlled experimental conditions. Many psychologists feel that existential psychology represents a disastrous break with the scientific establishment, thereby endangering the scientific status of psychology that was won with so much difficulty.

To this criticism existential psychology would reply that there are many kinds of scientific and philosophical viewpoints. Any science, including psychology, always makes a commitment to a particular philosophy whether this is understood or not. Objective, positivistic psychology rests upon Cartesian philosophy; existential psychology is based upon Heidegger's ontology. They are both equally philosophical and both equally scientific.

Existential psychology is openly hostile to the kind of experimentation that treats a person as an object or thing, to be pushed and pulled around in a laboratory. This kind of scientific manipulation and exploitation not only degrades humans but the results obtained from such experimentation are often either artificial or trivial. Understanding of the whole person obtained through phenomenological analysis versus prediction and control of behavior by experimental investigations pretty well sums up the rival positions of existential psychology and "scientific" psychology. [A lively discussion of the relative merits and deficiencies of phenomenology and behaviorism by such prestigious psychologists as B. F. Skinner, Carl Rogers, Sigmund Koch, and R. B. MacLeod is found in the book *Behaviorism and phenomenology* edited by T. W. Wann (1964).]

The one existential concept that arouses the greatest opposition from "scientific" psychology is an individual's freedom to be what he or she wants to be. This concept, if true, would naturally invalidate a psychology based upon a strict deterministic conception of behavior. For if humans are really free to choose their existence, then total prediction and control are impossible and experimentation is of limited value.

Existential psychology rejects—by implication, at least—the evolutionary doctrine that has been one of the main pillars of American psychology. The existentialist asserts that humans are unique among all the creatures of the earth; they cannot be placed in the phylogenesis of the animal world without destroying their humanness. A person is not an animal like other animals; that is why it is unacceptable to generalize the findings of experimentation with animals to humans. Existential psychology does recognize that human existence has a ground—that is, an inheritance or destiny—but people are free to make of this ground pretty much whatever they choose, which other species are not able to do.

Existential psychology has been accused of being subjectivistic or solipsistic. Even Karl Jaspers, one of the leading existentialists, thought there was a danger of it lapsing into pure subjectivity. Boss insists that *Dasein* is neither idealism (Berkeley) nor subjectivism. Things are not created by a person's mind nor are they independent of a person. People and the things they disclose or luminate are mutually dependent on each other for their existence.

As mentioned earlier, existential psychology has been criticized for employing a vocabulary that is regarded by many psychologists as being poetic and esoteric. Closely related to this criticism is the one that existential psychologists are merely putting old wine into fancy new bottles. They are using new words to describe familiar concepts. American psychologists, even many of those who are favorably inclined toward existential thought, then attempt to back-translate the new terms into a familiar idiom. This irritates the European existential psychologist, who maintains that existential psychology is an entirely new scientific enterprise—although having a long philosophical lineage—and that any attempt to assimilate it to one of the older psychological viewpoints is an egregious error. The co-optation of existentialism by American humanistic psychology, for example, is resented by its founders.

There is a strong flavor of ethical concern in the writings of existentialists to which many psychologists object. The concept of transcendence, like that of sublimation (Freud), implies that humans have a "lower" and a "higher" nature, and that they should overcome their "baseness" if they are to become truly human. Existentialists constantly refer to an individual's responsibility for his or her own existence which opens the door to moralizing and to punishment when a person does not act responsibly. Some existential psychologists even use religious concepts such as "God" and "Godhead," which arouses the suspicion that they are trying to sneak religion into psychology. Existential psychologists, or some of them, might reply that this is exactly what psychology needs if it is to have any real meaning for people.

Whatever the future of existential psychology may be—and at the present time it appears to have sufficient vigor and vitality to last a long time—it has already served at least one very important function. That function is to rescue psychology from being drowned in a sea of theories that have lost contact with the everyday world and with the "givens" of experience. "Return to the things themselves" admonished Husserl, the father of modern phenomenology. It is refreshing and revitalizing to observe, describe, and analyze behavior and experience without being weighted down by abstract and overgeneralized preconceptions and hypotheses. (A hypothesis can be confirmed or disconfirmed but it cannot result in new insights.) Existentialism is helping to revitalize a science that many feel has become theoretically moribund. It has done this by insisting on using a strictly phenomenological methodology. It has tried to see what is actually there and to describe human existence in concrete terms.

On the other hand, since a human being seems to be the theorizing animal, existential psychology may not be able to avoid developing its own theory of humans. This theory may also prove to be just as constraining as it believes other theories have been. Boss, for one, is fully cognizant of this possibility. He writes,

I can only hope that existential psychology will never develop into a theory in its modern meaning of the natural sciences. All that existential psychology can contribute to psychology is to teach the scientists to remain with the experienced and experienceable facts and phenomena, to let these phenomena tell the scientists their meaning and their references, and so do the encountered objects justice—in short, becoming more "objective" again (*personal communication*).

Whatever the future of existential psychology may be, whether it solidifies into a theory or withers away by being co-opted by special interests, it is clear that now it offers a profoundly new way of studying and comprehending human beings. For this reason, it merits the closest attention by serious students of psychology.

BIBLIOGRAPHY
PRIMARY SOURCES

Binswanger, L. The existential analysis school of thought. In R. May, E. Angel, and H. F. Ellenberger (Eds.). *Existence*. New York: Basic Books, 1958a, 191–213.

Binswanger, L. Insanity as life-historical phenomenon and as mental disease: The case of Ilse. In R. May, E. Angel, and H. F. Ellenberger (Eds.). *Existence*. New York: Basic Books, 1958b, 214–236.

Binswanger, L. The case of Ellen West. In R. May, E. Angel, and H. F. Ellenberger (Eds.). *Existence*. New York: Basic Books, 1958c, 237–364.

Binswanger, L. *Being-in-the-world: selected papers of Ludwig Binswanger*. New York: Basic Books, 1963.

Boss, M. *The analysis of dreams*. New York: Philosophical Library, 1958.

Boss, M. *Psychoanalysis and Daseinsanalysis*. New York: Basic Books, 1963.

Boss, M. *Existential foundations of medicine and psychology*. New York: Aronson, 1977.

REFERENCES

Barrett, W. *Irrational man; a study in existential philosophy*. Garden City, N.Y.: Doubleday Anchor Books, 1962.

Binswanger, L. *Sigmund Freud: reminiscences of a friendship*. New York: Grune and Stratton, 1957.

Binswanger, L. The existential analysis school of thought. In R. May, E. Angel, and H. F. Ellenberger (Eds.). *Existence*. New York: Basic Books, 1958a, 191–213.

Binswanger, L. Insanity as life-historical phenomenon and as mental disease: The case of Ilse. In R. May, E. Angel, and H. F. Ellenberger (Eds.). *Existence*. New York: Basic Books, 1958b, 214–236.

Binswanger, L. The case of Ellen West. In R. May, E. Angel, and H. F. Ellenberger (Eds.). *Existence*. New York: Basic Books, 1958c, 237–364.

Binswanger, L. *Being-in-the-world: selected papers of Ludwig Binswanger.* New York: Basic Books, 1963.

Boring, E. G. *A history of experimental psychology.* (2nd ed.) New York: Appleton-Century-Crofts, 1950.

Boss, M. The psychopathology of dreams in schizophrenia and organic psychoses. In M. DeMartino (Ed.) *Dreams and personality dynamics.* New York: C. C. Thomas, 1959.

Boss, M. *The analysis of dreams.* New York: Philosophical Library, 1958.

Boss, M. *Psychoanalysis and Daseinsanalysis.* New York: Basic Books, 1963.

Boss, M. *A psychiatrist discovers India.* London: Oswald Wolff, 1965.

Boss, M. *Existential foundations of medicine and psychology.* New York: Aronson, 1977.

Boss, M. *"I dreamt last night . . ."* New York: Gardner Press, 1978.

Buber, M. *I and Thou.* (2nd ed.) New York: Scribner, 1958.

Bugental, J. F. T. *The search for authenticity: an existential-analytic approach to psychotherapy.* New York: Holt, Rinehart and Winston, 1965.

Frankl, V. E. *The doctor and the soul.* New York: Bantam Book, 1969.

Fromm, E. *Escape from freedom.* New York: Rinehart, 1941.

Heidegger, M. *Being and time.* New York: Harper and Row, 1962.

Jaspers, K. *Man in the modern age.* London: Routledge and Kegan Paul, 1951.

Köhler, W. *Gestalt psychology: an introduction to new concepts in psychology.* New York: Liveright, 1947.

Laing, R. D. *The politics of experience.* New York: Ballantine Book, 1968.

MacLeod, R. B. Phenomenology: a challenge to experimental psychology. In T. W. Wann (Ed.). *Behaviorism and phenomenology: contrasting bases for modern psychology.* Chicago: Univ. of Chicago Press, 1964, 47–78.

May, R. (Ed.). *Existential psychology.* (2nd ed.) New York: Random House, 1969.

May, R., Angel, E., and Ellenberger, H. F. (Eds.). *Existence.* New York: Basic Books, 1958.

Needleman, J. A critical introduction to Ludwig Binswanger's existential psychoanalysis. In L. Binswanger, *Being-in-the-world: selected papers of Ludwig Binswanger.* New York: Basic Books, 1963, 1–145.

Spengler, O. *The decline of the west.* One volume ed. New York: Knopf, 1932.

Straus, E. W. *The primary world of senses: a vindication of sensory experience.* Glencoe, Ill.: Free Press, 1963.

Straus, E. W. *Phenomenological psychology: the selected papers of Erwin W. Straus.* New York: Basic Books, 1966.

Van Kaam, A. *Existential foundations of psychology.* Pittsburgh, Pa.: Duquesne Univ. Press, 1966.

Wann, T. W. (Ed.). *Behaviorism and phenomenology: contrasting bases for modern psychology.* Chicago: Univ. of Chicago Press, 1964.

EASTERN PSYCHOLOGY

10

Attempts to forge a systematic understanding of human personality and behavior did not originate with contemporary Western psychology. Our formal psychology, about a hundred years old, is merely a recent version of an endeavor probably as old as human history. The theories of personality discussed in other chapters are the product of European and American culture, and are only one set of the innumerable "psychologies" that people in many times and places have articulated. While the psychologies of some cultures and epochs have been at best loose collections of folk wisdom combined with imaginative myths, other peoples have developed theories of personality as sophisticated and as well grounded in empirical observations as our own.

One of the richest sources of such well-formulated psychologies are Eastern religions. Quite separate from the vagaries of cosmology and the dogma of beliefs, most major Asian religions have at their core a psychology little known to the masses of adherents to the faith, but quite familiar to the appropriate "professionals," be they yogis, monks, or priests. This is the practical psychology that the most dedicated practitioners apply to discipline their own minds and hearts.

Just as there is a multitude of personality theories in Western civilization, there are numerous Eastern psychologies. But while there are major differences of belief and world view among the religions that contain the Eastern psychologies, there is far less difference among the psychologies themselves. Among their common features are a phenomenological method: all seek to describe the nature of a person's immediate experience. Indeed, some of these systems center around techniques of meditation that allow one simply to observe the stream of their awareness, giving one a detached window on their flow of experience. Further, all these psychologies find fault with humans as they are, positing an ideal mode of being that anyone can attain who seeks with diligence to do so. The path to this transformation is always via a far-reaching change in one's personality, so that these ideal qualities may become stable traits. And finally, all the Eastern psychologies agree that the main means to this transformation of self is meditation.

In Buddhism, until this century the largest religion in the world, these psychological principles were enunciated by its founder, Gautama Buddha (536–438 B.C.). In the 2500 years since he lived, his basic psychological insights were developed into different systems of theory and practice by each branch of Buddhists. Among the dozen or so that exist today, the most influential are the Therevadans in the countries of Southeast Asia, the Ch'an School of China (suppressed since the Communist takeover), Zen in Korea and Japan, and the sects of Tibet. In India two of the foremost codifiers of the psychological principles of the Hindu schools of yoga were Patanjali (Prabhavanda and Isherwood, 1969) and Shankara (Prabhavanda and Isherwood, 1970). In the Moslem world the Sufis have acted as the applied psychologists (Shah, 1971). Among Jews the Kabbalists have been the group most concerned with psychological transformation (Halevi, 1976; Scholem, 1961). An excellent survey of these religions, their history, and beliefs is Huston Smith's *The Religions of Man* (1958).

The similarities among these psychologies contrast with the ostensible differences among faiths in their belief systems and theologies. One of the most systematic and intricately laid out of these psychologies is that of classical Buddhism. Called in the Pali language of Buddha's day *Abhidhamma* (or *Abhidharma* in Sanskrit), which means "the ultimate doctrine," this psychology elaborates Gautama Buddha's original insights into human nature. [The best available dictionary of Abhidhamma terms is by Nyanatiloka (1972).] Since it stems from Buddha's basic teachings, *Abhidhamma,* or a psychology very much like it, is at the core of all the various branches of Buddhism. From its fullest development during the first millennium after Buddha's death, it has been preserved largely unchanged by the Therevadan Buddhists as part of their scriptures, the Pali Canon. The basic texts of Abhidhamma are found in nearly identical form—although translated—in the Buddhist scriptures of Tibet and China. In this chapter we will look in depth at Abhidhamma as a personality theory.

Many Abhidhamma principles represent the psychological teachings common to all Eastern faiths rather than those limited to Buddhism. As a prototype of Asian psychology Abhidhamma presents us with a set of concepts for understanding mental activity that differs markedly from the concepts of the theories reviewed in other chap-

Fifteenth century bronze Buddha from Thailand.

ters. This Asian psychology has proved remarkably durable, surviving longer than two thousand years; Western personality theories are quite young by comparison. Virtually every Eastern meditation system transplanted to the West—Transcendental Meditation, Zen, and the like—stems from this psychology or another much like it. But these recent arrivals are by no means the first dissemination of Eastern psychological theory to the West.

Western thinkers since the time of the Greeks and Romans have been influenced by Eastern philosophies. After all, Alexander (356–323 B.C.) and his armies founded kingdoms that spread well into north India, and both technologies and ideas travelled across Eurasia on the silk routes, centuries old even in Alexander's time. Plotinus (205–270 A.D.) was one of the early philosophers whose thought closely paralleled the psychological views of Eastern thinkers of his day. A native of Egypt of Roman descent, Plotinus went to Persia and India in 242 to study their philosophies. His ideas became the hallmark of Christian mystics for centuries after. Plotinus mapped out a world of experience beyond the bounds of sense reality, compared to which the normal world was illusory. In his theory a person could develop toward perfection by divorcing their "soul"—that is, the awareness that perceives through the senses, but not including the senses themselves—from their body. In doing so a person transcends self-awareness, time and place, to experience the ineffable One in a state of ecstacy. Plotinus' version of ecstacy agrees with such classical Indian texts as Patanjali's *Yoga Sutras,* which says that the person who can transcend the ordinary limits of their body, senses, and mind will enter an altered state of ecstatic union with God. This same doctrine became part of Christian psychology, surfacing in one form or another within the influential writings of the Egyptian St. Antony (Waddell, 1971), St. John of the Cross (1958) and Meister Eckhardt (Blakney, 1941), to name a few.

With the rise of the natural sciences, the positivistic approach came to dominate Western science and philosophy. To progressive thinkers the mystical aspects of religion—if not religion itself—fell out of fashion. Western psychology has its roots in the positivist tradition, and by and large the early psychologists turned to concerns other than those of the religious mystics. By the nineteenth century Eastern thought had less impact on the fledgling psychologies of the time than on the philosophers and poets. The writings of the Transcendentalists, such as Emerson and Thoreau, and the poetry of Walt Whitman, are permeated with the words and concepts of the East. William James, America's most prominent nineteenth century psychologist, was keenly interested in religion, both Eastern and Western. He befriended Vivekananda, an Indian Swami who toured America after speaking at the First World Congress of Religions in 1893. Religion and the occult fascinated James; his book *Varieties of Religious Experience* (1961b) remains a classic on the psychology of religion. But because Eastern thought is largely religious, the scientific bent of modern psychology has lead the great majority of Western psychologists to ignore the teachings of their Eastern counterparts.

One reason why some Western psychologists have recently become interested in Eastern theories is that they deal in part with a range of experience that our own theorists have largely ignored. A well-known instance is the case of the Canadian psychiatrist R. M. Bucke. His experience occurred during a visit to England in 1872; one account tells us (Bucke, 1969:iii):

He and two friends had spent the evening reading Wordsworth, Shelley, Keats, Browning, and especially Whitman. They parted at midnight, and he had a long drive in a hansom. His mind, deeply under the influence of the ideas, images and emotions called up by the reading and the talk of the evening, was calm and peaceful. He was in a state of quiet, almost passive, enjoyment.

All at once, without warning of any kind, he found himself wrapped around, as it were, by a flame-colored cloud. For an instant he thought of fire—some sudden conflagration in the great city. The next [instant] he knew that the light was within himself.

Directly after there came upon him a sense of exultation, of immense joyousness, accompanied or immediately followed by an intellectual illumination quite impossible to describe.

Afterwards Bucke was to speak of his experience as a glimpse of "cosmic consciousness," a phrase Walt Whitman, the nineteenth century American poet, borrowed from the Vedantic philosophy of India, and which Bucke in turn appropriated. In using this Eastern concept to interpret his unusual psychological state, Bucke was one of the first to turn Eastward to understand aspects of the mind about which Western psychologies have little to say. The psychology of Bucke's time provided no labels save those of psychopathology for such states as he entered that night. The modern interest in Eastern psychologies may be due in part to the increasing frequency of experiences of altered states, like Bucke's, that our psychological theories do not deal with. Our present psychologies have little to say about such states—whether induced by drugs, meditation, or other means—that resonates with the experience of the person who undergoes them. Many Eastern psychologies offer ways to understand altered states that can make sense of these often confusing experiences.

While Eastern psychologies are concerned with states of consciousness and the laws that govern their alteration, they also contain articulate theories of personality. The goal of Eastern psychologies is to alter a person's consciousness so as to transcend the limits imposed by the habits that form the person's personality. Each personality type needs to overcome different obstacles to attain the liberation from these limits. We will review the theory of personality Abhidhamma offers after a survey of the impact of Eastern psychologies on Western thought.

EASTERN PSYCHOLOGIES AND WESTERN PERSONALITY THEORIES

Among modern personality theorists, C. G. Jung was probably the most knowledgeable about Eastern psychologies. Jung was a close friend of the Indologist Heinrich Zimmer and was himself an authority on the mandala, a central motif in much sacred art of the East. Jung wrote forewords to books by the Zen scholar D. T. Suzuki (1974), and by Richard Wilhelm (1962), translator of the *I Ching* and other Chinese Taoist texts. Jung also penned commentaries on Evans-Wentz' translations of *The Tibetan Book of the Great Liberation* (1968), and *The Tibetan Book of the Dead* (1960), two important works in the psychological compendium of Tibetan Buddhism. Jung's friend and neighbor, Herman Hesse, spread Eastern thought through his novels *Siddhartha* (1970) and *Journey to the East* (1971). Jung reached into matters alien to positivistic science by his extensive analysis of Eastern religions. Although he also warned of the dangers for a Westerner of being engulfed by Eastern traditions, Jung's writings form a major bridge between the psychologies of the East and West.

Apart from Jung, the Eastern psychologies have made their greatest inroads in the West through their influence on theorists such as the holistic outlooks of Angyal and Maslow, the humanists Buber and Fromm, the existentialist Boss, and the new wave of "transpersonal psychologists" (Tart, 1976). Maslow, for example, read extensively in Eastern literature, and Buber, Fromm, and Boss have each had a personal history of contact with Eastern teachers. Buber knew the works of the Hasidic masters, the mystics of Judaism. Fromm has had a longstanding dialogue with Buddhist teachers; his *Zen Buddhism and Psychoanalysis* (1970) was co-authored with D. T. Suzuki, an experienced Zen student and scholar, as well as with Richard DeMartino, a professor of religion.

Medard Boss, the influential Swiss existentialist (see Chapter 9), was invited to lecture on psychiatry in India, where he had an opportunity to meet Indian holy men. Feeling that Western therapies lack the ability to bring an illuminating insight of power comparable to that of Eastern methods, he looked to the traditions of India for guidance. Boss was little impressed with those Westerners he met who had donned the garb of Indian holy men; he found them to have inflated their egos with Indian formulas of wisdom, but otherwise to be unchanged, not having truly incorporated these formulas into their own existence. The Indian sages he met, however, impressed him deeply:

And yet there were the exalted figures of the sages and holy men themselves, each one of them a living example of the possibility of human growth and maturity and of the attainment of an imperturbable inner peace, a joyous freedom from guilt, and a purified, selfless goodness and calmness. . . . No matter how carefully I observe the waking lives of the holy men, no matter how ready they were to tell me about their dreams, I could not detect in the best of them a trace of a selfish action or any kind of repressed or consciously concealed shadow life (1965, pp. 187–188).

Boss came away from these meetings with the conviction that, in light of the teachings and behavior of the Eastern masters, the methods and aims of Western psychotherapy were inadequate. Compared with the degree of self-purification Eastern discipline demands, "even the best Western training analysis is not much more than an introductory course." Nevertheless, in Boss' view, the Western "yogis" in whom he was so disappointed could all have benefited by a psychoanalysis as preparation for their further training in Eastern disciplines. The Italian psychiatrist Alberto Assagioli would agree with Boss' assessment of the relationship between Western therapies and Eastern disciplines. Assagioli's (1971) "psychosynthesis" offers a wide-ranging set of therapeutic methods that start by dealing with a person's physical problems—especially psychosomatic disorders—proceed through his or her psychological disturbances, and finally culminate in spiritual exercises.

In the late 1960s Gardner and Lois Murphy published *Asian psychology* (1968), a collection of psychological writings selected from the ancient scriptures of India, China, and Japan. The editors envisioned the book as part of a series of volumes meant to articulate a "universal psychology—a psychology accepted by all men and used in dealing with ultimate things as well as with the things of the marketplace" (1968, v). What is universal about these psychologies from different lands is not the specifics of their theories of behavior but rather the attempt to develop a systematic science of the mind. The approach of the Asian psychologies is grounded in introspection and arduous self-examination, in contrast to Western psychologies that rely more on observation of behavior. The Murphys examined each excerpt from the Asian scriptures to determine what it had to say of a psychological nature. Each excerpt offers some sort of psychological insight, whether it is a view of how the mind works, a theory of personality, or a model of motivation. While appreciating the differences among Asian psychologies, the Murphys conclude that they are essentially a reaction to life viewed as full of suffering and frustration. The common means these psychologies recommend to overcome distress are discipline and self-control, which can bring the seeker a "sense of the unlimited ecstacy that could be found within a self which is freed of personal strivings" (1968, p. 228). In their epilogue, the editors note that the psychological interests of East and West are "coming together very fast indeed."

Alan Watts, though not himself a psychological theorist, did much to bring Eastern teachings to the awareness of Western psychologists as a guest lecturer at numerous medical schools, hospitals, and psychiatric institutes, and in a series of books, most importantly, *Psychotherapy East and West* (1961). Watts recognized that what he called Eastern "ways of liberation" resemble Western psychotherapy in that both are concerned with changing peoples' feelings about themselves and their relation to others and to the world of nature. Western therapies, for the most part, deal with disturbed people; Eastern disciplines with normal, socially adjusted people. Even so, Watts saw that the aims of the ways of liberation were compatible with the therapeutic goals of several theorists, notably Jung's individuation, Maslow's self-actualization, Allport's functional autonomy, and Adler's creative selfhood.

Richard Alpert, better known as Ram Dass, like Alan Watts, has bridged Eastern religions and Western psychology. Alpert, a developmental psychologist and psychotherapist at Harvard in the 1960s and an associate of Timothy Leary, was an early experimenter with psychedelics. He dropped out of academic life to pursue his interest in psychedelics, but became disillusioned with drugs, feeling they produced no lasting positive change in personality. He travelled to India in 1966, studied there with a yogi named Neemkaurari Baba, and returned to America the next year as "Ram Dass." Since then Ram Dass had done much to translate Eastern thought into Western psychological terms. Ram Dass feels that meditation and other spiritual disciplines can produce the kind of therapeutic personality change that drugs cannot. He also emphasizes the importance of spiritual growth and the emptiness of a life lived without spiritual awareness. In his book *Be here now* (1971), he tells the story of his transformation from psychologist to yogi; *The only dance there is* (1974) is the transcript of talks he gave to therapists at psychiatric hospitals. Both books have found a following among psychologists and sparked their interest in Eastern psychologies.

Some ten years after the appearance of Watts' book comparing Eastern disciplines and Western therapies, a book by Abraham Maslow (1971) was published posthumously that indirectly carried Watts' work a step further. Maslow, about a year before his death, had suffered a near-fatal heart attack. After recovering from this brush with death, he set about to organize and re-think his major contributions to personality theory. One product of his effort was an essay called "Theory Z" in which he postulated a degree of healthiness more "fully human" than any he had described heretofore. These "self-actualizing transcenders" are people who, by his description, sound like the ideal types of fully healthy people in Eastern psychologies. Although Maslow cites no single Eastern psychologist as a source for his ideas, he freely sprinkles Eastern concepts in his discussion, for example, calling a therapist at the level of Theory Z, among other terms, a "Taoistic guide," a "Guru," a "Boddhisattva," and a "Tsaddik," all names in Eastern traditions for a sage or saint. It is almost certain that Maslow developed his new concept of healthiness independently, assimilating bits of Eastern psychologies as they fit his own thinking. It seems unlikely that he studied any of the Eastern schools with the intention of borrowing their concepts.

The same posthumous volume contains an essay in which Maslow presents a new perspective on an earlier book *Religions, values, and peak-experiences* (1964). In this essay he cautioned against those who might exalt the "peak experience" as an end in itself or might turn away from the world in a romantic search: "The great lesson from the true mystics . . . that the sacred is *in* the ordinary, that it is to be found in one's daily life, in one's neighbors, friends, and family, in one's back yard, and that travel may be a *flight* from confronting the sacred—this lesson can be easily lost." Here again he echoes the Eastern psychologies by recognizing both the value and the hard work required for what he calls "the plateau experience":

. . . Plateau experiencing can be achieved, learned, earned by long hard work. . . . A transient glimpse is certainly possible in the peak experiences which may, after all, come sometimes to anyone. But, so to speak, to take up residence on the high plateau . . . that is another matter altogether. That tends to be a lifelong effort (1971, pp. 348–349).

A close collaborator of Maslow's, Anthony Sutich founded a psychology journal in 1969 devoted to the study of the kind of concepts

Maslow described. Sutich's *Journal of Transpersonal Psychology* has become the forum for psychologists with interests similar to Maslow's; "Theory Z" was first published there, and Maslow himself was a founding member of the Board of Editors. While there is no single spokesman for the transpersonal perspective, as a whole this group of psychologists is most open to studying and borrowing from Eastern psychologies. Sutich's statement (1969) in the first issue of the *Journal* expresses the far-ranging interests of transpersonal psychology:

Transpersonal Psychology is the title given to an emerging force in the psychology field by a group . . . who are interested in those ultimate human capacities and potentialities that have no systematic place in . . . behavioristic theory ("first force"), classical psychoanalytic theory ("second force"), or Humanistic psychology ("third force"). The emerging Transpersonal Psychology ("fourth force") is concerned specifically with . . . ultimate values, unitive consciousness, peak experiences, ecstasy, mystical experience, awe, being, self-actualization, essence, bliss, wonder, ultimate meaning, transcendence of the self, spirit, oneness, cosmic awareness . . . and related concepts, experiences, and activities (p. 1).

Because psychologists with a transpersonal orientation deal with phenomena such as "awe" and "unitive consciousness," they often turn to the Eastern psychologies for guidance, just as R. M. Bucke did a century ago. One area where some see Western psychologies as deficient relative to those from the East is in dealing with human spiritual aspirations or religious life. Charles Tart, a major investigator of altered states of consciousness (1969), edited a pioneering collection of these Eastern theories in *Transpersonal psychologies* (1976). Tart observes that Eastern psychologies do not share the assumptions of Western theories and so do not suffer the same limitations:

Orthodox, Western psychology has dealt very poorly with the spiritual side of man's nature, choosing either to ignore its existence or to label it pathological. Yet much of the agony of our time stems from a spiritual vacuum. Our culture, our psychology, has ruled out man's spiritual nature, but the cost of this attempted suppression is enormous. If we want to find ourselves, our spiritual side, it's imperative for us to look at the psychologies that have dealt with it (1976, p. 5).

Tart suggests that the realm of spiritual experience is connected to the realm of altered states of consciousness. To the extent that the Eastern psychologies help us predict or control such altered states, the psychologies are themselves state-specific sciences, that is, theories that derive from and apply to specific states of awareness. Tart's purpose in surveying the transpersonal psychologies of the East is not to offer them for wholesale adoption by Western psychology, but to consider them as guides for our own efforts. He proposes that we can use Eastern thought to build, in the mode of contemporary science, a more fully informed understanding of these spiritual realms and the altered awareness they bring. Tart cautions: "I have no doubt that many sacred scriptures contain a great deal of valuable information and wisdom, and I am certain that many spiritual teachers have a great deal to teach us that is of immense value, but even the greatest sorts of spiritual teachings must be adapted to the culture of the people they are presented to if they are really to connect with their whole psyches" (1976, p. 58). Tart envisions "the development of scientific tradition with the vast, uncharted (to science) sea of human potentials we can call man's spiritual potentialities."

Robert Ornstein, a psychologist with background and interest similar to Tart's borrows freely from Eastern psychologies in his books *The psychology of consciousness* (1973a) and *On the nature of human consciousness* (1973b). Ornstein's interest in Eastern psychologies is an outgrowth of his research on the different functions of each half of the brain. The left—and usually dominant—hemisphere is best at rational, linear thought; the right hemisphere excells at nonrational, intuitive insights. Our culture and our science, Ornstein notes, favor the left hemisphere's mode of knowing to the detriment of the right. He argues that a person who has access to the benefits of both modes would be more fully able to function well. Ornstein posits that what he calls "the traditional esoteric psychologies" cultivate in their serious students a fuller access to an intuitive, holistic mode of thought from which our own rational, scientific culture closes us off.

Tart and Ornstein, like many transpersonal psychologists, take their cue from William James' seminal observation: "Our normal waking consciousness . . . is but one special type of consciousness, whilst all about it, parted from it by the filmiest of screens, there lie potential forms of consciousness entirely different" (1950, p. 305). As psychologists like Maslow, Tart, and Ornstein explore such different states of consciousness, they discover new potentials for personality growth. Often, however, they find that the new ground they break has been explored and mapped long before by the psychologists of the East. Let us now turn to consider a still flourishing Eastern personality theory, that of Abhidhamma.

ABHIDHAMMA: AN EASTERN PERSONALITY THEORY

Abhidhamma was developed in India fifteen or more centuries ago, but present-day Buddhists continue to apply it in various forms as a guide to the workings of the mind. This psychological theory stems directly from the insights of Gautama Buddha in the fifth century B.C. Buddha's teachings have been refined and evolved into the various lineages, teachings, and schools of Buddhism, in a process of evolution akin to that by which, for example, Freud's thought developed into disparate schools of psychoanalysis. Like other Eastern psychologies, Abhidhamma contains an ideal type of the perfected personality around which its analysis of the workings of the mind is oriented. As Bhikku Nyanaponika, a modern Buddhist scholar-monk put it, "In the Buddhist doctrine, mind is the starting point, the focal point, and also, as the liberated and purified mind of the Saint, the culminating point" (1962, p. 12). In this section we will survey Abhidhamma theory and the avenues its students follow in meditation to fulfill its model of the healthy personality. [An excellent description of Abhidhamma is in Lama Govinda's *The psychological attitude of early Buddhist philosophy* (1969). For more detailed reviews of Abhidhamma see also Guenther (1976); Narada (1968); and Nyanaponika (1971).]

A possibly apocryphal tale is emblematic of Abhidhamma's extremely analytic attitude toward the person. A beautiful young woman had quarrelled with her husband, and was running away back home to her family. She passed by a monk, who, as he walked on his daily round for alms, saw the woman pass by him "dressed up like a celestial nymph." The monk, who at the time was reflecting on the nature of the human skeleton, looked up and noticed the whiteness of her teeth. A little later, her husband came by, in hot pursuit. He asked, "Venerable sir, did you by any chance see a woman?" Replied the monk:

> Whether it was a man or woman
> That went by I noticed not;
> But only that on this high road
> There goes a bag of bones.
>
> (Buddhaghosa, 1976:22)

Since the old monk in the story was meditating on one of 32 parts of the body—the skeleton—for him that aspect of the pretty woman loomed largest. Through keen observation in meditation the monk was able to become so detached from all the constituents of body and mind that no one of them held any greater value than any other. From this perspective a person's bones are as noteworthy as his or her thoughts. This degree of utter detachment reflects the spirit of Abhidhamma as it surveys and dissects the human personality.

What we denote by the word "personality" equates most closely in Abhidhamma to a concept of *atta,* or self. But a central premise of Abhidhamma is that there is no abiding self whatsoever, only an impersonal aggregate of processes that come and go. The semblance of personality springs from the intermingling of these impersonal processes. What appears to be "self" is the sum total of body parts, thoughts, sensations, desires, memories, and so on. The only continuous thread in the mind is *bhava,* the continuity of consciousness over time. Each successive moment of our awareness is shaped by the previous moment, and will in turn determine the following moment; it is *bhava* that connects one moment of consciousness to that which follows. We may identify the "self" with psychological activities such as our thoughts, memories, or perceptions, yet all these phenomena are part of a continued flow. The human personality, says Abhidhamma, is like a river that keeps a constant form, seemingly a single identity, though not a single drop is the same as a moment ago. In this view "there is no actor apart from action, no percipient apart from perception, no conscious subject behind consciousness" (Van Aung, 1972, p. 7). In the words of Buddha (Samyutta-Nikaya, 1972, I, 35):

> Just as when the parts are set together
> There arises the word "chariot,"
> So does the notion of a being
> When the aggregates are present.

The study of personality in Buddhism does not deal with a complex of postulated entities, such as "ego" or "unconscious," but with a series of events. The basic event is the ongoing relationship of mental states to sense objects—for example, a feeling of desire (the mental state) toward a beautiful woman (the sense object). A person's mental states are in constant flux from moment to moment; their rate of change is reckoned in microseconds. The basic method Abhidhamma offers for studying the mind's multitudinous changes is introspection, a close and systematic observation of one's own experience. Without careful introspection one might think that a state such as desire can persist without interruption for a long while, but Abhidhamma says this is not so. For example, even if one is in the throes of passionate lovemaking, where desire seems overwhelming, Abhidhamma has it that if one were to closely monitor each successive mental state, one would see that that desire is actually interspersed with innumerable other feelings that come and go. Not only do a person's mental states vary from moment to moment; so also do sense objects. While a person might think that during lovemaking all that he pays attention to is his lover, close scrutiny of his stream of consciousness would reveal that in addition a multitude of other objects occupy his mind and senses. These might include a variety of pleasant sensations, various sounds from near and far, and an assortment of smells, tastes, and sights. In addition, random memories, future plans, and other thoughts would mingle with these objects of the senses.

In Abhidhamma, in addition to the objects of the five senses, there are thoughts; that is, the thinking mind itself is counted as the "sixth" sense. Thus, just as a sound or sight can be the object of a mental state, so can a thought—for example, the thought "I should take out the garbage," might be the object of a mental state of aversion. Each mental state is composed of a set of properties, called mental factors, that combine to flavor and define that state. The Abhidhamma system discussed here enumerates 53 categories of such mental factors; in other branches of Buddhism the count varies up to 175. In any one mental state only a sub-set of the factors are present. The unique qualities of each mental state is determined by which factors it combines. The moment of dislike for taking out the garbage, for example, would have a more complex combination than simple aversion; a dozen or more other mental factors, such as misperception of what taking out the garbage is really like, would combine with aversion. Mental states come and go in a lawful and orderly manner. As in Western psychology, Abhidhamma theorists believe each mental state derives in part from biological and situational influences, in addition to a carryover from the preceding psychological moment. Each state in turn determines the particular combination of factors in the next mental state.

Mental factors are the key to what we in the West know as "karma," or in Pali, *kamma.* In Abhidhamma *kamma* is a technical word for the principle that every deed is motivated by underlying mental states. In Abhidhamma, as in many Eastern psychologies, a given behavior is in essence ethically neutral. Its moral nature cannot be determined without taking into account the underlying motives of the person as he or she performed it. The acts of someone who has a negative mix of mental factors—who acts, for example, from malice or greed—are evil, even though the act itself might seem to an observer neither good nor bad. The *Dhammapada,* a collection of verses spoken by Gautama Buddha, begins with a statement of the Abhidhamma doctrine of Karma:

All that we are is the result of what we have thought: it is founded on our thoughts, it is made up of our thoughts. If a man speaks or acts with an evil thought, pain follows him, as the wheel follows the foot of the ox that draws the wagon. . . . If a man speaks or acts with a pure thought, happiness follows him, like a shadow that never leaves him (Babbitt, 1965, p. 3).

The Abhidhamma distinguishes between mental factors that are *ku-sula*—pure, wholesome, or healthy—and *akusula*—impure, unwhole-some, or unhealthy. Most perceptual, cognitive, and affective mental factors fit into either the healthy or unhealthy category. The judg-ment of "healthy" or "unhealthy" was arrived at empirically, on the basis of the collective experience of large numbers of early Buddhist meditators. Their criterion was whether a particular mental factor fa-cilitated or interfered with their attempts to still their minds in medi-tation. Those factors that interfered with meditation were designated as "unhealthy," those that aided as "healthy."

In addition to healthy or unhealthy factors, there are seven neutral properties present in every mental state. Apperception (*phassa*) is the mere awareness of an object; perception (*sanna*), its first recognition as belonging to one or the other of the senses; volition (*cetana*), the con-ditioned reaction that accompanies the first perception of an object; feeling (*vedana*), the sensations aroused by the object; onepointedness (*ekaggata*), the focusing of awareness; spontaneous attention (*manasi-kara*), the involuntary directing of attention due to attraction by the object; and psychic energy (*jivitindriya*), which lends vitality to and unites the other six factors. These factors provide a basic framework of consciousness in which the healthy and unhealthy factors are em-bedded. The particular combination of factors that embeds in this framework varies from moment to moment. Let us now turn to sur-vey the unhealthy and healthy mental factors.

Unhealthy Factors

The central unhealthy factor, delusion, is perceptual: delusion (*moha*) is defined as a cloudiness of mind that leads to misperception of the object of awareness. Delusion is seen in Abhidhamma as basic igno-rance, the primary root of human suffering. This misperception of the true nature of things—the simple failure to see clearly, without bias or prejudice of any kind—is the core of all unhealthy mental states. Delusion, for example, leads to "false view" or misdiscern-ment (*ditthi*). False view entails placing something in the wrong cate-gory or miscategorization. The working of these factors is clear in the case of the paranoid, who misperceives as threatening someone who wishes him or her no harm, and so categorizes the other person as part of a fancied conspiracy against him or herself. The Buddha is quoted as saying that while a person's mind is dominated by false view, whatever he might do or aspire to could only "lead him to an undesirable, unpleasant, and disagreeable state, to woe and suffering" (*Anguttara Nikaya,* 1975, I, p. 23). Among the pernicious false views the Buddha explicitly criticized is one of the pervasive assumptions of many Western personality theories, namely, that there is a fixed "self" or "ego." In Abhidhamma there is no self as such but a "self-consuming process of physical and mental phenomena which continually arise and again disappear immediately" (Nyanatiloka, 1972, p. 25).

Perplexity (*vicikiccha*) denotes the inability to decide or make a correct judgment. When this factor dominates a person's mind he or she is filled with doubt and, at the extreme, can become paralyzed. Other unhealthy cognitive factors are shamelessness (*ahirika*) and remorselessness (*anottappa*); these attitudes allow a person to disregard the opinions of others and one's own internalized standards. When these factors hold sway, a person views evil acts without compunction, and so is apt to misbehave. Indeed, these factors are prerequisites for the mental states that underly any act of ill-will. Another unwholesome factor that might lead to wrongdoing is egoism (*mana*). This attitude of self-interest causes a person to view objects solely in terms of fulfilling their own desires or needs. The concatenation of these three mental factors in a single moment—shamelessness, remorselessness, and selfishness—is undoubtedly often the basis for much human evil.

The rest of the unhealthy mental factors are affective. Agitation (*uddhacca*) and worry (*kukkucca*) are states of distractedness, remorse, and rumination. These factors create a state of anxiety, the central feature of most mental disorder. Another set of unhealthy factors relate to clinging: greed (*lobha*), avarice (*macchariya*), and envy (*issa*) denote different kinds of grasping attachment to an object, while aversion (*dosa*) is the negative side of attachment. Greed and aversion are found in all negative mental states, and always combine with delusion. Two final unhealthy factors are contraction (*thina*) and torpor (*middha*). These factors lend a rigid inflexibility to mental states. When these negative factors predominate, a person's mind as well as their body is prone to sluggishness.

Healthy Factors   Each of the unhealthy factors is opposed by a healthy factor. These factors are either healthy or unhealthy; there is no middle ground. The means in Abhidhamma for attaining a healthy mental state is to replace the unhealthy factors with their polar opposites. The principle that allows this is akin to "reciprocal inhibition" as used in systematic desensitization, where relaxation inhibits its physiologic opposite, tension (Wolpe, 1958). For each negative mental factor there is a corresponding positive factor that overrides it. When a given healthy factor is present in a mental state, the unhealthy factor it suppresses cannot arise.

The central healthy factor is insight (*panna*), the opposite of delusion. Insight, in the sense of "clear perception of the object as it really is," suppresses delusion, the fundamental unhealthy factor. These two factors cannot coexist in a single mental state: where there is clarity, there cannot be delusion; nor where there is delusion in any degree can there be clarity. Mindfulness (*sati*) is the continued clear comprehension of an object; this essential partner of insight steadies and holds clarity in a person's mind. Insight and mindfulness are the primary healthy factors; when they are present in a mental state, the other healthy factors tend to be present also. The presence of these two healthy factors is sufficient to suppress all the unhealthy factors.

Some healthy factors require certain circumstances to arise. The twin cognitive factors of modesty (*hiri*), which inhibits shamelessness, and discretion (*ottappa*), the opposite of remorselessness, come to mind only when there is a thought of an evil act. Modesty and discretion are always connected with rectitude (*cittujjukata*), the attitude of correct judgment . Another healthy factor is confidence (*saddha*), a sureness based on correct perception. This group of mental factors—modesty, discretion, rectitude, and confidence—act together to produce virtuous behavior as judged both by personal and social standards.

The cluster of unhealthy factors formed by greed, avarice, envy, and aversion are opposed by the healthy factors of nonattachment (*alobha*), nonaversion (*adosa*), impartiality (*tatramajjhata*), and composure (*passadhi*), which reflect the physical and mental tranquility that arises from diminishing feelings of attachment. The above four factors replace a grasping or rejecting attitude with an even-mindedness toward whatever object might arise in a person's awareness. The unhealthy factors of greed, egoism, envy, and aversion, for example, might cause a person to crave a more prestigious job with higher pay and glamor, or to envy someone who had such a job, or to despise his or her own lesser position. The opposing healthy factors of composure, nonattachment, nonaversion, and impartiality, on the other hand, would lead the person to weigh the advantages of pay and prestige against such drawbacks as more pressure and stress, to assess fairly the strengths that have led another to have such a job and the weaknesses that make the person perform less well than he or she should. Finally, these four healthy factors would let one weigh whatever advantages one's own job might have, in what respects it might be unsuitable, what one's genuine capabilities are, and how to use them to get a better position within the limits of one's skills. Even more important, impartiality would lead one to regard the whole situation coolly, neither unhappy that one does not have a better job, nor despising one's own, nor resigned to accepting with despair an unsuitable job. These four healthy mental factors allow one to accept things as they are, but also to make whatever changes seem appropriate.

Body and mind are seen as interconnected in Abhidhamma. While every factor affects both body and mind, the final set of healthy factors are the only ones explicitly described as having both physical and psychological effects. These are buoyancy (*ahuta*), pliancy (*muduta*), adaptability (*kammannata*) and proficiency (*pagunnata*). When these factors arise a person thinks and acts with a natural looseness and ease, performing at the peak of his or her skills. They suppress the unhealthy factors of contraction and torpor, which dominate the mind in such states as depression. These healthy factors make one able to adapt physically and mentally to changing conditions, meeting whatever challenges may arise.

Table 10-1 lists the healthy and unhealthy factors. In the Abhidhamma psychodynamic, healthy and unhealthy mental factors are mutually inhibiting; the presence of one suppresses its opposite. But there is not always a one-to-one correspondence between a pair of healthy and unhealthy factors; in some cases a single healthy factor will inhibit a set of unhealthy factors—nonattachment alone, for example, inhibits greed, avarice, envy, and aversion. Certain key factors will inhibit the entire opposite set; for example, when delusion is present, not a single positive factor can arise along with it.

It is a person's *kamma* that determines whether he or she will experience predominantly healthy or unhealthy states. The particular combination of factors are the outcome of biological and situational

TABLE 10-1 *The healthy and unhealthy mental factors*	Unhealthy factors	Healthy factors
	Perceptual/Cognitive:	
	Delusion	Insight
	False View	Mindfulness
	Shamelessness	Modesty
	Recklessness	Discretion
	Egoism	Confidence
	Affective:	
	Agitation	Composure
	Greed	Nonattachment
	Aversion	Nonaversion
	Envy	Impartiality
	Avarice	Buoyancy
	Worry	Pliancy
	Contraction	Adaptability
	Torpor	Proficiency
	Perplexity	Rectitude

influences as well as the carryover from one's previous states of mind. The factors usually arise as a group, either positive or negative. In any given mental state the factors composing it arise in differing strengths; whichever factor is the strongest determines how a person experiences and acts at any given moment. Although all the negative factors may be present, the state experienced will be quite different depending on whether, for example, it is greed or torpor that dominates the mind. The hierarchy of strength of the factors, then, determines whether a specific state will be negative or positive. When a particular factor or set of factors occurs frequently in a person's mental states, then it becomes a personality trait. The sum total of a person's habitual mental factors determine their personality type traits, as we will see in the next section.

The Abhidhamma model for personality types follows directly from the principle that mental factors arise in differing strengths. If a person's mind is habitually dominated by a particular factor or set of factors, these will determine personality, motives, and behavior. The uniqueness of each person's pattern of mental factors gives rise to individual differences in personality over and above the broad categories of the main types. The person in whom delusion predominates is one of the common types, as are the hateful person, in whom aversion predominates, and the lustful person, in whom greed is strong. A more positive type is the intelligent person, in whom mindfulness and insight are strong.

Personality Types

The Abhidhamma view of human motivation stems from its analysis of mental factors and their influence on behavior. It is a person's mental states that move the person to seek one thing and avoid another. His or her mental states guide every act. If the mind is dominated by greed, then this will become the predominant motive, and one will behave accordingly, seeking to gain the object of one's greed. If egoism is a powerful factor, then the person will act in a self-aggrandizing manner. Each personality type is, in this sense, a motivational type also.

The Visuddhimagga (Buddhaghosa, 1976), an Abhidhamma-based manual for meditators that dates from the fifth century A.D., devotes a section to recognizing the main personality types, since each kind of person must be treated in a way that suits his or her disposition. One method it recommends for evaluating personality type is careful observation of how a person stands and moves. The lustful or sensual person, for example, is said to be graceful in gait; the hateful person drags the feet as he or she walks; the deluded person paces quickly. A typical rule of thumb for this analysis goes (Vajiranana, 1962, p. 99):

Of the lustful the footprint is divided in the middle,
Of unfriendly man it leaves a trail behind.
The print of the deluded one is an impression quickly made. . .

It goes on to note that a Buddha leaves a perfectly even footprint, since his mind is calm and his body poised.

The author of the Visuddhimagga recognized that every detail of life is a clue to character; this fifth century manual gives a remarkably complete behavioral profile for each personality type. The sensual person, it tells us, is charming, polite, and replies courteously when addressed. When such persons sleep, they make their beds carefully, lie down gently, and move little while asleep. They perform their duties artistically; sweep with smooth and even strokes, and do a thorough job. In general they are skillful, polished, tidy and circumspect workers. They dress neatly and tastefully. When they eat they prefer soft, sweet food that is well cooked and served in sumptuous fashion; they eat slowly, take small bites, and relish the taste. On seeing any pleasing object they stop to admire it, and are attracted by its merits, but do not notice its faults. They leave such an object with regret. But on the negative side they are often pretentious, deceitful, vain, covetous, dissatisfied, lascivious, and frivolous.

The hateful person, by contrast, stands stiffly. These persons make their bed carelessly and in haste, sleep with their bodies tense, and reply in anger when awakened. When they work they are rough and careless; when they sweep the broom makes a harsh, scraping noise. Their clothes are likely to be too tight and unfinished. When they eat their preference is for pungent food that tastes sharp and sour; they eat hurriedly without noticing the taste, though they dislike food with a mild taste. They are uninterested in objects of beauty, and notice even the slightest fault while overlooking merits. They are often angry, full of malice, ungrateful, envious, and mean.

The third type is distinct from these two. The deluded person stands in a slovenly manner. Their beds are untidy, they sleep in a sprawl, and arise sluggishly, grunting with complaints. As workers they are unskillful and messy; they sweep awkwardly and at random, leaving bits of rubbish behind. Their clothes are loose and untidy. They do not care what they eat, and will eat whatever comes their way; they are sloppy eaters, putting large lumps of food in the mouth and smearing the face with food. They have no idea whether an object is beautiful or not, but believe whatever others tell them, and so praise or disapprove accordingly. They often show sloth and torpor, are easily distracted, are given to remorse and perplexity, but can also be obstinant and tenacious.

The Visuddhimagga goes on to specify the optimal conditions that should be arranged for persons of each type when they begin to meditate. The first goal in their training is to counteract their dominant psychological tendencies, and so bring their mind into balance. For this reason the conditions prescribed for each type are not those they would naturally choose. The cottage given to the sensual person, for example, is an unwashed grass hut that ought to be "spattered with dirt, full of bats, dilapidated, too high or too low, in bleak surroundings, threatened by lions and tigers, with a muddy, uneven path, where even the bed and chair are full of bugs. And it should be ugly and unsightly, exciting loathing as soon as looked at" (p. 109). The Visuddhimagga goes on to detail the other conditions that suit the sensual person:

Suitable garments have torn-off edges with threads hanging down, harsh to the touch like hemp, soiled, heavy and hard to wear. And the right kind of bowl for him is an ugly clay bowl or a heavy and misshappen iron bowl as unappetising as a skull. The right kind of road for him on which to wander for alms is disagreeable, with no village near, and uneven. The right kind of village for him is where people wander about as if oblivious of him. Suitable people to serve him are unsightly, ill-favoured, with dirty clothes, ill-smelling and disgusting, who serve him his gruel and rice as if they were throwing it rudely at him. The right kind of food is made of broken rice, stale buttermilk, sour gruel, curry of old vegetables, or anything at all that is merely for filling the stomach (Buddhaghosa, 1976, pp. 109–110).

The suitable conditions for the hateful person, on the other hand, are as pleasant, comfortable, and easy as can be arranged. For the deluded person, things are to be made simple and clear, and quite as pleasant and comfortable as for the hateful person. In each case the environment is tailored to inhibit the kind of mental factor that usually dominates each personality type: the lustful person finds little to be greedy about, the hateful person little to despise, and for the deluded person things are clear. This program of environments designed to promote mental health is an ancient predecessor to what modern advocates of similar plans call "milieu therapy." The Buddha also saw that different types of people would take more readily to different kinds of meditation, and so he devised a wide variety of meditation methods tailored to fit different personality types.

The factors that form one's mental states from moment to moment determine one's mental health. The operational definition of mental disorder in Abhidhamma is simple: the absence of healthy factors, and presence of unhealthy factors. Each variety of mental disorder stems from the hold of certain unhealthy factors on the mind. The special

The Healthy Personality and Mental Disorder

character of each unhealthy factor leads to a particular disorder—egoism, for example, underlies the purely self-interested actions that we in Western psychology call "sociopathic" behavior; agitation and worry are the anxiety at the core of neuroses; aversion tied to a specific object or situation is a phobia.

The criterion for mental health is equally simple: The presence of the healthy factors, and absence of unhealthy factors, in a person's psychological economy. The healthy factors, besides supplanting unhealthy ones, also provide a necessary mental environment for a group of positive affective states that cannot arise in the presence of the unhealthy factors. These include loving-kindness (*karuna*) and "altruistic joy" (*mudita*)—that is, taking pleasure in the happiness of others.

The normal person has a mixture of healthy and unhealthy factors in the flow of their mental states. Each of us probably experiences periods of wholly healthy or unhealthy mental states as our stream of consciousness flows on. Very few people, however, experience only healthy mental states, and thus all of us are "unhealthy" in this sense. Indeed, one scripture quotes the Buddha as saying of normal people, "All worldlings are deranged." The goal of psychological development in Abhidhamma is to increase the amount of healthy states—and correspondingly, decrease unhealthy ones—in a person's mind. At the peak of mental health, no unhealthy factors arise at all in a person's mind. Although this is the ideal that each person is urged to seek, it is, of course, rarely realized.

One reason few people achieve the ideal mental health is due to *anusayas,* latent tendencies of the mind toward unhealthy mental states. *Anusayas* lie dormant in the person's mind until an opportune moment arises for them to surface. Seven of the unhealthy factors are particularly strong *anusayas:* greed, false view, delusion, aversion, doubt, pride, and agitation. While a person experiences a healthy mental state, these *anusayas* are in abeyance, but they are never far from taking over when the moment is ripe. The final criterion for full mental health is to have eradicated the *anusayas* from one's mind, thereby eliminating even the tendency toward unhealthy states of mind. The principle of *anusayas* is the closest approximation in Abhidhamma to the Western concept of the unconscious.

As a catalogue of the mental properties we experience from moment to moment, the Abhidhamma list of mental factors is by no means exhaustive. The possibilities for categorizing mental states are countless; the Abhidhamma theorists do not pretend to offer a total compendium. But theirs is a purposeful analysis; their categories are designed to help a person recognize, and so control, key states of mind so that he or she may ultimately rid themselves of unhealthy states. The practicing Buddhist embarks on a coordinated program of environmental, behavioral, and attentional control to attain his or her final goal, a plateau of purely healthy mental states. In the classical Buddhist path a person who sought this plateau of health would enter the controlled surroundings of a monastery, regulate his or her actions by taking the 227 vows of a monk or nun, and, most important, meditate.

Once people have become familiar with the categories of healthy and unhealthy mental factors so that they can see them at play in their own minds, they will find that simply knowing a state is unhealthy does little or nothing to end it. For example, if a person resents the predominance of unhealthy factors in the mind, or if he wishes they would go away, he is merely adding aversion and desire to the psychological mix. The strategy the Abhidhamma offers for attaining healthy states is neither directly to seek them nor to be averse to unhealthy states. The recommended approach is meditation.

Meditation: Means to a Healthy Personality

We shall discuss two methods of meditating. The first method consists of keeping one's mind concentrated; the second method involves adopting a neutral stance toward whatever comes and goes in the stream of awareness. The first method is called *concentration,* the second *mindfulness.* [The most complete description of the systems of meditation discussed here is Buddhaghosa's *Visuddhimagga* (1976). Other excellent commentaries on Buddhist meditation are Dhammaratana (1964) and Mahasi Sayadaw (1965).]

CONCENTRATION AND ALTERED STATES OF CONSCIOUS-NESS. In concentration the meditator aims to bring his or her attention to a single object or point of focus. In the course of developing concentration, the meditator seeks to surpass what we typically assume to be the normal limits for holding a single object in awareness. William James, after trying to hold one thought in mind, proclaimed that "No one can possibly attend continuously to an object that does not change" (1961a, p. 421). But this is precisely the goal of the meditator.

Concentration on an unhealthy factor, such as on lust, will lead to agitation, and so make the mind distracted. Concentration on a healthy factor facilitates deeper concentration. As the strength of concentration deepens, the meditator's mind will become increasingly stable, and the unhealthy factors—including agitation and distractedness—will be suppressed. With much practice—mainly in simply returning one's attention to the object of focus whenever one becomes distracted—the meditator can reach a point where these hindrances to concentration are overcome. When this occurs there comes a moment when concentration notably quickens and the mind is dominated by a set of healthy factors that anchor attention on the object of meditation. These factors include applied and sustained attention (*vicara* and *vitakka*), which keep the mind continuously focused on a single object; feelings of rapture (*piti*); energy (*viriya*) and equanimity (*uphekha*). However, at this stage—called "access" concentration—these factors fluctuate in strength. With continued one-pointed concentration the fluctuation changes to stability, and the meditator experiences a total break with normal consciousness. This altered state of consciousness is called *jhana* (*samadhi* in some other Buddhist and Hindu traditions). In jhana normal perceptions and thoughts cease altogether. In the first jhana the meditator is totally one-pointed on the object, so that the mind seems to merge with it. This sense of merging is accompanied by bliss, rapture, and the disappearance from the mind of all other thoughts and feelings.

There are seven levels of jhana beyond this first one, each marked by a more intense one-pointedness combined with a more subtle bliss. In the higher jhanas bliss is replaced by strong equanimity. On emerging from jhana there is an afterglow whereby unhealthy factors tend to be inhibited, and healthy ones dominate. The deeper the jhana, the more efficient the elimination of unhealthy mental factors from the meditator's mind. As the effects of jhana dissipate, unhealthy factors once again return and can dominate the meditator's mind. As with many other experiences of altered states, the effects of jhana recede so that a person's mind once again resumes its former habits.

MINDFULNESS MEDITATION: THE PATH TO PERSONALITY CHANGE. Unlike the method of concentration, in using mindfulness the meditator makes no effort to regulate flow of consciousness. While doing this type of meditation, one aims for full awareness of any and all contents of the mind. Instead of getting caught up in any one thought or feeling, the meditator seeks to maintain an attitude of being a neutral "witness" of it all. In its initial phase this approach entails mindfulness, where the meditator faces each experience, each mental event, as though it were occurring for the first time. He or she restricts attention to the bare noticing of each successive moment of awareness. If a subsequent train of association, categorization, or affective reaction arises in the mind, the meditator takes that too as an object of bare attention. One neither rejects nor pursues it, but drops it from awareness after one has noted it. The meditator gives each and every object of awareness equal value; he or she isolates nothing as cognitive figure, nor relegates anything to ground.

It is extremely difficult, especially in the beginning, to break one's habits of perception and thought in this way. The meditator continuously gets drawn into one train of thought or another, letting mindfulness lapse. Mindfulness works best when the meditator's concentration is strong enough to keep the mind steadily noting perception and thought, but not so strong that these processes stop. As the meditator's mindfulness progresses, the normal illusion of mental continuity and reasonableness breaks down; the person becomes aware of the random and discrete units from which the mind continually builds a reality. When mindfulness is so strong that it continues without a moment of forgetfulness, a second phase in this process begins, called insight (*vipassana*). The path of insight is marked by an increasingly fine and more accurate perception of the workings of the mind. The meditator realizes his mind is in constant flux, and witnesses the innumerable combinations of mental factors that flow through it. The mind's qualities of constant change and impersonality lead one finally to the desire to escape the world of experience. Insight then culminates in the total cessation of mental processes in *nibbana,* what we know as the "nirvanic" state. There is no experience whatsoever for the person in nirvana, not even of bliss or equanimity. It is a state even more empty than jhana.

In Abhidhamma, nirvana is said to bring radical and lasting alteration of one's mental states. This is the path to a healthy personality. Though a key step, nirvana is not the end of the Abhidhamma path. The significance for personality of nirvana is in its aftereffect. Unlike jhana, which has a short-lived effect on the meditator's personality, a person's post-nirvana personality is said to be irrevocably altered. A person's first experience of nirvana initiates a progression of changes that can finally lead to the point where unhealthy factors cease altogether appearing in the mental states. Not only are there no unhealthy factors in the states, but the person has also eradicated any and all *anusayas,* the latent tendencies that could potentially lead to an unhealthy factor arising in the mind. This transformation of consciousness is gradual. As the meditator's insight strengthens and he or she attains nirvana at increasingly profound depths, groups of the unhealthy factors become totally inhibited. Finally not a single unhealthy factor will appear in any of the person's mental states. A meditator who reaches this point is called an *arahat,* literally, "one worthy of praise."

Arahat: Ideal Type
of the Healthy
Personality

The *arahat* embodies the essence of mental health in Abhidhamma. An arahat's personality traits are permanently altered; all the motives, perceptions, and actions formerly engaged in under the influence of unhealthy factors will have vanished. Rune Johansson, in *The psychology of nirvana* (1970), has culled Abhidhamma sources for the personality attributes of the arahat. His list includes:

1. *absence of:* greed for sense desires; anxiety, resentments, or fears of any sort; dogmatisms such as the belief that this or that is "the Truth"; aversion to conditions such as loss, disgrace, pain or blame; feelings of lust or anger; experiences of suffering; need for approval, pleasure, or praise; desire for anything for oneself beyond essential and necessary items; and

2. *prevalence of:* impartiality toward others and equanimity in all circumstances; ongoing alertness and calm delight in experience no matter how ordinary or even seemingly boring; strong feelings of compassion and loving kindness; quick and accurate perception; composure and skill in taking action; openness to others and responsivity to their needs.

One of the few mentions of dreams in Abhidhamma suggests another unusual attribute of the arahat. People's dreams are said to be of four types. The first is due to some organic or muscular disturbance, and typically involves a strong physical sensation such as falling, flying, or being chased. Nightmares belong to this category. The second type of dream is due to one's activities during the day, and echoes these past experiences. Such dreams are generally mundane. The third kind of dream is of an actual event as it happens, akin to Jung's principle of synchronicity. The last type of dream is clairvoyant, an accurate prophecy of events yet to occur. When an arahat dreams, it is always such a clairvoyant dream (Van Aung, 1972). The Buddha was adept at interpreting symbols in his dreams, although there is no formal system for symbolic analysis in Abhidhamma. Just before his enlightenment, the Buddha had a series of vivid dreams that predicted his enlightenment, the teaching he would do afterward, the gathering of students to him, and the course of Buddhism after his death.

Although the *arahat* may seem virtuous beyond belief from the perspective of the other personality theorists we have reviewed, he embodies characteristics common to the ideal type in most every Asian psychology. The *arahat* is the prototypic saint, a prototype notable in the main by its absence in Western personality theory. Such a radical transformation of personality overreaches the goals and hopes of our psychotherapies. From the perspective of most Western personality theories the *arahat* must seem too good to exist; he or she lacks many characteristics they assume intrinsic to human nature. An arahat does, however, bear some resemblance to the fully actualized person described in the writings of Maslow and Rogers. But the arahat is an ideal type, the end-point in a gradual transformation that anyone can undertake, and in which anyone can succeed to whatever small measure. Thus the monk or lay meditator may not become a saint overnight, but may well experience himself changing so that he has a greater proportion of healthy mental states. [The reader who wishes to pursue an interest in Buddhist meditation or to compare this system to others will find a more detailed discussion and comparison in Goleman (1977).]

Abhidhamma stands silent on many issues of importance to Western personality theorists. It has nothing to say, for example, about the influence of childhood events on personality, nor does it have anything to say about the stages of life, from infancy through old age. One reason may be that the Buddhist perspective on the human lifespan differs radically from Western concepts. For the Buddhist, a human life is seen as one of a continuous chain of reincarnations. Just as each psychological moment shapes the next, each lifetime has its influence on the person's next incarnation. For this reason Buddhists place a special emphasis on a person's mental state at the moment of his or her death, since it is seen to be a large determinant in the person's psychological status at the moment of the person's next birth.

CURRENT STATUS AND EVALUATION

Abhidhamma is mute on other salient issues in Western personality theory as well. Sex differences in personality are not dealt with, nor do they seem to have been the basis of bias in early Buddhism. The Pali Canon, in recording the lives of the saints of Buddha's time, lists about as many female arahats as male. Other topics of interest to personality theorists that play no part in Abhidhamma are whether personality traits are inherited or due to upbringing, the role of culture in shaping personality, and the problem of the relationship of mind to body—although, as we have seen, Abhidhamma recognizes that mind and body are in some ways interlinked.

While we in the West tend to think of Eastern psychologies as other-worldly, Abhidhamma belies this stereotype. Buddha, in fact, said it was useless to conjecture about other realms of existence, and based his teaching on the experiences of ordinary people. His expressed mission was to save people from the miseries of life, and Abhidhamma is a theoretical statement of the nature of human suffering and what is entailed in ending it. This mission of social concern is emphasized in Mahayana Buddhism, the branch that spreads through the northern part of the Buddhist world from Tibet to Japan. Every Mahayana Buddhist takes a vow to help save all living beings from misery. Although the means for doing so varies from sect to sect within Mahayana, all sects accept the basic analysis of the human condition as expressed in Abhidhamma. A Mahayana version of Abhidhamma is translated by H. V. Guenther and L. S. Kawamura in *Mind in Buddhist psychology* (1975).

The Abhidhamma system of psychology is essentially phenomenological, a descriptive theory of internal states. Only a person who undergoes the required training and subsequent experience can fully put such a theory to the test. The Abhidhamma, when it deals with altered states in meditation also represents a "state-specific science" in Tart's (1972) definition: a body of knowledge obtained by analysis, experimentation, and communication within a specific state, in this case, the state of meditating. A major pitfall of both phenomenological theories and state-specific sciences is self-deception. A person may convince him or herself that their experience is one thing, while in fact it is another; in the absence of any other evidence to correct the person, their error will persist.

For this reason a theory such as Abhidhamma needs tests of its hypotheses, insofar as its predictions can be verified at all from the vantage point of an outside observer. This is relatively difficult with the subtle moment-to-moment changes of a person's mental factors. It is possible, however, to test the Abhidhamma descriptions of the changes that stem from intense one-pointedness on the one hand, or systematic mindfulness on the other. The Abhidhamma descriptions of *jhana* are altered states that occur only during meditation practice itself. Characteristics of the *arahat* represent trait effects, the personality changes that accompany the transition to a lasting altered state that endures apart from meditation *per se*.

Experimental studies done on Indian yogis, Japanese Zen masters, and American meditators bear on such an evaluation of the Abhidhamma version of meditation and its effects. In the early 1960s a group of investigators in India reported on electroencephalographic correlates of Indian yogis in deep meditation (Ananda et al., 1961). The yogis had entered the highly concentrated state they called "*samadhi*," in which a person feels ecstasy but is oblivious to environmental stimuli—the same state as *jhana* in Abhidhamma. During *samadhi* the yogis were exposed to several strong stimuli, including flashing lights, loud banging, and the touch of a hot test tube, but the EEG showed that none of these broke their meditative state. More recently, reports have come from Japan on EEG correlates of Zen masters meditating using a mindfulness technique (Kasamatsu and Hirai, 1966; Hirai, 1974). The masters were exposed to steady, repetitive stimuli, including clicks, neutral sounds, and affectively loaded words. Unlike the yogis, who did not show any response to even very strong stimuli, these Zen meditators exhibited a steady and continual registering of each sound. They responded as much to the last click in a long series as to the first, and responded equally to neutral sounds and emotionally loaded words. Each of these studies seems to corroborate Abhidhamma predictions for the outcome of different meditation strategies. The yogi who practices one-pointedness enters an altered state where all extraneous stimuli are blocked, as Abhidhamma predicts for *jhana*. On the other hand, the Zen monk who practices a mindfulness technique notes every stimulus with equal interest, again as Abhidhamma describes for this kind of meditation.

It is not such temporary effects that are of significance for personality, but the lasting changes. Many phenomena are capable of producing dramatic but short-lived changes in the person—psychedelic drugs are one example. But these changes must persist if they are to have any import for personality. The Abhidhamma proposes that meditation can produce certain lasting changes in personality. Recent empirical studies of personality in meditators bears on the major predicted change of a decrease in negative and increase in positive psychological states. For example, meditators, compared to nonmeditators, have been found to be significantly less anxious (Ferguson and Gowan, 1976; Goleman and Schwartz, 1976; Nidich et al., 1973), report fewer psychosomatic disorders, more positive moods, and are less neurotic on Eysenck's scale (Schwartz, 1973). Meditators also show an increased independence of situational cues, that is, an internal locus of control (Pelletier, 1974); are more spontaneous, have greater capacity for intimate contact, are more accepting of self, and have higher self-regard (Seeman et al., 1972); are better at empathizing with another person (Lesh, 1970; Leung, 1973); and show less fear of death (Garfield, 1974). Although these studies were not specifically designed to assess the Abhidhamma formulations of the impact of meditation on personality, their findings tend to bear out its major premise: that meditation reduces negative states while increasing positive ones.

In his textbook on psychology, William James noted the value of training one's attention: "The faculty of voluntarily bringing back a wandering attention, over and over again, is the very root of judgment, character, and will. No one is *compos sui* if he have it not. An education which should improve this faculty would be the education *par excellence*. But it is easier to define this ideal than to give practical directions for bringing it about" (1961a, p. 424). Although "voluntarily bringing back a wandering attention" is the basic step in meditation, James was apparently unaware that the training he recommended existed in Eastern psychologies. Even though James was familiar with some aspects of Eastern philosophy, it is no surprise that he was unaware of their psychologies. The majority of American personality theorists have been by and large ignorant of these Eastern psychologies. This is understandable in light of their inaccessibility, until recently, to those who do not read Pali, Sanskrit, or the other tongues in which they are found. In addition, when translated into English, these psychologies are rarely identified as such, being more often treated as religious doctrine. When called to the attention of the earlier personality theorists, like Freud, they were rejected out of hand.

Freud, a product of the positivism of nineteenth century science, was negative toward these Eastern teachings. For example, in his introduction to *Civilization and its discontents* (1930) Freud tells of receiving a letter from the French writer Romain Rolland, who had become a student of the great Indian saint Sri Ramakrishna. Rolland described a feeling of something "limitless and unbounded," which he saw as "the physiological basis of much of the wisdom of mysticism." Freud labelled this feeling of being at one with the universe "oceanic," and, admitting his puzzlement and failure to discover this oceanic feeling in himself, went on to reinterpret this fact of experience in a manner consonant with his own theory. Freud said the oceanic feeling was due to a sense of omnipotence that was a reaction formation to the infant's feeling of helplessness. This feeling of helplessness he saw as the genetic source of religion. In keeping with his antireligious bent, Freud noted: "The idea of men's receiving an intimation of their connection with the world around them through an immediate feeling which is from the outset directed to that purpose sounds so strange and fits in so badly with the fabric of our psychology that one is justified in attempting to discover a psychoanalytic—that is, a genetic—explanation of such a feeling" (1930, p. 65).

In reacting in this way to Rolland's unusual experience Freud articulated an attitude that has since become an assumption of many, if not most, of those who have followed in the psychoanalytic lineage he founded. The psychoanalyst Franz Alexander, for example, echoed Freud's sentiments in a paper entitled "Buddhistic Training as an Artificial Catatonia" (1961). Alexander, from the perspective of psychoanalysis, pronounced Buddhist meditation a "libidinal, narcissistic turning inward, a sort of artificial schizophrenia."

The work of Carl Jung shows him to be far more informed about the Eastern psychologies than Freud and Alexander. Despite his familiarity with the psychologies of the East, Jung was harshly critical of Europeans who tried to apply Eastern teachings to themselves. Jung felt that it was too easy to become fascinated with the exotic forms of the East as a means to avoid facing one's own problems. Wrote Jung:

People will do anything, no matter how absurd, in order to avoid facing their own souls. They will practice yoga and all its exercises, observe a strict regimen of diet, learn theosophy by heart, or mechanically repeat mystic texts from the literature of the whole world—all because they cannot get on with themselves and have not the slightest faith that anything useful could ever come out of their own souls (1968, pp. 99–101).

Jung himself studied the Eastern psychologies diligently, while he chastised those who indulged in them with more than a scholarly interest. He may have also wanted to draw criticism away from his own theories and methods. Jung's delving deep into the human psyche and using such tools as mandalas and I ching made him appear to some of his contemporaries as mad as any Eastern mystic. Jung retorted (rather testily) to these critics:

I have no wish to disturb such people at their pet pursuits, but when anybody who expects to be taken seriously is deluded enough to think that I use yoga methods and yoga doctrines or that I get my patients, whenever possible, to draw mandalas for the purpose of bringing them to the "right point"—then I really must protest and tax these people with having read my writings with the most horrible inattention (1968, pp. 101–102.)

Still another source of Jung's resistance toward Eastern psychologies stemmed from his own ideas about the function of religion. For Jung religions develop as a means for humans to know the archetypes, those potentialities for action and thought that inhere in the very structure of the human psyche. The Eastern religions, he felt, represented a higher level of development that reflected the maturity of the ancient civilizations of Asia; Europe and its indigenous faiths were younger, and so less sophisticated. Just as a person must go through each developmental stage to achieve full maturity, so must each race. It was unnatural, then, for Europeans to turn to disciplines such as yoga, for these methods reflected a uniquely Eastern history and experience.

Jung did not, however, reject the goal of the Eastern psychologies;

he simply objected to their method as unsuited to the Western mind. The altered state which a yogi seeks in the trance called *samadhi* Jung identified as an absorption in the collective unconscious, the deepest layer of the psyche and the realm of the archetypes. Jung believed that his own method of individuation led to the same goal as yoga: a shift away from the ego and toward the self. Yoga, said he, was an alternative route to the same end as his therapy, but a route for which Europeans were unfit. In his essay on "Yoga and the West," Jung (1958) shows his respect for this Eastern psychology, while at the same time he cannot endorse it as a method for the West: "I say to whomsoever I can: Study yoga—you will learn an infinite amount from it—but do not try to apply it, for we Europeans are not so constituted that we apply these methods correctly, just like that" (1958, p. 534). Rather than borrowing an unsuitable yoga from the East, said Jung, we should find our own path:

Instead of learning the spiritual techniques of the East by heart and imitating them in a Christian way—*imitatio Christi!*—with a correspondingly forced attitude, it would be far more to the point to find out whether there exists in the unconscious an introverted tendency similar to that which has become the guiding spiritual principle of the East. We should then be in a position to build on our own ground with our own methods (1958, p. 483).

Most Western personality theorists, however, have been oblivious even to the fact that Eastern psychologies like Abhidhamma exist. Even if these psychologies were brought to their attention, the likelihood is that most theorists would discount their validity on any of a number of counts. For the behaviorist, for example, a psychology such as those from the East would be rejected by virtue of its introspective, phenomenological nature. The behaviorist position is that inner experience cannot be studied scientifically and so no psychology can be found that is based on introspection. Behaviorism in its infancy fought early battles with Titchener's Introspectionists, who held tenets quite similar to Abhidhamma: that consciousness is directly observable, is composed of describable units, and that the task of the psychologist is to analyze it into its components. In stating the behaviorist position Watson (1913) was emphatic in his critique of the introspectionists, whom he contended had substituted "consciousness" for what was formerly called the soul: "The time seems to have come when psychology must discard all references to consciousness; when it need no longer delude itself into thinking that it is making of mental states the object of observation" (p. 163). This antiintrospectionist bent among behaviorists would certainly lead them to argue against the validity of Eastern psychologies.

As modern psychologists turn attention to the ancient Eastern psychologies like Abhidhamma, the biases against them, such as those held by behaviorists, should matter less and less. The Eastern psychologies come from a tradition that is largely religious and metaphysical, but which is also based on observation and direct experience. Western psychology, on the other hand, comes from a largely philosophical and scientific tradition. Each has its proper domain as well as its limitations; the psychologies of the East, like our own, are honorable theories of human behavior. The upsurge of interest in Eastern psychology shows that, at last, they are earning our respect.

BIBLIOGRAPHY
PRIMARY SOURCES

Buddhaghosa (B. Nyanamoli, trans.). *Visuddhimagga: the path of purification*. Berkeley: Shambhala, 1976.

Dhammaratana, U. *Guide through Visuddhimagga*. Varanasi, India: Mahabodhi Society, 1964.

Goleman, D. *The varieties of the meditative experience*. New York: Dutton, 1977.

Govinda, Lama Anagarika. *The psychological attitude of early Buddhist philosophy*. London: Rider, 1969.

Guenther, H. V. *Philosophy and psychology in the Abhidhamma*. Berkeley: Shambhala, 1976.

Mahasi Sayadaw (T. Nyanaponika, trans.). *The process of insight*. Kandy, Sri Lanka: The Forest Hermitage, 1965.

Narada, M. *A manual of Abhidhamma*. Kandy, Sri Lanka: Buddhist Publication Society, 1968.

Nyanaponika, M. (Ed.) *Pathways of Budhist thought*. London: George Allen and Unwin, 1971.

Nyanatiloka. *Buddhist dictionary*. Colombo, Sri Lanka: Frewin, 1972.

Vajiranana, P. *Buddhist meditation in theory and practice*. Colombo, Sri Lanka: Gunasena, 1962.

REFERENCES

Alexander, F. Buddhistic training as an artificial catatonia. In F. Alexander, *The scope of psychoanalysis*. New York: Basic Books, 1961.

Ananda, B., Chhina, G., and Singh, B. Some aspects of EEG studies in Yogis. *EEG Clin. Neurophysiol.*, 1961, **13,** 452–456. Reprinted in C. Tart (Ed.) *Altered states of consciousness*. New York: Anchor, 1972.

Anguttara nikaya (T. Nyanaponika, trans.). Kandy, Sri Lanka: Buddhist Publication Society, 1975.

Assagioli, A. *Psychosynthesis*. New York: Viking, 1971.

Babbitt, I. (trans.). *The Dhammapada*. New York: New Directions, 1965.

Blakney, R. B. *Meister Eckhart*. New York: Harper & Row, 1941.

Boss, M. *A psychiatrist discovers India*. London: Oswald Wolff, 1965.

Bucke, R. M. *Cosmic consciousness*. New York: Dutton, 1969.

Buddhaghosa (B. Nyanamoli, trans.). *Visuddhimagga: the path of purification*. Berkeley: Shambhala, 1976.

Dhammaratana, U. *Guide through Visudhimagga*. Varanasi, India: Mahabodhi Society, 1964.

Evans-Wentz, W. Y. (Ed.). *The Tibetan book of the great liberation*. New York: Oxford Univ. Press, 1968.

Evans-Wentz, W. Y. (Ed.). *The Tibetan book of the dead*. New York: Oxford Univ. Press, 1969.

Ferguson, P., and Gowan, J. TM: some preliminary findings. *J. Humanistic Psychol.*, 1976, **16,** 51–60.

Freud, S. Civilization and its discontents. In *Standard edition*. Vol. 21. London: Hogarth Press, 1961. (First German edition, 1930.)

Fromm, E., Suzuki, D. T., and DeMartino, R. *Zen Buddhism and psychoanalysis*. New York: Harper & Row, 1970.

Garfield, C. Consciousness alteration and fear of death. *J. Transpersonal Psychol.*, 1974, **7,** 147–175.

Goleman, D. *The varieties of the meditative experience*. New York: Dutton, 1977.

Goleman, D., and Schwartz, G. E. Meditation as an intervention in stress reactivity. *J. Clinical and Consulting Psychol.*, 1976, **44,** 456–466.

Govinda, Lama Anagarika. *The psychological attitude of early Buddhist philosophy*. London: Rider, 1969.

Guenther, H. V. *Philosophy and psychology in the Abhidhamma*. Berkeley: Shambhala, 1976.

Guenther, H. V., and Kawamura, L. S. *Mind in Buddhist psychology*. Berkeley: Dharma Publishing Co., 1975.

Halevi, Z. S. *The way of Kabbalah*. New York: Weiser, 1976.

Hesse, H. *Siddhartha*. New York: Bantam, 1970.

Hesse, H. *Journey to the east*. New York: Bantam, 1971.

Hirai, T. *Psychophysiology of Zen*. Tokyo: Igaku Shoin, 1974.

James, W. *The principles of psychology*. New York: Dover, 1950.

James, W. *Psychology: briefer course*. New York: Harper Torchbooks, 1961a.

James, W. *The varieties of religious experience*. New York: Crowell-Collier, 1961b.

Johansson, R. E. A. *The psychology of nirvana*. New York: Anchor, 1970.

Jung, C. G. Psychology and religion: west and east. In *Collected works*. Vol. 11. Princeton: Princeton Univ. Press, 1958.

Jung, C. G. Psychology and alchemy. In *Collected works*. Vol. 12. Princeton: Princeton Univ. Press, 1968.

Kasamatsu, A., and Hirai, T. An EEG study on the Zen meditation (Zazen). *Folio Psychiatrica and Neurological Japonica,* 1966, **20,** 315–336.

Lesh, T. V. Zen meditation and the development of empathy in counselors. *J. Humanistic Psychol.,* 1970, **10,** 39–54.

Leung, P. Comparative effects of training in external and internal concentration on two counseling behaviors. *J. Couns. Psychol.,* 1973, **20,** 227–234.

Mahasi Sayadaw (T. Nyanaponika, trans.). *The process of insight.* Kandy, Sri Lanka: The Forest Hermitage, 1965.

Maslow, A. *Religions, values, and peak-experiences.* Columbus, Ohio: Ohio State Univ. Press, 1964.

Maslow, A. *The farther reaches of human nature.* New York: Viking Press, 1971.

Murphy, G. and L. B. (Eds.). *Asian psychology.* New York: Basic Books, 1968.

Narada, M. *A manual of Abhidhamma.* Kandy, Sri Lanka: Buddhist Publication Society, 1968.

Nidich, S., Seeman, W., and Dreskin, T. Influence of transcendental meditation: a replication. *J. Counseling Psychol.,* 1973, **20,** 565–566.

Nyanaponika, M. *The heart of Buddhist meditation.* London: Rider, 1962.

Nyanaponika, M. (Ed.) *Pathways of Buddhist thought.* London: George Allen and Unwin, 1971.

Nyanatiloka. *Buddhist dictionary.* Colombo, Sri Lanka: Frewin, 1972.

Ornstein, R. *The psychology of consciousness.* San Francisco: W. H. Freeman, 1973a.

Ornstein, R. (Ed.). *On the nature of human consciousness.* San Francisco: W. H. Freeman, 1973b.

Pelletier, K. Influence of transcendental meditation upon autokinetic perception. *Perceptual and Motor Skills,* 1974, **39,** 1031–1034.

Prabhavanda, S., and Isherwood, C. *How to know God.* New York: Mentor, 1969.

Prabhavanda, S., and Isherwood, C. *Crest: jewel of discrimination.* New York: Mentor, 1970.

Ram Dass. *Be here now.* New York: Crown, 1971.

Ram Dass. *The only dance there is.* New York: Doubleday, 1974.

St. John of the Cross. (E. Allison Peers, trans.) *Ascent of Mount Carmel.* Garden City, N.Y.: Image Books, 1958.

Samyutta-Nikaya. (F. L. Woodward, trans.) London: Pali Text Society, 1972.

Scholem, G. G. *Jewish mysticism.* New York: Schocken, 1961.

Schwartz, G. E. Pros and cons of meditation: current findings on physiology and anxiety, self-control, drug abuse, and creativity. Paper presented at the meeting of the American Psychological Association, Montreal, September, 1973.

Seeman, W., Nidch, S., and Banta, T. A study of the influence of transcendental meditation on a measure of self-actualization. *J. Counseling Psychol.,* 1972, **19,** 184–187.

Shah, I. *The Sufis*. Garden City, N.Y.: Doubleday Anchor, 1971.

Smith, H. *The religions of man*. New York: Harper & Row, 1958.

Suzuki, D. T. *An introduction to Zen Buddhism*. New York: Causeway, 1974.

Sutich, A. Statement of purpose. *J. Transpersonal Psychol.*, 1969, **1,** 1.

Tart, C. (Ed.). *Altered states of consciousness*. New York: Wiley, 1969.

Tart, C. States of consciousness and state-specific sciences. *Science,* 1972, **176,** 1203–1210.

Tart, C. (Ed.). *Transpersonal psychologies*. New York: Harper & Row, 1976.

Vajiranana, P. *Buddhist meditation in theory and practice*. Colombo, Sri Lanka: Gunasena, 1962.

Van Aung, Z. (trans.). *Compendium of philosophy*. London: Pali Text Society, 1972.

Waddell, H. *The desert fathers*. Ann Arbor, Mich.: Univ. of Michigan Press, 1971.

Watson, J. B. Psychology as a behaviorist views it. *Psychol. Rev.,* 1913, **20,** 158–177.

Watts, A. *Psychotherapy East and West*. New York: Pantheon, 1961.

Wilhelm, R. (trans.). *The secret of the golden flower*. London: Routledge and Kegan Paul, 1969.

Wolpe, J. *Psychotherapy by reciprocal inhibition*. Stanford, Calif.: Stanford Univ. Press, 1958.

LEWIN'S FIELD THEORY

11

The older sciences of physics and chemistry have often influenced the course of newer sciences like psychology by furnishing them ways of thinking about and conceiving of natural phenomena. As new viewpoints develop in physics and chemistry it is almost inevitable, considering the basic unity of all sciences, that they should be taken over by the less mature sciences and applied in their special provinces. It is not surprising, therefore, that the field concept of physics, initiated by the work of Faraday, Maxwell, and Hertz on electromagnetic fields in the nineteenth century and culminating in Einstein's powerful theory of relativity in the twentieth century, has had an impact on modern psychological thought. It should be pointed out, however, as Deutsch does (1968), that it is the *method* of representing the world and not the actual physical concepts and facts themselves that has been incorporated into psychology.

The first important manifestation of the influence of physical field theory in psychology appeared in the movement known as Gestalt psychology that was initiated by three German psychologists, Max Wertheimer, Wolfgang Köhler and Kurt Koffka, in the years immediately preceding World War I. The chief tenet of Gestalt psychology is that behavior is determined by the psychophysical field consisting of an organized system of stresses or strains (forces) analogous to a gravitational or an electromagnetic field. How we perceive an object, for example, is determined by the total field in which the object is embedded.

Kurt Lewin

Although Gestalt psychology is a general psychological theory, it is primarily concerned with perception, learning, and thinking and not with personality. The field theory of personality to be presented in this chapter was originated by Kurt Lewin. Deeply influenced by Gestalt psychology as well as by psychoanalysis, his theory nonetheless is an entirely original formulation.

Kurt Lewin was born on September 9, 1890, in a small village in the Prussian province of Posen. The second of four children, his father owned and operated a general store. The family moved to Berlin in 1905, where Lewin completed his secondary schooling. He then entered the University of Freiburg, intending to study medicine, but soon gave up this idea and, after a semester at the University of Munich, returned to Berlin in 1910 to study psychology at the University there. His major professor was Carl Stumpf, a highly respected experimental psychologist. After obtaining the doctorate in 1914, Lewin served in the German army for four years as an infantryman, rising from private to lieutenant. At the end of the war, he returned to the University of Berlin as an instructor and a research assistant in the Psychological Institute. Max Wertheimer and Wolfgang Köhler, two of the three founders of Gestalt psychology, were also at the University of Berlin at this time. In 1926, Lewin was promoted to a professorship. While at the University of Berlin, Lewin and his students published a series of brilliant experimental and theoretical papers (De Rivera, 1976).

When Hitler came to power, Lewin was a visiting professor at Stanford University. He went back to Germany to settle his affairs, and then returned to the United States where he resided the rest of his life. He was professor of child psychology at Cornell University for two years (1933–1935) before being called to the State University of Iowa as professor of psychology in the Child Welfare Station. In 1945, Lewin accepted an appointment as professor and director of the Research Center for Group Dynamics at the Massachusetts Institute of Technology. At the same time, he became director of the Commission of Community Interrelations of the American Jewish Congress, which engaged in research on community problems. He died suddenly of a heart attack in Newtonville, Massachusetts, February 12, 1947, at the age of 56.

During his years in the United States, Lewin attracted a number of graduate students, many of whom have become prominent psychologists. As a person, Lewin was very democratic, friendly, energetic, and immensely stimulating. He made a lasting impression on everyone who came into contact with him.

Lewin is considered by many of his peers to be one of the most brilliant figures in contemporary psychology (G. W. Allport, 1947; Tolman, 1948). His theoretical writings (Lewin, 1935a, 1936a, 1938, 1951) and his experimental work have left an indelible mark upon the development of psychology. Lewin stood first and foremost for the application of field theory in all branches of psychology. For Lewin, field theory is not a new system of psychology limited to a specific content; it is a set of concepts by means of which one can represent psychological reality (1936a, pp. 6–7). These concepts should be broad enough to be applicable to all kinds of behavior, and at the same time specific enough to represent a definite person in a concrete situation. Lewin also characterized field theory as "a method of analyzing causal relations and of buiilding scientific constructs" (1951, p. 45).

The principal characteristics of Lewin's field theory may be summarized as follows: (1) behavior is a function of the field that exists at the time the behavior occurs, (2) analysis begins with the situation as a whole from which are differentiated the component parts, and (3) the concrete person in a concrete situation can be represented mathematically. Lewin also emphasizes underlying forces (needs) as determiners of behavior and expresses a preference for psychological as opposed to physical or physiological descriptions of the field. A field is defined as "the totality of coexisting facts which are conceived of as mutually interdependent" (Lewin, 1951, p. 240).

The concepts of field theory have been applied by Lewin to a wide variety of psychological and sociological phenomena including infant and child behavior (Lewin, 1951, Chapter X), adolescence (1951, Chapter VI), feeblemindedness (1935a, Chapter VII), minority group problems (1935b, 1946), national character differences (1936b), and group dynamics (Lewin, 1948). Lewin, like so many other personality theorists, was not an ivory-tower thinker who turned aside from the problems of the world. A person of broad humanitarian sympathies and democratic values, he attempted rather directly to ameliorate some of the problems facing mankind by undertaking the type of investigation known as action research. Action research has as its objective the changing of social conditions. Examples of action research performed by Lewin and his associates will be found in Bavelas and Lewin (1942) and Lewin (1943, 1946, 1947, 1948).

In the present chapter, we shall focus our attention upon Lewin's theory of the structure, dynamics, and development of the person. We shall have to consider the psychological environment as well, since people and their environment are interdependent regions of the *life space,* which is Lewin's term for the total psychological field. The influential areas of action research and group dynamics that Lewin fathered are not discussed here. These aspects of Lewin's thinking have been treated by Deutsch (1968) and research in the area of group dynamics has been surveyed by Gerard and Miller (1967). Applied group dynamics is the subject of a book by Schein and Bennis (1965).

The first step in defining the person as a structural concept is to represent him or her as an entity set apart from everything else in the world. This setting apart can be done in words as a dictionary definition does, for example, a person is an individual human being (Webster), or it can be done by making a spatial representation of the person. Because spatial representations can be treated mathematically and ordinary verbal definitions cannot be, Lewin prefers to define his structural concepts spatially. In this way, Lewin attempts to mathematize his concepts from the very beginning. One important advantage of this type of scientific strategy according to Lewin is that mathematical representations require precise formulation whereas verbal definitions are more likely to be inexact and ambiguous. Furthermore, mathematical representations can be made to divulge important information by performing various mathematical operations on them. Unknowns can be solved for, rational equations connecting different concepts can be written, and functional relationships can be formulated. Words, on the other hand, only lead to more words. Mathematics, Lewin reminds us, is the proper language of scientific discourse, although the type of mathematics employed by Lewin for representing psychological concepts is not the kind with which most people are familiar. Lewin's mathematics is nonmetrical in character and describes spatial relationships in other than Euclidean terms. It is essentially a mathematics for describing interconnections and intercommunications among spatial regions without regard to size or shape.

THE STRUCTURE OF PERSONALITY

The separation of the person from the rest of the universe is accomplished by drawing an enclosed figure. The boundary of the figure defines the limits of the entity known as the person. Everything lying inside the boundary is *P* (the person); everything lying outside the boundary is non-*P*. It does not make any difference whether the figure drawn is a circle, a square, a triangle, an octagon, or irregular shape just as long as it is completely bounded.

Before proceeding let us pause to consider what has been conceptualized by representing the person as an enclosed figure. Since absolute size and shape are irrelevant properties of the representation, the only significant feature of Figure 11-1 is that it portrays a completely bounded area lying within a larger area. Thus it follows that two properties of the person are conceptualized by drawing a circle on a piece of paper. These are (1) separation from the rest of the world by

FIGURE 11-1

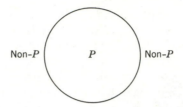

means of a continuous boundary, and (2) inclusion in a larger area. The first property is that of *differentiation,* the second of the *part-whole relationship*. In short, the person is represented as being separated from yet included within a larger totality. Such a conception is not at variance with common sense since the skin or the individual's garments are visible boundaries that set him or her off from the larger universe through which they move and of which they are so evident a part.

The Psychological Environment

Were we only interested in the person and not in the world of which he or she is a part, we could restrict our attention to the properties of the area circumscribed by the circle and ignore the boundary and its hinterland. To proceed in this manner, however, would be to overlook the important interactions between the person and the environment.

The next step, then, in the representation of psychological reality is to draw another bounded figure that is larger than and encloses the person. The shape and size of this enclosing figure are not important as long as it fulfills the two conditions of being bigger than and enclosing the person. For this representation Lewin prefers a figure that is roughly elliptical in form. An additional qualification is also necessary. The new figure cannot share any part of the boundary of the circle that represents the person. There must be a space left between the boundary of the person and the boundary of the larger figure. Aside from this restriction, the circle may be placed anywhere inside the ellipse. The sizes of the two forms relative to one another are immaterial.

We now have a picture of a circle enclosed by but not touching an ellipse (Figure 11-2). The region between the two perimeters is the *psychological environment, E.* The total area within the ellipse, including the circle, is the *life space, L.* The space outside the ellipse represents the nonpsychological aspects of the universe. For the sake of convenience, we shall call this region the physical world, although it is not restricted to physical facts alone. There are, for example, social facts as well in the nonpsychological world.

FIGURE 11-2

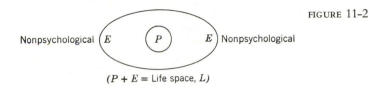

Nonpsychological (*E* *P* *E*) Nonpsychological

(P + E = Life space, L)

Although this simple exercise in drawing figures may appear to be inconsequential, it is absolutely indispensable for an understanding and appreciation of Lewin's theory. It is essential, Lewin maintains, to start with an over-all picture of psychological reality, a picture of the greatest general validity, and then proceed, step by step, to differentiate out of this broad panorama the details by which a precise understanding of the concrete psychological situation can be achieved. For it is Lewin's contention that if the general picture of psychological reality is inaccurate, the more detailed picture cannot be correct.

The circle-in-the-ellipse is not merely an illustration or a teaching device; it is a faithful representation of the most general structural concepts of Lewin's theory, namely, the person, the psychological environment, and the life space. The circle-in-the-ellipse is a map or conceptual representation of reality, and like any map its function is to guide its user through unfamiliar territory and in so doing to acquaint the person with new facts about reality.

Although we began with the person and subsequently surrounded him or her with a psychological environment, it would have been more in keeping with Lewin's rule of going from the general to the particular to have started with the life space and differentiated from it the person and the environment. For the life space is the psychologist's universe; it is the whole of psychological reality. It contains the totality of *possible* facts that are capable of determining the behavior of an individual. It includes *everything* that has to be known in order to understand the concrete behavior of an individual human being in a given psychological environment at a given time. Behavior is a function of the life space. $B = f(L)$. "The task of dynamic psychology is to derive univocally the behavior of a given individual from the totality of the psychological facts that exist in the life space at a given moment" (Lewin, 1936a).

The fact that the life space is surrounded by the physical world does not mean that the life space is a part of the physical world (Figure 11-3). Rather, the life space and the space beyond it are differentiated and separate regions of a larger totality. Whether this larger totality, the

The Life Space

FIGURE 11-3

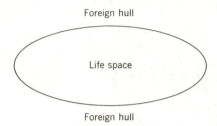

universe, is finite or infinite, chaos or cosmos, is of no concern to psychology except in one very important respect. Facts that exist in the region outside and adjacent to the boundary of the life space, a region that Lewin calls "the foreign hull of the life space," can materially influence the psychological environment. That is, nonpsychological facts can and do alter psychological ones. Lewin has suggested that the study of the facts in the foreign hull be called "psychological ecology" (1951, Chapter VIII). The first step in making a psychological investigation is to establish the nature of the facts that exist at the boundary of the life space since these facts help to determine what is and what is not possible, what might or might not happen in the life space. Lewin did this before he undertook to investigate the food habits of people and how they might be changed (1943; 1951, Chapter VIII).

Facts in the psychological environment can also produce changes in the physical world. There is two-way communication between the two realms. Consequently, it is said that the boundary between the life space and the outer world is endowed with the property of *permeability*. A boundary resembles a permeable membrane or mesh more than it does a wall or rigid barrier. Parenthetically, it should be noted that the physical world cannot communicate directly with the person, nor can the person communicate directly with the outer world. A fact must exist in the psychological environment before it can influence or be influenced by the person. This is evident from the diagram which depicts the person as being completely surrounded by the region of the psychological environment.

The implication of a permeable boundary between the life space and the physical world is of far-reaching significance. Since a fact in the nonpsychological world may radically change the whole course of events in the life space, prediction from a knowledge of psychological laws alone is usually futile. One can never be sure beforehand that a fact from the foreign hull may not penetrate the boundary of the life space and turn everything topsy-turvy in the psychological environment. A chance meeting, an unexpected telephone call, an automobile accident, have been known to change the course of one's life. Therefore, as Lewin emphasizes, it is more feasible for a psychologist to try to understand the momentary, concrete psychological situation by describing and explaining it in field-theoretical terms than it is to attempt to predict how a person is going to behave at some future time.

Another property of the life space should be noted. Although the person is surrounded by his psychological environment, he or she is not a part of or included in the environment. The psychological environment stops at the perimeter of the circle just as the non-psychological world stops at the perimeter of the ellipse. However, the boundary between the person and the environment is also a permeable one. This means that environmental facts can influence the person, $P = f(E)$, and personal facts can influence the environment, $E = f(P)$. Before considering the nature of this influence, a further differentiation within the structure of the person and of the environment must be made.

The Differentiated Person

Up to this point, the person has been represented as an empty circle. Such a representation would be appropriate if the person were a perfect unity, which one is not. Lewin maintains that the structure of the person is heterogeneous not homogeneous, that it is subdivided into separate yet intercommunicating and interdependent parts. To represent this state of affairs, the area within the circle is divided into zones.

One proceeds in the following manner. First, divide the person into two parts by drawing a concentric circle within the larger circle. The outer part represents the *perceptual-motor region* (P-M), the central part represents the *inner-personal region* (I-P). The inner-personal region is completely surrounded by the perceptual-motor area, so that it has no direct contact with the boundary separating the person from the environment (Figure 11-4).

The next step is to divide the inner-personal region into cells (Figure 11-5). The cells adjacent to the perceptual-motor region are called *peripheral* cells, *p;* those in the center of the circle are called *central* cells, *c.* Lewin is not explicit regarding the differentiation of the perceptual-motor area into smaller regions. He feels that the motor system acts as a unit since it can ordinarily perform only one action at a time. Similarly, the perceptual system usually functions in a unified manner, that is, a person can attend to and perceive only one thing at a time. It is clear, however, that the motor system should be separated from the perceptual system because they are independent systems. How this separation is to be conceptualized spatially is not divulged.

FIGURE 11–4
FIGURE 11–5

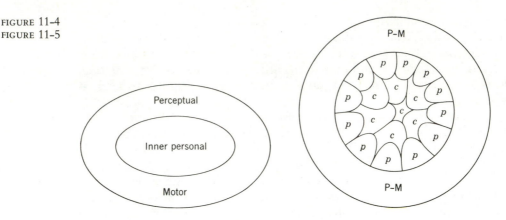

Perhaps the best solution and one that Lewin apparently adopts is to leave the perceptual-motor system unstructured, with the understanding that when the direction of influence is from the environment to the person the region surrounding the inner-personal sphere represents perceptual processes, and when the direction of influence is from the person to the environment this same region stands for the motor system. This would agree with the common-sense view that input involves perception and output involves motor action.

We now have an accurate conceptual representation of the structure of the person. The person is defined as a differentiated region in the life space. Now let us consider the psychological environment.

The Differentiated Environment   A homogeneous or undifferentiated environment is one in which all the facts are equally influential upon the person. In such an environment the person would have perfect freedom of movement since there would be no barriers to impede him or her. Such complete freedom of movement obviously does not represent the true state of affairs. Therefore, it is necessary to subdivide the environment into part regions (Figure 11-6).

There is one difference between the differentiation of the environment and the differentiation of the person. It is not necessary to distinguish between different *kinds* of environmental regions. The environment does not contain anything comparable to a perceptual-motor stratum or an inner-personal sphere. All of the regions of the environment are alike. Consequently, any crisscross pattern of lines will serve our present purpose. It should be pointed out, however, that in the concrete representation of a particular person in a concrete psychological situation at a given moment the exact number and relative positions of the environmental subregions, as well as the precise number and relative positions of the inner-personal sphere, must be known if one is to understand behavior. A complete and accurate structural analysis reveals the totality of possible psychological facts in the momentary situation. Dynamical analysis, the topic of the next section of this chapter, tells us which of the possible facts will actually determine the behavior.

The life space is now represented by a differentiated person surrounded by a differentiated environment. This differentiation has been accomplished by drawing lines which serve as boundaries between regions. It is not intended, however, that these boundaries should represent impenetrable barriers that divide the person and the environment into independent and unconnected regions. Permeability, as we have already pointed out, is one of the properties of a boundary. Since this is so, the life space consists of a network of interconnected systems.

Connections Between Regions

What is signified by saying that regions are connected? In order to answer this question, let us assume that each of the subregions of the environment contains one psychological fact, and that the same fact does not appear in more than one region at the same time. (Lewin's use of the word *fact* in this context may sound strange to some ears. A fact, for Lewin, is not only an observable thing like a chair or a football game; it is also something that may not be directly observable but which can be inferred from something that is observable. In other words, there are empirical or phenomenal facts and hypothetical or dynamic facts. Anything, either sensed or inferred, is a fact in Lewin's eyes. An event, on the other hand, is the result of the interaction of several facts. A chair and a person are each facts, but a person seating him or her self on a chair is an event.) Two regions are said to be connected when a fact in one region is in communication with a fact in another region. For example, the person is said to be connected

FIGURE 11-6

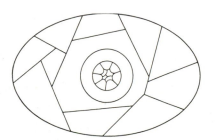

with the environment because a fact in the environment can alter, modify, displace, intensify, or minimize facts within the person. In ordinary language, the environment can change the person, and vice versa. Lewin also says that two regions are connected when the facts of one region are accessible to the facts of another region. Accessibility is the spatial counterpart of influence.

Our immediate problem, then, is how to represent the extent of influence or accessibility between regions. There are several ways of doing this. One way is to place the regions close together when the influence of one upon the other is great (Figure 11-7), and to place them far apart when the influence is weak (Figure 11-8). The number of regions intervening between *A* and *B* represents the extent of their influence upon one another. This type of representation may be called the *nearness-remoteness* dimension.

For example, a region that is buried deeply in the central portion of the inner-personal stratum may be many cells away from the perceptual–motor area. Under these circumstances an environmental fact will have a difficult time getting to the remote central region, and likewise a fact embedded in the central region will have little or no communication with the environment. They will be relatively independent of one another. On the other hand, a peripheral region of the inner-personal sphere that adjoins the perceptual motor system may be very accessible to environmental facts.

Two regions may be very close together, even to the extent of sharing a common boundary, and yet not influence or be accessible to each other at all. The degree of connectedness or interdependence is not only a matter of the number of boundaries that must be crossed; it also depends upon the strength of the resistance offered by the boundary. If the resistance is very great then it does not make any difference how close together the regions are; they will have very little influence upon one another. On the other hand, two regions may be far apart and still exert considerable influence upon each other if all of the intervening boundaries are very weak.

FIGURE 11-7
FIGURE 11-8

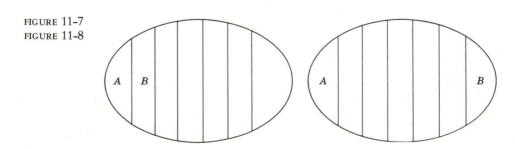

The resistance of a boundary, or its permeability, is represented by the width of the boundary line. A very thin line represents a weak boundary, a very thick line represents an impermeable boundary (Figure 11-9). This type of representation may be called the *firmness-weakness* dimension.

A boundary is not necessarily equally permeable from both sides. That is to say, a fact in region *A* may influence a fact in region *B* but a fact in region *B* may have virtually no influence over a fact in region *A*. There is no way to represent this difference in accessibility except to make two drawings, one in which the boundary line is thin, the other in which the boundary line is thick. This is conceptually proper since the influence of *A* upon *B* is a psychologically different situation from that of *B*'s influence on *A*.

A third way of representing the interconnections between regions is to take into account the nature of the medium of a region. The medium of a region is its floor or surface quality. Lewin has distinguished several properties of the medium, the most important of which is the *fluidity-rigidity* dimension. A fluid medium is one that responds quickly to any influence that is brought to bear upon it. It is flexible and pliant. A rigid medium resists change. It is stiff and inelastic (Figure 11-10). Two regions that are separated from each other by a region whose surface quality is extremely rigid will not be able to communicate with one another. It is analogous to a person trying to cross a swamp or make their way through heavy underbrush.

By utilizing the concepts of nearness-remoteness, firmness-weakness, and fluidity-rigidity, most of the possible interconnections in the life space can be represented. Let us take a few concrete examples. In Figure 11-11, the boundary of the life space is thick, while in Figure 11-12 the boundary is thin. Figure 11-11 depicts a situation in which the outside world has little influence on the life space and the life space has little influence on the outside world. The person is en-

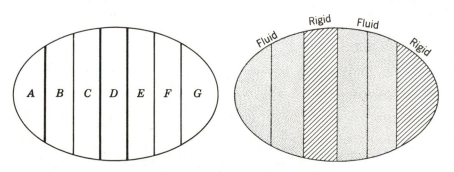

FIGURE 11-9
FIGURE 11-10

FIGURE 11-11
FIGURE 11-12

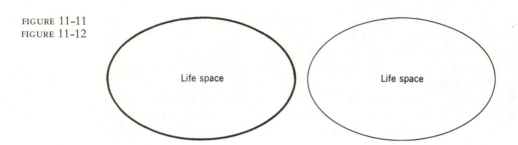

capsulated in their psychological environment; their contacts with physical reality are slight. One thinks of a deteriorated schizophrenic or a person who is asleep and dreaming. Figure 11-12 portrays just the opposite situation. The life space and the outer world are closely connected. Changes in the outer world affect the state of the life space and changes in the life space affect the outer world. This is the picture of a person whose psychological environment is closely attuned to the physical world. The slightest change in the "foreign hull" is immediately reflected in a change in the psychological environment.

Figures 11-13 and 11-14 show an inaccessible and an accessible person. One is firmly insulated from his environment by a thick wall, the other has free and easy exchanges with the psychological environment.

Figure 11-15 portrays a more complexly structured person. Cells p_1 and p_2 are closely connected, while p_2 and p_3 are cut off from one another by an impermeable boundary. Region c has little or no accessibility to any other region. It is as though this area were dissociated from the rest of the person. The crosshatched cell is impervious to influence because of the turgid quality of its surface, while the dotted area is easily influenced. Region p_4 is remotely connected to p_1, p_2, and p_3. Figure 11-16 portrays a complexly structured psychological environment.

It should be kept in mind that these drawings represent momentary

FIGURE 11-13
FIGURE 11-14

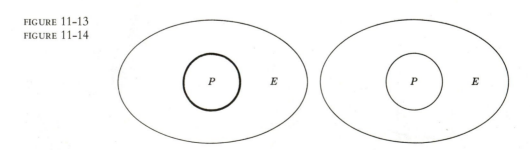

situations. There is nothing fixed or static about them, and they are constantly changing as a result of dynamic forces. One cannot characterize the person as being thus and so for any long period of time. A firm boundary can suddenly dissolve, a weak boundary grow tough. Regions that were far apart may come close together. A stiff medium softens while a pliant medium hardens. Even the number of regions can increase or decrease from moment to moment. Consequently, spatial representations are continually going out of date because psychological reality is forever changing. Lewin does not put much stock in fixed traits, rigid habits, or other constants of personality. Concepts of this sort are characteristic of Aristotelian thinking that Lewin deplores (1935a, Chapter I).

What determines how many regions there will be in the life space? The number of regions is determined by the number of separate psychological facts that exist at any given moment of time. When there are only two facts, the person and the environment, there are only two regions in the life space. If the environment contains two facts, for example, the fact of play and the fact of work, then the environment has to be divided into a play area and a work area. If there are a number of different kinds of play facts, for instance, the fact of playing football, the fact of playing chess, and the fact of playing darts, then the play area must be divided into as many subregions as there are separate play facts. Similarly, there may be different kinds of work facts each of which has to have its own separate region. Should it not make any difference to the person whether one plays football or chess or darts, just as long as one plays something, there will only be one play area and not three. For a person who is overcome by terror, the whole psychological environment may be filled with the one fact of terror. All other facts may disappear, leaving a perfectly homogeneous environment. As the person begins to regain composure, he or she may see that one part of their environment offers security. At this moment, the environment becomes differentiated into a safe area and

The Number of Regions

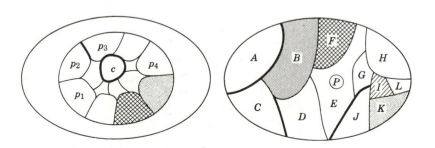

FIGURE 11-15
FIGURE 11-16

a danger area. In short, a new region is differentiated out of the life space whenever a new fact comes into existence; a region disappears whenever a fact disappears or merges with another fact. A psychological fact is coordinated with a psychological region.

The number of regions in the person is also determined by the number of personal facts that exist. If the fact of feeling hungry is the only one that exists, then the inner-personal sphere will consist of only one region. But if in addition to the fact of hunger there is also a need to finish a given job, the inner-personal region has to be divided into two regions.

As we shall see later, the principal facts of the inner-personal region are called *needs,* while the facts of the psychological environment are called *valences.* Each need occupies a separate cell in the inner-personal region and each valence occupies a separate region in the psychological environment.

The Person in the Environment
Earlier when we were discussing the placing of the person in the environment, we said it did not make any difference where the circle was placed inside the ellipse just as long as their two boundaries did not touch. This holds true only for an undifferentiated, homogeneous environment where all the facts are in one and the same region, that is, where all the facts are identical. As soon as the environment becomes differentiated into bounded regions, then it makes considerable difference where the circle is placed. For whatever region it is placed in, the facts of that region are closer to and have more influence on the person than do the facts of any other region. An understanding of a concrete psychological situation requires, therefore, that we know where the person is in his or her psychological environment. Physically the person may be sitting in a schoolroom, but psychologically he may be replaying a baseball game on the playground. Some facts that exist in the schoolroom, such as what the teacher is saying, may not impinge upon him at all, whereas others, for example, a note from a girl sitting at the next desk, may easily divert his thoughts from the ball game.

Locomotion and Communication
The way in which the regions that make up the life space are interconnected represents the degree of influence or accessibilty between regions. Precisely how does this influence or accessibility express itself? In the preceding example of the boy who is accessible to the note from the girl but inaccessible to what the teacher is saying, accessibility means that the boy can move more easily into the region of the girl than into the region of the teacher. When the girl performs the action of passing the boy a note, he may move out of the baseball

region and into her region. He has performed what Lewin calls a *locomotion*. Two regions are closely connected, accessible to one another, and mutually influential, if locomotions may be made easily between the regions.

A locomotion in the psychological environment does not mean that the person has to make a physical movement through space; in fact, most of the locomotions that are of interest to the psychologist involve very little physical movement. There are social locomotions such as joining a club, vocational locomotions such as being promoted, intellectual locomotions such as solving a problem, and many other types of locomotions.

We now see that an important property of the psychological environment is that it is a region in which locomotion is possible. "One can treat everything as environment in which, toward which, or away from which the person as a whole can perform locomotions" (Lewin, 1936a, p. 167). In performing a locomotion, the person traverses a path through the environment. The direction of the path and the regions through which it passes are determined in part by the strength of the boundaries and the fluidity of the regions, and in part by dynamic factors yet to be discussed.

The influence, then, of environmental regions upon one another is expressed by the ease with which the person can move from one region to another. Is locomotion also the mode by which regions of the person reveal their influence upon one another? Lewin says not. "The person himself cannot . . . be considered as a medium within which an object carries out locomotions from one part region to another" (1936a, p. 168). Regions of the person are said to *communicate* with one another. The perceptual region communicates with the peripheral cells of the inner-personal region, and they in turn communicate with the more centrally located cells. Inner-personal cells can communicate with one another and with the motor sphere. Which regions will communicate with one another and the path by which the communication is transmitted through a number of regions are determined in part by such structural features as the width of the boundaries and the nature of the medium, and in part by dynamic factors.

Locomotion and communication are said to be events since they result from an interaction of facts. A fact, it will be recalled, is represented by a region. Accordingly, an event represents an interaction between two or more regions. Lewin says that in deriving an event, for example, a locomotion or a communication, from the life space three principles should be followed. The first one which is called the *principle of relatedness* has already been mentioned. It states that an event is always the result of an interaction between two or more facts. One fact alone cannot cause an event. It is necessary to have at least two facts, for example, the person and the environment, before there can be any locomotion. The second principle, that of *concreteness,* says that only concrete facts can have effects. A concrete fact is one that actually exists in the life space. Potential or possible facts, that is, facts that may come into existence sometime in the future but that do not exist now, cannot be the cause of present events. Closely related to the principle of concreteness is the *principle of contemporaneity,* which states that only present facts can produce present behavior. Facts that once existed but no longer do cannot influence the present. The facts of infancy or childhood can have no bearing upon the behavior of the adult unless those facts have managed to remain in some sort of existence throughout the intervening years (Lewin, 1936a, pp. 18–36).

Restructuring of the Life Space

Locomotion and communication are not the only events that may occur as the result of one fact (region) impinging upon another fact (region). Other consequences may follow. The number of regions may be increased or decreased depending upon whether new facts are added or old facts are subtracted from the life space. The position of regions relative to each other may be altered. Two regions that were far apart may draw closer and regions that were close together may draw apart. Changes in the boundary may occur. A permeable boundary may become firm, a strong boundary may become weak. Finally, there may be alterations in the surface qualities of regions. A fluid region may stiffen up, a rigid region relax. All of these structural changes or events may be subsumed under the general heading, *restructuring of the life space* (Lewin, 1951, p. 251).

Levels of Reality

Thus far in our discussion of Lewin's structural concepts two dimensional spatial representations have sufficed. However, a third dimension is necessary in order to give a complete representation of the life space. This third dimension is co-ordinated with the concept of degrees of reality and unreality. Reality consists of an actual locomotion whereas unreality consists of an imaginary locomotion. There are various degrees or levels between actuality and pure imagination. For example, a person can join a club, change their job, or work out a problem, or he or she can plan to do things, or they can daydream about doing them. Planning or thinking is an intermediate level between the most realistic level of performance and the most unrealistic level of pure fantasy.

By and large, locomotions are easier to make as one moves up the ladder toward unreality; the boundaries become less firm and the surface qualities of the regions become more fluid.

Lewin believes that the concept of levels of reality applies not only to the structure of the environment but also to the structure of the person. Although he does not elaborate on this point, it appears that he means that communications between regions of the person can be more or less realistic. For example, an inner-personal cell may actually affect the motor region or it may do so in an imaginary way. A person may speak his or her mind or may only daydream about doing so.

Although neither the past nor the future can affect present behavior, according to the principle of contemporaneity, peoples' attitudes, feelings, and thoughts about the past and the future may have considerable influence upon their conduct. The hopes of the future may be much more important to a person than the hardships of the present. Just as expectations of things to come may lighten current burdens so may shadows from the past darken the present. The present, therefore, must be represented as containing both a psychological past and a psychological future (Lewin, 1951, pp. 53–56). This dimension may be long or short. It may be well-defined or hazy. Its structure may be simple or complex, and its boundaries may be weak or firm.

The Time Dimension or Perspective

Résumé

The principal structural concepts discussed in this section are a *life space* consisting of a *person* surrounded by a *psychological environment*. The person is differentiated into a *perceptual-motor region* and an *inner-personal region*. The inner-personal region is subdivided into a group of *peripheral cells* and *central cells*. The psychological environment is also differentiated into *regions*. The life space is surrounded by a *foreign hull* that is part of the nonpsychological or objective environment.

Regions of the person and of the environment are separated by *boundaries* that possess the property of *permeability*. The regions of the life space are *interconnected* so that a *fact* in one region can influence a *fact* in another region. When such an influence occurs between two facts it is called an *event*. The degree of connectedness or the extent of the influence between regions is determined by the *firmness* of the boundaries, the number of regions *intervening,* and the *surface qualities* of the regions.

Regions of the environment are said to be connected when the person can perform a *locomotion* between the regions. Regions of the person are said to be connected when they can *communicate* with one another.

Two other dimensions of the life space are those of *reality-unreality* and *past-future*.

Lewin represents (defines) the foregoing concepts in spatial terms so that they may be handled by a branch of mathematics known as *topology*. Topology deals with spatial relations. It is not concerned with size or shape, nor with magnitudes, distances, and other conventional characteristics of space. Topology involves such spatial relationships as "being included in," " part-whole," and "connectedness and disconnectedness." Since Lewin represents his structural concepts topologically he calls this part of his system *topological psychology* (1936a).

In order to represent dynamic concepts such as direction, distance, and force, Lewin had to invent a new kind of space that he called *hodological*. Hodology is the science of paths. A path is the same as a locomotion. The properties of Lewin's hodological space have also been expressed by linear graphs in which each region is represented by a point and each boundary between regions by a line connecting these points (Harary, Norman, and Cartwright, 1965).

We turn now to a discussion of Lewin's dynamic concepts which taken together constitute what Lewin calls *vector psychology*.

THE DYNAMICS OF PERSONALITY

A structural representation of the life space is like a road map. A good road map contains all of the information one needs to know to plan any sort of a trip just as a good structural representation of persons and their environment contains all of the facts one needs to know to account for any possible kind of behavior. But just as a road map cannot tell us what trip a person will actually decide to take, neither can a detailed picture of the life space tell us how a person is going to behave. Structural or topological concepts alone cannot explain concrete behavior in an actual psychological situation. For this kind of understanding dynamic concepts are needed.

Lewin's principal dynamic concepts are energy, tension, need, valence, and force or vector.

Energy

Lewin, in common with most personality theorists, assumes that the person is a complex energy system. The kind of energy that performs psychological work is called *psychical energy*. Since Lewin's theory is exclusively psychological in character, it is not necessary for him to deal with the question of the relation of psychical energy to other kinds of energy.

Psychical energy is released when the psychic system (the person) attempts to return to equilibrium after it has been thrown into a state of disequilibrium. Disequilibrium is produced by an increase of tension in one part of the system relative to the rest of the system, either as a result of external stimulation or internal change. When tension throughout the system becomes equalized again, the output of energy is halted and the total system comes to rest.

Tension is a state of the person, or speaking more precisely, it is a state of an inner-personal region relative to other inner-personal regions. When Lewin refers to the dynamic properties of a region or cell of the inner-personal sphere, he calls the region a *system.*

Tension

Tension has two important conceptual properties. The first property is that a state of tension in a particular system tends to equalize itself with the amount of tension in surrounding systems. If system *a,* for example, is in a state of high tension, and if the surrounding systems, *b, c, d, e,* and *f,* are in a state of low tension (Figure 11-17), then tension will tend to pass from *a* into *b, c, d, e,* and *f* until there is an equality of tension throughout the whole system (Figure 11-18).

The psychological means by which tension becomes equalized is called a *process.* A process may be thinking, remembering, feeling, perceiving, acting, or the like. For instance, a person who is faced with the task of solving a problem becomes tense in one of their systems. In order to solve the problem and thereby reduce the tension he or she engages in the process of thinking. Thinking continues until a satisfactory solution is found, at which time the person returns to a state of equilibrium. Or the intention may be one of remembering a name. The memory process goes into action, recalls the name, and enables the tension to subside.

Although tension always moves toward a condition of equilibrium, this conceptual property applies only to the system as a whole, and not necessarily to all of the part systems. A part system may actu-

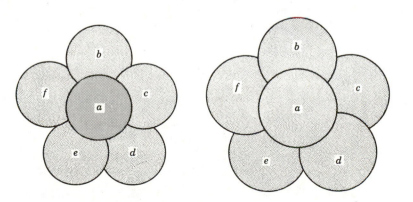

FIGURE 11-17
FIGURE 11-18

ally become more and more tense during the time that the whole system is returning to a balanced condition. This happens when a person has to take a circuitous route in solving a problem. During the detour, tension may mount in one of the subregions although the overall process will eventually bring the person back to a state of equilibrium. For example, someone may undertake a task, knowing full well that he or she will have to endure increasing tension, but at the same time anticipates that the end result will be a more perfect balance of forces.

A state of equilibrium does not mean that the system is without tension. Probably no organism can achieve a completely tension-free state and remain alive. Equilibrium means either that the tension throughout the total system is equalized or that a subsystem in which an unequal amount of tension exists is firmly walled off and isolated from the other inner-personal systems (Figure 11-19). Such a tense system may remain segregated for a long period of time and constitute a more or less permanent reservoir of energy. There may be a number of such firmly segregated tense systems in the personality, which furnish a continuous supply of energy for the operation of psychological processes.

A person who has established an equilibrium on a high tension level differs appreciably from a person who has established an equilibrium on a low tension level. In the former case, the pressure on the motoric will be greater and there is likely to be a continual seepage of energy into the motoric. Such a person will show a great deal of diffuse, restless activity.

A second conceptual property of tension is that it exerts pressure upon the boundary of the system. If the boundary is particularly firm, the diffusion of tension from one system to adjacent systems

FIGURE 11-19

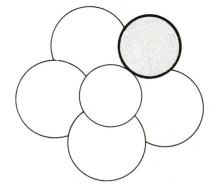

will be impeded, but if the boundary is weak tension will flow readily from one system into other systems. Ordinarily, a particular tension system shares its boundary with more than one other tension system. In such cases, the resistance of one part of the boundary may be weaker than that at other parts of the boundary. This will permit tension to pass in certain directions more freely than in other directions. In other words, dynamic communication between systems is a variable condition. Tension system *a* may be in close communication with tension system *b* so that exchanges of energy are easily made, whereas *a* may be remotely connected with *c, d, e,* and *f* so that exchanges of energy are difficult to make (Figure 11-20).

Dynamically speaking, a boundary is a region of resistance or a barrier. As a barrier it corresponds to a restraining force. Does the boundary itself have the property of being a tension system? Lewin thinks not. It is more likely that the force exerted at the region of the boundary of *a* against the force that is generated within *a* is determined by the states of tension in the surrounding systems. That is, the opposing force is really the tension being exerted on the boundary from adjacent systems (Figure 11-21).

An increase of tension or the release of energy in an inner-personal region is caused by the arousal of a need. A need may be a physiological condition such as hunger, thirst, or sex; it may be a desire for something such as a job or a spouse; or it may be an intention to do something such as completing a task or keeping an appointment. A need is, therefore, a motivational concept and is equivalent to such terms as motive, wish, drive, and urge.

Need

Lewin refrains from systematically discussing the nature, source, number, and kinds of needs because he is not at all satisfied with the concept. He feels that eventually the term *need* will be dropped from

FIGURE 11-20
FIGURE 11-21

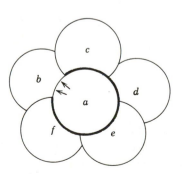

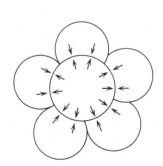

psychology in favor of a more suitable concept, one that is more observable and measurable. Nor does he feel that it is worthwhile to set forth a list of needs as so many psychologists do. In the first place, the list would be of almost infinite length, and in the second place, the only thing that really matters in the description of psychological reality is to represent those needs that actually exist in the momentary situation. These are the only needs that are producing effects. On an abstract level, it may be said that everyone is capable of feeling hungry but it is only when the hunger drive is actually disturbing the equilibrium of a person that it has to be taken into account.

It is apparent that Lewin is extremely pluralistic in his conception of needs. There are as many needs as there are specific and distinguishable cravings. One can have a need for the kind of rare steak that is served in only one particular restaurant or a need to hear a particular movement of a Sibelius symphony played by a specific orchestra. Lewin does not attempt to reduce a number of specific needs down to one general need, for as he says:

The problem of the emergence of needs lies at the crossroad of cultural anthropology, developmental psychology, and the psychology of motivation. Its investigation has been hampered by premature speculative attempts to systematize needs into a few categories (1951, p. 280).

Each need is a concrete fact, and unless it is described in all of its particularity and detail, one is not able to understand true psychological reality.

Lewin does say regarding needs that three states can be distinguished, a state of hunger, of satiation, and of oversatiation. "These states correspond to a positive, a neutral, and a negative valence of the activity regions which are related to a particular need" (1951, p. 282). Oversatiation means that the formerly desired object or activity has become distasteful through continued experience with it. Too much of anything produces surfeit and disgust.

Lewin also distinguishes between needs and *quasi-needs*. A need is due to some inner state, such as hunger, while a quasi-need is equivalent to a specific intention, like satisfying one's hunger by eating at a particular restaurant. Lewin feels that the needs of a person are determined to a large extent by social factors (1951, p. 289).

Tension and Motoric Action   Thus far, we have been concerned primarily with the internal dynamics of tension systems, that is, with the dynamic interdependence and communication between systems. What is the relation of tension to action? One might conjecture that energy flowing from an inner-personal region into the motoric would result directly in a psychological locomotion. Lewin, however, rejects such a position. Tension pressing on the outer boundary of the person cannot cause a locomotion. Therefore, instead of linking need or tension directly to action by way of the motoric, he links need with certain properties of the environment that then determine the kind of locomotion that will occur. This is a very ingenious way of connecting motivation with behavior.

Two additional concepts are required in order to accomplish this purpose. They are *valence* and *force*.

A valence is a conceptual property of a region of the psychological environment. It is the value of that region for a person. There are two kinds of value, positive and negative. A region of positive value is one that contains a goal object that will reduce tension when the person enters the region. For example, a region that contains food will have a positive valence for a person who is hungry (Figure 11-22). A region of negative value is one that will increase tension. For a person who is afraid of dogs any region that contains a dog will have a negative valence (Figure 11-23). Positive valences attract, negative valences repel.

A valence is coordinated with a need. This means that whether a particular region of the environment has a positive or negative value depends directly upon a system in a state of tension. Needs impart values to the environment. They organize the environment into a network of inviting and repelling regions. However, this network of valences depends also upon alien factors that do not fall within the scope of psychological laws. The presence or absence of the needed objects themselves obviously plays an important part in structuring the psychological environment. Whether food is present and recognizable, what kind of food it is and in what quantity, its availability and its proximity to objects that possess negative valence, are all non-

Valence

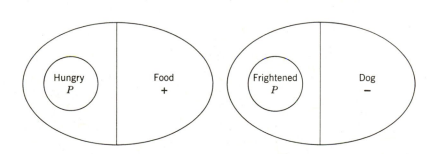

FIGURE 11-22
FIGURE 11-23

psychological factors that influence the valence of a region for a hungry person.

A valence is a variable quantity; it may be weak, medium, or strong. The strength of a valence depends upon the strength of the need plus all of the nonpsychological factors mentioned above.

A valence is not a force. It steers the person through his or her psychological environment but it does not supply the motive power for the locomotion. As we have already seen, neither does a system in a state of tension produce a locomotion. Another concept is needed. This is the concept of *force* or *vector*.

Force or Vector   A locomotion occurs whenever a force of sufficient strength acts upon a person. A force is coordinated with a need, but it is not a tension. A force exists in the psychological environment while a tension is a property of an inner-personal system.

The conceptual properties of force are direction, strength, and point of application. These three properties are represented mathematically by a *vector*. The direction in which the vector points represents the direction of the force, the length of the vector represents the strength of the force, and the place where the tip of the arrow impinges upon the outer boundary of the person represents the point of application. A vector is always drawn on the outside of a person (Figure 11-24) and never inside because psychological forces are properties of the environment and not of the person.

If there is only one vector (force) acting upon a person, then there will be a locomotion or a tendency to move in the direction of the vector. If two or more vectors are pushing the person in several different directions, the resulting locomotion will be the resultant of all of the forces.

Now we can see the relation of valence to vector. A region that possesses a positive valence is one in which the forces acting upon the person are directed toward this region. A region of negative valence is one in which the vectors are pointing in the opposite direction. In other words, the direction of a vector is directly determined by the

FIGURE 11-24

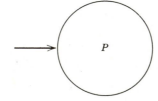

location of a region with either positive or negative valence. The strength of a vector is related to the strength of a valence, to the psychological distance between the person and the valence, and to the relative potency of other valences.

Parenthetically, it may be observed that the concept of need is the one concept with which all of the other dynamical constructs are coordinated. A need releases energy, increases tension, imparts value, and creates force. It is Lewin's central or nuclear concept around which the other concepts cluster.

We are now in a position to represent the specific path that a person   *Locomotion*
will transcribe in moving through his or her psychological environment. For example, a child passes a candy store, looks in the window, and wishes she had some candy. The sight of the candy arouses a need, and this need does three things. It releases energy and thereby arouses tension in an inner-personal region (the candy-wanting system). It confers a positive valence upon the region in which the candy is located. It creates a force that pushes the child in the direction of the candy.

Let us say that the child has to enter the store and buy the candy. This situation can be represented by Figure 11-25. Suppose, however, that the child does not have any money; then the boundary between her and the candy will be an impassable barrier. She will move as close to the candy as possible, perhaps putting her nose against the window, without being able to reach it (Figure 11-26).

She may say to herself, "If I had some money, I could buy some candy. Maybe mother will give me some money." In other words, a new need or quasi-need, the intention to get some money from her mother, is created. This intention, in turn, arouses a tension, a vector, and a valence that are represented in Figure 11-27. A thin boundary has been drawn between the child and the mother on the assumption that she has to go home, find her mother, and ask her for money.

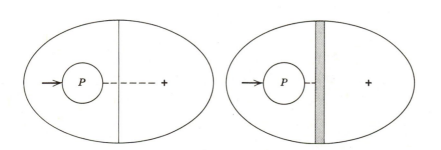

FIGURE 11-25
FIGURE 11-26

Another thin boundary has been drawn between the mother and the candy to represent the effort required to return to the store and make a purchase. The child moves to the candy by way of the mother.

If the mother refuses to give the child any money, she may think of borrowing it from a friend. In this case, the region containing the mother is surrounded by an impenetrable barrier, and a new path through the region containing the friend to the candy is transcribed (Figure 11-28).

This topological representation could be endlessly complicated by introducing additional environmental regions and boundaries of varying degrees of firmness, and additional needs with their coordinate tension systems, valences, and vectors.

In general, it may be said that any locomotion can be fully accounted for by the concepts of need, tension, force, valence, barrier, the properties of the medium, the dimension of reality-unreality, and the time perspective.

Dynamical Restructuring of the Psychological Environment   The dynamics of the psychological environment can change in four different ways. (1) The value of the region may change quantitatively, for example, from less positive to more positive, or it may change qualitatively, from positive to negative. New valences can appear and old ones can disappear. (2) Vectors may change in strength or in direction or in both respects. (3) Boundaries may become firmer or weaker, appear or disappear. (4) The material properties of a region, for instance, its fluidity or rigidity, may be altered.

Restructuring of the psychological environment may take place as a result of changes in the tension systems of the person, as a result of a locomotion, or as a result of cognitive processes. Cognitive resturcturing occurs when the person discovers a new way of solving a problem (insight), remembers something that he or she has forgotten, or perceives something about their environment that they had not noticed before. Restructuring can also result from the intru-

FIGURE 11-27
FIGURE 11-28

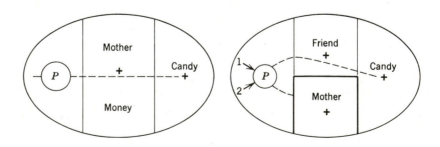

sion of alien factors from the foreign hull into the psychological environment.

The ultimate goal of all psychological processes is to return the person to a state of equilibrium. This goal can be reached in a number of ways, depending upon the particular process that is engaged. Although some of the processes have been described in the preceding discussion, it may be helpful to list all of them at this time.

Return to Equilibrium

Disequilibrium is defined as a state of unequal tension throughout the various systems of the person. For the sake of simplicity, let us assume that one inner-personal system is in a condition of heightened tension and all of the others have a low tension level. One way in which an equilibrium can be reached is for the tension of system *a* to diffuse throughout all of the other systems until the tension throughout the inner-personal sphere is equalized. Assuming that no energy is lost from the inner-personal sphere, the consequence of this diffusion is to raise the tension level of the total system and to increase the pressure on the boundary between the inner-personal stratum and the perceptual-motor stratum. Assuming that this process is repeated again and again, the result will be an accumulation of tension in the inner-personal sphere. Such a person is said to be under great inner tension. When the boundary of the inner-personal region is no longer able to resist the pressure on it, there will be a sudden breakthrough of energy into the motorium that will produce agitated behavior. This describes what takes place when a person has a temper tantrum or a fit.

If the boundary between the inner-personal system and the perceptual motor area is fairly permeable, the tension can be dissipated in restless activity. This is a fairly primitive mode of tension reduction that is seen chiefly during infancy. As the baby becomes hungrier, for example, it becomes more restless. Restlessness, it is said, helps one blow off steam.

The most prevalent method of returning to a state of equilibrium is by performing an appropriate locomotion in the psychological environment. An appropriate locomotion is one that brings the person into the region of a satisfying goal object. For instance, if a person is in a state of tension because he or she is unemployed, then finding a job will remove the tension. In such cases, perceptual and motor processes are instrumental in bringing about relief from tension. It may be necessary, of course, to restructure the environment to reach the desired goal, and this restructuring may involve complicated and time-consuming cognitive processes. A man who aspires to be president may spent years manipulating the environment before he is successful. Or he may never be successful, in which case he will remain in a permanent state of disequilibrium.

Tension may be reduced and equilibrium restored by a substitute locomotion. This process requires that two needs be closely interdependent so that the satisfaction of one need discharges the tension from the other need system. We will have more to say about this topic in a later section of this chapter.

Finally, tension may be reduced by purely imaginary locomotions. A person who imagines that he or she has performed some difficult feat or occupies a pre-eminent position gains a kind of vicarious satisfaction from merely daydreaming about success. We are even provided with a number of ready-made daydreams in the form of novels, plays, and movies.

Résumé   In this section, Lewin's principal dynamic concepts, those of need, psychical energy, tension, force or vector, and valence, have been presented and discussed. These dynamical constructs taken in conjunction with the structural constructs discussed in the last section determine the specific locomotions of the individual and the way in which he structures his environment. Locomotions and restructurings serve the purpose of reducing tension by satisfying needs.

THE DEVELOPMENT OF PERSONALITY   Although Lewin does not reject the idea that heredity and maturation play a role in development, nowhere in his writings does he discuss their possible influence in any detail, nor does he assign them any place in his conceptual representations. This is in keeping with Lewin's preference for a purely psychological theory. Since heredity and maturation fall within the realm of biological facts and consequently exist outside the life space along with physical and social phenomena, Lewin ignores them. On rare occasions, he intimates that organic changes can and do influence psychological development. In discussing the period of adolescence, for example, he observes that changes in the functions and structure of the body profoundly influence the psychic structure in the direction of greater uncertainty and instability (1951, Chapter VI).

Nor does Lewin have a learning theory as that term is usually understood in American psychology. He describes the kinds of changes that take place in behavior and ascribes them to such constructs as cognitive restructuring, differentiation, organization, integration, and motivation (1951, Chapter IV).

It is interesting to recall, however, that Lewin's earliest experimental work consisted of research on associative learning. Frequency of repetition and contiguity between the stimulus words to be associated were thought to be, at that time, important determinants of learning. Lewin discovered, however, that the items to be associated had to belong to the same tension system for a connection to be formed between them. Lewin's findings cast doubt upon the validity of associationistic theories of learning. Hilgard presents a fine account of this phase of Lewin's scientific work (1956, Chapter 8).

Moreover, Lewin has written an extensive paper on reward and punishment (1935a, Chapter IV) but his ideas on this subject have very little connection with such hedonistic formulations as those of the law of effect (Thorndike) or the principle of reinforcement (Hull). Lewin was interested in reward and punishment, not as habit-makers or habit-breakers, but as devices for controlling behavior in the concrete, momentary situation. Reward and punishment do not, in Lewin's analysis, stamp in or stamp out associations as Thorndike used to say; rather, they cause changes in the vectors, valences, and boundaries of the psychological environment and in the tension systems of the person.

Nor should one overlook the fact that Lewin and his students, notably Zeigarnik (1927), made a large contribution to our understanding of memory when they demonstrated that interrupted tasks were remembered better than completed ones. But all of this work does not constitute a theory of learning. We agree with Hilgard, who has made an analysis of Lewin's ideas as they bear upon the psychology of learning (1956, Chapter 8), that although many of Lewin's formulations are relevant to a theory of learning they do not constitute such a theory. Nor did Lewin ever claim that they did.

In his important paper, *Regression, retrogression and development* (1951), Chapter V), Lewin discusses some of the behavioral changes that occur during development, following which he tries to show how these changes can be represented by means of field constructs.

Behavioral Changes

VARIETY. It is pretty obvious that as one grows older the variety of one's activities, emotions, needs, information, and social relationships increases, at least up to a certain age. Thereafter, the versatility of one's behavior may show a contraction.

ORGANIZATION. Not only do activities become more versatile with age; they also show important changes in organization. A given unit of behavior displays increasing complexity. A young child can carry on a relationship with one other child at a time, but an older child can have relationships with a number of children at the same time. Behavior also becomes more hierarchical in structure. For example, a young child may play with blocks just for the pleasure he derives from the activity, but as he grows older playing with blocks may become a means to other goals as well, such as the desire for approval or the need to outdo another child. Behavior may also become more complicated in the sense that an older child can engage in several activities during a period of time. He can be crayoning a picture, talking to a friend, be interrupted to run an errand for his mother, return to his crayoning, talk with another friend, answer the phone, and return ro his crayoning. The young child is a good deal more distractible. He or she does one thing at a time, and when that is interrupted they are not likely to return to it.

EXTENSION OF AREAS OF ACTIVITIES. The older child has more freedom of movement than the baby. Older children can do things, for example, cross the street, go to school, visit friends, that younger children cannot do. Furthermore, time becomes more extended with age. The young child is pretty much a creature of the present; for it the future and to a lesser degree the past do not exist. As the child grows older, he or she begins to think about the past, make plans for the future, and see the present as consisting of a larger block of time.

INTERDEPENDENCE OF BEHAVIOR. It is a matter of common observation that the behavior of the infant involves diffuse reactions of the whole body. Lewin calls this behavior an example of *simple interdependence* or an *undifferentiated state*. With increasing maturity, specialized and independent forms of action become differentiated out of mass activity. The simple unity of infantile behavior yields to a plurality of actions. Some integration takes place when independent actions become organized hierarchically but real integration is achieved only through what Lewin calls *organizational interdependence*. Organizational interdependence consists of combining and integrating separate activities or needs into a larger whole. Playing the piano, building a tree house, or writing a story involves the bringing together of a lot of separate activities. Lewin points out that mass activity decreases with age, hierarchical organization increases with age, and the degree of unity based on organizational interdependence fluctuates with age.

DEGREE OF REALISM. A person customarily becomes more oriented to reality as he or she grows older. The young child does not readily distinguish between what is real and what is imaginary. Not until it learns to differentiate between them can it develop a sense of reality.

Having set forth some of the important changes that take place during development, namely, changes in variety, complexity, extensity, organization, integration, and realism, Lewin then proceeds to conceptualize these changes. The constructs he uses are the same as those discussed in preceding sections of this chapter, since behavior and development are both deemed to be functions of the same structural and dynamic factors (Lewin, 1951, p. 238).

DIFFERENTIATION. This is one of the key concepts in Lewin's theory of personality development and applies to all aspects of the life space. It is defined as an increase in the number of parts of a whole. For example, the number of regions in the inner-personal sphere increases with age. Compare the child and the adult in Figure 11-29. The adult has many more differentiated tension systems than the child. In a similar manner, the psychological environment becomes increasingly differentiated with age. The time dimension becomes differentiated into a remote past, a near past, a present, a near future, and a far future. Increasing maturity also brings an increasing differentiation of the reality-unreality dimension. By the time a person gets to be an adult he or she has learned, to some extent, to distinguish not only between the true and the false but also between different degrees of possibility and probability.

BOUNDARY PROPERTIES. Greater differentiation of the person and the psychological environment obviously means an increase in the number of boundaries. But not all boundaries are alike. They vary in strength. In general, the boundaries of the child are less firm than those of the adult. For example, the boundary between the child and its psychological environment is weaker than that between the adult

Developmental Concepts

FIGURE 11-29

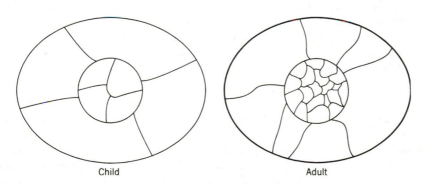

Child   Adult

and his or her environment. This accounts for the fact that the child is more subject to influences from the environment and can discharge inner tensions more easily than the adult. The child is more a part of the environment. As a matter of fact, during the very early weeks of life, there may be virtually no boundary at all between the infant and its psychological environment. The weakness of the boundaries in the inner-personal sphere of the child means that one need can substitute more easily for another need than is the case with the adult. A similar weakness of boundaries in the reality-unreality dimension and the time perspective is also characteristic of the child.

INTEGRATION. Differentiation and changing boundary properties can account for many of the facts of development, but they cannot explain the increasing organization and integration of behavior with age. Another concept is necessary, which Lewin calls *organizational interdependence*. In order to appreciate what is meant by this concept, it may help to contrast it with the simple interdependence of regions. Consider, for example, two neighboring and interdependent tension systems, *a* and *b*. When *a* is thrown into a state of heightened tension, energy flows from *a* into *b* until a state of equal tension exists between the two systems. Similarly, if the tension level of *b* is raised, energy will flow into *a*. The influence is mutual and reciprocal. This is the kind of relationship between tension systems that appears to exist in the baby. A disturbance in one region spreads to other regions of the inner-personal sphere and out through the motoric in a massive, diffuse discharge. The hungry baby is restless all over.

As the baby matures, the influence of neighboring tension systems upon one another appears to lose the characteristics of being mutual and reciprocal. In place of simple interdependence, the type of relationship that becomes established is that of leader and led. Tension system *a* leads tension system *b* in such a manner as to help *a* discharge its tension without necessarily leading to any final equality between the two. A simple example of this organizational interdependence is the way in which an inner-personal region can subordinate the motoric to its objectives, or when an inner-personal region regulates and controls what will be perceived.

Moreover, in organizational interdependence tension does not diffuse from region to region on the basis of proximity alone. Selectivity develops so that systems which are remote from one another may dominate or lead each other. A whole hierarchy of dominant-subordinate relationships can become established; region *a* may rule region *b, b* may rule *c,* and so on. This would explain, among other things, the ability of an older person to organize and execute a complicated plan of action, an ability in which children seem to be deficient.

Lewin likens the organizational unity of a person to an organization with one head. When the one head breaks up into several heads, unity decreases; when a new central head emerges, unity increases. Thus, the unity of the adult person waxes and wanes instead of developing in a straight-line manner.

Lewin does not discuss this subject at any length. Development is, for him, a continuous process in which it is difficult to recognize discrete stages. He does say that important developmental changes occur around the age of three, that this is followed by a period of relative stability until adolescence which is a period of dynamic reorganization culminating finally in the stability of adulthood (1951, Chapter VI). He also points out that the first regions to become differentiated in the baby are those that have to do with eating and elimination.

Lewin believes that the use of an age scale for describing development is not really adequate for understanding psychological growth. The age scale will eventually have to be dropped in favor of degrees of differentiation, organization, integration, and the like. Moreover, psychology must address itself to the task of discovering the coexisting and dynamically related facts which represent the conditions for the change at the time the change takes place. It is not enough to say that six-year-olds do things that three-year-olds do not do. One must account for the change using the concepts of field theory.

Stages of Development

Any theory of development must take into account the regressions that occur from time to time. Lewin has made some important contributions, both theoretical and experimental, to our understanding of regression (1951, Chapter V). In the first place, he distinguishes between retrogression and regression. Retrogression refers to a return to an earlier form of behavior in the life history of the person whereas regression refers to any change to a more primitive form of behavior, regardless of whether the person had ever behaved in that way previously. It is much easier to study regression than retrogression, as these terms are defined, because it is not necessary to establish whether the behavior took place previously in the lives of the subjects. Moreover, in studying regression, the experimenter can make use of age norms that have been established for various activities. For example, if two-year-old children play with toys in certain ways, while four-year-old children play with toys in different ways, one can ask under what conditions will four-year-olds regress to the play level of two-year-olds. Lewin and his associates have performed such

Regression

experiments and have found that frustration is one factor which produces regression (Barker, Dembo, and Lewin, 1941).

Résumé   Lewin's theoretical analysis of development employs such field concepts as differentiation, changes in boundary conditions, organization, and integration. In general, it may be said that with increasing maturity there is greater differentiation both of the person and of the psychological environment, increasing firmness of boundaries, and a more complicated network of hierarchical and selective relationships among the tension systems. For Lewin, development of behavior is a function of the person and the psychological environment.

CHARACTERISTIC RESEARCH AND RESEARCH METHODS   One widely acknowledged criterion of a "good" theory is the measure of its fruitfulness in stimulating research. In this respect, Lewin's theory is a very "good" theory indeed. Few other theories of personality have been responsible for generating so much experimentation. Lewin himself, although known as a brilliant theoretician, was always a working scientist. He took the lead in formulating empirical tests of many of his basic hypotheses, and his great enthusiasm for research has been transmitted to many generations of students in Germany and in the United States. The series of articles in the *Psychologische Forschung* between 1926 and 1930 is one of the most distinguished group of empirical studies in the psychological literature (De Rivera, 1976). Moreover, Lewin's ideas and his genius for devising simple and convincing demonstrations of his theoretical conceptions have acted as catalysts for many psychologists who were never personally associated with him. It is impossible to estimate the number of investigations that bear the imprint of Lewin's influence. Their number is surely legion. Whatever may be the fate of Lewin's theory in the years to come, the body of experimental work instigated by it constitutes an enduring contribution to our knowledge of personality.

The empirical investigations of Lewin and his many associates have always been theory-oriented. That is, experiments were undertaken to test propositions suggested by field theory; they were never done purely for the sake of collecting facts. A particular fact was only of significance to Lewin as it shed light upon the validity of a general principle or law.

The studies growing out of Lewin's conception of tension systems are a case in point. It will be recalled that the inner-personal sphere of personality consists of a number of regions or cells. Each cell is separated from its neighboring cells by boundaries whose chief property is that of offering resistance to the diffusion of energy from one cell into adjacent cells. The firmness of the boundaries can and does vary, with the result that a region may be in closer communication with one region than another. This means that when the tension level of a cell is increased by a need or intention, energy can pass more readily into a neighboring region where the barrier is weak than into one where the barrier is strong. This much is theory. How can it be tested in the crucible of empirical investigation?

Lewin devised the following experimental strategy (1935a, pp. 180–193). Suppose, for example, that a child is given an opportunity to build something with blocks. An intention to build a house, let us say, is induced in the child. An intention, it will be recalled, is coordinated with an inner-personal region in a state of tension. Before the child has an opportunity to complete the task and thus discharge the tension completely, it is interrupted and given another type of play material, such as some play-dough. A new intention, for instance, to model a horse, is induced which means conceptually that a second inner-personal region is thrown into a state of tension. The child is allowed to complete the second project. Then it is given an opportunity to return to the unfinished task of building a house out of blocks. If it does not resume the interrupted task, this indicates that the tension in the first system has been discharged by the completion of the second task. The second task is said to be a substitute for the first task. On the other hand, if the child resumes the interrupted task, that indicates that the tension in the block-building system has not been drained off by the completed activity of modeling a horse. That is, the completed activity has no substitute value for the interrupted activity. Each of these results can be depicted by the following conceptual representations (Figure 11-30).

In the left-hand figure, the two regions are separated by a strong, impermeable boundary, which prevents the discharge of tension from the blocks system by way of the play-dough system. The tension remaining in the blocks system causes the child to resume building with blocks. In the right-hand figure, the boundary is weak and the

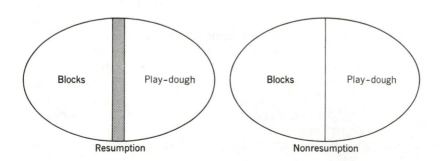

FIGURE 11-30

tension in the blocks system can be easily drained off through the play-dough system. Since no tension remains in the blocks system after the play-dough horse has been completed, the child has no desire to return to the blocks. The experimental design also requires that a control group, in which the children are interrupted but are given no substitute task, be used. The purpose of the control group is to make sure that at the time of interruption there actually is some tension in the system. Otherwise, no test of the substitute value of the completed task would be possible.

Experimental investigations that make use of this basic design are called studies of substitution. One of the earliest of the substitution experiments performed under the influence of Lewin's field theory was done by Kate Lissner (1933). She sought to determine what there was about the tasks themselves that had a bearing upon the substitute value of one task for another. She found, as might be expected, that the more similar the two tasks were, the greater was the substitutibility of one for the other. For example, if the interrupted task consisted of modeling a horse and the substitute task of modeling a snake, the amount of resumption was much less than if the substitute task consisted of drawing a picture or stringing beads. Unfortunately, there are no very good criteria for determining beforehand the amount of similarity between tasks. Two tasks may seem to be very much alike to an observer and yet be quite different in the eyes of the person doing them, or two tasks may appear to be very dissimilar and yet be very much alike to the performer. Lissner also discovered that if the substitute task is difficult it will have greater substitute value than if it is easy, other things being equal. Task difficulty is also hard to judge before the actual test is made. What is difficult for one person may be easy for another.

Another one of Lewin's students, Mahler (1933), found that the higher the degree of reality of the second task, the more substitute value it will have for the first task. Thus, if a child is interrupted in the middle of drawing a picture and is then permitted to tell how he or she would complete it if given the opportunity, there is less going back to the original task than if the child is told to think about or imagine how he or she would have finished it. Talking about an activity is assumed to be more realistic than thinking about it. However, as Sliosberg's work (1934) indicates, the degree to which the less real can be substituted for the more real depends upon the character of the situation. In a relaxed, play situation a fantasy may be as satisfying as actual motor activity, while in a more serious context the fantasy may have no substitute value whatsoever.

Köpke (cited in Lewin, 1935a, p. 185) has used the substitution experimental design for testing a special application of Lewin's theory of the person. Lewin suggested that the boundaries between the cells of the inner-personal sphere of the mentally retarded child should be firmer than those of the normal child. If this hypothesis is correct, there should be less substitutibility of tasks among retarded children than among normal ones. This is confirmed by Köpke's findings. Even with very similar tasks such as drawing a picture of a cat on red paper, and drawing the same animal on green paper, retarded children nearly always went back and finished the first task after they had completed the second task. This difference between the boundary properties of normal and retarded children is illustrated in the following figure (Figure 11-31).

The heavier boundaries of the retarded child's inner-personal region indicate that there is less communication between tension systems than is the case in the normal child. There are more cells in the representation of the normal child because Lewin postulates that the normal child is more differentiated than the deficient child. For other differences between the retarded and the normal child see Lewin (1935a, Chapter VII).

Perhaps the most ambitious and carefully formulated investigation of substitution based upon Lewin's theory and experimental design was carried out by Mary Henle (1942). Henle has numerous criticisms to make of previous studies of substitution, the most relevant for our purposes being the circularity involved in Lissner's interpretation of her findings. Henle makes the point that it adds very little if anything to our knowledge of substitutibility to say that one task has substitute value for another task because the two systems are in dynamic communication, when one has to find out by empirical test

FIGURE 11-31

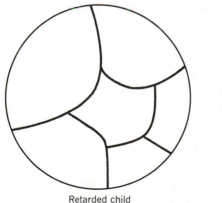

Retarded child

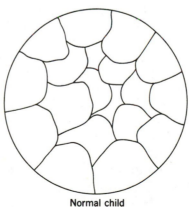

Normal child

whether one task will actually be a substitute for another task. In other words, to explain results after the results have been obtained is not a real test of the theory, since explanations based upon other theories might work just as well. One must be able to *predict* in advance what one expects to find if the theory is to have any unique explanatory power. Accordingly, Henle addresses herself to the significant problem of finding some principles by which one can predict beforehand what tasks will and what tasks will not substitute for each other.

Henle selected principles from the Gestalt theory of perception and learning. Gestalt theory asserts that such structural factors as similarity, proximity, homogeneity, closure, and figure-ground relationships are important in producing perceptual organization and in determining what is learned. Henle asks whether these principles may not be operative in task substitution.

Accordingly, she devised the following experiments based upon the principles of homogeneity and proximity. A series of five homogeneous tasks, one of them solving paper and pencil mazes, was administered to a number of subjects, all of whom were college students, under the following conditions. The subject was allowed to complete the first three mazes, was interrupted on the fourth maze, and completed the fifth one, following which he was permitted to go back and work on the uncompleted maze. Henle predicted that subjects would resume work on the interrupted task because the two last tasks, being units in a homogeneous series of mazes, do not stand out from the others. Consequently, tasks four and five do not form a pair that can be said to be in communication with one another. Virtually every subject did resume work on the interrupted maze.

Following the same line of reasoning, Henle predicted that in a heterogeneous series in which the fourth and fifth tasks were quite different from the first three, there should be less resumption than there was in the homogeneous series. This prediction was not borne out. For example, when the first three tasks consisted of making mosaic designs, and the interrupted fourth and the completed fifth tasks consisted of working jigsaw puzzles, the amount of resumption was similar to that for the homogeneous series. Henle acknowledges that failure to predict the results correctly in the second experiment nullifies the purported confirmation of the hypothesis by the first experiment, since the two predictions were made on the basis of the same principles.

Henle was puzzled by the results of the second experiment because in a previous one in which two tasks alone were used instead of a series of tasks, a fairly high proportion of the subjects did *not* resume the interrupted task. Why should there be this difference? Henle suggests three possibilities. In the first place, the interruption of a task in a series of tasks may make the interrupted task stand out from the other four. By becoming segregated, the interrupted task would lose its dynamic communication with the others. When there are only two tasks, the interrupted one does not stand out as much and maintains its relationship with the completed task. As a result there would be greater substitute value when only two tasks were used. If this is the reason, then the following procedure should elicit the required proof. Five tasks were used. The first three were alike and the last two were alike, thus constituting a heterogeneous series. Tasks one, three, and four were interrupted, so that task four, which was to be tested for amount of resumption, did not stand out by being interrupted since one and three were also interrupted. The results were the same as those found when only task four was interrupted. That is, most of the subjects resumed work on the interrupted fourth task after completing the fifth one. Apparently, interruption by itself does not make a task stand out and cause the tension system to lose its dynamic connection with neighboring systems.

A second possible factor that might have caused a disparity in the results for a series of tasks versus a pair of tasks was the greater attractiveness (valence) of the tasks used in the series compared to those used in pairs. It may be, Henle suggests, that substitutes will be accepted less readily when the subject is very much interested in the interrupted task. To test this conjecture, Henle used pairs of tasks varying in relative valence. One pair consisted of highly preferred tasks, a second pair of medium valence, and a third pair of low interest value. The results plainly showed that the greatest degree of resumption took place for the task of highest valence, the lowest for the task of little valence, and a moderate amount of resumption for the task of medium valence. A strong valence inhibits communication between tension systems and reduces substitute value. Or it may be that a task of high valence has greater tension behind it that is not sufficiently drained off by the completion of the second task, as would be the case with a task of low valence and correspondingly low tension.In either case, the contradictory results obtained for a pair of tasks of low valence versus a series of high valence would be explained by the difference in valence. Consequently, in planning experiments on structural factors such as proximity and similarity it is necessary to use tasks of equal valence in the different experimental conditions.

The third factor that Henle thought might have produced different results between the experiment using a pair of tasks and the experiment employing a series of five tasks is that of success. Her argument regarding the influence of success runs as follows. A subject tends to view an interrupted task as being more difficult than a completed one. When the subject has an opportunity to complete a number of tasks, when a series of five is presented, he or she gains confidence in their ability to do the work. Consequently, they tend to go back and complete the interrupted task. When there are only two tasks, the subject does not have an opportunity to build up much self-confidence by experiencing success and so is less likely to resume the difficult interrupted task.

Henle investigated the relevance of this factor in the following way. Subjects were allowed to complete three mazes of increasing difficulty, followed by an interrupted maze and a completed one. Practically all the subjects returned to work on the interrupted maze. When the first three mazes were so simple that they did not provide the subjects with feelings of success, a much smaller number of subjects resumed the interrupted task.

Having determined that task valence and task difficulty were important variables in substitution experiments, Henle proceeded to keep these two factors constant while varying the conditions of task homogeneity and task proximity.

A series of heterogeneous tasks consisting of three letter cancellation tests that were completed and two mosaic design tests, one of which was interrupted and the other completed, resulted in a great deal less resumption of the interrupted task than when a series of homogeneous tasks, for example, all letter cancellation tests or all mosaic design tests, was administered. Heterogeneity of tasks permits the last two to stand out and become dynamically interdependent, whereas homogeneity prevents communication from developing.

To test for the factor of proximity, the following two series of three tasks were used. In the first series, the sequence was task one completed, task two interrupted, and task three completed. Tasks two and three were similar and task one was different. In this series, the interrupted task was next to a similar completed task. Seventy-five percent of the subjects did *not* resume the interrupted task. This result shows that task three has a very high substitute value for task two. In the second series, the sequence was task one interrupted, task two completed, and task three completed. Tasks one and three were similar and two was different. In this series, the interrupted task was separated from its similar completed task. Only 36 percent of the subjects did *not* resume the interrupted task. The results of these two sets of experiments confirm the hypothesis that the boundary between two tension systems is made more permeable under conditions of task heterogeneity and task proximity.

The foregoing studies of substitution constitute only a small segment of the experimental work that has been instigated by Lewin's field theory. It is quite impossible to do justice to all of the research within the limits of a single chapter. We can only point out some of the areas of research that bear directly upon Lewin's theory of personality, and trust that the reader will become acquainted with them. They are level of aspiration (Lewin, Dembo, Festinger, and Sears, 1944), interrupted activities (Katz, 1938; Zeigarnik, 1927), psychological satiation (Karsten, 1928; Kounin, 1941), regression (Barker, Dembo, and Lewin, 1941), and conflict (Lewin, 1951, pp. 260–268; Smith, 1968). A convenient survey of the experimental work done by Lewin and his associates will be found in Lewin's chapter in the *Manual of child psychology* (1954) and Deutsch (1968). A detailed presentation of Lewin's ideas and the research they have stimulated will be found in Volume 2 of *Psychology: A study of a science* (Cartwright, 1959).

CURRENT STATUS AND EVALUATION

One indication of the vitality of a scientific viewpoint is the amount of controversy it arouses between proponents of the system and its critics. Watson's behaviorism, psychoanalysis, Hull's behavior theory, and Tolman's purposive behaviorism are examples of viewpoints that have divided psychologists into rival camps, and in each case the theory has exercised considerable influence upon the course that psychology has taken.

Lewin's field theory has been the object of considerable controversy for the past thirty years. During that time it has attracted a devoted group of adherents who, since the death of Lewin, have been carrying on the work that he started, especially in the study of group processes. Many of those who were associated with Lewin in the Research Center for Group Dynamics at the Massachusetts Institute of Technology are now working together at the University of Michigan. As Deutsch points out (1968), group dynamics has become an integral part of social psychology. The origin of the encounter group movement and its various offshoots, for example, at Esalen and in Synanon communities, have been traced by Burton (1974) to a workshop for community leaders on interracial tension conducted by Lewin in 1946.

Lewin's theory of the person has not fared as well. Lewin himself during the later years of his life devoted his energies largely to the study of group processes and to action research (Lewin, 1948). He became interested in applying field theory throughout the social sciences. Consequently, there have been no important advances in Lewin's theory of the person since the early 1940s. Many of his concepts, however, have become assimilated into the main stream of psychology. Vector, valence, tension system, barrier, and life space are no longer strange words to the ears of psychologists.

One significant innovation in studies that have a field theoretical orientation is the increased attention that is being paid to the influence of nonpsychological factors on the life space. Escalona and Leitch, for example (Escalona, 1954), in their studies of infant behavior show how such constitutional factors as sensitivity to various stimuli, physical activity, and tension tolerance affect the psychological environment of the child. An impressive investigation of psychological ecology is that done by Barker, Wright, and their associates at the University of Kansas (Barker, 1963, 1965; Barker and Wright, 1951, 1955). Their aim was to describe the behavior settings of all of the children in a small midwestern town in the United States. Barker and Schoggen (1973) have made a comparative study of the community factors that affect children's behavior in a small town in the United States and one in England.

As an outgrowth of Lewin's concept of psychological ecology and the pioneering studies of Barker and Wright, a new field of psychology has come into existence. Although Barker (1968) uses the term "ecological psychology" to describe this new field, it is more commonly referred to as "environmental psychology (Heimstra and Mc-Farling, 1974; Ittelson, Proshansky, Rivlin, and Winkler, 1974; Mehrabian and Russell, 1974). Broadly speaking, environmental psychology is concerned with all of the conditions, but especially those in the physical environment, external to the person that influence his or her behavior.

Lewin's influence on current thinking in psychology is exemplified by Atkinson's theory of achievement motivation (Atkinson, 1964; Atkinson and Feather, 1966). This theory represents an extension and elaboration of level of aspiration. Cantril (1965) has used level of aspiration methodology in his global studies of human concerns. Rokeach's investigation of the open and closed mind (1960) makes use of Lewinian concepts. The closed mind is less differentiated, has more rigid boundaries, and possesses a narrower time perspective than the open mind. Festinger (1957, 1964) has developed a theory of cognitive dissonance that elaborates Lewin's view that the situation prior to decision differs from the situation after a decision has been made.

Heider's influential theoretical analysis of social perception and interpersonal relations (1958) draws heavily upon Lewin's field-theoretical approach. Heider says, "though not many of the specific concepts of topology have been taken over, they have helped in the construction of new ones with which we have tried to represent some of the basic facts of human relations" (p. 4).

The criticisms of Lewin's field theory may be subsumed under four headings.

Lewin's topological and vectorial representations do not divulge anything new about the behavior they are supposed to explain. This objection has been formulated in various ways by different critics. Some like Garrett (1939) allege that Lewin's representations are cumbersome portrayals of fairly simple psychological situations, whereas Brolyer (1936–1937) calls them pictorial analogies or illustrative metaphors. London (1944) says that they are pictures of what is already known, that they do not add any new knowledge or insights. In Lindzey's review (1952) of Lewin's *Field theory in social science* he notes Lewin's tendency to employ after-the-fact illustrations more often than before-the-fact predictions made on the basis of propositions deduced from the basic theory. Householder (1939) also observes that Lewin formulates no laws and gives no account of the operations required for determining the constants of the equations from which predictions of the behavior of an individual in a given situation might be made. Spence (1944) denies that Lewin's experimental work has anything to do with his theory. "Lewin sets up a most attractive program for theory. Taken in conjunction with his interesting experiments the illusion is nicely created that there is some connection between them" (p. 54 fn.).

Tolman raises the same question in his appreciative article on Lewin at the time of his death. "Is it true as I have heard asserted—or as I myself have at times been tempted to believe—that the proper conceptualization of a given life space is possible only after the behaviors which are supposed to result from it have already been observed?" (Tolman, 1948, p. 3). More charitable than other critics, Tolman avers that the fault lies in Lewin's failure to make explicit certain steps in his thinking. Heidbreder (1937) in a very thoughtful review of Lewin's *Principles of topological psychology* asserts that Lewin did not intend that his topological diagrams should serve as models of reality. Rather, they are graphic methods of representing the logical structure of the relationships themselves. Heidbreder goes on to say that topological concepts may be peculiarly adapted to portray compactly and conveniently the complex network of relationships in a psychological situation.

Lewin has this to say about the criticism that his representations are merely pictures of known facts and do not permit one to predict in advance what behavior will occur.

Not infrequently it has been stated that theories which merely explain known facts are of no particular value. I cannot agree with this view. Particularly if the theory combines into one logical system known facts which previously had to be treated by separate theories; it would have a definite advantage as an organization device. Besides, agreement with the known facts proves the adequacy of this theory at least to a certain degree (Lewin, 1951, p. 20).

But then Lewin goes on to admit the validity of the criticism.

It is true, however, that it is a clearer test of the adequacy of the theory if one can make predictions from it and prove these predictions experimentally. The reason for this difference seems to be that empirical data generally allow for quite a range of different interpretations and classifications and that therefore *it is usually easy to invent a variety of theories covering them* [our italics] (1951, p. 20).

In the italicized portion of the last sentence, Lewin has put his finger on the reason why after-the-fact explanations are criticized and why a rigorous scientific methodology insists that empirical predictions should be made beforehand in order to test a theory.

Psychology cannot ignore the objective environment. This criticism of Lewin's field theory has been raised by Leeper (1943), Brunswik (1943), and Tolman (1948). The argument runs as follows. The life space is not a closed psychological system. On the one hand, the life space is influenced by the external world, and on the other hand, the life space produces changes in the objective world. In order to have an adequate psychological theory it is necessary, therefore, to formulate a "set of principles whereby such and such individual and group life-space configurations will produce such and such behaviors, [and] a set of principles whereby the independent variables of environmental situation and given personality make-up will produce such and such inner and outer life spaces" (Tolman, 1948, pp. 3–4). Tolman believes that Lewin's theory falls down especially in not conceptualizing how the external environment produces changes in the life space. Failure to provide such principles means that Lewin's field theory falls into the trap of subjectivism from which only intuition can rescue it. That is, one has to intuit what is in the life space instead of discovering by scientific operations the independent variables in the environment that produce a given life space. If one knows the independent variables that are responsible for producing a life space, one can predict and control the life space in an objective fashion.

Lewin's answer to this criticism consists of two parts. In the first place, he states that he does take into account those aspects of the objective environment that are affecting the life space of the person at the time (1951, pp. 57 ff.). It certainly seems to be true that when Lewin and his colleagues are doing research they specify the independent variables and the stimuli from the nonpsychological environment in much the same manner as any experimentalist does.

Secondly he proposes an area of investigation, psychological ecology, that will study the relation between psychological and nonpsychological factors (1951, Chapter VIII). Apparently, it is to be the main task of this discipline to make predictions about what variables in the objective environment are likely *at some future time* to influence the life space of the individual. Valuable as this new program may be for long-range predictions of what might happen in the unspecified future, it does not seem to answer the objection of Leeper, Brunswik, and Tolman. What they want is a conceptualization of the environmental factors, here and now, that are affecting the life space. What are the mediation processes by which physical and social facts are transformed into psychological facts?

A different criticism but one that is related to the problem of the relation of the physical world to the life space has been elaborated by Floyd Allport (1955). Allport believes that Lewin has confused the physical with the psychological, or as Allport prefers to call the life space, "the phenomenological" (direct awareness). In Lewin's writings, locomotions are sometimes physical, sometimes "mental"; boundaries are sometimes actual barriers in the external world and sometimes they are inner barriers. Lewin's model confuses the inner world of phenomenology with the outer world of physics, and the result, Allport asserts, is a hopeless muddle. Allport feels that this muddle is inevitable if one adopts a field-theoretical approach because of the great temptation to include within the same field factors that lie within the person (phenomenology) and factors that lie outside the person (physicalism). Only by keeping the two sets of factors conceptually separate to begin with is it possible to find the laws by which they interact with one another.

Lewin does not take into account the past history of the individual. Leeper (1943) and Garrett (1939), in particular, raise this objection. They feel that in order to have a complete explanation of any present behavior it is necessary to look into the individual's past for causative factors. This criticism carries considerable weight with those psychologists who believe that the person is a product of heredity, maturation, and learning.

It is true that Lewin's principle of contemporaneity seems to exclude the past, but Lewin denies that historical causation should be excluded from psychology. Concerning this matter Lewin writes as follows.

This principle [the principle of contemporaneity] has been stressed by the field theorists from the beginning. It has been frequently misunderstood and interpreted to mean that field theorists are not interested in historical problems or in the effect of previous experiences. Nothing can be more mistaken. In fact, field theorists are most interested in development and historical problems and have certainly done their share to enlarge the temporal scope of the psychological experiment from that of the classic reaction time experiment, which last only a few seconds, to experimental situations, which contain a systematically created history throughout hors or weeks (1951, pp. 45–46).

Lewin misuses physical and mathematical concepts. Although Lewin has taken great pains to point out that he has merely adopted the method of field theory as expounded in physics and not its content, and that he uses those aspects of topology that are appropriate for psychological representations, nevertheless he has been severely scolded for an undiscriminating and incorrect use of physical and mathematical concepts (London, 1944). The objection appears to be that words like force, vector, valence, tension system, path, boundary, space, region and other terms used by Lewin are taken out of their context in physics, chemistry, and mathematics and are misapplied as psychological constructs. Valence in psychology, for example, does not mean the same thing as it means in chemistry. Moreover, as both Leeper (1943) and Cantril (1935) have indicated, Lewin does not always define his terms carefully, which can and has led to confusion. For if the borrowed term is not rigorously defined in its new setting, its old meaning is apt to persist.

Probably the most trenchant criticism that has been made of Lewin's field theory is that it pretends to offer a mathematical model of behavior from which specific predictions can be made, when in fact no such predictions can be formulated. In the eyes of many mathematical psychologists, Lewin's so-called mathematical model has no utility whatsoever in generating testable propositions. Whatever mathematical manipulations Lewin indulged in, he performed after the observations had been made. In other words, he made his equations fit the data, rather than deriving equations deductively from his theory that could then be tested by observational techniques. Discovering a way of expressing one's findings in mathematical terms is an interesting exercise in translating verbal statements into numerical or nonmetrical ones, but it does not have any relevance for the development of a useful theory. Lewin's field theory is not a mathematical one despite the topological language used in setting forth the theory.

On the positive side, psychologists have found much to commend in Lewin's work. There is, first of all, the tremendous amount of investigatory activity that has been stimulated by Lewin's ideas. He opened many new doors for the psychologist, doors that have led into regions of the personality and social behavior that were previously closed to the experimenter. The work on substitution, level-of-aspiration, the effects of interruption on memory, regression, conflict, and group dynamics was initiated by Lewin. The importance of many of these psychological phenomena had been established by the observations of psychoanalysts but it remained for Lewin to provide a congenial theoretical atmosphere and to devise methods by which the phenomena could be investigated. The problem of human motivation, in particular, which had proved to be an intransigent area for research except for the experimental studies of biological drives in lower animals has become a vital area of experimentation, thanks to Lewin.

Lewin possessed the valuable talent of being able to make explicit and concrete some of the more implicit and elusive assumptions regarding personality. He saw, for example, the necessity of spelling out in detail the basic assumptions made by psychoanalytic theorists regarding the substitution of one activity for another. When this was done in terms of an organization of segregated tension systems whose boundaries possessed the property of permeability the way was provided for experimental attack. In a similar manner, the rather involved question of psychological conflict that has always played a central role in psychoanalytic theory was worked over by Lewin and emerged as a clear statement of what conflict is and how it may be studied experimentally. This capacity for fairly rigorous and clarifying thinking about significant concepts was one of Lewin's strong points, and he illuminated many problems that had languished in the shade of incomplete conceptualization and fuzzy theorizing. He was convinced that the science of psychology, if it was to be of use to humans, would have to penetrate and explore experimentally the significant dimension of human conduct. Although Lewin could be abstruse in his theorizing, he rarely failed to get down ultimately to concrete cases and practical prescriptions for research.

Moreover, he clearly recognized that a theory that would encompass the vital aspects of human behavior would have to be multidimensional in scope. In other words, it would have to be a field theory, one that embraced a network of interacting variables rather than pairs of variables. It was this field emphasis that was needed in the 1920s and 1930s to counteract the influence and prestige of an oversimplified and naive stimulus–response psychology. While Gestalt psychology was assaulting and overwhelming the ramparts of structural psychology that stood for mental analysis into elements, Lewin's topological and vector psychology was vying with a rather barren form of behaviorism that reduced human conduct to simple stimulus-response connections. Furthermore, the type of field theory that Lewin espoused was thoroughly psychological in character, which contrasted sharply with the more physical and physiological orientation of behaviorism, and even with the physicalistic bias of Gestalt psychology. Lewin's theory helped to make a subjective frame of reference scientifically respectable at a time when objectivism was the dominant voice in psychology. The so-called inner determinants of conduct, such things as aspirations, values, and intentions, had been summarily cast out by an "objective" psychology in favor of conditioned reflexes, rote learning, and the automatic stamping in and out of stimulus-response bonds. Behaviorism had almost succeeded in reducing a human being to an automaton, a mechanical puppet who danced to the tune of external stimuli or jerked to the promptings of internal physiological drives, a robot bereft of spontaneity and creativity, a hollow person.

Lewin's theory was one of those that helped to revive the conception of the individual as a complex energy field, motivated by psychological forces, and behaving selectively and creatively. The hollow man was replenished with psychological needs, intentions, hopes, and aspirations. The robot was transformed into a living human being. The crass and dreary materialism of behaviorism was replaced by a more humanistic picture of people. While "objective" psychology tailored many of its empirical propositions to be tested on dogs, cats, and rats, Lewin's theory led to research on human behavior as expressed in more or less natural settings. Children at play, adolescents in group activities, workers in factories, people planning meals, these were some of the natural life situations in which hypotheses derived from Lewin's field theory were empirically tested. With such vital research being done under the persuasive aegis of field theory, it is not surprising that Lewin's viewpoint became widely popular. The heuristic power of the theory, irrespective of its formal adequacy or its pretensions of being a mathematical model, justifies the high esteem in which Lewin's field theory is held in contemporary psychology. "Lewin's basic notions . . . have a wealth of implicit meaning which has not been exhausted, and they are therefore still full of promise for further development" (Heider, 1959, p. 119). Heider's appraisal of field theory remains valid. Lewin's theory of the person in his psychological environment is still very much alive.

Lewin, K. *A dynamic theory of personality*. New York: McGraw-Hill, 1935a.

Lewin, K. *Principles of topological psychology*. New York: McGraw-Hill, 1936a.

Lewin, K. The conceptual representation and measurement of psychological forces. *Contr. psychol. Theor.*, 1938, **1** (4).

Lewin, K. *Resolving social conflicts; selected papers on group dynamics*. Gertrude W. Lewin (Ed.). New York: Harper & Row, 1948.

Lewin, K. *Field theory in social science; selected theoretical papers*. D. Cartwright (Ed.). New York: Harper & Row, 1951.

BIBLIOGRAPHY
PRIMARY SOURCES

Allport, F. H. *Theories of perception and the concept of structure*. New York: Wiley, 1955.

Allport, G. W. The genius of Kurt Lewin. *J. Pers.*, 1947, **16,** 1–10.

Atkinson, J. W. *An introduction to motivation*. New York: Wiley, 1964.

Atkinson, J. W. and Feather, N. T. (Eds.). *A theory of achievement motivation*. New York: Wiley, 1966.

Barker, R. G. (Ed.). *The stream of behavior*. New York: Appleton-Century-Crofts, 1963.

Barker, R. G. Explorations in ecological psychology. *Amer. Psychol.*, 1965, **20,** 1–14.

Barker, R. G. *Ecological psychology*. Stanford: Stanford Univ. Press, 1968.

Barker, R. G., Dembo, T. and Lewin, K. Frustration and regression: an experiment with young children. *Univ. Ia. Stud. Child Welf.*, 1941, **18,** (1).

Barker, R. G., and Schoggen, P. *Qualities of community life*. San Francisco: Jossey-Bass, 1973.

Barker, R. G., and Wright, H. F. *One boy's day*. New York: Harper, 1951.

Barker, R. G., and Wright, H. F. *Midwest and its children*. New York: Harper, 1955.

Bavelas, A. and Lewin, K. Training in democratic leadership. *J. Abnorm. Soc. Psychol.*, 1942, **37,** 115–119.

Brolyer, C. R. Review of Lewin's *Principles of topological psychology*. *Character and Pers.*, 1936–37, **5,** 257–258.

Brunswik, E. Organismic achievement and environmental probability. *Psychol. Rev.*, 1943, **50,** 255–272.

Burton, A. (Ed.). *Operational theories of personality*. New York: Brunner/Mazel, 1974.

Cantril, H. Review of Lewin's *A dynamic theory of personality*. *J. Abnorm. Soc. Psychol.*, 1935, **30,** 534–537.

Cantril, H. *The patterns of human concerns*. New Brunswick, N. J.: Rutgers Univ. Press, 1965.

Cartwright, D. Lewinian theory as a contemporary systematic framework. In S. Koch (Ed.). *Psychology: a study of a science*. Vol. 2. New York: McGraw-Hill, 1959, 7–91.

REFERENCES

De Rivera, J. *Field theory as human science: contributions of Lewin's Berlin group.* New York: Halsted Press, 1976.

Deutsch, M. Field theory in social psychology. In G. Lindzey and E. Aronson (Eds.). *Handbook of social psychology.* Vol. I. Cambridge: Addison-Wesley, 1968, 412–487.

Escalona, S. The influence of topological and vector psychology upon current research in child development: an addendum. In L. Carmichael (Ed.). *Manual of child psychology.* New York: Wiley, 1954, 971–983.

Festinger, L. *A theory of cognitive dissonance.* Stanford, Calif.: Stanford Univ. Press, 1957.

Festinger, L. *Conflict, decision and dissonance.* Stanford, Calif.: Stanford Univ. Press, 1964.

Garrett, H. E. Lewin's "topological" psychology: an evaluation. *Psychol. Rev.,* 1939, **46,** 517–524.

Gerard, H. B., and Miller, N. Group dynamics. In P. R. Farnsworth (Ed.). *Annual Review of Psychology.* Vol. 18. Palo Alto, Calif.: Annual Reviews, 1967.

Harary, F., Norman, R. Z., and Cartwright, D. *Structural models: an introduction to the theory of directed graphs.* New York: Wiley, 1965.

Heidbreder, E. Review of Lewin's *Principles of topological psychology. Psychol. Bull.,* 1937, **34,** 584–604.

Heider, F. *The psychology of interpersonal relations.* New York: Wiley, 1958.

Heider, F. On Lewin's methods and theory. *Psychol. Issues,* 1959, **1** (3), 123.

Heimstra, N. W., and McFarling, L. H. *Environmental psychology.* Monterey: Brooks/Cole, 1974.

Henle, Mary. An experimental investigation of dynamic and structural determinants of substitution. *Contr. Psychol. Theor.,* 1942, **2** (3).

Hilgard, E. R. *Theories of learning.* (2nd Ed.). New York: Appleton-Century-Crofts, 1956.

Householder, A. J. Review of Lewin's *Principles of topological psychology. J. Gen. Psychol.,* 1939, **54,** 249–259.

Ittelson, W. H., Proshansky, H. M., Rivlin, L. G., and Winkler, G. H. *An introduction to environmental psychology.* New York: Holt, Rinehart and Winston, 1974.

Karsten, A. Psychische Sättigung. *Psychol. Forsch.,* 1928, **10,** 142–154.

Katz, E. Some factors affecting resumption of interrupted activities by preschool children. *Inst. Child Welf. Monogr. Ser.,* 1938, no. 16.

Kounin, J. S. Experimental studies of rigidity. *Character and Pers.,* 1941, **9,** 251–282.

Leeper, R. W. Lewin's topological and vector psychology; a digest and critique. *Univ. Ore. Publ. Stud. Psychol.,* 1943, no. 1.

Lewin, K. *A dynamic theory of personality.* New York: McGraw-Hill, 1935a.

Lewin, K. Psycho-sociological problems of a minority group. *Character and Pers.,* 1935b, **3,** 175–187.

Lewin, K. *Principles of topological psychology.* New York: McGraw-Hill, 1936a.

Lewin, K. Some social-psychological differences between the United States and Germany. *Character and Pers.,* 1936b, **4,** 265–293.

Lewin, K. The conceptual representation and measurement of psychological forces. *Contr. Psychol. Theor.,* 1938, **1** (4).

Lewin, K. Forces behind food habits and methods of change. *Bull. Nat. Res. Counc.,* 1943, **108,** 35–65.

Lewin, K. Action research and minority problems. *J. Soc. Issues,* 1946, **2,** 34–46.

Lewin, K. Frontiers in group dynamics. II. Channels of group life; social planning and action research. *Hum. Relat.,* 1947, **1,** *143*–153. (Reprinted in K. Lewin. *Field theory in social science,* Chapter VIII.)

Lewin, K. *Resolving social conflicts; selected papers on group dynamics.* G. W. Lewin (Ed.). New York: Harper & Row, 1948.

Lewin, K. *Field theory in social science; selected theoretical papers.* D. Cartwright (Ed.). New York: Harper & Row, 1951.

Lewin, K. Behavior and development as function of the total situation. In L. Carmichael (Ed.). *Manual of child psychology.* New York: Wiley, 1954, 918–970. (Reprinted in K. Lewin. *Field theory in social science,* Chapter X.)

Lewin, K., Dembo, T., Festinger, L., and Sears, P. S. Level of aspiration. In J. McV. Hunt (Ed.). *Personality and the behavior disorders.* New York: Ronald Press, 1944, 333–378.

Lindzey, G. Review of Lewin's *Field theory in social science. J. Abnorm. Soc. Psychol.,* 1952, **47,** 132–133.

Lissner, K. Die Entspannung von Bedürfnissen durch Ersatzhandlungen. *Psychol. Forsch.,* 1933, **18,** 218–250.

London, I. D. Psychologists' misuse of the auxiliary concepts of physics and mathematics. *Psychol. Rev.,* 1944, **51,** 266–291.

Mahler, W. Ersatzhandlungen verschisdemen Realitätsgrades. *Psychol. Forsch.,* 1933, **18,** 27–89.

Mehrabian, A., and Russell, J. A. *An approach to environmental psychology.* Cambridge, Mass.: MIT Press, 1974.

Rokeach, M. *The open and closed mind.* New York: Basic Books, 1960.

Schein, E. H. and Bennis, W. G. *Personal and organizational change through group methods: the laboratory approach.* New York: Wiley, 1965.

Sliosberg, S. Zur Dynamik des Ersatzes in Spiel- und Ernstsituationen. *Psychol. Forsch.,* 1934, **19,** 122–181.

Smith, N. W. On the origin of conflict types. *Psychol. Rec.,* 1968, **18,** 229–232.

Spence, K. W. The nature of theory construction in contemporary psychology. *Psychol. Rev.,* 1944, **51,** 47–68.

Tolman, E. C. Kurt Lewin, 1890–1947. *Psychol. Rev.,* 1948, **55,** 1–4.

Zeigarnik, B. Über das Behalten von erledigten und unerledigten Handlungen. *Psychol. Forsch.,* 1927, **9,** 1–85.

ALLPORT'S PSYCHOLOGY OF THE INDIVIDUAL

12

Three decades ago most of the best minds in psychology were pushing relentlessly toward increasing rigor and quantification or else were earnestly seeking to track unconscious motives to their hidden lair. In the very midst of these trends Gordon Allport serenely pursued his own way, advocating the importance of the qualitative study of the individual case and emphasizing conscious motivation. This reluctance to swim with contemporary currents of thought has resulted at times in Allport's formulations seeming archaic or old-fashioned, but on other occasions he has appeared to be the champion of new and outrageously radical ideas. In spite of his iconoclasms, he represents, perhaps better than any other contemporary theorist, the synthesis of traditional psychological thought and personality theory.

His systematic position represents a distillation and elaboration of ideas that are in part derived from such highly reputable sources as Gestalt psychology, William Stern, William James, and William McDougall. From Gestalt theory and Stern has come a distrust of the customary analytic techniques of natural science and a deep interest in the uniqueness of the individual, as well as the congruence of his or her behavior. James is reflected not only in Allport's brilliant writing style, a wide-ranging, relatively humanistic orientation toward human behavior, and an interest in the self but also in certain doubts concerning the ultimate power of psychological methods to represent adequately and to understand completely the enigma of human behavior. Similar to McDougall's position is Allport's heavy emphasis upon the importance of motivational variables, his ready acceptance of the important role played by genetic or constitutional factors, and his prominent use of "ego" concepts. In addition to these focal influences it is clear from Allport's writings that he deeply respects the

Gordon W. Allport

message of the past and he consistently shows a full awareness of, and sympathy for, the classical problems that psychologists in and out of the laboratory have struggled with during the past century.

Allport, one of four sons of a physician, was born in Indiana in 1897 but grew up in Cleveland where he received his early education in public schools. He completed his undergraduate work at Harvard University at the same time that his older brother Floyd was a graduate student in psychology at the same university. After securing an A.B. in 1919 with a major in economics and philosophy, Allport spent a year at Robert College in Istanbul teaching sociology and English. He then returned to Harvard and completed the requirements for the Ph.D. in psychology in 1922. During the next two years he studied in Berlin, Hamburg, and Cambridge, England. This extensive experience in foreign academic settings must have played some part in developing the stout interest in international affairs that has been so evident in Allport's activities during the past thirty years. It also led to Allport serving for a decade or more as one of the chief interpreters of German psychology in America. Returning from Europe he accepted an appointment as instructor in the Department of Social Ethics at Harvard University. Again there seems to be a continuity between this first American teaching appointment and Allport's persistent concern with problems imbued with social and ethical implications. At the end of two years he accepted an appointment as assistant professor of psychology at Dartmouth College but was invited to return to Harvard in 1930 where he remained until his death October 9, 1967, one month before his seventieth birthday. The year prior to his death he was appointed the first Richard Cabot Professor of Social Ethics. Allport was one of the central figures in the interdisciplinary movement that led to the formation of the Department of Social Relations at Harvard University, in an attempt to effect a partial integration of psychology, sociology, and anthropology. (For a brief autobiography see Allport, 1967.)

Against the background of these many years of college teaching it should come as no surprise that in much of his professional writing Allport displays a deliberate didactic intent. In contrast to most technical writers, whose primary goal appears to be the construction of irreproachable statements that defy the efforts of the critic to find a tooth-hold, Allport seems much more interested in expressing issues in a salient, provocative fashion. This sometimes leads to overstatement or else to focusing upon a particular issue to the relative exclusion of other pertinent questions. Thus, it might be said that Allport is one of the most hotly criticized of psychological theorists, but in

the same breath it should be mentioned that questions Allport
has raised have usually become matters of general concern
to psychologists.

During his career Allport received virtually every professional
honor that psychologists have to offer. He was elected president of
the American Psychological Association, president of the Eastern
Psychological Association, and president of the Society for the
Psychological Study of Social Issues. In 1963 he was awarded the gold
medal of the American Psychological Foundation, and in 1964 he received the award of the American Psychological Association for distinguished scientific contributions. The breadth and diversity of his
scholarly work are clearly evident in the dozen books and the innumerable monographs, articles, forewords, and reviews he wrote,
often in collaboration with other psychologists. He was also the co-
author of two widely used tests, *The A-S reaction study* and *A study of
values*. (Many of these publications are listed in the bibliography. The
complete list of his writings will be found in *The person in
psychology,* 1968.)

How can we characterize Allport's theoretical convictions? To
begin with, his writings reveal an unceasing attempt to do justice to
the complexity and uniqueness of individual human behavior. In
spite of the dazzling complexity of the individual, the main trends in a
person's nature display an underlying congruence or unity. Furthermore, for the normal individual at least, conscious determinants of
behavior are of overwhelming importance. The congruence of behavior and the importance of conscious motives lead Allport naturally
to an emphasis upon those phenomena often represented under the
terms *self* and *ego*. Consistent with this emphasis upon rational factors
is Allport's conviction that the individual is more a creature of the
present than the past. His concept of "functional autonomy," to be
discussed later, represents a deliberate attempt to free the theorist or
investigator from unnecessary preoccupation with the history of the
organism. In broad terms, his is a view of humans in which positive,
conscious elements of motivation are emphasized, and behavior is
seen as internally consistent and determined by contemporary factors.

For Allport there is a discontinuity between normal and abnormal,
child and adult, animal and human. Theories such as psychoanalysis
may be highly effective as representations of disordered or abnormal
behavior; however, they are of little utility in any attempt to account
for normal behavior. In similar vein, theories that provide a perfectly
adequate conceptualization of the infant or young child are not adequate as representations of adult behavior. Allport consistently opposed extensive borrowing from the natural sciences. His belief is

that methods of study and theoretical models that have proved useful in the physical sciences may only be misleading in the study of complex human behavior. This conviction is most clearly revealed in a discussion (Allport, 1947) of the various kinds of models currently popular in psychological theorizing. He considers the mechanical model, the animal model, and the model of the child, and concludes that none of these provides an adequate base from which to construct a useful theory of human behavior. Consistent with this distrust of borrowing is his belief that premature emphasis upon the importance of operationism, a detailed concern for specifying the measurement operations implied by each empirical concept, can serve to impede progress in psychology. Positivism that leads to the conception of an empty organism he finds "merely absurd." He is equally contemptuous of "intemperate empiricism" and has been severely critical of factor analytic studies of personality for this reason.

The application of psychological method and findings in an "action setting," where an effort is made to bring about the amelioration of some undesirable social condition, represents a deep and enduring interest for Allport. For many years he inveighed against encapsulating psychology within the walls of the laboratory, and his work in the fields of prejudice and international relations are among the more fruitful examples of the application of psychology to social issues. It is interesting to note that with many other theorists who have emphasized strongly the uniqueness and individuality of human behavior there is an underlying pessimism on Allport's part concerning the ultimate power of psychological method and theory to unravel the mystery of human behavior. The enigma posed by the complex individual is too great to be completely understood through the earthbound methods and conceptions of the psychologist. Thus, although Allport accepts the importance and inevitability of an experimental approach to psychological problems, he maintains reservations concerning the eventual success of this effort.

As we have indicated, a basic consistency of viewpoint is to be found in Allport's writing. However, he himself does not claim to be a systematist. He asserts that his work is oriented always toward empirical *problems* rather than toward the achievement of theoretical or methodological unity. He argues for an open personality theory rather than a closed or partially closed one. Allport considers himself to be a systematic pluralist working toward a systematic eclecticism. "A pluralist in psychology is a thinker who will not exclude any attribute of human nature that seems important in its own right" (1964, p. 75). In 1966, Allport proposed an epistemological position for research in personality that he labelled "heuristic realism." This position "accepts the common-sense assumption that persons are real beings, that each has a real neuropsychic organization, and that our job is to comprehend this organization as well as we can" (1966, p. 8). To him personality is a riddle to be solved in the most adequate way possible with the tools available in the middle of the twentieth century; so, too, the other problems he has set himself: rumor, radio, prejudice, the psychology of religion, the nature of attitudes, and other topics of human interest. To all these problem areas he applies concepts in an eclectic and pluralistic manner, striving for what to him seems the most adequate account that can be achieved in our present state of knowledge. Thus, questions of the formal adequacy of his theory are of no great significance to him.

THE STRUCTURE AND DYNAMICS OF PERSONALITY

In the preceding chapters we have usually considered separately the structure of personality and the dynamics of personality. However, in the case of Allport's theory, this distinction seems largely inapplicable. Personality structure is primarily represented in terms of traits, and, at the same time, behavior is motivated or driven by traits. Thus, structure and dynamics are, for the most part, one and the same.

It should also be noted that Allport published two major formulations of his viewpoint—the first in *Personality: A psychological interpretation* (1937); the second in *Pattern and growth in personality* (1961). Between 1937 and 1961, Allport made a number of conceptual and terminological changes in his theory. The present account is based upon his 1961 volume whenever that differs from the 1937 book and upon articles he published subsequent to 1961 that further modified or elaborated his theory.

Gordon Allport's eclecticism is nowhere better reflected than in the rich variety of concepts he was willing to accept as playing some useful role in the description of human behavior. He considered concepts as segmental as specific reflexes and as broad as cardinal traits or the proprium (self) to possess some importance in understanding behavior, and he saw the processes referred to by these concepts as operating within the organism in a hierarchical fashion so that the more general usually takes precedence over the more specific. In the most detailed statements of his theory, Allport (1937, 1961) suggested that each of the following concepts possesses some utility: conditioned reflex, habit, trait, self, and personality.

Although all of the above concepts are acknowledged and conceded a certain importance, the major emphasis of the theory is upon traits, with attitudes and intentions given an almost equivalent status. Indeed, Allport's theory is often referred to as a trait psychology.

Within this theory, traits occupy the position of the major motivational construct. What the need is to Murray, the instinct to Freud, the sentiment to McDougall, the trait is to Allport. Before proceeding to a more detailed consideration of the trait concept, let us examine Allport's definition of personality.

For Allport definitions are not matters to be treated lightly. Before arriving at his own definition of *personality* he listed and discussed half a hundred proposals by various authorities in the field (1937). He classified these in terms of whether they refer to: (1) etymology or early history of the term; (2) theological meanings; (3) philosophical meanings; (4) juristic meanings; (5) sociological meanings; (6) external appearance; (7) psychological meanings. After this detailed summary and critique, Allport attempted to combine the best elements of the previous definitions while avoiding their major shortcomings. First, he suggested that one might briefly define personality as "what a man really is." However, he agreed that this is too abbreviated to be very helpful and proceeded to the better known definition:

Personality, Character, and Temperament

Personality is the dynamic organization within the individual of those psychophysical systems that determine his unique adjustments to his environment (1937, p. 48).

Certain aspects of this definition merit special emphasis. The phrase "dynamic organization" emphasizes the fact that personality is constantly developing and changing, although at the same time there is an organization or system that binds together and relates the various components of personality. The term "psychophysical" reminds the reader that personality is "neither exclusively mental or exclusively neural. The organization entails the operation of both body and mind, inextricably fused into a personal unity" (1937, p. 48). The word "determine" makes clear that personality is made up of determining tendencies that play an active role in the individual's behavior. "Personality *is* something and *does* something. . . . It is what lies *behind* specific acts and *within* the individual" (1937, p. 48).

What has been said thus far makes it clear that for Allport personality is not merely a construct of the observer, nor is it something that exists only when there is another person to react to it. Far from this, personality has a real existence involving neural or physiological concomitants. The care and detail with which Allport developed his definition of personality are reflected in the frequency with which other theorists and investigators have borrowed from it.

Although the terms personality and *character* have often been used interchangeably, Allport shows that traditionally the word character has implied some code of behavior in terms of which individuals or their acts are appraised. Thus, in describing an individual's character the word "good" or "bad" is often employed. Allport suggests that character is an ethical concept and states that "we prefer to define character as personality evaluated, and personality as character devaluated" (1961, p. 32).

Temperament and personality have also frequently been confused. However, here again there is a clear basis for distinguishing between them in terms of common usage. Temperament ordinarily refers to those dispositions that are closely linked to biological or physiological determinants and that consequently show relatively little modification with development. The role of heredity is naturally somewhat greater here than in the case of some other aspects of personality. Temperament is the raw material along with intelligence and physique out of which personality is fashioned.

Given these important distinctions, it is now possible to consider those concepts that are more uniquely a part of Allport's theory.

Trait In his 1937 statement, Allport differentiated between individual and common traits but included both of them under a single definition. This resulted in some confusion and ambiguity, so in 1961 Allport made some terminological alterations and provided separate definitions for what he had formerly called individual and common traits. The term trait was reserved for common traits, and a new term *personal disposition* was introduced to take the place of individual trait. Allport also refers to personal dispositions as *morphogenic* traits.

A trait is defined as a

neuropsychic structure having the capacity to render many stimuli functionally equivalent, and to initiate and guide equivalent (meaningfully consistent) forms of adaptive and expressive behavior (1961, p. 347).

A personal disposition or morphogenic trait is defined as a

generalized neuropsychic structure (peculiar to the individual) with the capacity to render many stimuli functionally equivalent, and to initiate and guide consistent (equivalent) forms of adaptive and stylistic behavior (1961, p. 373).

It will be observed that the only real difference between these two definitions is that traits, unlike personal dispositions, are not designated as being peculiar to the individual. The implication is that a trait may be shared by a number of individuals. Nevertheless, a trait is just as much within an individual as a disposition is. Both are neuropsychic structures, both have the capacity to render many stimuli functionally equivalent, and both guide consistent forms of behavior.

One may wonder then why it is necessary to have two definitions. The answer lies in the implications for empirical research. With the concept of common traits, one may make what Allport calls comparative studies of the same trait as expressed in different individuals or groups of individuals. With the concept of personal dispositions, the investigator may study a person and determine what Allport calls that person's "unique patterned individuality." One approach falls within the tradition of psychometrically oriented differential psychology, the other within the tradition of clinical psychology. In Allport's own research and that of his students both approaches have been employed.

Although traits and dispositions really exist in the person they cannot be observed directly but have to be inferred from behavior. Allport writes:

A specific act is always the product of many determinants, not only of lasting sets, but of momentary pressures in the person and in the situation. It is only the repeated occurrence of acts having the same significance (equivalence of response) following upon a definable range of stimuli having the same personal significance (equivalence of stimuli) that makes necessary the inference of traits and personal dispositions. These tendencies are not at all times active, but are persistent even when latent, and have relatively low thresholds of arousal (1961, p. 374).

It is necessary not only to indicate what trait and disposition refer to but also to distinguish them from related concepts. *Habits* are also determining tendencies but traits or dispositions are more general both in the situations appropriate to them and in the responses to which they lead. Actually, the trait, to a considerable extent, represents the outcome of combining or integrating two or more habits. Somewhat more difficult is the distinction between trait or disposition and *attitude*. An attitude is also a predisposition; it too may be unique; it may initiate or guide behavior; and it is the product of genetic factors and learning. Nevertheless, there remain certain distinctions between the concepts. First, the attitude is linked to a specific object or class of objects while the trait or disposition is not. Thus, the generality of the trait is almost always greater than that of the attitude. In fact, as the number of objects increases to which the attitude refers, it comes to resemble a trait or disposition more and more. The attitude may vary in generality from highly specific to the relatively general, while the trait or disposition must always be general. Second, the attitude usually implies evaluation (acceptance or rejection) of the object toward which it is directed while the trait does not. In summarizing this, Allport suggests:

> Both *attitude* and *trait* are indispensable concepts in psychology. Between them they cover the principal types of disposition with which the psychology of personality deals. In passing, however, we should point out that since *attitude* has to do with people's orientations to definite facets of the environment (including people, culture, and society), it is the favored concept in *social psychology*. In the field of personality, however, we are interested in the structure of the person, and hence *trait* becomes the favored concept (1961, p. 348).

Finally, Allport distinguishes between traits (or personal dispositions) and *types* in terms of the extent to which they are tailored to the individual. A person can be said to possess a trait but not a type. Types are idealized constructions of the observer, and the individual can be fitted to them, but only at the loss of his or her distinctive identity. The personal disposition can represent the uniqueness of the person whereas the type must conceal it. Thus, for Allport, types represent artificial distinctions that bear no close resemblance to reality, and traits are true reflections of what actually exists. Allport acknowledges, however, that the postulation of types may stimulate research although the end of such research is the specification of complex traits.

CARDINAL, CENTRAL, AND SECONDARY DISPOSITIONS. As we have indicated, personal dispositions represent generalized predispositions to behavior. There remains the question of whether all dispositions possess roughly the same degree of generality, and if not, how to distinguish between the varying degrees. Allport suggests a distinction between cardinal, central, and secondary personal dispositions. A *cardinal disposition* is so general that almost every act of a person who possesses one seems traceable to its influence. This variety of disposition is relatively unusual and not to be observed in many people. More typical are the *central dispositions,* which represent tendencies highly characteristic of the individual, are often called into play, and are very easy to infer. Allport suggests that the number of central dispositions by which a personality can be fairly accurately known is surprisingly few—perhaps five to ten. The *secondary disposition* is more limited in its occurrence, less crucial to a description of the personality, and more focalized in the responses it leads to, as well as the stimuli to which it is appropriate.

Allport discusses other crucial questions regarding traits and dispositions. Do they serve to guide or direct behavior only, or do they also have a role in initiating or instigating behavior? There is no simple answer to this question. Some traits are clearly more impelling, have a more crucial motivational role, than others. Thus, among traits there is considerable variation in the extent to which they exert driving influences upon the individual. Further, we may reason that in one sense there is always a previous stimulation that is related to the activation of the trait, for example, an external stimulus or an internal state of some sort must always precede the operation of the trait. However, it is clear that most traits are not pallid reflectors of external stimuli. In fact, the individual actively seeks stimuli that make appropriate the operation of the trait. The person with a marked disposition toward sociability does not wait for a suitable situation in which to express this trait; rather he or she creates situations in which they can interact with people.

A further consideration is the *independence of traits* (dispositions). To what extent do they exist as systems of behavior that operate without regard for other systems? Is the operation of a particular trait always conditioned by and relative to other traits and their state? Allport argues that the trait is identifiable not by its rigid independence but rather by its focal quality. Thus, it tends to have a center around which its influence operates, but the behavior it leads to is clearly influenced simultaneously by other traits. There is no sharp boundary that delimits one trait from another. This intertwining of the various traits also accounts in part for the fact that it is not possible to devise completely satisfactory methods for classifying traits.

It is clear that the inferences involved in identifying a trait imply *consistency*. Thus, by definition, a disposition is known only by virtue of certain regularities or consistencies in the manner in which an individual behaves. Allport is quick to point out that his theory of traits does not necessitate a complete consistency. The mere fact that there are multiple, overlapping traits simultaneously active suggests that apparent inconsistencies in the organism's behavior may be expected relatively frequently. Further, the fact that dispositions are uniquely and individually organized implies that they may include elements that would appear inconsistent when viewed from a normative or external viewpoint. Thus, we may observe apparent inconsistency in behavior that actually reflects a uniquely organized internal consistency. It is less the observance of exact correspondence or consistency in behavior that is implied by Allport's theory than it is the existence of a subtle congruence that unites, frequently in a fashion difficult to detect, the various behavioral manifestations of the individual. It is not implied that every (or any) personality is perfectly integrated.

Dissociation and repression may exist in every life. But there is ordinarily more consistency than the customary methods of psychological investigation are equipped to discover.

An interesting and useful outgrowth of Allport's interest in traits is his painstaking categorization of roughly eighteen thousand terms taken from an unabridged dictionary. In collaboration with Odbert (1936) these terms were classified primarily in terms of whether they represented authentic traits of personality, present activities (temporary states), or evaluative terms.

Intentions   More important than all of the searching into the past or the history of the organism is the simple question of what the individual intends or is striving for in the future. The hopes, wishes, ambitions, aspirations, plans of the person are all represented under this general heading of intention, and here one of the characteristic differences between Allport and most other contemporary personality theorists is manifested. It is the contention of this theory that what the individual is trying to do (and by and large it is accepted that the person can tell us what he or she is trying to do) is the most important key to how the person will behave in the present. Whereas other theorists turn to the past for the key that will unlock the riddle of present behavior, Allport turns to the intended future. In this respect, he shows a strong similarity to certain views of Alfred Adler and Carl Jung, although there is no reason to believe that there was any direct influence from these sources.

The Proprium   Although Allport has been called an "ego" or even a "self" psychologist, this characterization is only partially accurate. In 1943 (*The ego in contemporary psychology*) and again in 1955 (*Becoming: basic considerations for a psychology of personality*) he reviewed the many meanings of ego and of self in psychological writings. In his earlier basic text (1937) he largely avoided the problems raised by these concepts; but finally came to ask directly the crucial question, "Is the concept of self necessary?" His answer is guarded. Anxious to avoid the confusion and special connotations of these terms, he proposes that all of the self- or ego-functions that have been described be called propriate functions of the personality. These (including bodily sense, self-identity, self-esteem, self-extension, sense of selfhood, rational thinking, self-image, propriate striving, cognitive style, and the function of knowing) are all true and vital portions of personality. They have in common a phenomenal warmth and a "sense of importance." Together they might be said to comprise "the proprium." It is in this region of personality that we find the root of the consistency that

marks attitudes, intentions, and evaluations. The proprium is not innate, but develops in time.

Allport identifies seven aspects in the development of the proprium or selfhood (1961, Chapter 6). During the first three years,
three of these aspects make their appearance: a sense of bodily self, a
sense of continuing self-identity, and self-esteem or pride. Between
the ages of four and six, two other aspects appear: the extension of
self and a self-image. Sometime between six and twelve, the child develops the self-awareness that it can cope with its problems by means
of reason and thought. During adolescence, intentions, long-range
purposes, and distant goals emerge. These are called *propriate strivings*.
These seven aspects of selfhood constitute the proprium.

By approaching the riddle of the self in this manner, Allport hopes
to avoid the question-begging position of many theorists to whom
the self or ego is like a homunculus, a "man within the breast" who
does the organizing, pulls the strings, and administers the personality
system. He admits the importance of all psychological functions that
have been ascribed to self and ego, but wishes at all costs to avoid the
factotum or "agent" type of theory. To him, self and ego may be
used adjectivally to indicate the propriate functions within the total
sphere of personality (many functions are not propriate but merely
"opportunistic") but he believes neither term needs to be used as a
substantive. There is no ego or self that acts as an entity distinct from
the remainder of personality.

Functional Autonomy

In approaching the complex and controversial problem of human
motivation, Allport specifies what he feels are the requirements for an
adequate theory. First, such a theory will acknowledge the *contemporaneity* of human motives. Whatever it is that moves us to think or act
moves us now. Second, it will be a pluralistic theory, allowing for
motives of many types. Allport is definitely not a reductionist who
seeks to reduce all motives to a few organic drives. Third, it will in-
vest cognitive processes such as planning and intention, with dynamic force. And finally the theory will allow for the concrete uniqueness of motives within an individual (1961, Chapter 10).

Such a theory, Allport believes, is contained in the concept of *functional autonomy*. This is easily the best known and most controversial
of the concepts introduced by Allport. In many respects it stands at
the center of his system, for a number of the distinctive features of his
theory derive quite naturally from this position. The principle simply
states that a given activity or form of behavior may become an end or
goal in itself, in spite of the fact that it was originally engaged in for
some other reason. Any behavior, complex or simple, although it

may originally have derived from organic or segmental tensions, may be capable of sustaining itself indefinitely in the absence of any biological reinforcement. The formal statement of the concept is as follows:

Functional autonomy regards adult motives as varied, and as self-sustaining contemporary systems, growing out of antecedent systems, but functionally independent of them (1961, p. 227).

The reader should carefully distinguish the principle of functional autonomy from the common notion that a given behavior may be continued for a motive different from the one originally giving rise to the behavior; for example, the hunter initially hunts in order to eat, but when there is ample food the hunter hunts to express inborn aggression. This formulation still refers the behavior back to a more primitive or pre-existing motive, which is just what Allport wishes to avoid. Functional antonomy implies that the hunter would continue to hunt even in the absence of all instrumental significance, that is, even if there were no aggression or other more basic needs served by this act. A hunter may simply "like" hunting.

In presenting this view, Allport (1937, 1961) indicates that it echoes certain earlier formulations; for example, Woodworth's (1918) well-known dictum that mechanisms may be transformed into drives, Stern's (1935) assertion that phenomotives may become genomotives, and Tolman's (1935) suggestion that "means-objects" may "set up in their own right." One might suggest that such formulations as Harlow's (1950) "manipulation drive," and "partial irreversibility" as proposed by Solomon and Wynne (1954), are intended to account for phenomena quite similar to those that played an important role in leading to the concept of functional autonomy.

In justification of the concept, Allport points to observations from a number of areas, all of which suggest a tendency on the part of an organism to persist in a particular response even though the original reason for engaging in the response is no longer present. He points to the circularity of child behavior and of neurotic behavior among adults, the repetitive elements in the Zeigarnik effect (the observation that incompleted tasks tend to be remembered better than completed tasks), the frequently observed temporal regularities or rhythms in behavior of both animals and humans, the motivating power of acquired interests and values that appear to have no anchoring in fundamental motives. There is also some evidence drawn from comparative psychology. A study by Olson (1929) revealed that when collodion was placed on the ears of rats they scratched continuously in an attempt to remove the foreign substance. Moreover, long after the collodion was removed and when there was no longer any evidence of skin irritation, they continued to scratch and with no apparent reduction in rate. Thus, the scratch began as a functional attempt to cope with a physical state but with sufficient repetition it appeared to become an integral part of the organism's behavior in spite of the fact that it no longer served a biological function. Some of the important research conducted by Selye (1952) and his collaborators suggests similarly that adaptive responses may set up in their own right even to the detriment of the organism. Similar to this are studies by Anderson (1941a, 1941b, 1941c, 1941d) of what he called "externalization of drive." In these studies rats were taught to navigate runways at high rates of speed under strong hunger drive and rewarded with food at the end of the runway. After a very large number of reinforced trials, the rats did not appear to show ordinary extinction of the response when placed in the same situation under low drive or in a satiated state; that is, even though they were no longer hungry they continued to travel through the runways at the same rapid rate. Thus, we again have the spectacle of an organism performing an act for clear biological reasons, and yet when these reasons are removed the behavior continues without apparent interruption. Anderson would reason that this phenomenon results from the fact that aspects of the stimulus situation have been conditioned to provide secondary reward; Allport would say, according to the principle of functional autonomy, that the behavior is continued simply because it had been repeated so often that it became an end or motive in itself, a part of the rat's "style of life."

Following Allport's original statement of this principle (1937), he was vigorously attacked by Bertocci (1940) who raised several serious questions. First of all, asked Bertocci, is it in fact true that any form of behavior if repeated often enough will become autonomous? Are there no limits or conditions to be placed on this generalization? Second, if any form of behavior is potentially capable of becoming an enduring motive, what is to prevent the individual from developing a kind of psychological anarchy in which conflicting and antithetical motives are built into the organism and tear the individual asunder?

Such questions as these led Allport to clarify and expand his position. He recognized two levels of functional autonomy; one he called *perseverative,* the other *propriate.* Perseverative functional autonomy includes addictions, circular mechanisms, repetitive acts, and routines. Their perseveration is accounted for in such terms as delayed extinction, self-maintaining circuits in the nervous system, partial reinforcement, and the coexistence of multiple determinants. Propriate functional autonomy refers to acquired interests, values, sentiments, intentions, master motives, personal dispositions, self-image, and life style. Allport admits it is not easy to explain how this type of functional autonomy comes about.

First, he suggests that "the self-structure demands it." For example

A young man intends to become a physician, a man of the world, a politician, or a hermit. None of these ambitions is innate. They are all acquired interests. We contend they do not exist *now* because of remote reinforcements. Rather, they exist because a self-image, gradually formed, demands this particular motivational focus (1961, p. 252).

He then asks whether it is the "self" that explains propriate functional autonomy, and says no because it implies that some "little man within the breast" shapes one's motives. Allport takes a strong stand against explanations in terms of a separate self because it smacks too much of the idea of a "soul" that guides a person's destiny.

What then is responsible for propriate motives and for their organization into a coherent and consistent pattern? Allport's answer is that it is the essential nature of humans for motives to change and grow in the course of life and for them to become unified. Readers may find in this answer an echo of Jung's *unity archetype*.

The fact that the proprium is a developmental phenomenon, derived from primitive states and past experience, does seem to imply a direct link with the past, in spite of functional autonomy. As the forms of behavior that will become autonomous are determined by an organization that owes much to the past of the organism, it appears that the past retains a central role. In the end, however, the most important issue here seems to be whether or not mature, adult motivations retain a functional tie to their origins in infancy or biology. Whatever ambiguity may exist concerning the exact status of the concept of functional autonomy, it is clear that Allport contends strongly that for most adult motives there is no longer any functional relation to the historical roots of the motive.

A further question that is often asked of this principle is whether all adult motives are functionally autonomous. Allport says not. There are drives such as hunger, breathing, and elimination, reflex actions, constitutional equipment such as bodily strength, habits that are not motivational at all but are merely instrumental acts, infantilisms and fixations, some neuroses and psychoses, and sublimations. Moreover, many adult activities need continuing primary reinforcement for their perseveration. However, the extent to which an individual's motivations are autonomous is a measure of the maturity of the individual.

Clearly the most important question that can be asked of any concept is what it will do for the person who utilizes it. The consequences of functional autonomy are clear, and it is in terms of these that psychologists should decide whether they wish to embrace the concept or not. Most important is the fact that *it permits a relative divorce from the past of the organism.* If the ongoing motives do not depend completely upon more basic or primary motives for their continuance, then the investigator may legitimately turn away from the past of the individual and focus upon the present and the future. The history of the individual becomes a matter of relative indifference if he or she is at present driven by desires and intentions independent of what motivated the individual at earlier periods. A further significant consequence of this principle is that it makes more or less inevitable the great, dazzling, unique *individuality* that is so much emphasized in Allport's theory. If potentially any form of instrumental behavior can become an end in itself, we know that there is sufficient heterogencity of behavior and environmental demand to lead to a bewildering complexity and uniqueness in motives. Insofar as the individual's adult motivational structure is freed from whatever communality may have existed at birth, we can expect that the motives of different individuals will show little similarity.

The Unity of Personality

Having decomposed psychological humans into a set of traits and dispositions, of attitudes and habits, of values, intentions, and motives, one is faced with the task of putting Humpty-Dumpty together again. Allport, while acknowledging that this is a very difficult task, seeks a solution with his usual doggedness and perspicacity. There are, in fact, a number of unifying concepts. In early infancy there is a high degree of dynamical unity that gradually gives way to differentiation. Differentiation is then offset by the learned process of integration. Allport calls this "the dialectic of dividing and uniting." Homeostatic mechanisms with which the organism is furnished preserve unity, or at least equilibrium, of a fundamental though static nongrowth kind. The mobilization of energies for carrying out an integrated course of conduct (the principle of convergence) is a form of unification although it is usually transient and focalized. Cardinal dispositions by definition confer unity on the personality, as does the recognition that traits and dispositions are interdependent. "They interlace like a tapestry." While acknowledging the contribution that each of these principles makes to the unification of personality, Allport ascribes the chief unifying role to the propriate functions.

THE
DEVELOPMENT
OF PERSONALITY

Thus far we have seen what personality is composed of and have examined in broad terms the dispositions that set behavior in action. In this section we are concerned with the way in which these structures emerge and the differences in the manner in which the individual is represented at various developmental stages. It is already clear from our discussion of functional autonomy that this theory proposes important changes between infancy and adulthood.

The Infant

Let us begin with the individual at birth. Where Allport is a radical when dealing with adult behavior, he is an arch-conservative when discussing infant behavior. In fact, until the child has lived the first two or three years of its life, Allport's formulations have little in the way of surprise value. It is only with the development of self-identity that things begin to assume a new and unexpected appearance. This is getting ahead of our story, however; let us return to the neonate as seen by this theory.

Allport considers the newborn infant almost altogether a creature of heredity, primitive drive, and reflex existence. It has not yet developed those distinctive attributes that will appear later as a result of transactions with the environment. Significantly, Allport does not consider the neonate to possess a personality. At birth the infant is innately endowed with certain physique and temperament potentialities, although fulfillment of these must wait upon growth and maturation. In addition, it is able to respond with some highly specific reflexes, such as sucking and swallowing, to rather clearly delimited kinds of stimulation. Finally, it displays mass action or gross undifferentiated responses in which most or all of the individual's muscular apparatus seems to be involved.

Given this equipment, how is the child set into action or motivated? Initially, Allport assumes that there exists a general stream of activity that is the original source of motivated behavior. At this point in development, the child is largely a creature of segmental tensions and pleasure-pain feelings. A biological model of behavior or a theory that rests heavily upon the importance of reward, the law of effect, or the pleasure principle, is perfectly acceptable as a guide for the earliest years of life. Thus, motivated by the need to minimize pain and to maximize pleasure and with these conditions determined largely by the reduction of visceral, segmental tensions, the child proceeds to develop.

In spite of the fact that the individual at birth lacks the distinctive qualities that later will go to make up its personality, this state is altered very early and in a gradual manner. Even in the first year of life, Allport considers that the infant begins to show distinctive qualities, for example, differences in motility and emotional expression, that tend to persist and merge into the more mature modes of adjustment learned later. Thus, some of the infant's behavior is recognizable as a forerunner of subsequent patterns of personality. Allport concludes that at least by the second half of the first year the infant is definitely beginning to show distinctive qualities that presumably represent enduring personality attributes. Nonetheless, he maintains that "In a sense the first year is the least important year for personality assuming that serious injuries to health do not occur" (1961, p. 78).

The process of development takes place along multiple lines. A wide variety of mechanisms or principles is considered appropriate by Allport to describe the changes that take place between infancy and adulthood. He discusses specifically differentiation, integration, maturation, imitation, learning, functional autonomy, and extension of self. He even accepts the explanatory role of psychoanalytic mechanisms and trauma although these processes do not have a central theoretical role in what he calls *normal* personality.

Transformation of the Infant

In respect to learning theory, Allport is completely eclectic. He holds that all the myriad observations that investigators have made, all the conclusions they have reached, and all the resulting theories of learning are probably true in a sense and to a degree. Thus, conditioning, reinforcement theory, and habit hierarchy are valid principles, especially when applied to animal, infant, and opportunistic learning. They are inadequate to account for propriate learning, which requires such principles as identification, closure, cognitive insight, self-image, and subsidiation to active ego-systems. Allport himself has made no systematic contribution to the theory of learning. Rather he has proposed functional autonomy as a basic fact in human motivation that must eventually be accounted for in terms of principles of learning that have not yet been adequately coordinated into a sufficiently broad theoretical scheme. Perhaps his chief contribution to the subject is his sharp criticism of theories of learning (for example, Allport, 1946) that claim more universal validity than he will concede.

Thus, we have an organism that at birth is a creature of biology, transformed into an individual who operates in terms of a growing ego, a widening trait structure, and a kernel of future goals and aspirations. Crucial to this transformation is, of course, the role played by functional autonomy. This principle makes clear that what is initially a mere means to a biological goal may become an autonomous motive that directs behavior with all the power of an innately endowed drive. In large part because of this discontinuity between the early and the later motivational structure of the individual, we have essentially two theories of personality. The one, a biological or tension-reduction model, is adequate at birth and becomes gradually less adequate until, with growing awareness of the self, the individual develops motives that bear no close relation to those that had previously motivated behavior. At this point a reorientation is necessary if we are to represent the individual adequately.

The Adult   We now have, in the mature individual, a person whose major determinants of behavior are a set of organized and congruent traits. These traits have arisen in a variety of means from the sparse motivational equipment that characterized the newborn infant. The exact path of development for these tendencies is of no special interest because they are no longer, according to the principle of functional autonomy, deriving their motive power from primitive sources, whatever they may have been. As Allport puts it: "What drives behavior, drives now," and we need not know the history of the drive to understand its operation. To a considerable extent the functioning of these traits is conscious and rational. Normal individuals know, as a rule, what they are doing and why they do it. Their behavior fits into a congruent pattern and at the core of this pattern lie the functions Allport terms propriate. A full understanding of the adult cannot be secured without a picture of his or her goals and aspirations. Their most important motives are not echoes of the past but rather beckonings from the future. In most cases, we will know more about what a person will do if we know their conscious plans than if we know their repressed memories.

Allport grants that the picture we have just outlined is somewhat idealized. Not all adults achieve full maturity. There are grown individuals whose motivations still smack of the nursery. Not all adults seem to guide their behavior in terms of clear, rational principles. However, the extent to which they avoid unconscious motivations and the degree to which their traits are independent of childish origins represents a measure of their normality and maturity. It is only in the seriously disturbed individual that we find adults acting without knowing why they act, whose behavior is more closely linked to events that took place in childhood than to events taking place in the here and now or in the future.

In contrast to most personality theorists, the bulk of whose interest is focused on the negative side of the adjustment register, Allport considers at some length the qualities that make for more than an "adequate" or "normal" adjustment (1961, Chapter 12). The *mature personality* must possess first of all an *extension of the self*. That is, his or her life must not be tied narrowly to a set of activities that are closely linked to their own immediate needs and duties. The person should be able to participate in and enjoy a wide variety of different activities. Satisfactions and frustrations should be many and diverse, rather than few and stereotyped. An important part of this extension of the self involves projection into the future—planning, hoping. For maturity, the individual must also be able *to relate him or her self warmly to others* in both intimate and nonintimate contacts and possess a fundamental *emotional security* and an *acceptance of self*. He or she should be *realistically oriented* both with respect to oneself (self-objectification) and with respect to outer reality. Two main components of self-objectification are *humor* and *insight*. It is clear that what we mean by insight is the capacity of the individual to understand him or her self, although it is not clear just how to secure an adequate standard against which to compare the individual's beliefs. A sense of humor implies not only the capacity to find enjoyment and laughter in the customary places but also an ability to maintain positive relations to oneself and loved objects, at the same time being able to see incongruities and absurdities connected with them. Finally, maturity implies that the individual possess a unifying *philosophy of life*. Although individuals should be able to be objective and even amused about the ordinary events in their life, there should nevertheless be an underlying thread of complete seriousness that gives purpose and meaning to everything they do. Religion represents one of the most important sources of unifying philosophies, although this is by no means the only source of such integrating themes.

In considering Allport's research, it is important to distinguish between that which has some direct bearing upon his theoretical convictions and that which has grown out of other orientations such as his concern with "action" research, for example, prejudice (Allport, 1954, 1968) and religion (Allport, 1950b, 1968). Likewise his use and development of methods of measuring personality as exemplified by the *A-S reaction study* and *A study of values* has been dictated only in part by his theoretical convictions. In spite of his pleas for "idiographic" methods and studies, much of his own work has been "nomothetic." In this section we shall begin with a consideration of the distinction between idiographic and nomothetic, follow this with a discussion of direct and indirect methods of measuring personality, and finally discuss studies of expressive behavior and a study of an individual case as the best examples of investigations that mirror central aspects of his theoretical position.

CHARACTERISTIC RESEARCH AND RESEARCH METHODS

Idiographic versus Nomothetic   Allport has emphasized that the investigator may choose to study behavior in terms of general principles, universal variables, and a large number of subjects; or may elect to focus on the individual case, using methods and variables that are adequate to the uniqueness of each person. In labeling these two approaches to the study of behavior, Allport borrowed from the German philosopher Windelband the terms *idiographic* (individual) and *nomothetic* (universal). Later, however, he (1962) suggested substituting new terms, *morphogenic* for idiographic and *dimensional* for nomothetic. There is a place in psychology for both approaches, argues Allport, but the emphasis, particularly in American psychology, has been so overwhelmingly upon nomothetic methods that a drastic reorientation is called for. This reorientation is particularly urgent as the morphogenic approach will lead to better prediction and understanding. In fact, it is only by knowing the person as a person that we can predict what *he* or *she* will do in any given situation.

This emphasis upon the morphogenic approach is a logical outgrowth of several features of Allport's theoretical position. First of all, his emphasis upon the uniqueness of each person places a heavy obligation upon the investigator to select methods of study that will not conceal and blur this individuality. Second, and closely related, is the emphasis upon the importance of personal dispositions (individual traits) as the primary determinants of behavior. If these dispositions are the "real" units of personality, and if they are characteristic of only a single person, then clearly the most effective approach to the study of behavior will be a method of studying the individual.

Allport recognizes the importance of developing valid methods of studying the individual case but it is to be noted that he and others have made only a beginning in evolving such methods. As we have observed before, in Allport's own work he has more frequently used dimensional methods than morphogenic ones.

The use of matching techniques employed by Allport and Vernon (1933) in their studies of expressive behavior is one method that preserves the patterned individuality of each subject. Two other methods, structural analysis and content analysis, were used by Allport and his students (1965) in investigating the traits of a woman from letters she wrote. Allport (1962) has called attention to morphogenic approaches devised by other investigators. These include Q methodology (Stephenson, 1953), individualized questionnaires (Shapiro, 1961), self-anchoring scales (Kilpatrick and Cantril, 1960), the role construct repertory test (Kelly, 1955), and inverse factor analysis. Allport's interest in personal documents (1942) is of course intimately related to this emphasis upon the morphogenic approach to behavior.

It seems fair to say, in summary, that Allport, consistent with his theoretical position, has strongly urged psychologists to devote more of their time and energy to the study of the individual case than has been their custom. Further, it appears that this emphasis has met with considerable favor on the part of contemporary psychologists, so that what was once a deviant position is today widely accepted.

Beginning in the 1930s psychology has seen an unprecedented expansion in and development of indirect methods of assessing personality. The main impact of psychoanalytic theory was felt in academic psychology during this period and naturally led to an increased interest in instruments that seemed sensitive to unconscious motives and conflicts. In the face of this trend, projective techniques became enormously popular, while techniques of self-report, including the interview and questionnaire, waned in their popularity. Allport is not entirely sympathetic with this trend. He writes:

Direct and Indirect Measures of Personality

At no point do these [projective] methods ask the subject what his interests are, what he wants to do, or what he is trying to do. Nor do the methods ask directly concerning the subject's relation to his parents or to authority figures. They infer this relationship entirely by assumed identification. So popular is this indirect, undercover approach to motivation that many clinicians and many university centers spend far more time on this type of diagnostic method than on any other. . . . it is probably true that most psychologists prefer to assess a person's needs and conflicts by going the long way around. The argument, of course, is that everyone, even a neurotic, will accommodate himself fairly well to the demands placed upon him by reality. Only in an unstructured projective situation will he reveal his anxieties and unmasked needs. . . . this uncompromising statement . . . seems to mark the culmination of a century-long era of irrationalism, and therefore of distrust. Has the subject no right to be believed? . . . This prevailing atmosphere of theory has engendered a kind of contempt for the "psychic surface" of life. The individual's conscious report is rejected as untrustworthy, and the contemporary thrust of his motives is disregarded in favor of a backward tracing of his conduct to earlier formative stages. The individual loses his right to be believed. And while he is busy leading his life in the present with a forward thrust into the future, most psychologists have become busy tracing it backward into the past. . . . It is not the well-integrated subject, aware of his motivations, who reveals himself in projective testing. It is rather the neurotic personality, whose facade belies the repressed fears and hostilities within. Such a subject is caught off guard by projective devices; but the well-adjusted subject gives no significantly different response (1953, pp. 108–110).

Allport's position on this issue is altogether consistent with the importance he attributes to conscious, rational determinants of behavior. His conviction that the normal individual behaves in terms of known, reasonable motives leads him to the assertion that projective techniques have a unique contribution to make only in the case of the neurotic or disturbed individual, where the importance of unconscious motives may, in fact, be considerable. Allport maintains that direct and indirect methods will give a consistent picture in the case of the normal individual, whereas there may be considerable discrepancy between direct and indirect methods for the seriously maladjusted individual. He generalizes:

. . . a normal, well-adjusted individual with strong goal-directedness may on projective tests do one of two things: 1) either give material identical with that of conscious report—in which case the projective method is not needed; or 2) give no evidence whatever of his dominant motives (1953, p. 111).

He concludes that indirect methods may reveal important unconscious determinants of behavior, but only if compared with the yield of direct methods. It follows that indirect methods should not be used except in conjunction with direct methods. For the normal person direct methods give a much fuller and more useful picture of the motivational structure of the subject than does the indirect method. Not to be overlooked in a comparison of these methods is the vastly greater efficiency and simplicity of the direct methods.

Allport's construction and use of questionnaire methods is consistent with the point of view we have just outlined. On the other hand, it must be remembered that his stress upon the use of personal documents as an approach to personality and his studies of expressive behavior represent contributions to the indirect assessment of personality.

Studies of Expressive Behavior   Beginning in the early 1930s Allport and his collaborators carried out a series of investigations concerned with demonstrating the significance and consistency of expressive behavior. In defining this area of study, Allport distinguishes between two components that are present in every human response. First, there is the adaptive or coping component, which is primarily concerned with the functional value of the act, the effect that it produces, or the end to which it leads. Second, there is the expressive component, which refers to the manner or style in which the act is performed. Millions of individuals perform the same adaptive acts, but no two individuals carry out these acts with exactly the same flavor or style. Considering the emphasis in Allport's theory upon the individual and unique elements in behavior, it seems fitting that he should be deeply interested in expressive behavior—the personal or idiosyncratic component that appears in even the most stereotyped responses.

Not only does Allport's theory seem to lead naturally to an interest in expressive behavior; it also promises that the study of this aspect of behavior will be of general significance. If all of the individual's behavior is congruent and interrelated, then even the most trivial of individual acts must be related to central aspects of the individual's make-up. Consequently, we may study the inconspicuous expressive acts in order to obtain information about the most central aspects of behavior. In comparing expressive and adaptive components, Allport states:

The expressive portion of conduct results, then, from deep-lying determinants, functioning, as a rule, unconsciously and without effort. The adaptive portion, on the other hand, is a more limited system, circumscribed by the purpose of the moment, closely dependent upon the stimulus and upon voluntary effort or upon habits of skill. The *reason* for a present act of conduct is to be sought in the present desires and intentions of the individual (though these in turn may arise from deep-lying personal traits and interests); but the *style of execution* is always guided directly and without interference by deep and lasting personal dispositions (1937, p. 466).

Thus, Allport, in consonance with his theory, studies expressive aspects of behavior as a means of securing ready access to important sources of motivation and conflict in the individual.

The style of behavior is not determined solely by personality factors. Allport accepts the role of sociocultural determinants, temporary states or moods, organic conditions, and other variables. The contributions of these multiple factors do not lessen the importance of expressive behavior as a source of evidence concerning personality; they serve only to make somewhat more complex the empirical task of the investigator or diagnostician. Expressive behavior may be classified in terms of the type of act involved, for example, facial expression, gait, voice, and handwriting. Allport argues that one should not attend to any one type of expressive behavior exclusively, since all are of significance and add to our knowledge of the individual.

The most extensive of Allport's investigations in this area was carried out in collaboration with Philip E. Vernon (Allport and Vernon, 1933) and was aimed particularly at the problem of consistency of expressive movement. In one part of this investigation, a group of twenty-five subjects of rather heterogeneous composition was studied in three different sessions, each session separated by a period of about four weeks. During each session, the subject responded to a large number of different tests providing measures of: speed of reading and counting; speed of walking and strolling; length of stride; estimation of familiar sizes and distances; estimation of weights; strength of handshake; speed and pressure of finger, hand, and leg tapping; drawing squares, circles, and other figures; various handwriting measures; muscular tension, and so forth. In addition, observer ratings were secured for various measures, such as voice intensity, speech fluency, amount of movement during natural speech, and neatness of appearance. It is obvious that the investigators had an extremely large number of derived measures that they were able to use in their analysis.

In their study of consistency, Allport and Vernon began by examining the repeat-reliability (consistency of measure on two different occasions) of the various expressive measures. In general, these reliabilities appeared to be reasonably high, the intercorrelations being roughly equivalent to repeat-reliabilities for conventional psychological measuring instruments. In the face of this consistency, the authors conclude: "Single habits of gesture, as we have measured them, are stable characteristics of the individuals in our experimental group" (1933, p. 98). Next they examined the relation between scores for the same tasks performed by different muscle groups, left and right side of the body, arms and legs, and so forth, and found about an equal amount of consistency. This finding is of considerable importance, as it tends to suggest a general or central integrating factor that produces a consistent style no matter what peripheral manifestation is chosen.

The most difficult of the group comparisons that the investigators attempted was the intercorrelation of the major variables from all of their tasks. A total of thirty-eight measures was intercorrelated. The first impression gained from the matrix of correlations was that the intercorrelations were more often positive than would be expected by chance. Thus, the initial evidence suggests that there is some generality underlying the individual scores. The data did not permit application of conventional factor analysis, so the investigators performed a kind of cluster analysis in which they identified groups of correlations or factors consisting of those variables that showed significant intercorrelations. They concerned themselves not only with the statistical significance but also with the psychological meaningfulness of the cluster in question.

In the end there appeared to be three group factors that accounted for most of the intercorrelations observed. The first of these was called the "areal group factor" and included such variables as: area of total writing, area of blackboard figures, area of foot squares, overestimation of angles, length of self-rating checks. This appears to be a kind of "motor expansiveness." The second cluster was called the "centrifugal group factor" and included such variables as: overestimation of distance from body with legs, extent of cubes, verbal speed, underestimation of weights, underestimation of distances toward the body with hands. The authors are less content with this factor than with the previous one, but they conclude: "The group factor is based chiefly on the centrifugal-centripetal measures. . . . Thus the group factor may be interpreted as a general 'outward-tendency,' freedom and 'extroversion' of expressive movement, the reverse of shut-in, restrained, and pedantic motility" (1933, p. 112). The third cluster was called the "group factor of emphasis" and included such measures as: voice intensity, movement during speech, writing pressure, tapping pressure, overestimation of angles, pressure of resting hand. The investigators conclude that this is a relatively heterogeneous factor but that a common factor of emphasis seems to underlie most of the measures. They suggest: "Mere physical pressure or tension would seem to be significant only as part of a wider and more psychological tendency to make emphatic movements" (1933, p. 112).

Allport and Vernon, not completely satisfied with their group comparisons, followed this analysis with four case histories in which the subjects' expressive movements are examined in the context of their known personalities. They say: ". . . we are forced to the striking conclusion that virtually no measurements contradict the subjective impression of the personalities. The measures faithfully record what common sense indicates. Even measures which do not correspond statistically fit into the picture in such a way as to be readily intelligible and psychologically congruent" (1933, p. 180). Further, it was found that judges were able to match, with more than chance success, handwriting samples and kymographic curves (indicating the pressure exerted while writing) with personality sketches. They make an interesting final statement: "There are degrees of unity in movement, just as there are degrees of unity in mental life and in personality. It is surely not unreasonable to assume that insofar as personality is organized, expressive movement is harmonious and self-consistent, and insofar as personality is unintegrated, expressive movement is self-contradictory" (1933, p. 182).

In a graphology study, a group of twenty-three undergraduate males, who had been studied extensively through the use of conventional psychological measures, as well as through ratings secured from various observers, provided a number of handwriting samples. These handwriting samples were then given to two collaborators (Downey and Lucas) who prepared personality sketches based solely upon a knowledge of the individual's handwriting. The experimenter then attempted to identify the personality sketches through his detailed knowledge of the subjects, working with the entire group of subjects, as well as with small subgroups. Using either method, his success in identifying the subjects correctly exceeded chance, although in absolute terms the accuracy was not great.

After a final consideration of the positive findings of their investigations, Allport and Vernon conclude:

From our results it appears that a man's gesture and handwriting both reflect an essentially stable and constant individual style. His expressive activities seem not to be dissociated and unrelated to one another, but rather to be organized and well-patterned. Furthermore, the evidence indicates that there is a congruence between expressive movement and the attitudes, traits, values, and other dispositions of the "inner" personality. Although the question of the organization of the personality as a whole is beyond the scope of this volume, it is clear that the foundations for an adequate solution of this important problem cannot be supplied by the anarchic doctrine of specificity but only by the positive and constructive theories of consistency (1933, p. 248).

A series of studies by Allport and Cantril (1934) attempted to assess the extent to which judges could estimate personality accurately on the basis of voice alone. Over 600 judges were employed in the judgment of 16 speakers. Three different techniques of judging were used: personality sketches, matching speakers to personality descriptions, and rating speakers on attributes that were independently measured. The attributes judged included: physical and expressive features, like age, height, complexion, appearance in photographs and handwriting; as well as interests and traits, for example, vocation, political preference, extroversion, ascendance.

The results of these studies were consistent in indicating that judges were able to relate the voice with personality characteristics and with certain physical characteristics with better than chance accuracy. A comparison of judgments based on the natural voice with those based on the radio voice revealed that under both conditions the judges were able to do better than chance, but that the natural voice led to slightly more accurate ratings than the radio voice. An examination of the different personal characteristics that were assessed revealed that the judges were both more consistent and more accurate in their estimates of interests and traits as opposed to physical features and handwriting. The authors conclude from this: "Not only are the more highly organized traits and dispositions judged more consistently than such outer characteristics as physique and appearance, but they are also judged more *correctly*" (Allport and Cantril, 1934, p. 51).

Another student of Allport's, C. W. Huntley (1940), conducted several interesting studies designed to examine expressive behavior with special reference to self-esteem. These studies grew out of the work of Werner Wolff (1933, 1943) and represent an attempt to examine some of Wolff's findings under carefully controlled experimental conditions. In the two studies that Huntley conducted, he asked the subjects to take a series of tests and during the test sessions managed to record without the subjects' awareness a number of "forms of expression." These included photographs of the back of the hands of the subjects and their profiles, as well as samples of their handwriting and voices. Six months after the original session, the subjects were recalled and asked to judge samples of their own and others' forms of expression. They were not told, of course, that any of the samples were their own. In each trial, they were presented with four samples: two from the opposite sex, one from the same sex, and the remaining sample the subject's own. The subject was then asked to give a free personality characterization of the owner of each sample and also asked to rank the samples in order of his preference for them, or else he was asked to rate each sample in terms of a series of specified attributes: originality, attractiveness, intelligence, and so forth. The two major findings concern recognition of own forms of expression and the evaluative reaction to recognized and unrecognized own forms. Huntley's study concurred with Wolff's in showing a surprisingly low incidence of complete recognition of samples of own expression. Further, the results of these studies showed that when the individual evaluated his own samples without recognizing them as his own there was a strong tendency to be extreme in the reaction. The evaluation was sometimes negative, but usually positive, and very seldom neutral. When there was a partial or dubious recognition of the samples as own, the judgments became markedly more favorable, and where there was complete recognition, the judgments tended to become neutral. There were also marked individual differences in the self-judgments, with some subjects being consistently extreme while others were moderate. More recently, some of Wolff's and Huntley's findings have been re-examined by Lindzey (Lindzey, Prince, and Wright, 1952) who was also a student of Allport's.

Allport, generalizing from the results of his own and others' investigations, states:

The expressive features of the body are not independently activated. Any one of them is affected in much the same way as any other. Hence, to a degree Lavater is justified in saying that "one and the same spirit is manifest in all."

The consistency, however, is never found to be perfect. One channel of expression is not an exact replica of all others. If this were so, monosymptomatic methods of psychodiagnostics would be fully justified. The complete personality would be betrayed equally well in every feature. Handwriting would tell the whole story, so too would the eyes, the hands, or the limbs. The amount of agreement that has been demonstrated does not justify so simple an interpretation of the case.

The unity of expression turns out, as we would indeed expect, to be entirely a question of degree, just as the unity of personality itself is a matter of degree. The expressive features of the body should not be expected to reflect more consistency than the personality itself possesses (nor should they be expected to reflect *less*). Expression is patterned in complex ways precisely as personality itself is patterned. There are major consistencies and secondary consistencies, much congruence and some conflict and contradiction. Psychodiagnostics must then proceed as any other branch of the psychology of personality proceeds, to the study of *complex* phenomena at a *complex* level (1937, pp. 480–481).

Letters from Jenny   In the 1940s, Allport came into possession of 301 letters written by a middle-aged woman, Jenny Masterson (a pseudonym), to a young married couple over a period of twelve years. Allport recognized the psychological import of these particular letters and used them for many years in his classes in personality at Harvard to stimulate class discussion. They were published in an abridged form in the *Journal of Abnormal and Social Psychology* (anonymous, 1946).

Allport and his students have done several types of analyses of these letters in order to determine Jenny's outstanding traits. Baldwin (1942) was the first to make use of the letters. He devised a method that he called *personal structure analysis*. The first step consisted of reading the letters in order to identify the prominent topics and themes that Jenny wrote about. Baldwin found that she often wrote about her son, Ross, money, nature and art, and, of course, her own feelings. The next step was to find the relationships among these topics by noting how often they occurred together. When Jenny wrote about Ross, for instance, how frequently was he mentioned along with money, art, women, and so forth? A number of statistically significant clusters or constellations emerged from this analysis. Two such clusters revolved around seeing Ross in a favorable and in an unfavorable light. When he was referred to favorably in a letter, the themes of nature and art, and of Jenny's memories of her past life were also more likely to occur in the same letter than would be expected by chance. When Ross was written about unfavorably, other topics mentioned were Ross's selfishness, Jenny as self-sacrificing, and other women as unfavorable. Allport remarks that Baldwin's study shows "that quantification of the structure of a single personality is possible by means of statistical aids applied to content analysis"

(1965, p. 199), but he also wonders "whether this rather laborious mode of classifying ideational clusters adds anything new to the interpretations reached through a common sense reading of the material" (pp. 198–199).

Allport himself used a more common sense approach to the analysis of Jenny's traits as revealed in her letters. He asked thirty-six people to read Jenny's letters and characterize her in terms of her traits. They used a total of 198 trait names. Since many of these names were synonymous or highly related it was possible for Allport to group them under eight headings and a residual group of thirteen terms. The eight categories are

1. Quarrelsome–suspicious

2. Self-centered

3. Independent–autonomous

4. Dramatic–intense

5. Aesthetic–artistic

6. Aggressive

7. Cynical–morbid

8. Sentimental

There was considerable agreement among the judges, almost all of them perceiving as most prominent in Jenny's personality the traits of suspiciousness, self-centeredness, and autonomy.

Allport acknowledges that a list of traits is not a structure. "Surely her personality is not an additive sum of eight or nine separate traits" (p. 195). Accordingly, he asked the judges whether they could perceive any one unifying theme that marks almost all of her verbal behavior and received such a diversity of replies that it was impossible to decide upon one cardinal trait. Allport also admits that psychoanalysts would be critical of his trait analysis since it does not get at the underlying dynamics (motivations) of Jenny's behavior. He defends his position, however, by pointing to the consistency of Jenny's behavior so that one is able to predict her future conduct by what she did in the past.

Allport's evaluations of these content-analysis studies are summed up in the following statement:

Content analysis (whether longhand or automated) provides no golden key to the riddle of Jenny. It does, however, objectify, quantify, and to some extent purify commonsense impressions. By holding us close to the data (Jenny's own words) it warns us not to let some pet insight run away with the evidence. And it brings to our attention occasional fresh revelations beyond unaided common sense. In short, by bringing Jenny's phenomenological world to focus it enables us to make safer first-order inferences concerning the structure of personality that underlies her existential experience (1965, p. 204).

CURRENT STATUS AND EVALUATION

In contrast to many theorists, Allport has never developed a school of followers, although traces of his influence may be found in the work of former students such as A. L. Baldwin, J. S. Bruner, H. Cantril, G. Lindzey, D. G. McGranahan, T. Pettigrew, and M. B. Smith. Most of the developments in his theory have depended upon Allport's own contributions, which have been continuous for nearly a half-century. Beginning with an interest in an appropriate unit for the description of personality that led to his conception of the trait, and a simultaneous concern over the developmental transformation that motives undergo, which culminated in the concept of functional autonomy, he has progressively modified the theory so as to place increasing emphasis upon intentionality and ego (propriate) functions.

Although few psychologists have embraced this theory in its total form, it has nevertheless had considerable influence. One bit of evidence for the theory's utility is supplied by a questionnaire circulated by the Division of Clinical and Abnormal Psychology of the American Psychology Association (Schafer, Berg, and McCandless, 1951). This questionnaire was sent to practicing clinical psychologists and asked them to indicate what personality theorist was of most direct value to them in their day-to-day clinical work. The overwhelming majority of the respondents mentioned Freud as being most influential, but the second most frequently mentioned theorist was Allport.

One of the most interesting current developments in connection with this theory is the manner in which it has become of interest to psychoanalytic theorists. Allport's emphasis upon active propriate (ego) functions and the concept of functional autonomy are highly congruent with recent developments in psychoanalytic ego psychology. Thus, in spite of the fact that he has been one of the most unremitting critics of orthodox psychoanalysis, Allport has, in the end, proved to be one of the most fashionable of psychological theorists among psychoanalysts.

Whatever the ultimate systematic status of this theory, it is clear that its plentiful novel features must have consequences for future developments in psychological theorizing. In an area where there are so few well-established regularities and where the major variables almost certainly are not yet clearly identified, it seems important to maintain a healthy diversity in the theoretical positions guiding research. From this point of view, Allport has occupied a crucial role in pyschological theorizing, as his views give persuasive emphasis to problems and concepts often neglected in contemporary psychological theory.

One of the striking phenomena of the past sixty years in psychology has been the demise and subsequent rebirth of self and ego concepts. Perhaps no other psychologist has had so influential a role in restoring and purifying the ego concept as Allport. Not only has he placed the concept in historical context but he has also attempted persistently to show the functional necessity of employing some such concept in a discriminating way in any attempt to represent normal, complex, human behavior. A further novel feature of Allport's position has been his emphasis upon the importance of conscious determinants of behavior, and, as a corollary to this, his advocacy of direct methods of assessing human motivation. As we have already indicated, this position has been distinctly unpopular among contemporary psychologists, and yet it is a point of view that should be represented if we are to avoid a one-sided approach to our subject matter. More in keeping with current modes in psychology is the ardent plea that Allport has made for the detailed study of the individual case. Although others have shared this conviction, Allport, with his monograph on the use of personal documents in psychology (1942), his stress upon idiographic methods, his *Letters from Jenny,* and his publication of case histories as editor of the *Journal of Abnormal and Social Psychology,* is clearly one of the most important figures in a movement that has led to current acceptance of the individual case as a legitimate object of psychological investigation.

We have already mentioned the fact that Allport represents one of the few theorists who provides an effective bridge between academic psychology and its traditions on the one hand and the rapidly developing field of clinical and personality psychology on the other hand. This continuity not only serves to enrich each of the subdisciplines with the insights of the other but also helps to maintain an intellectual continuity that is important for the long-term development of psychology. A final novelty in Allport's position is contained in his emphasis upon the future and the present to the relative exclusion of the past. With the influence of psychoanalysis so pervasive, it is easy for the investigator or practitioner to forget about the importance of situational and ongoing determinants of behavior in favor of historical determination. Consequently, it has indeed been helpful to have Allport's writings as a constant reminder that the past is not the whole of the functioning individual.

So much for the positive side of the register. Let us examine the negative. In many respects, this theory is singularly vulnerable to criticism, and there has been no dearth of active critics, such as Bertocci (1940), Coutu (1949), Seward (1948), and Skaggs (1945). As we suggested earlier, Allport has usually been more concerned with presenting his viewpoint vividly and effectively than in protecting himself from criticism. The formal inadequacy of the theory has led to much negative comment. Just what is the axiomatic base of his position? What is assumed and what is open to empirical test? Just how are the assumptions made by the theory interrelated, and where are the careful empirical definitions that permit the investigator to translate concepts into observation terms? Intimately related to these questions, but vastly more important, is the issue of the variety and quantity of investigation to which the theory has led. It must be admitted that, with the possible exception of the field of expressive behavior, this theory has not been an efficient generator of propositions for empirical test. Like most other personality theories, it is more at home when attempting to account for known relations than it is in attempting to make predictions about unobserved events. Thus, although Allport's own writings and investigations have led to a large amount of related research, for example, prejudice, social and religious attitudes, and rumor, we must admit that his theory falls down sadly as a formal device for generating research.

Many psychologists feel that one reason the theory has difficulty in making predictions is that the concept of functional autonomy is not susceptible to empirical demonstration, let alone to making predictions about unobserved events. We have already referred to some embarrassment created for this concept when the notion of propriateness is introduced as a criterion for determining what becomes autonomous. The basis of functional autonomy is a failure to observe the expected extinction or dropping out of a given response, and no matter how long we observe a given response that has failed to extinguish, there is always the possibility of criticism. The detractor may say we should have watched longer in order to observe extinction, or may account for the apparent autonomy of the response in terms of some underlying motivation that is not adequately understood by the investigator. It is always possible to account for any concrete example of functional autonomy in terms of other theoretical formulations, but so, too, can examples of other theoretical principles be accounted for in terms of alternative principles. Perhaps the most serious criticism of this principle is that Allport provides no adequate account of the process or mechanism underlying functional autonomy. He tells us that the phenomenon takes place but provides no satisfactory explanation of how or why.

Another feature of the theory that has come under heavy critical fire is Allport's assumption of partial discontinuity between normal and abnormal, between infant and adult, and between animal and human. Most psychologists are so firmly convinced that we have gained increased knowledge of normal behavior from studying abnormal subjects that any attempt to imply that the abnormal is discontinuous from the normal seems nothing short of heretical. In fact, the extent to which psychologists have borrowed conceptions developed through observation of lower animals makes the assumption of discontinuities within the human species all the more difficult to accept. Consistent with his view of normal, adult, human behavior as distinct from abnormal, child or lower animal behavior is Allport's preference for a model of a human that emphasizes positive or normatively prized aspects of behavior. The influence of psychoanalysis and comparative psychology has been so strong that a theory which insists upon emphasizing socially acceptable motives rather than primitive needs, such as sex and aggression, sounds mildly Victorian at present. Allport himself would say that he does not deny the importance of biological or of unconscious motives but wishes to give due place to the role of socialized motives and rational processes, which he believes a transitory era of irrationalism has neglected. However that may be, many critics of the theory maintain that Allport's position represents humans in terms that are altogether too similar to those that the ordinary individual uses in accounting for his or her behavior.

No contemporary psychologist can dwell heavily upon "uniqueness" without incurring the wrath of many of their colleagues who are oriented toward abstracting and measuring behavior. What Coutu (1949) has called "the fallacy of the unique personality" represents a major disagreement between Allport's beliefs and those of most contemporary social scientists. It is their conviction that individuality can be accounted for in terms of adequate common or general principles and that to focus upon the individual and unique at psychology's present state of development can only lead to sterile speculation.

Sanford (1963) has also been severely critical of the "uniqueness" concept. He insists that science cannot take account of unique events, that it looks for uniformities and statistical regularities and it attempts to generalize. He observes that clinicians and others who are most intimately involved with the study of individual personalities have not followed Allport's recommendation that they concentrate on trying to understand the uniquely patterned organization of a person. Rather they attempt to discover general principles in the analysis of the individual case. Allport's reply to this criticism is that one can find uniformities in a person's life, and one can make generalizations for

that person. The fact remains, however, that aside from Jenny, Allport did not follow his own advice. (Even in the case of Jenny there
was little attempt made to establish her uniqueness as a human being.)
His research has been of the nomothetic type.

A further objection to the theory, intimately related to its failure to
generate empirical propositions, is the theory's inability to specify a
set of dimensions to be used in studying personality. Individual traits,
by definition, cannot be stated in a general form, and consequently,
the investigator, if he or she takes the idiographic approach, must
begin anew the task of devising variables for each subject studied.
Obviously, this is a discouraging state of affairs for the person interested in research.

Finally, those among contemporary psychologists who are impressed with the contribution of sociocultural determinants to behavior—and this is a sizable group—find no easy way to give these factors adequate representation in Allport's theory. They maintain that
the theory gives full attention to the interrelatedness of all behavior,
but fails to recognize the interrelatedness of behavior and the environmental situation within which it operates. Allport gives too much
credit to what goes on inside the organism and not enough credit to
the seductive and constraining impact of external forces.

Allport in his characteristic openminded manner has listened to this
criticism and has replied to it. He acknowledged in his important
paper *Traits revisited* (1966) that "my earlier views seemed to neglect
the variability induced by ecological, social and situational factors" (p.
9). "This oversight," he goes on to say, "needs to be repaired
through an adequate theory that will relate the inside and outside systems more accurately." Allport does not, however, attempt to provide such a theory, and in fact seems to imply that such a theory will
not invalidate or replace his viewpoint. He does not believe that traits
can be accounted for in terms of interaction effects. Environmental
situations and sociocultural variables may be distal causal forces but
"the intervening factor of personality is ever the proximal cause of
human conduct." It is the duty of psychology, Allport maintains, to
study the person-system because it is the person who accepts, rejects,
or remains uninfluenced by the social system. Allport's tolerant eclecticism is seen in this solution to the person-society controversy.

The personality theorist should be so well trained in social science that he can view
the behavior of an individual as fitting any system of interaction; that is, he should be
able to cast this behavior properly in the culture where it occurs, in its situational
context, and in terms of role theory and field theory. At the same time he should not
lose sight of the fact that there is an internal and subjective patterning of all these contextual acts (1960a, p. 307).

Perhaps the most remarkable attribute of Allport's theoretical writings is that in spite of their pluralism and eclecticism they have managed to create a sense of novelty and to exert a broad influence. His work stands as a monument to a wise and sensitive scholar who was committed to representing the positive aspects of human behavior in terms that respected the uniqueness of every living organism.

BIBLIOGRAPHY
PRIMARY SOURCES

Allport, G. W. *Personality: A psychological interpretation.* New York: Holt, 1937.

Allport, G. W. *The nature of personality: selected papers.* Cambridge, Mass.: Addison-Wesley, 1950a. (Includes the most important of Allport's papers published prior to this date.)

Allport, G. W. *Becoming: basic considerations for a psychology of personality.* New Haven: Yale Univ. Press, 1955.

Allport, G. W. *Personality and social encounter.* Boston: Beacon, 1960b.

Allport, G. W. *Pattern and growth in personality.* New York: Holt, Rinehart and Winston, 1961.

Allport, G. W. *The person in psychology: selected essays.* Boston: Beacon, 1968.

REFERENCES

Allport, G. W. *Personality: A psychological interpretation.* New York: Holt, 1937.

Allport, G. W. Motivation in personality: Reply to Mr. Bertocci. *Psychol. Rev.,* 1940, **47:** 533–554.

Allport, G. W. *The use of personal documents in psychological science.* New York: Soc. Sci. Res. Council, Bull. 1942, **49.**

Allport, G. W. The ego in contemporary psychology. *Psychol. Rev.,* 1943, **50,** 451–478.

Allport, G. W. Effect: a secondary principle of learning. *Psychol. Rev.,* 1946, **53,** 335–347.

Allport, G. W. Scientific models and human morals. *Psychol. Rev.,* 1947, **54,** 182–192.

Allport, G. W. *The nature of personality: selected papers.* Cambridge, Mass.: Addison-Wesley, 1950a. (Includes the most important of Allport's papers published prior to this date.)

Allport, G. W. *The individual and his religion.* New York: Macmillan, 1950b.

Allport, G. W. The trend in motivational theory. *Amer. J. Orthopsychiat.,* 1953, **23,** 107–119.

Allport, G. W. *The nature of prejudice.* Cambridge, Mass.: Addison-Wesley, 1954.

Allport, G. W. *Becoming: basic considerations for a psychology of personality.* New Haven: Yale Univ. Press, 1955.

Allport, G. W. The open system in personality theory. *J. Abnorm. Soc. Psychol.,* 1960a, **61,** 301–310.

Allport, G. W. Personality and social encounter. Boston: Beacon, 1960b.

Allport, G. W. *Pattern and growth in personality.* New York: Holt, Rinehart and Winston, 1961.

Allport, G. W. The general and the unique in psychological science. *J. Personality,* 1962, **30,** 405–422.

Allport, G. W. Imagination in psychology: some needed steps. In *Imagination and the university,* Toronto: University of Toronto Press, 1964.

Allport, G. W. *Letters from Jenny.* New York: Harcourt, Brace, Jovanovich, 1965.

Allport, G. W. Traits revisited. *Amer. Psychologist,* 1966, **21,** 1–10.

Allport, G. W. Autobiography. In E. G. Boring and G. Lindzey (Eds.). *A history of psychology in autobiography,* Vol. 5, New York: Appleton-Century-Crofts, 1967, 1–25.

Allport, G. W. *The person in psychology: selected essays.* Boston: Beacon, 1968.

Allport, G. W., and Allport, F. H. *A-S reaction study.* Boston: Houghton Mifflin, 1928.

Allport, G. W., and Cantril, H. Judging personality from voice. *J. Soc. Psychol.,* 1934, **5,** 37–55.

Allport, G. W., and Odbert, H. S. Trait-names: a psycho-lexical study. *Psychol. Monogr.,* 1936, **47,** no. 211, 1–171.

Allport, G. W. and Pettigrew, T. F. Cultural influence on the perception of movement: the trapezoidal illusion among Zulus. *J. Abnorm. Soc. Psychol.,* 1957, **55,** 104–113.

Allport, G. W., and Vernon, P. E. *A study of values.* Boston: Houghton Mifflin, 1931. (Rev. ed. with P. E. Vernon and G. Lindzey, 1951.)

Allport, G. W., and Vernon, P. E. *Studies in expressive movement.* New York: Macmillan, 1933.

Anderson, E. E. The externalization of drive: I. Theoretical considerations. *Psychol. Rev.,* 1941a, **48,** 204–224.

Anderson, E. E. The externalization of drive: II. The effect of satiation and removal of reward at different stages in the learning process of the rat. *J. Genet. Psychol.,* 1941b, **59,** 359–376.

Anderson, E. E. The externalization of drive: III. Maze learning by non-rewarded and by satiated rats. *J. Genet. Psychol.,* 1941c, **59,** 397–426.

Anderson, E. E. The externalization of drive: IV. The effect of pre-feeding on the maze performance of hungry non-rewarded rats. *J. Comp. Psychol.,* 1941d, **31,** 349–352.

Anonymous. Letters from Jenny, *J. Abnorm. Soc. Psychol.,* 1946, **41,** 315–350; 449–480.

Baldwin, A. L. Personal structure analysis: a statistical method for investigating the single personality. *J. Abnorm. Soc. Psychol.,* 1942, **37,** 163–183.

Bertocci, P. A. A critique of G. W. Allport's theory of motivation. *Psychol. Rev.,* 1940, **47,** 501–532.

Coutu, W. *Emergent human nature.* New York: Knopf, 1949.

Harlow, H. F., Harlow, M. K., and Meyer, D. R. Learning motivated by a manipulation drive. *J. Exp. Psychol.*, 1950, **40,** 228–234.

Huntley, C. W. Judgments of self based upon records of expressive behavior. *J. Abnorm. Soc. Psychol.*, 1940, **35,** 398–427.

Kelly, G. A. *The psychology of personal constructs.* New York: Norton, 1955, Vol. 1.

Kilpatrick, F. P., and Cantril, H. Self anchoring scale: a measure of the individual's unique reality world. *J. Ind. Psychol.*, 1960, **16,** 158–170.

Lindzey, G., Prince, B., and Wright, H. K. A study of facial asymmetry. *J. Pers.*, 1952, **21,** 68–84.

Olson, W. C. *The measurement of nervous habits in normal children.* Minneapolis: Univ. of Minnesota Press, 1929.

Sanford, N. Personality: Its place in psychology. In S. Koch (Ed.). *Psychology: A study of a science.* New York: McGraw-Hill, 1963, Vol. 5.

Schafer, R., Berg, I., and McCandless, B. Report on survey of current psychological testing practices. *Supplement to Newsletter, Division of clin. abn. Psychol., Amer. Psychol. Ass.*, 1951, **4,** no. 5.

Selye, H. *The story of the adaptation syndrome.* Montreal: Acta, 1952.

Seward, J. P. The sign of a symbol: A reply to Professor Allport. *Psychol. Rev.*, 1948, **55,** 277–296.

Shapiro, M. B. The single case in fundamental clinical psychological research. *Brit. J. Med. Psychol.*, 1961, **34,** 255–262.

Skaggs, E. B. Personalistic psychology as science. *Psychol. Rev.*, 1945, **52,** 234–238.

Solomon, R. L., and Wynne, L. C. Traumatic avoidance learning: The principles of anxiety conservation and partial irreversibility. *Psychol. Rev.*, 1954, **61,** 353–385.

Stephenson, W. *The study of behavior: Q-technique and its methodology.* Chicago: Univ. of Chicago Press, 1953.

Stern, W. *Allgemeine Psychologie auf personalistischer Grundlage.* The Hague: Nijhoff, 1935. (Engl. translation by H. D. Spoerl. *General psychology: from the personalistic standpoint.* New York: Macmillan, 1938.)

Tolman, E. C. Psychology versus immediate experience. *Phil. Sci.*, 1935, **2,** 356–380.

Wolff, W. The experimental study of forms of expression. *Character & Pers.*, 1933, **2,** 168–176.

Wolff, W. *The expression of personality.* New York: Harper, 1943.

Woodworth, R. S. *Dynamic psychology.* New York: Columbia Univ. Press, 1918.

SHELDON'S CONSTITUTIONAL PSYCHOLOGY

13

For the individual on the street physical characteristics of fellow humans illumine manifold aspects of personality. It is "well-known" that fat men are jolly and indolent, that lean individuals are shy and morose, that red hair betokens a swift and violent anger. A large dictionary of such diagnostic statements could be compiled and this is precisely what early investigators such as Lavater (1804) and Gall and Spurzheim (1809) did. Other students of human behavior (Rostan, 1824; Viola, 1909; Sigaud, 1914; Naccarati, 1921; Kretschmer, 1921) have advanced similar findings and have frequently attempted to introduce empirical control into the demonstration of such relations. Thus, the layperson and many scholars of the past share the belief that behavior is related in important respects to observable aspects of the individual's physical make-up. In surprising contrast, we find few psychologists in this country who hold this conviction.

Acceptance of a theory or body of evidence is not solely dependent upon the empirical findings that can be summoned to substantiate it. There are many overriding considerations including the extent to which the formulations fit with the guiding preconceptions or convictions of the time and culture. The difficulty encountered by Galileo in his attempt to develop a concept of the universe that reversed the church-supported, Aristotelian view is merely a dramatic instance of a process that goes on continually in a milder form among all empirical disciplines. Various scholars have written persuasively about the reluctance of most contemporary psychologists to give a fair hearing to the extrasensory research (parapsychology) of Rhine and his collaborators. To this instance could be added many others, perhaps including constitutional psychology. The resistance of most American psychologists to consider the possibility of an intimate tie between body and behavior seems linked to a number of factors. One important by-product of American democracy, the Protestant ethic, and the dogma of the self-made person has been the rejection of formulations implying that behavior may be innately conditioned, immutable, a "given." Because it is commonly accepted that physical characteristics are linked closely to genetic factors, the suggestion that physical and psychological characteristics are intimately related seems to imply a championing of genetic determinism. It is not surprising that such a conception has been unable to muster much support in the face of the buoyant environmentalism of American psychology. In general, it seems fair to say that American psychologists have largely neglected the study of that important class of variables having to do with the physical description of the body.

In the face of this indifference or hostility to the possibility of important associations between structural and behavioral characteristics, the work of William H. Sheldon stands as a unique contribution on the contemporary scene. In the present chapter we shall attempt to place Sheldon's work in brief historical perspective and then describe his formulations and investigations. In some respects it may seem unwise to focus so heavily upon the work of a single man when over the years so many have worked in this area. However, Sheldon's work is empirically far superior to that of his predecessors and for the contemporary psychologist it is largely the research of Sheldon and his collaborators that makes this a topic of significance.

A word should be said concerning the sense in which we intend to use the term constitutional. There are two definitions frequently encountered in psychology. In the first, the term is used to refer to those factors that are given, or present, at birth. Here, constitutional is simply a shorthand means of referring to the contributions of genes plus the uterine environment. The second usage equates the term to the most basic "make-up of the body." Thus Sheldon suggests that: ". . . constitution refers to those aspects of the individual which are relatively more fixed and unchanging—morphology, physiology, endocrine function, etc.—and may be contrasted with those aspects which are relatively more labile and susceptible to modification by environmental pressures, i.e., habits, social attitudes, education, etc." (1940, p. 2). As this definition implies, constitutional psychology then becomes ". . . the study of the psychological aspects of human behavior as they are related to the morphology and physiology of the body" (Sheldon, 1940, p. 1). It is clear that these two usages have much in common because both physical structure and biological function are commonly assumed to be closely related to prenatal determinants of behavior.

For the purposes of this chapter we shall naturally adopt the definition proposed by Sheldon. There remains the question whether the term constitution implies an equal emphasis upon physical structure and biological function. Logically it should include both. Thus, the individual who studied the relation between behavior and measurable aspects of the autonomic nervous system or the endocrine system should be considered a "constitutional psychologist" just as much as the student of physique. In point of historical fact, however, the term is ordinarily used to refer to those theorists or investigators who have emphasized the relation between structural aspects of the body (physique or body build) and behavior. Thus, for present purposes the *constitutional psychologist is one who looks to the biological substratum of the individual for factors that are important to the explanation of human behavior.* Since more is known about morphology than about the other aspects of this substratum, our discussion will thus dwell mostly on the dependence of behavior upon physique or body build.

Recent developments in such areas as psychophysiology, psychopharmacology, behavior genetics, and brain function and behavior suggest that in the relatively near future we confidently may expect to see the development of a variety of constitutional psychology that will be as much concerned with the role of physiological function in behavior as with anatomical structure and behavior. The exciting new findings that are emerging in the neurosciences underline the importance of constitutional psychology in its role as a bridge between the biological and behavioral.

Before examining the formulations of Sheldon, let us look at some of the important work that preceded his. Our historical account necessarily must be very brief: however, the interested reader will find excellent supplementary accounts in Allport (1937) Sheldon (1940, 1944), and Rees (1968, 1973).

CONSTITUTIONAL PSYCHOLOGY OF THE PAST

Theories that suggest a relation between physique and behavior antedate by many centuries the birth of academic psychology. Not only did these formulations begin in the dim past but more surprisingly many of them show a remarkable correspondence to formulations that are still popular. The individual who is generally credited with having begun work in this area is Hippocrates who suggested not only a typology of physique but also a temperament typology and a conception of humors that is highly congruent with the current emphasis upon the importance of endocrine secretions as determinants of behavior (cf. Hoskins, 1941). He suggested a twofold classification of physiques, dividing subjects into those who were short and thick and those who were long and thin. Although this division may sound rudimentary, it is nevertheless not far removed from many of the classifications that have been proposed during the past century. He also suggested that these body types were accompanied by characteristic disease afflictions. The short and thick body build was especially prone to apoplexy; the long and thin build was frequently accompanied by tuberculosis. Here is the birth of constitutional medicine, a field in which Sheldon was active. Further, Hippocrates suggested that men could be divided into four basic temperament types that corresponded to Empedocles' four basic elements—air, water, fire, and earth. There were also four humors (liquid substances) within the body, the relative predominance of which determined the temperamental type to which the individual would belong. Thus, we have here the suggestion of classifying individuals in terms of temperament, and further the implication that liquids within the body (endocrine secretions?) have a determining effect upon the temperament an individual will display.

With Ernst Kretschmer (1921) constitutional psychology embarked upon its modern course. Kretschmer was a German psychiatrist whose contributions to European psychiatry are of first magnitude, although he is best known in this country for his studies of the relation between physique and mental disorder. In his psychiatric practice he became convinced that there were important relationships between physique and manifest behavior, especially the type of behavior displayed in the two major forms of mental disorder; manic-depressive psychosis and schizophrenia. Schizophrenia is the most common of all psychotic disorders and is characterized by a loss of affect or emotional responsiveness and a withdrawal from normal interpersonal relations, and is frequently accompanied by delusions and hallucinations. The manic-depressive psychosis in its extreme manifestation is characterized by mood swings such that individuals in one phase may be so overactive and excitable (manic) that they have to be forcibly restrained to prevent their harming themselves and others, yet at another time may be so inactive, lethargic, and depressed that they have to be cared for as though they were infants.

Given this general pattern of interest, Kretschmer set out to accomplish three things: (1) to devise a means of objectively classifying individuals in terms of a limited number of physique categories; (2) to relate physique, as measured by the pre-established categories, to the two major forms of psychosis, schizophrenia and manic depression; (3) to relate physique to other forms of behavior falling in the normal range.

In the measurement of physique Kretschmer was surprisingly systematic and painstaking. In an effort to achieve repeatability and consistency of measurement he devised an elaborate check list representing the major parts of the body, with a cluster of descriptive phrases for each of these areas. This check list was then filled out with the subject standing naked in front of the investigator. As the result of a complex analysis of these ratings and objective measurements Kretschmer arrived at a conception of three fundamental types of physiques.

The first type is called *asthenic* and refers to a frail, linear physique. In Kretschmer's words:

. . . there is typically . . . *a deficiency in thickness combined with an average unlessened length*. This deficiency in the thickness development is present in all parts of the body,—face, neck, trunk, extremities—and in all the tissues—skin, fat, muscle, bone, and vascular system throughout. On this account we find the average weight, as well as the total circumference and breadth measurements, below the general value for males . . . a lean narrowly-built man, who looks taller than he is, with a skin poor in secretion and blood, with narrow shoulders, from which hang lean arms with thin muscles, and delicately boned hands; a long, narrow, flat chest, on which we can count the ribs, with a sharp rib angle, a thin stomach . . . (1925, p. 21).

The second physique type is the *athletic* which is a muscular vigorous physique.

The male athletic type is recognized by the strong development of the skeleton, the musculature and also the skin. . . . A middle-sized to tall man, with particularly wide projecting shoulders, a superb chest, a firm stomach, and a trunk which tapers in its lower region, so that the pelvis, and the magnificent legs, sometimes seem almost graceful compared with the size of the upper limbs and particularly the hypertrophied shoulders (1925, p. 24).

The third type is the *pyknic* physique which is characterized by plumpness and corresponds to Rostan's digestive type. Kretschmer suggests that:

The pyknic type . . . is characterized by the pronounced peripheral development of the body cavities (head, breast and stomach), and a tendency to a distribution of fat about the trunk . . . middle height, rounded figure, a soft broad face on a short massive neck, sitting between the shoulders; the magnificent fat paunch protrudes from the deep vaulted chest which broadens out towards the lower part of the body (1925, p. 29).

In addition to the three types outlined above an additional type was added—the *dysplastic*. This includes the small group of cases where there are strikingly deviant aspects to the individual's build so that they appear to even the casual observer as "rare, surprising and ugly."

Given this system of physique classification, Kretschmer set out to compare psychiatric patients. He studied 260 psychotics made up of 43 manic-depressive men and 42 manic-depressive women, and 125 schizophrenic men and 50 schizophrenic women. When these patients were classified according to his scheme Kretschmer found the distribution presented in Table 13-1. From these findings Kretschmer concludes that there is a "clear biological affinity" between manic-depressive psychosis and the pyknic body build and a similar association between schizophrenia and the asthenic, athletic, and certain dyplastic body builds.

Kretschmer also makes plain his conviction that psychotic states are directly continuous with normal behavior. Given the relationship between physique and psychosis, and given also Kretschmer's assumption of continuity between normal and abnormal, it is easy to see that Kretschmer would expect a relation between physique and patterns of behavior in normal subjects. This relationship remains merely an assertion, however, for Kretschmer provides no direct evidence to support his contention.

Although it is evident that Kretschmer made a considerable contribution to constitutional psychology, it is also evident that his work is not beyond criticism. The most important objection is that he failed to control adequately for differences in age between manic-

TABLE 13-1
*Incidence of physique types
in two types of psychosis*

	Number of cases	
	Manic-depressive	Schizophrenic
Asthenic	4	81
Athletic	3	31
Asthenic-athletic mixed	2	11
Pyknic	58	2
Pyknic mixture	14	3
Dysplastic	—	34
Deformed and uncategorized	4	13
	85	175

Adapted from Kretschmer (1925), p. 35.

depressives and schizophrenics. Thus, the common observation that with increasing age most of us increase in weight and are more likely to resemble pyknics, and the further evidence that manic-depressive psychosis typically occurs later in life than schizophrenia, might account for the relation he observed between physique and psychosis. In addition, various investigators have encountered considerable difficulty in assigning physiques to Kretschmer's categories in an objective and repeatable fashion.

The work we have described, especially that of Ernst Kretschmer, provides an indispensable backdrop against which Sheldon's formulations and procedures evolved. Although it is true that Sheldon's work is vastly superior in many respects to that of his predecessors, it is unlikely that his achievements could have been accomplished without the imaginative and painstaking efforts of these earlier figures. Let us turn now to a consideration of Sheldon's background, his theory, and his investigation.

WILLIAM H. SHELDON

Sheldon was born in the year 1899 in Warwick, Rhode Island, where he grew up in a farm setting. The rural atmosphere of his early life and his close relationship with his father, who was a naturalist and animal breeder, had a lasting effect upon his values and upon his view of human behavior. Even today his writing shows clear evidence of his interest in the animal world and many of his ideas concerning determinants of human behavior seem to have grown out of a close familiarity with the ways and the breeds of animals. He was educated in public schools and attended Brown University where he received his A.B. in 1919. Subsequently he received an A.M. from the University of Colorado and a Ph.D. in psychology from the University of Chicago in 1926. In 1933 he received his M.D., also from the University of Chicago. From 1924 to 1926 he was an instructor in psychology at the University of Chicago and then was an assistant professor for one year at both the University of Chicago and Northwestern University. He was next an assistant professor at the University of Wisconsin from 1927 until 1931. After securing his medical degree he interned at a children's hospital in Chicago and secured a fellowship that enabled him to spend two years in psychiatric study abroad. Much of his time during this period was spent in Zurich with Carl Jung but he also visited Freud and Kretschmer. On his return to this country in 1936 he went to the University of Chicago as a professor of psychology. In 1938 he moved to Harvard University where he remained for a number of years and where his

William H. Sheldon

collaboration with the distinguished experimental psychologist, S. S. Stevens, developed. Following a period of wartime Army service, Sheldon accepted in 1947 a position as Director of the Constitution Laboratory, College of Physicians and Surgeons, Columbia University, where he remained until his retirement. In this position he succeeded George Draper, a pioneer in constitutional medicine; and like Draper he studied the relation between organic disease and physical structure. Until his death on September 16, 1977, he resided in Cambridge not far from Harvard's Memorial Hall where much of his major research and writing were carried out.

Sheldon's professional writings follow a remarkably consistent main stream. With only two interesting excursions, they represent an attempt to identify and describe the major structural components of the human body (*The varieties of human physique,* 1940), the major components of temperament (*The varieties of temperament,* 1942), and the application of these findings to the area of delinquency (*Varieties of delinquent youth,* 1949). Sheldon returned to the problem of description of physique in his *Atlas of men* (1954) and in several publications dealing with refinements of his method of somatotyping (Sheldon, 1971; Sheldon, Lewis, and Tenney, 1969). His first book (*Psychology and the Promethean will,* 1936, 1974) is a provocative essay on the role of religion in modern life. He also outlines in this volume what he considers to be the principal sources of conflict in modern humans. The other book not closely related to constitutional psychology is a technical volume that deals with the taxonomy of coins (*Early American cents, 1793–1814,* 1949, 1976), in which Sheldon proves himself as adept at classifying old coins as human physiques. Up until the time of his death Sheldon was actively working on an "Atlas of Women," an "Atlas of Children," and a volume concerned with physique and organic disease.

The breadth of Sheldon's training makes it difficult to isolate specific figures who have influenced his professional development. However, in both writing and investigation he shows clearly his indebtedness to predecessors in the field of constitutional psychology, especially Kretschmer and Viola. Futhermore, although he has pungently expressed reservations concerning the nature of Freud's impact upon psychology, there is evidence of some influence from this quarter and from the work of Carl Jung. The writings of William James, who was Sheldon's godfather, have exerted a detectable influence upon him. Sheldon's medical training and early interests in animal breeding are clearly reflected in his professional concern over biological and hereditary factors in behavior. Finally, the procedural and measuremental sophistication of S. S. Stevens manifestly had its effects upon Sheldon during the period of their collaboration.

In Sheldon's theory we find a clear and vigorous exposition of the crucial importance of the physical structure of the body as a primary determinant of behavior. Moreover, he identifies a set of objective variables that can be used as a bridgehead for describing physique and behavior. In an area where the use of types—what Whitehead has referred to as a "half-way house on the road to measurement"—has been the rule, Sheldon introduces and stoutly defends the notion of continuous variables. Furthermore, his techniques for assessing the structural characteristics of the body involve the use of standard photographs and a much more carefully specified and reproducible procedure than that of his predecessors.

Underlying this emphasis upon physique and its measurement is a strong conviction that biological-hereditary factors are of immense importance in determining behavior and a belief that the riddle of the human organism will be unraveled only with the aid of increased understanding of these factors. A fully rounded psychology cannot exist in a biological vacuum. Thus, in a psychological world that is focused upon environmental transactions we find Sheldon looking away from the external world and gazing instead at the physical structure that silently underlies all behavioral phenomena. It is his assumption that here, in the physique, the psychologist may find the constants, the firm substructures that are so desperately needed to introduce regularity and consistency into the study of human behavior. All this is implied in the following statement:

It has been growing increasingly plain that the situation calls for a biologically oriented psychology, or one taking for its operational frame of reference a scientifically defensible description of the *structure* (together with the behavior) of the human organism itself. This is perhaps tantamount to saying that psychology requires a physical anthropology for its immediate foundation support. More than that, it requires a physical anthropology couched in terms of components, or variables, which can be measured and quantified at both the structural and behavioral ends—the anthropological and psychological ends—of the structure-behavior continuum which is a human personality (Sheldon, 1949, p. xv).

William Sheldon was not only a student of physical structure and a believer in the importance of biological factors but also a singularly provocative protagonist. His writing style is direct and unconventional. He was a scholar who delighted in extreme statements and who could weave compelling word images to defend these statements. Thus, we have the desirable combination of a tireless investigator and a polemically oriented individual defending a position that is poorly represented in American psychology today.

One of the fascinations of Sheldon's theory of personality lies in its simplicity and specificity. In contrast to many personality theories, which provide an unlimited number of blank checks that can be written for puzzling behavioral equations, Sheldon defines a discrete number of physical and temperamental variables that he considers of primary importance in representing human behavior. Although he does not close the door to further elaboration or refinement, neither is he apologetic about the present fruitfulness of these variables.

Consistent with the approach of most other constitutional psychologists, Sheldon attempts to identify and provide suitable measures for the physical components of the human body. It is important to realize that he is not simply looking for a means of classifying or describing physiques. His goal is much more ambitious—to provide a "biological identification tag." He assumes that genetic and other biological determinants play a crucial role in the development of the individual. He believes also that it is possible to get some representation of these factors through a set of measures based upon the physique. In his view there is a hypothetical biological structure (morphogenotype) that underlies the external, observable physique (phenotype) and plays an important role not only in determining physical development but also in molding behavior. The *somatotype* represents an attempt to assess the morphogenotype, although it must approach this goal indirectly, and in its derivation leans heavily upon measurements of the phenotype (physique).

We shall consider here Sheldon's approach to the measurement of the physical aspects of the individual, and following this we shall examine his efforts to identify the most important components underlying behavior.

Although Sheldon was well aware of his predecessors' attempts to type or measure physique, he began his efforts inductively. The first problem he faced was to secure a large number of physiques that could be examined and re-examined. In order to make this procedure practical and efficient he devised a photographic technique that involved taking pictures from the front, side, and rear of individuals posed in a standard position before a standard background. This procedure has come to be called the *Somatotype Performance Test* and is described in full detail in Sheldon's *Atlas of men* (1954).

In his first important study of the human physique, Sheldon secured roughly four thousand standard photographs of male college

THE STRUCTURE OF PHYSIQUE

Dimensions of Physique

Fig. 13-1 Illustrative Somatotypes ★

7-1-1

1-1-7

1-7-1

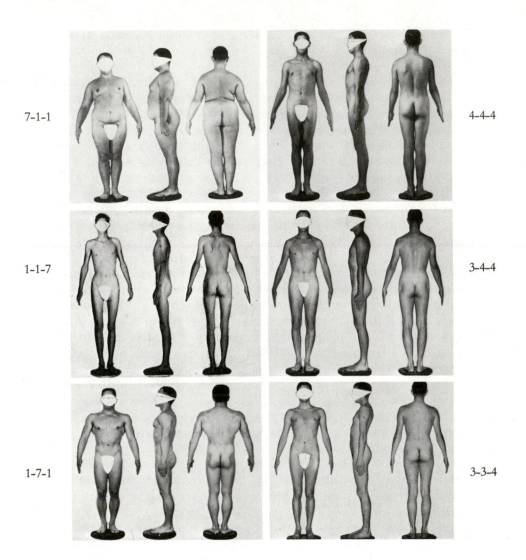

4-4-4

3-4-4

3-3-4

★ Adapted from Sheldon, 1954

students. These pictures were then inspected carefully by several judges with the intent of teasing out the principal variables that account for or form the basis of physique variation. Once a given characteristic was suspected of being a primary component, it was appraised in terms of the following criteria: (1) Was it possible to rank all four thousand subjects in terms of this characteristic? (2) Could different judges reach agreement independently in ranking physiques in terms of this characteristic? (3) Was it impossible to account for this variable in terms of some combination of the other variables that had already been identified?

After a considerable period of carefully examining and judging these pictures Sheldon and his associates concluded that, with a list of three, they had exhausted the possibilities of discovering new components. These three dimensions became the core of the technique for assessing the physical structure of the body, and their careful delineation and measurement occupied the next phase of Sheldon's investigation.

Primary Components of Physique

The first component was *endomorphy*. The individual who is high in this component and low in both of the others is characterized by softness and a spherical appearance. Consistent with the softness and rounded quality is an underdevelopment of bone and muscle and a relatively low surface-mass ratio. Such an individual has a low specific gravity and floats high in the water. The fact that the digestive viscera are highly developed in this physique and that the functional elements of those structures develop primarily from the endodermal embryonic layer accounts for the use of the term endomorphy.

The second component was referred to as *mesomorphy*. A physique heavily developed in this component, and showing a decrement in both the other components, is hard and rectangular, with a predominance of bone and muscle. The mesomorphic body is strong, tough, resistant to injury, and generally equipped for strenuous and exacting physical demands. The athlete, adventurer, or professional soldier might best be endowed with this type of physique. The dominant portions of this physique have derived primarily from the mesodermal embryonic layer, hence the term mesomorphic.

The third component was labeled *ectomorphy*. An individual who is at the upper extreme in this component and low in the other components is linear and fragile, characterized by flatness of the chest and delicacy of the body. He is usually thin and lightly muscled. Relative to his mass the ectomorph has more surface area than the other types of physique; he shows a preponderance of surface over mass. He also has the largest brain and central nervous system in proportion to his size. From this, Sheldon reasons that his physique is made up, more so than the other physiques, of tissues that have derived from the ectodermal embryonic layer. The ectomorph, because of his large proportionate surface area, is overexposed to external stimulation. This is a physique poorly equipped for competitive and persistent physical action.

Intervening between a general definition of the primary components of physique and the final delineation of the somatotype are the details of an objective measurement technique. A suitable measurement procedure was derived from an intricate mixture of judges' ratings or rankings and an elaborate network of physical measurements. Each of the four thousand subjects was ranked and rated in terms of each of the primary components. It was possible to take a great many anthropometric measurements, most of them consisting of diameters of various parts of the body, and determine how effectively these measures differentiated between individuals who were high or low in the judges' rankings for each of the components. Those physical measurements that differentiated accurately between subjects the judges had ranked differently on the three primary components were retained, and all other measurements were rejected. This resulted eventually in the retention of a cluster of seventeen anthropometric measures, all of which were diameters expressed as ratios to the height of the individual. It was soon discovered that these diameters could be measured at least as accurately from photographs as from the body of the subject. Thus, the technique substituted measures derived from standard photographs for the previous practice of taking measurements directly from the subject's body.

At this point a total of four thousand subjects had been ranked by judges in terms of the extent to which each of the primary components was present in their physical make-up. In addition, all subjects had been assigned a score of from one to seven for each of the components. Thus, for every rating or score on each variable there existed a number of concrete illustrations in the form of individuals in the original sample who had been assigned this rating. In addition, for every individual there was a set of physical measurements that had been shown to differentiate between individuals with different ratings on the three components. It was then possible for Sheldon to develop a process whereby, given the seventeen physical measurements, the appropriate ratings on each of the three components could be objectively derived. At one point in the research a collaborator, S. S. Stevens, developed a machine, which, although it required a human operator, reduced the assignment of scores to a relatively simple, though numerous, set of manipulations. Using an operator who was unfamiliar with the somatotyping procedure, except for the instructions necessary to operate the machine, it was possible to demonstrate for one hundred cases a correlation of .94 between the ratings assigned by the machine and those arrived at by the more customary observational technique. Sheldon reports (1954) that, in general, individuals who were accustomed to somatotyping the college group customarily found correlations of .90 or above between their independent somatotype ratings.

The physical measurements not only lead to an over-all score for each of the components; they also provide *ratings for* these components for *five different areas of the body:* head-neck, chest-trunk, arms, stomach-trunk, and legs. A complete description of the process of somatotyping the male body is contained in Sheldon's *Atlas of men* (1954) which includes representative somatotype photographs of over one thousand men derived from a total sample of 46,000 photographs.

Although the development of a machine for computing the somatotype served certain useful demonstrational purposes, Sheldon considers that such an approach to somatotyping is much too slow, mechanical, and inflexible. In practice the procedure most commonly used in arriving at the somatotype begins with tables providing the distribution of known somatotypes for the various ratios derived from dividing the subject's height by the cube root of his weight. These tables are available for five-year age groups from eighteen to sixty-five. Thus, if we know an individual's height, weight, and age it is possible to go to an appropriate table where we will find suggested a small number of somatotypes (usually not more than four or five) as most typical. It is then possible to select the most appropriate somatotype by examining the actual physical measurements or by simple inspection. This process of inspection can be facilitated by the file of photographs that appears in the *Atlas of men* where the pictures are conveniently ordered so that the user can quickly find photographs of any desired somatotype.

Sheldon has since developed a method of assigning somatotype ratings that is almost wholly objective. The method combines three variables in a highly objective manner and in almost all cases produces an actuarial estimate of the somatotype. The three variables employed are the somatotype Ponderal Index (height/cube root of weight), the Trunk Index (ratio of upper torso (thoracic trunk) to lower torso (abdominal trunk) derived primarily from the front view of the standard somatotype photograph), and mature height. Even before the method had been fully described, it was utilized in several empirical studies (Livson and McNeil, 1962; McNeil and Livson, 1963). These investigators report that correlations between the old and new methods of somatotyping range upward from .70.

In his major publication of recent years, Sheldon has presented (Sheldon, Lewis, and Tenney, 1969) a full discussion of these basic somatotype variables together with a series of tables (The Basic Tables for Objective Somatotyping) that permit one to establish the correct somatotype given scores on the three variables. An abbreviated version of this monograph (Sheldon, 1971) provides the historical context of this work and a brief summary of the new procedure.

The *somatotype* of the individual is the patterning of the primary components of physique as expressed by three numerals derived from the seventeen measures mentioned above, or some equivalent set of operations, viewed against an adequate history of the individual. The first of these numerals always refers to endomorphy, the second to mesomorphy, and the third to ectomorphy. The numerals range from 1 to 7 with 1 representing the absolute minimum of the component and 7 the highest possible amount. Thus, an individual rated 7-1-1 is extremely high in endomorphy and very low in mesomorphy and very low in ectomorphy. An individual rated 4-6-1 is about average in endomorphy and very high in mesomorphy but markedly deficient in ectomorphy.

In Figure 13-1 we present a series of illustrative somatotypes. In addition to the three polar or extreme physiques, where one component is completely dominant, we also present several examples of a more typical or balanced physique. Most individuals will fall into one of the relatively balanced somatotypes.

To many readers it seemed that Sheldon implied in his early writing that the somatotype could be adequately derived from a single set of somatotype photographs. Later, however, he clearly indicated that information concerning the weight history of the individual and, ideally, a series of photographs separated in time are needed for a more precise measure of the somatotype (Sheldon, 1949, 1954). These subsequent qualifications seem related to a more explicit treatment of the underlying *morphogenotype*. As we mentioned earlier, the somatotype is viewed as a means of estimating or approximating the basic and unchanging biological determinants of behavior (morphogenotype) through measures in large part based upon the external observable body (phenotype). In Sheldon's words:

The principal problem of constitutional research, to date, has been to try to throw a preliminary taxonomic illumination on the behavior of the morphogenotype in man.

But you cannot deal directly with a morphogenotype. All you can see, or touch, or measure and weigh is a phenotype. The phenotype is the living body as it is presented to sensory perception at a given moment. The phenotype by definition has no fourth dimension, no continuance in time. . . . But to work directly with the genotype is impossible since at present the latter is but a conceptual abstraction. It was necessary therefore to introduce another concept, the somatotype, which is neither phenotype nor genotype but is the reflection of the continuity which apparently exists between these two aspects of organic life. . . . To somatotype is to try to reflect light on the *fixed* end of the continuum by repeatedly recording the *varying* end of it which is presented to the senses in successive examinations of the phenotype (1954, p. 19).

Thus, the somatotype is a compromise between the morphogenotype and the phenotype. It is more than the individual's present physique but it is clearly less than the biologically determined structure of the body independent of environmental influences. Sheldon suggests that if we are seriously interested in getting a best estimate of the underlying morphogenotype we should have, ideally, not only a complete history of the individual but also a record of his or her ancestors and descendants. Further, the somatotype photographs should be taken at regular intervals throughout the individual's life in addition to as many biological tests as are feasible. The ordinary somatotype does not, of course, approach this ideal; but presumably it does move in this direction and away from a simple static description of the present physique. Consistent with this view is Sheldon's definition of the somatotype:

The somatotype is by definition a prediction of the future succession of phenotypes which a livng person will present, if nutrition remains a constant factor or varies only within normal limits. We define the somatotype more formally as a *trajectory or pathway through which the living organism will travel under standard conditions of nutrition and in the absence of grossly disturbing pathology* (1954, p. 19).

In the four thousand cases that Sheldon first studied he was able to identify 76 distinct somatotype patterns. Although he admitted the probability that additional patterns would be discovered, he did not expect the frequency of these to even approach the 343 that were theoretically possible. His acumen in this particular instance is documented by the fact that after examining over forty thousand male physiques he was able to report a total of only 88 different somatotypes. However, with his new method of determining the somatotype, this picture has changed dramatically, and he reported a total of 267 observed somatotypes (Sheldon, Lewis, and Tenney, 1969).

Sheldon is clearly aware of the extent to which the somatotype is an abstraction from the full-blown complexity of any concrete physique. The primary components serve to set limits upon a classified physique but within any single somatotype classification there is still room for tremendous variation. This variation is in part intercepted or accounted for by a series of secondary components. Sheldon considers the primary components to anchor the physique and permit an adequate classification, but there remain additional dimensions that will be of interest to the investigator who wishes to describe physiques more fully. It is to these additional components that we turn now.

The Secondary Components   One of the most important of the secondary components is *dysplasia*. Borrowing the term from Kretschmer, Sheldon uses it to refer to "any inconsistent or uneven mixture of the three primary components in different regions of the body" (1940, p. 68). Thus, it is a measure of disharmony between different areas of the physique, for example, head and neck of one somatotype and legs of another. The measure of dysplasia is arrived at by taking the separate somatotype ratings for the five regions of the body and summing the differences for each of the components among the five areas of the body. In other words, it represents the amount of discrepancy in the somatotype as computed for each of the five areas of the body. One can derive separate dysplasia scores for each of the three components as well as a total score. Preliminary findings indicate that there is more dysplasia associated with the ectomorphic component than with either of the other two components, and also more dysplasia observed in the female physique than in the male physique. Sheldon (1940) also reports that there is more dysplasia among psychotics than among college students.

Another secondary component is called *gynandromorphy*. This represents the extent to which the physique possesses characteristics ordinarily associated with the opposite sex and is referred to as the "g index." The male individual who is high in this component possesses a soft body, broad pelvis, and wide hips as well as other feminine features including long eyelashes and small facial features. The thoretical range on this variable is from 1, no sign of characteristics of the opposite sex, to 7, hermaphroditism. In his study of delinquency Sheldon (1949) distinguishes between primary and secondary gynandromorphism. The primary measure represents the physique as "seen at a distance" or as inferred from the somatotype photograph. The secondary measure is inferred from a physical examination or direct observation of the person and includes physical movement, voice, and facial expression.

Perhaps most important of all the secondary components, and certainly most elusive, is the *textural aspect*. Sheldon indicates his conviction that this component is of great significance and likens the person who is high in this dimension to a purebred animal. He suggests,

. . . within each somatotype there is a fairly clear gradation from very coarse to very fine physical texture . . . there is a high correlation between the *t*-index and the fineness of the hair of the head . . . coarseness of texture might correlate with the gross size of the individual cells of various parts of the body (1940, pp. 76–77).

In a later publication he suggests that this is simply a measure of "aesthetic pleasingness," and in attempting to answer the question "pleasing to whom?" he suggests:

High *t* component is structure pleasing to any person of average aesthetic perception or of average appreciation of beauty of form and of proportion. Beyond this simple statement, objectification of the definition of *t* is difficult in the same way, and possibly for the same reason, that the definition of delinquency is difficult. In the final analysis, it is *you* to whom delinquency must be a disappointing performance . . . and to whom high *t* must be pleasing (1949, p. 22).

Sheldon reasons that the *t* component is an evaluation of the "aesthetic success of that particular biological experiment which the individual himself is" (1949, p. 21), and concludes that this kind of evaluation of humans cannot be avoided by a society that wishes to survive, or a social science that intends to deal with the most important of social problems.

There is an important distinction between primary and secondary *t* component that corresponds to the distinction drawn earlier between primary and secondary gynandromorphy. Primary *t* is inferred from the somatotype photograph itself whereas the secondary component is inferred from close and direct contact with the individual. The author provides (Sheldon, 1954) illustrations of somatotypes that have been rated as falling in each of the categories from 1 to 6 for both the textural aspect and gynandromorphy. In neither case has a physique been observed that deserves the highest rating on these variables.

We have not outlined all of the secondary components but those we have described are the most important. They will suffice to illustrate for the reader the manner in which Sheldon is able to supplement and enrich the description of physique provided by the primary components.

Female Somatotyping   The bulk of the initial work that was done with Sheldon's physical dimensions was carried out with males. It is evident that in our society the sanctions against studying the naked human body are more stringent in the case of the female than in the case of the male. Consequently, it is quite natural that the initial work in this area should have been executed with male subjects. In his first volume on physique Sheldon (1940) states that the evidence then available indicates that the same seventy-six somatotypes seemed to occur among women as had been observed among men, although probably with different frequencies. He also suggests that endomorphy, and endomorphy combined with ectomorphy, are more common among women; while mesomorphy, and mesomorphy combined with endomorphy, are more common among men.

Sheldon reported (1954) that considerable work has been carried out in the area of female somatotyping, and that an 'Atlas of Women" will be published in the future. The more extensive findings that he now possesses confirms his earlier observation that female physiques are much more endomorphic than male physiques. He also indicates that women show less range on the components than men; nevertheless there are a small number of female somatotypes without parallel in the male series.

Constancy of the   One of the points where common sense and the generalizations of the
Somatotype   constitutional theorist seem to diverge is in regard to the degree to which a classification or description based upon objective measures of the physique can be expected to remain constant. The usual changes introduced by aging and diet variation seem compelling evidence to most people of the changeability of the somatotype. However, Sheldon, in his early writings, along with other constitutional psychologists is equally firm in his conviction that ". . . apparently no nutritional change can cause the measurements of a person of one somatotype to simulate those of another somatotype" (1944, p. 540). It is possible for nutritional factors to produce changes in the individual measurements, but these will not change the actual somatotype. Instead, they will appear as deviations from the normal or original somatotype. This generalization is presented by Sheldon in the face of measurements that have been carried out before and after shifts in weights of as much as one hundred pounds. He summarizes:

> . . . it has been possible to follow the development of several hundred individuals over a period of about a dozen years, and while many have shown sharp fluctuations in weight, we have discovered no case in which there has been a convincing change in the somatotype. In order for the somatotype to change, the skeleton must change,

as well as the shape of the head, the bony structure of the face, the neck, wrists, ankles, calves, and forearms, and the relations of stature to measurements made at places where fat does not accumulate. The deposit or removal of fat does not change the somatotype, for it does not change significantly any of the measurements except those where the fat is deposited. . . . It can be said that the case has yet to occur in which a nutritional disturbance has caused a physique either to become unrecognizable or to simulate another somatotype strongly enough to cause any justifiable confusion (1940, p. 221).

Sheldon suggests that just as a starved mastiff does not become a poodle, so a starved mesomorph does not become an ectomorph. Only in certain diseases, such as acromegaly and muscle-wasting diseases, does the actual structure of the body change, and such disorders are readily identifiable through inspection and thus should not lead to unexpected changes in the somatotype. The constancy of the somatotype is so general that Sheldon maintains that even the index of dysplasia does not fluctuate with weight changes.

One type of physique that frequently leads to the belief that there has been a dramatic change in somatotype is the PPJ or Pyknic Practical Joke. Here we have an individual endowed with a rating, say a 4, in the endomorphic component, and a slightly higher mesomorphic component, a 5 let us say. Given such a physique, the individual is likely to appear lean and athletic in late adolescence and early adulthood, but with the passage of years the first component asserts itself, and the joke becomes evident as the person becomes very heavy and round. In spite of the anthropometric change in the physique the somatotype has remained the same. Another factor that makes it difficult to assess accurately the constancy of the somatotype is the much greater skill that is required to measure the somatotype in late adolescence or early adulthood. By the time the individual is thirty his or her somatotype is vividly revealed, but earlier in life it takes a more skilled observer to detect it, although the signs are nonetheless objectively present.

Some evidence in favor of the hypothesis of constancy is provided by the similarity in the distribution of types of somatotypes found in different age groups. For example, Sheldon (1940) reports that men forty years of age show roughly the same frequencies of the various somatotypes that college students display. It seems probable that if age led to systematic changes in the somatotype these would be reflected in shifts in the frequency with which the various kinds of somatotypes are observed in different age groups.

Subsequently, Sheldon (1954) seemed to have modified, or at least elaborated, his views regarding the constancy of the somatotype. As we have already noted, the most recent definition of somatotype includes a provision of nutritional constancy as well as absence of pathology; furthermore, there has appeared a heavy emphasis upon the importance of an adequate history of the individual focused about the weight during development, especially just before pubescence, for an adequate somatotyping. Thus, the former impression of a somatotype derived from three standard photographs that is impervious to environmental change has been replaced by a more general and explicit conception that recommends that the somatotype be derived from successive photographs in conjunction with a history of the individual and leaves open the question of the extent to which this somatotype may be modifiable. Sheldon's position on this topic is well summarized by the following quotation:

> Is there a degree of dependability (or predictability) in the somatotype as in practice it is actually gauged? That is to say, when we have to depend on only two or three adult phenotype presentations, and a good history, can a predictive somatotype be assigned which will "stay put"? Some would like to answer that question in the categorical affirmative, fearing that any other answer might elicit an unhealthful complacency among "environmental determinists," a few of whom perhaps come near to believing, as they proclaim, that the somatotype is "nothing but nutrition." But only a good longitudinal study, carried on for at least one human lifetime, would adequately document such an answer (1954, p. 20).

More recently he presented brief summaries of a number of diverse studies (Sheldon, Lewis, and Tenney, 1969) indicating remarkable temporal stability in the Trunk Index. In view of the central role occupied by the TI in determining the somatotype in Sheldon's modified procedure, it is not surprising that he has once again asserted the unchanging nature of the somatotype. It is too soon for other investigators to have examined the constancy of the somatotype when it is determined by Sheldon's new technique.

THE ANALYSIS
OF BEHAVIOR
(PERSONALITY)

Given a stable means of assessing the physical aspects of the human build, the constitutional psychologist must still devise or borrow some method of assessing behavior in order to explore the relation between physique and personality. In the present case, Sheldon began with the assumption that although there were manifold surface dimensions or variables in terms of which behavior could be described, underlying these was a small number of basic components that could be expected to account for all the surface complexity and variety. He set out to devise a technique for measuring these basic components that would borrow from the wisdom of past investigations of personality and combine with this his own clinical knowledge and inductive experience.

Initially the literature of personality, especially that having to do with specifying human traits, was carefully inspected, and a list of 650 traits was extracted. The list was increased by adding variables derived from the investigator's own observations and then was sharply reduced through combining overlapping dimensions and eliminating those that seemed of no significance. In the end Sheldon and his co-workers had a total of 50 traits that seemed to them to represent all of the specific phenomena that had been dealt with by the original 650 traits.

Dimensions of Temperament

    The next step was to select a group of thirty-three young men, for the most part graduate students and instructors, who were studied for one year through the medium of observation in their everyday professional activities and in clinical interviews. Each subject was rated by the investigator on a seven-point scale for each of the fifty traits, and the resultant scores were intercorrelated with the intent of discovering clusters of positively correlated traits that could be considered to represent the same underlying variable. It was decided arbitrarily that in order for a trait to be included within a cluster or component it must show a positive correlation of at least .60 with each of the other traits in the cluster and show a negative correlation of at least −.30 with all traits found in other clusters.

The results of the correlational analysis revealed three major clusters or groups of traits that included twenty-two of the original fifty items. The first group included traits of relaxation, love of comfort, pleasure in digestion, dependence on social approval, deep sleep, need of people when troubled. The traits spanned by the second cluster included assertive posture, energetic characteristic, need of exercise, directness of manner, unrestrained voice, quality of seeming older, need of action when troubled. Finally, there was a third group of traits, including restraint in posture, overly fast reaction, sociophobia, inhibited social address, resistance to habit, vocal restraint, poor sleep habits, youthful intentness, need of solitude when troubled.

Primary Components of Temperament

    At this stage Sheldon was satisfied that at least tentatively he had identified components of behavior sufficiently basic to warrant further study. He set about improving and enlarging the lists of traits for each component in order to devise a sensitive and reliable measure for the three components. He attempted to add traits and reflected the constitution of the individual and thus were not highly variable in the face of environmental or cultural variation. A series of eight trial studies of various combinations of the old and new traits was completed before the investigator arrived at the last stage. A final intercorrelation study with one hundred subjects, using seventy-eight traits, resulted in the selection of twenty traits for each of the three clusters (a total of sixty traits), all of which met the criteria of correlating at least .60 with all other traits in the same cluster and showing a negative correlation of at least −.30 with all traits in other clusters. The traits that were finally selected are summarized in Table 13-2.

The first component of temperament was named *viscerotonia*. An individual high in this component is characterized by general love of comfort, sociability, and gluttony for food, people, and affection. He or she is relaxed in posture, reacts slowly, is even-tempered, tolerant in their relations to others, and is generally an easy person to interact with. Sheldon suggests: "The personality seems to center around the viscera. The digestive tract is king, and its welfare appears to define the primary purpose of life" (1944, p. 543).

The second component was called *somatotonia*. A high score on this component is ordinarily accompanied by love of physical adventure, risk-taking, and a strong need for muscular and vigorous physical activity. The individual is aggressive, callous toward the feelings of others, overmature in appearance, noisy, courageous, and given to claustrophobia. Action, power, and domination are of first importance to such an individual.

The third component was labeled *cerebrotonia*. An elevated score on this component implies restraint, inhibition, and the desire for concealment. The individual is secretive, self-conscious, youthful in appearance, afraid of people, and happiest in small enclosed areas. He or she reacts overquickly, sleeps poorly, and prefers solitude, particularly when troubled. Such an individual consistently attempts to avoid attracting attention to him or her self.

The three general dimensions, together with the twenty defining traits for each dimension, make up the *Scale for Temperament* that is an elaborate rating procedure for arriving at scores for each of the primary components. Sheldon recommends in using the Scale that where possible:

Observe the subject closely for at least a year in as many different situations as possible. Conduct a series of not less than twenty analytic interviews with him in a manner best suited to the situation, and to the temperaments and interests of the two principals. . . . After each interview . . . turn to the score sheet and assign a rating on as many of the traits as possible. . . . Repeat the observations, interviews, and revisions of ratings until reasonably satisfied that all of the sixty traits have been adequately considered and evaluated (1942, p. 27).

TABLE 13-2
The scale for temperament

Viscerotonia	Somatotonia	Cerebrotonia
( ) 1. Relaxation in posture and movement	( ) 1. Assertiveness of posture and movement	( ) 1. Restraint in posture and movement, tightness
( ) 2. Love of physical comfort	( ) 2. Love of physical adventure	2. Physiological over-response
( ) 3. Slow reaction	( ) 3. The energetic characteristic	( ) 3. Overly fast reactions
4. Love of eating	( ) 4. Need and enjoyment of exercise	( ) 4. Love of privacy
5. Socialization of eating	5. Love of dominating. Lust for power	( ) 5. Mental overintensity. Hyperattentionality. Apprehensiveness
6. Pleasure in digestion	( ) 6. Love of risk and chance	( ) 6. Secretiveness of feeling, emotional restraint
( ) 7. Love of polite ceremony	( ) 7. Bold directness of manner	( ) 7. Self-conscious mobility of the eyes and face
( ) 8. Sociophilia	( ) 8. Physical courage for combat	( ) 8. Sociophobia
9. Indiscriminate amiability	( ) 9. Competitive aggressiveness	( ) 9. Inhibited social address
10. Greed for affection and approval	10. Psychological callousness	10. Resistance to habit and poor routinizing
11. Orientation to people	11. Claustrophobia	11. Agoraphobia
( ) 12. Evenness of emotional flow	12. Ruthlessness, freedom from squeamishness	12. Unpredictability of attitude
( ) 13. Tolerance	( ) 13. The unrestrained voice	( ) 13. Vocal restraint and general restraint of noise
( ) 14. Complacency	14. Spartan indifference to pain	14. Hypersensitivity to pain
15. Deep sleep	15. General noisiness	15. Poor sleep habits, chronic fatigue
( ) 16. The untempered characteristic	( ) 16. Overmaturity of appearance	( ) 16. Youthful intentness of manner and appearance
( ) 17. Smooth, easy communication of feeling, extraversion of viscerotonia	17. Horizontal mental cleavage, extraversion of somatotonia	17. Vertical mental cleavage, introversion
18. Relaxation and sociophilia under alcohol	18. Assertiveness and aggression under alcohol	18. Resistance to alcohol and to other depressant drugs
19. Need of people when troubled	19. Need of action when troubled	19. Need of solitude when troubled
20. Orientation toward childhood and family relationships	20. Orientation toward goals and activities of youth	20. Orientation toward the later periods of life

Note: The thirty traits with parentheses constitute collectively the short form of the scale. From Sheldon (1942), p. 26.

Thus, after a long period of observation the investigator assigns ratings of from 1 to 7 for sixty specific traits each of which Sheldon defines in detail. The total score for the twenty traits within each component is then computed by adding the individual ratings, and this is converted to an over-all rating for each variable by consulting a table (Sheldon, 1942, p. 95) or averaging the ratings. For a particularly careful analysis it is possible to assign half scores, thus expanding the seven-point range to a thirteen-point range.

There are also secondary components for describing behavior although these are not so numerous or so carefully worked out as those for the assessment of physique. For this reason we shall omit their description here. The interested reader will find the most complete account of these components in Sheldon (1949).

THE RELATION OF PHYSIQUE TO BEHAVIOR (PERSONALITY)

We have now seen how Sheldon identified what he considered to be the basic components of physique (structure) and temperament (function), and we have also observed how he devised instruments to measure these components. It remains to survey his attempts to relate these two classes of variables.

In one sense we might consider the earlier studies simply preliminary steps to the more significant goal of estimating the degree of relationship between physique and temperament. In another sense, it is obvious that the measures of somatotype and temperament possess an independent value not derived from the outcome of the study to be reported here. An adequate means of measuring physique is of value to many investigators who may have no interest in constitutional psychology as such; for example, physical anthropologists, applied psychologists, physiologists, pathologists. Similarly, a set of objective and sensitive measures of important dimensions of behavior would be a boon to almost all psychologists, whether or not they are interested in the relation between physique and behavior.

Most of Sheldon's research revolves around the question of how much association exists between physique and personality. However,

TABLE 13-3 *Correlation between physique components and temperament components*		*Viscerotonia* r	*Somatotonia* r	*Cerebrotonia* r
	Somatotype	($n=200$)	($n=200$)	($n=200$)
	Endomorphy	+0.79	−0.29	−0.32
	Mesomorphy	−0.23	+0.82	−0.58
	Ectomorphy	−0.40	−0.53	+0.83

Adapted from Sheldon (1942), p. 400.

we shall limit ourselves for the present to the description of a single representative study that related physique and temperament among normal college students. We shall discuss briefly, in a later section of the chapter, studies bearing on delinquency and mental disorder.

Over a period of five years Sheldon (1942) carried out a study of two hundred male, white subjects who were college students or college graduates involved in academic or professional activities. These subjects were rated on the temperament dimensions, as defined in the Scale of Temperament, after a long period of observation. Following this the subjects were somatotyped according to the procedure already described.

The most significant findings in this study concerned the degree of association between the temperament variables and the physique variables as estimated by a correlation technique. The results in Table 13-3 indicate very clearly that the correlation between the parallel physique and temperament dimensions is significant and surprisingly high, while the correlation between all other combinations of the physique and temperament variables is significantly negative. These results are unambiguous in suggesting that *there is a close correspondence between temperament as measured by observer ratings and physique as derived from measures taken from somatotype photographs.* Sheldon suggests:

These are higher correlations than we expected to find, and they raise some questions of great interest. If we were to regard the product-movement correlation as a measure of the degree to which two variables are made up of common elements, correlations of the order of +.80 would suggest that morphology and temperament, as we measure them, may constitute expressions at their respective levels of essentially common components. . . . If we *have* already reached basic factors in personality, the correlations are not higher than should be expected, for then with the two techniques we are but measuring the same thing at different levels of its expression (1942, p. 401).

Sheldon concludes that if these measures, on further study, prove to have the basic status that he hopes for, they will provide a frame of reference in terms of which psychology can contribute to the study of individual differences in all areas of behavior. Such a possibility would facilitate the interpenetration of psychology with both biology and the social sciences.

We find, then, that Sheldon's research has led to a surprisingly strong confirmation of the constitutional psychologist's expectation that there is a marked continuity between the structural or physical aspects of the individual and his or her functional or behavioral qualities. In fact, the magnitude of the correlations observed between the physique and temperament components is sufficient to dwarf the correlations reported in similar studies attempting to relate personality and environmental or experiential determinants. Let us turn now to the interpretation of this relationship.

SOME
THEORETICAL
FORMULATIONS

It is important to realize that constitutional theory is more inductive and less of a theory than many other brands of psychological theory. Much more central to the position than a set of axioms are the primary components that have been described and the empirically derived relations among them. Sheldon himself seems to be essentially a naturalist with a taxonomic bent. Thus, he is at his best in making shrewd observations concerning regularities in behavior and in trying to group together or classify individuals who are similar in some important respect. He has shown little interest in formalizing or systematizing his viewpoint and this may well be a self-conscious choice as the following quotation seems to imply:

If we seem to overemphasize the constitutional factor throughout this book by largely omitting the factor of environmental influence, it does not mean that we consider the latter unimportant. It means only that we are presenting here the neglected side of the picture, without which a general psychology seems fatuous or anomalous. The problem of synthesis lies on beyond. In these two volumes [1940, 1942] . . . we have attempted to do no more than write in the foundation for the constitutional side of this structure as a whole. That, in itself, has been sufficiently difficult.

Constitutional psychology we regard as only a contribution to general psychology, not a substitute. Its place in the total scheme is possibly comparable to the description of the skeleton in anatomy. If such a point of view does not seem to have been maintained dispassionately in all of the sections of the present book, let the shortcoming be charged (in the reader's generosity) to counteremphasis (Sheldon, 1942, p. 438).

Factors Mediating the
Physique-
Temperament
Association

We accept here the existence of a marked relation between measures of physique and measures of important behavioral attributes, and inquire into what has led to this striking congruence. One may reason that an individual who is endowed with a particular type of physique is likely to find certain kinds of responses particularly effective while an individual with another type of physique will find it necessary to adopt other modes of response. This conception suggests that *the success or reward that accompanies a particular mode of responding is a function not only of the environment in which it occurs but also of the kind of person (type of physique) making the response.* The individual with a frail ectomorphic body cannot successfully adopt a bluff, aggressive, domineering manner in relation to most people, whereas it may be perfectly possible for the oversized mesomorph to do so. Further, the child with a small stomach, or low thresholds for pain, may be exposed to characteristic experiences that are strikingly different from those typical for individuals of different physical characteristics. Given a particular physique and a normal environment, the individual finds certain kinds of responses are relatively often rewarded and certain other kinds of responses are usually punished. This implies that the individual will develop patterns of behavior that will show similarity to the behavior of other people, who because of sharing the same kind of physiques have had similar sets of experiences.

The limitations that physique places upon behavior may be either direct or indirect. Height, weight, and comparable physical attributes place direct and unmistakable limits upon how an individual may expect to perform adaptively in a given environment. In addition, possession of a particular type of physique makes it likely that an individual will be exposed to certain types of environmental experience, while another variety of physique would normally lead to quite a different set of experiences. For example, it is known (McNeil and Livson, 1963) that females with a linear physique are slower to reach physiological maturation than girls with a less linear physique, and it is clearly a matter of substantial psychological importance just when an individual matures and becomes an adult.

Another possibility is that *the relation between physique and temperament is mediated by commonly accepted stereotypes or the social-stimulus value* within the culture in regard to the sort of behavior to be expected of individuals with different kinds of physique. Thus, we may suggest that the individual with a particular physique occupies a social role, which includes a set of behavioral specifications, and in the normal course of events the individual will conform to these specifications. Expectations on the part of the culture will lead the individual with a distinctive physique to show distinctive patterns of behavior and this behavior will tend to be shared by other individuals with the same type of physique who have been exposed to similar expectations. This formulation does not account for the origin of the stereotype, nor does it have much to say concerning the individual whose physique is in the midrange and fits no convenient stereotype.

Still another means of explaining the observed relation is in terms of experience of *environmental influences that tend to produce particular kinds of physique and at the same time produce certain behavioral tendencies.* Thus, we might reason that exposure of the child to an overprotective mother would predispose the child to obesity and at the same time would produce identifiable personality characteristics. If we accept Landauer and Whiting's (1964) findings in regard to the relationship between traumatic early experience and enhanced adult stature and also believe that these early experiences shape behavior we would again expect to find an association between physical attributes and personality characteristics. This line of reasoning merely assumes that there are certain events that influence the development of both physical and personality characteristics and that, as a consequence, we observe significant association between these two domains. This formulation avoids the notion of biological determinism and suggests that both physique and behavior are largely determined by environmental influences.

A final alternative is to account for the relation between body build and behavior in terms of the *common operation of biological factors.* Thus, one may argue that both physique and behavioral tendencies are largely determined by hereditary factors and among these factors are certain associative links that result in particular kinds of physical attributes being linked with particular behavioral attributes. The individual who possesses certain physical qualities may be expected to display specifiable behavioral tendencies because the same gene or genes influence both sets of attributes. The two major twin studies that involved the study of physical attributes (Newman, Freeman, and Holzinger, 1937; Osborne and DeGeorge, 1959) found strong evidence for the important role of genetic factors in determining physique. This finding, coupled with many studies showing the role of genetic variation as a determinant of behavior, makes it altogether reasonable to expect that genes, either alone or in combination, will have multiple or pleiotropic effects that include both behavior and physique.

It is primarily the first two modes of explanation, selective experience and cultural determination, that Sheldon appears to emphasize although he is also willing to acknowledge the operation of genetic determination. The third formulation, implying that both physique and behavior are the outcome of environmental factors, is least compatible with the assumptions of constitutional psychologists, Sheldon included.

Biological and Genetic Orientation

Many personality theorists have chosen to place a heavy emphasis upon the psychobiological nature of human behavior (Murray, Murphy, Freud); however, few have shown much willingness to adapt their procedural methods to this assumption. In many respects the details of Sheldon's position may be considered to stem from a conviction that biological factors are of overwhelming importance in accounting for human behavior and his consequent decision to attempt the measurement of important elements of this biological foundation of behavior. As we have seen from his distinction between the somatotype and the morphogenotype, the measurement of physique is merely a means of estimating the underlying biological factors that have such a heavy influence upon the course of life. All things considered, it seems safe to say that Sheldon's position revolves more closely about biological determinants of behavior than does that of any other contemporary personality theorist.

Although our discussion of the possible factors mediating the association between physique and behavior made clear that Sheldon does not overemphasize the potential role of genetic factors in the determination of behavior, nevertheless he is hopeful that somatotype measurement may permit a more accurate measurement of some genetic factors and thus enable us to estimate realistically the indirect effect of genetic factors upon behavior.

Sheldon seems consistently concerned with the problem of context and, as one would expect of a devoted naturalist, he is reluctant to examine any one aspect of behavior to the exclusion of all (or most) other aspects. In general, his concern over considering all aspects of the total organism is much greater than his concern over the environmental context within which behavior occurs. Such a position stems quite naturally from his great interest in biological determinants of behavior.

Organismic and Field Emphasis

Although Sheldon succeeded in isolating and measuring dimensions for describing physique and temperament, he does not believe that it is fruitful to examine these dimensions one by one. The *pattern* of relations between the variables is much more important than the absolute level of any single component. He is constantly aware of the essential uniqueness of each individual in both behavior and physical appearance. In spite of his willingness to fracture this unique totality with his component measurements, he still considers the outcome of such measurement only a first step toward describing the organism. It is his conviction that the sensitive, globally oriented observer is capable of contributing knowledge that the skilled and objective psychometrist cannot yet hope to unearth. A fundamental concern over the dangers of premature quantification and too heavy an emphasis upon objectivity runs through all of Sheldon's writings.

In view of what has been said concerning Sheldon's interest in biological determinants of behavior, it should come as no surprise to discover that Sheldon has shown somewhat less concern over the details of development than most other personality theorists. While he freely admitted that early childhood events of a particular kind may presage certain types of adult adjustment, he was not convinced

Development of the Individual

that the childhood even plays a causative role in such relationships. It is quite likely, he suggested, that there may be biological predispositions that lead to particular kinds of childhood or infantile experience, and further that these same predispositions may lead to specifiable forms of adult behavior. In other words, the apparent relation between early events and subsequent behavior may be largely a reflection of the consistent operation of biological factors over a long period of time.

Sheldon is interested in the developmental process, at least to the extent of expressing his conviction that it could be made much more efficient and less frustrating for the participants if those who were guiding the child would take the trouble to consider the child's somatotype. In this manner one could avoid instilling in the child aspirations and expectations inconsistent with its physical and temperamental potential. This view makes it clear that Sheldon does not consider the development of the individual to be completely fixed by his or her biological inheritance as represented in the morphogenotype. Rather, he sees the person as endowed with potentials that set limits upon and mold the possibilities for future growth. However, the particular experiences to which the person is exposed will have a crucial role in determining whether the person eventually realizes the full extent of these potentials.

Unconscious Processes The importance of unconscious determinants of behavior is accepted by Sheldon but he is inclined to equate these determinants to underlying biological factors. Presumably if the individual knew more about the structure of his body and the biological factors at work within it, he would be more conscious of the forces that impel his behavior. Sheldon (1949) suggests that the unconscious *is* the body and implies further that the reason there is so much difficulty in verbalizing the unconscious is simply because our language is not geared to systematically reflecting what goes on in the body. Thus, he considers that the psychoanalyst who is exploring the unconscious is approaching obliquely, and in a rather inefficient manner, the same thing that Sheldon attempts to reach more directly and objectively through his somatotyping.

CHARACTERISTIC RESEARCH AND RESEARCH METHODS More than most personality theorists Sheldon's formulations are embedded in empirical studies. We have already gained a rather representative view of his investigations in the process of noting how he set about the formulation and measurement of physique and temperament. In the present section we shall deal briefly with two further studies in which he investigated mental disorder and delinquency against the background offered by somatotype measurement.

Constitutional psychology not only gives promise of providing new vistas of understanding in the study of normal human behavior; it also offers the possibility of understanding better, and perhaps alleviating or preventing, various psychological and social abnormalities. Consistent with this conviction are Sheldon's studies of mental disorder that are reported in one brief paper (Wittman, Sheldon, and Katz, 1948) and in a chapter continued in his volume dealing with delinquency (Sheldon, 1949). After examining the state of psychiatric diagnosis he concluded that it would not be possible to approach the study of physique in relation to mental disorder without first providing a measure of mental disorder that was more objective and sensitive than the customary diagnostic techniques.

In the same manner that Sheldon had introduced continuous variables in place of discrete categories in the measurement of physique, so too in the measurement of mental disorder he proposed to substitute dimensions in place of disease entities. On the basis of observation of many psychiatric patients over a number of years he developed a conception of mental disorder as subject to description in terms of three primary dimensions. These three dimensions correspond roughly to three of the diagnostic categories frequently used in psychiatric diagnosis: the first psychiatric component (affective) at its height represents extreme manic-depressive psychosis (fluctuation between extreme elation and depression); the second psychiatric component (paranoid) at its height represents paranoid psychosis (strong delusional system marked by ideas of persecution and self-reference); and the third psychiatric component (heboid) represents the hebephrenic form of schizophrenic psychosis (extreme withdrawal). The three psychiatric components represent respectively a deficiency in the temperament components of cerebrotonia, viscerotonia, and somatotonia.

Sheldon frankly admits that his work in this area is still in a highly tentative state but promises that a future volume will give a full report of his research on this problem and describe a measurement technique and findings that are more definitive than those presently available. He has reported one study that is suggestive of the value of this approach to mental disorder. The research was conducted at the Elgin State Hospital in Illinois in collaboration with Phyllis Wittman (Wittman, Sheldon, and Katz, 1948; Sheldon, 1949). Wittman collected a large amount of descriptive material from the psychiatric files in this hospital, and after refining and pruning the material arrived at a list of 221 behavioral items that appeared to be important in the psychiatric description of patients. She then classified these items in terms of the three psychiatric components mentioned above and called the result-

Physique and Mental Disorder

ing list of items the *Check List of Psychotic Behavior*. A group of 155 male psychotic patients were then selected and were independently somatotyped by Sheldon and rated on the items on the check list by Whittman and a staff psychiatrist, neither of whom actually saw the patients. Average scores for the three psychiatric variables were derived from the check list for each of the raters and intercorrelated. These rater reliability correlations ranged from +0.78 to +0.91 indicating that the ratings were being made with reasonable objectivity. Wittman's ratings for the psychiatric components were then correlated with Sheldon's independent ratings for the physique components with the results summarized in Table 13-4.

Sheldon's exploratory work had led him to expect that there would be only moderate intercorrelations between the two sets of variables and this, of course, is what he observed. In general, the results confirm the expected relations although out of the nine correlations three reversed the direction that he would have predicted in advance of the study. The correlation between the first, second, and third components of the somatotype and the corresponding psychiatric components are, however, all positive and moderately high. These findings appear to imply that psychiatric diagnosis and somatotype are definitely associated, although the nature of this relationship seems somewhat more complex than that observed between physique and temperament.

Sheldon suggests that the components he devised for representing psychotic behavior have their parallels in less severe forms of maladjustment and may even be reflected in an obverse or superior form of adjustment. Thus, he discusses in a hypothetical vein the manner in which various kinds of exceptional achievement can be considered to represent unusually rich development of the potentialities implied by the various patterns of the psychiatric components. The psychiatric components are seen as a supplement to the somatotype and temperament ratings and serve to increase somewhat the spectrum of behavior that these components can adequately represent. Sheldon believes

TABLE 13-4 *Correlations between somatotype and psychiatric components* (n = 155)	1st Psychiatric component (affective)	2nd Psychiatric component (paranoid)	3rd Psychiatric component (heboid)
Endomorphy	+0.54	−0.04	−0.25
Mesomorphy	+0.41	+0.57	−0.68
Ectomorphy	−0.59	−0.34	+0.64

From Sheldon (1949), p. 69.

that eventually customary methods of psychiatric diagnosis may give way to a method of description and classification that leans more heavily upon objective techniques including the Somatotype Performance Test. This will imply a close linkage with biological determinants of behavior. This general point of view is elaborated and some additional findings presented in Sheldon's recent publication with Lewis and Tenney (1969).

Sheldon's eight-year study of delinquent youth was conducted to provide a kind of background against which to compare his findings from the study of normal college youth. The investigation was carried out at the Hayden Goodwill Inn, a resident rehabilitation home for boys in Boston, Massachusetts. During the three years from 1939 to 1942 approximately four hundred young men were studied by Sheldon and his collaborators and, from this sample, two hundred were selected for a follow-up study after the war on the basis of completeness of information and clear evidence of delinquency. All of the subjects were examined by means of the Somatotype Performance Test and assigned somatotype ratings as well as ratings on the secondary components of physique. They were also rated in terms of the psychiatric components and in addition detailed life histories were compiled that included information about their mental and educational performance, family background, medical history, delinquent behavior, and characteristic behavior.

Physique and Delinquency

The core of Sheldon's report of this research is a series of what he calls psychological biographies, which represent thumbnail sketches of the life history of the individual, together with somatotype photographs. These biographies are arranged in terms of a classification that divides the young men into groups according to mental deficiency, psychopathy, alcoholism, excessive femininity, and degree of criminality. In addition to these classified biographical sketches, which leave the task of generalizing largely upon the shoulders of the reader, Sheldon presents diagrams of the distribution of somatotypes for his delinquent population in comparison to the group of college students. It is clear that while the college students show a clustering around the mid-range somatotypes (4-4-4) with a scatter fairly evenly divided over the remainder of the diagram, the delinquents are heavily bunched in the "northwest region"—they tend to be endomorphic mesomorphs. There is obviously a much greater elevation of mesomorphy in the delinquent group and a marked absence of individuals high on the ectomorphic component. Sheldon also presents similar diagrams for each of the subgroups into which the delinquents had been divided. These plots suggest that although the characteristic delinquent physique is endomorphic mesomorphy, there is considerable variation among the delinquent subgroups in somatotype. The various subgroups of delinquents are also compared in terms of the secondary components, the psychiatric components, and a variety of demographic and life history data.

Sheldon at the culmination of his study appears convinced that there are important behavioral and constitutional differences not only between delinquents and normals but also between the subvarieties of delinquents. Further, he speculates concerning the possible role of asthenia (weakness), dysplasia (uneven distribution of somatotype), and burgeoning (gross and nonfunctional enlargement of the physique) as biological determinants characteristic not only of delinquents but also of their parents. This observation leads him to relatively pessimistic conclusions concerning what is happening to the biological stock of this nation as a result of selective differences in reproductive rates favoring social and economic groups that typically display asthenia, dysplasia, and burgeoning.

Several independent investigators have subsequently produced findings that are strongly supportive of Sheldon's major findings in regard to physique and delinquency. It appears that when compared with nondelinquent controls delinquent subjects are high in mesomorphy whether they are English or American subjects and whether they are males or females (Epps and Parnell, 1952; Gibbens, 1963; Cortes, 1961). The most extensive of the studies conducted in this area was carried out by Glueck and Glueck (1950, 1956) and involved the comparison of 500 delinquents with 500 carefully matched nondelinquents. These investigators found that approximately 60 percent of the delinquent youth were classified as primarily mesomorphic while only 30 percent of the nondelinquent subjects were assigned the same classification. In addition, almost 40 percent of the normal subjects were classified as primarily ectomorphic while fewer than 15 percent of the delinquents were so classified. In general, the Gluecks found relatively firm evidence that the delinquents were characterized by "northwest" physiques.

CURRENT STATUS AND EVALUATION   Few psychologists have shown the singleness of purpose and the dedication that Sheldon displayed in pursuing empirical paths all of which lead from a core idea. He has now published a consistent and integrated set of four volumes with several more related volumes in preparation. Thus, Sheldon himself has already shown remarkable energy and persistence in his attempts to arrive at a means of representing biological factors through the description of physique. More significantly, his research produced a host of related investigations on the part of interested or indignant psychologists, psychiatrists, and anthropologists. The reader will find references to a representative group of these studies at the end of this chapter, and papers by Lindzey (1967) and Rees (1968, 1973) summarize relevant research in several significant areas. Although few of these investigators have been much concerned with the theoretical formulations that could or should accompany these findings, they have nevertheless made valuable empirical contributions. Recent years have seen a flurry of research concerned with chromosomal abnormalities (for example, XYY), physique, and deviant behavior although the findings at this point fail to support any single or simple conclusion (Kessler and Moos, 1970). There has also been an increased interest in physical attractiveness as a major determinant of social behavior (Berscheid and Walster, 1974). Both these areas of investigation are highly congruent with Sheldon's approach to understanding human behavior.

In any attempt to appraise the over-all significance of Sheldon's work it is necessary to consider it in the context of existing psychological theories. As we have already suggested, American psychology has been singularly insular in regard to the contribution of biological or hereditary factors as determinants of behavior. Even though some personality theorists have chosen to dwell upon these factors, they have, in general, shown little inclination to implement their theoretical assertions with procedural techniques for assessing the crucial biological factors. Thus we may largely credit Sheldon with reminding psychologists that the behaving human has a physique, and further that this physique provides valuable clues to an underlying set of determinants, which in the end may prove quite as coercive and pervasive as environmental factors. The increasing collaboration between biological and behavioral scientists and the growing awareness on the part of psychologists of the importance of biological factors has served to make Sheldon's position far more acceptable today than it was a decade or so ago.

Aside from the matter of general emphasis upon biological factors and the role of heredity, there is the further fact that Sheldon seems to have isolated and demonstrated a set of empirical relations that are important data for any theory of personality. One may quarrel over the degree of relation between physique and personality, or even over the factors that mediate this relation, but present evidence leaves little doubt, at least in the authors' minds, that something important is afoot here. Prior to Sheldon's forceful appearance on the scene, such a relationship was customarily dismissed in this country as representing little more than superstition or speculation.

In addition to contributions that are directly in the domain of personality theory, it is clear that Sheldon's somatotyping procedure exists as an important contribution to the person who would study the human organism. It not only serves as an admirable link between the anatomical, potentially biological, and the behavioral; it also provides a measuring technique for the individual who is solely interested in the structure of the human body. The human engineer, the physical anthropologist, and others who are not psychologists may derive from this technique unique assistance in their problems.

Undeniably, the substitution of continua for dichotomies, or variables for categories, represents an important measurement advance. For people interested in measuring physique, things are likely to go more smoothly when they can provide values for a number of components rather than force an individual into one of three, four, or five categories. Likewise, Sheldon's development of the dysplastic index as a quantified measure of somatotype discrepancy between the different areas of the body represents an advance over the "wastebasket status" it enjoyed in the system of Kretschmer. In this same area, his development of the photographic technique made it possible to introduce a degree of precision and control that could never have been hoped for when measurements were derived directly from the human body.

The positive contributions of Sheldon's work are evident and can be stated simply. Likewise the negative. Perhaps the most frequent criticism leveled at Sheldon's constitutional theory is that it is no theory at all. It is almost impossible to deduce propositions from the theory; in fact, as we have already discovered, the theory consists largely of one general assumption (the continuity between structure and behavior) and a set of descriptive concepts for scaling physique and behavior. In fairness to Sheldon we must remember that he has occasionally indicated that his position is not to be considered an attempt at a general theory but rather it is intended to account for a limited range of variables and perhaps to offset certain biases that are generally operative among individuals studying human behavior. Thus, he has suggested that it is the task of a more general theory to embrace the variables and findings of his work. It is hard to argue with this point of view although one may regret that such an attitude is not more consistently present in Sheldon's writings.

Some investigators have accepted the basic premise of Sheldon's work but have recommended other methods of measurement and, in some cases, other variables as superior to those advocated by Sheldon. Parnell (1958) has advanced a three variable system (fat, muscularity, linearity), which is dependent upon a number of objective indices such as subcutaneous fat, bone length, and length and girth of arm and calf. Still another system has been devised by Lindegard (1953, Lindegard and Nyman, 1956) that involves four factor-analytically derived variables—length, sturdiness, muscularity, and fat. Ratings on these variables are derived from a series of anthropometric and performance (strength) tests. It is interesting that in spite of the differences in method employed, and the differences in the means used in deriving the variables, there is a strong congruence between the variables proposed by Sheldon and those advocated by these other investigators.

A further criticism that psychologists level against Sheldon's work has to do with the procedural flaws inherent in his investigation. Many aspects of his work are open to such attack, but these criticisms have usually focused about the inordinately high correlations he reported between physique and temperament variables.

Humphreys (1957) has been particularly vigorous in his criticism of these correlations and even argues that Sheldon's own findings in regard to the intercorrelation of his physique variables indicate the existence of two independent physique components instead of three. However, this picture has again been altered by Sheldon's most recent publication in which he indicated "the correlations between endomorphy and mesomorphy approach zero in both sexes. In males the mean for this correlation hovers around−0.05; in females, around +0.05. The ectomorphy-endormorphy correlations, and the ectomorphy-mesomorphy correlations, always negative, now average about−0.40 in both instances" (Sheldon, Lewis, and Tenney, 1969, p. 848).

Although Sheldon considers at great length the problem of rater bias and contamination of data (1942, pp. 411–425), no amount of discussion will eliminate the fact that in his study of temperament the same individual (Sheldon) made the somatotype and temperament ratings. More important, Sheldon, with his experience in this area, could undoubtedly classify the individual quite accurately in terms of somatotype while making the temperament ratings. Thus the magnitude of his correlations may reflect the strength of the investigator's preconceptions rather than an actual association between physique and temperament. In defending himself against this criticism, Sheldon has pointed out that his temperament ratings were made prior to his physique ratings. As we know that the physique ratings are highly objective, this reduces somewhat the likelihood of one set of ratings having been contaminated by the other, although the possibility remains of implicit physique ratings having influenced the temperament ratings. Further, he insists that it is ridiculous to ask an individual to perform temperament ratings without having seen the persons being rated. The very nature of the temperament ratings demands that the observer have a deep and intimate knowledge of the person being rated, and if he cannot observe this person how can he make sensitive ratings? In Sheldon's view, his critics insist that in order to avoid the possibility of bias he must introduce sufficient ignorance to destroy the likelihood of unearthing significant findings. It is clear that there is something to be said for both sides of this argument and it is also evident that there is little chance of Sheldon and his psychologist critics reaching agreement on this issue.

This criticism leads directly to a further objection to the temperament study. Correlations of the magnitude reported by Sheldon are simply not consistent with all that is known and generally assumed about human behavior. The measurement error inevitable in the type of instrument he used to assess temperament, and the complexity of the factors that *must* have some role in determining behavioral phenomena, combine to make it seem unlikely to most psychologists that behavior and physique should be so closely linked as these findings seem to imply. In replying to this assertion, Sheldon points out that he conceives of behavior as falling on a continuum ranging from those aspects that are most clearly determined by environmental or experiential events to those aspects that are most closely related to the biology and structure of the individual. In his study he deliberately selected aspects of behavior that seemed to him close to the constitutional or biological and therefore it should come as no surprise that there was a close relationship between his behavioral and structural measures. Naturally the magnitude of this relationship might depreciate if other aspects of behavior were related to physique. Sheldon's point is well taken, but it still leaves him open to criticism for having failed to make this sufficiently clear in his publications and thus having omitted certain important limits that should be placed upon the generality of his findings.

One may observe that in several studies concerned with the relationship between physique and behavior (for example, Child, 1950; Walker, 1962) there has been substantial support for Sheldon's position in the form of highly significant and predicted associations between physical and behavioral dimensions. Equally important, however, is the much weaker relationship between these two sets of variables observed by these investigators. Granted all of the important variations in method and sample used in the various studies, these other investigators were unable to unearth correlation findings that even vaguely approximate those reported by Sheldon.

Frequently critics have insisted that the somatotype is not invariant in the face of nutritional or other environmental changes and there is some evidence to support this contention (Lasker, 1947; Newman, 1952). As we have seen, Sheldon's distinction between the somatotype and the phenotype, and his insistence upon the necessity of successive measures and nutritional constancy to permit adequate diagnosis of the somatotype, take much of the sting from such criticisms. Nevertheless, by giving up the invariance of his physique classification Sheldon detracts somewhat from its potential utility. Apparently realizing this Sheldon recently reasserted the constancy of the somatotype as measured by his modified technique "It [somatotype] cannot change, since maximal stature and maximal massiveness are simply items of historical fact, and TI is constant through life" (Sheldon, Lewis, and Tenny, 1969, p. 848). There has not yet been time for these observations to be repeated by other investigators.

Psychologists who value quantitative methods highly look upon the results of several factor analytic studies of physique (Eysenck, 1947; Howells, 1952; Thurstone, 1946; Rees, 1968, 1973), which have produced factors different from Sheldon's primary components, as raising serious questions concerning his findings. Actually, these studies have generally used as their basic data physique measures that differ in important respects from those employed by Sheldon, making comparison of these findings very difficult. Further, there is sufficient disagreement concerning factor analysis as an empirical tool (see Chapter 14) to make it unwise to decide the status of Sheldon's work on this ground alone.

Many observers feel that in spite of appearing to follow an inductive path in developing his concepts and measures, Sheldon shows heavy evidence of having been influenced by preconceptions. Thus, his physique variables exhibit a surprising correspondence to those characteristically employed by his predecessors and, more important, it is a genuinely remarkable coincidence that his temperament variables should turn out to mirror these physique variables so exactly. These critics feel that bias in the observer accounts for this correspondence rather than the natural state of things. They suggest further that some of his temperament ratings come dangerously close to the physique in the aspect of behavior to which they refer. A number of these criticisms have been advanced forcefully by Humphreys (1957). We have already seen that Sheldon accepts this close parallel between physique and temperament ratings in his explanation of why the relation between these measures should be so high.

What has been the outcome of the empirical research stimulated by Sheldon's work? Have the numerous studies provided results that, in general, confirm or disagree with Sheldon's reported results? A careful summary and appraisal of these investigations would take more space than we can afford, particularly since most investigators have introduced sufficient variation in their procedures so that it is difficult to make a simple comparison with Sheldon's research. Thus, all we can hope to present here is a global impression. We believe that if readers will examine carefully the numerous studies cited at the end of this chapter and the surveys by Lindzey (1967) and Rees (1968,1973) they will come away convinced that Sheldon is eminently correct in his assertion that there is a highly significant association between physique and personality. However, it will also be apparent that virtually none of these investigators has found an association between physique and personality that approaches the magnitude reported by Sheldon. Even accepting the fact that the lower correlations reported by almost all other investigators may be partly due to less sensitive measurement technique, the difference between these findings and Sheldon's is so large as to suggest that "truth" lies in a moderate position. Thus, our belief is that an over-all appraisal of the many studies conducted since Sheldon began his work will lead the reader to accept the existence of a significant and interesting relation between physique and personality, but will leave him unconvinced that the relation is so close as Sheldon seems to imply.

In any final evaluation of Sheldon's theory it is important to consider the wealth of empirical studies that have been conducted by Sheldon and stimulated by his writings. Ultimately the value of a theory can best be measured by its empirical impact and no one can deny that Sheldon's findings and formulations have provoked dozens or perhaps hundreds of related studies. Although few if any of these studies represent attempts to test derivations from a set of postulates, this is indeed a pallid criterion compared to the more vigorous query of how many such studies provide findings of ultimate significance. On the latter score it seems safe to say that Sheldon's work is of assured interest to posterity; whatever its shortcomings may be it has led to findings with which the future must reckon.

BIBLIOGRAPHY
PRIMARY SOURCES

Sheldon, W. H. (with the collaboration of S. S. Stevens and W. B. Tucker). *The varieties of human physique: an introduction to constitutional psychology.* New York: Harper, 1940.

Sheldon, W. H. (with the collaboration of S. S. Stevens). *The varieties of temperament: a psychology of constitutional differences.* New York: Harper, 1942.

Sheldon, W. H. (with the collaboration of E. M. Hartl and E. McDermott). *Varieties of delinquent youth: an introduction to constitutional psychiatry.* New York: Harper, 1949.

Sheldon, W. H. (with the collaboration of C. W. Dupertuis and E. McDermott). *Atlas of men: a guide for somatotyping the adult male at all ages.* New York: Harper, 1954.

Sheldon, W. H., Lewis, N. D. C., and Tenney, A. M. Psychotic patterns and physical constitution: A thirty-year follow-up of thirty-eight hundred psychiatric patients in New York State. In D. V. Siva Sankar (Ed.). *Schizophrenia: current concepts and research*. New York: PJD Publications, 1969, pp. 838–912.

Sheldon, W. H. The New York study of physical constitution and psychotic pattern. *J. Hist. Behav. Sci.*, 1971, **7**, 115–126.

REFERENCES

Allport, G. W. *Personality: a psychological interpretation*. New York: Holt, 1937.

Berscheid, E. & Walster, E. A little bit about love. In T. L. Houston (Ed.). *Foundations of interpersonal attraction*. New York: Academic, 1974, pp. 355–381.

Child, I. L. The relation of somatotype to self-rating on Sheldon's temperamental traits. *J. Pers.*, 1950, **18**, 440–453.

Child, I. L., and Sheldon, W. H. The correlation between components of physique and scores on certain psychological tests. *Character and Pers.*, 1941, **10**, 23–34.

Coffin, T. E. A three-component theory of leadership. *J. Abnorm. Soc. Psychol.*, 1944, **39**, 63–83.

Cortes, J. B. *Physique, need for achievement, and delinquency*. Unpublished doctoral dissertation. Harvard Univ., 1961.

Epps, P. and Parnell, R. W. Physique and temperament of women delinquents compared with women undergraduates. *Brit. J. Med. Psychol.*, 1952, **25**, 249–255.

Eysenck, H. J. *Dimensions of personality*. London: Routledge and Kegan Paul, 1947.

Fiske, D. W. A study of relationships to somatotype. *J. Appl. Psychol.*, 1944, **28**, 504–519.

Gall, F. J., and Spurzheim, J. G. *Recherches sur le Système nerveux*. Paris: Schoell, 1809.

Gibbens, T. C. N. *Psychiatric studies of Borstal lads*. London: Oxford Univ. Press, 1963.

Glueck, S., and Glueck, E. *Unraveling juvenile delinquency*. New York: Harper, 1950.

Glueck, S., and Glueck, E. *Physique and delinquency*. New York: Harper, 1956.

Hoskins, R. G. *Endocrinology: the glands and their functions*. New York: Norton, 1941.

Howells, W. W. A factorial study of constitutional type. *Amer. J. Phys. Anthrop.*, 1952, **10**, 91–118.

Humphreys, L. G. Characteristics of type concepts with special reference to Sheldon's typology. *Psychol. Bull.*, 1957, **54**, 218–228.

Janoff, I. Z., Beck, L. H. and Child, I. L. The relation of somatotype to reaction time, resistance to pain, and expressive movement. *J. Pers.*, 1950, **18**, 454–460.

Jones, M. C. Psychological correlates of somatic development. *Child Development*, 1965, **36**, 899–912.

Kessler, S., and Moos, R. H. The XYY karyotype and criminality: a review. *J. Psychiat. Res.*, 1970, **7**, 153–170.

Kline, N. S., and Tenney, A. M. Constitutional factors in the prognosis of schizophrenia. *Amer. J. Psychiat.*, 1950, **107**, 432–441.

Kline, N. S., and Oppenheim, A. N. Constitutional factors in the prognosis of schizophrenia: further observations. *Amer. J. Psychiat.,* 1952, **108,** 909–911.

Kretschmer, E. *Physique and character.* New York: Harcourt, 1925. (Translated by W. J. H. Spratt from *Körperbau und charakter.* Berlin: Springer, 1921).

Landauer, T. K., and Whiting, J. W. M. Infantile stimulation and adult stature of human males. *Amer. Anthrop.,* 1964, **66,** 1007–1028.

Lasker, G. The effects of partial starvation on somatotype: an analysis of material from the Minnesota Starvation Experiment. *Amer. J. Phys. Anthrop.,* 1947, **5,** 323–341.

Lavater, J. C. *Essays on physiognomy: for the promotion of the knowledge and the love of mankind.* London: Whittingham, 1804.

Lindegard, B. Variations in human body-build. *Acta Psychiatrica et Neurologica.* Supplementum. 1953, **86,** 1–163.

Lindegard, B. and Nyman, G. E. Interrelations between psychologic, somatologic and endocrine dimensions. *Lunds Universities Arsskrift,* 1956, **52,** 1–54.

Lindzey, G. Behavior and morphological variation. In J. N. Spuhler (Ed.). *Genetic diversity and human behavior.* Chicago: Aldine, 1967, pp. 227–240.

Livson, N. and McNeil, D. Physique and maturation rate in male adolescents. *Child Development,* 1962, **33,** 145–152.

MacKinnon, D. W. and Maslow, A. H. Personality. In H. Helson (Ed.). *Theoretical foundations of psychology.* New York: Van Nostrand, 1951, pp. 602–655.

McNeil, D. and Livson, N. Maturation rate and body build in men. *Child Development,* 1963, **34,** 25–32.

Naccarati, S. The morphologic aspect of intelligence. *Arch. Psychol.,* 1921, no. 45.

Newman, N. H., Freeman, F. N., and Holzinger, K. J. *Twins: a study of heredity and environment.* Chicago: Univ. Chicago Press, 1937.

Newman, R. W. Age changes in body build. *Amer. J. Phys. Anthrop.,* 1952, **10,** 75–90.

Osborne, R. H. and DeGeorge, F. V. *Genetic basis of morphological variations.* Cambridge, Mass.: Harvard Univ. Press, 1959.

Parnell, R. W. *Behavior and physique: an introduction to practical and applied somatometry.* London: Arnold, 1958.

Paterson, D. G. *Physique and intellect.* New York: Century, 1930.

Rees, L. Constitutional factors and abnormal behavior. In H. J. Eysenck (Ed.). *Handbook of abnormal psychology.* San Diego, Calif.: Knapp, 1973, pp. 487–539.

Rees, L. Constitutional psychology. In D. L. Sills (Ed.). *International Encyclopedia of the social sciences. Vol. 13.* New York: Macmillan, 1968, pp. 66–76.

Rostan, L. *Cours élémentaire d'hygiene.* 2nd ed. Paris: Béchet jeune, 1824.

Sanford, R. N., Adkins, M. M., Miller, R. B., Cobb, E. A., et al. Physique, personality and scholarship. *Monogr. Soc. Res. Child Developm.,* 1943, **8,** no. 1.

Seltzer, C. C. The relationship between the masculine component and personality. *Amer. J. Phys. Anthrop.,* 1943, **3,** 33–47.

Seltzer, C. C., Wells, F. L., and McTernon, E. B. A relationship between Sheldonian somatotype and psychotype. *J. Pers.,* 1948, **16,** 431–436.

Sheldon, W. H. *Psychology and the Promethean will.* New York: Harper, 1936.

Sheldon, W. H. (with the collaboration of S. S. Stevens and W. B. Tucker). *The varieties of human physique: an introduction to constitutional psychology.* New York: Harper, 1940.

Sheldon, W. H. (with the collaboration of S. S. Stevens). *The varieties of temperament: a psychology of constitutional differences.* New York: Harper, 1942.

Sheldon, W. H. Constitutional factors in personality. In J. McV. Hunt (Ed.). *Personality and the behavior disorders.* New York: Ronald Press, 1944, pp. 526–549.

Sheldon, W. H. (with the collaboration of E. M. Hartl and E. McDermott). *Varieties of delinquent youth: an introduction to constitutional psychiatry.* New York: Harper, 1949.

Sheldon, W. H. *Early American cents, 1793–1814.* New York: Harper, 1949.

Sheldon, W. H. (with the collaboration of C. W. Dupertuis and E. McDermott). *Atlas of men: a guide for somatotyping the adult male at all ages.* New York: Harper, 1954.

Sheldon, W. H. *Prometheus revisited.* Cambridge, Mass.: Schenkman, 1974.

Sheldon, W. H. *Penny Whimsey.* New Ed., Somerville, Mass.: Quarterman, 1976.

Sheldon, W. H., Lewis, N. D. C., and Tenney, A. M. Psychotic patterns and physical constitution: A thirty-year follow-up of thirty-eight hundred psychiatric patients in New York State. In D. V. Siva Sankar (Ed.). *Schizophrenia: current concepts and research.* New York: PJD Publications, 1969, pp. 838–912.

Sigaud, C. *La forme humaine.* Paris: Maloine, 1914.

Smith, H. C. Psychometric checks on hypotheses derived from Sheldon's work on physique and temperament. *J. Pers.,* 1949, **17,** 310–320.

Smith, H. C., and Boyarsky, S. The relationship between physique and simple reaction time. *Character and Pers.,* 1943, **12,** 46–53.

Thurstone, L. L. Factor analysis and body types. *Psychometrika,* 1946, **11,** 15–21.

Viola, G. *Le legge de correlazione morfologia dei tippi individuali.* Padova, Italy: Prosperini, 1909.

Walker, R. N. Body build and behavior in young children. Body build and nursery school teachers ratings. *Monogr. Soc. Res. Child Developm.,* 1962, **27,** Serial No. 84.

Wittman, P., Sheldon, W. H., and Katz, C. J. A study of the relationship between constitutional variations and fundamental psychotic behavior reactions. *J. nerv. ment. Dis.,* 1948, **108,** 470–476.

CATTELL'S FACTOR THEORY

CATTELL'S FACTOR THEORY · 14

In the present chapter we will be concerned both with a particular empirical method, the technique of factor analysis, and with a theoretical position whose development has been heavily dependent on the use of that method, the personality theory of Raymond B. Cattell. Other theorists working in the area of personality have also used this technique; H. J. Eysenck, J. P. Guilford, Cyril Burt, L. L. Thurstone, and W. Stephenson must be ranked among the important pioneers. Factor analysis is of course widely used as an everyday empirical tool by contemporary investigators of a host of theoretical orientations. However, Cattell's theory is by far the most comprehensive and fully developed theory of personality based on factor analysis, and therefore, it will be described at length in this chapter, followed by a brief consideration of theories of Eysenck and Guilford. Before we begin, however, we need to acquaint ourselves briefly with the method of factor analysis itself.

The essential ideas of factor analysis were introduced by Spearman (1904), a distinguished English psychologist who is best known for his work with mental abilities (Spearman, 1927). He suggested that if we examine any two related tests of ability we may expect to find two types of factors contributing to performance on these tests. First there is a general factor (for example, verbal fluency, general intelligence, educational level) that is important for both tests. Second, there is a specific factor (for instance, visual memory, spatial perception, specific information) that is unique to each test. The method of factor analysis was developed as a means of determining the existence of general factors and aiding in their identification. Spearman's technique for isolating single factors was revised with Thurstone's (1931) introduction of multiple factor analysis. This opened the way to studying much more complex problems and has since remained the principal method of factor analysis. The cogency of Thurstone's arguments, coupled with findings from Spearman's own laboratory, led almost all workers in this area to accept the fact that there were not only general factors, common to all tests or measures under scrutiny, and specific factors, which were limited to a single test but also group factors, which were involved in more than one test but at the same time were not completely general. Factor analysis today places particular emphasis upon these group factors.

A detailed understanding of factor analysis is not necessary for purposes of the exposition involved in this chapter; however, it is essential that the reader appreciate the general logic behind the technique. The factor theorist typically begins the study of behavior with a large number of scores for each of a large number of subjects. These scores may be derived from questionnaires, ratings, situational tests, or any other source that provides a significant and quantifiable measure of behavior. Ideally these measures should deal with many different aspects of behavior. Given these surface indices, the investigator then applies the technique of factor analysis to discover what the underlying factors are that determine or control variation in the surface variables. Thus, he or she hopes to identify a small number of basic factors whose operation accounts for most of the variation in the very large number of measures with which the investigator began.

The outcome of the factor analysis not only isolates the fundamental factors but also provides for each measure or set of scores an estimate of the extent to which this measure is contributed to by each of the factors. This estimate is customarily referred to as the *factor loading* or *saturation* of the measure and is simply an indication of how much of the variation on this particular measure is to be attributed to each of the factors. The psychological meaning of a factor and the name or label that is attached to it are largely determined by the nature of the particular measures that have high loadings on this factor. Having identified the basic factors, it is possible for the factor theorist to attempt to devise means of measuring these factors more efficiently than can be done by means of the original measures.

Thus, the factor theorist commences with a wide array of behavioral measures, identifies the factors underlying these measures, and then attempts to construct more efficient means of assessing these factors. The factors of the factor analyst are in conception little different from the components or underlying variables of other personality theorists. They are merely attempts to formulate variables that will account for the diverse complexity of surface behavior. It is in the technique employed in deriving these variables that the novelty of this approach lies.

The reader should remember that although group or common factors are of particular interest to the factor analyst these are not the only types of factors. Burt (1941) has provided a widely accepted description of the kinds of factors that can be derived from the application of factor analysis. He suggests that there are universal or *general factors* that contribute to performance on all measures, and there are also particular or *group factors* that play a role in more than one but not in all measures. Further, there are singular or *specific factors* that contribute to only one of the measures, and finally there are accidental or *error factors* that appear on a single administration of a single measure and are to be attributed to faulty measurement or lack of experimental control.

One other issue that has proved somewhat controversial among factor analysts should be mentioned here—the distinction between *orthogonal* and *oblique* systems of factors (and the related notion of *second-order factors*). One may specify in the factor analysis that the factors extracted are to be uncorrelated with one another (in a geometrical sense, at right angles to one another, or "orthogonal"), or one may allow correlated, or "oblique" factors to emerge. The former procedure has been preferred by some factor analysts in the personality realm, for example, Guilford (1959), because of its simplicity and efficiency. But others, including Cattell, have argued for oblique factors, on the ground that true causal influences in the personality realm may well be somewhat intercorrelated, and that only by the use of an oblique factor system can an undistorted picture emerge.

The use of oblique factors has an additional implication. If factors are obtained that are correlated with one another, it is possible to reapply the same factor-analytic methods to the correlations among the factors, yielding so-called *second-order* factors. For instance, the factoring of ability tests often leads to such first-order factors as "verbal fluency," "numerical ability," "spatial visualization," and so on, which themselves tend to be interrelated. One can then proceed to factor the correlations among these first-order factors, perhaps finding a single second-order "general intelligence" factor, or perhaps broad "verbal" and "nonverbal" factors, or the like.

Similar to any other procedure, factor analysis can be abused and the wisest investigators in this area emphasize the fact that it is no substitute for good ideas or detailed knowledge of the phenomena under investigation. Thus, Thurstone (1948) in discussing the work of his psychometric laboratory states:

. . . we spend more time in designing the experimental tests for a factor study than on all of the computational work, including the correlations, the factoring, and the analysis of the structure. If we have several hypotheses about postulated factors, we design and invent new tests which may be crucially differentiating between the several hypotheses. This is entirely a psychological job with no computing. It calls for as much psychological insight as we can gather among students and instructors. Frequently we find that we have guessed wrong, but occasionally the results are strikingly encouraging. I mention this aspect of factorial work in the hope of counteracting the rather general impression that factor analysis is all concerned with algebra and statistics. These should be our servants in the investigation of psychological ideas. If we have no psychological ideas, we are not likely to discover anything interesting because even if the factorial results are clear and clean, the interpretation must be as subjective as in any other scientific work (p. 402).

A thorough and sophisticated treatment of the factor-analytic method is contained in a text by Harman (1967). A novice may find easier going in books by Gorsuch (1974), Muliak (1972), or Comrey (1973).

So much for the logic of factor analysis. For an important illustration of the diverse ways in which this method can be applied in the theoretical and empirical analysis of personality, we turn to a consideration of the personality theory of Raymond B. Cattell.

CATTELL'S
THEORY OF
PERSONALITY

In Raymond Cattell we find an investigator whose deep interest in quantitative methods has not narrowed the spectrum of his interest in psychological data and problems. For him, factor analysis has been a tool that he has used to enlighten a variety of problems all of which have been ordered within a systematic framework. His theory represents a major attempt to bring together and organize the findings of factor analytic studies of personality. He pays some attention to the findings of investigators using other methods of study, although the core of his position rests upon the results of factor analysis because it is here that he derives the variables that he considers most important in accounting for human behavior. He resembles Gordon Allport in that his position may accurately be labeled a "trait theory," and Kurt Lewin in his ability to translate psychological ideas into explicit mathematical forms. However, among the theorists discussed in this volume, perhaps the one Cattell most resembles is Henry Murray. Both take a broad view of personality, and have developed large, inclusive theoretical systems incorporating many different classes of variables.

Raymond Bernard Cattell

Both have been concerned with an empirical mapping of wide reaches of the personality domain, and this has in both cases resulted in large numbers of constructs, with operational links to data, and often with strange names. In addition, both theorists place heavy emphasis on motivational constructs: "needs" for Murray, "dynamic traits" for Cattell; both make substantial use of psychoanalytic formulations; and both give a systematic theoretical status to the environment as well as to the person. An outstanding difference between them is, of course, Cattell's heavy commitment to a particular statistical methodology, factor analysis.

Raymond Bernard Cattell was born in Staffordshire, England, in 1905 and received all of his education in England. He secured his B.Sc. from the University of London in 1924 in chemistry, and his Ph.D. in psychology under Spearman from the same institution in 1929. He was a lecturer at University College of the South West, Exeter, England, from 1928–1931 and director of the City Psychological Clinic at Leicester, England, from 1932–1937. This unusual combination of an academic post followed immediately by extensive experience in a clinical setting undoubtedly provides a partial explanation for Cattell's subsequent breadth of interest. In 1937 he was awarded a D.Sc. by the University of London for his contributions to personality research. He served as research associate to E. L. Thorndike at Teachers College, Columbia University, during the year 1937–1938 and following this was the G. Stanley Hall professor of psychology at Clark University until moving to Harvard University as a lecturer in 1941. In 1944 he accepted a position at the University of Illinois, where he remained, as research professor in psychology and director of the Laboratory of Personality and Group Behavior Research, until his retirement in 1973. Since 1973 he has been visiting professor at the University of Hawaii. In 1953, Cattell was awarded the Wenner-Gren prize of the New York Academy of Science for his work on the psychology of the researcher. He was instrumental in founding the Society for Multivariate Experimental Psychology in 1960, and served as its first president.

Like all other theorists who emphasize the method of factor analysis, Cattell is deeply indebted to the pioneer work of Spearman and the extensive developments by Thurstone. His theoretical formulations are closely related to McDougall's, whose interest in ferreting out the underlying dimensions of behavior and emphasis upon the self-regarding sentiment is seen in modern dress in Cattell's writings. The details of many of Cattell's theoretical ideas, especially those related to development, are quite intimately related to the formulations of Freud and subsequent psychoanalytic writers.

Over a period of forty years Cattell has published an amazing number of books and articles that not only span the field of personality research and mental measurement but also touch upon topics within the traditional fields of experimental psychology, social psychology, and human genetics. The simple statistics of this output are staggering. As of about 1964 the count by the students and associates who edited his collected papers was: twenty-two books and monographs; a dozen intelligence, personality, and clinical tests, with associated handbooks; twenty-two chapters in books edited by others, and about 235 scientific articles (1964, p. ix). Moreover the output by Cattell and his associates has shown no signs of slackening during the years since 1964.

Out of this wealth of publication we may single out a few that constitute major landmarks in Cattell's systematic treatment of personality. The first of these volumes is entitled *Description and measurement of personality* (1946) and attempts to outline from a cross-sectional viewpoint a descriptive foundation for an adequate theory of personality. The second is called *Personality: a systematic, theoretical, and factual study* (1950) and tries to build upon the foundation established in the earlier book a synthetic view of the major phenomena of personality, including both a developmental and a cross-sectional perspective. The third in a series, and perhaps the most complete and detailed presentation to date of Cattell's theoretical views, is *Personality and motivation structure and measurement* (1957). A semi-popular account of his theory and research in the area of personality is contained in *The scientific analysis of personality* (1966a). Major surveys of much of his empirical and theoretical work may be found in three recent books: *Personality and mood by questionnaire* (1973a), *Motivation and dynamic structure* (Cattell and Child, 1975), and *Personality and learning theory* (in press).

A panoramic overview of the development of Cattell's varied interests in psychology may be obtained from the sixty-two papers collected in *Personality and social psychology* (1964). Cattell is also the author of numerous psychological tests including *The culture free test of intelligence* (1944), *The O-A personality test battery* (1954), and *The 16 personality factor questionnaire* (with D. R. Saunders and G. F. Stice, 1950).

THE NATURE OF PERSONALITY: A STRUCTURE OF TRAITS

The system of constructs proposed by Cattell is among the most complex of any of the theories we shall consider. Although these concepts derive their characteristic flavor and, in many cases, their empirical definition from studies using factor analysis, some of them represent derivations from experimental findings or simple observational studies of behavior. This state of affairs is considered by Cattell to be only an expedient, however, as the following quotation reveals:

Our knowledge of dynamic psychology has arisen largely from clinical and naturalistic methods and secondarily from controlled experiment. Findings of the former, and even of the latter, are in process of being placed on a sounder basis by the application of more refined statistical methods. In particular, experiments and clinical conclusions need to be refounded on real conceptions as to what traits (notably drives) are really unitary, and this requires a foundation of factor-analytic research (1950, p. 175).

Cattell considers that the detailed task of defining personality must await a full specification of the concepts that the theorist plans to employ in his study of behavior. Thus, he deliberately provides only a very general definition:

Personality is that which permits a prediction of what a person will do in a given situation. The goal of psychological research in personality is thus to establish laws about what different people will do in all kinds of social and general environmental situations. . . . Personality is . . . concerned with *all* the behavior of the individual, both overt and under the skin (1950, pp. 2–3).

It is clear that this emphasis upon personality study including "all" behavior is not an attack upon the necessary abstracting or segmenting that takes place in the usual empirical study. It is simply a reminder that the meaning of small segments of behavior can be fully understood only when seen within the larger framework of the entire functioning organism.

Cattell views personality as a complex and differentiated structure of *traits,* with its motivation largely dependent upon a subset of these, the so-called *dynamic traits*. When we have examined Cattell's multifarious trait concepts and certain related notions, such as the *specification equation* and the *dynamic lattice,* we will have a fairly broad grasp of his conception of personality. A discussion of his treatment of personality development, a consideration of his views of the social context of personality, and a brief look at some of his characteristic research methods will complete the picture.

Traits   The trait is by far the most important of Cattell's concepts. In fact, the additional concepts that we shall examine are for the most part viewed as special cases of this general term. Except perhaps for Gordon Allport, Cattell has considered this concept and its relation to other psychological variables in greater detail than any other current theorist. For him a trait is a "mental structure," an inference that is made from observed behavior to account for regularity or consistency in this behavior.

Central to Cattell's point of view is the distinction between *surface traits,* which represent clusters of manifest or overt variables that seem to go together, and *source traits,* which represent underlying variables that enter into the determination of multiple surface manifestations. Thus, if we find a number of behavioral events that seem to go together we may prefer to consider them as one variable. In a medical setting, this would be referred to as a syndrome but here it is labeled a surface trait. Source traits on the other hand are identified only by means of factor analysis which permits the investigator to estimate the variables or factors that are the basis of this surface behavior.

It is evident that Cattell considers source traits more important than surface traits. This follows not only because the source traits promise greater economy of description, as there are presumably fewer of them, but more importantly because:

. . . the source traits promise to be the real structural influences underlying personality, which it is necessary for us to deal with in developmental problems, psychosomatics, and problems of dynamic integration. . . . as research is now showing, these source traits correspond to real unitary influences—physiological, temperamental factors; degrees of dynamic integration; exposure to social institutions—about which much more can be found out once they are defined (1950, p. 27).

Surface traits are produced by the interaction of source traits and generally can be expected to be less stable than factors. Cattell admits that surface traits are likely to appeal to the common-sense observer as more valid and meaningful than source traits because they correspond to the kinds of generalizations that can be made on the basis of simple observation. However, in the long run it is the source traits that prove to have the most utility in accounting for behavior.

Clearly, any single trait may represent the outcome of the operation of environmental factors, hereditary factors, or some mixture of the two. Cattell suggests that while surface traits must represent the outcome of a mixture of these factors it is at least possible that source traits may be divided into those that reflect heredity, or more broadly, constitutional factors and those derived from environmental factors. The traits that result from the operation of environmental conditions are called *environmental-mold traits;* those that reflect hereditary factors are called *constitutional traits.*

If source traits found by factorizing are pure, independent influences, as present evidence suggests, a source trait could not be due both to heredity and environment but must spring from one or the other. . . . Patterns thus springing from *internal* conditions or influences we may call *constitutional source traits*. The term "innate" is avoided, because all we know is that the source is physiological and *within the organism,* which will mean inborn only in a certain fraction of cases. On the other hand, a pattern might be imprinted on the personality by something external to it. . . . Such source traits, appearing as factors, we may call *environmental-mold* traits, because they spring from the molding effect of social institutions and physical realities which constitute the cultural pattern (1950, pp. 33–34).

Traits may also be divided in terms of the modality through which they are expressed. If they are concerned with setting the individual into action toward some goal they are *dynamic traits;* if they are concerned with the effectiveness with which the individual reaches the goal they are *ability traits*. Or they may be concerned largely with constitutional aspects of response such as speed, energy, or emotional reactivity, in which case they are referred to as *temperament traits*. In addition to these major trait modalities, Cattell has in recent writings placed increasing emphasis on more transient and fluctuating structures within the personality, including *states* and *roles*. In discussing Cattell's views of personality structure we will find it convenient to discuss first the relatively stable and enduring ability and temperament traits, then the dynamic traits, which tend to be intermediate in stability, and finally the more changeable roles and states.

ABILITY AND TEMPERAMENT TRAITS. In Cattell's view, there are three major sources of data about personality: the life record, or *L-data;* the self-rating questionnaire, or *Q-data;* and the objective test, or *T-data*. The first of these, *L*-data, may in principle involve actual records of the person's behavior in society, such as school records and court records, although in practice Cattell has usually substituted ratings by other persons who know the individual in real-life settings. Self-rating (*Q*-data) by contrast, involves the person's own statements about his or her behavior, and thus can provide a "mental interior" to the external record yielded by *L*-data. Objective test (*T*-data) is based on a third possibility, the creation of special situations in which the person's behavior may be objectively scored. These situations may be pencil-and-paper tasks, or they may involve apparatus of various kinds. Cattell and his associates have been extremely fertile in devising and adapting these tests: a compendium (Cattell and Warburton, 1967) lists over 400 of them.

Cattell has sought to locate general traits of personality by conducting separate factor analytic studies using all three of the above data sources, on the assumption that if the same source traits emerged from all three, this would provide strong persumptive evidence that the source traits were true functional unities and not mere artifacts of method. The outcome of some twenty or thirty factor analyses carried out by Cattell and his associates over the past several decades leads to the conclusion that a similar factor structure emerges from behavior rating data and questionnaire data, but that rather different factors tend to emerge from objective test data. The populations sampled in these studies have included several age groups (adults, adolescents, and children) and several countries (U.S., Britain, Australia, New Zealand, France, Italy, Germany, Mexico, Brazil, Argentina, India, and Japan), so presumably the factors have some generality. It should be noted that other investigators, using somewhat different procedures, have found different sets of replicable factors in the personality domain (Guilford and Zimmerman, 1956; Norman, 1963; Comrey and Jamison, 1966); but even if Cattell's factors constitute merely one of a number of sets of dimensions along which personality may be described, they are at least a set around which considerable empirical data have been accumulated.

A critical determiner of the outcome of a factor analysis is the starting point, the surface variables one begins with, and Cattell has placed considerable stress on the importance of adequately sampling the whole *personality sphere* at the start of exploratory research. Cattell began his behavior rating study with Allport and Odbert's (1936) list of around 4500 trait names from an unabridged dictionary. These were condensed to somewhat under 200 by grouping near-synonyms and eliminating rare and metaphorical terms. The remaining trait names were intercorrelated and further reduced by empirical clustering procedures to yield thirty-five surface traits. Ratings on these thirty-five traits provided the basis for the initial *L*-data factor analysis.

The main personality factors that Cattell considers well established in both *L* and *Q*-data are listed in Table 14-1. Many of the factor titles, it will be noted, illustrate Cattell's characteristic fondness for inventing new terms. Some of the factor titles are essentially descriptive, others reflect Cattell's hypotheses concerning the origin or underlying nature of the factor. Parmia, for instance, stands for "parasympathetic immunity," Premsia is a contraction of "protected emotional sensitivity," Autia suggests an autistic, or self-absorbed quality in persons extreme on this factor, and so on. Popular labels for the factors are also supplied in Table 14-1. Cattell regards the factor names as approximate and tentative in any case, and in practice typically refers to factors by identifying letters or numbers. Besides the twelve factors shown in Table 14-1, a number of additional questionnaire and rating factors have been proposed by Cattell. These include the four alphabetically missing factors *D, J, K,*

TABLE 14-1 *Major personality factors found in both L and Q data*[a]	Letter symbol	Technical title	Popular label
	A	Affectia-Sizia	Outgoing-reserved
	B	Intelligence	More intelligent-less intelligent
	C	Ego strength	Stable-emotional
	E	Dominance-Submissiveness	Assertive-humble
	F	Surgency-Desurgency	Happy-go-lucky-sober
	G	Super ego strength	Conscientious-expedient
	H	Parmia-Threctia	Venturesome-shy
	I	Premsia-Harria	Tender-minded-tough-minded
	L	Protension-Alaxia	Suspicious-trusting
	M	Autia-Praxernia	Imaginative-practical
	N	Shrewdness-Artlessness	Shrewd-forthright
	O	Guilt proneness-Assurance	Apprehensive-placid

[a] Adapted from Cattell (1966a), p. 365.

and *P;* seven factors (designated Q_1 through Q_7) found primarily in Q- rather than L-data; and twelve factors from the domain of psychopathology (Cattell, 1973a).

These rating and questionnaire factors fall chiefly in the class of temperament traits, although *B* (intelligence) would be classed as an ability factor. Factors derived from objective tests spread more broadly across the ability, temperament, and dynamic realms. One example of an objective test factor in the temperament realm is shown in Table 14-2. As is characteristic of Cattell's *T*-data factors, a curious array of measures show up together, although some coherence is evident. The themes of emotionality and conformity appear to run through a good many of the measures in Table 14-2. Cattell has reported that the factor correlates well with psychiatric ratings of anxiety and with the Taylor Manifest Anxiety Scale (Cattell and Scheier, 1961).

TABLE 14-2 *A typical T-data factor, (T) 24, anxiety*[a]	*Measures loaded*
	Willingness to admit common frailties
	Tendency to agree
	Annoyability
	Modesty on untried performance
	High critical severity
	Few questionable reading preferences
	High emotionality of comment
	Many anxiety tension symptoms checked

[a] Based on Hundleby, Pawlik, and Cattell (1965).

This particular factor is interesting for another reason as well. It will be recalled that the factors found by Cattell in *L-* and *Q*-data tended to be generally similar, but that the *T*-data factors on the whole did not match these. It turns out, however, that some of the *T*-data factors seem to correspond to *second-order* factors in questionnaire and rating data. The *T*-data factor just described appears to align itself very well with a second-order temperament factor, also labeled Anxiety, which loads the first order factors *C-,* low ego strength; *O,* guilt proneness; *H-,* shyness; and *L,* suspiciousness. Another case of such correspondence involves a test data factor that loads measures of fluency, confidence, and inaccuracy, and that shows close agreement with a second-order questionnaire and rating factor of extraversion-introversion (or, as Cattell prefers, Exvia-Invia). This second-order factor loads *F,* happy-go-lucky; *A,* outgoing; and *H,* venturesome.

Thus Cattell suggests that part of the lack of correspondence across data sources may merely mean that the different measurement approaches are sampling data at rather different levels of generality, so that a one-to-one match of factors is not found, but rather a modest degree of across-level alignment. In any event, it is clear that Cattell's initial hope of finding identical factor structures in all three data sources so far has been realized only partially.

THE SPECIFICATION EQUATION. Given that one may describe the personality in terms of ability, temperament, and other kinds of traits, how is one to put this information back together in a particular case to predict the response of an individual in some particular situation? Cattell suggests that we can do this by means of a *specification equation,* of the form:

$$R = s_1 T_1 + s_2 T_2 + s_3 T_3 + \ldots + s_n T_n$$

This simply means that the given response may be predicted from the characteristics of the given person (the traits T_1 to T_n), each weighted by its relevance in the present situation (the situational indices s_1 to s_n). If a particular trait is highly relevant to a given response, the corresponding s will be large; if the trait is totally irrelevant, the s will be zero; if the trait detracts from or inhibits the response, the sign of s will be negative. The form of the equation implies that each trait has an independent and additive effect on the response. The model is an extremely simple one. Cattell does not deny that more elaborate models may ultimately be needed; he merely suggests that simple linear models often provide fairly good approximations to more complex ones, and provide a logical place to begin.

It is sometimes bemoaned that the factor analyst reduces the personality interactions to additive ones, whereas, in fact, they may be multiplicative or catalytic in some sense. It cannot be doubted that there are likely to be instances where one factor does not merely add itself to another, but greatly facilitates the second factor. . . . Related to this is the general assumption of linearity, whereas again it is likely that in some cases the relation of the factor to the performance will be curvilinear. Properly regarded, these limitations are stimuli to fresh inquiry, but not criticisms of the factor-analytic method as such. One must walk before he can run. The fact is that the factor-analytic model in its present simple form certainly seems to give better predictions and greater constancy of analysis than any other design that has been tried. As it progresses, it will doubtless become modified to meet the special needs of the possibilities just indicated (Cattell, 1956, p. 104).

The specification equation implies both a multidimensional representation of the person and of the psychological situation. The person is described by their scores on a set of traits—a trait profile. The psychological situation is described by a set of situation indices, as another profile. Put together, these yield the prediction. Catell points out that the specification equation can be regarded as a multidimensional version of Kurt Lewin's formulation of behavior as a function of person and environment: $B = f(P, E)$. In the specification equation, the person P is differentiated into a series of T's and the psychological environment E into a series of s's.

The specification equation formulation lends itself readily to applied use. Thus, in an employment situation, one might maintain a file of jobs described as profiles of s's. A job applicant can then be tested and described as a profile of T's, which can be combined in turn with the various sets of s's to find the job placement in which this individual would be expected to perform best. Or, in an academic setting, a specification equation could be developed to predict academic achievement from ability and personality variables (compare Cattell and Butcher, 1968).

DYNAMIC TRAITS. The important dynamic traits, in Cattell's system, are of three kinds: *attitudes, ergs,* and *sentiments. Ergs* correspond roughly to biologically based drives, *sentiments* to acquired attitude structures. We will now examine these three kinds of dynamic traits, their interrelationship in the *dynamic lattice,* and their role in conflict and adjustment.

Attitudes. An attitude, for Cattell, is the manifest dynamic variable, the observed expression of underlying dynamic structure from which ergs and sentiments and their interrelationships must be inferred. An attitude of a particular individual in a particular situation is an interest of a certain intensity in some course of action with respect to some object. Thus the attitude of a young man "I want very much to marry a woman" indicates an intensity of interest ("want very much") in a course of action ("to marry") toward an object ("a woman"). The attitude need not be verbally stated; indeed Cattell would prefer to measure the strength of the young man's interest by a variety of devices, direct and indirect. These might include his rise in blood pressure to a picture of a bride, his ability to remember items from a list of good and bad consequences of marrying, his misinformation concerning the matrimonial prospects of a male in our society, and so forth. Cattell and his co-workers have in fact intercorrelated some sixty or seventy different devices for measuring attitude strength in a series of studies aimed at developing an efficient test battery for measuring conscious and unconscious components of attitudes (see, for example, Cattell, Radcliffe, and Sweney, 1963). Five attitude component factors, designated Alpha through Epsilon, have been described and speculatively related to psychoanalytic concepts (Id, ego, repressed complexes, and so on). In practice, however, two second-order components of attitude strength are usually measured—one concerned with the relatively conscious and integrated aspects of an attitude (as measured, for instance, by information tests), and one concerned with less integrated or unconscious aspects (as measured, for example, by wishful thinking or forgetting tests). To obtain a single score for the strength of an attitude, the scores for the two components can simply be added together.

Attitudes, of course, are as numerous as one cares to specify. Cattell in his research has mostly worked with a sample of about fifty varied attitudes and interests. A possible limitation on the generality of his research in this area lies in the fact that much of it leans heavily on this somewhat arbitrarily selected sample of attitudes.

Ergs. In simplest terms an erg is a constitutional, dynamic, source trait. It is this concept that permits Cattell to give adequate representation to the importance of innately determined but modifiable impellents of behavior. His heavy emphasis upon ergic motivation reflects his conviction that hereditary determinants of behavior have been underestimated by contemporary American psychologists. He defines an erg as:

An innate psycho-physical disposition which permits its possessor to acquire reactivity (attention, recognition) to certain classes of objects more readily than others, to experience a specific emotion in regard to them, and to start on a course of action which ceases more completely at a certain specific goal activity than at any other. The pattern includes also preferred behavior subsidiation paths to the preferred goal (1950, p. 199).

As Cattell indicates, this definition has four major parts that refer to perceptual response, emotional response, instrumental acts leading to the goal, and the goal satisfaction itself. If the last two parts are combined the definition consists of a cognitive, affective, and conative component, just as in McDougall's famous definition of instinct. Actually, the erg serves a function within Cattell's theory of personality that is quite similar to the function that the concept of instinct or propensity fulfilled within McDougall's theory.

Cattell considers ten ergs to have been reasonably well established by his factor-analytic researches (Cattell and Child, 1975). These ergs are: hunger, sex, gregariousness, parental protectiveness, curiosity, escape (fear), pugnacity, acquisitiveness, self-assertion, and narcissistic sex. (The last of these derives its title from a psychoanalytic notion; the content of the factor has to do with general self-indulgence—smoking, drinking, laziness, and so on.)

Sentiments. A sentiment is an environmental-mold, dynamic source trait. Thus, it is parallel to the erg, except that it is the result of ex-

FIGURE 14-1
Portion of a dynamic lattice illustrating subsidiation
(Cattell, 1950, p. 158).

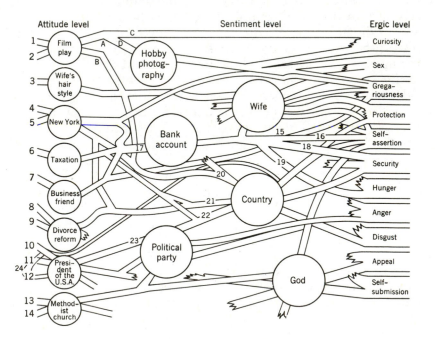

periential or sociocultural factors, not constitutional determinants. In
Cattell's words, sentiments are ". . . major acquired dynamic trait
structures which cause their possessors to pay attention to certain objects or classes of object, and to feel and react in a certain way with
regard to them" (1950, p. 161). Again both the definition and the use
of the concept are highly congruent with the parallel concept in Mc-
Dougall's theory, which was also called the sentiment.

Sentiments, in Cattell's view, tend to be organized around important cultural objects, such as social institutions or persons, toward
which elaborate constellations of attitudes accrue during an individual's life experience. Among sentiments found in the researches of
Cattell and his associates with young adult (mostly male) populations
are: career or profession, sports and games, mechanical interests, religion, parents, spouse or sweetheart, and self. The last named, the
self sentiment, is one of the stablest and most consistently reported in
different studies, and, as we shall see, plays a particularly important
role in Cattell's theorizing.

The dynamic lattice. The various dynamic traits are interrelated in a
pattern of *subsidiation* (Cattell has borrowed the term from Murray).
That is to say, certain elements are subsidiary to others, or serve as
means to their ends. In general, attitudes are subsidiary to sentiments,
and sentiments are subsidiary to ergs, which are the basic driving
forces in the personality. These various relationships may be expressed in the *dynamic lattice,* pictorially represented in Figure 14-1.
This represents a portion of the motivational structure of a hypothetical American male. At the right in the diagram are the basic biological
impulses, the ergs. In the middle of the diagram are sentiment structures, each subsidiary to several ergs. Thus the sentiment toward wife
is built upon the expression of the ergs of sex, gregariousness, protection, and self-assertion; the sentiment toward God expresses the
ergs of self-submission and appeal, and so forth. At the left of the
diagram are attitudes toward particular courses of action with respect
to the designated objects—to see a particular film, for instance, or to
travel to New York. Note that each attitude is subsidiary to, and
hence expresses, one or more sentiments, and through them, a
number of ergs; sometimes attitudes express ergs directly as well.
Thus the desire to see the film is linked to sentiments toward the
man's hobby of photography and toward his country (perhaps the
movie has a patriotic theme). There appears also to be a cross-link to
his wife and her hair style (maybe it looks better in the dark). There is
also a direct expression of the erg of curiosity, in addition to the indirect one via photography. Note that through the sentiments to
hobby, wife, and country, the desire to see this movie may express to

a greater or lesser degree the ergs of curiosity, sex, gregariousness, protection, self-assertion, security, and disgust—in some cases along multiple paths. Note also that sentiments may sometimes be subsidiary to other sentiments—as bank account to wife, or political party to country.

These multiple and overlapping paths between ergs and sentiments and the expressed attitudes provide the basis for inferring ergs from sentiments. If one observes that a certain subset of attitudes tends to vary in strength together across individuals, or within an individual over time, one infers an erg or sentiment structure underlying them. In fact that is what Cattell does: measures of a number of attitudes are obtained (by the methods described earlier) and factored, and the factors interpreted as representing ergs or sentiments.

The self. The self is one of the sentiments, but an especially important one, since nearly all attitudes tend to reflect the self sentiment in greater or lesser degree. It in turn is linked to the expression of most or all of the ergs or other sentiments. In some studies (see, for example, Cattell and Horn, 1963) related but distinct superego and ideal self sentiments have emerged as well. In any event, the sentiment or system of sentiments focused around the self is considered by Cattell to play a crucial role in the integration of the personality, but interrelating the expression of the various ergs and sentiments.

In the first place, the preservation of the self as a physically healthy and intact going concern is obviously a prerequisite for the satisfaction of any sentiment or erg which the individual possesses! So also is the preservation of the social and ethical self as something which the community respects. . . . Dynamically, the sentiment towards maintaining the self correct by certain standards of conduct, satisfactory to community and super-ego, is therefore a *necessary instrumentality* to the satisfaction of most other of our life interests.

The conclusion to which this leads is that the self-sentiment must appear in the dynamic lattice . . . far to the left and therefore among the latest of sentiments to reach a ripe development. It contributes to all sentiment and ergic satisfactions, and this accounts also for its dynamic strength in controlling, as the 'master sentiment', all other structures (Cattell, 1966a, p. 272).

One may note in Cattell's treatment of self the influence of the psychoanalytic concepts of ego and superego, as well as Allport's ego and McDougall's concern with the sentiment of self-regard.

Conflict and adjustment. Cattell has suggested that a useful way of expressing the degree of conflict that a particular course of action presents for a person is by way of a specification equation that expresses the involvement of the person's dynamic source traits (ergs and sentiments) in the action. Thus, to take our earlier example, suppose that a particular young man's interest in marrying has the following specification equation, in which E's stand for ergs and M's for sentiments:

$$I_{marry} = 0.2E_{curiosity} + 0.6E_{sex} + 0.4E_{gregariousness} - 0.3E_{fear} + 0.3M_{parents} - 0.4M_{career} + 0.5M_{self}$$

Marrying, for this man, promises potential rewards for his sex, gregariousness, and curiosity ergs; he thinks his parents would approve and it would be good for his self-esteem. He is, however, somewhat fearful of the prospect of such a marriage, and it represents a potential threat to his career interests. The exact strength of his attitude at any given moment will of course depend on the current strengths of the various motivational factors, but one can make certain general observations about the role of attitudes in the personality based on their situational indices. For example, if the terms in the specification equation for an attitude are predominantly positive, the attitude will tend to be fixed as a stable feature of the individual's motivational structure; whereas if they are predominantly negative, it will tend to be abandoned. A fixed attitude will represent a source of conflict to the extent that it contains negative terms in its specification equation. In fact, Cattell suggests that a possible index of the degree of conflict inherent in a particular attitude is the ratio of the sum of negative situational weights to the sum of positive situational weights for the dynamic source traits involved. In the example above, this ratio would be $(0.3 + 0.4)/(0.2 + 0.6 + 0.4 + 0.3 + 0.5) = 0.7/2.0 = 0.35$, representing a moderate degree of conflict. If the man's parents were disapproving, this would become a more conflictual attitude for him, as indicated by a ratio of $1.0/1.7$ or 0.59. The degree of conflict inherent in a total personality would be represented by this type of ratio computed over all of the person's stable attitudes (in practice, estimated from a sample of them). The degree of adjustment or motivational integration within the person could then simply be expressed as $1 - C$, where C is the conflict index. Cattell has factor-analyzed a variety of conflict measures to find components of conflict (Cattell and Sweney, 1964), in a fashion essentially parallel to his work with components of attitudes discussed earlier.

States, roles, and sets. The concepts to be discussed in this section constitute a recent development in Cattell's theorizing, and in consequence, some of Cattell's formulations are not yet firmly crystallized. However, the general outlines of his theoretical treatment can be sketched (Cattell, 1963a; 1966b; 1973a).

Certain patterns within the personality come and go to a much greater extent than others: mood states change, a person steps into or out of a particular role, momentary mental sets are adopted toward aspects of the environment. These factors all influence behavior, hence they must be included in the specification equation, which winds up as a series of ability terms, plus temperament terms, plus erg and sentiment terms, plus state terms, plus role terms, plus set terms, each with its appropriate situational index defining its relevance. The personality is still a profile, but a profile involving all the kinds of factors that may affect response at a particular moment in time. For ability, temperament, and dynamic traits, while moment-to-moment fluctuation may occur, considerable prediction is possible from stable or average levels of the trait. For the more unstable factors we are discussing now, however, the person's momentary condition is crucial to prediction.

Cattell's proposed theoretical solution is to split the situation (and the situational indices of the later terms in the equation) into two components: one representing the *focal stimulus,* the aspect of the situation to which the person is directly responding, and the other representing the *background conditions,* which determine the current state of the organism. The background conditions may include ambient or contextual stimuli that influence mood, role cues, organismic conditions, and the like. These background conditions play the formal role of *modulators,* temporarily changing the psychological meaning of the situation in a systematic way, so that the response of the individual may be different, depending on whether one is in or out of a particular role, in an anxious or nonanxious state, and so on.

Although roles and sets have so far not received extensive empirical exploration by Cattell and his associates, a good deal of work has been done with states—in particular, with the state of anxiety (Cattell and Scheier, 1961). It will be recalled that anxiety has also been studied by Cattell as a trait. These two approaches are in no sense incompatible: a person's level of anxiety may be characteristic as a trait, and yet fluctuate considerably with situational and organismic influences as a state.

States are investigated by factor analysis as are traits, the difference being that traits are usually studied by correlations among test scores, and states by correlations among *changes* in test scores—over time or in response to particular situations. Thus if the same persons tend to be high on, say, annoyability and lack of confidence, this will help define a trait factor, but if both measures tend to increase or decrease together, this will help define a state factor.

A number of other state factors besides anxiety have been investigated by Cattell and his co-workers. These include depression, stress, fatigue, and general autonomic activity. Recent studies suggest that a dozen or more different state factors may be identifiable (Cattell, 1973a, Chapter 6).

It is possible to study personality development at a purely descriptive level, by charting the change in personality structures over the life span. Alternatively, one may study development at a theoretical level, in terms of the genetic and environmental influences involved, and the laws of maturation and learning that describe their interaction in shaping the developing individual. Cattell has done both.

    In his investigations of temperament and dynamic traits, Cattell and his associates have carried out factor-analytic studies at both adult and child levels, in an effort to develop devices capable of measuring the same personality factors at different ages. In general, he has tended to find similar factors at ages ranging from four years to adulthood. As all psychologists know, it is difficult to be sure that purported measures of the "same" trait at different ages are in fact measuring the same thing, a difficulty produced by the fact that one expects a particular aspect of the personality to be expressed through somewhat different behavior at different ages. Cattell has suggested that one way of dealing with this predicament is to carry out bridging studies with intermediate age groups; thus he has compared separately-factored adult and eleven-year-old versions of his personality questionnaire by giving both to an intermediate group of sixteen-year-olds (Cattell and Beloff, 1953). The results of such studies have been somewhat equivocal; usually there are a number of fairly good matches, but others that are less convincing (Cattell, 1973a, Chapter 3). Further work along these lines would appear to offer promise of producing genuinely comparable personality measuring instruments across a range of ages, and thus the possibility of a true mapping of developmental trends in personality traits. Cattell has discussed evidence for age trends on temperament factors, such as rises over the age range eleven to twenty-three in H(adventurousness) and C(ego strength), and drops in O(guilt proneness) and L(suspiciousness) (Sealy and Cattell, 1966).

THE DEVELOPMENT OF PERSONALITY

Cattell has for a number of years been actively interested in assessing the relative weight of genetic and environmental influences on source traits. He has developed a method for this purpose, which he calls Multiple Abstract Variance Analysis, or MAVA (1960). MAVA involves gathering data on the resemblances between twins and siblings reared together in their own homes or adopted into different homes,

Heredity-Environment Analysis

and then analyzing the data to estimate the proportions of individual variation on each trait that are associated with genetic differences, with environmental differences, and with at least some of the correlations and interactions between heredity and environment. A preliminary version of MAVA has been tried out by Cattell and his coworkers on a limited scale (Cattell, Blewett, and Beloff, 1955; Cattell, Stice, and Kristy, 1957) and a larger study is still in progress. One tendency observed in the initial studies is of some theoretical interest: the heredity-environment correlations appeared to be predominantly negative. Cattell interprets this as evidence for a *law of coercion to the biosocial mean,* that is, a tendency for environmental influences to oppose systematically the expression of genetic variation, as when parents (or other social agents) attempt to bring different children to the same norm of behavior by encouraging the bashful ones and reining in the more obstreperous.

Learning   Cattell distinguishes at least three kinds of learning that play important roles in personality development. The first two are the familiar classical and instrumental (operant) conditioning of the experimental psychologist. Cattell's treatment of these is fairly conventional: classical conditioning is held to be of importance in attaching emotional responses to environmental cues, and instrumental conditioning for establishing means to the satisfaction of ergic goals. Instrumental conditioning plays a substantial role in building up the dynamic lattice, which, it will be recalled, consists of subsidiation (that is, means-end) relations (attitudes and sentiments serve as the means of achieving ergic goals). A form of instrumental conditioning of special interest in personality learning is what Cattell calls *confluence learning,* in which a behavior or attitude simultaneously satisfies more than one goal. Thus one attitude comes to be linked to several sentiments, and one sentiment to several ergs, giving the dynamic lattice its characteristic structure.

The third kind of learning is called *integration learning*. It appears to be essentially a more elaborate form of instrumental learning. In integration learning, the individual learns to maximize total long-term satisfaction by expressing some ergs at any given moment, and suppressing, repressing, or sublimating others. Integration learning is a key aspect of the formation of the self and superego sentiments.

According to Cattell, *personality learning* is best described as a multidimensional change in response to experience in a multidimensional situation. A way of studying personality learning empirically is by means of a procedure called *adjustment path analysis*. One begins with two things: first, with information about trait changes occurring in a number of people, possibly in response to a period of ordinary life adjustments; and second, with a theoretical analysis of various possible paths of adjustment (such as regression, sublimation, fantasy, neurotic symptoms) that people may take in response to conflictual life situations. If one can then estimate the frequency with which each of these individuals has taken each of the adjustment paths, one can solve a matrix equation to find out what the average effect of taking each path is on changing each of the traits. This is of theoretical interest in itself, and has the practical value that given new, but comparable individuals, and information about their trait changes, one can now estimate the frequency with which they have taken each of the various adjustment paths, by solving the equation in the opposite direction.

Cattell much earlier had provided a theoretical analysis of adjustment paths, as a series of *dynamic crossroads* or *chiasms* that are successively met in the expression of a blocked drive—from simple rage, to conflict and anxiety, to neurotic symptom formation. This theoretical analysis draws on psychoanalytic ideas to a considerable extent, although it has some novel features. The procedure of adjustment path analysis may provide a way of assessing the empirical value of the dynamic crossroads formulation.

Integration of Maturation and Learning

Cattell has attempted to bring together personality changes due to environmental influences and genetically based maturation into a single theoretical scheme (Cattell, 1973b). He has coined the term *threptic* to designate changes due to environmental influence, including learning as well as other changes induced by such external agents as general stimulation, diet, drugs, and the like. He proposes as a goal the splitting of developmental change curves for various traits into genetic and threptic components, and various subcomponents of these. His general strategy for achieving this is the comparative use of the MAVA method mentioned earlier. The comparisons may involve various ages, or various cultural or subcultural groups. Thus, if the threptic variation of a trait in the population is large during the preschool years, diminishes during the years children are in the public schools receiving a relatively standard educational exposure, and increases again in adulthood, one could draw different conclusions about the forces acting on the trait than if the genetic and threptic components were constant over this age span. Likewise if genetic and threptic components varied substantially among different religious groups or ethical traditions (or did *not* so vary) one again could learn something about the forces acting on the development of the trait in question.

Such an analysis has many complexities, as the genetic and threptic sources of influence on a trait may be correlated in various ways, and may interact over time. Thus genetic influences may lead to certain behaviors that may provoke particular kinds of threptic influences that may in turn either enhance or inhibit the further development of the trait. Cattell's treatment of these issues has for the most part been at a schematic and theoretical level, but he has suggested a number of statistical approaches toward resolving them empirically (Cattell, 1973b).

The Social Context   Thus far we have focused upon individuals and their development in interaction with the immediate environment. Here we shall suspend this restriction and consider the efforts Cattell has made to give adequate emphasis to sociocultural determinants of behavior.

Cattell suggests that objective dimensions may be used to describe groups in much the same manner as traits are used to describe individuals. These dimensions represent the group *syntality* (Cattell, 1948), which is the equivalent of the individual personality. Thus, an important task for the individual who would study personality in relation to the sociocultural matrix is the description of the syntality of the various groups that influence the individual personality. It is only through an adequate representation of *both* the individual personality and the group syntality that one can hope to gain detailed knowledge concerning the interaction between these two structures.

There are many social institutions that exert a molding or modifying influence upon personality but by far the most important of these is the family. In addition to this primary source of influence there are other institutions whose role is worth consideration, such as: occupation, school, peer group, religion, political party, and nation. These institutions may produce effects upon personality in one of three ways. First, there may be a deliberate intention to produce a particular kind of character or personality. That is, the definition of socially desirable behavior may include specification of personality traits and the institution may involve a self-conscious attempt to produce these characteristics. Second, situational or ecological factors may produce effects that are not intended by the society or the institutions. Third, as a result of patterns of behavior established through the first or second processes, the individual may find further modification of personality necessary in order to express or gratify important motives.

Thus, an adequate understanding of personality development must include a specification of the contribution of various social institutions ranging from the family to the nation or cultural group. Further, this step can be taken only when the appropriate dimensions for describing and differentiating these groups and institutions have been isolated. We find that factor analysis plays just as crucial a role in the description of the syntality as it did in the description of the individual personality. Early work in the study of the syntality of small groups (Cattell and Wispe, 1948; Cattell, Saunders, and Stice, 1953) has led to the description of a number of factors with such labels as extrovert responsiveness versus withdrawal; informed, realistic relaxedness versus industrious, rigid aggressiveness; vigorous unquestioned purposefulness versus self-conscious unadaptedness; diffidence in internal communication; and so forth. Given group syntality variables such as these and means of measuring them objectively, it becomes possible to examine relationships between groups varying along such dimensions and individual personalities described by the source traits we have already considered.

Cattell (1949) has also provided a set of dimensions for describing the syntality of nations. In this case, ten factors were derived from the study of seventy nations by means of seventy-two diverse measures. Of these ten factors only eight seemed to possess clear significance; these were size, cultural pressure, enlightened affluence, thoughtful industriousness, vigorous and self-willed order, bourgeois-Philistinism, Buddhism-Mongolism, and cultural integration and morale. Many, although not all of these dimensions of national syntality have re-emerged in subsequent factorings of economic and cultural variables within and across nations (Cattell and Adelson, 1951; Cattell, 1953; Cattell and Gorsuch, 1965).

Cattell has drawn together his ideas on the relationship between individual personality and group syntality in a series of twenty-eight propositions, which are reported in a major theoretical article (1961) and a chapter (1966b). He concludes that the relationship between the individual personalities of the group members and the syntality of the group is mediated by variables of *group structure,* of which the most fully discussed is *role.* A subset of syntality dimensions are *synergy* dimensions, which are to the group what dynamic traits are to the individual. Moreover, a specification equation can be written for group synergy in terms of the interests of the individual members belonging to the group.

CHARACTERISTIC RESEARCH AND RESEARCH METHODS

In this section we shall mention very briefly certain distinctive aspects of Cattell's views concerning personality research. In addition, we shall summarize an investigation that illustrates the flexibility with which Cattell employs his favorite tool of factor analysis—in this case, to a study of the dynamic traits of a single individual. The reader will recall that we already have a considerable familiarity with Cattell's research as a result of frequent references to his empirical work in discussing his theoretical concepts.

We have mentioned earlier Cattell's conviction that *large-scale research* will produce the most significant advances of the future in this area. Coupled with this is his belief that most psychologists have unwisely shunned the necessity of *careful description* of personality in favor of moving toward impressive generalization and the study of developmental phenomena. Much of his work, particularly that concerned with identifying source and surface traits, can be considered simply an attempt to fulfill this task of description and provide a firm base upon which future investigation and generalization can build.

One of the most novel features of Cattell's writing has been his consistent emphasis upon the different types of correlational studies that the investigator may pursue. First, he points out, there are *R-technique* studies that represent the customary approach of the psychologist. Here, a large number of individuals are compared in terms of their performance on two or more tests. The fundamental question is whether individuals who score high on one test tend to do so on the other test, and the resulting coefficient represents the extent to which scores on the tests covary or go together. Second, there is the *P-technique* where scores for the same individual on a number of measures are compared for different occasions or at different times. Here we are asking how consistent the individual's behavior is, and the resulting statistic is an index of how closely different aspects of the same individual's behavior covary or go together. Third, there is the *Q-technique* where two individuals are correlated on a large number of different measures. In this case, the resulting coefficient represents a measure of similarity or covariance between two individuals; if such correlations are carried out on a number of persons the investigator may secure a typology or a clustering together of persons who are similar on these measures. (*Q-technique,* by the way, has no special relationship to *Q-data;* the use of the same letter is merely coincidental.) A fourth technique, really a variant of the first, is called *differential R-technique,* which is like ordinary *R*-technique, except that the measurements are repeated twice and the *changes* between them correlated and factored. As we have noted, this method is especially useful in the study of psychological states.

In addition to the above techniques, Cattell has described and discussed quite a number of other theoretically possible designs (the interested reader should consult the treatment of the "data box" in Cattell, 1966b). However, the four designs we have mentioned are the ones that have been most employed in practice.

In the preceding section the distinction was drawn between *R*-technique and *P*-technique. In the former, the usual factor-analytic procedure, correlations are calculated over many persons, and the factors obtained are common traits. In *P*-technique, however, the correlations are calculated over many repeated measurements on a single person, and the factors can represent unique traits of that individual. As Cattell puts it:

A Factor-Analytic Study of a Single Individual

Thus an R-technique discovery of the pattern of the dominance source trait might show that for most people it expresses itself with highest loading in, say, reaction to insults and in interference with subordinates, whereas for a particular individual analyzed by P-technique it might prove also to have a high loading in, say, piano playing, because that individual happens to have learned to express dominance by pounding a piano (Cattell and Cross, 1952, p. 250).

To illustrate the possibility of a factor analytic approach to the unique individual we will describe a study carried out by Cattell and Cross (1952) in which twenty attitudes of a twenty-four-year-old male graduate student in drama were measured twice a day over a forty-day period, and then intercorrelated over the eighty occasions and factor-analyzed. The resulting factors should represent the dynamic source traits of this person, and one can observe how they are similar to or different from those of people in general obtained through *R*-technique studies, and how their day-to-day fluctuations reflect the events of the person's life during the period studied.

This type of study presents special problems of method. In addition to securing a cooperative and dependable subject, one must have measures that can be given over and over again to the same individual without showing large effects due to the repeated testing itself and one must work with traits showing appreciable day-to-day fluctuation.

The twenty attitudes were selected from the sample of attitudes used in Cattell's *R*-technique studies, and were measured by three techniques: a preference measure, in which the subject made choices from pairs of statements, each describing a course of action relevant to some attitude; a fluency measure, in which the subject was asked to state in thirty seconds as many satisfactions as he could think of that could be derived from a course of action relevant to an attitude; and a retroactive inhibition measure, carried out in conjunction with the fluency task, in which six three-digit numbers were exposed to the subject before a fluency measurement and the amount of interference with the attitude was observed. A combined score for each attitude on each occasion was obtained and the attitudes were intercorrelated over occasions and factored. Seven of the eight interpretable factors were judged to correspond to six ergs and one sentiment found in previous *R*-technique studies: sex, self-assertion, parental protectiveness, appeal, and narcissism, in addition to the self-sentiment. The extra factor was identified as fatigue, which has since shown up as a state factor in several studies from Cattell's laboratory.

Thus the common factor structure from the population serves reasonably well to describe this particular person, at any rate, no massive unique factors emerged from the analysis. One can speculate—and the authors do—about the possible significance of some of the deviations of this individual's loadings from the population pattern, but it is not altogether clear that these deviations exceed those one would expect to find between one *R*-technique study and another, with a sample size of eighty.

Having identified factors, it is possible to estimate scores on them for each session, and a plot of these over the period of the experiment, shown in Figure 14-2, displays some interesting reflections of the events of the subject's life, as recorded in a diary he kept during the experiment. Some of the major incidents are indicated on the baseline of Figure 14-2—rehearsals for a play in which he was to act a leading role, a severe cold, the nights of the play itself, a fairly serious accident occurring to his father, a letter in which an aunt reproached

FIGURE 14-2
Changes in strength of dynamic source traits in one individual over eighty test sessions
(Cattell, 1966a, p. 229).

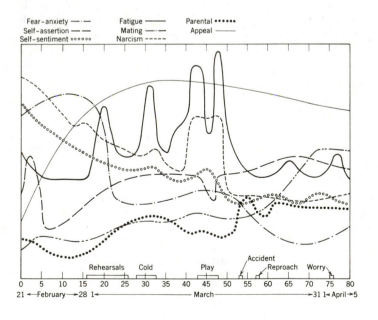

him for not giving up his own interests to help his family, and worry over apparent hostility from a faculty adviser. One may note especially the sharp peaks in fatigue during rehearsals and the play itself; the drop in anxiety after the play, when he was beginning to get caught up in his studies, and have some time for dating (witness the rise of the sex erg); the rise in parental feelings at the time of his father's accident—and the rather interesting drop later, at the time of his aunt's reproach; and finally, the oscillations of the self-related source traits (self-assertion, narcissism, self-sentiment) at the critical period of the play performances.

We may fittingly round out our discussion of Cattell's personality research by simply *mentioning* some additional areas in which he has carried out extensive investigations: humor (Cattell and Luborsky, 1947); music preferences (Cattell and Saunders, 1954); intelligence (Cattell, 1963b); creativity (Cattell and Butcher, 1968); leadership (Cattell and Stice, 1954); projective techniques (Cattell and Wenig, 1952); psychopathology (Cattell and Tatro, 1966); typology (Cattell and Coulter, 1966); and response sets ("instrument factors"— Cattell, 1968).

SOME RELATED FORMULATIONS

Two major contributors in this area in addition to Cattell are H. J. Eysenck and J. P. Guilford. A third theorist, William Stephenson, might logically be added; his work with Q-technique is, however, discussed in Chapter 8, so we need only note here that the factoring of different expressions of the same individual provides yet another way of studying personality by factor analysis.

H. J. Eysenck

Some aspects of the work of this energetic and prolific British psychologist are discussed in the chapter on S-R theories. Here we will only consider his personality factors. Eysenck views personality as organized in a hierarchy. At the most general level are broad dimensions, or *types*. At the next level are *traits*—Cattell's source traits would presumably fall here. Below this is a level of *habitual responses,* and at the bottom of the hierarchy are *specific responses,* the behavior actually observed. At the type level, Eysenck analyzes personality along three broad dimensions: *neuroticism, extraversion-introversion,* and *psychoticism.* His most extensive empirical work has been done with the first two of these factors. Cattell, it will be recalled, found second-order factors in his rating and questionnaire data, which he believes to correspond roughly with Eysenck's two major personality dimensions. Eysenck shares this view, but finds his own level of analysis a theoretically more meaningful and empirically more dependable one (Eysenck, 1953). Eysenck, like Cattell, has used ratings, questionnaires, situational tests, and physiological measures in investigating his personality factors. He also has been interested in hereditary influences on personality (again like Cattell), and has done studies in this area with both neuroticism (Eysenck and Prell, 1951) and extraversion-introversion (Eysenck, 1956).

An important methodological innovation of Eysenck's in factor analysis is the technique of *criterion analysis,* in which a factor is adjusted in the analysis in such a way as to give maximal separation to a particular criterion group. Thus in defining his neuroticism factor, Eysenck aligned the factor to distinguish with maximum clarity between a group of neurotic and a group of nonneurotic soldiers (Eysenck, 1952).

In his recent work, by linking his personality factors with certain basic learning processes, Eysenck has generated a whole new range of research possibilities (see Chapter 15). The use of factor analysis within a defining theoretical framework must be considered a major characteristic of Eysenck's approach (Eysenck and Eysenck, 1968).

J. P. Guilford   Guilford is perhaps best known among psychologists for his work on intelligence and creativity, and for his texts on statistics and psychometric methods. However, his factor analyses of personality traits go back at least to the early 1930s, when he published a paper showing that items that were expected to measure the single trait of introversion-extraversion in fact defined several distinct personality factors (Guilford and Guilford, 1934). An eventual outgrowth of this research was the personality inventory called the *Guilford-Zimmerman Temperament Survey* (Guilford and Zimmerman, 1949), which measures ten factorially defined traits—general activity, restraint versus rhathymia (happy-go-lucky disposition), ascendance, sociability, emotional stability, objectivity, friendliness, thoughtfulness, personal relations, and masculinity. Some overlap will be noticed between this list and Cattell's. Empirical investigations in which Cattell's 16PF Questionnaire and the Guilford-Zimmerman inventory have been given to the same subjects (Cattell and Gibbons, 1968) suggest that the two factor systems intercept much the same personality realm, but the factors for the most part do not match up on a one-to-one basis. To some extent, presumably, this has resulted from the fact that Guilford prefers to use orthogonal factors, whereas Cattell allows his factors to be oblique in respect to one another.

Guilford has summarized his views on personality in the book *Personality* (1959), in which he strongly emphasizes factor-analytic studies: "As a single, logical model for unifying the facts of individual differences, there is at present no rival to the model provided by factor theory" (p. viii). Guilford, like Eysenck, views personality as a hierarchical structure of traits, from broad *types* at the top, through *primary traits,* to *hexes* (rather specific dispositions, like habits), and, at the lowest level, *specific actions.* Guilford also recognizes major subareas within the personality. Three of these: *ability dimensions, temperament dimensions,* and *hormetic dimensions,* correspond roughly to Cattell's ability, temperament, and dynamic traits. In addition, Guilford adds a class of *somatic dimensions,* and an additional category of *dimensions of pathology* to cover personality disturbance. Guilford likes to organize the dimensions in any one of these areas into two- or three-dimensional rectangular tables, or matrices, in which a particular factor is seen as a more general function or quality being expressed in a certain area of behavior. Thus, in the temperament domain, a "positive-negative" dimension yields in general behavior a "confidence versus inferiority" factor, in the emotional area a "cheerfulness versus timidity" factor. It should be noted that these organizing principles are not themselves discovered by factor analysis, but represent interpretations or schemas into which already discovered factors can be ordered, and which can direct the search for new factors to fill in empty spaces in the tables. In the ability domain, the schema is Guilford's well-known "structure of intellect" model (1956).

It is clear that Cattell has developed over the years a large, diversified, and complex theory of personality. Purely as an intellectual achievement it must be considered on a par with the other theories described in this book. It is equally clear that Cattell and his co-workers have produced a volume of empirical data related to their theory that exceeds that inspired by most of the personality theories we have discussed. And yet reviews of Cattell's work invariably seem to display a mixture of admiration and uneasiness, sometimes the former predominating (Sells, 1959), sometimes the latter (Gordon, 1966). An insightful appraisal by Goldberg (1968) suggests that this ambivalence may involve a confusion between Cattell the strategist and Cattell the tactician:

CURRENT STATUS AND EVALUATION

Virtually all previous criticism of Cattell has focused upon Cattell the tactician and has brushed aside Cattell the strategist—a fault akin to ignoring Freud on the grounds that free association is a poor measurement technique. Cattell has been roundly criticized because his efforts to chart 'the whole domain of personality structure' have prevented him from focusing concerted attention on any one delimited portion of the total task (p. 618).

And this seems accurate. The very breadth of Cattell's theoretical interests has tended to send him off to a new project before the old one was really solidly nailed down. Great chunks of Cattell's theoretical structure rest on shaky empirical underpinnings (Becker, 1960). But great chunks of any comprehensive personality theory *must* rest on shaky empirical underpinnings—at least during the lifetime of the theorist, if he does much of the work himself. Good personality research is slow and expensive. It is greatly to Cattell's credit that so much of his theory has as much empirical grounding as it does.

Cattell's theory cannot be said to be popular in the sense that Freud's, Rogers', or Sullivan's or even Allport's or Murray's theories have been popular, although it has attracted a small and active band of adherents. Partly this is because the somewhat forbidding technical machinery of factor analysis, including the debates over its controversies, is likely to put off the casual reader. Partly it is because the sometimes exaggerated empirical claims and occasional denigration of alternative approaches are not well calculated to win over the sophisticated reader. This is a great pity, because it is exactly the latter who should find the most to appreciate in Cattell's wealth of theoretical ideas and in the glittering treasure trove of raw fact that his laboratory has gathered over the years. In any case, it must be remembered that Cattell's theory is still actively developing—no final evaluation is necessary or appropriate at this time.

Theories of personality based upon factor analysis reflect current psychological emphasis upon quantitative methods and in turn are reflected in large numbers of specially designed personality studies. Guilford, Eysenck, and Cattell, as well as others working in this area, have shown a ready inclination to convert their theoretical ideas into empirical steps. In contrast to other personality theories, there is no tendency for theory to develop as an armchair abstraction while the empirical appraisal lingers far behind. In fact, there is scarcely any clear separation of theory and experiment. This empirical vigor seems assured for the future not only because of the demonstrated talents of those working in the area but also because individuals attracted to these formulations will almost certainly possess a similar orientation. In other words, the nature of the position guarantees that individuals who occupy it will be highly empirical. Further, the contemporary fascination of psychologists with the quantitative makes it unlikely that there will be any dearth of scholars interested in advancing and developing this body of thought and empirical findings.

In an area of psychology that has been characterized by sensitivity and subjectivity, factor theorists have introduced a welcome aura of tough-mindedness and emphasis upon the concrete. Where many personality theorists have been content to elaborate concepts and assumptions to a point where the investigator is trapped in a morass of conflicting and unclear implications, factor theorists are inclined to put forward their faith in terms of a simple and lucid set of dimensions or factors. Thus, simplicity and explicitness are cardinal virtues of this brand of theory.

Not only is the factor theorist economical and explicit in formulations but he or she is also operational. More than almost any other brand of psychological theory this position has included a detailed concern for clear and unambiguous empirical definition. The factor theorist has borrowed much of the traditional skill of the psychometrician in devising adequate means of measurement and has tended to ask embarrassing but important questions concerning unidimensionality, internal consistency, and repeatability that surely have had a beneficial effect upon colleagues who are less concerned with the details of measurement.

Whereas most personality theorists have arrived at their conception of the crucial personality variables through a process that is largely intuitive and unspecified, these theorists provide an objective and replicable procedure for the determination of underlying variables. Although one may quarrel with the assertion that the variables are determined by the factor analysis instead of by the tests that are inserted into the factor analysis, there is no possibility of objecting to the claim that factor analysis at least provides a test of whether the variable that had already been conceived of, and was represented in the initial measure, actually exists. In other words, even if factor analysis depends upon prior ideas, and surely it does, it provides a means of assessing the fruitfulness of these ideas. In contrast, many personality theorists have originated hosts of personality variables without ever submitting them to the empirical crucible.

Most personality theories owe more to the clinical setting than to the computation room. Consequently, it is not surprising to find that many psychologists have treated factor theory as an interloper on the personality scene. One of the most frequent and vigorously voiced criticisms alleges that factor theorists create systems of artifacts that have no true relation to any single individual and consequently distort and misrepresent reality. This point of view is stated effectively by Allport (1937):

An entire population (the larger the better) is put into the grinder, and the mixing is so expert that what comes through is a link of factors in which every individual has lost his identity. His dispositions are mixed with everyone else's dispositions. The factors thus obtained represent only *average* tendencies. Whether a factor is really an *organic* disposition in any one individual life is not demonstrated. All one can say for certain is that a factor is an empirically derived component of the *average* personality, and that the average personality is a complete abstraction. This objection gains point when one reflects that seldom do the factors derived in this way resemble the dispositions and traits identified by clinical methods when the individual is studied intensively (p. 244).

As we have seen, factor analysis *can* deal with the unique individual, but the last point still stands. The essence of this objection is that the derived factors are not psychologically meaningful and, consequently, that they do not fit with the observations of other students of human behavior. Thus, most psychologists simply do not find the factors of the factor analyst useful in describing individual behavior. The reader should note that the factor analyst is placed in a rather precarious position here, for if the factors fit closely with prior observations of human behavior the investigator is accused of having labored long and hard to produce the obvious. If the factors do not show this correspondence, the analyst is accused of adding confusion to an already confused scene. Our discussion of Cattell's surface and source traits makes clear that the factor analyst does not necessarily anticipate that his factors will show any exact correspondence with the results of simple observation of behavior. Indeed, it is the intent of such theorists to go beyond simple observation and dredge up variables that have not yet been inferred. Furthermore, the factor theorist would assert, with the passage of time and the accumulation of additional empirical findings these factors will become as meaningful as and more useful than those psychological variables now in common use. Whether this will prove to be the case remains to be seen.

Another popular criticism is that what comes out of factor analysis is no more than what is put in. The factor analyst objects to subjectivity and eliminates it in the place where it is usually encountered, but actually is simply moving subjectivity or intuition back to the point where one decides what tests or measures will be introduced into the matrix of correlations. The criticism seems clearly valid where the theorist maintains that the method of factor analysis, applied to any collection of variables, suffices to produce the fundamental dimensions of personality. However, this would not be the stand of many factor theorists. For example, Eysenck's method of criterion analysis requires the investigator to hypothesize the nature of the psychological factor before embarking upon his study, and Cattell's concept of sampling a defined personality sphere provides a rational basis for a more broadly exploratory approach.

Other critics point to the inevitable subjectivity involved in naming the factors that result from factor analysis. Particularly if the elements composing the factor are very diverse, as is often the case, the investigator may have to resort to as much imagination and ingenuity in arriving at an overall caption for the variable as a clinician would ordinarily employ in describing a single intensively studied case. The last two points may be generalized as a claim that the concern for rigor and empirical control, professed by the factor analyst, is not evenly spread over the research process. Thus, these critics assert that whereas the factor analysis may be carried out with great care and attention to detail, the same amount of attention is not always paid to the steps that have led to the scores from which the factors are derived or the process by means of which the eventual factor is interpreted.

The many disagreements among factor analysts concerning the computational or interpretive steps involved in factor analysis provide a ready target for the detractor. If this method is so objective and rational, why is it that those who know most about it are least agreed as to just how the process should go? If the factor analysts cannot agree, why should the less sophisticated public accept the word of any single factor theorist as definitive? Although many of the earlier methodological controversies among factor analysts have now been largely resolved, several important issues remain unsettled, such as the relative merits of orthogonal and oblique rotation, and how many factors one should extract from a given correlation matrix.

Many psychologists have felt that factor theories are not theories at all. Some of the systems simply specify important variables or factors but with no indication of the developmental process or provision of the detailed assumptions concerning behavior that would be necessary to permit predictions concerning unobserved data. As we have seen, this criticism does not apply to Cattell's position; nor does it apply to Eysenck or Guilford, both of whom place factors within a theoretical framework.

The necessary emphasis upon quantitative scores reduces the kinds of problems and variables that the factor analyst can presently deal with. Thus, many personality theorists would argue that early stress upon quantification results in artificial and premature congealing of an area that is still in an exploratory stage. These critics assert that although factor analysis purports to be concerned with discovering the underlying dimensions of personality in a completely general sense, in fact, the kinds of data that must be employed place tremendous restrictions upon the nature of the variables that may be derived.

Whatever the shortcomings of factor theories may be, it is clear that their emphasis upon explicitness and adequate standards of measurement represents a very healthy influence. One might contend that the *content* of factor theories may or may not make a fruitful contribution to future theories of personality, but the *style* or mode of approach of these theorists will surely have an impact upon the way in which future theory will develop.

BIBLIOGRAPHY
PRIMARY SOURCES

Cattell, R. B. *Description and measurement of personality.* New York: World Book Co., 1946.

Cattell, R. B. *Personality: a systematic, theoretical, and factual study.* New York: McGraw-Hill, 1950.

Cattell, R. B. *Personality and motivation structure and measurement.* New York: Harcourt, Brace, Jovanovich, 1957.

Cattell, R. B. (Ed.). *Handbook of multivariate experimental psychology.* Chicago: Rand McNally, 1966b.

Cattell, R. B. *Personality and mood by questionnaire.* San Francisco: Jossey-Bass, 1973a.

Cattell, R. B., and Child, D. *Motivation and dynamic structure.* New York: Wiley, 1975.

Eysenck, H. J. *The structure of human personality.* New York: Wiley, 1953.

Guilford, J. P. *Personality.* New York: McGraw-Hill, 1959.

REFERENCES

Allport, G. W., and Odbert, H. S. Trait-names: a psycho-lexical study. *Psychol. Monogr.,* 1936, **47,** Whole No. 211.

Allport, G. W. *Personality: a psychological interpretation.* New York: Holt, 1937.

Becker, W. C. The matching of behavior rating and questionnaire personality factors. *Psychol. Bull.,* 1960, **57,** 201–212.

Burt, C. L. *The factors of the mind.* New York: Macmillan, 1941.

Cattell, R. B. *The culture free test of intelligence.* Champaign, Ill.: Inst. Pers. and Abil. Test., 1944.

Cattell, R. B. *Description and measurement of personality.* New York: World Book Co., 1946.

Cattell, R. B. Concepts and methods in the measurement of group syntality. *Psychol. Rev.,* 1948, **55,** 48–63.

Cattell, R. B. The dimensions of culture patterns by factorization of national character. *J. Abnorm. Soc. Psychol.,* 1949, **44,** 443–469.

Cattell, R. B. *Personality: a systematic, theoretical, and factual study.* New York: McGraw-Hill, 1950.

Cattell, R. B. *Factor analysis: an introduction and manual for psychologist and social scientist.* New York: Harper, 1952.

Cattell, R. B. A quantitative analysis of the changes in the culture pattern of Great Britain 1837–1937, by P-technique. *Acta Psychol.,* 1953, **9,** 99–121.

Cattell, R. B. *The O-A Personality Test Battery.* Champaign, Ill.: Inst. Pers. and Abil. Test., 1954.

Cattell, R. B. Personality and motivation theory based on structural measurement. In J. L. McCary (Ed.). *Psychology of personality*. New York: Grove Press, 1956.

Cattell, R. B. *Personality and motivation structure and measurement*. New York: Harcourt, Brace, Jovanovich, 1957.

Cattell, R. B. The multiple abstract variance analysis equations and solutions: for nature-nurture research on continuous variables. *Psychol. Rev.,* 1960, **67,** 353–372.

Cattell, R. B. Group theory, personality and role: a model for experimental researches. In F. A. Geldard (Ed.). *Defence psychology*. Oxford: Pergamon Press, 1961.

Cattell, R. B. Personality, role, mood, and situation-perception: a unifying theory of modulators. *Psychol. Rev.,* 1963a, **70,** 1–18.

Cattell, R. B. Theory of fluid and crystallized intelligence: a critical experiment. *J. Educ. Psychol.,* 1963b, **54,** 1–22.

Cattell, R. B. *Personality and social psychology*. San Diego: Knapp, 1964.

Cattell, R. B. *The scientific analysis of personality*. Chicago: Aldine, 1966a.

Cattell, R. B. (Ed.). *Handbook of multivariate experimental psychology*. Chicago: Rand McNally, 1966b.

Cattell, R. B. Trait-view theory of perturbations in ratings and self ratings (*L* (*BR*)- and Q-Data). *Psychol. Rev.,* 1968, **75,** 96–113.

Cattell, R. B. *Abilities: their structure, growth and action*. Boston: Houghton Mifflin, 1971.

Cattell, R. B. Unraveling maturational and learning developments by the comparative MAVA and structured learning approaches. In J. R. Nesselroade and H. W. Reese (Eds.). *Life-span developmental psychology*. New York: Academic Press, 1973b.

Cattell, R. B. *Personality and learning theory*. New York: Springer (in press).

Cattell, R. B., and Adelson, M. The dimensions of social change in the U.S.A. as determined by P-technique. *Soc. Forces,* 1951, **30,** 190–201.

Cattell, R. B., and Baggaley, A. B. A confirmation of ergic and engram structures in attitudes objectively measured. *Austral. J. Psychol.,* 1958, **10,** 287–318.

Cattell, R. B., and Beloff, J. R. Research origins and construction of the IPAT Junior Personality Quiz. *J. Consult. Psychol.,* 1953, **17,** 436–442.

Cattell, R. B., Blewett, D. B., and Beloff, J. R. The inheritance of personality. *Amer. J. Hum. Genet.,* 1955, **7,** 122–146.

Cattell, R. B., and Butcher, H. J. *The prediction of achievement and creativity*. Indianapolis: Bobbs-Merrill, 1968.

Cattell, R. B., Coan, R. W., and Beloff, H. A re-examination of personality structure in late childhood, and development of the High School Personality Questionnaire. *J. Exper. Educ.,* 1958, **27,** 73–88.

Cattell, R. B., and Coulter, M. A. Principles of behavioral taxonomy and the mathematical basis of the taxonome computer program. *Brit. J. Math. Stat. Psychol.,* 1966, **19,** 237–269.

Cattell, R. B., and Cross, K. P. Comparison of the ergic and self-sentiment structure found in dynamic traits by R- and P-techniques. *J. Pers.,* 1952, **21,** 250–271.

Cattell, R. B., and Dreger, R. M. *Handbook of modern personality theory*. New York: Hemisphere (in press).

Cattell, R. B., and Gibbons, B. D. Personality factor structure of the combined Guilford and Cattell personality questionnaires. *J. Pers. Soc. Psychol.,* 1968, **9,** 107–120.

Cattell, R. B., and Gorsuch, R. L. The definition and measurement of national morale and morality. *J. Soc. Psychol.,* 1965, **67,** 77–96.

Cattell, R. B., and Horn, J. An integrating study of the factor structure of adult attitude-interests. *Genet. Psychol. Monog.,* 1963, **67,** 89–149.

Cattell, R. B., and Luborsky, L. B. Personality factors in response to humor. *J. Abnorm. Soc. Psychol.,* 1947, **42,** 402–421.

Cattell, R. B., Radcliffe, J. A., and Sweney, A. B. The nature and measurement of components of motivation. *Genet. Psychol. Monog.,* 1963, **68,** 49–211.

Cattell, R. B., and Saunders, D. R. Musical preferences and personality diagnosis: I. A factorization of one hundred and twenty themes. *J. Soc. Psychol.,* 1954, **39,** 3–24.

Cattell, R. B., Saunders, D. R., and Stice, G. F. *The 16 personality factor questionnaire,* Champaign, Ill.: Inst. Pers. and Abil. Test., 1950.

Cattell, R. B., Saunders, D. R., and Stice, G. F. The dimensions of syntality in small groups. *Hum. Rel.,* 1953, **6,** 331–356.

Cattell, R. B., and Scheier, I. H. *The meaning and measurement of neuroticism and anxiety*. New York: Ronald, 1961.

Cattell, R. B., and Stice, G. F. Four formulae for selecting leaders on the basis of personality. *Hum. Rel.,* 1954, **7,** 493–507.

Cattell, R. B., Stice, G. F., and Kristy, N. F. A first approximation to nature-nurture ratios for eleven primary personality factors in objective tests. *J. Abnorm. Soc. Psychol.,* 1957, **54,** 143–159.

Cattell, R. B., and Sweney, A. B. Components measurable in manifestations of mental conflict. *J. Abnorm. Soc. Psychol.,* 1964, **68,** 479–490.

Cattell, R. B., and Tatro, D. F. The personality factors, objectively measured, which distinguish psychotics from normals. *Behav. Res. and Therapy,* 1966, **4,** 39–51.

Cattell, R. B., and Warburton, F. W. *Objective personality and motivation tests*. Urbana, Ill.: Univ. of Illinois Press, 1967.

Cattell, R. B., and Wenig, P. W. Dynamic and cognitive factors controlling misperception. *J. Abnorm. Soc. Psychol.,* 1952, **47,** 797–809.

Cattell, R. B., and Wispe, L. G. The dimension of syntality in small groups. *J. Soc. Psychol.,* 1948, **28,** 57–78.

Comrey, A. L. *A first course in factor analysis*. New York: Academic Press, 1973.

Comrey, A. L., and Jamison, K. Verification of six personality factors. *Educ. Psychol. Measmt.,* 1966, **26,** 945–953.

Eysenck, H. J. *The scientific study of personality*. London: Routledge and Kegan Paul, 1952.

Eysenck, H. J. *The structure of human personality*. New York: Wiley, 1953.

Eysenck, H. J. The inheritance of extraversion-introversion. *Acta Psychol.,* 1956, **12,** 95–110.

Eysenck, H. J., and Eysenck, S. B. G. A factorial study of psychoticism as a dimension of personality. *Multivar. Behav. Res.,* 1968, Clinical Psychol. Special Issue, 15–31.

Eysenck, H. J., and Prell, D. B. The inheritance of neuroticism: an experimental study. *J. Ment. Sci.,* 1951, **97,** 441–465.

Goldberg, L. R. Explorer on the run. *Contemp. Psychol.,* 1968, **13,** 617–619.

Gordon, J. E. Archetypical, Germanic, factorial, brilliant and contradictory. *Contemp. Psychol.,* 1966, **11,** 236–238.

Gorsuch, R. L. *Factor analysis.* Philadelphia: Saunders, 1974.

Guilford, J. P. The structure of intellect. *Psychol. Bull.,* 1956, **53,** 267–293.

Guilford, J. P. *Personality.* New York: McGraw-Hill, 1959.

Guilford, J. P., and Guilford, R. B. An analysis of the factors in a typical test of introversion-extraversion. *J. Abnorm. Soc. Psychol.,* 1934, **28,** 377–399.

Guilford, J. P., and Zimmerman, W. S. *The Guilford-Zimmerman temperament survey: manual of instructions and interpretations.* Beverly Hills, Calif.: Sheridan Supply Co., 1949.

Guilford, J. P., and Zimmerman, W. S. Fourteen dimensions of temperament. *Psychol. Monogr.,* 1956, **70,** Whole No. 417.

Harman, H. H. *Modern factor analysis.* 2nd ed. Chicago: Univ. of Chicago Press, 1967.

Hundleby, J. D., Pawlik, K., and Cattell, R. B. *Personality factors in objective test devices.* San Diego: Knapp, 1965.

Muliak, S. A. *The foundations of factor analysis.* New York: McGraw-Hill, 1972.

Norman, W. T. Toward an adequate taxonomy of personality attributes: replicated factor structure in peer nomination personality ratings. *J. Abnorm. Soc. Psychol.,* 1963, **66,** 574–583.

Sealy, A. P., and Cattell, R. B. Adolescent personality trends in primary factors measured in the 16PF and the HSPQ questionnaires through ages 11 to 23. *Brit. J. Soc. Clin. Psychol.,* 1966, **5,** 172–184.

Sells, S. B. Structured measurement of personality and motivation: a review of contributions of Raymond B. Cattell. *J. Clin. Psychol.,* 1959, **15,** 3–21.

Spearman, C. "General intelligence" objectively determined and measured. *Amer. J. Psychol.,* 1904, **15,** 201–293.

Spearman, C. *Abilities of man.* New York: Macmillan, 1927.

Thurstone, L. L. Multiple factor analysis. *Psychol. Rev.,* 1931, **38,** 406–427.

Thurstone, L. L. Psychological implications of factor analysis. *Amer. Psychologist,* 1948, **3,** 402–408.

STIMULUS-RESPONSE THEORY   15

We shall present here the personality theory that is most elegant, most economical, and shows the closest link to its natural science forebears. Stimulus-response (S-R) theory, at least in its origins, can accurately be labeled a laboratory theory in contrast to other theories with which we have dealt where the role of clinical or naturalistic observation has been much more important. Consistent with these origins is the position's explicitness, economy of formulation, and the serious efforts made to provide suitable empirical anchoring for the main terms of the theory.

Actually there is no single S-R theory, but rather a cluster of theories all resembling each other more or less, but at the same time each possessing certain distinctive qualities. These systems began as attempts to account for the acquisition and retention of new forms of behavior that appeared with experience. It is thus no surprise to find that the learning process is given predominant emphasis. Although innate factors are not ignored, the S-R theorist is primarily concerned with the process whereby the individual mediates between an array of responses and the tremendous variety of stimulation (internal and external) to which he or she is exposed.

Although there is no need to engage in a detailed discussion of the complex origins of S-R theory, it would scarcely be appropriate to introduce this theory without mentioning the contributions of Ivan Pavlov, John B. Watson, and Edward L. Thorndike. The distinguished Russian physiologist Ivan Pavlov (1906, 1927) discovered a type of learning that has become known as classical conditioning. Pavlov was able to demonstrate that through the simultaneous presentation of an unconditioned stimulus (meat paste) and a conditioned stimulus (sound from a tuning fork), the conditioned stimulus would eventually elicit a response (salivation) that originally could be elicited only by the unconditioned stimulus. The act of salivating to the sound of the tuning fork was referred to as a conditioned response.

This process of classical conditioning, in the hands of a number of American psychologists, became a means of building an objective psychology that dealt only with observables. John B. Watson (1916, 1925) was the leader of this movement. He rejected the then dominant conception of psychology as a unique type of science, aimed at discovering the structure of consciousness by introspection. Psychology, he proposed, should study *behavior,* using the same types of objective techniques as other natural sciences. He seized upon Pavlov's principle of conditioning and, combining this with ideas he had already developed, presented to the world a position he called "behaviorism." This objective and environmentalistic point of view quickly came to typify American psychology and even today it is closely linked with the most distinctive features of psychology in this country. At the same time that these developments were proceeding, Edward Thorndike (1911, 1932) was demonstrating the importance of reward and punishment in the learning process, and his "law of effect" has become one of the cornerstones of modern learning theory. Despite the crucial nature of Pavlov's contributions, learning theory with its heavy stress upon objectivity, its emphasis upon careful experimentation, and its strong functional flavor exists as one of the most singularly American theories of all the positions we shall consider.

Psychologists have devoted more thought and activity to the construction of learning theory than to any other contemporary theoretical enterprise. As a result of the ideas and investigations of Edward L. Thorndike, John B. Watson, Edward C. Tolman, Edwin R. Guthrie, Clark L. Hull, Kenneth W. Spence, and others, the dominant theoretical interest of American psychologists shifted during the third decade of this century toward the learning process. During the next two decades, most major theoretical issues in psychology were debated within the framework of learning theory. Theorists such as Thorndike, Hull, Spence, and Guthrie described the learning process as involving the *associative linkage* between *sensory* and *motor* processes. Much of the controversy centered about this theoretical conception of the learning process. Edward Tolman, one of the major theorists of this period, shared the view that the empirical task of the learning theorist is to identify the environmental forces that determine behavior but conceived of learning as the development of organized *cognitions* about sets of *sensory,* or stimulus, events. Lewin also made steps toward developing a cognitive type of theory, although he was not deeply and continuously concerned with the learning process. Much of the experimental work stimulated by these theoretical debates involved the investigation of relatively simple forms of learning, particularly as they occurred in animals. In the last ten to fifteen years, experimental psychologists have shown an increasing interest in studying language, memory, and complex thought processes in humans. Reflecting this shift in emphasis, sophisticated cognitive and information processing theories that bear little resemblance to simple association theories have been developed. The interested reader will find an excellent summary of all the major types of learning theory, including cognitive theories and related formulations, in Hilgard and Bower (1975).

As the title of this chapter implies, we are concerned here with formulations that are based on S-R association theory or whose intellectual lineage, although showing the influence of recent thought on cognitive processes, owes much to the S-R behaviorist tradition. More specifically, we shall pay particular attention to attempts to generalize or apply the theoretical position of Clark Hull (1943, 1951, 1952) to phenomena of interest to the personality psychologist. What are the reasons for concentrating our interest on the formulations influenced by Hull and his writings? First of all, this theoretical position is one of the most elegant and highly developed of any comprehensive theory. The viewpoint has been stated more explicitly, has been more adequately formalized, and has fostered a greater wealth of related empirical investigation than any comparable theory. Second, and most important, it is largely the intellectual descendants of Hull and Spence who have made the most serious and systematic attempts to apply their laboratory-developed theories to the understanding of personality. A feature that has made Hullian theory particularly attractive is its attention to the role of motivation in determining behavior and the processes by which learned motives are acquired.

B. F. Skinner, a major figure in the field of learning, has also had a marked impact on many areas of psychology including personality functioning. His contributions will be considered in a separate chapter.

Contrary to the theories we have already discussed, the rudiments of the S-R position were developed in connection with data that possess little seeming similarity to the data of major interest to the personality psychologist. It may be an overstatement to say that the white rat has had more to do with shaping this theory than have human subjects, but it is certainly true that members of lower species have had infinitely more to do with the theory's development than in the case of the other theories we have considered. One must not, however, overemphasize the importance of the place of origin of this theory. A theory should be evaluated in terms of what it does rather than where it comes from. Hull, the intellectual father of this position, made explicit his intent of developing a general theory of *human* behavior at the very beginning of his theoretical strivings. It was only for reasons of strategy that he chose to develop his initial ideas against the relatively stable background provided by animal behavior in carefully controlled experimental situations. Thus, the essence of this theory did not develop from the study of lower organisms because of any conviction that all behavioral problems could be solved in this manner. Rather, it was hoped that the simplicity of the lower organism would permit the establishment of certain fundamentals which, when elaborated through the study of complex human behavior, might prove to be the core of a satisfactory theory of behavior. This readiness to change and extend the peripheral part of the theory, at the same time maintaining certain core assumptions and concepts, is clearly demonstrated in the work of many of Hull's students. Consistent with this point of view we shall make no effort here to outline the details of Hull's theory but rather will focus upon attempts that have been made to modify or elaborate the theory so as to deal with behavior of crucial interest to the personality psychologist. The outstanding example of such a derived theory is contained in the work of Dollard and Miller, and our chapter will give predominant attention to this position. The writings of many others deserve mention but space limitations will allow us to summarize briefly the views of only several other individuals: Eysenck and Wolpe, Seligman and Bandura.

Before turning to the details of these theories, a word should be said concerning the Institute of Human Relations at Yale University. This institution was established in 1933 under the direction of Mark May in an effort to bring about closer collaboration and integration among psychology, psychiatry, sociology, and anthropology. The Institute embraced all of these traditionally separate departments. The first decade of its existence represents one of the most fruitful periods of collaboration in the behavioral sciences that has occurred in any American university. Although Clark Hull provided the theoretical underpinning for this group, its activities were by no means focused primarily on experimental psychology. Indeed, social anthropology, the study of the social aspects of humans in nonliterate societies, contributed an important element to the intellectual framework of this group and there was an intense interest in psychoanalytic theory that contributed to many of the theoretical and research ideas of members of the group. During this ten-year period a remarkable group of young men received training either as graduate students or young staff members and upon all of them this experience seems to have exerted a powerful and enduring influence. Among the outstanding members of this group were Judson Brown, John Dollard, Ernest Hilgard, Carl Hovland, Donald Marquis, Neal Miller, O. H. Mowrer, Robert Sears, Kenneth Spence, and John Whiting. It was the Institute of Human Relations, directed by Mark May, infused with the ideas of Clark Hull, and vitalized by the productive scholarship of the individuals just mentioned, that resulted in the developments with which we are concerned in this chapter.

THE REINFORCEMENT THEORY OF DOLLARD AND MILLER

This theory represents the efforts of two individuals, sophisticated in both laboratory and clinical investigation, to modify and simplify Hull's reinforcement theory so that it can be used easily and effectively to deal with events of major interest to the social and clinical psychologist. The details of the theory have been shaped not only by the formulations of Hull but also by psychoanalytic theory and by the findings and generalizations of social anthropology. As we shall see, the concept of habit, which represents a stable S-R connection, is crucial to this position. In fact, most of the theory is concerned with specifying the conditions under which habits form and are dissolved. The relatively small number of concepts that are employed for this purpose have been used with great ingenuity by the authors to account for phenomena of central interest to the clinician, for example, repression, displacement, and conflict. In many instances the authors have attempted to derive from psychoanalytic writing and clinical observation substantive wisdom concerning behavior which in turn they have incorporated within their S-R concepts. Thus, a good deal of theory application consists of the translation of general observation, or vague theoretical formulation, into the more aseptic terms of S-R theory. Although translation is not in itself a particularly important goal, this effort has frequently made possible new insights and predictions concerning unobserved empirical events, and these functions represent the highest order of theoretical contribution.

In some respects John Dollard and Neal Miller provide striking contrasts; in other regards their backgrounds show great similarity. They are different in that Miller has advanced important ideas and findings primarily within the domain of experimental psychology, and Dollard has made significant anthropological and sociological

John Dollard.

contributions. However, both have been influenced heavily by their experiences at the Institute of Human Relations and consistent with this is their indebtedness to Hull and Freud. Perhaps the fruitfulness of their collaboration has derived from this common core of conviction upon which each has erected unique empirical and theoretical strengths.

John Dollard was born in Menasha, Wisconsin, on August 29, 1900. He received an A.B. from the University of Wisconsin in 1922 and subsequently secured his M.A. (1930) and Ph.D. (1931) in sociology from the University of Chicago. From 1926 until 1929 he served as assistant to the president of the University of Chicago. In 1932 he accepted a position as assistant professor of anthropology at Yale University and in the following year became an assistant professor of sociology in the recently formed Institute of Human Relations. In 1935 he became a research associate in the institute and in 1948 a research associate and professor of psychology. He became professor emeritus in 1969. He was trained in psychoanalysis at the Berlin Institute and became a member of the Western New England Psychoanalytic Society. Dollard's convictions concerning, and personal dedication to, the unification of the social sciences is reflected not only in his publications but also in the remarkable fact that he has had academic appointments in anthropology, sociology, and psychology all at the same university. It should be noted that this interdisciplinary activity occurred at a time when the individual disciplines were much less cordial to integration than they are at present. Dollard has written numerous technical articles in the social sciences that have ranged from ethnology to psychotherapy. He has authored a number of books that reflect this same wide-ranging interest. *Caste and class in a Southern town* (1937) is a highly regarded field study concerned with the role of the black in a southern community and represents one of the early examples of culture and personality analysis. This was followed by a related volume, *Children of bondage* (1940), which was coauthored with Allison Davis. He published two volumes concerned with the psychological analysis of fear: *Victory over fear* (1942) and *Fear in battle* (1943); and a significant monograph concerned with the use of life history material, *Criteria for the life history* (1936). He has published jointly with Frank Auld and Alice White *Steps in psychotherapy* (1953), a book presenting a method of psychotherapy that includes the detailed description of an individual in treatment, and, with Frank Auld, *Scoring human motives* (1959).

Neal E. Miller was born in Milwaukee, Wisconsin, on August 3, 1909, and received his B.S. from the University of Washington in

1931. He received his M.A. from Stanford University in 1932 and his Ph.D. in psychology from Yale University in 1935. From 1932 until 1935 he served as an assistant in psychology at the Institute of Human Relations and in 1935–1936 he was a Social Science Research Council traveling fellow during which time he secured a training analysis at the Vienna Institute of Psychoanalysis. From 1936 until 1940 he was an instructor and subsequently assistant professor at the Institute of Human Relations. He became a research associate and associate professor in 1941. From 1942 to 1946 he directed a psychological research project for the Army Air Force. In 1946 he returned to Yale University, becoming the James Rowland Angell professor of psychology in 1952. He remained at Yale until 1966, when he became professor of psychology and head of the Laboratory of Physiological Psychology at Rockefeller University. Aside from his collaboration with John Dollard, Miller is best known in psychology for his careful experimental and theoretical work on the acquisition of drives, the nature of reinforcement, and the study of conflict. His early research

Neal E. Miller.

was purely behavioral in nature but since the mid 1950s, Miller has become concerned with the physiological mechanisms underlying drive and reinforcement and other related phenomena. This work is presented in detail in journal publications, although much of it is summarized in three excellent handbook chapters (Miller, 1944, 1951a, 1959). The respect that his contributions have commanded is reflected in the honors he has received. These include membership in the prestigious National Academy of Science, election to the presidency of the American Psychological Association (1959), receipt of the Warren medal from the Society of Experimental Psychologists (1957), and receipt of the President's Medal of Science (1965), a distinction he shares with only two other behavioral scientists.

In 1939 several staff members of the Institute of Human Relations, including Dollard and Miller, published a monograph titled *Frustration and aggression* (1939). This was an early and interesting example of the kind of application with which we are concerned in this chapter. The authors attempted to analyze frustration and its consequence in terms of S-R concepts. In their monograph they present a systematic formulation of this position, together with a considerable amount of new investigation and predictions concerning yet-to-be-observed events. This work not only illustrates the integration of S-R concepts, psychoanalytic formulation, and anthropological evidence but it also provides evidence for the fruitfulness of this union, as it has led to a host of related empirical studies. Miller and Dollard have jointly written two volumes representing the attempt to apply a simplified version of Hull's theory to the problems of the social psychologist (*Social learning and imitation,* 1941) and to the problems of the clinical or personality psychologist (*Personality and psychotherapy,* 1950). It is primarily the contents of these volumes, particularly the latter one, which will form the basis for the exposition to follow.

The core of their position is a description of the learning process. Miller and Dollard clearly express their general view of this process and its constituent elements in the following passage:

What, then, is learning theory? In its simplest form, it is the study of the circumstances under which a response and a cue stimulus become connected. After learning has been completed, response and cue are bound together in such a way that the appearance of the cue evokes the response. . . . Learning takes place according to definite psychological principles. Practice does not always make perfect. The connection between a cue and a response can be strengthened only under certain conditions. The learner must be driven to make the response and rewarded for having responded in the presence of the cue. This may be expressed in a homely way by saying that in order to learn one must want something, notice something, do something, and get something. Stated more exactly, these factors are drive, cue, response and reward. These elements in the learning process have been carefully explored, and further complexities have been discovered. Learning theory has become a firmly knit body of principles which are useful in describing human behavior (1941, pp. 1–2).

The learning principles that Dollard and Miller have applied to everyday life have been discovered in controlled laboratory investigations that typically have involved animals as subjects. Knowledge of these laboratory principles, as well as of certain theoretical notions concerning them, is therefore critical to an understanding of their personality theory. A description of a hypothetical experiment, patterned after pioneering studies of Miller and his colleagues (Miller, 1948; Brown and Jacobs, 1949), and a theoretical analysis of its result will serve as a means of introducing this necessary background.

An Illustrative Experiment   In this hypothetical experiment, each subject (the ubiquitous laboratory rat) is placed in a rectangular box with a grid floor. The box is divided into two square compartments by a low "fence" or hurdle over which the rat can easily jump. A buzzer is sounded and simultaneously a pulsing electrical charge is sent through the grid floor. The electric shock is omitted with control subjects. The animal can be expected to show a variety of vigorous responses to the shock and eventually will scramble over the hurdle into the other compartment. The shuttlebox apparatus is arranged so that as soon as the subject goes over the hurdle dividing one compartment from the other, the buzzer and shock are terminated. Over the next sixty minutes, this procedure is repeated at irregular intervals, and it is observed that the time between the onset of the buzzer and shock and the subject's hurdle-jumping response becomes progressively shorter and shorter. On the next day, each subject is again placed in the shuttlebox for an hour. During this session, the buzzer is periodically sounded and remains on until the animal enters the other compartment but it is never again accompanied by shock. Despite the absence of the shock, the subject continues to jump over the hurdle whenever the buzzer sounds and may even continue to improve its performance.

After several such sessions, a new feature is introduced into the apparatus. Jumping the hurdle no longer is followed by cessation of the buzzer. If, however, the rat depresses a lever attached to the base of the hurdle, the buzzer is turned off. Again, the animals are observed to exhibit vigorous activity, largely confined to jumping back and forth across the hurdle. In the course of moving about the rat might depress the lever. Gradually hurdle-jumping begins to disappear and the time between the buzzer onset and the lever press gets shorter and shorter and eventually it occurs promptly as the buzzer sounds. The behavior of these subjects is in marked contrast to the unshocked control animals who show no similar systematic changes in their behavior in any of the experimental sessions. Obviously, as a result of the buzzer-shock pairings the experimental subjects have learned or acquired new responses while the control subjects have not.

Actually several types of learning have taken place. The first is *classical conditioning,* the form of learning originally discovered by Pavlov. Classical conditioning involves a procedure in which an initially neutral stimulus (*conditioned stimulus* or CS) is paired with an *unconditioned stimulus* (US), which regularly elicits a characteristic behavior pattern, the *unconditioned response* (UR). After repeated CS-US pairings, the CS, presented by itself or in anticipation of the US, elicits a characteristic reaction known as the *conditioned response* (CR). Typically, the CR is similar to the UR, though rarely identical.

An outline of the classical conditioning that has occurred in our illustrative experiment, according to Miller's theory, is shown below in Figure 15-1. However, first consider the consequences of the shock per se. Between the observable US (shock) and the overt behavior (R_{emot}) it produces, a chain of internal events occurs. The shock elicits a number of internal *responses* associated with pain (symbolized here as r_{emot}). These r_{emot} give rise, in turn, to an internal pattern of *stimuli*. In addition to having the same capacity as external sources of stimulation to set off or "cue" still further responses, these internal stimuli consequent on r_{emot} are said to have *drive* (D) properties and hence are identified as *drive stimuli* or s_D.

Drive is a motivational concept in the Hullian system and is said to impel or activate behavior but not to determine its direction. In this instance, the drive is an innate or primary one, based on pain. There are, of course, a number of primary drives, in addition to pain, such as hunger, thirst, and sex. The latter examples, in contrast to pain, are deprivation states, brought about by withholding some kind of stimulus, such as food, and reduced by providing the organism with the

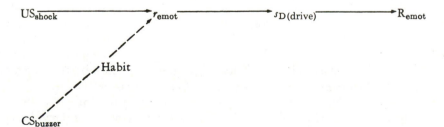

FIGURE 15-1
Theoretical analysis of the processes involved in the classical conditioning of an emotional response based on pain.

appropriate stimulus, instead of by removing noxious stimulation. Actually, Miller postulates that any internal or external stimulus, if intense enough, evokes a drive and impels action. As this statement implies, drives differ in strength and the stronger the drive the more vigorous or persistent the behavior it energizes. In our experiment, for example, the vigor of the overtly observable emotional behavior that occurs in subjects in response to the US and later, of the learned hurdle-jumping response is influenced by the level of shock that is given.

Initially the buzzer elicits none of the emotional behaviors associated with the shock. But after repeated presentations of the buzzer with the shock, the buzzer gains the capacity to elicit internal r_{emot}, similar to those originally evoked by the painful US; a conditioned response (CR) has been acquired. In the Hullian system that Dollard and Miller utilize, the learning that has taken place is described as an associative connection between the conditioned stimulus (buzzer) and the response (r_{emot}) and is represented by the theoretical concept, *habit*. As will be discussed in more detail shortly, Hull postulated that for a habit to be established, not only must the stimulus and response occur close to each other temporally and spatially but also the response must be accompanied by a reinforcement or reward. Assuming that the latter condition is met, the strength of the S–R habit increases with the number of occasions on which the stimulus and the response have occurred together.

The repeated presentations of the buzzer and shock in the first session of our experiment with the subject's escape from shock acting as the reinforcer is sufficient to set up a relatively strong habit. Once the classically conditioned r_{emot} has been established, presentation of the buzzer alone not only elicits r_{emot} but also sets into operation the rest of the chain of events originally associated with the administration of shock. Thus, the distinctive pattern of internal stimulation s_D, will be aroused and in combination with the buzzer it will act as a cue to elicit overt behavior similar to that previously evoked by the shock. Further, these observable responses are energized or activated by the drive properties of s_D. Since the drive is elicited by a *learned* response to a previously neutral stimulus, it is identified as an acquired or *secondary* drive, in contrast to the *primary* drive evoked by responses to painful stimulation.

In order to distinguish between the $r_{emot} \rightarrow s_D$ sequence elicited by shock and the classically conditioned sequence elicited by the buzzer, the latter has been given the distinctive label of anxiety or *fear*. Thus fear is both a learned *response*—the conditioned form of the pain response, to use Mowrer's phrase—and a learned or secondary *drive*.

But as we have said, the experimental subjects have learned more than these fear reactions. During the first session, they quickly learned to jump over the hurdle as soon as the buzzer and shock were presented, even though initially the stimulation elicited a variety of vigorous responses of which hurdle-jumping was not the most prominent. The key to why this response dominated the others lies in its consequences: only hurdle-jumping was followed by discontinuation of the shock and the train of internal events it provoked. Although there are exceptions, events that reduce or eliminate drive stimuli typically strengthen or increase the probability of appearance of any responses they regularly accompany and are called reinforcers. Conversely, responses unaccompanied by events that reduce drive stimuli tend not to be repeated. Since only hurdle-jumping was followed by reinforcement—cessation of the shock—this response was strengthened instead of others.

The development of the capacity of the buzzer-shock combination to elicit hurdle-jumping is an example of a kind of learning in which, in contrast to classical conditioning, the occurrence of the reinforcer is contingent on the response having been made; the response is instrumental in producing the reinforcing event. The type of learning that occurs under these conditions is termed *instrumental* or, as Skinner would call it, operant conditioning. During the first session of our experiment two types of response were learned: the classically conditioned fear response, and the instrumental hurdle-jumping response that brought about cessation of the US (thus reinforcing, via drive reduction, both of these responses).

After the first session, the shock was discontinued and only the buzzer was employed. Since no shock was given, cessation of shock no longer occurred. The procedure in which the reinforcers used to establish a response are withdrawn is known as *experimental extinction* and typically produces a rapid reduction in the strength of the learned response. For example, hungry rats who have learned to perform a distinctive instrumental act to obtain food quickly cease to make the response after the food is discontinued. But cessation of shock in our experiment did *not* lead to disappearance of the hurdle-jumping response (or, theoretically, of r_{emot}); for many subjects, the response even continued to increase in strength, as indexed by a decrease in time to respond with successive presentations of the buzzer. Miller suggests that this "extinction" procedure leads to little or no weakening of the learned responses because, in actuality, these responses *continue* to be reinforced. The CS elicits not pain but the learned fear sequence, and it is this that activates the instrumental habit underlying the hurdle-jumping. Occurrence of the instrumental response turns off the buzzer, and the drive stimuli associated with fear are therefore reduced in intensity. Thus both the classically conditioned fear reaction and the instrumental hurdle-jumping continue to be reinforced.

Experimental extinction of the hurdle-jumping response *did* occur, however, when it became ineffective in terminating the buzzer and the fear it elicited. Goaded by this fear, the animals learned instead the now effective lever-pressing response. Thus the subjects continued to perform the response that had allowed them in the past to escape a painful stimulus only as long as it continued to permit them to reduce fear. When conditions changed, they learned a *new* instrumental response, motivated by the learned fear drive and reinforced by fear reduction.

Actual experiments of similar design have indicated that instrumental responses that allow a subject to escape or avoid an anxiety-evoking CS may slowly weaken with successive presentations of the latter. But if a substantial number of CS–US presentations have been given during the initial training period or the noxious US has been intense, the instrumental response may continue with little or no visible decreases in strength for hundreds of presentations of the CS (Miller, 1948). Dollard and Miller have pointed to a strong analogy between the experimental animal who persists in becoming frightened by harmless events such as the sound of a buzzer and the irrational neurotic fears and anxieties that can be observed in human subjects. If the observer has seen the initial learning process, there is nothing mysterious about the animal's fear of the buzzer and its efforts to escape; if the observer has seen the learning process preceding the neurotic symptom there is nothing surprising or senseless about the way in which the human subject behaves. It is only when the observer steps in after the fear has been learned that the subject's behavior appears strange or irrational.

Another learning principle of which Dollard and Miller make important use in their theory of personality may be illustrated by a variation in the procedure of our hypothetical experiment. After a first session in which the buzzer-shock pairings occur, a second session is conducted in which only a buzzer is presented. But now the buzzer signals vary in intensity, sometimes being the same as in the first session, and at other times louder or softer than during training. At the onset of a buzzer signal, the subjects jump the hurdle when the sound of the same intensity that had originally been paired with shock comes on. But they also tend to respond to the other sounds, with the strength of the response tendency being inversely related to the similarity of these buzzer intensities to the one used in the first session. These behaviors illustrate a *gradient of stimulus generalization:*

when a stimulus has gained the capacity to elicit a response by virtue of being paired with an unconditioned stimulus, other stimuli will have automatically gained some degree of this capacity, depending on their similarity to the original stimulus. A related phenomenon, which is more difficult to demonstrate concretely, is *response generalization:* a stimulus acquires the capacity to elicit not only the response that has typically followed it but also a number of similar responses.

It has been argued that without the capacity for stimulus and response generalization, organisms would exhibit little or no learning. Although, for convenience, one often refers to the "same" stimulus reoccurring and eliciting the "same" response, rarely if ever are individuals confronted with exactly the same stimulus situation on two or more occasions and the responses are never completely identical. Even in meticulously controlled experiments, it is more accurate to state that a range of stimuli are presented that elicit the capacity to evoke a range of responses.

Generalization gradients, however, have been demonstrated to extend far beyond the limits of stimulus and response variation that occurred in the training situation, the strength of the generalization tendency being related not only to the degree of similarity to the original learning situation but to such factors as the amount of original learning and the intensity of the drive that underlies the response. However, the generalization gradient can be narrowed by differential reinforcement. Continuing with our illustrative experiment, shocking the animal whenever the buzzer of the original intensity is presented and omitting the shock whenever the buzzer intensity is different will gradually lead to the extinction of hurdle-jumping to all but the training stimulus. The procedure has led to *stimulus differentiation.*

As this account makes clear, the fate of a stimulus-response connection is heavily influenced by the outcome of the responses—the stimulus events that closely follow it. Certain outcome events result in strengthening the connection, that is, in increasing the probability that the response will occur more vigorously or quickly on the next occasion the stimulus is presented. These events are classified as positive reinforcers or rewards. We have also seen that the *cessation* of other types of events, often noxious in nature, may also act to reinforce responses. Dollard and Miller have looked for a general principle that would allow them to determine whether any given stimulus should be considered a reinforcer. Following Hull (1943), they suggested the drive-reduction hypothesis, which states that an event that results in a sudden reduction in drive stimuli acts to reward or reinforce any response it accompanies. In what Miller (1959) describes as its strong form, the drive-reduction hypothesis further states that the reduction of drive stimuli is not merely a *sufficient* condition for reinforcement to occur but a *necessary* condition.

The strong version of the drive reduction hypothesis, adopted by Dollard and Miller, implies that the learning of an S-R association or habit will take place only if the response has been reinforced. The hypothesis that reinforcement is necessary for learning to occur has generated considerable controversy. Some theorists, such as Guthrie (1959), have insisted that the mere contiguity of a stimulus and response is sufficient; others have formulated two-factor theories in which it is proposed that some kinds of learning require reinforcement in addition to contiguity and others do not (see, for example, Mowrer, 1947; Spence, 1956; and Tolman, 1949).

Criticism has also been aimed at the assumption that reduction in drive stimuli produces the reinforcement effect. Miller himself has indicated on several occasions (see, for example, Miller, 1959) that although he has found the drive reduction hypothesis to be more appealing than any of the extant rival hypotheses, he has little confidence in its ultimate correctness. More recently, he tentatively presented what he considers to be a plausible alternative to the drive reduction hypothesis (Miller, 1963). There may be, he suggests, one or more "go" or "activating" mechanisms in the brain that are triggered by events resulting in drive stimulus reduction. These "go" mechanisms serve to intensify or energize ongoing responses elicited by the stimulus cues, and these vigorous responses are learned on the basis of pure contiguity. Activation of a "go" mechanism is itself a response and, similar to other responses, may also be conditioned by contiguity. Thus, a previously neutral stimulus may acquire the capacity to set off a "go" mechanism by virtue of having previously occurred in conjunction with activation of the mechanism.

Currently, the dominant approach among learning theorists is to accept the contiguity position or to bypass the issue entirely. Fortunately, Dollard and Miller have suggested that the major arguments in their S-R analysis of personality are unaffected by their specific hypotheses about reinforcement, so that it is possible to embrace the essential aspects of their theory without accepting their speculations about it. All that is necessary, they state, is that one assumes that events resulting in sudden reduction of drive stimuli reinforce the responses with which they are contiguous in the sense of making these acts more prepotent. Since the experimental evidence demonstrates that, with a few possible exceptions, drive reducing stimuli do have reinforcing effects, this assumption should find easy acceptance.

Dollard and Miller have consistently shown less interest in the structural or relatively unchanging elements of personality than in the process of learning and personality development. Granted that structural aspects are not emphasized, what concepts do they employ to represent the stable and enduring characteristics of the person? Habit is the key concept in the learning theory espoused by Dollard and Miller.

A *habit,* we have seen, is a link or association between a stimulus (cue) and a response. Learned associations or habits may be formed not only between external stimuli and overt responses but between internal ones as well. The bulk of their theory is concerned with specifying the conditions under which habits are acquired and extinguished or replaced, with little or no attention given to specifying classes of habits or listing the major varieties of habits that people exhibit.

Although personality consists primarily of habits, their particular structure will depend on the unique events to which the individual has been exposed. Further, this is only a temporary structure—the habits of today may alter as a result of tomorrow's experience. Dollard and Miller are content to specify the principles governing habit formation and leave to the individual clinician or investigator the task of specifying the habits that characterize any particular person. They take great pains to emphasize, however, that an important class of habits for humans are elicited by verbal stimuli, whether they are produced by the persons themselves or by someone else, and that responses are also frequently verbal in their nature.

It must also be pointed out that some habits may involve internal responses that in turn elicit internal stimuli with drive characteristics. (We have already examined fear as one example of a learned, response-produced drive). These secondary drives must also be considered enduring portions of personality. Primary drives and innate S-R connections also contribute to the structure of personality. Typically, however, they are not only less important in human behavior than secondary drives and other types of habits but also define what individuals have in common, as members of the same species, rather than their uniqueness.

THE STRUCTURE OF PERSONALITY

Dollard and Miller are explicit in defining the nature of motivation and they specify in considerable detail the development and elaboration of motives; but there is again no interest in taxonomy or classification. Instead they have focused on certain salient motives, such as anxiety. In their analysis of these they have attempted to illustrate the general process that can be expected to operate for all motives.

THE DYNAMICS OF PERSONALITY

The effect of drives on the human subject is complicated by the large number of derived or acquired drives that eventually make their appearance. In the process of growth the typical individual develops a large number of secondary drives that serve to instigate behavior. "These learned drives are acquired on the basis of the primary drives, represent elaborations of them, and serve as a facade behind which the functions of the underlying innate drives are hidden" (1950, pp. 31–32).

In the typical modern society secondary drive stimulation largely replaces the original function of primary drive stimulation. Acquired drives such as anxiety, shame, and the desire to please impel most of our actions. As this implies, the importance of the primary drives in most instances is not clear from casual observation of the socialized adult. It is only in the process of development, or in periods of crisis (failure of the culturally prescribed modes of adaptation), that one can observe clearly the operation of primary drives.

It should be obvious also that most of the reinforcements in the ordinary life of human subjects are not primary rewards but originally neutral events that have acquired reward value by virtue of having consistently been experienced in conjunction with primary reinforcement. A mother's smile, for example, becomes a powerful acquired or *secondary reward* for the infant, with its repeated association with feeding, diapering, and other caretaking activities that bring pleasure or remove physical discomfort. Secondary rewards often serve, by themselves, to reinforce behavior. Their capacity to reinforce is not sustained indefinitely, however, unless they continue to occur on occasion in conjunction with primary reinforcement. How these changes take place leads us to the general question of the development of personality.

THE DEVELOPMENT OF PERSONALITY

The transformation of the simple infant into the complex adult is a matter of little interest to some theorists, but this process is elaborated by Dollard and Miller. We shall present their treatment of this problem beginning with a brief consideration of the innate equipment of the infant and following this with a discussion of the acquisition of motives and the development of the higher mental processes. In addition we shall briefly consider the importance of the social context of behavior and developmental stages. In conclusion we shall illustrate the application of learning principles to repression, conflict, and other "neurotic" phenomena.

Innate Equipment

At birth and shortly thereafter the infant is endowed with only a limited array of behavioral equipment. First, it possesses a small number of *specific reflexes,* which are, for the most part, segmental responses made to a highly specific stimulus or class of stimuli. Second, it possesses a number of *innate hierarchies of response,* which are tendencies for certain responses to appear in particular stimulus situations before certain other responses; for example, it may be innately determined that when exposed to certain noxious stimuli the child will first try to escape from the stimuli before crying. This assumption implies that so-called random behavior is not random at all but is determined by response preferences which early in the organism's development are largely the result of innate factors but with development are influenced by a complex mixture of experience and these innate hierarchies. Third, the individual possesses a set of *primary drives* which, as we have already seen, are in the typical case internal stimuli of great strength and persistence and usually linked to known physiological processes.

Thus, we have initially an individual who is capable of a few, relatively segmental, or differentiated, responses to specific stimuli. This individual also possesses a group of primary drives that under certain organic conditions impel him or her to act or behave but which do not direct this activity. The only initial guidance of responses stems from an innate hierarchy of response tendencies that imposes a gross or general control over the order in which particular responses will appear in specified situations. Given this initial state our theory of development must account for: (1) the extension of present responses to new stimuli or stimulus situations; (2) the development of new responses; (3) the development of new or derived motives; (4) the extinction or elimination of existing associations between stimuli and responses. All of these developments, Dollard and Miller believe, can be understood by appealing to learning principles.

The Learning Process

We have noted that Dollard and Miller suggest that there are four important conceptual elements in the learning process. These are drive, cue, response, and reinforcement. Let us now amplify some of our earlier remarks about these concepts.

A *cue* is a stimulus that guides the response of the organism by directing or determining the exact nature of the response. "Cues determine when he will respond, where he will respond, and which response he will make" (Dollard and Miller, 1950, p. 32). Cues may vary in kind or in intensity. Thus, there are visual cues and auditory cues, but there are also weak flashes of light and blinding flashes of light. Or, there are auditory cues associated with the ringing of a bell and auditory cues associated with the human vocal cords, but there are also gentle, barely detectable, ringing sounds and there are shattering, clanging, ringing sounds. The cue function of stimuli may be associated with variation either in intensity or kind, although in most instances it is variation in kind that serves this function. Any quality that makes the stimulus distinctive may serve as the basis for the cue and in the usual case distinctiveness is more easily based upon variation in kind than intensity. Stimuli may operate as cues not only singly but also in combination. That is, the distinctiveness may depend not upon the difference in individual stimuli but rather upon the pattern or combination of several different stimuli, for example, the same individual letters may be used in different combinations to spell two or more words which will have completely different effects upon the reader. We have already suggested that any stimulus may also become a drive if it is intense enough; thus the same stimulus may have both drive and cue value—it may both arouse and direct behavior.

An exceedingly important part in the learning process must be assigned to *response* factors. As Dollard and Miller point out, before a given response can be linked to a given cue, the response must occur. Thus, a crucial stage in the organism's learning is the production of the appropriate response. In any given situation certain responses will be more likely to appear than others. This order of preference, or probability of response, when the situation is first presented is referred to as the *initial hierarchy of responses*. If this initial hierarchy appears to have occurred in the absence of any learning it may be referred to as the *innate hierarchy of responses,* which we have already mentioned as part of the primitive equipment of the individual. After experience and learning have influenced the individual's behavior in this situation, the derived order of response is labeled the *resultant hierarchy*. These concepts simply remind us that in any environmental setting the potential responses an individual may make have a different probability of occurring and can be ranked in terms of this probability.

With development, the hierarchy of response becomes intimately associated with language because particular responses become linked to words and consequently speech may mediate or determine the particular hierarchy that will operate. Thus, the same situation referred to as "dangerous" or as a "frolic" will evoke vastly different response hierarchies. The particular hierarchy displayed is also heavily influenced by the culture in which the individual has been socialized as the prescriptions of all cultures include notions of what the preferred or most likely response is to situations of social importance.

Once a response has been made, its subsequent fate is determined by the events that follow its occurrence. Responses that have been successful in bringing about primary or secondary reinforcement will be most likely to recur the next time the situation is encountered. Not infrequently a situation arises in which none of the responses the individual can make readily is reinforcing. These occurrences not only lead to the dropping out or extinction of ineffective behavior but play a crucial role in the development of new responses and a wider range of adaptive behavior. These *learning dilemmas,* as Dollard and Miller term them, necessitate new responses, or invoke responses that are more distant on the hierarchy of response, and this is the crux of learning new responses. If the individual's old responses are perfectly adequate to reduce all of the person's drive tensions, there is no reason to produce new responses and his or her behavior remains unmodified.

We have already seen that the infant is born with a limited range of primary drives that develop into a complex system of secondary drives with growth and experience. The learning processes underlying the acquisition of secondary drives are, in general, the same and have already been illustrated in our earlier presentation of an experiment in which the learned drive of fear or anxiety was acquired. Let us return briefly to a consideration of the processes by which such acquired drives are developed.

Secondary Drive and the Learning Process

Strong stimuli, such as shock, may elicit intense internal responses, which in turn produce still further internal stimuli. These internal stimuli act as *cues* to guide or control subsequent responses and serve as a *drive* that activates the organism and keeps the person active until reinforcement occurs or some other process, such as fatigue, intervenes. The overt responses that result in reinforcement are the ones that are learned. A previously neutral cue that has regularly occurred in conjunction with a drive producing stimulus may gain the capacity to elicit some part of the internal responses initially elicited only by the drive. These learned internal responses then automatically set off drive stimuli. A secondary drive has been established and will motivate the organism to new learning that leads to reinforcement just as will primary drives.

Dollard and Miller assert that the strength of the learned internal responses setting off drive stimuli, and hence the acquired drive itself, is a function of the same factors that determine the strengths of S-R connection or habit. Thus, the intensity of the primary drive involved in the reinforcement leading to the drive-producing internal response, and the number and pattern of reinforced trials, are important determinants of their intensity. If, in our illustrative experiment, a weak shock and few trials are employed, the rat will develop a much weaker fear of the buzzer than if a strong shock and a long series of trials are employed. The gradient of stimulus generalization also applies. The fear response will generalize to cues resembling the learned cue, with those cues that are most similar being feared the most. In general, situations in which the drive-producing internal response is not followed by reinforcement will gradually lead to extinction of that response. They may also be eliminated by a process known as *counterconditioning* in which a strong incompatible response is conditioned to the same cue. If, for example, a fear-provoking stimulus is paired with a pleasant event, such as eating, it may lose its capacity to act as a conditioned stimulus for the fear reaction (at least if the fear is relatively mild) and become a cue for the eating response instead.

The stimuli associated with acquired drives can serve as cues in the same manner as any other stimulus. The individual may learn to respond with the word "afraid" in fear-evoking situations, that is, label the secondary drive, and this response-produced cue will then mediate the transfer of responses learned in the original fear-producing situation to the present situation. This transfer, involving a response that serves as a cue, is called *secondary generalization.* Individuals can learn to discriminate different intensities of drive stimulation just as in the case of other stimuli, so that the cue value of the acquired drive may depend on the intensity of the drive.

To summarize, internal responses that produce drive stimuli may become attached to new and originally neutral cues in accordance with the same learning principles that govern the formation and dissolution of other habits. The drive stimuli that these conditioned internal responses set off function just as any other cue and may elicit, for example, responses that have been learned in other situations in which the same drive stimuli were aroused. Finally, these response-produced stimuli serve as a secondary drive in the sense that they will instigate or impel the organism to respond and their reduction will reinforce or strengthen those responses associated with the reduction. In other words, secondary drives operate just like primary drives.

Higher Mental Processes   The individual's interactions with the environment are of two varieties: those that are direct and guided by a single cue or cue situation and those that are mediated by internal processes. It is the latter class of responses that is of interest here, those mediated by *cue-producing responses.* Following Hull, Dollard and Miller distinguish between responses that are instrumental, possess some immediate effect upon the environment, and those that are cue-producing, whose main function is to mediate or lead the way to another response. Obviously, language is involved in most cue-producing responses although it need not be spoken language.

One of the most important cue-producing responses is the labeling or naming of events and experiences. The individual may immediately increase the generalization or transfer between two or more cue situations by identifying them as having the same label. For example, by identifying two completely different situations as "threatening," the individual may greatly increase the likelihood that he or she will behave in the same manner in both situations. Or the individual may build up a sharp discrimination between two similar situations by giving them different names; for instance, two individuals who are objectively very much alike may be labeled respectively as "friend" and "enemy" with the result that they will be responded to in a highly individual manner. Within any culture there will be critical generalizations and discriminations that are emphasized and thus made easier by the structure of the language. The often repeated examples of tribes where a given commodity, such as cattle or coconuts, is of great importance and where the language contains a tremendous number of differentiated labels for such objects illustrate this principle.

Not only may words serve to facilitate or inhibit generalization, they may also serve the important function of arousing drives. Further, words may be used to reward or reinforce. And, most important of all, they serve as time-binding mechanisms, permitting the individual to instigate or reinforce present behavior in terms of consequences that are located in the future but susceptible to verbal representation in the present. It is clearly the verbal intervention in the drive-cue-response-reinforcement sequence that makes human behavior so complex and difficult to understand and at the same time accounts for much of the difference between humans and lower species.

Reasoning is essentially a process of substituting internal, cue-producing responses for overt acts. As such, it is vastly more efficient than overt trial and error. Not only does it serve the function of testing symbolically the various alternatives, it also makes possible the substitution of anticipatory responses that may be more effective than any of the overt response alternatives originally available. It is possible through the use of cue-producing responses (thoughts) to begin at the goal situation and work backward until the correct instrumental response has been identified, a feat that would not ordinarily be possible in motor learning. Planning is a special variety of reasoning, where the emphasis is upon future action.

In order for either reasoning or planning to take place the individual must first be able to inhibit or delay the direct instrumental response to the drive stimulus and cue. It is this inhibition that offers the cue-producing responses an opportunity to operate and this response of "not-responding" must be learned just as any other new response. It is also necessary that the cue-producing responses be efficient and realistic and finally that they lead to appropriate instrumental or overt acts.

The ability to use language and other response-produced cues is greatly influenced by the social context in which the individual develops. In the words of Dollard and Miller:

> The problem solutions painfully acquired during centuries of trial and error, and by the highest order of creative reasoning by rare geniuses, are preserved and accumulate as a part of the culture. . . . People receive an enormous amount of social training in putting words and sentences together in ways that lead to the adaptive solution of problems (1950, p. 116).

It is a rare and creative act to originate the Pythagorean theorem but it is not much of a trick to learn it at an appropriate time and place when it is already known. Thus, language provides the key by means of which wisdom from the past is transmitted to the present.

In view of the immense importance of language it is quite appropriate that the child should be trained to pay attention to and respond to verbal cues and eventually to produce them. The use of verbal symbols for communication with other people presumably precedes their use in thought and a great deal of the child's interactions with its environment are concerned with how to produce these cues under appropriate circumstances as well as how to understand those that are produced by others.

Language, as we have implied, is a social product and if we grant significance to the language process it seems reasonable that the social milieu within which the individual functions must be of importance. Let us turn now to a consideration of this factor.

The Social Context   It is very likely that any theory or theorist influenced by social anthropology will highlight the role of sociocultural determinants of behavior, and the present theory is no exception to this rule. Dollard and Miller consistently emphasize the fact that human behavior can be understood only with a full appreciation of the cultural context within which behavior occurs. The psychology of learning provides us with an understanding of the *principles of learning* but the social anthropologist or the equivalent provides us with the *conditions of learning*. And one of these specifications is as important to a full understanding of human development as the other.

No psychologist would venture to predict the behavior of a rat without knowing on what arm of a T-maze the feed or the shock is placed. It is no easier to predict the behavior of a human being without knowing the conditions of his "maze," i.e., the structure of his social environment. Culture, as conceived by social scientists, is a statement of the design of the human maze, of the type of reward involved, and of what responses are to be rewarded. It is in this sense a recipe for learning. This contention is easily accepted when widely variant societies are compared. But even within the same society, the mazes which are run by two individuals may seem the same but actually be quite different. . . . No personality analysis of two . . . people can be accurate which does not take into account these cultural differences, that is, differences in the types of responses which have been rewarded (Miller and Dollard, 1941, pp. 5–6).

As this passage implies, the learning theorist enriches the data of the social anthropologist through providing principles that help to account systematically for the importance of cultural events, while the anthropologist provides the learning theorist with the information he needs in order to fit his principles with the actual experience of human subjects. In one sense, this viewpoint argues that the empirical definition of psychological variables is impossible without the wisdom and data of the anthropologist.

Thus, the position of Dollard and Miller cedes a kind of transcultural generality to the principles of learning (or at least some of them) but at the same time grants, and even emphasizes, that the exact form of behavior displayed by a given individual will be tremendously influenced by the society of which he is a member.

Dollard and Miller assume that unconscious conflict, learned for the most part during infancy and childhood, serves as the basis for most severe emotional problems in later life. They agree with psychoanalytic theorists in considering experiences of the first half dozen years of life crucial determinants of adult behavior.

Critical Stages of Development

It is important to realize that neurotic conflict is not only learned by the child but it is learned primarily as a result of conditions created by the parent. This unfortunate capacity of the parent for impairing the child's development stems in part from the fact that cultural prescriptions concerning the child are contradictory or discontinuous and in part from the fact that the child during infancy is not well equipped to cope with complex learning demands even if they are consistent. Thus, society demands that the child learn to be aggressive in some situations and submissive in other very similar situations, a difficult discrimination at best. Worst of all, this demand may be made a a time

when the child does not have at its command all the symbolic functions contributed by language so that such discriminations may simply overreach its learning capacity with resultant frustration and emotional upheaval. A similar set of overwhelming conditions may occur
in adulthood under exceptional circumstances such as war. As might
be expected, such conditions frequently lead to neurosis.

A crucial aspect of childhood experience is the extreme helplessness of the child. It is chiefly in infancy that it is more or less unable to
manipulate its environment and thus is vulnerable to the depredations
of impelling drive stimuli and overwhelming frustrations. In the ordinary process of development the person will devise mechanisms to
avoid situations that are severely frustrating. In infancy the child has
no choice but to experience them.

It is not surprising, then, that acute emotional conflicts occur in childhood. The infant has not learned to wait, not knowing the world's inescapable routines; to hope,
and thus to assure itself that the good moment will return and that the evil occasion
will pass; to reason and plan, and thus to escape present disorder by constructing the
future in a controlled way. Rather, the child is urgently, hopelessly, planlessly impelled, living by moments in eternal pain and then suddenly finding itself bathed in
endless bliss. The young child is necessarily disoriented, confused, deluded, and hal-
lucinated—in short, has just those symptoms that we recognize as a psychosis in the
adult. Infancy, indeed, may be viewed as a period of transitory psychosis. Savage
drives within the infant impel to action. These drives are unmodified by hope or
concept of time. The higher mental processes (the Ego) cannot do their benign work
of comforting, directing effort, and binding the world into a planful sequence. What
is gone may never return. The present pain may never fade. These are the tumultu-
ous circumstances in which severe unconscious mental conflicts can be created. Only
when the child has been taught to speak and think at a rather high level can the impact
of the raw, drastic character of these circumstances be reduced (Dollard and Miller,
1950, pp. 130–131).

Consistent with this view is the prescription that during the early
stages of life the parent's primary role is to maintain drive stimuli at a
low level. The parent should be permissive, gratifying, and make few
learning demands until the child's language skills have developed.

Granted the fact that every culture makes many demands upon the
individual who is to live effectively within it, still there are certain of
these demands that are particularly likely to produce conflict and
emotional disturbance. Dollard and Miller identify four situations in
which cultural prescription, as interpreted by the parent, is particularly likely to have disastrous consequences for normal development.
These are the feeding situation in infancy, toilet or cleanliness train-

ing, early sex training, and training for control of anger and aggression.

Dollard and Miller suggest that their analysis of these conflict situations is a restatement of the formulations of Freud in terms of their own conceptual scheme. For this reason, we shall not attempt to reproduce here all that they have to say about these critical stages, but shall simply consider briefly their analysis of the feeding situation to illustrate the use they make of learning concepts in this setting. The important things for the reader to grasp are that this theory assumes events early in development to be of central importance in their effects upon behavior and, beyond this, that the operation of these events is seen as perfectly consistent with the learning process we have already outlined.

Drive stimuli associated with hunger are among the first strong activity impellents to which the individual is exposed. Consequently, the techniques the individual devises to reduce or control these stimuli may be expected to have an important role as a model for the devices used later in life to reduce other strong drive stimuli. In this sense, the theory proposes that the feeding situation serves as a small-scale model that in part determines the large-scale adjustments of the adult. Thus, Dollard and Miller suggest that the child who cries when it is hungry and finds that this leads to feeding may be taking the initial steps that will result in an active, manipulative orientation toward drive reduction. On the other hand, the child who is left to "cry himself out" may be laying down the basis for a passive and apathetic reaction to strong drive stimuli. Further, if hunger stimuli are permitted to mount without restriction the child may come to associate mild hunger stimuli with the intensely painful, overpowering stimuli that he has subsequently experienced on so many occasions; and in this manner it may come to "overreact" to relatively mild drive stimuli, that is, the mild drive stimuli acquire a secondary drive strength that is equivalent to the very intense drive stimuli. Another dangerous consequence of permitting the child to be exposed to intense hunger drive stimuli is that it may develop on this basis a fear of being alone. If, when the child is alone, it is exposed to very painful hunger stimuli and if these stimuli are reduced only when the parent finally appears, it may happen that this strong reinforcement (reduction of hunger stimuli) will habituate the response that immediately preceded the appearance of the parent—a fear response. Thus, in the future when the child or adult is alone he or she will respond with this previously reinforced fear response and will show a typical pattern of fear of the dark or of being alone.

Perhaps the most important aspect of the feeding situation is that its relative success may be expected to have a great deal to do with future interpersonal relations. This follows from the fact that the feeding experience is associated with the first intimate interpersonal relation—that between mother and child. If the feeding is successful and characterized by drive reduction and gratification, the child comes to associate this pleasant state with the presence of its mother and this relation by a process of stimulus generalization comes to be linked with other people so that their presence becomes a goal or a secondary reward. If the feeding is unsuccessful and accompanied by pain and anger the reverse can be expected. Weaning and digestive disturbances are especially likely to have unfortunate consequences for the child as they introduce pain and discomfort into the situation and complicate a learning situation that is already demanding the full capacity of the infant.

An interesting addendum to this analysis of the feeding situation is provided by the results of a set of ingenious experiments conducted with monkeys by Harry Harlow and his colleagues (see, for example, Harlow, 1958; Harlow and Zimmerman, 1959) after the appearance of the Dollard and Miller volume. Harlow doubted their assumption about the importance of feeding in the development of the mother-child relationship and suggested that bodily contact was far more critical. Evidence supporting Harlow's views was shown in experiments in which infant monkeys were reared in complete isolation except for the presence of two inanimate "mothers," one of which was made of wire and held the bottle from which the infant obtained all of his nourishment, and the other of which was padded with terry cloth and provided a warm, comfortable surface to which the young monkey could cling. The young animals spent much of their time in physical contact with their terry cloth surrogate-mother or playing in her vicinity. When frightened, they sought her protection and in other ways, behaved toward the terry cloth structure in much the same way that infant monkeys do toward their actual mothers. The wire "mother," in sharp contrast, was almost completely ignored when the monkeys were not feeding.

What should be noted about these findings is that they do not challenge the essential form of the Dollard and Miller account of the development of affectional attachments. They do suggest that in specifying the *conditions* of learning, Dollard and Miller may have exaggerated the importance of the reduction of hunger and thirst and underestimated the significance of the mother's rocking, stroking, and holding of her infant while she is feeding it or ministering to it in other ways.

We have observed that Dollard and Miller represent language as playing a crucial role in human development. In view of this, it is quite natural that those determinants of behavior that elude language, or are unconscious, should play a key role in behavioral disturbances. The theory is quite consistent with psychoanalytic formulations in accepting unconscious factors as important determinants of behavior; however, the account offered by Dollard and Miller of the origin of these unconscious processes shows little similarity to the Freudian version.

Unconscious determinants can be divided into those that have never been conscious and those that although once conscious are so no longer. In the first category are included all those drives, responses, and cues learned prior to the advent of speech and which consequently were not labeled. Also in this group belong certain areas of experience for which our society provides only meager or inadequate names. Kinesthetic and motor cues and responses are generally overlooked by conventional labels and for this reason are not easily discussed and may be considered largely unconscious. In a similar vein, certain areas of sexual and other kinds of tabooed experience are not usually accompanied by appropriate designations and thus are only poorly represented in consciousness. In the second category belong all those cues and responses that were formerly conscious but that through repression have become unavailable to consciousness. The process involved in the first category is clear enough and it is to the phenomenon of repression that we shall devote our attention.

Repression is a process of avoiding certain thoughts and this avoidance is learned and motivated in exactly the same manner as any other learned response. In this case, the response of *"not-thinking"* of certain things leads to drive reduction and reinforcement, and thus becomes a standard part of the individual's repertoire. There are certain thoughts or memories that have acquired the capacity to arouse fear (secondary drive stimuli) and the response of "not-thinking" or ceasing to think of them leads to a reduction in the fear stimuli and thus the response of "not-thinking" is reinforced. Whereas in the initial learning the individual first thinks of the fearful act or event and then experiences the fear and gives up the thought with the consequent reinforcement, after experience the response of "not-thinking" becomes anticipatory and occurs before the individual has actually reconstructed the event or wish. "Not-thinking" as an anticipatory response not only keeps the fear-evoking thoughts from consciousness but it also interferes with the normal extinction process. That is, if the response does not occur it can hardly be extinguished even if the original source of reinforcement has since vanished.

Dollard and Miller clearly consider repression to exist on a con-

Unconscious Processes

tinuum ranging from slight tendencies not to think about certain things to the strongest avoidance of threatening material. They also consider that this tendency can be traced largely to childhood training which often tends to produce fear of certain thoughts. Once the fear of the thought is developed, the process of repression is readily understandable in terms of the reduction of drive stimuli by "not-thinking." Children are often punished for the use of certain tabooed words; thus the spoken verbal symbol alone is sufficient to elicit the punishment without the act. Or the child may announce its intention of doing something wrong and be punished before any act has been committed. In other cases, the child may think certain things which it does not even express verbally but which the parent infers correctly from expressive behavior or other cues and for which the child is punished. Frequently the child is punished for acts that have been carried out in the past, so that the punishment accompanies the thought of the act and not the act itself. All of these and other experiences tend to build up a generalization from the act or overt behavior that leads to punishment to the mere thought or symbolic representation of this act. Not only can the individual generalize from the overt act to the thought but also he or she can discriminate between the two. In the well-adjusted individual this is an exceedingly important and efficient process. Such a person realizes that certain thoughts must never be expressed in certain contexts yet will feel relatively free to think these thoughts privately.

The extensity and severity of repression depend upon many factors; among them are possible variations in the innate strength of the fear response; the degree of dependence upon the parents, and thus the intensity of the threat of loss of love to which the child can be exposed; and the severity of traumas or fear-producing situations to which the child has been exposed.

The crucial importance of consciousness has to do with the significance of verbal labels in the learning process, particularly in connection with the operation of the higher mental processes. We have already indicated that the processes of generalization and discrimination can be made more efficient by means of verbal symbols and if labeling is eliminated the individual clearly operates at a more primitive intellectual level. Thus, the person must become more concrete and stimulus bound, and their behavior comes to resemble that of the child or lower organism where the mediating role of language is not highly developed.

Conflict No human being operates so effectively that all of his tendencies are congruent and well-integrated. Consequently, all personality theories must deal directly or indirectly with the problems posed for the organism by conflicting motives or tendencies. Conflict behavior is represented by Miller and Dollard in terms of five basic assumptions that are extensions of the principles we have already discussed.

They assume *first* that the tendency to approach a goal becomes stronger the nearer the individual is to the goal and this is referred to as the *gradient of approach. Second,* they assume that the tendency to avoid a negative stimulus becomes stronger the nearer the individual is to the stimulus and this is referred to as the *gradient of avoidance.* These assumptions can be derived primarily from the principle of stimulus generalization, which we have already described. The *third* assumption is that the gradient of avoidance is steeper than the gradient of approach. This implies that the rate at which avoidance tendencies increase with approach to the goal is greater than the rate at which approach tendencies increase under the same conditions. *Fourth,* it is assumed that an increase in the drive associated with the approach or avoidance will raise the general level of the gradient. Thus, there will still be an increase in the strength of approach or avoidance as the goal is approached but these tendencies will now have a greater strength at each stage of approach. *Fifth,* it is assumed that when there are two competing responses the stronger will occur. Given these assumptions, in addition to the concepts we have already discussed, Miller and Dollard are able to derive predictions concerning the manner in which an individual faced with the various types of conflict will respond.

One of the most important types of conflict is concerned with the opposition between approach and avoidance tendencies aroused simultaneously by the same object or situation; let us say that a young man is strongly attracted to a woman and yet finds himself embarrassed and uncomfortable (afraid) in her presence. As the first three assumptions above tell us, the avoidance response (getting away from the woman) falls off more sharply than the approach response as the subject moves away from the goal (woman). This is represented graphically in Figure 15-2, where the broken lines, representing the avoidance responses, are angled more sharply than solid lines that represent the approach responses. Therefore the avoidance tendency may be higher or more intense than the approach response near to the goal (woman) but when the subject has moved away a certain distance (in the diagram to a point beyond the intersection of the gradients) the approach response will be stronger than the avoidance response (having left the woman he may call or write to arrange another date). It is at the point where the two gradients intersect (let us say, when the man enters the same room with the woman) that the individual should show a maximum of hesitation and conflict, as it is here that the two competing responses are approximately evenly balanced.

When the approach response is stronger than the avoidance response the individual will approach without conflict and vice versa when the avoidance response is stronger. It is only when the two are evenly matched in strength that the individual will have difficulty in mustering an appropriate response.

If either the approach or the avoidance response is increased in strength, this will have the effect of raising the entire level of that gradient as shown in the diagram by the upper gradients of approach and avoidance. This will naturally lead to a different point of intersection between the two gradients. Thus, if the approach tendency is increased in strength the two gradients will intersect closer to the goal, which implies that the individual will come nearer to the goal before he will hesitate in conflict. The closer he comes to the goal the stronger will be the avoidance response, and therefore the more intense will be his conflict. That is, the closer he approaches the woman the more attracted he is and at the same time the more uncomfortable and embarrassed. Conversely, if the tendency to approach is weakened (if he likes the woman less) he will not come so close to the goal before the gradients intersect (he will not keep his date with the woman) and his conflict or disturbance will be weaker because the intensity of the avoidance responses and approach responses will be less at this point. If the tendency to avoid is increased in strength (if his discomfort increases), this will result in the two gradients intersecting at a point farther removed from the goal (he may think about but never actually arrange another date) and thus will reduce the intensity

FIGURE 15–2
*Graphic representation of
conflict situations*
(Adapted from Miller,
1951b.)

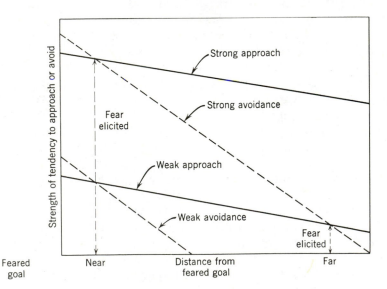

of the conflict. In general, the closer to the goal the point of intersection of the two gradients, the stronger the two competing tendencies and therefore the more intense the conflict. One should note that if the strength of the approach response can be raised to a point where it is stronger than the avoidance response at the goal (in Figure 15-2 this is represented by the strong approach and weak avoidance gradients), the individual will go directly to the goal and the conflict will be overcome. Thus, if the man is so strongly attracted to the woman that he is able to stay in close proximity to her even though uncomfortable the conflict will eventually be resolved.

Response generalization may also determine what an individual does when confronted with an approach-avoidance conflict. Dollard and Miller tentatively suggest that the same assumptions made about stimulus generalization may also hold for response generalization, namely that the approach gradient for responses of varying degrees of similarity to the one elicited by the instigating stimuli falls off more rapidly than the avoidance gradient. Thus a child may be intensely angry at its parents after they have forbidden some favorite activity but too fearful or guilty about direct expressions of aggression to call them names or lash out at them physically. However, the child's avoidance tendencies may have fallen off sufficiently to permit it to show its displeasure more obliquely by stomping off to its room and slamming the door.

A second type of conflict is encountered when the individual is faced with two competing avoidance responses. For example, a small boy may be afraid to climb and at the same time wish to avoid being called a coward by his playmates. Thus, the nearer he comes to the one goal (the higher he climbs), the stronger the avoidance response and the more likely he will be to retreat. However, as he retreats he comes closer to the other goal (being called a coward) and the second avoidance response increases while the first decreases. Thus, the individual should show vacillation, turning first from one goal and then from the other, that is, climbing to a certain height and then descending. If the strength of one of the avoidance responses is increased, this will change the point of intersection so that the place where the individual will turn back from his goal will be made more distant. It will also increase the intensity of the conflict as now both gradients will be stronger at the point of intersection. Again, if one of the responses is stronger than the other at the goal, the individual will simply continue to withdraw from the most feared situation until he is past the competing situation and the conflict will be overcome: he either climbs to the necessary height or accepts the fact that he is to be called a coward.

Miller and Dollard do not consider the competition between two approach responses to represent a realistic dilemma. They point out that once the individual has started to move toward one of the positive goals the strength of this response will increase (according to first assumption) and the strength of the competing response will decrease. Therefore, the individual will go directly to this goal. Even if the person begins exactly balanced between the two goals, variations in the stimulus situation or within the organism will upset this balance slightly and once this is done the individual will then continue to move toward the nearest goal. Where individuals appear to be in conflict between two positive alternatives there are always hidden or latent avoidance responses operating.

For a more detailed description of this theory of conflict the reader should consult Miller (1944, 1951b, 1959) where a number of experimental studies which have tested various derivations from this position are summarized. In general, the results of these studies provide strong evidence for the utility of the theory.

How Neuroses Are Learned

Dollard and Miller share with psychoanalytic theorists an abiding concern with the neurotic individual. Consequently, they devote a substantial portion of their theory to the conditions that lead to the development of neuroses and to the psychotherapeutic procedures that can be used to overcome them.

At the core of every neurosis is a strong unconscious conflict, with the origins of the conflict almost always being found in the individual's childhood. "Neurotic conflicts," Dollard and Miller assert, "are taught by parents and learned by children" (1950, p. 127). We have already described the four critical training situations that lend themselves so easily to parental mishandling and lay the groundwork for future problems: the feeding situation, toilet or cleanliness training, sex training, and training in the control of aggression. All too frequently the child develops intense anxiety or guilt about the expression of its basic needs in these areas, and a conflict has been established that is likely to continue in some form into adult life.

Just as the experimental animal in our laboratory study learns any instrumental response of which it is capable that allows it to escape an anxiety-provoking stimulus, so the human in real-life conflict attempts to escape or avoid feelings of anxiety and guilt by all manner of "instrumental responses." One highly available and thus frequently used mode of reaction is "not thinking." The individual represses memories and thoughts that are capable of making him or her anxious or guilty and refuses to try to understand their conflict and the circumstances that brought it about. The person is aware that something is wrong and is often miserable, but does not (because he or she will not) understand why.

Since neurotic conflicts are unconscious, the individual cannot bring problem-solving abilities to bear on problems or recognize that the conditions that brought him or her into conflict may no longer exist. For example, the adult whose parents in his early years had constantly threatened him with loss of love and approval at the least sign of anger shown toward them may so completely inhibit any expression of aggression that he never discovers that others do not share these parental attitudes. As long as conflicts remain unconscious they are not only likely to continue to exist but to lead to the development of still further reactions or *symptoms*. These symptoms may be the fairly direct consequences of the emotional turmoil caused by the conflict, but frequently they are behaviors allowing individuals temporary escape from their fears and anxieties. As Dollard and Miller describe them:

Although in many ways superficial, the symptoms of the neurotic are the most obvious aspects of his problems. These are what the patient is familiar with and feels he should be rid of. The phobias, inhibitions, avoidances, compulsions, rationalizations, and psychosomatic symptoms of the neurotic are experienced as a nuisance by him and by all who have to deal with him. . . . [He] believes that the symptoms *are* his disorder. It is these he wishes to be rid of and, not knowing that a serious conflict underlies them, he would like to confine [any] therapeutic discussion to getting rid of the symptoms.

The symptoms do not solve the basic conflict in which the neurotic person is plunged, but they mitigate it. They are responses that tend to reduce the conflict, and in part they succeed. When a successful symptom occurs it is reinforced because it reduces neurotic misery. The symptom is thus learned as a "habit" (Dollard and Miller, 1950, p. 15).

As an illustration of the relationships among conflict, repression, symptoms, and reinforcement, Dollard and Miller presented in some detail "The Case of Mrs. A." A highly condensed version of this case follows.

Mrs. A was a young woman who sought psychiatric help because of a number of fears that had exhausted her husband's patience and led him to threaten to sue for divorce. Her most intense fear was that if she did not count her heartbeats, her heart would stop. In addition she became anxious and upset in a number of public places and was growing increasingly fearful about leaving her apartment alone. Over the course of the therapeutic sessions, the nature of Mrs. A's problems gradually became clarified. Her most severe conflict was about sex. Although she had strong sexual appetites, her childhood training had led her to feel so guilty and anxious about them that she denied any sexual feelings and expressed only revulsion. Although she consciously tried to be a well–behaved wife, her sexual needs indirectly expressed in irresponsible behavior, such as going out to bars on drinking parties with other women, in which she seemed almost to court seduction. She was unaware of the motivations for this behavior and was constantly surprised by its consequences.

An analysis of her phobic reactions to being in public places revealed that when she was out alone, she unconsciously became fearful and guilty about the possibility that she would be approached sexually and tempted to succumb. Her fear and guilt about sexual temptation could be lessened by going home or partially avoided by not going out by herself. Her compulsive counting of heartbeats also served to keep her sexual anxieties at a minimum. Any stimuli, including her own thoughts, with sexual connotations would arouse her anxiety. But these thoughts could be banished or prevented from occurring by devoting her attention to her heartbeats. As soon as she started to count she began to "feel better," so that the habit was reinforced by anxiety reduction.

The types of symptoms exhibited by Mrs. A are examples of *learned* reactions to affectively unpleasant states. Dollard and Miller suggested that in addition to this type of learned behavior, there are symptoms of a psychosomatic nature that are *innate*. Physiological responses, mediated primarily by the so–called autonomic nervous system, are elicited automatically by a number of strong drive states without having to be learned. These innate autonomic responses are frequently aroused by primary drives but may also be produced by secondary or learned drives. The wet palms, queasy stomach, and pounding heart of the anxious student awaiting an important examination provide an all too familiar example.

It has long been believed that in contrast to skeletal responses, such as movements of the arms and legs, the physiological reactions elicited by the autonomic nervous system are not under the individual's voluntary control. The evidence available to Dollard and Miller also suggested that although the visceral and glandular responses controlled by the autonomic nervous system could be *classically* conditioned, they could not be *instrumentally* conditioned. Instrumental or operant conditioning, as noted in an earlier discussion, is a form of learning in which the occurrence of reinforcement is contingent on the appearance of a specified response, and the failure of a reward to follow the response leads to its extinction. Autonomic responses, according to the traditional view accepted by Dollard and Miller, were not influenced by their consequences, being neither strengthened by the occurrence of reinforcers nor weakened by their nonoccurrence.

Miller subsequently conducted a series of exquisitely controlled animal studies whose results seemed to challenge this view. An experiment by Miller and Banuazizi (1968) involving visceral responses in rats is representative of these investigations. Two types of internal responses were monitored: heart rate and intestinal contractions. For one set of animals, intestinal contractions were selected to be conditioned. For half of the subjects, reward was given each time spontaneous contractions *above* a certain amplitude happened to occur. For the other half, reward was given for contractions *below* a certain magnitude. Contractions systematically increased over the course of training in subjects rewarded for large amplitude responses and *decreased* in those rewarded for small responses. No systematic change in heart rate was found in either group. In another set of animals, there was a spontaneous occurrence of either a fast or a slow heart rate in the appropriate direction but none in intestinal contractions. The limitation of the conditioning effect to the specific type of response that was followed by reinforcement was seen as providing particularly impressive evidence that autonomic responses can be instrumentally conditioned in the same manner as skeletal responses.

These revolutionary findings suggesting that autonomic response can be instrumentally conditioned raised a number of intriguing possibilities. As Miller (1969) pointed out, psychosomatic symptoms in the human being might be learned in exactly the same way as other symptoms. An even more fascinating possibility is that instrumental conditioning techniques might be used therapeutically to mitigate the intensity of somatic symptoms (for example, high blood pressure) whether induced by organic or psychological factors. (An interesting account of Miller's experiments and some therapeutic applications based on his findings, written for a nonprofessional audience, may be found in Jonas' 1973 book, *Visceral learning*). However, Miller (Miller and Dworkin, 1974) has reported the puzzling finding that his recent experiments have not been as successful in demonstrating instrumental conditioning, suggesting that the existence of the phenomenon may not have been as definitively established as was thought earlier.

Psychotherapy

Dollard and Miller are concerned not only with the development of neuroses but also with their treatment. The essence of their approach to psychotherapy is straightforward.

If neurotic behavior is learned, it should be unlearned by some combination of the principles by which it was taught. We believe this to be the case. Psychotherapy establishes a set of conditions by which neurotic habits may be unlearned and nonneurotic habits learned. . . . the therapist [acting] as a kind of teacher and the patient as a learner (Dollard and Miller, 1950, pp. 7–8).

The actual therapeutic procedures that Dollard and Miller advocate are quite traditional. The therapist should be a sympathetic, permissive listener who encourages the patient to express all his or her feelings and to free associate. Whatever the patient's thoughts, the therapist remains nonpunitive and tries to help the patient understand these feelings and how they developed.

The most novel contribution of Dollard and Miller lies in their learning theory analysis of what occurs in successful psychotherapy. Unrealistic fears and guilt have failed to extinguish because the person has been all too successful in developing techniques to avoid or escape thought and situations that stir up these unpleasant emotions. In the therapeutic situation, an attempt is made to set up the conditions that will result in extinction. The individual is encouraged to express prohibited thoughts and emotions, and to experience the fear and guilt evoked by them. Since no unpleasant consequences follow these expressions, extinction of the neurotic fear can be expected to occur. In the initial stages of therapy, patients are likely to discuss only moderately distressing problems of which they have allowed themselves to be consciously aware. But as the unrealistic fear and guilt associated with these problems begin to fade, the extinction effect generalizes to similar but more disturbing problems and thus weakens their motivation to repress or in other ways to avoid confronting them. Gradually, patients become more and more able to face their core conflicts and the significance of their symptomatic behavior. The therapist constantly assists patients in this process by encouraging the use of verbal labels that will help them to discriminate between thought and action, their inner fears and outer realities, and between the conditions of their childhood, in which they learned their fears and conflicts, and the conditions of their adult world.

As repressions are lifted and discriminations developed, patients become able to use their higher mental processes to devise constructive solutions to their problems. As they find more successful ways of behaving, their fears are extinguished still further and their symptoms disappear. Their new ways of responding are strongly reinforced by more positive rewards and take the place of the old, self-defeating symptoms. The whole process of unlearning and relearning that takes place in therapy is likely to be slow and frequently agonizing, but even more so was the learning that initially drove the patient to the therapist.

This theoretical account of the therapeutic process developed by Dollard and Miller has a variety of testable implications, a number of which have received support in studies analyzing the therapy protocols of actual cases. One of these studies, involving *displacement,* a complex type of conflict phenomenon, is described in the following section.

Miller and Dollard have reported a considerable quantity of investigation that illustrates or tests derivations from their theoretical position. In their volume *Social learning and imitation* (1941) a number of studies on human and lower animal subjects are summarized that represent attempts to confirm predictions derived from their theory. Miller, as we have mentioned, has conducted a number of experimental studies relevant to various aspects of the theory and has prepared several extensive summaries of them (1944, 1951a, 1959). Here we shall discuss a cluster of studies that deal with the concept of displacement. These investigations not only demonstrate an interest in bridging the gap between psychoanalytic theory and S-R concepts but also provide experimental evidence for the operation of a number of the concepts we have already discussed.

The concept of displacement occupies a central position in psychoanalytic theory, where it is ordinarily used to refer to the capacity of the organism to redirect responses or impulses to a new object when they are denied expression toward their original object. In terms of the theory of Dollard and Miller, this phenomenon can be accounted for quite readily by the concept of stimulus generalization. Miller, in a series of experiments, has attempted to demonstrate the empirical phenomenon, show the continuity of stimulus generalization and displacement, and provide a theoretical account that will permit new predictions concerning these events.

An initial study by Miller and Bugelski (1948) attempted to demonstrate displacement with human subjects. These investigators administered a set of questionnaires that assessed attitudes toward Mexicans and Japanese to a group of boys who were attending a summer camp. While they were filling out these questionnaires, the boys were forced to miss a highly prized social event and a comparison was made of the attitudes expressed toward the minority groups before and after this frustration. The results showed that following the frustration there was a significant increase in negative attitudes expressed toward the two minority groups. This increase in hostility was interpreted as a displacement of the hostility aroused by the experi-

**CHARACTERISTIC
RESEARCH AND
RESEARCH
METHODS**

menters through their interference with the attendance of the boys at
the social event. In psychoanalytic terms, the subjects were displacing
the hostility felt toward the experimenters upon the minority group
members; in S-R terms, they were generalizing a response from one
stimulus object to a similar stimulus object. At any rate, the study
showed that the phenomenon in question did occur among human
subjects and could be produced experimentally.

Miller reasoned that both psychoanalytic theory and S-R theory assume that a given response may be generalized not only from one
stimulus to another but also from one drive to another. Freud very
early postulated a considerable amount of interchangeability or sub-
stitutability between drives or instincts and for the S-R theorist
drives are only one kind of stimulus; therefore, it is perfectly natural
that there should be drive generalization as well as stimulus generalization. In order to test this prediction, a group of rats was trained
under the motivation of thirst, and with the reward of drinking, to
run down an alley. These same animals were then divided into two
groups, both of which were satiated on water, but one group was
deprived of food and the other satiated on food. The prediction was
that the response of running down the maze (which had been learned
to thirst) would generalize or displace to the hunger drive. Consequently, the food-deprived rats should run down the maze faster
than the nonhungry rats. The results of the study showed a clear confirmation of this prediction. It was also possible to show experimentally that the response of running down the maze, which was
originally reinforced by reduction of thirst drive stimuli, extinguished when the animals continued to run down the maze with no
reduction of drive stimuli. Likewise consistent with S-R theory was
the observation that when the response had been partially extinguished, an interval with no trials produced spontaneous recovery, or
a return to a higher level of response probability. The investigator
also demonstrated response generalization from the drive of hunger
to the relatively remote drives of pain and fear. The greater dissimi-
larity between fear and hunger made this appear a more stringent test
of the prediction of drive generalization than the previous study.

Given these experimental findings, Miller incorporated them as
derivations from a series of five assumptions that resemble very
closely those we discussed in connection with the analysis of conflict. The principal difference between the two sets of assumptions
is that those bearing on conflict concern the distance between the
subject and the goal, whereas the present assumptions focus about
the similarity between the original stimulus object and certain substitute objects.

This model accepts the fact that whenever displacement takes place there is a response competing with the direct response that is stronger than the direct response. Thus, the aggressive response of the child toward its father is not strong enough to overcome the fear response elicited by the same object. For this reason the child cannot express its aggression directly toward the father. Moreover, the model assumes that the direct response to the original stimulus generalizes to similar stimuli and that the competing response shows the same stimulus generalization. The more similar the new stimulus is to the original stimulus, the greater will be the degree of generalization. However, the gradient of generalization for the competing (inhibiting) response falls off or decreases more rapidly than the gradient of generalization for the direct response. Thus, while the competing response may be much stronger than the direct response in the face of the original stimulus, by the time the two responses have been generalized to stimuli of a certain degree of remoteness the order of strength may become reversed, that is, the child may show fear rather than anger to the father but show anger rather than fear to a fatherlike doll.

These assumptions not only permit the derivation of the empirical phenomena we have already summarized, displacement or stimulus and drive generalization; they also lead to a number of additional predictions, some of them referring to relations that have yet to be tested under controlled empirical conditions. Miller has reported several studies that present further empirical evidence relevant to this theory, most of which is confirmatory (Miller and Kraeling, 1952; Miller and Murray, 1952; Murray and Miller, 1952).

The empirical studies we have outlined above, and the theoretical reasoning that has accompanied them, demonstrate quite clearly how much tidier the formulations and investigations of these theorists have been than those of most personality investigators. We see revealed also the preference for paradigmatic studies involving animal subjects but with appropriate bridging studies carried out on human subjects. It is evident that these investigations not only make a contribution to the understanding of displacement or stimulus generalization but also lead to a large number of testable assertions that, when the appropriate empirical steps have been taken, may add weight to or challenge the effectiveness of this theory.

The pioneering theories of Dollard and Miller, along with those of such individuals as O. Hobart Mowrer (1950, 1953) and Robert R. Sears (1944, 1951) have been highly influential in stimulating further efforts to extend learning principles into the realm of personality development and psychotherapy. We cannot hope to do justice to the

SOME RELATED FORMULATIONS

many investigators and theorists who have contributed to this enterprise. The work of two pairs of individuals, Joseph Wolpe and Hans Eysenck, and Martin Seligman and Albert Bandura will serve, however, to illustrate the directions in which learning theory approaches to personality have developed.

The views of Wolpe and Eysenck are interesting to contrast with those of Dollard and Miller. Dollard and Miller, we have seen, were heavily influenced by psychoanalytic thought and they accepted as valid many of the insights provided by the Freudians. They attempted to combine two traditions by bringing to the rich literature of psychoanalytic theory the power and precision of the concepts of learning theory. Wolpe and Eysenck have rejected this type of approach, and put forward the view that a simple set of learning principles established in the laboratory is sufficient to account for the acquisition of many personality phenomena. They find traditional methods of psychotherapy to be equally wanting on both theoretical and practical grounds. Eysenck (1952a; Eysenck and Wilson, 1974) has, in fact, argued that there is no definitive evidence that psychoanalysis and other similar forms of psychotherapy have any efficacy at all. In the place of these methods are substituted radically different types of techniques, which have come to be called behavior therapies (Skinner and Lindsley, 1954; Eysenck, 1959). These behavior therapies, several of which were developed by Wolpe, are based on the direct application of principles developed in the learning laboratory to neurotic problems.

Wolpe, a psychiatrist whose medical training was received at the University of Witwatersrand in South Africa (M.B., 1939; M.D., 1948), has had many years of practical experience in conducting psychotherapy. Except for several interruptions spent in military service or in advanced training, he was in private practice in his native country from 1940 to 1959. During the last decade of this period he also served as a lecturer in psychiatry at the University of Witwatersrand, where he conducted laboratory studies of experimental neuroses in animals and developed a number of behavior therapy techniques. These studies resulted in a number of articles published in psychiatric and psychological journals. He spent the 1956–1957 academic year as a fellow at the Center for Advanced Study in the Behavioral Sciences in Stanford, California. While at the Center he worked on a book, *Psychotherapy by reciprocal inhibition,* published in 1958, in which he summarized and extended his ideas about the development and treatment of the neuroses. In 1960 Wolpe moved to the United States as a professor of psychiatry, first at the University of Virginia Medical School and then, in 1965, at the Temple University Medical School. His continued work on behavior therapy has culminated in a number of publications, including the books *The conditioning therapies* (1966, in collaboration with A. Salter and L. Reyna), *Behavior therapy techniques* (1966, with A. A. Lazarus), *The practice of behavior therapy* (1973), and *Theme and variations: A behavior therapy casebook* (1976).

Eysenck was born in Germany where he received his early education. In 1934 under the impact of the Nazi movement he left Germany and eventually came to England where he secured his Ph.D. in psychology at the University of London in 1940. During the war years he served as psychologist at the Mill Hill Emergency Hospital and following the war was appointed reader in psychology at the University of London and director of the Psychological Department at the Institute of Psychiatry, which is associated with Maudsley and Bethlehem Royal Hospitals and where much of his research has been carried out. In 1954, he was appointed professor of psychology of the University of London, a position he still holds along with his directorship at the Institute of Psychiatry.

Although most of Eysenck's work has been centered in the clinical-personality area, he has also conducted investigations concerning such topics as attitudes, humor, aesthetics, and intelligence. His wide-ranging interests have led to a prodigious number of publications: over twenty books and more than 300 articles and handbook chapters. The theories presented in *The causes and cures of neuroses* (1965), which he wrote with S. Rachman, and in *Case Studies in Behavior Therapy* (1976) are of major concern to us in this chapter. Many of the central concepts in his theory of the neuroses were based on work reported in several earlier books, most notably *Dimensions of personality* (1947), *The dynamics of anxiety and hysteria* (1957), and *The structure of human personality* (1960).

Wolpe and Eysenck have not worked together in a close collaborative relationship, but they have come to share many of the same views and to be stimulated by the ideas of each other. As might be expected from his background in psychiatry, Wolpe has largely confined his interest in personality to the psychoneuroses, and was originally committed to a psychoanalytic interpretation of their etiology. He described the events that led him to reject this position in favor of a learning theory approach in the Preface to his major work, *Psychotherapy by reciprocal inhibition:*

The theory of neurosis and the methods of psychotherapy described in this book stem directly from modern learning theory. The chain of events leading to the writing of it may be dated from the year 1944, when as a military medical officer I had plenty of time for reading. Then a staunch follower of Freud, I was one day surprised to find in Malinowksi's *Sex and repression in savage society* persuasive evidence against the assumption that the Oedipus theory had *universal* application. The ripple this roused in me soon subsided since the point did not seem vital; but a month or so later I chanced to read in C. W. Valentine's *Psychology of early childhood* an account of observations on young children that threw doubt on the validity of the Oedipus theory even for Western society. This time my faith in the "sure stronghold" of Freudianism was seriously shaken, and a paragraph in a newspaper to the effect that the Russians do not accept psychoanalysis was enough to motivate me to find out what they do accept; the answer was Pavlov. This answer did not directly yield much enlightenment, but Pavlov led to Hull, and Hull to the studies of experimental neurosis that suggested the new methods of psychotherapy (p. vii).

Quite a different route led Eysenck to his common interest with Wolpe in the application of learning theory to the etiology and treatment of neuroses. From the beginning of his career, Eysenck was convinced that most personality theories are both overly complex and too loosely formulated. Influenced by the theoretical contributions of European typologists such as Carl Jung and Ernst Kretschmer, his early work was aimed at the goal of identifying primary dimensions of personality. In a series of studies carried out on a large group of normal and neurotic subjects (Eysenck, 1947), he was able to discover, by means of factor analytic techniques, two fundamental dimensions of personality: *neuroticism* and *introversion-extraversion*. By comparing individuals high and low on the two primary variables on various other measures, Eysenck evolved full and complex statements concerning the attributes of the individuals who fell at the extremes of one or both of the neuroticism and introversion–extraversion dimensions. In a later program of research, Eysenck (1952b) extended to three the fundamental dimensions leading to personality types by adding the variable of *psychoticism*.

Drawing heavily upon the work of Pavlov and Hull, Eysenck subsequently expanded this essentially descriptive system to include more explanatory types of principles. Many of the testable implications of his hypotheses have been formally investigated in laboratory studies with some success. At the heart of his theory is the assumption that people differ, on a hereditary basis, in the reactivity of their autonomic nervous system and in the speed and firmness with which they build up conditioned responses. These individual differences are associated respectively with the personality dimensions of neuroticism and introversion–extraversion. The autonomically reactive individual is prone, given the appropriate environmental conditions, to develop neurotic disorders, while the individual who forms conditioned responses easily will exhibit introverted behavior. The person who is unfortunate enough to be at the extreme in both conditionability and autonomic reactivity almost inevitably develops strong conditioned fears, phobias, compulsions and obsessions, and other neurotic symptoms.

Individuals whose difficulties stem from excessive neurotic anxieties are suffering from what Eysenck calls *disorders of the first kind.* There are also, according to his theory, *disorders of the second kind.* These disorders are due to the *absence* of conditioned responses that lead to the acquisition of socially desirable habits and are most likely to occur in extraverted individuals low in conditionability. The psychopath, Eysenck suggests, is a major example of an individual exhibiting a disorder of the second kind. Unlike the ordinary person, such an individual has failed to acquire sufficiently strong fear or guilt reactions about antisocial impulses to inhibit their expression. Space limitations unfortunately prohibit us from further exposition of Eysenck's notions about the etiology of these disorders of the second kind and the behavior therapies that may be used in their treatment. We therefore return to our discussion of disorders of the first type—those based on too strong rather than too weak anxiety reactions.

Both Eysenck and Wolpe agree that although individuals may differ in the degree to which they are constitutionally predisposed to develop neurotic anxiety, all neurotic behavior is learned. Their conception of this behavior departs sharply from classical psychoanalytic theory, as they take pains to point out. The differences are succinctly described in the following passage:

When we observe people behaving in a manner which is apparently 'abnormal', self-destructive, or maladjusted, we have two very obvious and well-established ways of regarding their behaviour. The first is the *medical model;* according to this such people are ill. They suffer from some form of disease, and the observed behaviour is simply a symptom (or set of symptoms) of this disease. Treatment would consist of curing the underlying illness; this would make the symptoms disappear automatically. . . . The acceptance of Freud's teaching . . . owes much to his clever use of the medical analogy—the patient's complaints are but symptoms, the underlying disease is the 'complex' which must be eradicated by 'interpretive' psychotherapy before the symptoms can disappear for good. 'Symptomatic' treatment, on this account, is useless; relapses and symptom substitutions will show the strength of the surviving complex. . . .

In distinct contrast to the medical model we have the *behavioural model,* which forms the basis of behaviour therapy (Eysenck and Rachman, 1965). This model postulates very simply that all behaviour is *learned,* and that 'abnormal' behaviour is learned according to the same laws as 'normal' behaviour. The principles of learning and conditioning apply equally to both, enabling us to understand the genesis of both normal and abnormal behaviour. Thus the 'symptoms' the patient complains of are simply items of behaviour which the patient has learned; there is no underlying 'cause' or 'complex' which produces and sustains the 'symptoms', and makes them reappear once they have been eliminated by 'purely symptomatic' treatment. It also follows from this way of looking at the problem that behaviours, once learned, can also be unlearned, or 'extinguished', as the Pavlovian would say (Eysenck, 1976, 331–333).

Psychoanalytic theory postulates that an unconscious conflict between instinctual forces and ego defensive processes is at the heart of neurosis. Here, too, Wolpe and Eysenck vigorously disagree. The core phenomenon is simply a conditioned fear reaction. A review of certain experiments done with animals leads Wolpe, at least, to suggest that while exposing an individual to a situation that simultaneously elicits strong competing responses *may* result in neurotic fear or anxiety, conflict is neither the necessary ingredient in the genesis of neuroses nor the most frequent one. More commonly, Wolpe and Eysenck insist, the core phenomenon is simply a conditioned fear reaction, brought about by the conjunction on one or more occasions of an initially neutral stimulus with a physically or psychologically painful event. If the trauma is sufficiently intense and the person particularly vulnerable, only one such experience may be required to establish an anxiety reaction of great strength and persistence.

Once learned, conditioned anxieties are elicited not merely by the original conditioned stimulus, but also, because of stimulus generalization, by other stimuli. The anxiety reactions evoked by these various stimuli lead the individual to make still further responses that not infrequently lead to rapid anxiety reduction. On these occasions, still further stimuli that happen to be present at the time the drive reduction occurred will acquire the capacity to elicit the anxiety. In this manner, fear reactions may spread to stimuli that bear little or no resemblance to those involved in the original conditioning.

Wolpe and Eysenck are less impressed with the adaptive significance of neurotic behavior accompanying anxiety reactions than are many personality theorists. They agree that individuals suffering from neurotic anxieties often develop responses that allow at least temporary escape or avoidance of these unpleasant emotions. But not all symptoms have this function. Some neurotic behavior, for example, consists of responses that happen to have been going on at the time of the original trauma and have therefore become associated or "hooked up" with the conditioned stimulus along with the conditioned anxiety reaction. Still other responses may later be added to the syndrome of neurotic responses because they are, by coincidence, going on at the time anxiety reduction occurs and thus reinforced. Such fortuitous behavior does not always have the effect of reducing the person's anxiety and may even increase the anxiety.

Wolpe's theories about human neuroses were heavily influenced by the results of a series of experiments he conducted with cats during the late 1940s which were stimulated by earlier investigations by the psychiatrist Jules Masserman (1943). In one study, Masserman had shown that animals first trained to receive food at a given location and then given shocks at that location developed intense anxiety reactions or "experimental neuroses." The experiment was designed to demonstrate that conflict, as is claimed in psychoanalytic theory, is a critical component in the production of neuroses and its results have frequently been cited in support of this contention. Wolpe repeated the conditions of the Masserman experiment but added another group of animals. This second group experienced shock in the experimental apparatus, but had not had the prior approach training with food given to the conflict group. The emotional behavior elicited by the cues of the experimental setting was observed to be similar in both groups, a finding that led Wolpe to believe that anxiety is typically the essential element in the formation of neuroses and that conflict need not necessarily be present.

Wolpe also attempted to "cure" his experimental animals of their neuroses by various methods. A highly successful technique, demonstrated in one study, was to feed the animals in a laboratory room only slightly similar to the one in which the shocks had been experienced, then in a somewhat more similar room, and so forth. Eventually the animals were able to eat and carry on other activities in the training setting without any visible signs of emotional upset.

Wolpe patterned this method after a procedure first reported many years before in a study of children's fears by Mary Cover Jones (1924). Jones successfully used a technique (which, in its basic elements, subsequently came to be labeled *counterconditioning*) in which children were given attractive food while a feared object was at some distance from them. The object was progressively brought closer and closer to the child until it eventually became a signal for food instead of a stimulus that elicited fear.

Such findings led Wolpe to formulate the following principle: "If a response antagonistic to anxiety can be made to occur in the presence of anxiety-evoking stimuli so that it is accompanied by a complete or partial suppression of the anxiety responses, the bond between these stimuli and the anxiety responses will be weakened" (Wolpe, 1958, p. 71). Wolpe saw this principle as a specific instance of the still more general principle of *reciprocal inhibition*. As Wolpe uses the term, reciprocal inhibition refers to the situation in which "the elicitation of one response appears to bring about a decrement in the strength of evocation of a simultaneous response" (Wolpe, 1958, p. 29).

Wolpe believed that human neuroses, developed in the course of everyday living, obey essentially the same laws as the experimental neuroses of his laboratory animals. It followed that therapies based on the principle of reciprocal inhibition should be successful with human clinical cases. Eating did not seem to be an appropriate response to pit against anxiety reactions with adults, so Wolpe's problem was to find an alternative. He suggested the use of several responses that are antagonistic to anxiety and has devised or adopted therapeutic techniques based on each of them. The most widely used of these techniques are assertiveness training and systematic desensitization. Assertiveness training, originally suggested by Salter (1949), is a method of deconditioning the anxiety of individuals who are too inhibited and timorous in interpersonal situations to respond appropriately. The therapist attempts to persuade the individual that acting assertively (which Wolpe defines as "the proper expression of any emotion other than anxiety towards another person," 1973, p. 81) is to his or her advantage, and to teach the individual appropriate behavior by such devices as role-playing in imaginary situations that are bothersome in real life and having the individual practice assertive responses. Systematic desensitization employs deep muscle relaxation to oppose anxiety. Since desensitization is the most highly developed of Wolpe's techniques and is most closely associated with his name, it will be the only behavior therapy discussed in any detail.

Systematic desensitization is closely modeled after the type of counterconditioning procedures Wolpe used to treat shock-induced neuroses in his experimental animals. Patients are initially given training that allows them to relax at will each of their major muscle groups. The second task that must be accomplished before therapy can begin is to identify the individual's problem areas and the situations that arouse emotional discomfort. This information is gathered in initial interviews and together the patient and the therapist construct one or more *anxiety hierarchies* in which a series of related situations are ranked according to the amount of anxiety they elicit.

Therapy consists of having the individuals relax, and then imagine as vividly as possible each scene on their anxiety hierarchy *while maintaining their relaxation*. The patients begin with imagining the least anxiety-provoking item on their hierarchy, and are instructed to stop immediately if they begin to feel at all anxious. They then repeat this scene until they can picture it for a number of seconds and remain completely relaxed. When extinction of the anxiety reaction to the scene has been accomplished, they go on to the next item. Extinction of the weak anxiety reactions to the first scene generalizes to this next item, thus making extinction to this scene easier to accomplish, and so forth through the entire list of anxiety-provoking situations.

In his 1958 volume, Wolpe reported that of about two hundred individuals that he and his colleagues had treated by desensitization and other reciprocal inhibition techniques, approximately ninety percent were "cured" or showed much improvement, a figure much higher than has been reported for more conventional therapies. Further, considerably fewer sessions were required to bring about these results than are typically required by ordinary psychotherapy. Wolpe has also reported that although interviewing the individual seeking help to determine the stimuli eliciting anxiety and setting up appropriate hierarchies requires considerable clinical acumen, relatively untrained, inexperienced persons can successfully supervise desensitization sessions.

Wolpe's data encouraged other clinicians to use desensitization to treat a variety of neurotic anxieties and scores of case studies reporting successful outcome began to appear in the literature. Both Wolpe and Eysenck recognized that as encouraging as these reports were, scientific rigor demanded that conclusions about the relative efficacy of systematic desensitization in comparison to other therapeutic techniques be based on the results of carefully controlled experimental studies. Over the past decade, ten to fifteen years, a great number of such experiments have been conducted, many of them published in the journals, *Behaviour Research and Therapy,* established in the early 1960s with Eysenck as editor, and *Behavior Therapy and Experimental Psychiatry,* established several years later with Wolpe as editor. The results of these studies have not only confirmed that desensitization can be used with beneficial effects in treating many types of problems, often in conjunction with other behavioral techniques, but also that the procedure may be superior to more traditional therapeutic techniques.

The success of desensitization prompted a number of investigators to undertake serious experimental tests of Wolpe's theoretical propositions and to propose alternate theories to explain desensitization's effectiveness and extensions or modifications of the technique. One major outcome has been the development of behaviorally oriented procedures aimed at cognitive restructuring or modification of the destructive thoughts accompanying anxiety reactions (e.g., Meichenbaum, 1976). A consequence of these developments is that the area is currently characterized by healthy theoretical debate and that behavior therapists have at their disposal a number of techniques, including systematic desensitization, each of which, singly or in combination, may be particularly useful with different individuals or kinds of complaints. The ingenuity with which behavior therapists have used behavioral techniques in treating individuals with a variety of seriously disruptive problems is illustrated in Eysenck's *Case studies in behaviour therapy* (1976).

In his influential research and writing, Martin Seligman focuses upon a narrower set of phenomena than Eysenck and Wolpe but shows the same willingness to apply principles originally discovered in the laboratory with animals to the emotional problems of human beings. Seligman observes that in the natural world, unpleasant, traumatic events may occur that the person or the animal can do little or nothing to control. When the organism discovers that nothing can be done to escape or ward off aversive events—that reinforcement and behavior are not contingent on each other—a reaction may be acquired that Seligman calls *learned helplessness.* One of the consequences of helplessness is *emotional disruption,* far greater in intensity than is shown by those who experience the same unpleasant events but have some degree of control over them. Helplessness also leads to a decrease in *motivation,* the organism behaving passively and appearing to "give up," doing little to attempt to escape the noxious stimulus. Even more serious, helplessness may lead to a *cognitive deficit* that interferes with the organism's capacity to perceive the relation between response and reinforcement in other situations in which control is possible. Seligman noted the similarity between learned helplessness, which he and others have demonstrated experimentally in the laboratory with a number of animal species, including humans, and the psychopathological phenomenon of *depression.* The behaviors exhibited by the depressed individual bear a striking resemblance to those associated with learned helplessness and, he proposes, have similar origins. The methods that are effective in reducing experimentally induced helplessness may also be beneficial in treating depressive reactions. Experimental studies of learned helplessness may thus serve as a laboratory model of depression as it occurs in the natural world.

Seligman did his graduate study in experimental psychology at the University of Pennsylvania, receiving his degree in 1967. He started his academic career as an Assistant Professor at Cornell University, moving back to the University of Pennsylvania in 1970 where he is now Professor of Psychology. In 1975 he was a Visiting Fellow at Maudsley Hospital, University of London. His theorizing and extensive experimental work on learned helplessness and depression are summarized in his book, *Helplessness* (1975), and in two recent articles, Learned helplessness and depression in animals and man (published in *Behavioral approaches to therapy,* 1976) and Learned helplessness: Theory and evidence (written with S. F. Maier and published in *Journal of experimental psychology: General,* 1976). In recognition of the significance of his contributions, he received in 1976 the American Psychological Association's Early Career Award.

Consider the following experiment (Overmier and Seligman, 1967). An experimental animal—a dog—is placed in a shuttlebox. Periodically, a tone comes on, and soon after, the dog experiences a painful but physically harmless shock. At the onset of the shock, the dog whines and runs about, at one point happening to jump over the barrier while the shock is still being administered. When the dog crosses the barrier, both the shock and the tone cease. With successive trials, the dog jumps over the barrier to escape the shock more and more quickly. Eventually, the animal waits quite calmly in front of the barrier, nimbly jumping over it as soon as the tone comes on, therby completely avoiding the shock.

Another dog is first placed in a restraining hammock and given a number of brief shocks it can do nothing to escape or avoid. When put into the shuttlebox a day later, the animal initially acts much like the dog that had not had the initial experience with uncontrollable shock, but quickly differences become apparent. Even if the animal accidentally jumps the barrier, it does not learn on subsequent trials to cross the barrier to escape or avoid the shock. Instead the dog ceases to be active, sitting or lying down, whimpering, until the tone and the shock end.

Almost all dogs without prior shock experience learn the barrier-jumping response to escape or avoid aversive stimulation. In contrast, most animals initially given uncontrollable shock respond apathetically to the shock in the shuttlebox situation and show little or no learning of the barrier-jumping response. This learned helplessness effect is not unique to dogs but has been demonstrated in cats (Thomas and Balter, in press), fish (Padilla, Padilla, Ketterer, and Giacolone, 1970), rats (e.g., Seligman and Beagley, 1975), and in man (e.g., Hiroto, 1974; Hiroto and Seligman, 1975; Klein, Fencil-Morse, and Seligman, 1976).

In one particularly illuminating experiment, Hiroto and Seligman (1975) not only demonstrated learned helplessness in the human subject but also showed that uncontrollable, unpleasant events inducing helplessness need not be physically noxious. Three groups of college students were presented with a shuttlebox arrangement in which they could escape or avoid loud noise by moving their hand from one side of the box to the other. Prior to this task, one group of students had been given discrimination learning problems that were solvable, and another group problems that, unknown to the students, were unsolvable. The third group received no problems. The individuals who had been given solvable or no problems quickly learned to escape or avoid the noise in the shuttlebox situation while those given the unsolvable problems (and thus subjected to unavoidable failure) did not learn. Seligman (1976) views these results as primarily revealing a motivational deficit in those who had been exposed to uncontrollable events, that is, as demonstrating a failure to initiate responses that would ward off undesirable outcomes. In complementary experiments, the cognitive deficit that is one of the symptoms of learned helplessness was highlighted. Miller and Seligman (1975) first instructed two groups of students to learn to escape unpleasant noise that came on periodically. The students in one group were able to discover a response that terminated the noise. The other group received exactly the same noise but were led to believe that termination was automatic and unrelated to their responses (that reinforcement and their behavior were unrelated or noncontingent). A third group received no pretreatment. All students were then given a series of anagrams to solve. The group that had previously experienced inescapable noise reached fewer solutions than the other two.

In addition to exhibiting motivational and cognitive deficits, organisms subjected to uncontrollable aversive events often exhibit marked emotional disturbance. In humans, for example, subjects allowed to terminate noxious stimulation by performing some instrumental act report less emotional stress and physical upset than yoked subjects given the same stimulation but forced to endure it passively (e.g., Glass and Singer, 1972). In lengthy experiments with animals, yoked subjects have been found to be more likely to develop ulcers and to show weight loss, loss of appetite, and other symptoms of severe emotional stress than the subjects whose responses controlled the duration of the noxious events (e.g., Weiss, 1971).

If subjects have been exposed only briefly to inescapable stress, learned helplessness is only a transitory phenomenon that wears off quickly and, in human experiments, is exhibited only in the laboratory setting. Investigations with animals demonstrate, however, that repeated exposure may lead, not only to the severe emotional reactions just described, but also to prolonged motivational and cognitive deficits. Animals with no prior experience coping with trauma seem particularly susceptible to learned helplessness. Animals brought up in benign laboratory environments, for example, are far more prone to exhibit learned helplessness after exposure to inescapable stress than animals that have experienced the rough and tumble of the natural world (Seligman and Maier, 1967; Seligman and Groves, 1970).

Humans tested in the laboratory also differ in their suceptibility to the helpless syndrome. The life experiences that make some people particularly likely to become helpless are not known but differences have been shown to be related to people's answers on a personality test (Rotter, 1966) measuring belief in internal versus external locus of control of reinforcement (Hiroto, 1974; Dweck and Reppucci, 1973). "External" individuals, those who believe that what happens to them in life is a matter of luck and beyond their control, are more likely to become helpless after being exposed to unescapable noxious events than "internal" individuals, those who regard their destiny as largely being in their own hands.

A rather simple "cure" has been found for the transient kind of helplessness induced in human subjects in the laboratory: giving the subjects experience in successfully mastering some task soon after they have been exposed to the unescapable aversive stimuli (e.g., Klein and Seligman, 1976). For individuals exhibiting helplessness in real life situations, more complicated therapeutic methods may be required. Dweck (1975), for example, devised treatment procedures for "helpless" children—those who had been observed by their school teachers and principals as expecting to fail and as doing badly in their school work when failure threatened. These children were also found to be more likely than their nonhelpless peers to attribute their intellectual successes and failures to forces outside themselves or to attribute their failures to lack of ability (both uncontrollable causes) rather than to their lack of effort (a controllable cause). The children were put through an extended program, lasting over a large number of sessions, in each of which they were given problems to solve. In one group, the children were taught to take responsibility for their failures and to attribute them to lack of sufficient effort. In a second group, the children were provided with only success experiences. In a posttreatment test, the children were given difficult problems and inevitably were unable to solve a number of them. After failure, the performance of those who had been allowed only to succeed deteriorated, as in the school setting, but the performance of children trained to take personal responsibility held up or actually improved.

Seligman has noted striking parallels between learned helplessness, induced in the laboratory, and the phenomenon of reactive depression, so-called because the state is presumably brought on by some emotionally upsetting event such as loss of a job, death of a loved one, or failure in some valued activity. Most people suffer from mild bouts of depression from time to time, but for many, the state may be severe and long lasting and carry with it the possibility of suicide. Depressed individuals are typically slowed down in their speech and body movements; they feel unable to act or to make decisions; they appear to have "given up" and to suffer from what one writer (Beck, 1967) describes as a paralysis of will. When asked to perform some task, those who are depressed are likely to insist that it is hopeless to try because they are incapable of being successful and to describe their performance as much worse than it actually was. All of these symptoms resemble learned helplessness. Underlying depression, Seligman (1975) proposes, ". . . is not a generalized pessimism, but *pessimism specific to the effects on one's own skilled actions*" (p. 122). This belief that reinforcement is not contingent on one's actions is, of course, the core of learned helplessness. Thus, according to Seligman's theory, depression represents a type of learned helplessness and is precipitated by the same causes: experiencing traumatic events that one's best efforts have done nothing to ward off and that one feels powerless to control.

In one experimental test of the learned helplessness model of depression, Miller and Seligman (1976) had groups of mildly depressed and nondepressed students perform two series of tasks, one involving skill and the other involving chance, and before each task, had the student state their expectancy of succeeding. On the skill task, the nondepressed students adjusted their expectancies up and down, depending on whether they had succeeded or failed on the previous problem, but on the chance task showed little change in their expectancies. The depressed students also showed little change after success and failure on the chance task, but also on the task involving skill. Nondepressed students who had been pretreated with inescapable noxious stimuli showed the same pattern. Helplessness, induced in the laboratory, and naturally occurring depression were thus shown to have the same effect of reducing the expectation that one's own effort can influence outcome.

The helplessness exhibited by mildly depressed college students in the laboratory can be alleviated by giving them a series of success experiences (Klein and Seligman, 1976). Treatment procedures for the more severely depressed, based on the learned helplessness model, are just beginning to be developed. Several techniques, related to those devised by Wolpe, have been found to be promising, such as training depressed individuals to become more assertive (Taulbee and Wright, 1971) or to perform a graduated series of task assignments requiring more and more effort (Burgess, 1968). The crux of successful therapy with depressives, Seligman advises, is to restore their sense of efficacy, to get them to perceive that they can control outcomes by their own behavior.

Albert Bandura shares the view that learning principles are sufficient to explain and predict behavior and behavior change. However, he takes issue with learning approaches to personality that draw their principles exclusively from studies of single organisms in an impersonal environment or that picture human behavior as being passively controlled by environmental influences. He reminds us that humans are capable of thought and self-regulation that permit them to control their environment as well as to be shaped by it. Furthermore, many aspects of personality functioning involve the interaction of the individual with others so that an adequate theory of personality must take into account the social context in which behavior is originally acquired and continues to be maintained. Bandura's intent has therefore been to extend and modify traditional learning theory by developing principles of *social learning*. As Bandura describes it:

Social learning theory approaches the explanation of human behavior in terms of a continuous reciprocal interaction between cognitive, behavioral, and environmental determinants. Within the process of reciprocal determinism lies the opportunity for people to influence their destiny as well as the limits of self-direction. This conception of human functioning then neither casts people into the role of powerless objects controlled by environmental forces nor free agents who can become whatever they choose. Both people and their environments are reciprocal determinants of each other (Bandura, 1977b, p. vii).

Bandura received his graduate training in clinical psychology at the University of Iowa which awarded him the Ph.D. in 1952. At Iowa the Hullian tradition was strong; its faculty consisted of such individuals as Kenneth Spence, Judson Brown, and Robert Sears, all of whom had received their doctoral training at Yale and made notable contributions of their own in extending Hull's theory. After a year of postdoctoral clinical training, Bandura accepted, in 1953, a position at Stanford University, where he is now David Starr Jordan Professor of Social Science. He has served as chairman of the Stanford Department of Psychology and in 1974 was elected to the presidency of the American Psychological Association.

Bandura's research has ranged widely over many problems central to social learning theory, in the course of which his theory has been refined and expanded. This research includes the study of imitation and identification (Bandura, 1962; Bandura and Huston, 1961; Bandura, Ross, and Ross, 1961, 1963a and b), social reinforcement (Bandura and McDonald, 1963), self-reinforcement and monitoring (Bandura and Kuppers, 1964; Bandura and Whalen, 1966; Bandura, Jeffery, and Gajdos, 1975; Bandura, Mahoney, and Dirks, 1976), and behavior change through modeling (Bandura, Blanchard, and Ritter, 1969; Bandura and Menlove, 1968; Bandura, Jeffery, and Wright, 1975). With the late Richard Walters as junior author, Bandura wrote *Adolescent aggression* (1959), a detailed report of a field study in which social learning principles were used to analyze the personality development of a group of middle class delinquent boys, followed by *Social learning and personality development* (1963), a volume in which he and Walters presented the social learning principles they had developed and the evidence on which the theory was based. In 1969 Bandura published *Principles of behavior modification,* in which he outlined the application of behavioral techniques based on learning principles to the modification of behavior and in 1973, *Aggression: A social learning analysis.* In his most recent, and theoretically ambitious book, *Social learning theory* (1977), he has "attempted to provide a unified theoretical framework for analyzing human thought and behavior" (p. vi).

In common with most learning theory approaches to personality, social learning theory is based on the premise that human behavior is largely acquired and that the principles of learning are sufficient to account for the development and maintenance of that behavior. However, previous learning theories not only have paid insufficient attention to the social context in which this behavior arises but also to the fact that much important learning takes place vicariously. That is, in the course of observing others' behavior, individuals learn to imitate that behavior or in some way model themselves after others. In their 1941 book, *Social learning and imitation,* Miller and Dollard had recognized the significant role played by imitative processes in personality development and had sought to develop explanations of certain kinds of imitative behavior. But few others interested in personality had attempted to incorporate the phenomenon of observational learning into their learning theories and even Miller and Dollard seldom referred to imitation in their later publications. Bandura has sought not only to redress this neglect but to extend the analysis of observational learning beyond the limited types of situations considered by Miller and Dollard.

The critical role Bandura assigns to imitation in personality development is best seen then in his analysis of its contribution to the acquisition of novel responses. In a series of experiments done with children, Bandura and his colleagues have demonstrated that subjects allowed to observe an unusual set of responses performed by another individual (the *model*) tend to exhibit these same responses when placed in a similar setting. In one representative study (Bandura, Ross, and Ross, 1961), nursery school children, tested one at a time, watched an adult model perform a series of particular aggressive acts, physical and verbal, toward a large toy doll. Other children saw a nonaggressive adult who sat quietly in the experimental room and paid no attention to the doll. Later, the children were mildly frustrated and then placed alone in the room with the doll. The behavior of the groups tended to be congruent with the adult model's. The children who had seen an aggressive adult themselves performed more aggressive acts than a control group given no prior experience with a model and made more responses than the control children that were quite exact imitations of the model's behaviors. Further, the children who had observed a nonaggressive adult made even *fewer* aggressive responses than the control subjects.

As this experiment illustrates, children can learn novel responses merely by observing others. Of equal importance, it shows that learning can take place without the children having had the opportunity to make the response themselves and without either the model or themselves having been rewarded or reinforced for the behavior.

The capacity to perform novel responses observed some time before but never actually practiced is made possible by the human's cognitive abilities. The stimuli provided by the model are transformed into images of what the model did or said or looked like, and even more important, are transformed into verbal symbols that can later be recalled.

These symbolic, cognitive skills also allow individuals to transform what they have learned or to combine what they have observed in a number of models into new patterns of behavior. Thus by observing others, one may develop novel, innovative solutions and not merely slavish imitations.

Mere exposure to others' behavior does not necessarily lead people to learn these responses or, once they have learned them, actually to perform these responses in appropriate situations. For learning to take place, the onlooker must *attend* to the cues provided by the model. A number of factors determine whether the model compels the observer's attention. Of major importance are the consequences of the model's behavior. If the model's behavior has been rewarded, imitation is more likely than if it has been punished (Bandura, Ross, and Ross, 1963b; Walters, Leat, and Mezei, 1963). Thus, not only is direct reinforcement a potent determinant of an individual's behavior, but so also is *vicarious reinforcement*—the consequences the individual observes as following another's behavior. Equally significant are the characteristics of the models themselves, attributes such as their age, social status, sex, warmth, and competence, determining the degree to which they will be imitated. The characteristics of the observers also determine how much imitative behavior takes place in a given situation. Highly dependent children, for example, have been found to be more influenced by the behavior of a model than the less dependent (Jakubczak and Walters, 1959).

The characteristics of both model and observer often jointly determine what will occur. A particularly informative study showing the interplay of model and observer was performed by Hetherington and Frankie (1967) with young children and their parents. The investigators first determined by observing the parents the degree of warmth and nurturance each expressed toward the child and which parent was dominant in matters of child-care. Subsequently, the child watched each parent play with toys and games supplied by the investigator, following which the child was allowed to play with the same materials and the amount of his or her imitative behavior recorded. Children of both sexes were much more likely to imitate a warm, nurturant parent than a cool or punitive one, but the largest effect was found with girls whose mothers were warm. By and large, the dominant parent also commanded more imitative behavior although when the father was dominant, girls imitated the mother somewhat more than the father.

In human cultures, novel behavior is very frequently acquired by observing the behavior of others. Often the instruction is quite direct, the child, in particular, learning what he or she sees others do. But individuals may also be influenced by models presented in more symbolic forms. Pictorial presentations, such as those in movies and television, are highly influential sources of models. Bandura, Ross, and Ross (1963a), for example, found that children who watched the aggressive behavior of a live adult model were no greater in their tendency to imitate than children shown a movie of the same behavior or even an animated cartoon.

Bandura suggests that exposure to models, in addition to leading to the acquisition of novel behavior, has two other types of effects. A model's behavior may simply serve to elicit the performance of similar responses already in the observer's repertoire. This facilitating effect is especially likely to occur when the behavior is of a socially acceptable nature. The second way a model may influence an observer occurs when the model is performing socially proscribed or deviant behavior. The observer's inhibitions about performing the behavior may be strengthened or weakened by watching the model, depending on whether the model's behavior has been punished or rewarded.

Rosekrans and Hartup (1967), for example, demonstrated that children who saw a model's aggressive behavior being consistently rewarded subsequently showed a high degree of imitative aggression while those who saw it consistently punished exhibited practically no imitative behavior. Children exposed to a model sometimes rewarded and sometimes punished displayed an intermediate amount of aggression.

The types of vicarious learning we have been discussing involve actions falling into the general category of instrumental or operant responses. Bandura (1969) has pointed to another kind of learning based on the observation of a model that is crucial in social learning theory, namely the vicarious acquisition of *classically conditioned emotional responses*. Not only may observers exposed to the emotional reactions of a model experience similar reactions, but they may also begin to respond emotionally to stimuli that produced these reactions in the model. In an illustrative experiment, Bandura and Rosenthal (1966) had each subject watch as a model, introduced as an actual subject, was presented with a series of buzzer signals. Following each occurrence of the buzzer, the model simulated a variety of pain reactions that the subject was falsely told were elicited by an intense shock delivered immediately after the buzzer. As indicated by a physiological measure of emotional responsivity, the subjects came to exhibit a conditioned emotional response to the buzzer, even in test trials in which the model was absent and despite the fact that they never directly experienced the painful unconditioned stimulus supposedly administered to the model.

As in other learning theories, reinforcement has a prominent place in Bandura's social learning theory but it is assumed to influence what is *performed* rather than what is learned. By noting the rewarding or punishing consequences of their own actions or the actions of others, people develop cognitive expectations about behavioral outcomes and about what they must do to achieve desirable outcomes or to avoid unpleasant ones. Reinforcement comes to guide behavior primarily through anticipation of its future occurrence; individuals regulate their behavior according to the outcomes they expect it will produce.

External rewards and punishments, however, are not the only source of reinforcement. Many actions are regulated by self-imposed consequences. Human beings develop their own values about what activities are important to perform and personal standards of behavior. These internalized standards lead them to evaluate their own actions and to reward or punish themselves by self-approval or self-criticism. When individuals fail to meet their self-imposed standards, they typically take corrective action to perfect their behaviors and to bring them to an acceptable level. By this process of monitoring, behavior becomes self-regulatory and is not constantly at the mercy of external forces. People thus achieve behavioral consistency and do not automatically change their behaviors to gain the approval or avoid the disapproval of the particular social group in which they happen to find themselves.

The reciprocal influence that Bandura describes as existing between the person and the environment is illustrated in his contention that self-reinforcement systems are themselves acquired by the same learning principles responsible for the acquisition of other types of behaviors. Thus, what individuals come to reward and punish in themselves may reflect the reactions that their behavior has elicited from others. Parents, peers, and other socializing agents set behavioral standards, rewarding the individual for living up to them and expressing their displeasure when the person fails. These externally imposed norms may be "taken over" by the individual and form the basis for later self-reinforcement systems. It might thus be expected, Bandura notes, that individuals who as children were praised and admired for rather low levels of accomplishment will grow up to administer self-rewards more generously than those who were held to higher standards of excellence and, indeed, there is evidence to suggest that this is so (Kanfer and Marston, 1963).

Extensive evidence indicates that self-evaluative standards can also be acquired vicariously by observing others. In one representative experiment, Bandura and Kupers (1964) had children observe a model who set either a high or a low standard of achievement for self-reward. Later observation of the children performing the same task showed that those exposed to the model with low standards rewarded themselves more indulgently than those who observed the stricter model.

As with other behaviors, characteristics of the model influence whether or not an observer will attend and attempt to emulate the model's self-reinforcement standards. Under certain conditions, children, for example, are more likely to model themselves after peers than adults (Bandura, Grusec, and Menlove, 1967b) or after models whose achievement standards are within their reach rather than those who set them beyond the child's capacity (Bandura and Whalen, 1966).

As might be anticipated from this description of the major principles of social learning theory, Bandura is committed to the view that techniques based on learning theory can be highly effective in modifying undesirable behavior. In fact, one of Bandura's books, *Principles of Behavior Modification* (1969), is almost exclusively devoted to a discussion of such techniques, including several novel methods he and his associates have developed for eliminating unrealistic fear reactions (Bandura, Grusec, and Menlove, 1967a; Bandura, 1968; Bandura and Menlove, 1968).

These latter techniques, which grew out of experimental work on modeling and observational learning, assume that emotional responses can not only be acquired by both direct and vicarious experience with traumatic events but also that under the proper circumstances, they can be both directly and vicariously *extinguished*. Thus, persons with unrealistic or exaggerated fears should be able to reduce their defensive and emotional reactions by watching a model interact fearlessly with the anxiety-provoking object or event and reduce them still further by practicing the model's behavior in a nonthreatening situation under the latter's guidance. Numerous experiments using various modeling techniques with both children and adults have yielded highly encouraging results. A study performed by Bandura, Blanchard, and Ritter (1969) is of particular interest since it incorporates several features of Wolpe's desensitization techniques into the modeling conditions and also includes, for purposes of comparison, a conventional desensitization condition. Adolescents and adults suffering from a severe snake phobia were assigned to one of three treatment groups. Members of the desensitization group were presented with a graded series of imaginal scenes involving snakes while deeply relaxed. In the second group a symbolic modeling condition was used in which the subjects watched a film showing models in progressively closer interactions with a large snake, also while maintaining a relaxed state. The third group observed a live model perform similar responses with an actual snake. After each of these interactions these latter subjects were asked to perform the same behavior as the model, initially with the model's assistance and later alone.

All subjects were asked to try to perform a graded series of tasks involving snakes both before and after treatment. While control subjects, who were given only these two test series and no intervening treatment, showed essentially no change in their behavior, a marked increase in approach behavior was noted in the desensitization and symbolic modeling groups following treatment. The most successful technique, however, was participant modeling, that is, the one in which subjects were exposed to an actual model and given guided experience in interacting with the phobic object.

Bandura's (1977b) theoretical analysis of behaviorally oriented therapies differs in crucial respects from Wolpe's and Eysenck's. He

agrees with the latter that one of their beneficial outcomes is the reduction of anxiety reactions. Emotional distress, however, is not the
key element causing inability to deal effectively with a feared object
or event, nor is its elimination at the heart of the behavior change
brought about by therapy. What creates a problem for the individual
is the belief that he or she is unable to cope successfully with a situation. The change brought about by therapeutic techniques, whatever
their particular form, results from the development of a sense of *self-
efficacy,* the expectation that one can, by one's personal efforts, master
situations and bring about desired outcomes. Anxiety and other similar forms of emotional arousal serve primarily as signals of impending
threat with which it may not be possible to cope. Elimination of negative emotions, by desensitization to symbolic stimuli, relaxation, or
other similar techniques, helps to remove one of the factors contributing to the individual's disbelief in their personal efficacy. Vicarious experience, such as observing a model successfully perform a
dreaded activity, may also be beneficial, allowing individuals to acquire more realistic expectations about the outcomes of their responses and by persuading them that if they try, they will also be able
to learn effective coping behaviors.

Neither fear reduction nor vicarious experience, however, are
likely to be sufficient to bring about an adequate sense of personal
mastery. The most effective method is to induce successful performance accomplishments in the actual situation rather than in some
symbolic representation of it. By permitting the individual to experience repeated successes, strong efficacy expectations are likely to develop, particularly if one can attribute success to one's own efforts
rather than to the intervention of some outside agency. Bandura
suggests that participant modeling is a particularly useful technique
since it not only allows the individual to perform with positive outcome tasks leading to the desired goal but also permits the introduction of other devices to induce the individual to persist until a sense of
mastery is achieved. These include initial observation of a model, the
performance of a graded series of tasks with the assistance of the
model at carefully spaced intervals, and a gradual phasing out of supportive aids, leaving the individual progressively dependent on his or
her own efforts (Bandura, Jeffery, and Wright, 1974).

It can be observed that Seligman's theory of learned helplessness,
discussed early in this chapter, has elements in common with this
theory. Indeed, Bandura suggests that learned helplessness may be
subsumed as a special case within his more general theory of self-efficacy. In Seligman's view, learned helplessness, which is postulated
to underlie depressive reactions, develops when individuals come to

perceive no contingency between reinforcing events and their own actions. Therapies that lead to a change in the person's expectations about the relationship between behavior and behavioral outcomes may be expected to eliminate helplessness or, in Bandura's terms, perception of a lack of self-efficacy. However, according to Bandura, the latter deficiency may develop in ways other than the particular experiences that Seligman has specified and may consist of the belief, not that the world is uncontrollable, but that one personally lacks the resources to control it.

Impressive evidence supporting the hypothesis that procedures bringing about behavioral change do so by increasing the strength of self-efficacy has been provided by Bandura, Adams, and Beyer (1977) in a study of severely snake phobic adults. As has consistently been found in prior experiments, subjects treated by the participant modeling technique that gave them successful mastery experiences with the phobic object were able in a post-treatment test to interact more closely with an unfamiliar snake than those who had been given only the vicarious experience of observing a model. Of critical significance to Bandura's theory was the relationship between the outcome of therapy and the participants' expectations of efficacy. When asked at the conclusion of treatment how certain they were that they would be able to perform each of the tasks in the test series, individuals in the participant modeling group indicated stronger expectations (and later were more successful in test performance) than those given only vicarious experience. Furthermore, the strength of each individual's efficacy expectations was highly accurate in predicting later behaviors, whatever treatment group the person happened to be in.

The basic principles by which learning theorists hoped to explicate personality phenomena have been based primarily on the data of carefully controlled laboratory experiments. Despite the many virtues of the experimental approach the bulk of these investigations have suffered from the limitation of involving animal subjects far simpler than the human being, and, even when human subjects have been used, of setting up conditions that bear little resemblance to the environmental circumstances in which the human personality develops and functions. One of the major contributions of Bandura's social learning theory has been his extensive effort to introduce into experimental settings conditions more analogous to our real life social environment and to incorporate into his theory principles that acknowledge that human beings have cognitive, symbolic capacities that allow them to regulate their own behavior and to some degree control their own environment rather than to be completely controlled by it.

CURRENT
STATUS AND
EVALUATION

The application of S-R learning principles to behavioral events outside the laboratory has taken place mostly during the past thirty to thirty-five years. In this interval a very large amount of relevant empirical research has been accumulated. Furthermore, several generations of able psychologists have been trained who possess the technical skill and theoretical conviction necessary to increase enormously the existing stock of such empirical evidence. Thus, the recent past has witnessed not only an empirical boom in this area but also the appearance of a large number of individuals actively concerned with extending and modifying the concepts we have discussed. Altogether it seems clear that this brand of personality theory is supported by an unusually vigorous group of adherents, and contrary to the belief or wish of many holistic theorists, there is little apparent danger that this theoretical school will vanish in the near future as a result of indifference.

Our discussion of the theory and research of Dollard and Miller has made manifest a number of virtues. The major concepts within this theory are clearly expounded and customarily linked to certain classes of empirical events. There is a scarcity of vague allusion or appeal to intuition in the works of these theorists. The hard-headed, positivistic reader will find much to admire in their writings. Moreover, this evident objectivity does not prevent many S-R learning theorists from being ready and eager to embrace a wide range of empirical phenomena with their conceptual tools. Although their formulations began in the laboratory, they have shown no timidity about advancing with them upon the most complex of behavioral phenomena.

A highly significant contribution of S-R theory to the personality scene is contained in the careful detail with which this position represents the learning process. Obviously the transformation of behavior as a result of experience is a crucial consideration for any adequate theory of personality, and yet many theories have largely overlooked this question or have brushed by it with a few stereotyped phrases. In this sense at least, S-R theory provides a model to be emulated by other theoretical positions.

The readiness of Dollard and Miller to extract wisdom from social anthropology and clinical psychoanalysis represents, for many, another attractive feature of their particular position. They make more explicit use of sociocultural variables than almost any of the other theories we have discussed and we have seen that their theory owes much to the impact of psychoanalysis. The readiness and sophistication with which sociocultural variables are introduced in the theory may be related to the fact that this theory has been applied by cultural anthropologists more widely than any other theory of personality except psychoanalysis.

This willingness to incorporate the hypotheses and speculations of other types of theories, such as psychoanalysis, while appealing to many inside as well as outside the learning group, has not found universal favor among those who advocate the application of learning principles to personality phenomena. Psychologists such as Bandura, Wolpe, and Eysenck, to say nothing of those who take the Skinnerian approach, not only find little necessity for going beyond the principles established in the learning laboratory but may actively disagree with the views of more traditional personality theorists, particularly those of a psychoanalytic persuasion.

Although divided on this issue, S-R theorists have characteristically emphasized the function of a theory as a guide to investigation and the necessity of submitting theoretical differences to experimental test. In these respects, members of this group have a definite superiority over most other personality theorists. In general, these theorists have a better sense of the nature and function of theory in an empirical discipline than any other group of personality theorists. In their writing, as compared with the writing of other theorists, there is less reification, less sterile argument over words, and more readiness to look at theories as sets of rules that are used only when they are demonstrably more useful than other sets of rules. This methodological sophistication is undoubtedly responsible for the relative explicitness and formal adequacy of these theories.

In many ways S-R theory typifies an experimental, objective approach to human behavior. As such, it has been a prime critical target for the many psychologists who are convinced that an adequate understanding of human behavior must involve more than a slavish application of the experimental methods of physical science. These critics feel that although their personal theoretical positions may be vulnerable because they rest on empirical observation that is not adequately controlled, the observations, at least, are relevant to the events with which they purport to deal. In the case of S-R theory, the bulk of the careful investigation is not only concerned with simple instead of complex behavior, but more important, has often been carried out with an animal species that is phylogenetically far removed from and manifestly different in many crucial respects from the human organism. What good are rigor and careful specification in the experimental situation if the investigator is subsequently forced to make a tenuous assumption of phylogenetic continuity in order to apply his findings to important events? We have already seen that S-R theorists consider that learning principles established in laboratory studies of animals must be justified with experimental studies employing human subjects. Thus, there is an essential agreement here concerning the importance of coordinating research; the question becomes one of how much confidence can be placed in the theory until such studies are carried out in considerable quantity.

A related criticism frequently leveled at learning theory approaches asserts that most of the positive features of this position, including its careful definitions, explicitness, and wealth of research exist only when the theory is applied to animal behavior or very restricted domains of human behavior. As soon as the theory is applied to complex human behavior it is in the same situation as other theories of personality, with ad hoc definitions, and reasoning by analogy, representing the rule instead of the exception. This criticism suggests that the rigor and relative formal adequacy of S-R theories are illusory as they exist only when their principles are applied within a very limited scope. Once a learning theory is generalized, concepts that were clear become ambiguous and definitions that were tight become flaccid.

Perhaps the most important critical objection to S-R approaches is the assertion that they do not provide adequate prior specification of stimulus and response. Traditionally, learning theorists have been concerned almost exclusively with the *process* of learning and have not attempted to identify the stimuli occurring in the natural environment of the organisms they study or to develop a suitable taxonomy for these stimulus events. Further, these learning processes have been investigated in restricted, controlled settings in which it is relatively simple to specify the stimuli eliciting observable behavior. The challenge to the personality theorist is to understand the human organism operating in the real-world environment and it can be cogently argued that if psychologists cannot fully define the stimulus for behavior their task has barely begun. Roughly the same arguments can be made about the response. In fairness it must be admitted that theorists such as Miller and Dollard are well aware of this problem. Miller, in a jocular vein, has suggested that S-R theory might better be labeled "hyphen theory" as it has had more to say about the connection between the stimulus and the response than about either the stimulus or the response itself. Miller and Dollard have made attempts to overcome this deficiency, as have Bandura and others, by specifying at least some of the social conditions under which human learning takes place in addition to the abstract principles governing that learning.

Related to this criticism is the fact that S-R theory has remarkably little to say about the structures or acquisitions of personality, which is undoubtedly why many theorists have found psychoanalytic theory useful in their thinking and investigation. This objection also maintains that, with its preoccupation with the process of learning, S-R theory is only a partial theory and that the relatively stable components of personality are an essential element in any attempt to understand human behavior.

Certainly the most frequently voiced criticisms of S-R theory point to the simplicity and molecularity of the position. Holists feel that this theory is the very essence of a segmental, fragmented, and atomistic approach to behavior. They claim that so little of the context of behavior is seen that one cannot hope to understand or predict human behavior adequately. There is no appreciation of the importance of the whole and the patterning of the parts is overlooked in favor of their microscopic examination. In these objections it is difficult to sort out the polemical and affective components from their legitimate intellectual accompaniment. In defense of learning theory, it is certainly clear that there is nothing in the S-R position to imply that variables must operate singly or in isolation. Interaction of variables is perfectly acceptable, so at least this degree of holism is congruent with S-R theory.

Still other psychologists accuse S-R theorists of having neglected language and thought processes and claim that their concepts are inadequate to explain the acquisition and development of these complex cognitive functions. Any acceptable theory of human learning, they contend, must incorporate these cognitive phenomena. It is only in recent years, however, that adequate theories of language and cognition have been developed (most of them, admittedly, outside of the S-R animal learning tradition). There is no barrier, in principle, to the discoveries of cognitive theories being incorporated into learning theory accounts of personality development. Bandura's social learning theory is a major step in this direction.

In summary, S-R theory is a theoretical position that in many respects is singularly American. It is objective, functional, places much emphasis on empirical research, and is only minimally concerned with the subjective and intuitive side of human behavior. As such it provides a striking contrast to many of the theories we have discussed that are deeply indebted to European psychology. Undoubtedly its tough-minded, empirical strengths have made and will continue to make unique contributions to this area of psychology.

BIBLIOGRAPHY
PRIMARY SOURCES

Bandura, A. *Principles of behavior modification.* New York: Holt, Rinehart and Winston, 1969.

Bandura, A. *Social learning theory.* Englewood Cliffs, N. J.: Prentice-Hall, 1977.

Dollard, J., and Miller, N. E. *Personality and psychotherapy: an analysis in terms of learning, thinking and culture.* New York: McGraw-Hill, 1950.

Eysenck, H. J. *The dynamics of anxiety and hysteria.* London: Routledge and Kegan Paul, 1957.

Eysenck, H. J., and Rachman, S. *The causes and cures of neuroses.* San Diego: Knapp, 1965.

Miller, N. E., and Dollard, J. *Social learning and imitation.* New Haven: Yale Univ. Press, 1941.

Seligman, M. E. P. *Helplessness: On depression, development, and death.* San Francisco: W. H. Freeman, 1975.

Seligman, M. E. P. Learned helplessness and depression in animals and man. In J. T. Spence, R. C. Carson, and J. W. Thibaut (Eds.). *Behavioral approaches to therapy.* Morristown, N. J.: General Learning Press, 1976.

Wolpe, J. *Psychotherapy by reciprocal inhibition.* Stanford: Stanford Univ. Press, 1958.

Wolpe, J. *The practice of behavior therapy.* Second edition. New York: Pergamon Press, 1973.

REFERENCES   Bandura, A. Social learning through imitation. In M. R. Jones (Ed.). *Nebraska symposium on motivation.* Lincoln: Univ. of Nebraska Press, 1962.

Bandura, A. Modeling approaches to the modification of phobic disorders. In *Ciba Foundation Symposium. The role of learning in psychotherapy.* London: Churchill, 1968.

Bandura, A. *Principles of behavior modification.* New York: Holt, Rinehart and Winston, 1969.

Bandura, A. *Aggression: A social learning analysis.* Englewood Cliffs, N. J.: Prentice-Hall, 1973.

Bandura, A. Self-efficacy: toward a unifying theory of behavioral change. *Psychological Review,* 1977a, **84,** 191–215.

Bandura, A. *Social learning theory.* Englewood Cliffs, N. J.: Prentice-Hall, 1977b.

Bandura, A., Adams, N. E., and Beyer, J. Cognitive processes mediating behavioral change. *Journal of Personality and Social Psychology,* 1977, **35,** 125–139.

Bandura, A., Blanchard, E. B., and Ritter, B. The relative efficacy of desensitization and modeling approaches for inducing behavioral, affective, and attitudinal changes. *J. Pers. Soc. Psychol.* 1969, **13,** 173–199.

Bandura, A., Grusec, J. E., and Menlove, F. L. Vicarious extinction of avoidance behavior. *J. Pers. Soc. Psychol.,* 1967a, **5,** 16–23.

Bandura, A., Grusec, J. E., and Menlove, F. L. Some social determinants of self-monitoring reinforcement systems. *Journal of Personality and Social Psychology,* 1967b, **5,** 449–455.

Bandura, A., and Huston, A. C. Identification as a process of incidental learning. *J. Abnorm. Soc. Psychol.,* 1961, **63,** 311–318.

Bandura, A., Jeffery, R. W., and Wright, C. L. Efficacy of participant modeling as a function of response induction aids. *Journal of Abnormal Psychology,* 1974, **83,** 56–64.

Bandura, A., Jeffery, R. W., and Gajdos, E. Generalizing change through participant modeling with self-directed mastery. *Behaviour Research and Therapy,* 1975, **13,** 141–152.

Bandura, A., and Kupers, C. J. The transmission of patterns of self-reinforcement through modeling. *J. Abnorm. Soc. Psychol.,* 1964, **69,** 1–9.

Bandura, A., Mahoney, M. J., and Dirks, S. J. Discriminative activation and maintenance of contingent self-reinforcement. *Behaviour Research and Therapy,* 1976, **14,** 1–6.

Bandura, A., and McDonald, F. J. The influence of social reinforcement and the be-*havior of models in shaping children's moral judgments. J. Abnorm. Soc. Psychol.,* 1963, **67,** 274–281.

Bandura, A., and Menlove, F. L. Factors determining vicarious extinction of avoidance behavior through symbolic modeling. *J. Pers. Soc. Psychol.,* 1968, **8,** 99–108.

Bandura, A., and Perloff, B. Relative efficacy of self-monitored and externally-imposed reinforcement systems. *Journal of Personality and Social Psychology,* 1967, **7,** 111–116.

Bandura, A., and Rosenthal, T. L. Vicarious classical conditioning as a function of arousal level. *J. Pers. Soc. Psychol.,* 1966, **3,** 54–62.

Bandura, A., Ross, D., and Ross, S. A. Transmission of aggression through imitation of aggressive models. *J. Abnorm. Soc. Psychol.,* 1961, **63,** 575–582.

Bandura, A., Ross, D., and Ross, S. A. Imitation of film-mediated aggressive models. *J. Abnorm. Soc. Psychol.,* 1963a, **66,** 3–11.

Bandura, A., Ross, D., and Ross, S. A. Vicarious reinforcement and imitative learning. *J. Abnorm. Soc. Psychol.,* 1963b, **67,** 601–607.

Bandura, A., and Whalen, C. K. The influence of antecedent reinforcement and divergent modeling cues on patterns of self reward. *J. Pers. Soc. Psychol.,* 1966, **3,** 373–382.

Bandura, A., and Walters, R. H. *Adolescent aggression.* New York: Ronald Press, 1959.

Bandura, A., and Walters, R. H. *Social learning and personality development.* New York: Holt, Rinehart and Winston, 1963.

Beck, A. T. *Depression.* New York: Hoeber, 1967.

Brown, J. S., and Jacobs, A. The role of fear in the motivation and acquisition of responses. *J. Exp. Psychol.,* 1949, **39,** 747–759.

Burgess, E. The modification of depressive behavior. In R. Rubin and C. Franks (Eds.). *Advances in Behavior Therapy.* New York: Academic Press, 1968.

Davis, A., and Dollard, J. *Children of bondage.* Washington, D.C.: American Council on Education, 1940.

Dollard, J. *Caste and class in a southern town.* New Haven: Yale Univ. Press, 1937.

Dollard, J. *Criteria for the life history.* New Haven: Yale Univ. Press, 1936. (Reprinted, New York: Peter Smith, 1949.)

Dollard, J. *Victory over fear.* New York: Reynal & Hitchcock, 1942.

Dollard, J. *Fear in battle.* New Haven: Yale Univ. Press. 1943.

Dollard, J., and Auld, F. *Scoring human motives.* New Haven: Yale Univ. Press, 1959.

Dollard, J., Auld, F., and White, A. *Steps in psychotherapy*. New York: Macmillan, 1953.

Dollard, J., Doob, L. W., Miller, N. E., Mowrer, O. H., and Sears, R. R. *Frustration and aggression*. New Haven: Yale Univ. Press, 1939.

Dollard, J., and Miller, N. E. *Personality and psychotherapy: an analysis in terms of learning, thinking and culture*. New York: McGraw-Hill, 1950.

Dweck, C. S. The role of expectations and attributions in the alleviation of learned helplessness. *Journal of Personality and Social Psychology*, 1975, **31,** 674–685.

Dweck, C. S., and Reppucci, N. D. Learned helplessness and reinforcement responsibility in children. *Journal of Personality and Social Psychology*, 1973, **25,** 109–116.

Eysenck, H. J. *Dimensions of personality*. London: Routledge and Kegan Paul, 1947.

Eysenck, H. J. The effects of psychotherapy. *J. Consult. Psychol.*, 1952a, **16,** 319–324.

Eysenck, H. J. *The scientific study of personality*. London: Routledge and Kegan Paul, 1952b.

Eysenck, H. J. *The dynamics of anxiety and hysteria*. London: Routledge and Kegan Paul, 1957.

Eysenck, H. J. Learning theory and behavior therapy. *J. Ment. Sci.*, 1959, **105,** 61–75.

Eysenck, H. J. *The structure of human personality*. London: Methuen, 1960.

Eysenck, H. J. *Case studies in behaviour therapy*. London: Routledge and Kegan Paul, 1976.

Eysenck, H. J., and Rachman, S. *The causes and cures of neuroses*. San Diego: Knapp, 1965.

Eysenck, H. J., and Wilson, G. D. *The experimental study of Freudian theories*. New York: Barnes & Noble, 1974.

Glass, D. C., and Singer, J. E. *Urban stress: Experiments on noise and social stressors*. New York: Academic Press, 1972.

Guthrie, E. R. Association by contiguity. In S. Koch (Ed.). *Psychology: a study of a science,* Vol. 2. New York: McGraw-Hill, 1959.

Harlow, H. F. The nature of love. *Amer. Psychologist,* 1958, **13,** 673–685.

Harlow, H. F., and Zimmerman, R. R. Affectional responses in the infant monkey. *Science,* 1959, **130,** 421–432.

Hetherington, E. M., and Frankie, G. Effects of parental dominance, warmth, and conflict on imitation in children. *Journal of Personality and Social Psychology,* 1967, **6,** 119–125.

Hilgard, E. R., and Bower, G. *Theories of learning*. Fourth edition, Englewood Cliffs, N. J.: Prentice-Hall, 1975.

Hiroto, D. S. Locus of control and learned helplessness. *Journal of Experimental Psychology,* 1974, **102,** 187–193.

Hiroto, D. S., and Seligman, M. E. P. Generality of learned helplessness in man. *Journal of Personality and Social Psychology,* 1975, **31,** 311–327.

Hull, C. L. *Principles of behavior.* New York: Appleton-Century-Crofts, 1943.

Hull, C. L. *Essentials of behavior.* New Haven: Yale Univ. Press, 1951.

Hull, C. L. *A behavior system.* New Haven: Yale Univ. Press, 1952.

Jakubczak, L. F., and Walters, R. H. Suggestibility as dependency behavior. *J. Abnorm. Soc. Psychol.,* 1959, **59,** 102–107.

Jonas, G. *Visceral learning: toward a science of self-control.* New York: Viking, 1973.

Jones, M. C. A laboratory study of fear: The case of Peter. *Pedagog. Sem.,* 1924, **31,** 308–315.

Kanfer, F. H., and Marston, A. R. Determinants of self-reinforcement in human learning. *Journal of Experimental Psychology,* 1963, **66,** 245–254.

Klein, D. C., Fencil-Morse, E., and Seligman, M. E. P. Learned helplessness, depression, and the attribution of failure. *Journal of Personality and Social Psychology,* 1976, **33,** 508–516.

Klein, D. C., and Seligman, M. E. P. Reversal of performance deficits and perceptual deficits in learned helplessness and depression. *Journal of Abnormal Psychology,* 1976, **85,** 11–26.

Koch, S. Clark L. Hull. In *Modern learning theory.* New York: Appleton-Century-Crofts, 1954, 1–176.

Maier, S. F., and Seligman, M. E. P. Learned helplessness: Theory and evidence. *Journal of experimental psychology: General,* 1976, **105,** 3–46.

Masserman, J. H. *Behavior and neuroses.* Chicago: Chicago Univ. Press, 1943.

Meichenbaum, D. Cognitive behavior modification. In J. T. Spence, R. C. Carson, and J. W. Thibaut (Eds.). *Behavioral approaches to therapy.* Morristown, N. J.: General Learning Press, 1976.

Miller, N. E. Experimental studies of conflict. In J. McV. Hunt (Ed.). *Personality and the behavior disorders.* Vol. 1. New York: Ronald Press, 1944, 431–465.

Miller, N. E. Theory and experiment relating psychoanalytic displacement to stimulus response generalization. *J. Abnorm. Soc. Psychol.,* 1948, **43,** 155–178.

Miller, N.E. Learnable drives and rewards. In S. S. Stevens (Ed.). *Handbook of experimental psychology.* New York: Wiley, 1951a, 435–472.

Miller, N. E. Comments on theoretical models: illustrated by the development of a theory of conflict behavior. *J. Pers.,* 1951b, **20,** 82–100.

Miller, N. E. Liberalization of basic S-R concepts: Extensions to conflict behavior, motivation and social learning. In S. Koch (Ed.). *Psychology: a study of a science,* Vol. 2. New York: McGraw-Hill, 1959.

Miller, N. E. Some reflections on the law of effect produce a new alternative to drive reduction. M. Jones (Ed.). *Nebraska Symposium on Motivation,* 1963, 65–112.

Miller, N. E. Learning of visceral and glandular responses. *Science,* 1969, **163,** 434–445.

Miller, N. E., and Banuazizi, A. Instrumental learning by curarized rats of a specific visceral response, intestinal or cardiac. *J. Comp. Physio. Psychol.*, 1968, **65,** 1–7.

Miller, N. E., and Bugelski, R. Minor studies in aggression: II. The influence of frustrations imposed by the in-group on attitudes expressed toward out-groups. *J. Psychol.*, 1948, **25,** 437–442.

Miller, N. E., and Dollard, J. *Social learning and imitation*. New Haven: Yale Univ. Press, 1941.

Miller, N. E., and Dworkin, B. R. Visceral learning: Recent difficulties with curarized rats and significant problems for human research. In P. A. Obrist (Ed.). *Contemporary Trends in Cardiovascular Psychophysiology*. Chicago: Aldine, 1974.

Miller, N. E., and Kraeling, D. Displacement: greater generalization of approach than avoidance in a generalized approach-avoidance conflict. *J. Exp. Psychol.*, 1952, **43,** 217–221.

Miller, N. E., and Murray, E. J. Displacement and conflict; learnable drive as a basis for the steeper gradient of avoidance than of approach. *J. Exp. Psychol.*, 1952, **43,** 227–231.

Miller, W. R., and Seligman, M. E. P. Depression in humans. *Journal of Abnormal Psychology,* 1975, **84,** 228–238.

Miller, W. R., and Seligman, M. E. P. Learned helplessness, depression and the perception of reinforcement. *Behaviour Research and Therapy,* 1976, **14,** 7–17.

Mowrer, O. H. A stimulus-response analysis of anxiety and its role as a reinforcing agent. *Psychol. Rev.*, 1939, **46,** 553–566.

Mowrer, O. H. On the dual nature of learning—a reinterpretation of "conditioning" and "problem-solving." *Harv. Educ. Rev.*, 1947, **17,** 102–148.

Mowrer, O. H. *Learning theory and personality dynamics*. New York: Ronald Press, 1950.

Mowrer, O. H. *Psychotherapy theory and research*. New York: Ronald Press, 1953.

Murray, E. J. A case study in a behavioral analysis of psychotherapy. *J. Abnorm. Soc. Psychol.*, 1954, **49,** 305–310.

Murray, E. J., and Berkun, M. M. Displacement as a function of conflict. *J. Abnorm. Soc. Psychol.*, 1955, **51,** 47–56.

Murray, E. J., and Miller, N. E. Displacement; steeper gradient of generalization of avoidance than of approach with age of habit controlled. *J. Exp. Psychol.*, 1952, **43,** 222–226.

Overmier, J. B., and Seligman, M. E. P. Effects of inescapable shock upon subsequent escape and avoidance learning. *Journal of Comparative and Physiological Psychology,* 1967, **63,** 28–33.

Padilla, A. M., Padilla, C., Ketterer, T., and Giacolone, D. Inescapable shocks and subsequent avoidance conditioning in goldfish (*Carrasius auratus*) *Psychonomic Science,* 1970, **20,** 295–296.

Pavlov, I. P. The scientific investigation of the psychical faculties or processes in the higher animals. *Science,* 1906, **24,** 613–619.

Pavlov, I. P. *Conditioned reflexes*. (Trans. by G. V. Anrep.) London: Oxford Univ. Press, 1927.

Rosekrans, M. A., and Hartup, W. W. Imitative influences of consistent and inconsistent reponse consequences to a model on aggressive behavior in children. *Journal of Personality and Social Psychology*, 1967, **7,** 429–434.

Rotter, J. B. Generalized expectancies for internal versus external control of reinforcement. *Psychological Monographs*, 1966, **81** (1, Whole No. 609).

Salter, A. *Conditioned reflex therapy*. New York: Creative Age, 1949.

Schlosberg, H. The relationship between success and the laws of conditioning. *Psychol. Rev.*, 1937, **44,** 379–395.

Sears, R. R. Experimental analysis of psychoanalytic phenomena. In J. McV. Hunt (Ed.). *Personality and the behavior disorders*. Vol. 1. New York: Ronald Press, 1944, 306–332.

Sears, R. R. Social behavior and personality development. In T. Parsons and E. A. Shils (Eds.). *Toward a general theory of action*. Cambridge, Mass.: Harvard Univ. Press, 1951, 465–478.

Seligman, M. E. P. *Helplessness: On depression, development, and death*. San Francisco: W. H. Freeman, 1975.

Seligman, M. E. P. Learned helplessness and depression in animals and man. In J. T. Spence, R. C. Carson, and J. W. Thibaut (Eds.). *Behavioral approaches to therapy*. Morristown, N. J.: General Learning Press, 1976.

Seligman, M. E. P., and Beagley, G. Learned helplessness in the rat. *Journal of Comparative and Physiological Psychology*, 1975, **88,** 534–541.

Seligman, M. E. P., and Groves, D. Non-transient learned helplessness. *Psychonomic Science*, 1970, **19,** 191–192.

Seligman, M. E. P., and Maier, S. F. Failure to escape traumatic shock. *Journal of Experimental Psychology*, 1967, **74,** 1–9.

Seligman, M. E. P., Maier, S. F., and Geer, J. The alleviation of learned helplessness in the dog. *Journal of Abnormal and Social Psychology*, 1968, **73,** 256–262.

Seligman, M. E. P., Rosellini, R. A., and Kozak, M. J. Learned helplessness in the rat: Time course, immunization, and reversibility. *Journal of Comparative and Physiological Psychology*, 1975, **88,** 542–547.

Skinner, B. F. Two types of conditioned reflex and a pseudo type. *J. Gen. Psychol.*, 1935, **12,** 66–77.

Skinner, B. F., and Lindsley, O. R. Studies in behavior therapy, status reports II and III, Office of Naval Research, Contract N5, ori-7662 1954.

Spence, K. W. *Behavior theory and conditioning*. New Haven: Yale Univ. Press, 1956.

Taulbee, E. S., and Wright, H. W. A psycho-social-behavioral model for therapeutic intervention. In C. D. Spielberger (Ed.). *Current topics in clinical and community psychology*. *III*. New York: Academic Press, 1971, 92–125.

Thomas, E., and Balter, A. Learned helplessness: Amelioration of symptoms by cholinergic blockage of the septum. *Science* (in press).

Thorndike, E. L. *Animal intelligence: experimental studies*. New York: Macmillan, 1911.

Thorndike, E. L. *The fundamentals of learning*. New York: Teachers College, 1932.

Tolman, E. C. There is more than one kind of learning. *Psychol. Rev.*, 1949, **56,** 144–155.

Walters, R. H., Leat, M., and Mezei, L. Inhibition and disinhibition of responses through empathic learning. *Can. J. Psychol.*, 1963, **17,** 235–243.

Watson, J. B. The place of the conditioned reflex in psychology. *Psychol. Rev.*, 1916, **23,** 89–116.

Watson, J. B. *Behaviorism*. New York: Norton, 1925.

Weiss, J. M. Effects of coping behavior in different warning signal combinations on stress pathology in rats. *Journal of Comparative and Physiological Psychology*, 1971, **77,** 1–13.

Wolpe, J. *The practice of behavior therapy*. Second edition. New York: Pergamon Press, 1973.

Wolpe, J. *Theme and variations: A behavior therapy casebook*. New York: Pergamon Press, 1976.

Wolpe, J., and Lazarus, A. A. *Behavior therapy techniques*. New York: Pergamon Press, 1966.

Wolpe, J., Salter, A., and Reyna, L. (Eds.). *The conditioning therapies*. New York: Holt, Rinehart, and Winston, 1966.

SKINNER'S OPERANT REINFORCEMENT THEORY

16

In the early part of this century the strident but powerful voice of John B. Watson had enormous impact on both academic psychology and the general public. During the past two decades B. F. Skinner has exerted a comparable influence and has advocated some of the same reforms. Skinner is an ardent behaviorist convinced of the importance of objective method, experimental rigor, and the capacity of elegant experimentation and inductive science to solve the most complex behavioral problems. He is ready and eager to apply his concepts and methods to the major concerns of our time—both practical and theoretical. An effective polemicist who has never deviated from his path to avoid a confrontation, Skinner has had a steadily increasing influence on psychology and related fields.

This position could perfectly well have been considered under the heading of Stimulus-Response theory in view of the fact that Skinner utilizes these concepts in his analysis of behavior. However, the fact that he himself rejects this label in identifying his theory, in addition to several significant differences between his position and the Hull-Spence theory, suggests the desirability of a separate treatment. One distinguishing feature is Skinner's distaste for formal theory and his rejection of Hull's postulate-theorem approach to theorizing. Another distinctive aspect of his position is a heavy emphasis on the study of responses that are not necessarily elicited by any stimulus (operants) but are strongly under the influence of the consequences of

B. F. Skinner

the responses (reinforcement). Equally unusual is Skinner's focus on the study of individual subjects instead of generalized or group trends.

The son of a small-town lawyer, Skinner was born in 1904 and raised in Susquehanna, Pennsylvania, in a warm and stable family setting. It is interesting to note what the subsequent inventor of the "Skinner box," the "baby box," and various teaching machines observes in regard to his childhood:

I was always building things. I built roller-skate scooters, steerable wagons, sleds, and rafts to be poled about on shallow ponds. I made see-saws, merry-go-rounds, and slides. I made slingshots, bows and arrows, blow guns and water pistols from lengths of bamboo, and from a discarded water boiler a steam cannon with which I could shoot plugs of potato and carrot over the houses of our neighbors. I made tops, diabolos, model airplanes driven by twisted rubber bands, box kites, and tin propellers which could be sent high into the air with a spool-and-string spinner. I tried again and again to make a glider in which I myself might fly.

I invented things, some of them in the spirit of the outrageous contraptions in the cartoons which Rube Goldberg was publishing in the *Philadelphia Inquirer* (to which, as a good Republican, my father subscribed). For example, a friend and I used to gather elderberries and sell them from door to door, and I built a flotation system which separated ripe from green berries. I worked for years on the design of a perpetual motion machine. (It did not work.) (Skinner, 1967, p. 388).

As an undergraduate he attended a small liberal arts school, Hamilton College, where he majored in English and determined to become a writer. Encouraged in various ways, including a letter from Robert Frost appraising three of Skinner's short stories, he decided to spend a year or two in fulltime literary endeavor, while living at home. This period turned out to be relatively unproductive and following a brief interval in Greenwich Village and Europe he gave up writing and turned to Harvard and psychology. Although Skinner abandoned a career in creative writing, he did not give up his interest in literature, as a number of his subsequent articles testify (Skinner, 1961).

At this time Harvard was an informal but stimulating setting for a young psychologist. Skinner does not appear to have followed in the path of any particular faculty member although he had significant encounters with many including E. G. Boring, Carroll Pratt, and Henry A. Murray. At least as significant as these interactions were the influences of his fellow graduate student Fred Keller and the distinguished experimental biologist W. J. Crozier. Skinner received his Ph.D. in 1931 and spent five post-doctoral years working in Crozier's laboratory, the last three of which were as a Junior Fellow, Harvard's most prestigious position for a young scholar. Crozier was one of a number of rigorous biologists who influenced Skinner's thought. Ohers include Jacques Loeb, C. S. Sherrington and Ivan Pavlov. Among major psychologists in his intellectual lineage are John B. Watson and E. L. Thorndike. Skinner has identified a number of philosophers of science whose writings contributed to his behavioristic position including Bertrand Russell, Ernst Mach, Henri Poincaré, and Percy Bridgman.

His first academic position was at the University of Minnesota where he moved in 1936. The nine subsequent years at Minnesota were remarkably productive and established Skinner as one of the major experimental psychologists of his time. During this period of intense scientific activity he found time to begin a novel, *Walden two* (1948), which described the evolution of an experimental society based on psychological principles. Following a brief stay at Indiana University he returned to Harvard where he has since remained. During these years Skinner was accorded many honors including the Distinguished Scientific Award of the American Psychological Association, membership in the National Academy of Sciences, and serving as the William James Lecturer at Harvard. He is one of only three behavioral scientists who have received the President's Medal of Science.

Skinner's most important single publication is easily his first volume, *The behavior of organisms* (1938), which continues to be a major source of intellectual influence many years after publication. His volume entitled *Science and human behavior* (1953) provides an introduction to his position and illustrates its application to a wide variety of practical problems. A detailed analysis of language in terms of his concepts is contained in *Verbal behavior* (1957) and an early example of programmed learning is offered by Holland and Skinner (1961). His most important articles prior to 1961 are contained in a collection of papers entitled *Cumulative record* (1961). An interesting account of his intellectual development is provided in his autobiography (Skinner, 1967) and his book *The technology of teaching* (1968) has detailed his approach to learning in the school setting. *Contingencies of reinforcement* (1969) involves a restatement of Skinner's scientific position including its relevance for broad social problems. In *Beyond freedom and dignity* (1971), probably his most controversial book, Skinner argues that the concepts of *freedom* and *dignity* are hindrances to the improvement of modern society. His recent book *About behaviorism* (1974) summarizes Skinner's views on the brand of psychology that is practically synonymous with his name. *Particulars of my life* (1976) is the first half of Skinner's two-volume autobiography. He is currently writing the second volume as well as another book.

In addition to his capacity to influence (and to infuriate!) with the written word, Skinner has had a major impact upon psychology by means of a large number of gifted students who have carried on and extended his work. Among the best known of these are Nathan H. Azrin, Donald S. Blough, William K. Estes, Norman Guttman, Richard J. Herrnstein, Ogden R. Lindsley, William H. Morse, and Herbert Terrace.

What can we say in general terms regarding Skinner's position and its distinctive features? First of all, it would be difficult to find a theorist who was less enthusiastic about being cast in the role of theorist than Skinner. In spite of his enormous theoretical influence he has until recently *questioned the contribution of theory to scientific development* and has looked on his own work as illustrating an informed and systematic empiricism that operates without theoretical derivation. He has consistently opposed any attempt to fill in the gap between observed events with inferred or hypothesized variables. His intent has been to gather behavioral laws with no "explanatory fictions" at all. This point of view is particularly well illustrated in two papers entitled "Are theories of learning necessary?" (1950) and "A case history in scientific method" (1956).

One may also note that this *theory owes as much to the laboratory* as any other theory discussed in this volume. Skinner's principles are derived from precise experimentation, and he shows more careful respect for well-controlled data than any comparable theorist. It is an easy matter to state that rewards have something to do with learning, and it is not particularly difficult to demonstrate repeatedly under carefully controlled conditions that this is true in a number of different settings. It is another matter, however, to identify precisely highly regular relations between particular patterns of reinforcement and carefully specified response measures. In his studies of *reinforcement schedules* Skinner has done just this and has provided findings that have a regularity and specificity that rival those of any physical scientist. He has shown that particular patterns (schedules) of reinforcement generate characteristic and highly replicable changes in rate of responding, both in sustained responding and in extinction.

Skinner differs markedly from the average experimental psychologist in his *concern for the individual subject*. His results are typically reported in terms of individual records. It is not enough that his studies produce average results that concur with expectation and future observation. The behavioral law or equation must apply to each subject observed under appropriate conditions. Attention to the individual applicability of every finding or law is particularly valuable in a discipline where the investigator often does not look beyond group data to see whether there are many, if any, individual subjects whose behavior conforms to group generalizations.

Although many psychologists have focused on responses that appear largely under stimulus control (reflexes, for example), Skinner has chosen to direct his attention toward emitted instead of elicited responses. This *emphasis upon operants* rather than respondents, to use Skinner's terminology, constitutes another distinctive feature of his approach to the study of behavior. He also believes that psychology should properly *focus on simple behavioral events* before attempting to understand and predict the complex events.

Although he has emphasized the study of individual organisms and simple responses, Skinner assumes that the findings of this research have broad generality. In his words: "I suggest that the dynamic properties of operant behavior may be studied with a single reflex (or at least with only as many as are needed to attest to the general applicability of the results)" (Skinner, 1938, pp. 45–46). Skinner believes that the same general principles of behavior will be uncovered regardless of what organism, stimulus, response, and reinforcer the experimenter chooses to study. Thus, the pigeon and the laboratory provide a paradigm that can then be extrapolated and extended to the widest variety of other organisms and situations.

Consistent with the last observation is the fact that Skinner's approach to the study of behavior, his laws, and technology have been used in a *broad range of applied settings*. Skinner and his students have dealt significantly with practical problems such as missile control (Skinner, 1960), space technology (Rohles, 1966), behavioral assay of psychoactive drugs (Boren, 1966), educational technology (Skinner, 1968), the development of experimental cultures or societies (Skinner, 1961), the treatment of psychotics, autistic children, and the mentally retarded (Krasner and Ullmann, 1965), and child development (Bijou and Baer, 1966). Consequently, although in one respect Skinner is the "purest" of all the theorists under consideration he is also a theorist whose work has had very wide application in diverse behavioral domains.

We have seen something of the origins and general qualities of Skinner's austere formulations, and we shall now examine his conceptions and their application in somewhat more detail.

SOME GENERAL CONSIDERATIONS	Let us begin with an examination of some of the basic assumptions and attitudes that underlie Skinner's work. Although *the assumption that behavior is lawful* is implicit in all psychological research it is often not make explicit, and many of its implications remain unrecognized.

Skinner, like Freud, deserves recognition for his constant emphasis on the orderliness of behavior, and, perhaps more significantly, for communicating his belief in this lawfulness to a large segment of society. By means of his writings and refined experiments, Skinner has persuaded many that the principle of determinism applies to human beings and raises serious questions concerning our conception of a human being as a free agent with certain goals in life. For example, Skinner continually points out that once we accept this principle the apportioning of blame or responsibility for actions has little meaning. One individual commits serious crimes, another performs deeds in the service of humanity. Both classes of behavior result from the interplay of identifiable variables that completely determine behavior. An individual's behavior is entirely a product of, and can be understood purely in terms of, the objective world. In principle, and Skinner believes in practice also, an individual's actions can be considered just as lawful as the movement of one billiard ball when it is struck by another ball.

Of course, all personality theorists covertly assume that behavior is lawful. But Skinner has drawn out the implications of this assumption so that the ordinary person can understand them. The following quotation clearly illustrates Skinner's views:

Science is more than the mere description of events as they occur. It is an attempt to discover order, to show that certain events stand in lawful relations to other events. No practical technology can be based upon science until such relations have been discovered. But order is not only a possible end product; it is a working assumption which must be adopted at the very start. We cannot apply the methods of science to a subject matter which is assumed to move about capriciously. Science not only describes, it predicts. It deals not only with the past but with the future. Nor is prediction the last word: to the extent that relevant conditions can be altered, or otherwise controlled, the future can be controlled. If we are to use the methods of science in the field of human affairs, we must assume that behavior is lawful and determined. We must expect to discover that what a man does is the result of specifiable conditions and that once these conditions have been discovered, we can anticipate and to some extent determine his actions.

This possibility is offensive to many people. It is opposed to a tradition of long standing which regards man as a free agent, whose behavior is the product, not of a specifiable antecedent condition, but of spontaneous inner changes of course. Prevailing philosophies of human nature recognize an internal 'will' which has the power to interfere with causal relationships and which makes the prediction and control of behavior impossible. To suggest that we abandon this view is to threaten many cherished beliefs—to undermine what appears to be a stimulating and productive conception of human nature. The alternative point of view insists upon recognizing coercive forces in human conduct which we may prefer to disregard. It challenges our aspirations, either worldly or otherworldly. Regardless of how much we stand to gain from supposing that human behavior is the proper subject matter of science, no one who is a product of Western civilization can do so without a struggle. We simply do not want such a science (Skinner, 1953, pp. 6–7).

In *Beyond freedom and dignity* (1971), Skinner suggests that, in analyzing behavior, the layperson typically attributes a causal role to the environment for some behaviors but not for others. If a supervisor is in the factory, it is easy to attribute a worker's good performance to the supervisor's presence. We give more credit to a worker who is equally industrious in the absence of the supervisor, because in this case the causes of behavior are less obvious. Thus the amount of credit we give a person tends to be inversely related to the conspicuousness of the causes of his or her behavior. Skinner argues that the worker's behavior is lawful whether or not its causes are obvious to the casual observer, and giving credit to the individual for their actions only impedes the search for the factors controlling their behavior.

The assumption that all behavior is lawful clearly implies the possibility of behavioral control. All that is required is to manipulate those conditions that influence or result in a change in behavior. There can be some disagreement about whether control necessarily implies understanding or explanation, but on a purely practical level Skinner prefers to use the term control because its meaning is clear. Skinner is not much interested in those aspects of behavior that are strongly resistant to change, those governed primarily by hereditary endowment for example. The types of behavior that he studies are those that seem most plastic, and for which one can assume that change can be brought about by manipulation of those kinds of environmental variables that normally interact with the person. Skinner's interest in behavior stems not only from a curiosity about how behavior works, but also from an intense desire to go about the job of manipulating it. The word control is used in part because it correctly reflects this conviction. Skinner has frequently argued that the ability to manipulate behavior, if handled properly, can be used for the betterment of all.

The question now arises as to how control is most likely to be achieved. Skinner believes that a *functional analysis* is most appropriate. By a functional analysis Skinner means *an analysis of behavior in terms of cause and effect relationships,* where the causes themselves are controllable, that is, stimuli, deprivations and so on. Psychologists often use the terms independent variable and dependent variable in this context. An independent variable is one that is manipulated by the experimenter, and a dependent variable is a variable that may change as a result of this manipulation. Skinner contrasts the functional analysis of behavior with an analysis that seeks only to establish correlations between dependent variables instead of causal relationships. In the establishment of correlations, as in the classification of traits, we might find, for example, that people who are very aggressive tend also to be very intelligent. But we do not claim to show how the aggressive disposition or the intelligence can be encouraged or discouraged. We are only connecting effect with effect and are not disovering antecedent variables that give rise to either characteristic. Thus, although we may be able to predict behavior to some degree because we can measure intelligence and predict aggressiveness, we are given no indication of which variables to manipulate in order to heighten or reduce aggressiveness.

Skinner has consistently argued that behavior can best be studied by considering how it is related to antecedent events. This is an argument accepted by many psychologists. Skinner has also argued that in a functional analysis of behavior *there is no necessity to talk about mechanisms operating within the organism*. He believes that behavior can be explained and controlled purely by the manipulation of the environment that contains the behaving organism, and that there is no need to take the organism apart or make any inferences about the events that are going on inside the organism. This argument is not popular among psychologists outside of Skinner's sphere of influence.

To begin to understand his position it is helpful to see what Skinner says about some of the commonly used causal explanations of behavior that rely on internal events as the antecedent in a cause and effect relationship. Suppose a man walks into a restaurant, briskly calls the waiter, and orders a hamburger. When the hamburger is delivered he wolfs it down, without pausing to reply to conversation addressed to him. We ask why is the man eating? One common explanation of his behavior is that he is hungry. But how do we know that the man is hungry? We only know that the man engages in a number of activities that tend to be associated and that tend to occur following the same kinds of environmental conditions. But in using this description we are not recognizing an event of being hungry that is antecedent to eating; instead, the act of hurried eating is part of what we mean by being hungry. The term "being hungry" may simply describe the collection of activities that are associated with an identified independent variable (food consumption), much as the term "playing baseball" is a term used to encompass the activities of pitching, batting, fielding, and so on. Each of these activities could be explained by pointing to the sequence of events prior to the baseball game. But the activities are not explained simply by describing them as part of the playing of baseball. We do not say that an individual is pitching simply because he is playing baseball. Playing baseball is not an event antecedent to pitching, rather pitching is a part of "playing baseball."

Objecting to this line of reasoning we might claim that the term "being hungry" is used to label an event antecedent to eating (number of hours since last meal), and that "being hungry" is a cause of eating. In this sense, "being hungry" can be used as a causal link between food deprivation and the behavior that occurs in the restaurant. We then have the problem of how this causal link is to be identified and what properties are to be ascribed to it.

Two solutions to this problem are common. One solution is to give the event of "being hungry" a place in a mental universe, to assign it nonphysical status. This is frequently done, and gives rise to the conception of the outer person and the inner person. The outer person, or behavioral person as he might be called, is driven and controlled by the inner metaphysical person. The conception is illustrated in day to day statements such as "He failed to perform adequately because of mental fatigue," or "She failed because she was not attending to the task." Or even more clearly, "He managed to do it only through a tremendous exercise of will power." These statements give the impression of providing an explanation of behavior because they seem to refer to events that are antecedent to the behavior under consideration. Of course, it is true that these events are supposed to occur in a nonphysical world; the way in which they are able to influence physical events is not made at all clear. The more serious objection to this type of explanation is that when the events are looked at more closely it is found that they have no identifying properties other than their capacity to produce the behavior to be explained. The same kind of explanation is put forward by primitive people when they account for the movement of the sun by some human controlling force, when the only evidence they have for the existence of the controlling force is the movement of the sun itself. A controlling force can be manufactured to explain the occurrence of any conceivable event. The emptiness of this type of explanation is most easily seen when we ask ourselves how much more confidently an effect can be predicted now that the cause of it is isolated. Then we find that there is no isolation, the cause is not separable from the effect, for there is no property of the cause other than its production of the effect.

Usually an explanation of behavior in terms of a mental event is put forward when there is ignorance of the physical events important in the production of the behavior. Skinner believes it is a most harmful type of explanation simply because it has a misleading appearance of being satisfactory and therefore tends to retard the investigation of those objective variables that might yield genuine behavioral control.

Another status we might ascribe to "being hungry" is physiological. We might look for stomach contractions, the concentration of sugar in the blood, the activation of brain centers, and so forth. In a physiological explanation the causal antecedents of behavior could be isolated; and there would be no claim that mental events influence physical events. Skinner does not take such a firm stand against physiological explanations; he believes that behavior might ultimately be predicted by tracing the effects of an environmental variable through the entire sequence of physiological events by which it is followed. However, Skinner emphasizes that a science of behavior does not necessarily require a knowledge of physiological processes in order to be viable; he believes that even when we do understand these processes practical control of behavior will be exercised by the manipulation of "traditional" independent variables that lie outside the organism. Thus Skinner sees no reason why we should not treat the human organism as an unopened—but not empty—box with various inputs and outputs, and he believes that such a treatment will yield the most efficient control of those outputs. As we shall see when we look at Skinner's experimental work, his views are given strong support by the success of his approach thus far.

As we have noted, Skinner has a program for a descriptive science, for to link dependent variables to independent variables with no intervening steps leads only to laws or universal hypotheses, and not to theories. The distinction between these is not always very clear, but in one of his discussions that deals with whether theories are necessary in science Skinner attempts to explain what constitutes a theory. The following quotation shows that he uses the term to describe a system that relates one set of observations to another set of observations by an inferred set of events or constructs that are described in terms other than those describing the observations, and that are themselves not presently observed.

Certain basic assumptions, essential to any scientific activity, are sometimes called theories. That nature is orderly rather than capricious is an example. Certain statements are also theories simply to the extent that they are not yet facts. A scientist may guess at the result of an experiment before the experiment is carried out. The prediction and the later statement of result may be composed of the same terms in the same syntactic arrangement, the difference being the degree of confidence. No empirical statement is wholly nontheoretical in this sense because evidence is never complete, nor is any prediction probably ever made wholly without evidence. The term theory will not refer here to statements of these sorts but rather to any explanation of an observed fact which appeals to events taking place somewhere else, at some other level of observation, described in different terms, and measured, if at all, in different dimensions (1953, p. 26).

Skinner's approach is based on the assumption that behavior is orderly, and that our primary purpose is to control it. Moreover, this control can be achieved best by lawfully relating independent variables or inputs into the organism to dependent variables or outputs of the organism, and then controlling subsequent behavior by the manipulation of those same inputs (environmental events) in such a way as to obtain a particular output (response).

THE STRUCTURE OF PERSONALITY
Of all the personality theorists to be considered in this volume Skinner has shown much the greatest indifference to structural variables. This is not surprising in view of what has already been said concerning his general approach to the study of behavior.

Skinner focuses primarily on modifiable behavior. Consequently, he takes little interest in the behavioral characteristics that seem to be relatively enduring. This attitude is mainly a consequence of his emphasis on control of behavior. Prediction and explanation may be achieved by knowledge of the enduring and modifiable aspects of personality. But control is achieved only through modification; control implies that the environment can be varied in order to bring about different behavior patterns. However, Skinner never asserts that all the factors that determine behavior lie in the environment. In the first place, he argues that an organism's sensitivity to reinforcement itself has a genetic basis, having evolved because of the survival advantages of being able to learn about important events in the environment. Secondly, Skinner states that, in any given species or individual, some behaviors may be more easily conditioned than others. He also recognizes that some behaviors may have a completely genetic basis, so that experience will have no effect on them. Skinner sees a parallel between the hereditary and environmental bases of behavior—he suggests that the process of evolution shapes the innate behaviors of a species just as an individual's learned behaviors are shaped by the environment. Nevertheless, he warns that genetic explanations of behavior should be viewed with caution, both because the evolutionary factors that determined the form of an innate behavior are not observable, and because many behaviors thought to be innate might actually have been shaped by experience (Skinner, 1969). It should be clear that Skinner does not claim that an individual's behavior is only a product of the environment. He simply deemphasizes the practical importance of biological variability, because, in a purely behavioral science, this variability cannot easily be placed under behavioral control.

In selecting response variables, Skinner is primarily concerned with their simplicity and their lawful or regular association with environmental variation. The major classification of behavior that Skinner has suggested is the distinction between *operant* and *respondent*. This distinction primarily involves the difference between responses that are elicited and those that are emitted. As we have seen, the focus of Skinner's concern is on the operant that is emitted in the absence of any eliciting stimulus. A respondent, on the other hand, is elicited by a known stimulus and is best illustrated by a response such as the pupillary reflex or the knee-jerk reflex where there is a known and relatively invariable response associated with a specified stimulus. We shall have more to say about this distinction subsequently.

THE DYNAMICS OF PERSONALITY

Although Skinner shuns structural concepts he shows only a mild distaste for dynamic or motivational concepts. He recognizes that a person does not always exhibit the same behavior to the same degree when in a constant situation, and he believes that general recognition of this is the principal reason for the development of our concept of motivation. Inasmuch as behavior tends to be highly variable in some situations, an internal force is assumed to account for this variability. We see, for instance, that a child does not always eat the food presented to it, and therefore we say that its eating depends not only on the presence of the food but also on variation in the degree of hunger. On the other hand, we find that the knee-jerk reflex is elicited with about the same vigor on each occasion that the knee is struck. Thus we feel no need to postulate a variable knee-jerk drive because there is no unexplained variability in the vigor or frequency of the reflex.

As we have already suggested, Skinner believes that even when behavior shows this type of variability it is still unnecessary and often misleading to postulate an internal energizing force, for when this is done the question still remains as to how the intensity of this force is governed. For example, one asks for the cause of the child's hunger. An answer to this question is necessary, because only then can we estimate the intensity of the force so that a prediction can be made about the vigor of the associated behavior. Skinner points out that a satisfactory answer must at some stage involve discovery of an environmental variable to which the internal force is linked, just as hunger, for example, is linked to the deprivation of food. Why bother to account for behavioral variability in terms of an internal state, whose intensity must be calculated on the basis of knowledge about variation in the environment? Why not simply concern oneself with the environmental variable and account for the behavior directly? Following this argument, Skinner goes on to treat the variability in the vigor of behavior just as he treats any other aspect of behavior—as a direct causal consequence of the variation in an independent variable.

The argument just presented might lead one to believe that those variables that govern the *drive* or motivational states of other theorists assume no special position in Skinner's system. But this is incorrect, for they do have a special property, but it is not the property of being internal causes of behavior. We find that certain variables affect the probability of occurrence of whole groups of behavior patterns. For example, consider the case of thirst. Thirst can be increased by several different operations and in turn may influence a number of different responses. The temperature of the room in which an animal is enclosed can be increased, thereby causing the animal to discharge water by sweating more profusely; or the time elapsed since the animal was previously allowed to drink can be increased; or the animal can be induced to eat foods that have high salt contents. Each of these operations will increase the animal's thirst. By this we mean that each of these operations increases the likelihood that the animal will engage in one or more of a group of activities all of which are affected by any of this same group of operations. Thus, the animal will perform a learned response more vigorously if it produces water, a response such as pressing a lever, or running through a maze, for example, and it will drink more vigorously, choose water instead of food, or any other responses that have been followed by water in the past. These examples show that in saying that certain operations increase thirst we are only saying that these operations tend to increase the occurrence of specific responses. In summary, Skinner uses a term such as thirst simply as a convenient verbal device that acquires meaning through its ability to encompass the relation between a group of independent and dependent variables—and the term acquires no meaning other than that. Skinner does not ascribe a causal status to thirst; the causal status is ascribed to the operations that result in drinking behavior. It is important to note that unlike many other reinforcement theorists Skinner does not consider drives to represent a class of stimuli.

There are other terms that can be treated like drives because they are utilized for linking a group of independent variables to a group of dependent variables. These terms belong to the area of *emotion*. Skinner makes no real distinction between drives and emotions, and he uses these terms and justifies their use in the same way. Consider the example of an angry person. We do not know that a person is angry because we have had access into her mind, or because we have observed that certain glands are secreting certain substances. Instead, we have noted that such a person exhibits particular behavioral characteristics. She adopts a stern expression, speaks curtly, is disposed to aggressive behavior, and so on. Similarly, we know that a person is afraid because he stammers, starts easily, is tense, and shows various aversive responses. Such behavior might be observed when we see a student waiting outside a professor's office following a poor performance in an examination. We note aspects of the student's behavior, and then, because of our observation of some other associated behavior, or because we know the student's examination score, we judge the student to be afraid. The student need not be afraid when we see him stammering. He could be stammering because of an inherent defect in his vocal apparatus. But we judge him to be afraid because of the particular independent (environmental conditions) and dependent (response) variables with which the stammering is associated. To exhibit this particular association is to be afraid.

Thus, Skinner employs a set of concepts that might be called dynamic or motivational. These concepts, similar to the motivational concepts in other theories, are employed to account for the variability of behavior in otherwise constant situations. However, in Skinner's system they occupy a distinct category because they relate groups of responses to groups of operations, not because they are equated with energy states, purpose, or any other condition that implies they are causal antecedents of behavior.

Most of Skinner's position is concerned with behavioral change, learning, and modification of behavior; consequently one can say that his theory is most relevant to the development of personality. With many other theorists, Skinner believes that an understanding of personality will develop from a consideration of the behavioral development of the human organism in continuing interaction with the environment. Consistently, this interaction has been the focus of a large number of carefully managed experimental studies. A key concept within Skinner's system is the principle of reinforcement; indeed, Skinner's position is often labeled *operant reinforcement theory*.

To reinforce behavior is simply to carry out a manipulation that changes the probability of occurrence of that behavior in the future. The finding that certain operations change the probability of occurrence of responses in a lawful manner is credited primarily to two early leaders in the study of behavioral modification, I. P. Pavlov and E. L. Thorndike. Pavlov discovered the principle of reinforcement as it applies to classical conditioning. It can be illustrated with a famous example. Suppose that on a number of occasions a bell is sounded in

THE DEVELOPMENT OF PERSONALITY

the presence of a hungry dog, and suppose also that on each of these occasions the sound of a bell is immediately followed by the presentation of meat to the dog. What do we observe? On each presentation of the bell and meat combination the dog salivates. But at first the dog salivates only when the meat is presented and not before. Later, however, salivation begins to occur as soon as the bell is sounded—before the presentation of the meat. At this stage the salivary response is conditioned to the sound of the bell, and we find that the presentation of the meat immediately following the sound of the bell is the critical operation responsible for this conditioning. Thus the presentation of the meat is a reinforcing operation. It strengthens the likelihood that the salivary response will occur when the bell is sounded on a later occasion. Furthermore, because its presentation increases the chances of salivation it is classified as a positive reinforcer.

Following the development of a strong conditioned response, an experimenter might wish to see what happens when the conditioned stimulus is consistently presented without its being followed by the reinforcing stimulus. In the example outlined above the bell would be sounded but no meat would follow. What happens then is that the conditioned response extinguishes. That is, its frequency of occurrence and its magnitude decline with successive soundings of the bell, until finally no salivation is elicited by the bell at all. The conditioned response is then completely extinguished. *Extinction is the decrease in responding that occurs when the reinforcement following the response no longer occurs.*

Skinner points out that a characteristic of classical conditioning is the fact that a readily identifiable stimulus can be located that elicits the response even before conditioning begins. For instance, in the example considered above, the stimulus provided by the meat elicits salivation. As we have noted, Skinner calls such a response a *respondent* to emphasize the strong eliciting role played by the preceding stimulus. Another characteristic of this situation is that the reinforcer is manipulated in temporal association with the stimulus to which the response is being conditioned, while the response, if any, comes later. Conditioning is most effectively carried out when the reinforcer follows the conditioned stimulus, regardless of whether the response has occurred or not.

Skinner accepts the existence of classical conditioning and its dependence on the principle of reinforcement, but he is less concerned with it than with another type of learning that also relies on the principle of reinforcement. The other type of learning, which was first systematically investigated by Thorndike, is called instrumental or *operant* conditioning.

Many early investigators believed that all learning involved the process of classical conditioning. But Skinner noted that there was much that could not be fitted into this paradigm. There are some responses that, unlike respondents, do not appear to be tied to a readily identifiable eliciting stimulus—such responses as painting a picture, or crossing a street, for example. These responses seem to be spontaneous and voluntary. Another property of this kind of behavior, that again differentiates it from respondent behavior, is that its frequency of occurrence is changed according to the event that follows. More specifically, the strength of one of these responses increases when the response occurs and is followed by reinforcement. This peculiarity of this class of responses gives rise to Skinner's use of the term "operant." *An operant is a response that operates on the environment and changes it.* The change in the environment affects the subsequent occurrence of the response. In operant conditioning, therefore, the reinforcer is not associated with an eliciting stimulus as it is when respondents are conditioned. Instead it is associated with the response. When a salivary response is conditioned to the sound of a bell, the presentation of the meat does not depend on the prior occurrence of the response. On the other hand, when an operant response is conditioned, it is essential that the reinforcer be presented *after* the occurrence of the response. Only in this way does the frequency of the response increase.

Let us take a very simple example of operant conditioning. We can teach a child to ask for candy frequently by giving candy whenever it asks for candy. We positively reinforce the response of asking for candy. We can also extinguish the response of asking for candy by simply not presenting the candy when the child asks for it. We then find that the frequency of occurrence of asking for candy declines. There is another way that we can reduce the occurrence of the response. When the child asks for candy we can punish it by slapping it. When we perform an operation like this, of adding something to the situation that reduces the probability of responding, we say that we have punished the response. A *punishing stimulus* is an aversive stimulus, which, when occurring after an operant response, decreases the future likelihood of that response.

The general principles that Skinner relies on to account for the modification of behavior have now been explained. These principles derive from a massive amount of carefully controlled research, and they have been found to have wide applicability. It may seem that they are overly simple and that they have nothing to do with the development of personality. However, Skinner argues persuasively that a personality is nothing but a collection of behavior patterns, and that when we ask about the development of personality we ask only about the development of these behavior patterns. Skinner believes that we can predict, control, and explain these developments by seeing how the principle of reinforcement has worked to account for the present-day behavior of an individual as a result of the reinforcement of previous responses.

Because the principle of reinforcement is so important, it is necessary to consider the development of a particular response in detail and show how it can be manipulated with the use of the operant techniques. Suppose that we put a hungry pigeon into a small well-illuminated chamber that is isolated from the external environment by sound-proofed and opaque walls. Such a chamber is frequently called a Skinner box (although not by Skinner) and it represents an important engineering accomplishment. It shields the subject from much uncontrolled environmental variation, and it also permits mechanical or automated control of both stimulus events and the recording of responses.

On one wall of this chamber, about ten inches from the floor, is a transluscent disc that can be illuminated from behind by a red light. The disc is connected by an electrical switch to the external apparatus that records and controls the events occurring in the box. The apparatus is wired so that whenever pressure is applied to the disc a response is recorded and food is delivered to the pigeon in a hopper fixed to the wall of the chamber just below the disc. The pigeon can apply suitable pressure to the disc by pecking it, and this is the response we want to develop and control.

In order for the pigeon to peck the disc for the first time we *shape* its behavior. The probability of the pigeon pecking the disc on a "random" basis is very small indeed, and clearly we cannot increase the probability by the action of the food reinforcer until that response has first occurred. The pecking response is shaped by reinforcing successive approximations to the pecking response. First we train the bird to eat from a food hopper when it is opened. This behavior is readily conditioned and the sight of the open hopper becomes a stimulus for eating. Then, we present food only when the bird is near the disc. This increases the probability that the bird will again stand near the disc. Then we present food only when the bird raises its head when standing near the disc; then when its beak is in a striking position with respect to the disc, and so forth. Eventually, by means of these successive approximations the bird will peck the key for the first time. Food is, of course, delivered immediately. Shortly after this the bird will probably peck the disc again, and food can again be delivered. If reinforcement is then presented on each occasion that the bird pecks, pecking will soon be occurring quite rapidly. This is referred to as a *continuous reinforcement* schedule. However, if the food hopper is no longer operated when the bird pecks, then the rate of pecking declines, and in a very short time it is reduced to a rate similar to that observed when the bird was first put into the chamber. Pecking scarcely occurs at all; the previously reinforced response has been extinguished.

Suppose that instead of never operating the hopper, we operate it on fewer occasions. For example, the apparatus may be programmed so that food is available if the pigeon pecks following a certain period of time such as five minutes. If the reinforcement is contingent on an interval of time it is referred to as *interval reinforcement;* if this interval is unchanging (for example, every five minutes or every ten minutes), we have a *fixed interval* reinforcement schedule. Instead of providing reinforcement following a constant interval of time the investigator may wish to reinforce according to an intermittent or *variable interval* schedule. Here, although the reinforcement may be available on the average at five minute intervals the actual interval will vary randomly around this average. Thus, at each moment there is a low and constant probability that food will be available. Under these conditions the pigeon responds with a steady rate of pecking. Most of these pecks are not reinforced but those that are reinforced serve to maintain the over-all response rate. If the food hopper is disconnected so that pecking is no longer reinforced, the pecking response again extinguishes. This time it does so at a much slower rate than when reinforcement was continuous and many more pecks are emitted before extinction is complete.

A schedule of reinforcement can also be established in which temporal factors are unimportant and where the number of rewards obtained by the bird depends only on its own behavior (responses). This is called a *ratio reinforcement* schedule. Here the reinforcement is determined only by the number of pecks that have been emitted since the last reinforcement. In the very first example, each peck was reinforced. It is a simple matter to change this so that only every tenth peck is reinforced or every twentieth or any other number. This would be referred to as *fixed ratio* reinforcement. Or perhaps the number might vary on a random basis, just as the time intervals varied in the previous example, so that reinforcement might on the average be given after every fifth peck but in actuality be randomly distributed around this average. On some trials the reward might follow the second or third peck while on others it would follow the seventh or eighth. This would be called a *variable ratio* schedule. These ratio schedules are analogous to the situation of a piece worker or person working on a commission where the payoff depends only on the efficiency and effort of the worker. A variable ratio schedule is at the heart of all gambling systems and devices. It is worth noting that the extinction process is much slower with ratio schedules than it is with interval schedules. Also significant is the fact that variable or intermittent reinforcement tends to make a learned response more resistant to extinction.

The importance of these various schedules is that on the one hand they show correspondence to many learning situations of interest to the personality investigator or theorist and on the other hand they relate to particular patterns of acquisition and extinction of the responses being learned. A great deal of systematic work has been done by Skinner and his associates in describing the effects of a wide variety of schedules. We have already commented on some of the differences between the various schedules and there are many more generalizations available for the interested reader (Ferster and Skinner, 1957; Skinner, 1969).

In attempting to understand the generality and significance of the reinforcement principle it is important to note that it is not necessary for a response to physically produce the reinforcement for it to be reinforced. Ordinarily, for experimental purposes, an experimental apparatus is set up so that a reinforcer is produced by a response through its effects on the apparatus. This ensures that it is the one particular response in which we are interested that is reinforced. We could, however, simply deliver "free" reinforcements quite independently of the subject's behavior. Suppose we operate the food hopper every ten or fifteen seconds. When the hopper first operates the bird will be involved in some particular movement sequence, perhaps pacing in a circle in the center of the chamber. The fact that the hopper comes up immediately following a set of movements such as this ensures that the set of movements will be repeated shortly—although that behavior did not produce the reinforcer it was immediately followed by the reinforcer. It can easily be seen that this difference would not be relevant to the laws relating responses to reinforcement, because from the pigeon's point of view there is no way to ever determine whether a response is simply followed by the operation of the hopper, accidentally as it were, or whether a response caused the operation of the hopper. Suppose the probability of pacing round the cage is increased. This means that this behavior sequence is likely to be occurring when the hopper is operated next time, and so the sequence will again be reinforced. In this manner, pacing behavior may acquire considerable strength. It is unlikely that pacing will be followed by the operation of the hopper on every occasion that it occurs, but as we have previously seen, the intermittent reinforcement of responses actually contributes to the production and maintenance of extremely stable behavior.

This type of conditioning, in which there is no causal relation between the response and the reinforcer, is sometimes referred to as "superstitious behavior." Skinner believes that it accounts for many of the superstitions held by humans. The members of a primitive tribe may practice rain-making by the performance of some ritualized dance. On some occasions rain does happen to follow the performance. Thus the rainmaking dance is reinforced and tends to be repeated. The natives believe that a causal connection exists between the dance and the production of rain. Actually the dance is accidentally conditioned, the rain occasionally happens to follow the dance. The same type of behavior can be seen with superstitious people who carry lucky charms, rabbits' feet, and other talismans. It may even be the case that the generally superstitious person is distinguished from the less superstitious person by the fact that many instances of accidental conditioning have, by chance, figured to a relatively large extent in that person's life history. Another example that may be viewed in the same light is the supposed power of prayer. Occasionally prayers are "answered." Accidental conditioning can account for an increased frequency of praying without supposing that prayers actually produce any effect.

The fact that a chance reinforcement following a response is sufficient to ensure the strengthening of that response is not generally recognized, and, as a result, serious consequences sometimes arise. For example, a nurse might work in a hospital ward with mentally disturbed children. One child might appear to be relatively normal and quiet for most of the time, and the nurse turns her attention to other patients or duties. But perhaps when this occurs, the child begins to scream and violently bang its head against the wall. At this the nurse is quite likely to rush over to the child, kiss and embrace it, utter soothing words, and in general respond in an affectionate manner as she tells the child not to engage in such behavior. Under these conditions, we should not be surprised if the frequency with which the child engages in the abnormal behavior increases instead of decreases during its stay in the ward. It is fairly clear that the response of screaming and banging the head against the wall is reinforced by affection, kind words, and physical contact, actions that have for some time been established as positive reinforcers. The nurse misunderstands the effect of her own behavior. Parents do the same thing when they give attention to a normal child only when it cries for attention, or seeks attention in some irritating or anti-social way.

Let us turn again to one of the simplest cases of operant conditioning, in which the pecks made by a pigeon to a red disc are reinforced by the presentation of food in a hopper. Suppose that when the pecking response is firmly established, and the food-filled hopper has been presented a number of times, a new response is made available—perhaps the depression of a small foot pedal. The foot pedal is inserted into the chamber, and the apparatus is programmed so that one depression of the pedal causes the *empty* food hopper to be presented. At the same time the red disc is covered up so that the pigeon is unable to see or peck at it. Following this kind of operation it is consistently found that the pigeon presses the foot pedal a very large number of times. What has happened is that the presentation of the hopper acquired reinforcing properties in the first part of the experiment when it was consistently experienced as part of the stimulus complex associated with food. Because of this association the hopper becomes a *conditioned* or *secondary reinforcer*. The hopper is a reinforcer because its presentation increases the rate of emission of a response, in this case the depression of a pedal, and it is a conditioned reinforcer because its power to do this depends on its association with another reinforcer. The maintenance of the reinforcing properties of the hopper also depend on a continuing association of the hopper with another reinforcer; if food is permanently omitted from the hopper its conditioned reinforcing properties extinguish and the rate of pedal pressing declines. However, these properties can easily be restored by once again pairing the hopper with food.

Skinner believes that conditioned or secondary reinforcers are of great importance in the control of human behavior. It is obvious, at least in the affluent Western societies, that not every action is maintained by the presentation of the unconditioned or primary reinforcers such as food, water, and sex. On the basis of animal experimentation, which has demonstrated that stimuli can acquire reinforcing properties, it is possible to reason that much of human behavior relies on conditioned reinforcement. The most common example of a conditioned reinforcer is money. Money is a good example not only because it clearly has no intrinsic value of its own but also because it is a generalized conditioned reinforcer. It has been paired with a number of different unconditioned or primary reinforcers, and consequently is reinforcing under a wide variety of drives. The extremely generalized reinforcing effect of money is ultimately based on the fact that it is associated with a large number of other reinforcers. Learning theorists today do not play down the role of conditioned reinforcement as they did in the recent past. It is an explanatory concept that is heavily relied on. Thus the notion of conditioned reinforcement is important in Skinner's system, and, as we shall see later, he uses it effectively to account for the maintenance of many responses that occur as part of our social behavior.

The notion of *stimulus generalization* is also important in Skinner's system, as it is in all of the personality theories that derive from learning theory. In the pigeon experiments that we have described, the bird pecked at a red disc. A further experiment that can be carried out after the response to the red disc has become stabilized is the manipulation of the color of the disc across the wavelength spectrum. If this is done there occurs a very orderly change in the rate of pecking. As the color projected on the disc moves further away from the color at which the bird was trained to peck, so the rate of responding declines. With colors that are very near to red in the spectrum the bird's rate of pecking is almost as high as the rate of pecking to red.

Other aspects of the situation besides the color of the disc could be changed and in most cases the same effect would be obtained. Perhaps the brightness of the lights that illuminate the chamber might be changed or the shape of the stimulus. Again a decline in response rate would occur systematically as the stimulus shifted more and more away from its original state. This phenomenon is important for several reasons. First, it shows that a response may be emitted in a situation that is slightly different from the one in which it was originally reinforced. Second, it demonstrates that the strength of that response suffers some decrement in such a changed situation, and, if the situation is sufficiently different from the training situation, the response fails to occur. No person is ever in exactly the same situation twice. However, a situation in the real world may be slightly different from another situation and still be likely to yield the same reinforcement for the same response. Hence it is adaptive for the original stimulus situation to generalize to the new situation. If animals did not show stimulus generalization learning could never be exhibited. On the other hand, it is clearly not adaptive for an animal to completely generalize from one situation to all others. Very different situations do call for different behavioral responses. If perfect stimulus generalization occurred and the animal were to transfer a response to all situations regardless of their similarity to the original situation, inappropriate responses would constantly occur. Indeed there would be no learning and no reason to suppose that one response would occur instead of another. Thus it is important that the person shows *stimulus discrimination*.

One should note that Skinner does not define either stimulus generalization or stimulus discrimination in terms of perceptual or other internal processes. He defines each of them in terms of response measures in a well-controlled experimental situation. To the extent that the response is maintained in a new situation there is some degree of stimulus generalization. To the extent that the response is decreased or weakened there is stimulus discrimination. The animal discriminates (fails to respond in the presence of the new stimulus) to the extent that it fails to generalize (does respond to the new stimulus).

Stimulus discrimination can usually be enhanced by alternately presenting the animal with one stimulus, for example, the red disc, in the presence of which responding continues to be reinforced, and then presenting the animal with another stimulus, for example, a green disc, in the presence of which responding is nonreinforced. Responding in the presence of the red disc is then maintained by the action of the reinforcer, while responding in the presence of the green disc, although perhaps starting out at some high generalized rate, is extinguished. The procedure simply shows that the stimulus control of pecking may be considerably enhanced by appropriate training.

Most aspects of personality are demonstrated in a social context, and social behavior is a very important characteristic of human behavior in general. We shall now consider social behavior in humans in order to grasp the flavor of how Skinner uses the findings of his refined experimental work with lower animals to reach certain conclusions about personality development in humans. First, we should note that Skinner assigns no special significance to social behavior as distinct from other behavior. Social behavior is characterized only by the fact that it involves an interaction between two or more persons. Apart from this, it is not considered distinct from other behavior because Skinner believes that the principles that determine the development of behavior in an environment surrounded by inanimate or mechanical objects also determine behavior in an environment surrounded by animate objects. In each case the developing organism interacts with the environment, and as a part of that interaction receives feedback that positively or negatively reinforces or punishes that behavior. Perhaps social responses and the reinforcers appropriate to them are somewhat more subtle or difficult to identify than is behavior occurring in nonsocial situations, but this in itself indicates no important difference of principle between the two types of response.

One interesting point about social behavior, however, is that the reinforcers that a person receives usually depend entirely on the person's behavioral output. In discussing conditioning in the pigeon, we noted that ratio schedules were constructed so that the pigeon's rate of reinforcement could increase indefinitely with a greater and greater output of responses. Social behavior is most frequently reinforced according to the ratio principle. A child is rewarded for remaining quiet with candy, or with a conditioned reinforcer such as affection or a smile, and the more the child remains quiet, the more he or she is reinforced. In adult society one is normally reinforced for being polite. A shake of the hand or a friendly greeting are both likely to produce the social reinforcement of a friendly gesture on the part of another, and in some cases may lead to a better job, or perhaps an increase in social status.

When we talk about certain aspects of a person's personality in the context of social behavior, we ordinarily refer to general types of behavior instead of to specific responses. But so far, in looking at Skinner's system, we have only considered the development of particular responses such as a lever press or uttering a particular word or phrase. How is this involved in the understanding of a submissive, an anxious, or an aggressive personality? Skinner would argue that the terms normally used to describe personality traits have meaning only because they are ultimately reducible to the description of a range of specific responses that tend to be associated together in a certain type of situation. Thus in determining whether a person is socially dominant, we note his conversation in a group setting, observe him in interaction with a series of individuals, secure his responses to a number of specific items describing relevant situations, and so forth, and arrive at an over-all rating or judgment. Each of the *particular* responses tells us something about a person's dominance. The fact that specific responses tend to be associated in certain situations probably depends on their selective reinforcement as a group. A person acquires the general trait of dominance because some group, perhaps his or her family, has placed a high premium on a class of responses in its delivery of reinforcement.

Responses tend also to be associated with one another by virtue of the fact that they are functionally interchangeable. A person one meets for the first time may shake one's hand, or give a verbal greeting. In either case that person is behaving in a friendly manner and is likely to be reinforced in the same way no matter which response is emitted. At previous times, each response in that type of situation may easily have been reinforced equally often. Because of this, each response will be likely to occur on the present occasion, and the difference in their controlling stimuli that makes for the emission of one instead of the other may be so subtle that in practice the occurrence of the one particular response cannot be predicted. In these cases we would only go so far as to predict the general characteristics of the behavior that we expect to occur.

It is of interest to note that the same situation does not necessarily produce the same behavior in different individuals. An example of this is the person seeking a raise from their employer. One person may present himself in an aggressive manner, another may do it in a very friendly, or even obsequious, manner. If we looked into the background of the person who reacts aggressively in the superior's office we should find that aggressive behavior had been reinforced most frequently in the history of that individual, and probably reinforced in a larger variety of situations. In the case of the other individual aggressive behavior might have been punished by aversive consequences, and obsequious behavior might have been positively reinforced. To the extent that the previous situations, which generated these behaviors, are similar to the situation in which the employees ask for a raise we expect these two different and opposite categories of behavior to be in evidence. Of course, in this situation only one of the approaches may work—perhaps only the person with an obsequious manner gets the raise. That person's behavior will then be reinforced, while that of the aggressive individual will be nonreinforced. However, the aggressive manner of the nonreinforced individual may undergo little change. Most behavior outside the laboratory is reinforced only intermittently, and, as we saw in the case of the pigeon, intermittent reinforcement generates very stable and persistent behavior. Almost definitely, the history of reinforcement in the aggressive individual will have been intermittent and the amount of extinction of the aggressive behavior, which occurs as a result of this one nonreinforcement, will probably be very slight. Also, when the two individuals ask for a raise under other circumstances, perhaps from another employer, the aggressive approach might be the successful one, thus reversing the contingencies of reinforcement. This raises another complicating factor. One individual may show a much greater capacity for discrimination between the two types of employer, and the person's behavior might eventually become adjusted so that it is more often appropriate to differing situations. This person might be said to have the ability to assess people and adjust his or her own behavior in accordance with his assessment. In Skinner's system the processes involved in this would be those of differential reinforcement and discrimination.

Not surprisingly a number of clinical psychologists have adopted the basic attitudes and approach characteristic of Skinner. They have found that this framework can be used to understand normal development and it can also be applied to the study and control of pathological behavior. Abnormal behavior is assumed to be the same in its principles of development as normal behavior. In putting forward a program for the treatment of abnormal behavior, Skinner repeatedly asserts that the goal is simply to replace abnormal behavior with normal behavior, and this can be achieved by the direct manipulation of behavior. In dealing with abnormal behavior, Skinner does not appeal to the actions of repressed wishes, an identity crisis, conflicts between ego and superego, or other constructs—all of which he would label as explanatory fiction. Rather, he attempts to modify the undesirable behavior by manipulation of the environment in a manner determined by the techniques of operant and respondent conditioning.

Suppose that a soldier, initially of average courage, is shot and wounded in battle. Then he is hospitalized, and when he recovers he is again sent to the front line. When this happens the soldier develops a paralyzed arm, or perhaps becomes blind. A physical examination reveals no deficiency in either the nerves and muscles of the arm, or of the relevant sensory equipment. However, this apparently uncaused physical disability has the effect of releasing the soldier from his obligation to go to the front line, for blindness or paralysis ensures that the man is sent to a hospital or committed to relatively inactive duty.

Skinner would analyze this situation very simply. The injury received by the soldier is aversive, and so has negatively reinforcing properties. That is, it is a stimulus whose *withdrawal* increases the strength of the response that it immediately follows. That the injury is a stimulus of this type seems to be fairly obvious because it is reasonable to expect, for instance, that when the soldier is in the hospital he will behave in a manner appropriate to ridding himself of the injury as quickly as possible. In carrying out the doctor's orders the soldier effectively escapes from the injury. It can also be expected, given the principle of classical or respondent conditioning, that the stimuli associated with the onset of the injury will have come to possess some of its negative properties. A stimulus that is associated with the onset of a negative reinforcer becomes a conditioned negative reinforcer.

We can return to a simple animal experiment for an analogy. Suppose a rat is enclosed in a cage with a grid floor that can be electrified. The rat is shocked through the grid floor every so often and the shock is turned off only when the rat jumps over a little hurdle dividing the cage. Very soon we find that the response of jumping over the hurdle quickly follows the onset of the electric shock. This happens because each jump over the hurdle, which at first occurs only after much random action, is reinforced by the termination of a negative reinforcer, and having thus been reinforced occurs more readily on subsequent occasions. A conditioned negative reinforcer can be set up very easily. A buzzer is introduced into the situation so that its onset precedes each shock by several seconds. This will be sufficient to ensure that the buzzer acquires conditioned reinforcing properties. But to make the analogy with the case of the soldier more complete, the experimental program is changed so that a jump over the hurdle, following the onset of the buzzer, terminates the buzzer and switches off the shock that would have occurred subsequently. In this situation the rat is likely to end up by jumping over the hurdle on almost every occasion that the buzzer is presented. This leads to avoidance of shock. However, we can analyze the behavior of the rat without referring to avoidance at all by supposing that the buzzer has become a conditioned negative reinforcer through the process of classical conditioning, and that jumping over the hurdle is the response reinforced by termination of the negative reinforcer. Just as we can describe the rat as escaping from the shock in the original situation, so we can describe it as escaping from the buzzer in the modified situation.

Insofar as the case of the soldier is analogous to this, it can be seen that the stimuli associated with the injurious event that occurred in battle would acquire negative reinforcing properties. Thus, the soldier would be likely to engage in behavior that is followed by the termination of these stimuli. One type of behavior that would be reinforced in such a way would be the response of simply refusing to enter into the battle area. This could be interpreted as showing escape from the battle associated stimuli, but in ordinary language it would probably be described as avoidance of possible future injury.

It is very likely that such escape behavior would lead to social rejection and/or a court martial—with aversive consequences that in themselves would constitute punishment, such as a long prison term, or perhaps even the death penalty. Thus, when the soldier begins to take the obvious escape route of disobeying orders, his behavior, although leading to an escape from the aversive stimuli associated with his injury, would in itself produce other aversive stimuli based on the consequences of the court martial or social rejection. Behavior followed by an increase in aversive stimulation tends to be reduced in frequency—we say that such behavior declines in frequency because it is punished. The path that involves the disobeying of orders is not, therefore, likely to be taken. What will happen is that some behavior will emerge that terminates both sets of conditioned negative reinforcers, and this behavior will be reinforced and maintained. A paralysis of the arm or blindness satisfies these conditions because in most armies a soldier is not held responsible for these behavior patterns and their emergence is not punished. The fact that this type of route is taken follows directly from a consideration of the principles formulated by Skinner.

Notice that in the above analysis there is no reference to what the soldier is thinking, feeling, or trying to do. Neither is there any mention of conscious or unconscious processes, or physiological processes. The analysis makes use of the laws of respondent (classical) and operant conditioning, and depends only on observed operations and behavior. It does not have recourse to variables operating at other than a behavioral level, or to any kind of hypothetical theoretical construct.

The question now arises as to how the soldier is to be cured. There are several general ways of doing this that can be used to eliminate many different varieties of abnormal behavior. Let us return to the rat experiment. Suppose that the apparatus is now programmed so that the buzzer continues to be regularly presented, but it is no longer ever followed by the electric shock, regardless of the animal's behavior. When this change is first introduced and the buzzer is presented, the rat jumps the hurdle and terminates the buzzer sound. But after a few trials no jump occurs—and no shock occurs. The situation can be analyzed in this way. When the buzzer is regularly presented and is not followed by shock, as occurs when the rat terminates the sound of the buzzer and avoids the shock, or when the shock has been discontinued, then the conditioned aversive properties of the buzzer become reduced. Remember that in discussing classical conditioning it was pointed out that the conditioned salivary response extinguished if the sound of the bell was not followed by the presentation of meat. Similarly, in the present situation, the classically conditioned negative reinforcing properties of the sound of the buzzer will extinguish when it is not followed by shock. Then, since the conditioned reinforcing properties of the sound of the buzzer are being reduced, the operant response of terminating it is less likely to occur, because this response is being reinforced only by termination of a negative reinforcer whose strength is gradually weakening. The problem with this method is that extinction of such an avoidance response is often extremely slow. The animal may jump the hurdle for hundreds or thousands of trials after the shock is discontinued (Solomon, Kamin, and Wynne, 1953). Similarly, if the soldier were exposed to the stimuli associated with the battle without subsequent unconditioned negative reinforcement, these stimuli would lose their negatively reinforcing properties, and the paralysis or blindness should extinguish. However, the soldier is very unlikely to volunteer to return to the battlefield.

An alternative approach to this problem is to prevent the avoidance response from occurring, a procedure sometimes called *flooding* (Baum, 1970). If a barrier is constructed so that the rat cannot jump the hurdle, the buzzer will be presented without the shock, and the conditioned aversive properties of the buzzer will quickly extinguish. In the same way, requiring the soldier to return to the battle despite his paralysis or blindness should cause the aversive properties of the stimuli of the battlefield to extinguish if no further unconditioned aversive events occur.

Another way to cure the soldier is to shape some other response that is not considered to be abnormal and that terminates the conditioned negative reinforcer. The soldier could, for instance, be allowed to discharge himself from the army without fear of a penalty. Following this, the paralysis of his arm would presumably disappear. Or, the soldier could be told that he would be placed on inactive duty regardless of the condition of his arm. This would be functionally equivalent to a discharge. In either case the soldier escapes from the conditioned negative reinforcer without having to make the responses that result in paralysis.

One cure that would probably not succeed would be to punish the soldier. Suppose the soldier were to be punished whenever the paralysis showed signs of becoming worse. In that case the paralysis might disappear, but only to be replaced by some other response that was equally abnormal. The reason for the occurrence of a new response would be the same as that which accounted for the occurrence of the paralysis. It would be a response such as blindness or loss of speech whose strength would be increased because its occurrence was followed by the termination of negative reinforcement (being returned to battle). Punishment would be unlikely to work because it would not result in the substitution of a normal response for an abnormal response, nor would it extinguish the conditioned reinforcing properties of the stimuli associated with battle.

It has often been said, in criticism of Skinner, that this type of analysis of abnormality, and its cure by psychotherapy, is the analysis and cure of symptoms instead of causes. The internal causes, mental or physiological, are neglected and only the symptom is treated. Such therapy seems to disregard underlying forces which then exert their influence through some other behavioral outlet. However, when these cures are inadequate they are so because the psychotherapist has failed to understand properly the principles of behavior modification, or has failed to look adequately into the patient's history to determine the antecedents of the undesirable behavior. Indeed the existing evidence in regard to symptom substitution under these conditions indicates that such an outcome is not very likely (Krasner and Ullmann, 1965).

We have already examined a number of respects in which the work of Skinner and his followers deviates from the contemporary norm. Among these characteristics are the intensive study of individual subjects, the automated control of experimental conditions and recording of subjects' responses, and a focus on simple behavioral events that can be modified with appropriate environmental manipulation. Here we shall expand on certain aspects of this approach and provide a few illustrations of research programs carried out by Skinner and his students. There are several excellent source books for the person wishing to examine the research of Skinner and his followers in more detail, including volumes edited by Honig (1966) and Honig and Staddon (1977), Skinner's own *Cumulative record* (1961), and a personality text (Lundin, 1969).

Skinner's emphasis on individual subjects in experimentation has already been noted. Associated with this is the elimination of undetermined influences that might affect the subject's behavior. Other experimenters who work with animals, and whose primary interest is in the learning process, typically use large groups of animals in their experiments. This enables them to be little concerned with uncontrolled variables, provided they are randomly distributed. Skinner argues that if there are uncontrolled variables that affect behavior they should not be neglected, for they merit study as much as any other variables. Furthermore, Skinner feels that our aim should be directed to the control of behavior in the individual subject. If large groups of animals have to be used in an experiment, then for Skinner this is an admission of failure. If the effects of an intentional manipulation of an independent variable obviously are being masked by a great deal of "noise" or "random" variability, this clearly shows that control is not being adequately exercised. Under such conditions, Skinner would put aside the idea of manipulating the original independent variable, at least for the moment, and proceed instead to try to uncover the hidden variables that are causing the variability. Such an investigation can provide some understanding of controlling variables in their own right, and, if successful, can give one an idea of how to reduce the variability that has intruded. Attention can then be turned back to the effects of the original variable, and experimentation can proceed under more orderly conditions.

Once the stability of a response has been obtained, a typical operant reinforcement theorist would determine a baseline against which to assess the changes in responding that might occur as a result of the manipulation of an independent variable. Usually, the baseline measure consists of a record of the rate of emission of a simple response such as pecking a disc, or, in the case of the rat, pressing a lever. For example, an experimenter might train a pigeon to peck at a disc and then maintain responding with an intermittent reinforcement schedule. This has been found to produce baseline rates of responding that are stable, durable, and also fairly sensitive to the effects of introduced variables. One variable that might be introduced, for example, is a brief period of intense noise superimposed during the pecking. The effects of this would be measured as a change in the ongoing pecking rate. Probably, the pecking rate would decline during the first presentation of the noise, but with successive presentations it would decline less and less, and then finally would not be affected at all. The experiment would be reported as showing the effects of the independent variable of noise on the dependent variable of the pecking response. This simple example illustrates the general method of experimentation typically employed.

In practice it might have proved impossible to generate stable rates of responding in individual subjects. But Skinner has been extremely successful in achieving this end. Because of his emphasis on individual subject experimentation, he has managed to reduce substantially uncontrolled sources of influence on experimental subjects. This has been partly due to the use of the soundproofed and light controlled Skinner box for housing subjects during experimentation. This simple device very effectively isolates the organism from influences that are not directly controlled by the experimenter.

One area in which Skinner's influence has become pronounced is that of *psychopharmacology,* or the study of drugs and behavior. The Skinner box has proved to be an admirable tool for all types of precise work involving the observation of behavior following the administration of pharmacological agents. Suppose the behavioral effects of a particular drug are being investigated. A rat is first trained to press a bar in the Skinner box by reinforcing bar pressing according to some intermittent reinforcement schedule. After a number of sessions of such training the rate of bar pressing becomes stable. It does not vary much between sessions or within sessions. The drug is then administered to the rat before the beginning of a new session, and *during the course of that one session,* the time of onset of drug effects, its effect on behavior, and the duration of that effect can all be determined. Moreover, all this can be done with one experimental subject, although ordinarily there would be replications. In psychopharmacological studies the effects of drugs on timing behavior, perception, fear, avoidance and appetitive responding among others have all been studied. The Skinner box allows an experimenter to investigate these independently under very similar basic conditions. Up to the present time no method of animal experimentation has even approached that used by the Skinnerians for isolating particular aspects of behavior and studying the effects of drugs on them.

One drug that has been extensively investigated with this method is chlorpromazine, a drug widely used in the treatment of psychotics. This drug has been tested for its effect on the rate of bar pressing when that response is reinforced by the avoidance of an electric shock. The rate of bar pressing decreases. The most obvious conclusion to be drawn from this is that chlorpromazine reduces fear. This conclusion fits in nicely with some of the usual theories of the properties of the drug. However, in similar studies that differ only in the respect that responding is reinforced by the production of food pellets, exactly the same effect is obtained. Bar pressing is depressed (Boren, 1966). Presumably no fear or punishment is involved in such a study, and results thus suggest that it is not reasonable to assert that chlorpromazine selectively removes fear. Instead it seems to act as a general depressant and all types of responding are reduced. The picture is further complicated by the fact that this drug, similar to many other drugs, changes its mode of action with different dosages. In very small dosages chlorpromazine increases response rates.

Another interesting example is the study by Blough (1957) showing that the threshold for visual perception in the pigeon is lowered following the administration of LSD. The general technique for determining a visual threshold illustrates the ingenuity that the Skinnerians have shown in obtaining sophisticated experimental control. An experimental organism, for example, a pigeon, is presented with a stimulus panel that can be illuminated from behind by a spot of light that can be varied in its intensity. The idea of the experiment is to get the pigeon to "tell the experimenter when it can see the spot and when it cannot see the spot." This can be done in such a manner that the bird not only gives this information but also causes the intensity of the spot to vary continuously around its visual threshold. Two response discs are inserted into the wall of the chamber, one of these discs is labeled "disc A," the other is labeled "disc B." The bird is trained to peck at disc A when the spot is visible and at B when the spot is not visible. Pecks at A drive the intensity of the light downward, by means of a controlling apparatus, and pecks at B drive the intensity upward. Continuous responding is maintained by a schedule of intermittent reinforcement. Reinforcement is made available following a peck at B when the experimenter occasionally shuts off the light from the stimulus panel. Under these conditions, the experimenter knows that the bird fails to see the spot. Effectively, therefore, the bird pecks at A to "turn out the light" and at B "to get the food." Using this method, a very good measure of the bird's threshold can be obtained. Whenever the spot is no longer visible the bird stops pecking at A and begins pecking at B. Pecks at B then increase the physical intensity of the spot and again makes it visible, and the bird reverts to pecking at A. Thus the bird's responses track the changes in light intensity about a threshold, and also control the light intensity so that it deviates little from this threshold. In Blough's experimentation with LSD, the time of onset of the drug following its administration before effects were observed the fact that the drug lowered the threshold, and the duration of the effectiveness of the drug were all determined.

A significant example of the application of operant conditioning techniques in a mental hospital setting is provided by a series of studies by Ayllon and Azrin (1965, 1968). These investigators, working with a group of chronic psychotics who were judged to be unresponsive to conventional methods of therapy and unlikely to be discharged, were able to establish a "token economy" that was effective in manipulating the behavior of the patients in a socially desirable manner. The general procedure involved identifying some form of response such as feeding oneself satisfactorily or carrying out a work assignment and then associating the desired response with a reinforcer. The term "token economy" refers to the fact that tokens were introduced to serve as conditioned reinforcers bridging the gap between the time when the desired response was emitted and when the unconditioned reinforcement (cigarettes, cosmetics, clothing, attending a movie, social interaction, privacy, and so on) was presented. Ayllon and Azrin were able to show that when a particular type of response, such as completing a work assignment, was associated with the conditioned reinforcement (token payment) this response could be maintained at a high rate but that when the reinforcement was removed the rate of response immediately fell off although it could be reinstated by restoring the reinforcement contingency. In their words:

The results of the six experiments demonstrate that the reinforcement procedure was effective in maintaining desired performance. In each experiment, the performance fell to a near-zero level when the established response-reinforcement relation was discontinued. On the other hand, reintroduction of the reinforcement procedure effectively maintained performance both on and off the experimental ward (1968, p. 268).

Token economies have also been used extensively in classroom settings wih such populations as normal children, delinquents, and severely retarded children. Tokens may be awarded for proper classroom behaviors like remaining seated, paying attention, and completing assignments. The tokens can later be exchanged for candy, movies, periods of free play, or whatever reinforcers a particular child happens to value (Kazdin and Bootzin, 1972). The results of these and many other studies make it clear that the systematic and skillful use of reinforcement can produce dramatic and beneficial behavioral changes even in the very seriously disturbed. Moreover, these changes are highly lawful and conform precisely to what the principles of operant conditioning lead us to expect.

Many of these principles have been employed by Lovaas and his colleagues in their attempts to teach language to autistic children (Lovaas, et al., 1966). Autistic children usually do not engage in any form of communication, and they display bizzare and often self-destructive behaviors. Lovaas uses punishment to eliminate self-mutilative behaviors and extinction procedures to eliminate other undesirable but less dangerous behaviors. The language-training program is based on the concepts of shaping, reinforcement, generalization, and discrimination. For example, a child may initially be rewarded with a piece of candy for any vocalizations. Such vocalizations are then shaped into a word—*doll,* for example. Once several words are learned in this way, discrimination training is used to teach the child to produce each word (*doll, truck,* etc.) in the presence of the appropriate stimulus object. The child is taught by several different instructors in an effort to promote the generalization of language habits to other individuals. These procedures are slow and tedious, but more and more complex language skills can be taught in this way. Such training programs are not free from problems, and follow-up reports have been mixed. In general, children who lived with their families continued to improve, whereas those placed in institutions sometimes returned to their autistic behaviors. Despite these difficulties, all children showed some improvement in behavior as a result of their training (Lovaas, et al., 1973).

One of the most unusual applications of the operant approach was carried out by Skinner (1960) himself in an attempt to devise a means of controlling the flight of a missile. During World War II and for ten years thereafter, a variety of studies were carried out under governmental support that were intended to demonstrate the feasibility of employing pigeons as the means of guiding a missile to a predetermined target. This fantasy from science fiction involved nothing more than using operant techniques to train one or more pigeons. The subjects were taught to respond by pecking at a patterned stimulus that represented the missile target—a ship, a section of a city, or a profile of land. When the missile was on target the pigeon would peck in the center of the display area, where the image was presented, and this would continue the missile on its current course. When the missile deviated, the pecks of the pigeon, following the image of the target, would move to another area of the display and this would activate a control system that would adjust the course of the missile. Thus, let us say, when the target moves to the left and the pigeon would peck an area left of the center the missile would turn to the left. The investigators found that following appropriate schedules of reinforcement the pigeons would peck accurately, rapidly, and for amazingly long periods of time. In order to minimize the possibility of error they even devised multiple guidance systems that involved three or seven pigeons. Although the pigeons never guided any real missiles onto real targets, their simulated performance was such that Skinner could accurately state:

The use of living organisms in guiding missiles is, it seems fair to say, no longer a crackpot idea. A pigeon is an extraordinarily subtle and complex mechanism capable of performances which at the moment can be equalled by electronic equipment only of vastly greater weight and size, and it can be put to reliable use through the principles which have emerged from an experimental analysis of its behavior (Skinner, 1960, p. 36).

CURRENT
STATUS AND
EVALUATION

There is no question that at the present time Skinner's operant reinforcement theory is remarkably robust. Whether we use the criterion of number of devoted followers, amount of carefully executed research, or breadth of application the theory not only compares favorably with alternative positions but also shows an accelerating increase in its impact. One concrete example of this growing interest is the flourishing *Journal of Experimental Analysis of Behavior,* which was established in 1958 and is devoted to the publication of experimental contributions derived from or bearing on Skinner's position. Articles examining a wide range of practical applications of the Skinnerian approach fill the volumes of the *Journal of Applied Behavior Analysis,* established in 1968. Equally significant is the Division for the Experimental Analysis of Behavior of the American Psychological Association, which includes more than a thousand psychologists, elects its own officers, and arranges for speakers and programs of research papers at the annual convention of the APA. There are also a number of graduate training programs where the bulk of the students are trained in the techniques and approach of operant reinforcement theory. It is obvious that at present this position is strongly represented within American psychology and that its influence is on the increase.

We have already agreed that Skinner's position shares much in common with other S-R theories and thus it should come as no surprise that many of the same virtues and criticisms apply to both theories. Among the many shared, positive features are the firm anchoring in well-controlled laboratory data, the detailed specification of the learning process, and a willingness to resolve differences by means of experimentation rather than exhortation.

Not only has Skinner's influence led to a vast amount of relevant experimental research, it has also led to a fascinating series of applications. One might argue that no other theory of personality has had so substantial an impact upon such a *diverse array of area of application.* As we have seen, operant conditioning has become widely applied in clinical settings—both in individual psychotherapy and in establishing ameliorative group settings. In the area of animal training, whether for entertainment purposes or serious scientific and engineering goals, Skinner and his students have proven to be by far the most adept and accomplished. Indeed, one may fairly argue that only this group has been able to take untrained animals and in a systematic and predictable manner shape their behavior in the view of the general public. In many business and industrial settings operant techniques have proven valuable, including particularly the pharmacological industry where the assessment of drug effects on behavior has advanced with the very substantial participation of the techniques and the students of Skinner. Perhaps most extensive of all is the influence that operant conditioning has had on education through the development of teaching machines and programmed learning material. These methods, resting on the basic elements of Skinner's approach to learning (building complex responses out of many simple responses and associating reinforcement closely in time with the response to be learned), have become commonplace in educational systems all the way from preschool settings to post-graduate studies.

It is clear that Skinner would rank with the most idiographic of personality theorists in his emphasis on the importance of *studying individuals in detail* and stating laws that apply fully to single subjects instead of only to group data. Related to this emphasis on the individual is the fact that the findings reported by Skinner and his students present a degree of lawfulness or precise regularity that is virtually unparalleled among psychologists. This combination of elegant laboratory technique and precise experimental control with the study of individual subjects represents a unique achievement. Generally those who have emphasized study of the individual have been short on rigor and experimental finding.

A notable achievement of this group is their systematic study of *schedules of reinforcement.* Their voluminous findings in this area have provided the empirical basis for predicting the acquisition and extinction of learned responses with a much greater degree of exactness than had been previously possible. Moreover, their classifications of different types of schedules has made possible generalizations to a wide variety of situations and subjects. Recent research in this tradition has pursued still greater precision through mathematical analyses of the rates of behavior under different reinforcement schedules (Herrnstein, 1970). It should be noted that the results of the research on schedules of reinforcement are of crucial importance for all learning theorists and investigators whether or not they adopt Skinner's approach.

The forcefulness, clarity, and explicitness of Skinner's position has made it relatively easy to identify those aspects of the theory that are laudable as well as those features that appear objectionable. No one could ever accuse Skinner of trying to avoid controversy or to smooth over differences with his contemporaries. If there are significant differences between Skinner and other major theorists one may be sure that these differences have been highlighted and his position stoutly defended.

Perhaps the criticism most widely leveled at Skinner and his students is that *his theory is no theory* at all and, moreover, that he has little appreciation for the nature and role of theory in the building of science. As we have seen, Skinner typically has been in full agreement with this characterization of his position. He has felt it is not a theory and he does not believe that science, particularly at the stage occupied by psychology, is likely to be aided by devoting time to theory building. Thus, for those who believe that there is no such thing as "no theory," that one can choose only between good and bad or between explicit and implicit theory, there has been an irreducible gap between their conception of the scientific process and that which is espoused by Skinner. This gap has been substantially reduced with the publication of *Contingencies of reinforcement* (1969) in which he has quite explicitly accepted his role as a systematic theorist.

In a paper published in 1950 I asked the question "Are theories of learning necessary?" and suggested that the answer was "No." I soon found myself representing a position which has been described as a Grand Anti-Theory. Fortunately, I had defined my terms. The word "theory" was to mean "any explanation of an observed fact which appeals to events taking place somewhere else, at some other level of observation, described in different terms, and measured, if at all, in different dimensions"—events, for example, in the real nervous system, the conceptual system, or the mind. I argued that theories of this sort had not stimulated good research on learning and that they misrepresented the facts to be accounted for, gave false assurances about the state of our knowledge, and led to the continued use of methods which should be abandoned.

Near the end of the paper I referred to "the possibility of theory in another sense," as a critique of the methods, data, and concepts of a science of behavior. Parts of *The Behavior of Organisms* were theoretical in that sense, as were six published papers, in the last of which I insisted that "whether particular experimental psychologists like it or not, experimental psychology is properly and inevitably committed to the construction of a theory of behavior. A theory is essential to the scientific understanding of behavior as a subject matter." Subsequently I was to discuss such a theory in three other papers and in substantial parts of *Science and Human Behavior* and *Verbal Behavior* (Skinner, 1969, vii–viii).

In his system, Skinner has consistently rejected as an explanatory device any of the forms of ghostly mental machinery which many of us, deliberately or inadvertently, use to account for human behavior. In doing this he has performed a great service. But as we have seen Skinner also rejects the idea of introducing any type of inferred mechanisms into his system, even those that can be adequately tested by deriving noncontradictory explanations and explicit predictions. From this, one may anticipate that Skinner will have difficulty predicting the behavior that occurs in a situation consisting of combinations of novel stimuli or new configurations of familiar stimuli. This is because Skinner can only base his expectations of future behavior on the laws of behavior that already have been formulated. In other words, the laws of behavior can only be extrapolated to instances of the same type of behavior that they cover in the general case, because the system contains no theoretical statements that imply more empirical assertions than those on which they have been built.

Skinner's system is one that avoids asking what goes on inside the box, and therefore Skinner cannot make predictions in situations that are not directly covered by the laws of the system. However, Skinner fully recognizes this fact and defends the attitude that gives rise to it. In his classic paper "Are theories of learning necessary?" Skinner (1950) points out that although theorizing might lead us to novel expectations this in itself is no virtue unless those expectations are confirmed. And, although it is likely that someone will eventually come up with a workable theory that provides the correct expectations, this may be after many years of unproductive research that has involved the testing of nonfruitful theories in various trivial ways. Any new situation will eventually be investigated anyway and so there is certainly no *need* for theorizing. Behavior in such a situation will eventually be brought into the system even in the absence of a theory.

As we have seen, Skinner is a believer in the value of a molecular approach to the study of behavior. He searches for simple elements of behavior to study and he is certain that the whole is no more than the sum of its parts. Consequently, it is no surprise to discover that holistic psychologists of all varieties are convinced that Skinner's approach to the study of behavior is *too simplistic and elemental* to represent the full complexity of human behavior. These critics argue that human behavior shows characteristics that necessarily exclude significant areas of it from Skinner's analysis. Essentially, this is because behavior is much more complex than the kind of analysis that Skinner makes leads one to suppose. Skinner attempts to explain complex behavior by assuming that many response elements are built into larger units, and he also assumes that complexity develops from the simultaneous operation of many variables. But it is exactly Skinner's method of integrating behavioral elements that is questioned. At the very least, many observers feel that Skinner's system fails to account for the "richness" and "complexity" of behavior that is so characteristic of the human.

Human language is one example of the type of behavior many feel is not susceptible to analysis by Skinner's concepts. Some powerful arguments and data have been advanced to show that the nervous system, if it develops normally, is particularly receptive to the acquisition of a set of rules that generates theorems that we call sentences. This implies that a language is not acquired through long chains of stimulus-response terms, each one being learned by repetition and reinforcement, but instead is generated from a set of axioms and rules that can produce an appropriate sentence even when that sentence has not been emitted previously. Similar to geometry, the rules of language may generate theorems or sentences that have no historical relationship to other sentences occurring in the past. Linguists, such as Chomsky (1959), have particularly emphasized this point. These arguments, which are intimately bound up with the idea that certain response patterns cannot be analyzed into elemental sequences, have been advanced most prominently in connection with language, but some psychologists believe they are equally relevant to the analysis of many other types of behavior.

It is clear, from what has been said, that Skinner generally experiments with relatively simple organisms, with relatively simple histories, and under relatively simple environmental conditions. Rarely is the subject exposed to variations in more than one variable at a time. Critics sometimes say that this is an *artificial* type of *experimentation,* that such simple situations never occur outside the laboratory, and that because of this, behavior must necessarily be really much more complex than the Skinner box would lead us to believe. In reply, Skinner argues very effectively that science characteristically proceeds in a piecemeal manner. It almost always looks to simple phenomena first, and builds up complex phenomena in a step by step manner through an appropriate manipulation and integration of the laws that have been derived from the most simple or clear cases in which they operate. The following quotation from Skinner is instructive.

Have we been guilty of an undue simplification of conditions in order to obtain this level of rigor? Have we really "proved" that there is comparable order outside the laboratory? It is difficult to be sure of the answers to such questions. Suppose we are observing the rate at which a man sips his breakfast coffee. We have a switch concealed in our hand, which operates a cumulative recorder in another room. Each time our subject sips, we close the switch. It is unlikely that we shall record a smooth curve. At first the coffee is too hot, and sipping is followed by aversive consequences. As it cools, positive reinforcers emerge, but satiation sets in. Other events at the breakfast table intervene. Sipping eventually ceases not because the cup is empty but because the last few drops are cold.

But although our behavioral curve will not be pretty, *neither will the cooling curve for the coffee in the cup*. In extrapolating our results to the world at large, we can do no more than the physical and biological sciences in general. Because of experiments performed under laboratory conditions, no one doubts that the cooling of the coffee in the cup is an orderly process, even though the actual curve would be very difficult to explain. Similarly, when we have investigated behavior under the advantageous conditions of the laboratory, we can accept its basic orderliness in the world at large even though we cannot there wholly demonstrate law (Skinner, 1957, p. 371).

In this statement Skinner is agreeing that very simple processes are studied in the behavioral laboratory and that these never occur in such simple form outside the laboratory, but he is also suggesting that this is the way in which all sciences are practiced—and they seem to have suffered no disadvantage.

Another frequently encountered criticism concerns the *heavy proportion of* Skinner's early *work* that was *carried out on a pigeon or a rat* and the readiness with which derived principles and laws have been generalized to humans with little or no concern for species differences and communalities. It is a fact that Skinner and his disciples have frequently behaved as though every animal of each species, including the human species, can, by appropriate control, be induced to produce any behavior pattern. They have not sufficiently recognized the fact that the typical organism is not a *tabula rasa* whose final state is determined only by the stimulus–response–reinforcement pattern that is the essence of Skinner's system. The critics assert that there are at least some behavioral processes that do not fit into this paradigm. Harlows' (1962) work with the social development of rhesus monkeys and some of the European ethologists' work with instinctive behavior are typical of the illustrations used in these arguments, as is the linguistic work we have already discussed. Recently some psychologists have emphasized the role of biological factors in learning, questioning whether "general laws of learning" are possible at all (Seligman and Hager, 1972). This does not mean, of course, that the application of Skinner's work to human behavior is inappropriate. There is an enormous wealth of evidence to back up Skinner's argument that the concepts he uses have extensive application to the behavior of man. The question is how much and where, not whether.

Starkly simple, elegantly precise, and eminently practical, it is not surprising that Skinner's formulations have attracted more than their proportionate share of adherents. These ideas and related empirical findings are already an important part of modern psychology, and there is every reason to expect this enduring influence to increase in the future.

BIBLIOGRAPHY
PRIMARY SOURCES

Skinner, B. F. *The behavior of organisms.* New York: Appleton-Century-Crofts, 1938.

Skinner, B. F. *Science and human behavior.* New York: Macmillan, 1953.

Skinner, B. F. *Cumulative record.* New York: Appleton-Century-Crofts, 1961.

Skinner, B. F. *Contingencies of reinforcement: a theoretical analysis.* New York: Appleton-Century-Crofts, 1969.

REFERENCES

Ayllon, T., and Azrin, N. The measurement and reinforcement of behavior of psychotics. *J. Exp. Anal. Behav.,* 1965, **8,** 357–383.

Ayllon, T., and Azrin, N. *The token economy: a motivational system for therapy and rehabilitation.* New York: Appleton-Century-Crofts, 1968.

Baum, M. Extinction of avoidance responding through response prevention (flooding). *Psychol. Bull.,* 1970, **74,** 276–284.

Bijou, S., and Baer, D. M. Operant methods in child behavior and development. In W. Honig (Ed.). *Operant behavior: areas of research and application.* New York: Appleton-Century-Crofts, 1966, 718–789.

Blough, D. S. Effect of lysergic acid diethylamide on absolute visual threshold in the pigeon. *Science,* 1957, **126,** 304–305.

Boren, J. J. Some effects of Adiphenine, Benactyzine, and Chlorpromazine upon several operant behaviors. *Psychopharmacologia,* 1961, **2,** 416–424.

Boren, J. J. The study of drugs with operant techniques. In W. K. Honig (Ed.). *Operant behavior: areas of research and application*. New York: Appleton-Century-Crofts, 1966, 677–717.

Chomsky, N. Review of Skinner's *Verbal behavior*. *Language*, 1959, **35**, 26–58.

Ferster, C. B., and Skinner, B. F. *Schedules of reinforcement*. New York: Appleton-Century-Crofts, 1957.

Harlow, H. F., and Harlow, M. K. Social deprivation in monkeys. *Scientific American*, 1962, **207**, 136–146.

Herrnstein, R. J. On the law of effect. *J. Exper. Anal. Behav.*, 1970, **13**, 243–266.

Holland, J. G., and Skinner, B. F. *The analysis of behavior: a program for self-instruction*. New York: McGraw-Hill, 1961.

Honig, W. K. (Ed.). *Operant behavior: areas of research and application*. New York: Appleton-Century-Crofts, 1966.

Honig, W. K., and Staddon, J. E. R. (Eds.). *Handbook of operant behavior*. Englewood Cliffs, N. J.: Prentice-Hall, 1977.

Kazdin, A. E., and Bootzin, R. R. The token economy: an evaluative review. *J. Appl. Behav. Anal.*, 1972, **5**, 343–372.

Krasner, L., and Ullmann, L. P. (Eds.). *Research in behavior modification*. New York: Holt, Rinehart & Winston, 1965.

Lovaas, O. I., Berberich, J. P., Perloff, B. F., and Schaefer, B. Acquisition of imitative speech in schizophrenic children. *Science*, 1966, **151**, 705–707.

Lovaas, O. I., Koegel, R., Simmons, J. Q., and Long, J. S. Some generalization and follow-up measures on autistic children in behavior therapy. *J. Appl. Behav. Anal.*, 1973, **6**, 131–165.

Lundin, R. W. *Personality: a behavioral analysis*. New York: Macmillan, 1969.

Rohles, F. H. Operant methods in space technology. In W. K. Honig (Ed.). *Operant behavior: areas of research and application*. New York: Appleton-Century-Crofts, 1966, 531–564.

Seligman, M. E. P., and Hager, J. L. (Eds.) *Biological boundaries of learning*. New York: Appleton-Century-Crofts, 1972.

Skinner, B. F. The generic nature of the concepts of stimulus and response. *J. Genetic Psychol.*, 1935, **12**, 40–65.

Skinner, B. F. *The behavior of organisms*. New York: Appleton-Century-Crofts, 1938.

Skinner, B. F. The operational analysis of psychological terms. *Psychol. Review*, 1945, **52**, 270–277.

Skinner, B. F. "Superstition" in the pigeon. *J. Exper. Psychol.*, 1948, **38**, 168–172.

Skinner, B. F. *Walden two*. New York: Macmillan, 1948.

Skinner, B. F. Are theories of learning necessary? *Psychol. Review*, 1950, **57**, 193–216.

Skinner, B. F. *Science and human behavior*. New York: Macmillan, 1953.

Skinner, B. F. A case history in scientific method. *American Psychol.*, 1956, **11,** 221–233.

Skinner, B. F. *Verbal behavior.* New York: Appleton-Century-Crofts, 1957.

Skinner, B. F. *Cumulative record.* New York: Appleton-Century-Crofts, 1959.

Skinner, B. F. Pigeons in a Pelican. *American Psychol.*, 1960, **15,** 28–37.

Skinner, B. F. The design of cultures. *Daedalus,* 1961, **90,** 534–546.

Skinner, B. F. Behaviorism at fifty. *Science,* 1963, **140,** 951–958.

Skinner, B. F. Autobiography. In E. G. Boring and G. Lindzey (Eds.). *History of psychology in autobiography, Vol. V.,* New York: Appleton-Century-Crofts, 1967, 387–413.

Skinner, B. F. *The technology of teaching.* New York: Appleton-Century-Crofts, 1968.

Skinner, B. F. *Contingencies of reinforcement: a theoretical analysis.* New York: Appleton-Century-Crofts, 1969.

Skinner, B. F. *Beyond freedom and dignity.* New York: Knopf, 1971.

Skinner, B. F. *About behaviorism.* New York: Knopf, 1974.

Skinner, B. F. *Particulars of my life.* New York: Knopf, 1976.

Solomon, R. L., Kamin, L. J., and Wynne, L. G. Traumatic avoidance learning: the outcomes of several extinction procedures with dogs. *J. Abnorm. Soc. Psychol.*, 1953, **48,** 291–302.

Verplanck, W. S. et al. *Modern learning theory.* New York: Appleton-Century-Crofts, 1954.

PERSONALITY THEORY IN PERSPECTIVE

17

We have now reached the end of our tour through fifteen major types of personality theory. The reader who has faithfully completed the journey must surely be impressed with the diversity and complexity of these viewpoints. Each type has proved to have certain distinctive features and in each case we have found something about the position to approve or admire. It seems appropriate at this point to pause and attempt to identify general trends that exist in spite of the tremendous differences among personality theories. It is important that students should have a sense of the individuality and distinctiveness of each viewpoint but it is equally important that they be aware of whatever common qualities may exist in the midst of this welter of conflicting assertion and individual expression.

In this, our final chapter, we return to the personality theories under consideration in pursuit of the goal of generality and our discussion is organized around the dimensions proposed in the initial chapter as appropriate for comparing theories of personality. We also present a small number of issues that seem to us important in determining future developments in this area. As a concluding note we consider the advisability of attempting a synthesis of personality theories in order to arrive at a general theory that will be maximally acceptable to all persons working in this area and at the same time more useful than any existing theory.

THE
COMPARISON OF
THEORIES OF
PERSONALITY

In comparing the theories we will focus upon differences in content rather than differences in form. Our principal reason for overlooking formal differences derives from our conviction that at this stage of development there is little basis for choice among these theories on such grounds. All are in need of considerable improvement before they can be considered even minimally adequate in terms of formal criteria such as explicitness of statement and adequacy of definition. Although there are some detectable differences between the theories on these criteria, these differences are less interesting and important than the existing differences in substance or content. Something should be said, however, concerning the relative fruitfulness of the various viewpoints as generators of research and we will return to consider this issue when we have completed our discussion of the substantive differences between the theories.

Our discussion of contemporary personality theory reveals that the importance of conceiving of the human organism as a striving, seeking, *purposive* creature is less central today than it was three or four decades ago. During the first third of this century this was an issue that provided a dramatic cleavage between various psychological theorists. McDougall, Watson, Tolman, and other leading figures focused much of their attention upon the question of whether humans were necessarily purposive. While it is still true that some contemporary theorists, such as Allport, Murray, Goldstein, Rogers, Angyal, and Adler, place a heavy emphasis upon the purposive nature of behavior, there is little strong resistance to this point of view. Even theorists such as Miller and Dollard, Skinner, and Sheldon, who do not appear to view purpose as a crucial consideration in understanding behavior, make no attempt to pose this as a central distinction between their own position and other theories. One may suspect that the relatively general question concerning human purposive nature has been replaced by a series of more specific questions concerning such matters as the role of reward, the importance of the self, and the centrality of unconscious motivation. In general, then, most personality theorists seem to conceive of humans as purposive creatures but even where this is not taken for granted it does not seem to be a matter of hot dispute.

The relative importance of *unconscious determinants* of behavior as opposed to the importance of conscious determinants persists as a key factor in the distinction between the various theories of personality. Although this remains a central issue, the exact grounds for disagreement between theorists seem to have shifted considerably in recent years. Originally the debate focused about the reality or existence of unconscious motivation but today the question seems to be less a matter of whether such factors exist than a matter of under what conditions and how strongly they operate. Clearly Freud's theory gives the heaviest emphasis to unconscious factors and a variety of theories influenced by the orthodox psychoanalytic position such as Murray's and Jung's also give a heavy weighting to such factors. At the other extreme we find theories such as Allport's, Lewin's, Goldstein's, Skinner's, Rogers', and existentialism where unconscious motives are deemphasized or ceded an important role only in the abnormal individual. It is true that personality theorists have displayed a trend toward increased acceptance of the role of unconscious motives but there remains a great deal of variety among the theorists in the extent to which this role is emphasized.

The centrality of *reward* or reinforcement as a determinant of behavior is most vividly emphasized in the reinforcement theories of Skinner and of Miller and Dollard and in Freud's pleasure principle. Cattell, Murray, and Sullivan also accept the law of effect, with certain reservations, as a primary condition of learning. In contrast Allport, Angyal, Binswanger, Boss, Goldstein, and Rogers are relatively explicit in demoting reward to a secondary role. In general, contemporary formulations seem less often than in the past to imply that man is motivated by a conscious attempt to maximize pleasure and minimize pain. They stress the function of reward as a determinant of behavior regardless of whether the individual is aware of its role or not. There seems to be a growing tendency for personality theorists to deal explicitly with the issue of reward, either assigning it central importance or else subordinating it to other principles.

Contiguity, the spatial and temporal linking of two events, is less explicitly emphasized by most personality theorists than reward. In spite of the tremendous historical importance of Pavlov's studies of conditioning we find that of the theorists we have considered none appears to have made this factor one of the cornerstones of his theoretical position. Indeed, E. R. Guthrie who made simple association the core of his position appears to have left no immediate theoretical descendants. Miller and Dollard, and Skinner clearly subordinate contiguity to reward. Freud's theory appears to assign some importance to association in the process of symptom formation and symbolic transformation, as the nature of the symptom or symbol may be partially determined by associative links in the past. For the most part, however, personality theorists either do not deal explicitly with association or else assign it a minor role in the determination of behavior. This state of affairs probably reflects the feeling of most of these theorists that association alone is not a sufficient explanation of behavior and that the operation of association as a minor factor in the determination of behavior is too obvious to need emphasis. It is also true that personality theorists are very much engrossed with the motivational process, and simple association without the binding effects of motives seems irrelevant if not heretical to someone focused upon motivation.

The considerable variation among theories in their concern with the *learning process* is anchored at one end by the detailed exposition provided by Skinner and by Miller and Dollard and at the other end by the absence of any specific treatment of learning in the theories of Binswanger, Boss, Jung, Rogers, Sheldon, Erikson, and Eastern psychology. Allport and Cattell devote considerable attention to this process but for the most part their ideas represent attempts to pull together principles that have been developed by other theorists. Lewin has made some original contributions to the understanding of learning, but he has never centered his conceptual efforts in this area. Most personality theorists have been content to view development in terms of global principles such as maturation, individuation, identification, self-actualization, or the like, rather than attempting to provide a detailed picture of the learning process.

Although one can distinguish fairly sharply some of the theories treated in this book with regard to their emphasis on the *concrete aspects of behavior versus formalization into general laws* and principles, a number of them do not fit easily in either category. Angyal, Lewin, Miller and Dollard, and Skinner certainly aspire to a high degree of formalization, whereas Binswanger and Boss, and Sheldon stay closer to the actual behavior itself and are less likely to engage in high-level systematizing. Despite Jung's insistence on the "facts" of behavior, he did develop a number of very general principles. However, when it comes to specifying the other theories on this dimension, it is found that they are both particular *and* general. The outstanding example of this mixture of the concrete and the abstract is Freud's theory. His metapsychology is an attempt to formulate the general principles that seemed inherent in his observations of the concrete behavior of specific individuals. This mixture is also found in the theories of Adler, Allport, Cattell, Erikson, Fromm, Murray, Rogers, and Sullivan. It is as though these theorists were loath to lose the specific behavior of an individual while formulating laws about people in general. They are—to use Allport's terms—both idiographic and nomothetic.

Although there may be some neglect of the learning process, there is an abundance of interest in the products of learning or *personality structure*. One of the most distinctive features of personality theories is their numerous and distinctive schemes for representing personality structure. Among those who have been most detailed in their treatment of the acquisitions of personality are Allport, Cattell, Freud, Jung, Murray, and Sheldon. Historically there has been a tendency for those theorists who were most concerned with the learning process to be least concerned with the acquisitions of learning and vice versa. At present, however, those theorists who are sharply deficient in their treatment of either learning or structure tend to compensate for this deficiency by borrowing a set of formulations from another theory whose conceptual focus includes this neglected area. The best illustration of this trend is provided by the efforts of Miller and Dollard to incorporate into their learning theory the structural concepts of psychoanalysis. There is no doubt that the sophisticated personality theorist today accepts a responsibility for dealing with both the process of learning and the outcomes of this process.

We have already pointed to the fact that as a group American psychologists have minimized the role of *hereditary factors* as determinants of behavior. Yet many of the theorists we have considered clearly and explicitly emphasize the importance of such factors. Sheldon is convinced of the centrality of genetic determinants and hopes that his approach to the study of behavior will shed light on the details of the relation between genetic and behavioral events. Cattell has displayed both theoretical and empirical interest in the role of heredity in behavior. His investigations have actually tended to supply strong support for his theoretical convictions on this score. Jung's theory is deeply committed to the importance of the genetic and Freud considers hereditary factors of prime importance. Murray, Allport, and Erikson also accept the significance of heredity although they place somewhat less emphasis upon this issue than the previously mentioned theorists. Although heredity is recognized in a general way by the existential theorists, its role is diminished by their insistence that a person has the freedom to become what he or she wants to become. Incidentally, this is the only theory of personality treated in this book to acknowledge free will as a major determinant of behavior. No other theory remotely suggests that there is such a thing as free will. Skinner, who is consistently and bluntly critical of the concept of free will, appears quite neutral in regard to the importance of genetic variation. Of the personality theorists we have considered it seems that Eastern psychology, Fromm, Horney, Lewin, Rogers, and Sullivan place the least emphasis upon such factors. We find, then, somewhat surprisingly, that the majority of personality theorists have accepted or emphasized the importance of hereditary factors and several have coupled this theoretical emphasis with relevant empirical research.

The contrast between Freud's and Lewin's theoretical positions nicely illustrates the variation among personality theorists in their emphasis upon the significance of contemporary factors as opposed to the significance of *events taking place early in development*. Erikson's approach, the stimulus-response theory of Miller and Dollard, Murray's personology, and Sullivan's interpersonal theory resemble Freud's theory in their emphasis upon early experience, and Allport's, Rogers', and existential theories resemble Lewin's position in stressing the contemporaneous. The real and important theoretical differences existing here are sometimes concealed by the implication that the theorists who emphasize early experience do so only out of a fascination with history or the past and not because of the predictive power or current significance of such events. The defenders of the importance of the ongoing present maintain that the past can be of significance now only through the operation of factors in the present. Thus, if we fully understand the present there is no need to deal with the past. Actually, there is no real disagreement over the fact that the past influences the present only through the operation of present factors, forces, or attributes (ideas, archetypes, memories, dispositions). The individual who emphasizes the importance of past events maintains, however, that the past is indispensable in order to understand development and also to provide information about forces that are operating in the present. The chief disagreement between these two theoretical camps centers about the question of whether factors influencing present behavior can be assessed adequately from viewing present behavior or whether knowledge concerning past events may not provide special information of a crucial nature. On this issue personality theorists seem rather evenly divided.

The most extreme emphasis upon the *continuity of development* appears in the theories of Erikson, Freud, Miller and Dollard, and Skinner although to a lesser degree the same theme is present in the theories of Adler, Angyal, and Sullivan. These theories clearly imply that events taking place in the present are systematically linked to events that took place in the past and that development is an orderly and consistent process accountable in terms of a single set of principles. In contrast, Allport, Lewin, and to some extent Rogers, explicitly stress the lack of continuity in development and the relative independence of the functioning adult from the events of childhood or infancy. Jung too emphasizes the disjunctiveness of development although he sees the major discontinuity as occurring at middle age when biological motives are largely replaced by cultural and spiritual needs. All of these theorists suggest that somewhat different principles may be needed to account for what takes place at different stages of development. Not all theories of personality display much interest in the process of development but most of those that do seem to conceive of development as a continuous process to be represented in terms of a single set of theoretical principles.

We have already agreed that one of the features that distinguished personality theory historically from other varieties of psychological theory was an emphasis upon holism. Consistent with this observation is the fact that most contemporary personality theorists may be accurately classed as *organismic*. As a group they emphasize the importance of considering the individual as a total, functioning unit. Thus Allport, Angyal, Goldstein, Jung, Murray, Rogers, and Sheldon all stress the fact that an element of behavior is not to be understood when studied in isolation from the remainder of the functioning person including the person's biological make-up. Only Skinner, and Miller and Dollard seem willing to resist convention on this issue and question the importance of studying the "total individual." The importance of the *field* is emphasized by Adler, Angyal, Binswanger, Boss, Lewin, Murray, and Sullivan. Only Lewin and Murray, however, have attempted to provide a detailed set of variables in terms of which the field can be analyzed. This lack of interest in the details of analysis is a logical outgrowth of the holistic convictions of field theorists that lead them to be wary of specific sets of variables. Almost no one *denies* that the situation within which behavior occurs is important, although Freud, Jung, Miller and Dollard, Sheldon and Skinner give this matter less explicit attention than other theorists with whom we have dealt. It is evident, that the usual contemporary personality theory places heavy emphasis upon the importance of studying behavior "organically" without attempting to isolate small segments of behavior for microscopic study. At the same time there is a growing tendency for the personality theorists to provide a full representation of the situation or context within which behavior occurs.

An individual who adopts a holistic position may be recommending one of two approaches to the representation of behavior. He or she may simply be suggesting that a successful theory must be complex, multivariate, and include reference to the situation within which a behavioral event occurs, as well as to other behavioral events of the actor. On the other hand, he or she may be suggesting that all of the individual's behavior is so tightly cemented together and, further, that it is so closely linked to its environmental context, that any attempt to abstract elements or variables for study is doomed to failure. The first point of view accepts the complexity of behavior and suggests that a reasonably complex model of behavior is necessary to achieve much efficiency in predicting behavior. The second point of view takes the complexity of behavior as a point of emphasis and insists that "all" aspects of the individual and his or her situation must be given their due before progress can be made. It is easily understandable that those theories representing the latter position have customarily placed a heavy emphasis upon the distinctiveness or *uniqueness* of the individual. As the theory insists that the observer consider more and more different facets of the individual, the person's behavior, and the context of this behavior, the distinctiveness of each individual and indeed each act must become obvious and a matter of concern. Allport's theory is by far the most thoroughgoing in its stress upon the importance of giving a full consideration to individuality. In fact, as we have seen, this emphasis led Allport to propose that more attention be given to the idiographic method of studying behavior. This same general point of view is given central emphasis in the theories of Adler, Binswanger, Boss, Lewin, and Murray. The theories of Skinner, and Miller and Dollard are most explicit in denying the crucial significance of the uniqueness of behavior. Although there are a number of personality theorists who deal centrally with the uniqueness of behavior, this seems less typical of modern personality theory than the organismic emphasis.

It is commonly recognized that S–R theorists and Skinner deal with rather small *units of behavior* whereas the organismic theorists are more concerned with units that embrace the whole person. Cattell, Lewin, and Sheldon favor smaller units and Allport, Binswanger and Boss, Eastern psychology, and Rogers favor larger units in describing behavior. The remaining theorists range more widely over the molecular-molar spectrum. Freud, for example, could analyze behavior into very small units when the need arose; but he also had the facility of dealing with the whole person as a unit. Much the same can be said about Erikson.

Although virtually all of the theories described in this volume recognize that the structure of personality can be dislocated or even shattered by anxiety, conflict, frustration, stress, and physical traumas some of them attribute greater powers of resiliency and *homeostasis* to the individual than do others. Goldstein, in particular, has shown how even a badly brain-damaged patient can achieve some degree of stability by coming to terms with the environment. For Freud and Erikson, the ego and its integrative and defensive mechanisms play a stabilizing role and both Jung and Alder recognized the importance of compensation as a homeostatic device. In Rogers' theory the concepts of self and organism provide a strong measure of stability to personality, as does the biosphere in Angyal's theory. Murray has a number of integrative concepts. Other theories, for example, those of Cattell,

Sheldon, and Sullivan, without explicitly disavowing homeostatic mechanisms in the personality, tend to remain silent on this issue.

The significance of the *psychological environment*, or the world of experience as opposed to the world of physical reality, is accepted by most personality theorists and is a matter of focal emphasis for several. Binswanger, Boss, Lewin, and Rogers are the most explicit and thoroughgoing in their development of this point of view. In fact, they have been accused of largely ignoring the world of reality as a result of their preoccupation with the world of experience. This point of view also receives considerable attention in many of the psychoanalytic theories, and in Murray's theory. Although no one questions that the manner in which the individual perceives a given event has some influence upon the way in which he or she will respond to this event, we find that this process receives little attention in the theories of Cattell, Miller and Dollard, Sheldon, and Skinner. All in all, it is probably fair to say that personality theorists are more impressed with the importance of the psychological environment than with the importance of the physical environment.

We have seen that there are several senses in which the *self* concept is employed by personality theorists. Either the self is seen as a group of psychological processes that serves as a determinant of behavior or else it is conceived of as a cluster of attitudes and feelings the individual has about him or her self. In one form or the other, however, the self occupies a prominent role in most current personality formulations. Not only are there specific theories that are identified as self theories but a large number of other theories employ this concept as a focal theoretical element. Among the theorists who, in some way, make prominent use of the ego or self concept are Adler, Allport, Angyal, Cattell, Freud, Goldstein, Jung, and Rogers. Only Eysenck, Skinner, Miller and Dollard, and Sheldon seem to conceive of behavior in such a manner that the self is not ceded an important role. It is true that many of the current formulations of the self have avoided or lessened the subjectivity that inhered in early conceptions. There has been a definite trend in the direction of providing operations whereby the self or aspects of it can be measured. One might say that in the early days of psychological theorizing the self tended to have mystical or vitalistic implications whereas the comtemporary self seems to have lost these qualities as it gained at least a partial quantification. Clearly personality theorists today are characterized by an increased interest in the self and attendant processes.

The importance of *group membership determinants* of behavior is a matter for concerted emphasis primarily within those theories that have been heavily influenced by sociology and anthropology. Illustrative of this are the positions of Adler, Erikson, Fromm, Horney, Lewin, and Sullivan. It is quite natural that those theorists who have stressed the "field" within which behavior occurs should also manifest an interest in the social groups to which the individual belongs. Consistent with this is the fact that all of the above theorists with the exception of Miller and Dollard may be considered field theorists. None of the theorists we have examined believes that group membership factors are unimportant although Allport, Angyal, Binswanger, Boss, Goldstein, Jung, Sheldon, and Skinner have chosen not to focus upon these factors. In general, it seems that there is a growing tendency for personality theorists to give explicit attention to the sociocultural context within which behavior occurs.

We have observed that it is customary for personality theorists to attempt some form of *interdisciplinary anchoring* of their theories. Most of these efforts center about the possibility of interpenetrating psychological concepts with the findings and concepts of the biological sciences. Illustrative of this tendency are the theories of Allport, Freud, Goldstein, Jung, Murray, and Sheldon. Skinner and the existentalists are perhaps the most determined to pursue theory development at a purely psychological level. None of the personality theorists we have discussed, except possibly Lewin, seems primarily oriented toward linking their formulations with the disciplines of anthropology and sociology. However, Dollard and Miller, Freud, and Murray show a balanced interest in establishing theoretical links with both biology and the social sciences and Erikson shows a special interest in relating his theory to the field of history. From this it is clear that personality theorists as a group are more oriented toward the biological than toward the social sciences. There is, however, some evidence for an increased interest in the findings and theories of sociology and anthropology.

The diversity and *multiplicity of motivation* in the human is given a full recognition in the theories of Allport, Cattell, Lewin, and Murray. In each of these theories there is a firm emphasis upon the fact that behavior can be understood only with the identification and study of a large number of motivational variables. The theories of Cattell and Murray provide the only detailed attempts to translate this multiplicity into a set of specific variables. Adler, Angyal, Binswanger, Boss, Erikson, Freud, Fromm, Goldstein, Horney, Rogers, Sheldon, and Skinner seem willing to approach the study of human behavior with a much more abbreviated set of motivational concepts. Thus, although personality theorists share a detailed concern with the motivational process, they are divided between those who choose to represent motivation in terms of a relatively small number of variables and those who consider a very large number of such variables necessary.

Parallel to the attribute of the multiplicity of motives is the *complexity of mechanisms* that are evoked by the various theorists to explain human conduct. At one extreme of complexity are the theories of Cattell, Freud, Jung, and Murray; at the other extreme of conceptual parsimony are the theories of Adler, Binswanger and Boss, Goldstein, Horney, Rogers, and Skinner. Both Adler and Horney employ the creative self as an overarching principle of personality. For Goldstein it is self-actualization, for Binswanger and Boss it is being-in-the-world, for Rogers it is the organism, and for Skinner it is reinforcement. The remaining theories fall somewhere between these extremes of complexity and simplicity.

A large number of personality theorists demonstrate detailed and continuous concern with the actualized, mature or *ideal personality*. This is a primary feature of the theories of Rogers, Binswanger and Boss, Eastern psychology, Allport, and Jung. It is also prominent in the writings of Freud, Adler, Horney, Murray, Angyal, and Goldstein. Those theorists who have shown the least interest in specifying or accounting for maturity and self-actualization include Lewin, Cattell, Miller and Dollard, and Skinner.

As we have observed there is considerable variation among personality theories in their relevance to *abnormal behavior*. Not only have some theories been based largely upon the study of neurotic or other disturbed individuals but also many theories have a good deal to offer in the way of proper methods of altering or treating the various forms of psychopathology. The origins of psychoanalysis in the observation of patients undergoing psychotherapy is well known as is the profound impact that this theory has had upon the understanding and treatment of all varieties of behavior deviation. Much the same association can be seen between behavior disorder and the theories of Jung, Adler, Horney, Sullivan, and Angyal. There is a strong association between abnormal behavior and Eastern psychology and Goldstein's theory but in the first case the special tie is with altered states of consciousness and in the second, it is the study and understanding of individuals who have experienced brain damage. The theorists who have shown the least concern with the world of psychopathology are Lewin, Allport, and Cattell.

Our discussion to this point has been quite general and little attempt has been made to assess each theory in connection with each issue. We have been more concerned with the over-all status of contemporary personality theory than we have with a detailed comparison of the specific theories. Table 17-1 provides a partial correction

TABLE 17-1
Dimensional comparison of theories of personality

	Purpose	Unconscious determinants	Reward	Contiguity	Learning process	Formal analysis	Personality structure	Heredity	Early developmental experience	Continuity of development	Organismic emphasis	Field emphasis	Uniqueness	Molar units	Homeostatic mechanisms	Psychological environment	Self concept	Group membership determinants	Biology (Interdisciplinary emphasis)	Social science (Interdisciplinary emphasis)	Multiplicity of motives	Complexity of mechanisms	Ideal personality	Abnormal behavior
Freud	H	H	H	M	M	M	H	H	H	H	M	L	M	M	M	H	H	M	M	H	L	L	H	H
Erikson	H	M	H	M	L	M	H	H	H	H	M	L	M	M	H	H	H	H	H	H	L	H	H	M
Jung	H	H	M	L	L	M	H	H	M	H	H	L	M	M	H	H	H	L	M	L	M	H	H	M
Adler	H	H	M	L	L	M	M	H	H	H	H	H	H	M	H	M	M	M	H	H	M	H	H	H
Fromm	H	M	L	L	M	M	M	H	M	M	M	L	M	M	M	H	H	M	L	H	H	H	H	H
Sullivan	H	M	M	H	L	L	M	L	M	H	M	M	M	M	H	M	M	M	M	H	L	L	M	H
Horney	H	H	M	M	L	L	M	L	H	M	M	M	H	M	L	H	M	H	L	H	M	M	H	M
Murray	H	H	M	L	M	M	L	H	L	H	H	M	M	M	H	M	M	M	L	M	M	H	H	H
Goldstein	H	L	M	L	L	M	M	M	L	H	H	H	H	M	H	H	M	L	H	L	L	H	H	H
Angyal	H	M	L	L	M	L	H	M	L	H	H	H	M	M	M	H	H	M	L	L	L	H	H	M
Rogers	L	L	L	L	L	L	L	L	L	H	H	H	H	L	H	H	H	L	M	L	L	H	H	M
Binswanger & Boss	H	L	M	L	L	H	H	L	H	L	L	M	M	M	H	H	M	L	M	M	L	L	H	H
Eastern Psychology	M	L	M	M	L	M	M	L	M	M	M	H	M	H	H	H	M	M	M	M	H	H	H	M
Lewin	M	L	M	L	M	M	M	L	H	M	M	H	H	L	M	H	M	H	L	L	H	H	H	H
Allport	H	L	L	L	L	M	H	M	L	H	H	H	H	L	M	H	H	L	L	L	H	H	H	L
Sheldon	L	M	L	M	L	L	H	H	L	H	H	H	H	L	L	L	L	L	H	L	L	M	L	M
Cattell	M	M	M	M	M	L	H	H	M	M	L	M	L	L	L	L	L	L	L	H	H	H	M	M
Miller & Dollard	L	M	H	L	H	L	H	M	M	H	L	L	L	L	L	L	L	L	L	L	L	M	L	L
Skinner	L	L	H	H	H	H	M	H	M	H	L	L	L	L	L	L	L	L	L	L	L	L	L	M

Key: H, high (emphasized), M, moderate, L, low (deemphasized).

for this generality through indicating for the individual issues whether each of the theories emphasizes, occupies a moderate position, or deemphasizes this issue. Obviously these judgments are broad and approximate. Their lack of precision is due to the extremely general categories used in the rating and also to the complexity of the theories that, in certain instances, makes it impossible to know with certainty just how a particular theorist stands on a given issue. In any case, the justification for these ratings has been presented in the preceding chapters along with appropriate references to the original sources. Consequently, there is no need for readers to accept our judgments uncritically as they can freely make their own ratings using the same sources of data we have employed.

In Table 17-1 the symbol H indicates that the theory emphasizes the importance of this issue or this set of determinants, M indicates that the theory occupies a middle ground, L suggests that the issue or position is deemphasized within this theory.

We may note—without additional discussion—that to our knowledge four multivariate analyses have been performed on the data presented in previous editions of *Theories of personality*. The first such study was carried out by Desmond Cartwright (1957) and appeared shortly after the first edition was published. Using factor analysis, four factors were extracted. Factor A includes the attributes of *purpose* and *group membership determinants*. Theories highly saturated with this factor are those of Adler, Fromm, Horney, Rogers, and Sullivan. Factor B comprises the attributes of *structure, heredity,* and *biology.* Angyal, Eysenck, Freud, Jung, Murray, and Sheldon are high on this factor. *Purpose, organismic emphasis,* and *self-concept* are the principal attributes comprising Factor C. Theories loaded with this factor are those of Allport, Angyal, Goldstein, and Rogers. The fourth factor consists of *structure* and *heredity* and is of importance only with respect to the factor theories.

A few years later, Taft (1960) reported the results of a cluster analysis of the data in Table (first edition). Five main clusters emerged. Cluster I includes Adler, Fromm, Horney, Murray, and Sullivan, and the name suggested for this cluster is *functionalist social field theories.* The second cluster, called *developmental approach to unconscious complexes and personality structures,* includes only the three original psychoanalytic theorists, Freud, Adler, and Jung. Angyal, Goldstein, Jung, and Rogers form a cluster labeled *innate organismic self-actualization.* Cluster IV is identified as *continuous development in interaction with social environment.* Theories heavily loaded with this factor are those of Adler, Freud, Murray, and Sullivan. The last cluster includes Allport, Cattell, Eysenck, Freud, Jung, and Sheldon and is labeled *constitutional personality structures.*

Schuh (1966) performed a cluster analysis for both the attributes and the theorists. We shall report only his results for the theorists. They fall into four clusters. The first cluster consists of Adler, Fromm, and Horney and is named *social emphasis.* The second cluster composed of Allport, Angyal, Goldstein, Miller and Dollard, and Rogers is called *self emphasis.* The third cluster includes Eysenck, Freud, Lewin, Murray, and Sheldon, and the fourth Cattell, Jung, and Sullivan. These two clusters were not named since no common features could be found by which to characterize the diverse viewpoints.

The most recent study (Evans and Smith, 1972) involved the factor analysis of both attributes and theorists and a comparison with the results of Schuh. In spite of the addition of new dimensions and theorists in the revised version of this book, as well as the use of a different method of analysis, Evans and Smith found considerable similarity between their findings and those reported earlier. Their first theorist factor was comprised of Binswanger and Boss, Miller and Dollard, Cattell, Rogers, Goldstein, Angyal, and Allport and corresponds to Schuh's second factor, which was called *self emphasis.* Their second factor included Fromm, Horney, Adler, and Freud and corresponds to Schuh's first cluster, which was referred to as social emphasis in the previous study and *psychoanalytic emphasis* in the more recent report. The third factor consisted of Sheldon, Murray, Lewin, and Freud and corresponds to Schuh's third cluster. Evans and Smith label it *biological emphasis.* A fourth factor is called *learning emphasis* and is composed of Binswanger and Boss, Skinner, Miller and Dollard, Murray, and Allport. The authors report comparable congruences in their findings and those of Schuh when the analyses of the attributes were compared.

This brings us to the question of how well the various theories have functioned as *generators of research.* We have already agreed that this is the most important evaluative comparison that can be made among theories; unfortunately it is likewise the most difficult comparison to make with assurance. All of the theories have had some function as generators of investigation but the varied nature of the studies that have resulted, as well as the complexity of the relationship between the theory itself and pertinent research, makes anything other than a rough judgment impossible.

Granted the subjectivity and the tentative nature of our verdict, we propose that theories may be divided into three clusters in terms of how fruitful they have been as stimulants to research. In the first group belong the theories that have led to a large quantity of investigation that has been carried out in a variety of areas by a diverse group of investigators. Here we place Freud's theory, stimulus-response theory, Skinner's position, and Lewin's theory. In each case the message of the theory has transcended the bounds of one small group working in close collaboration so that issues related to the theory have been explored in a variety of different settings and by individuals who represent rather heterogeneous backgrounds. Psychoanalytic research is perhaps the best example of this, for the nature of individuals carrying out research that is conceived to be relevant to Freud's theory ranges from those who are directly in the mainstream of the medical-psychoanalytic tradition to persons who belong to an experimental or biological tradition. There are numerous sources that document the very great quantity of such research, for example, Hall and Lindzey (1968), Hilgard (1952), Sears (1943). The theory has not only had tremendous impact upon psychological research but has also had a considerable impact upon anthropological and sociological investigation as well as more limited influence upon the other social sciences, literature, the fine arts, and religion. This influence was modified and expanded by Erikson and the appearance of a substantial volume of work is psychohistory and psychobiography.

It is equally clear that Lewin's theory has led to a great deal of relevant research and that much of this has been carried out by individuals who have not been students of Lewin. Although the impact of this theory upon areas outside of psychology has been appreciably less than that of Freud's theory, within psychology its impact has extended to areas where Freud's influence has been little felt. It is evident that in both social psychology and personality psychology Lewin's theory ranks with the most influential in the quantity and quality of research that it has generated.

Hull's stimulus-response theory, as modified by Miller and Dollard and others, has clearly led to a very great quantity of research dealing with a broad range of topics. It has been applied in psychopathology, social behavior, and educational psychology as well as within the usual areas of animal and human learning. Even within social anthropology the theory has had more influence than any other theory except Freud's. Further, the amount of experimental investigation that has been carried out relevant to this theory is much greater than in the case of any other theory we have considered. It is true that there is somewhat more homogeneity of background among investigators here than in the case of Lewin's and Freud's theories. However, even here much of the research has been carried out by individuals who have had little direct contact with Hull.

As we have noted, Skinner, his students, and those he has influenced have produced a vast quantity of research. Although many of these studies have been conducted by experimental psychologists, there has been an increasing tendency for investigators in the clinical and personality areas to conduct research directly derived from Skinner's conceptions. Even in fields such as sociology there is clear evidence of research and formulation that is heavily influenced by operant conditioning ideas. Perhaps the most dramatic evidence of this research productivity is provided by the large and expanding *Journal of Experimental Analysis of Behavior,* which is devoted exclusively to controlled investigations growing out of this tradition.

The second cluster includes those theories that have been accompanied by a large bulk of studies that are either quite limited in scope or else have been carried out by individuals intimately involved with the theory and its development. In this group we would place the theories of Allport, Cattell, Goldstein, Jung, Murray, Sheldon, Sullivan, and Rogers. As the individual chapters made clear, each of these theories is accompanied by, or grew out of, a large body of relevant research. In most cases, however, the research deals with a limited range of problems or else the application of a small number of techniques. Further, in the usual instance the research has been carried out by a small number of closely knit investigators. The third group consists of those theories where there is little evidence of accompanying investigation. Here we place Adler, Angyal, Binswanger and Boss, Fromm, and Horney.

It is reassuring that, in spite of the limitations of theories of personality as generators of research, the large majority of such theories has been accompanied by a considerable quantity of research. Whatever procedural limitations may be inherent in these investigations, the fact remains that they document the interest of the theorists in examining the effectiveness of their theories in the face of empirical data. It is hard to believe that in the long run this attitude will not lead to progressive changes that will result in more effective theories.

SOME REFLECTIONS ON CURRENT PERSONALITY THEORY

What of the future development of personality theory? Are there qualities missing at present from the theoretical scene that should be added? Are there specifiable shortcomings in the theoretical approach of most psychologists? Are there issues that today are of ascending importance and point the way to probable future progress? It seems to us there are, although it must be admitted not all, or perhaps most, psychologists would agree with us as to their precise identity.

We believe the field of personality would benefit enormously from an *increased sophistication* on the part of psychologists *concerning the na-*

ture and function of theoretical formulation. While there are many aspects to this sophistication, perhaps the most important has to do with understanding the central importance of theories as a means of generating or stimulating research. Psychologists should give up the idea that they have discharged their obligations if they provide a theoretical formulation that takes into account or makes consistent what is already known in a given empirical area. If the theory does nothing more than organize known facts we might as well remain at a descriptive level and forsake theorizing. The plea here is simply that theories be evaluated in terms of their capacity to generate new research. Psychologists should also show themselves more willing to accept the fact that assumptions concerning behavior that do not have eventual consequences for the kind of predictions to be made, or the type of data to be collected, are valueless and a waste of time, effort, and print. Let theorists focus attention upon formulations that have some meaningful relation to the business they are about —studying behavior.

Related to this need for increased sophistication in methodology is the need for more sensitive *discrimination between effective literary style and powerful theorizing.* It is obvious that from the point of view of the reader the more literately and persuasively a theorist can present his or her system the better. It should be equally obvious, however, that the elegance of presentation is of no importance as a measure of whether the theory will prove an empirically useful tool. Currently many psychologists seem to evaluate a theory in terms of how compelling the creator of the theory is in presenting the theory. Although a vivid and effective style plays an important role in arousing interest in a theory, evaluation of the fruitfulness of the theory should rest upon uniquely different grounds. The essence of this point is that the value of theorists should be equated to the research utility of their theory rather than to their literary brilliance.

Personality theory and research are in need of *an increase in both radicalism and conservatism.* One might choose to express this alternatively as an increase in both creative imagination and in critical evaluation. The successful theorist must develop dispassionate willingness to do radical violence to common assumptions concerning behavior. One should, so far as possible, be able to free oneself from common preconceptions concerning the nature of behavior. Once having displayed a capacity to innovate or create a theory that is not tied tightly to existing conceptions of behavior, the theorist should then display a rigid conservatism in extending, formalizing, applying, and testing the consequences of this point of view. In other words, theorists should be convention-breakers but once they have established a new set of conventions they should be willing to explore exhaustively the implications of these conventions. It is impossible to test the consequences of a theory unless the theorist is willing to remain in one position long enough for verification procedures to be instituted and completed. This does not mean that the person should cling to their formulations stubbornly in the face of empirical disconfirmation. It does mean that given a stable body of theory, change should be introduced as a result of controlled empirical evidence rather than because of whim or passing observation. It is of crucial importance that the theorist and his or her followers devote themselves to empirical investigation instead of polemic or verbal argument. It is of little significance which personality theorist is the most effective protagonist in a debate but it is of crucial significance which personality theory is most useful in generating important and verifiable empirical consequences.

It is high time that the personality theorist was *freed from obligation to justify theoretical formulations that depart from normative or customary views of behavior.* It is all too common to find that a given theory is criticized for the fact that it emphasizes too strongly the negative aspects of behavior or overemphasizes the importance of sexual motives. It is true that a common-sense view of behavior sees humans as possessing both good and bad attributes and further considers them to possess not only sexual motives but other motives as well. This, however, is a complete *non sequitur* so far as the development of a theory of behavior is concerned. The theorist has complete freedom, as we have just emphasized, to depart from customary preconceptions about behavior and is required only to make statements about behavior that are empirically useful. The question of whether these statements please or offend the average individual is of no importance. It is quite possible that the most fruitful theories of behavior will prove eventually to be highly offensive to an average member of our society. Of course the opposite alternative is also perfectly possible. The point we are making here is not that theorists must deny customary views of behavior or that they must accept such views. They are at liberty to do either. Their position is neutral in regard to these views and they may conform or deviate as they wish with the evaluation of their decision resting upon criteria altogether removed from the normative acceptability or deviance of their theory. Many other criticisms of theoretical formulations that are frequently encountered have an equally dubious status. Thus, the suggestion that a given theory is too molecular, too rational, or too mechanistic simply reflects preconceptions about behavior that the particular critic possesses. These remarks serve more to reveal the position of the critic than to evaluate the theory. In the final analysis *the only telling criticism of an existing theory is an alternative theory that works better.* If one says that a given theory is too molecular it remains for someone to demonstrate that an alternative theory employing larger units of analysis is able to do all the first theory can do and more besides.

One may argue that at present in psychology there is altogether *too little value placed upon empirical research that bears directly upon existing theories* and altogether too much value placed on the contribution of new theoretical formulation or speculation provided after a given set of findings has been observed. There is more prestige associated in the minds of many psychologists with the creation of a new but trivial theory, possessing little demonstrated superiority over existing theories, than there is in the execution of research that bears crucially upon an important theory already in existence. Psychologists in their awe for theory and their failure to discriminate between after-the-fact explanation and before-the-fact prediction have created a set of conditions where there is a maximum of interest in developing new theories and a minimum of interest in examining the consequences of existing theories.

An annoying and possibly malignant characteristic displayed by some contemporary personality theorists is the tendency toward what might be called *theoretical imperialism.* We refer here to the attempt, once a particular theoretical position has been developed, to try and persuade the reader that this is the only feasible manner in which a theory of behavior can be formulated. Thus, numerous psychologists assert that the only defensible theoretical mode is one that involves continuous interaction with physiological processes, others suggest that only "molar" formulations are fruitful, and still others imply that the social context must be the center of the theorist's attention. The point is not that these theorists are necessarily wrong in their faith but only that theoretical formulation is a "free enterprise" if ever there was one. No theorist has the right to tell fellow theorists their business. He or she is fully entitled to state their own convictions and link them with as much empirical evidence of their utility as possible. He or she may even wish to couple the theory and evidence with rational arguments that the theorist finds convincing as to why this approach will prove in the end to be fruitful. But to imply that this is the way in which theoretical progress *must* be made is nonsense and can only serve to confuse the student in the field. Let the theorist present the theory in the most forceful manner possible but let the theorist respect the fact that there is no such thing as theoretical certainty.

All personality theories make at least weak assumptions concerning the existence of some form of personality structure. Thus, although some theorists are more concerned with the relative importance of external or situational factors than others, all agree there is some degree of constancy to personality that generalizes across different periods of time and different situations. Theoretical differences between *trait theorists* such as Allport or Cattell and *situational determinists* such as Hartshorne and May (1928, 1929) led to active debate and programs of research in the two decades prior to World War II. In the past decade or so this issue has once again appeared as a major topic of theoretical contention and research (Bem and Allen, 1974; Endler and Magnusson, 1976; Mischel, 1968; Magnusson and Endler, 1977). As we have seen most clearly in the case of Allport and Cattell, trait theorists believe that individuals can be compared in terms of a number of traits or enduring dispositions and with knowledge of the individual's relative position or score on a given trait it is possible to predict a good deal about the person's behavior in a variety of different environmental settings. The believer in situational determinism is convinced that most behavior is a consequence of the environmental setting or situation in which the individual is behaving. Thus, behavior is elicited by stimuli rather than being emitted because of an enduring trait or disposition. An intermediate position asserts that the individual's dispositions or traits influence the situations in which one finds oneself and the stimuli in the environment to which one attends. This *interactionist position* assigns a significant role to both situational variables and to traits or dispositions. There seems little doubt that this theoretical-empirical issue will continue to be of prime importance in decades to come.

Recent years have witnessed some preference for theorists to proceed in more modest steps than those implied by a single general theory that embraces all or most of human adaptive behavior. These more limited or *mini-theories* have sometimes been concerned only with a particular domain or area of behavior, such as decision making or motor skills, or they may have dealt with a particular complex of behavior such as schizophrenia or sexual development. Some theorists have directed their attention toward mathematical models of cognition or learning; others have been more concerned with the neurophysiological substrate of behavior, but in all cases the theorists have focused upon a particular dimension or mode of representation of behavior to the relative exclusion of many other aspects of behavior. These modest or circumscribed theoretical approaches must ultimately be considered by and contribute to inclusive or general personality theories.

As we have already noted, recent years have been accompanied by extensive and significant developments in the broad area of *psychobiology or behavioral biology*. The systematic investigation of genetic determinants of behavior has been promoted both by the development of new methods and findings and also by some evidence of a lessening of the traditional American focus upon environment to the relative exclusion of biology (Manosevitz, Lindzey, and Thiessen, 1969). Much the same can be said concerning hormones and behavior, brain behavior associations, and psychophysiology (Thompson, 1975). All in all, there has been a broadening and deepening of our knowledge of the manner in which biological factors influence and are influenced by behavior and this information is only now beginning to enter significantly into the attempt to account for the complex behavior of humans. The tremendous vitality of the neurosciences and the well-publicized concern with extending evolutionary theory to areas of complex human behavior such as aggression, altruism, cooperation, competition, and mating patterns (Barash 1977; Emlen and Oring, 1977; Wilson, 1975), all point to the increasing likelihood that biology will have much more to say about the future of personality theories than it has had to do with past theories.

There have been revolutions of method and concept not only in psychobiology but also in the area of *computers and quantitative analysis*. Computers are used extensively for quantitative analysis, often permitting psychologists to carry out calculations that literally would have been impossible prior to the introduction of computers. Thus, such theories as Cattell's and Guilford's have been enormously enhanced in the scope and power of the analyses that can be carried out. It is also true that many theories such as Skinner's and S-R theory, which are close to the laboratory, have been greatly facilitated because computers are now an essential part of many experimental laboratories controlling the conduct of experiments as well as carrying out analyses of data during the study itself, which in turn may influence the next phase of the study. This not only makes the experiments more efficient but also permits many studies to be conducted that otherwise would not have been possible.

The use of computers to simulate thought or other psychological processes has also become a major theoretical exercise in its own right. Indeed, the field of artificial intelligence—essentially the use of computers to perform cognitive tasks of the sort that are usually considered evidence of human thought or intelligence—has become a lively area of research involving mathematicians, electrical engineers, and psychologists as well as computer scientists. A general assumption underlies artificial intelligence research: whether the computer is used to play chess, administer therapy, or engage in complex reasoning. The assumption is that in order to produce the equivalent of human reasoning, or any other form of behavior, we must first understand the underlying processes involved in human behavior. There are at least some psychologists who see computer programs and simulation of human behavior as the theoretical path of the future (Simon, 1969). Whatever the shortcomings of this procedure may be, it certainly forces precision and explicitness upon the theorist.

The reader should be careful not to construe what has been said as indicating a sense of discouragement with the present state of personality theory. It is true that there is much that can be presented in the way of criticism of current theories, particularly when they are compared with absolute or ideal standards. More significant, however, is the fact that when these theories are compared with theories existing three or four decades ago the signs of rapid progress are unmistakable. It was primarily during the past thirty-five years that the bulk of relevant empirical research appeared and it was likewise during this period that sophistication concerning the contribution of neighboring disciplines developed. At the same time, the theories have tended to become more explicit in their statement and much more attention is paid to the problem of providing adequate empirical definitions. Further, the range of ideas or conceptions concerning behavior has broadened immensely. In general, we believe that whatever the formal shortcomings of these theories may be, the ideas contained within them have had a remarkably broad and generative influence upon psychology. Nor does there seem to be any reason to expect that this influence will diminish in the future.

THEORETICAL SYNTHESIS VERSUS THEORETICAL MULTIPLICITY

We have seen that although there are similarities and convergences among theories of personality, the diversities and disagreements remain striking. In spite of clustering about certain modal theoretical positions there has been, as yet, little progress in the direction of developing a single widely accepted theoretical position. One may indeed wonder at the apparently endless ingenuity of psychologists in devising new ways of viewing or ordering the phenomena of behavior. Sears in a survey of the personality literature was moved by this state of affairs to remark:

> Any theory is valid only to the extent that it proves useful in predicting or providing for control of behavior; there is no right or wrong in the matter, but only convenience. Since no theory yet has proved brilliantly efficacious in ordering the data of molar behavior for these purposes, it is perhaps not surprising that so many psychologists find themselves goaded into new attempts to construct a systematic set of personality variables (Sears, 1950, p. 116).

Granted that this theoretical multiplicity exists, and granted also that the factors leading to this state are evident, is it not undesirable to have so many conflicting viewpoints in a single empirical area? Would it not be better to provide a single viewpoint that incorporated all that was good and effective from each of these theories so that we could then embrace a single theory that would be accepted by all investigators working in this area? Surely many of the theories we have discussed contain strengths that are not present in other theories. Can we not combine these individual strengths so as to create a uniquely powerful theory that will give us added insight into human behavior and generate predictions concerning behavior that are more comprehensive and verifiable than those presently generated by any single theory of personality?

Although this line of reasoning is intriguing and finds much support among contemporary psychologists, there are, nevertheless, a number of serious objections that can be raised to it. First, this point of view assumes that the existing personality theories possess a sufficient degree of formal clarity so that their exact nature can be established and the synthesizer can then readily identify common components and disparate elements. As we have seen this is anything but the case. Many of the theories are stated so imprecisely that it would be extremely difficult to make any direct comparison of their elements with the elements of another theory. This suggests that synthesis of necessity must be a somewhat haphazard process as the elements involved in the synthesis are only dimly outlined. Second, the argument assumes that there are no unresolvable conflicts between the content of the various theoretical positions or, if such conflicts exist, that they can readily be settled through an examination of the "facts of the matter." It is evident that there are many points where the theories are in flat disagreement. Further, these points of disagreement are frequently related to empirical phenomena that are far from being adequately studied. In fact, many of these theoretical differences are concerned with empirical issues of the most elusive variety, so that the "facts of the matter" are by no means clear. Third, it assumes that all or most of these theories have a unique and positive contribution to make to a powerful theory of behavior. The truth of the matter is that some of these theories are a long way from possessing demonstrated empirical utility. The amount of empirical testing of the derivable consequences of psychological theory is minute compared to the range of problems with which the theories purport to deal. Fourth, this point of view assumes that a state of theoretical harmony and agreement is healthiest at present. At a stage where the relevant empirical findings are so scanty, and where no single position seems to have a convincing superiority over all others, one may argue quite reasonably that, rather than investing all of our time and talent in a single theory, it would be wiser to explore actively the area through the simultaneous use of a variety of theoretical positions. When so little is known with certainty why place all of the future's hopes in one theoretical basket? Is it not better to let theoretical development follow a natural and unfettered course with the reasonable expectation that as stable empirical findings multiply, and the individual theories become more formalized, an integration may be arrived at naturally, and upon a firm empirical base, rather than as an artificially contrived process with personal taste and belief as the primary determinants of the process? Fifth, one must recognize that several of the theories we have discussed are highly eclectic. For example, Gordon Allport's final position is one that incorporates much from many other theories we have discussed. Likewise, Bandura's social learning theory has gradually come to display much in common with cognitive approaches to understanding behavior—once considered the very antithesis of the S-R tradition from which his theory emerged. Thus, over time there has appeared a natural merging and intermixing of theoretical formulation even though it has not resulted in any single position of consensus.

What of the didactic value of presenting to the student a single organized view of personality rather than the welter of contradictory ideas that we have seen presented in this volume? Presumably it is good mental hygiene to give the student a single clearly outlined theoretical position but it is certainly poor preparation for serious work in the field. If students believe that there is only one useful theory, it is easy for them to feel that they have reality firmly in their grasp and consequently to overlook the importance of empirical study and the possibility of theoretical changes imposed by the outcome of such study. Why should students be given a false sense of harmony? Let them see the field as it really exists—different theorists making different assumptions about behavior, focusing upon different empirical problems, using different techniques for research. Let them understand also that these individuals are united in their common interest in human behavior and their ultimate willingness to permit empirical data to make the final decision concerning theoretical right and wrong.

Related to the above argument is the compelling consideration that theories are useful chiefly to the person who embraces them and attempts in a sympathetic and sensitive manner to extract their consequences. The notion of a general synthesis or integration usually communicates to the student the need to be cautious, take all points of view into consideration, and to avoid emotional involvement with a particular, one-sided position. Before embracing any particular theory let us compare it with others, see that it is just as good in all respects, and read what the critics have had to say about it. Contrary to this conception, we recommend strongly that students should, once they have surveyed the available theories of personality, adopt a vigorous and affectionate acceptance of a particular theoretical position without reservation. Let the individual be enthusiastic and imbued with the theory before beginning to examine it critically. A theory of personality is not going to say or do much for the individual who approaches it aloofly, with criticisms and reservation. It will dictate problems to the devotee and stimulate him or her to do research but it will not do the same for the cool and detached observer. Let the students reserve their critical capacity and their detailed scholarly apparatus to make certain that the research they carry out is so well executed that the findings "fall where they may." If the individual does extract consequences from the theory and engage in relevant research, he or she will have ample opportunity for discouragement and despair concerning the adequacy of the theory and may well end up convinced of its lack of utility. At least he will have had the opportunity of discovering just what the theory *can* do for him.

It is our strong conviction that this is not the appropriate time or circumstance for an attempted synthesis or integration of personality theories. In simplest terms we feel that it is unwise to attempt a synthesis of theories whose empirical utility remains largely undemonstrated. Why make a conceptual arrangement in terms of aesthetic reaction and internal consistency when the important issue is how these elements fare in the face of empirical data? Far more fruitful, we believe, than any attempt at a master theory is the careful development and specification of a single existing theory with simultaneous attention to relevant empirical data. The ultimate answer to any theoretical issue lies in well-controlled empirical data, and the nature of such data will be adequately defined only as the theories themselves are better developed. It is one thing to change a theory in the light of empirical data that force upon the theorist some essential change, and quite another to change a theory because of some conflicting rational or evaluative issue. Our faith is that almost any theory if it is systematically extended and coupled with extensive empirical research offers greater hope for advance than an amalgamation of existing theories some of which are poorly stated and precariously related to empirical data.

BIBLIOGRAPHY   Barash, D. *Sociobiology and behavior.* New York: Elsevier, 1977.

Bem, D., and Allen, A. On predicting some of the people some of the time. *Psychological Review,* 1974, **81,** 506–520.

Cartwright, D. S. Factor analyzing theories of personality, *Counseling Center Discussion Papers,* Univ. of Chicago, Vol. III, No. 24, Sept. 1957, 8 pp.

Emlen, S. T., and Oring, L. W. Ecology, sexual selection, and the evolution of mating systems. *Science,* 1977, **197,** 215–223.

Endler, N. S., and Magnusson, D. (Eds.). *Interactional psychology and personality.* Washington, D.C.: Hemisphere, 1976.

Evans, J. D., and Smith, H. W. A factor-analytic synthesis of personality theories: basic dimensions reconsidered. *J. Psychology,* 1972, **82,** 145–149.

Hall, C. S., and Lindzey, G. The relevance of Freudian psychology and related viewpoints for the social sciences. In G. Lindzey and E. Aronson (Eds.). *Handbook of social psychology,* Vol. 1. Cambridge, Mass.: Addison-Wesley, 1968, 245–319.

Hartshorne, H., and May, M. A. *Studies in the nature of character: studies in deceit.* New York: Macmillan, 1928.

Hartshorne, H., and May, M. A. *Studies in the nature of character: studies in self control.* New York: Macmillan, 1928.

Hilgard, E. R. Experimental approaches to psychoanalysis. In E. Pumpian-Mindlin (Ed.). *Psychoanalysis as science.* Stanford, Calif.: Stanford Univ. Press, 1952, 3–45.

Magnusson, D., and Endler, N. S. (Eds.). *Personality at the crossroads,* Hillsdale, N.J.: Erlbaum, 1977.

Manosevitz, M., Lindzey, G., and Thiessen, D. D. *Behavioral genetics: method and research.* New York: Appleton-Century-Crofts, 1969.

Mischel, W. *Personality and assessment.* New York: Wiley, 1968.

Schuh, A. J. A synthesis of personality theories by cluster analysis. *J. Psychology,* 1966, **64,** 69–71.

Sears, R. R. *Survey of objective studies of psychoanalytic concepts.* New York: Soc. Sci. Res. Council, Bull. No. 51, 1943.

Sears, R. R. Personality. In C. P. Stone and D. W. Taylor (Eds.). *Annual review of psychology.* Vol. 1. Stanford, Calif.: Annual Reviews, 1950, 105–118.

Simon, H. A. *The sciences of the artificial.* Cambridge, Mass.: M.I.T. Press, 1969.

Taft, R. A statistical analysis of personality theories. *Acta Psychologia,* 1960, **17,** 80–88.

Thompson, R. F. *Introduction to physiological psychology.* New York: Harper & Row, 1975.

Wilson, E. O. *Sociobiology.* Cambridge: Mass., Harvard Univ. Press, 1975.

NAME INDEX

SUBJECT INDEX